Christian Mission and Service in Western India

Christian Mission and Service in Western India

Contribution of Bombay-Poona Jesuit Mission (1914-1962)

Cornelius Ekka

Jesuit Conference of India

&

Christian World Imprints

First Published in 2021 by

Jesuit Conference of India
225 Jor Bagh
New Delhi-110003
Email jcsa.treas@gmail.com

&

Christian World Imprints
C-3, Wazirpur Industrial Area
Delhi-110052
cwidelhi2017@gmail.com
www.ChristianWorldImprints.com
Phone: +91 11 41526079

ISBN: 978-935148-510-0

Cover design by: Tapeshwar Prasad

Cover Picture legend: Photos of De Nobili College, Pune; St. Vincent's High School, Pune; Catholic Church, Sonegaon, Maharashtra

Printed in India.

DEDICATED

To the loving memory of Fr. Dr. Cornelius Ekka, SJ, Member of Madhya Pradesh Jesuit Province and Faculty of Vidyajyoti College of Theology, Delhi, who suddenly departed to his heavenly abode in his prime age soon after completing his thesis from which this book has emerged.

Fr. Ekka himself had dedicated his thesis:

To my departed loving parents for teaching what **LIFE** means!
To
My sister and brother with their loving families for teaching me what **LOVE** means!
To
All my friends and well-wishers who through their words and deeds have taught me what **CARE** and **CONCERN** mean!
And to the
Lord and Creator
For giving me **ALL** these!

Cornelius Ekka: A Profile

Late Cornelius Ekka (1969-2017) hailed from Benjora village in Jashpur District, Chhattisgarh. He was born on 18th May, 1969, to Barnabas and Christina Ekka, as the third of three children. He is survived by an elder brother and sister.

He did his Primary schooling in Benjora village, Secondary schooling at Boy's Middle School, Ambakona, and Higher Secondary schooling at Loyola Higher Secondary School, Kunkuri. He joined the Madhya Pradesh Province of the Society of Jesus on 20th June 1990 at Khrist Milan Ashram, Namna, Ambikapur. After his graduate studies (B.Sc. Maths from 1993 to 1996 from Govt. Motilal Vigyan Mahavidyalaya, Bhopal) he pursued his ecclesiastical studies: Bachelor of Philosophy at Jnana Deepa Vidyapeeth, Pune from 1996 to 1998 and Bachelor of Theology from Vidyajyoti College of Theology, Delhi from 2000 to 2003. He was ordained a priest on 7th May, 2004 at Ambakona, Jashpur District, Chhattisgarh.

He did a Master's in Theology (M.Th.) from Vidyajyoti College of Theology, Delhi from 2007 to 2010 and pursued his doctoral studies in Christian History at the *Faculty of Theology, Leopold-Franzens-University, Innsbruck, Austria, from 2011 to 2017. He* was awarded Ph. D in 2017 for his thesis, "*The German Swiss Jesuits in India (1914-1962)–A Historico-Missiological Study.*"

Cornelius was a faculty member of Vidyajyoti College of Theology, Delhi (Tutor, 2008-10; Lecturer, 2010 & 2017) where he taught Church History, Tribal Messianic Movements, Trinity and Tribal Theology.

A student of Christian History, he has published a few articles, notable among them being "Contribution of the Laity for the Spread of Christian Faith in Jashpur-Raigarh-Ambikapur" in *Indian Church History Review* (Vol. XLII, No. 2, Dec 2008, pp. 89-117). A very promising scholar, his life was sadly cut short by a massive heart attack on 17th October, 2017 shortly after he resumed his full teaching career at Vidyajyoti College of Theology, Delhi.

Contents

Publisher's Note

Fr. Dr. Cornelius Ekka, SJ who passed away unexpectedly on 17th October, 2017, within five months of his rejoining the faculty of Vidyajyoti College of Theology in Delhi, was promising scholar of Church History. His passing away in his prime youth shocked his students, staff and all Jesuits of Madhya Pradesh Province.

I am grateful to the successive Provincials of Madhya Pradesh Jesuit Province for making the services of Cornelius available to common house of formation of Jesuit Conference of South Asia, especially at Vidyajyoti College of Theology, Delhi.

It is to be highly appreciated that Cornelius undertook a study outside the familiar geographical region of his home state Chhattisgarh, India and outside his indigenous cultural background: on the German-Swiss Jesuit Mission in western India. This was all the more challenging because most of the original sources were in German and Latin. In the true research tradition in Anthropology, he was an 'outsider' to the area of study. But as a Jesuit he had the advantage of being an 'insider' so that he could sift through the labyrinth of sources, and choose the most relevant ones to reconstruct the story of the Poona Mission of the Society of Jesus. The laborious work that he undertook on '*Bombay-Poona Jesuit Mission (1914-1962)', especially researching on the* archival materials available in Rome, Innsbruck and Munich, need to be told to the larger public.

It is precisely because of this that the Jesuit Conference of India (JCI), Delhi feel extremely privileged to publish this work in collaboration with Christian World Imprints, Delhi to make Cornelius' work known to the academic world: it's a labour of love in honour of our Jesuit companion and scholar.

We are honored to get the services of Dr. Jose Kalapura, S.J. - a scholar in Christian and Jesuit History in India, – to make the required revision of the original thesis, to make it reader-friendly and to write an informed introduction to the book; this helps the reader to locate the book and thus to appreciate it better. Thank you dear Dr. Kalapura for this generous service in honour of our companion. May you be rewarded with 'blessings' from the Lord.

I thank Prof Bernhard Kriegbaum of Leopald-Franzens University of Innsbruck, his doctoral guide, for writing the Foreword and Tribute for this book.

My appreciation for Christian World Imprints, Delhi for joining hands with us to make Cornelus' work known to the larger public. May the Lord bless our efforts. I am deeply indebted to Vidyajyoti College of Theology, Delhi for the logistical support rendered, especially by Dr. (Fr) Rajkumar, SJ towards the publication of the book.

It is hoped that this study will add to the existing body of literature on Christian missions in India in general, and to Jesuit Studies in particular. It is envisaged that this volume will be valuable for students and scholars in Social Sciences, especially in Christian History, Missiology, Jesuit History, Theology and Social Work.

Dr. George Pattery, SJ
President, Jesuit Conference of India

Foreword and Tribute

When an Indian Jesuit companion introduced Fr. Cornelius to me eight years ago in order to write a dissertation on Church History with me, I presented him with two possible topics to choose from. One topic was relatively easy to work on, since all the sources were in print and could have been easily ordered from the Innsbruck University Library. The topic was of course not very relevant. The trouble of archival work and handling of handwritten source material would have been omitted and the dissertation could have been completed significantly faster.

It is characteristic of Fr. Ekka that he did not choose this simple subject, but the much more difficult one, namely the story of the Jesuit mission in the Poona province. There was no preliminary work on this topic, and most of the work had to be collected and processed from different archives in Rome, Zurich and Munich. Among them were numerous documents that were difficult to read and were written in different languages that the author had to learn for this purpose, apart from German. Nonetheless, and although I pointed out these difficulties to Fr. Ekka right from the start, he decided to work on this topic and wrote his dissertation with flying colours. After initial difficulties, which are not atypical at the beginning of doctoral thesis, he got along better and better with the work.

I was particularly amazed by the breadth of his interest, which led him to ever new questions that I hadn't expected and that surprised me again and again. Especially he made efforts to be more objective, when he needed to make judgements from his findings about people. He did not allow his ethnic or social cultural background to affect them. In striving for the greatest possible objectivity, Fr. Ekka also did not spare the Society of Jesus, whose mistakes and inadequacies in missionary activity, he does not cover up or deny. For him, however, it was clear that only those who do nothing make no mistakes, everyone else has to look for ways and means, whereby mistakes are inevitable. Cornelius was a happy and a hearty Jesuit. He loved his vocation and was committed to all that was entrusted to him by the Society of Jesus. He was good companion and a joyful person. All through the study, he maintained a good disposition towards his work, and that makes this book more balanced and meaningful.

To be precise, the author presents a special chapter in the history of Mission in India in 20th century. It's about the Jesuit mission which founded the Poona Province, soon after the end of the first World War. This history covers up to second Vatican Council, which marks a remarkable period of mission engagement of the Catholic Church in the western part of India. It is also noteworthy, that this part of the history of Catholic mission of Poona Province is written, not by a foreigner, but by an Indian himself and hence the Indian cultural and religious nuances are retained well and receive a higher quality description.

I was extremely pleased that this work is now also available in print and is therefore easily accessible to the public instead of gathering dust in university libraries in Europe. I believe that this book not only helps Indian Catholicism to recognize its own past a little better, but it could also help the interested Indian reader, regardless of religion, to understand Catholicism and mission of the Jesuits better.

I therefore wish this publication every success, an attentive and open-minded readership and a positive response from the public.

Prof. Dr. Bernhard Kriegbaum SJ
Dept., of Biblical and Historical Theology
Leopold-Franzens-University
Innsbruck (Austria), Sept 9, 2020

Acknowledgements

Jesuit mission histories have always been an area of fascination for me. One of the primary reasons for the same is the personal experience of transformation that a Jesuit mission has brought about in my community.

I belong to the third generation of Catholics in my family. As late as 1930s, my family along with my entire community practiced a non-Christian religion (akin to animism). Although the religion of my ancestors had a number of positive aspects, it was no less infested with superstitious beliefs. On account of the lack of education there was ignorance, illiteracy, lack of awareness about its rights and many other such evils. Consequently, my community suffered practically every conceivable aspect of dehumanization and subjugation ranging from virtual slavery under the feudal rulers to the loss of human dignity under various forms of oppression. Indeed they were the grim yet undeniable realities of the everyday-existence of my community.

Amidst such a situation, the Flemish-speaking Belgian Jesuit missionaries preached the Catholic Faith to my community. This included not only a promise of an eternal life in the after-life alone, but the same also embraced a here-and-now dimension of liberation as well. Such a claim is substantiated from the fact that the missionaries not only preached the faith but also advocated integral human development by introducing educational system and many social welfare schemes, which in turn gradually helped in bringing awareness about social equality, justice, freedom from superstitions, ignorance, illiteracy, etc. Consequently my community has begun to experience liberation at various levels of its existence. Given such a background, I firmly believe that a gradual process of transformation was set in motion in my community only because the generation of my grandparents embraced Catholicism.

Precisely this is one of the primary reasons for choosing such a topic for my doctoral dissertation. It is hoped that this study will unearth quite a significant treasure of knowledge on the Jesuit missions in India.

A doctoral dissertation by definition implies acquirement of skill and scholarship in the area of research at the end of the study. Yet, my opinion has always been that theology study should not be an intellectual exercise alone but also a process of deepening in the kind of experiences I have stated above. The topic I have selected offers me this possibility. Unfortunately I had not an iota of idea that the collection of a sufficient quantity of primary literature, for various reasons, would be a herculean task. In the initial stage often I had to face a virtual vacuum of primary literature in various archives, especially at Munich, Bombay and Poona. Often due to the virtual absence of materials (i.e., pertaining to the decades between the two World Wars) in the above-mentioned archives that the collection of primary literature turned out to be a daunting task. In spite of all these challenges, the entire journey was invariably characterized by a silver-lining, thanks to the constant support from various persons.

At the completion of my doctoral studies, therefore, as I thank the Lord most profoundly for his unconditional love, enlightenment and guidance all along my way; with grateful heart I recall many generous persons who have sacrificed their precious time and energy in helping me achieve this goal. My most sincere thanks go to my research guide o. Univ.-Prof. (em.) Dr. Bernhard Kriegbaum, SJ, of Leopold-Franzens University, Innsbruck, Austria, for his patience, support, encouragement and efficient guidance. His readiness to go through the text, critical comments and suggestions helped me crystalize my ideas. My sincere thanks are due also to Professor Dr. Roman A. Siebenrock, my second guide for his critical feedbacks and suggestions. I gratefully acknowledge their contributions in what has been achieved.

I owe a debt of gratitude also to my Superiors, both former and present, in India for giving me this chance to pursue a study at Innsbruck. I gratefully acknowledge the continual support of the staff of Vidyajyoti College of Theology in Delhi. My stay in Innsbruck would not have been possible, were it not for the generosity of the Austrian Province of the Society of Jesus. I sincerely thank Fr. Gemot Wisser SJ, its former Provincial as well as the present one, Fr. Bernhard Btirgler SJ for their support and encouragement. My sincere thanks to Fr. Markus Inama SJ, the present Rector of Jesuitenkolleg, Innsbruck, for his continual support. I gratefully acknowledge also the contribution of the former Rector, late Fr. Severin Leitner SJ. The community members have always been wonderful companions. My thanks to them all.

I am deeply indebted to Fr. Klaus Vathroder SJ and Fr. Anton Kurmann SJ, the Jesuit Mission Procurators of Germany and Switzerland respectively, for their help in making it possible to visit the archives for the purpose of collection of primary literature. Without their generous help, the research would have been inconceivable. My sincere thanks are due also to Fr. Brian Mac Cuarta SJ, the Director of the central archive of the Society of Jesus in Rome (ARSI) for his immense support and extra considerations in making exceptions pertaining to the rules of the archives. I am grateful for the permission to have access to the records and documents that belong to the restricted period, namely after 1939 (the year of the death of Pius XI). His assistants and colleagues Fr. Raul Gonzalez SJ and Fr. Robert Danieluk SJ too deserve sincere thanks for their friendly approach and ever readiness to help me. Fr. Lisbert D'Souza SJ, the South Asian Assistant to the Superior General went an extra mile in suggesting and paving the way to obtain a permission from the Superior General to do a research on the restricted period in the shortest time possible. It was a very kind gesture on his part. My sincere thanks to him.

Dr. Clemens Brodkorb, the archivist at the German Jesuit Province Archive in Munich (ADPSJ), Dr. Esther Schmid Heer, the librarian at the Swiss Province Archive and Library (ABSPGJ) and the co-workers at the Swiss Jesuit Province Archive (AMPSJ) in Zurich too have been ever willing to help me. Similarly the Jesuits and co-workers at the libraries and archives at Goa, Poona and Bombay were very generous in helping me out. May they be richly rewarded for their availability and generosity!

The community of San Pietro Canisio (Cassa dei Scrittori), Rome was exceptionally hospitable to make my stay during the visits to the archives homely and pleasant. Similarly the communities of the German and Swiss Jesuit Provincialates in Munich and Zurich respectively, the community at Berchmanskolleg Munich, St. Xavier's College (Mumbai), Sanjeevan Ashram (Provincialate), Pune and

Xavier Centre for Historical Research, Goa have been very kind to give me accommodation during my visits. I wish to say a word of special thanks to Professors (em.) Dr. Franz Weber for his extraordinary generosity in helping me out in reading the entire manuscript and giving his most valuable suggestions. Finally, I wish to say a word of thanks to all those who have helped me in some way or the other.

Cornelius Ekka, SJ
Innsbruck, 2017

List of Tables

List of Photos/Illustrations

List of Maps

Abbreviations

I. Archives and Archival Sources

ABSPGJ	Archiv und Bibliothek der Schweizer Provinz der Gesellschaft Jesu, Zurich
ADPSJ	Archiv der deutsche Provinz der Gesellschaft Jesu, Munich
AMPSJ	Archiv der Missionsprokur der Schweizer Jesuiten, Zurich
ARSI	Archivum Romanum Societatis Iesu, Rome
ASPF	Archivio Storico de Propaganda Fide, Rome
HIHCB	Heras Institute of Indian History and Culture, Bombay
PJPA	Pune Jesuit Province Archives, Pune
RLGGM	Registro Lettere dei Generali Assistentia Germanica Missiones [Epistolae Praepositi Generalis ad Miss. Assist. Germaniae]

II. Bulletins, Newsletters, Journals and Magazines

ASM	Aus der Stella Matutina
CMAPF	Catholic Missions and the Annals of the Propagation of the Faith
DS	Der Sonntag
EPW	Economic and Political Weekly
HG	Hitguj [Monthly Newsletter of Poona Province]
IADJ	Indien: Arbeitsfeld deutscher Jesuiten
IB	Indische Bilder
IB MR	International Bulletin of Missionary Research
IJFM	International Journal of Frontier Missions
IJHSSS	International Journal of Humanities & Social Science Studies

JJCI	Jeevadhara: A Journal of Christian Interpretation
KM	Die Katholische Missionen LCC La Civilta Cattolica
MB	Missions-Boetl [Pullach, Munich : Berchmannskolleg, 1929-1931]
MSHI	Messengers of the Sacred Heart for India
MJBKS	Missionsjahrbuch der katholischen Schweiz
MDPGJ	Mitteilungen aus den Deutschen Provinz der Gesellschaft Jesu
NJ	*Navajuni*
NZM	Neue Zeitschrift fur Missionswissenschaft
PA	Pacific Affairs
PI	*Promotio Iustitiae*
RL	Rays of Light
SBH	Seethaler-Bote, Hochdorf
SIQR	Studies: An Irish Quarterly Review
SSJ	Studies in the Spirituality of the Jesuits
SXCM	St. Xavier's College Magazine
TAER	The American Ecclesiastical Review
TCH	The Christian Herald
TDR	The Dublin Review
TEX	The Examiner
TUT	The Indian Journal of Theology
TUPS	The Indian Journal of Political Science
TMC	The Missionary Chronicle
TS	Theological Studies
UB	Unser Bocholt
VJTR	Vidyajyoti Journal of Theological Reflection
WMKK	Die Weltmission der katholischen Kirche
WL	The Woodstock Letters
ZMR	Zeitschrift fur Missionswissenschaft und Religionswissenschaft

III. Apostolic Letters/Exhortations, Encyclicals, Papal Bulls and Conciliar and Post-Conciliar Documents

AE *Ad Extremas*
AG *Ad Gentes*
DH *Dignitatis Humanae*
DSD *Deus Scientiarum Dominus*
EP *Evangelii Praecones*
EN *Evangelii Nuntiandi*
FD *Fidei Donum*
GS *Gaudium et Spes*
JW Justice in the World
LE Laborem Exercens
MBS Mit Brennender Sorge
MI *Maximum Illud*
MM *Mater et Magistra*
NA *Nostra Aetate*
OA *Octogesima Adveniens*
PP *Populorum Progressio*
PT *Pacem in Terris*
QA *Quadragesimo Anno*
RE *Rerum Ecclesiae*
RH *Redemptor Hominis*
RM *Redemptor Missio*
RN *Rerum Novarum*
SRS *Solicitudo Rei Socialis*

IV. Commentaries, Handbooks, Lexicons and Multi-Volume Editions

GCM Die Geschichte des Christentums, Vols. 11-13 (Herder/Mayeur, 1992)
HKGJ Handbuch der Kirchengeschichte, Vols. VI/2 - VII (1878-1985) (Herder/Jedin, 1973/1985)
HTKVCII Herders theologischer Kommentar zum zweiten Vatikanischen Konzil (Herder/Hunermann & Hilberath, 2004)

LTK Lexikon fur Theologie und Kirche (Herder/Kasper et al., 1996)

LTKVCII Lexikon fur Theologie und Kirche: Das zweite Vatikanische Konzil, Vol. I-III (Herder/Suso Brechter et al., 1968)

V. Jesuit Sources: Catalogues and Documents of General Congregations

ActRSJ Acta Romana Societatis Iesu

GC General Congregation of the Society of Jesus

CPGSSI Catalogus Provinciae Germaniae Superioris Societatis Iesu

(Allotting: Gebr. Geiselberger, 1920-1956).

CVAVAB (1883) Catalogus Vicariorum Apostolicorum necnon Patrum ac Fratru Societatis Jesu, Presbyterorum Seacularium atque Monialium

Vicariatu Apostolico Bombayensi (Bombay: Ex Typograph 'Examiner', 1883)

CABEPMAB (1917) Catalogus Archiepiscoporum Bombayensium et Episcoporum Poonensium Vicariorum Apostolicorum, Patrum et Fratru: Societatis Jesu, Praesbyterorum Seacularium atque Monialium Missione Apostolica Bombayensi (Bombay: Ex Typograph 'Examiner', 1917)

MAPS

1. Map of the Bombay Vicariate at the Time of the Arrival of the Jesuits (1854)

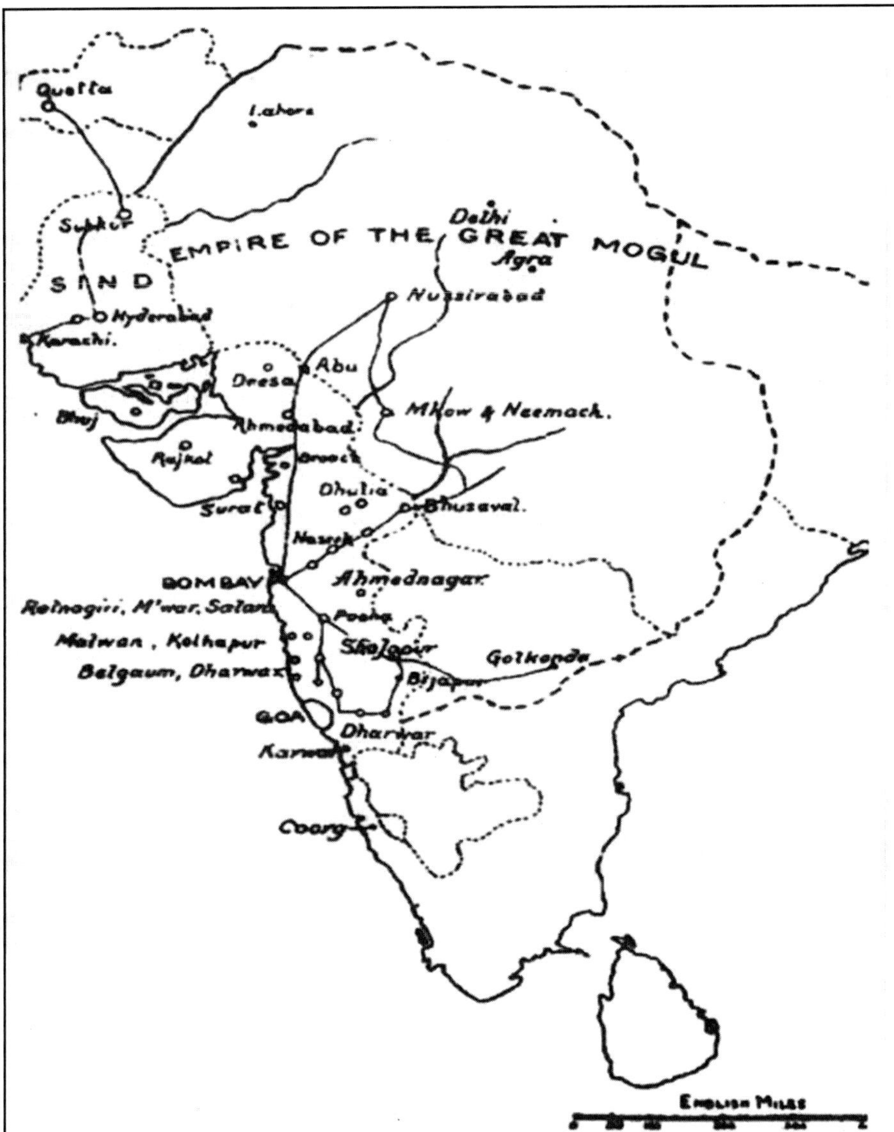

Source: Ernest R. Hull, *Bombay Mission History: With a Special Study of the Padroado Question* (Bombay: The Examiner Press, n.d.), xv.

2. Map of India

Source: https://www.google.at/search?q=india+states+and+union+territories+map, accessed on 17.11.2016.

3. Map of Maharashtra with Districts

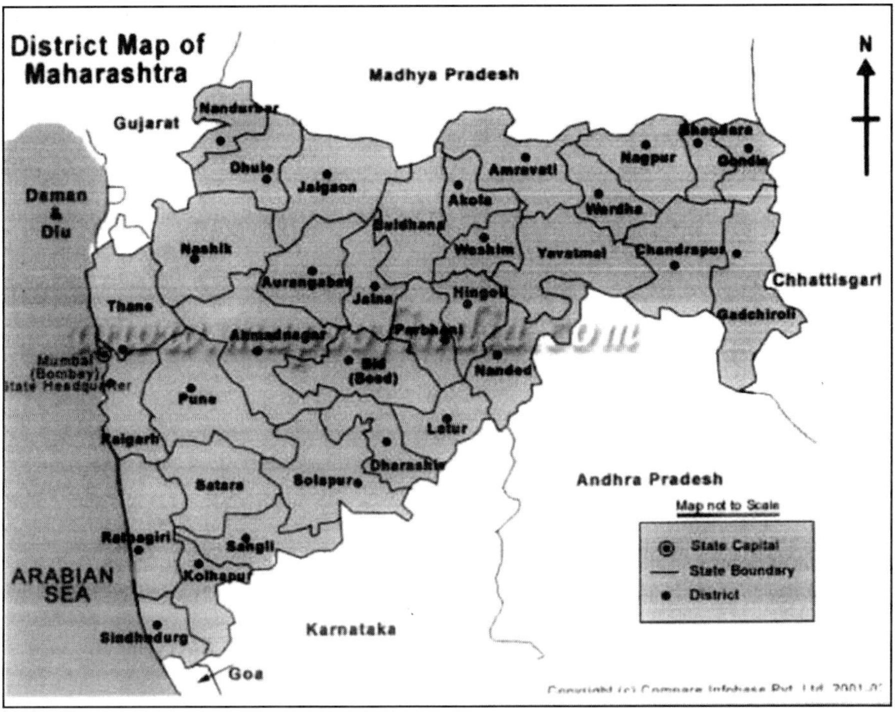

Source: http://wardha.nic.in/en/htmldocs/maps.html, accessed on 17.11.2016.

4. Map of Ahmadnagar District

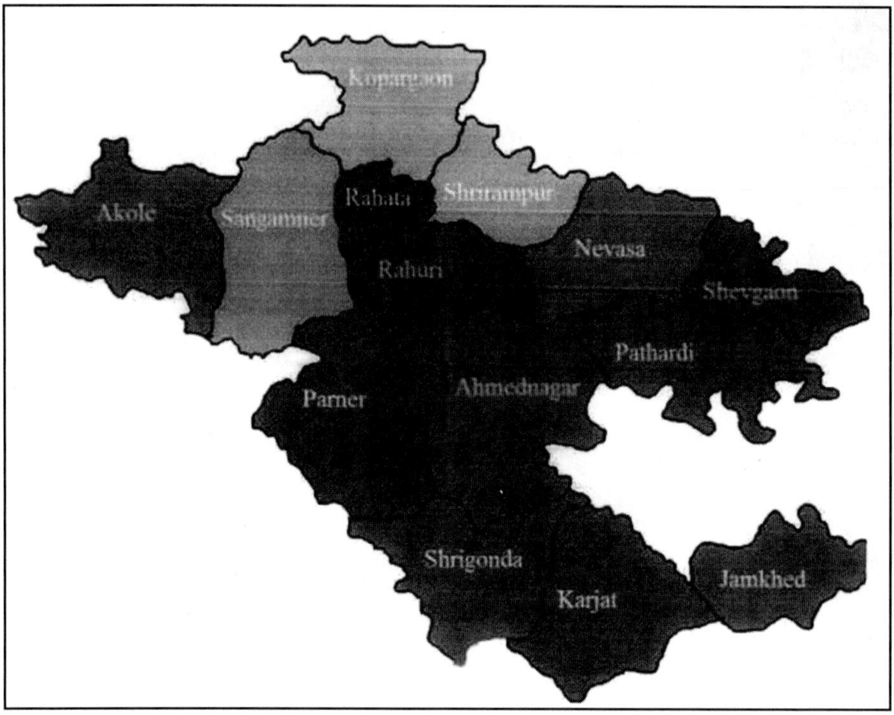

Source: https://en.wikipedia.org/wiki/Talukasof_Ahmednagardistrict#/media, accessed on 17.11.2016.

5. Map of Bombay-Poona Mission (1914)

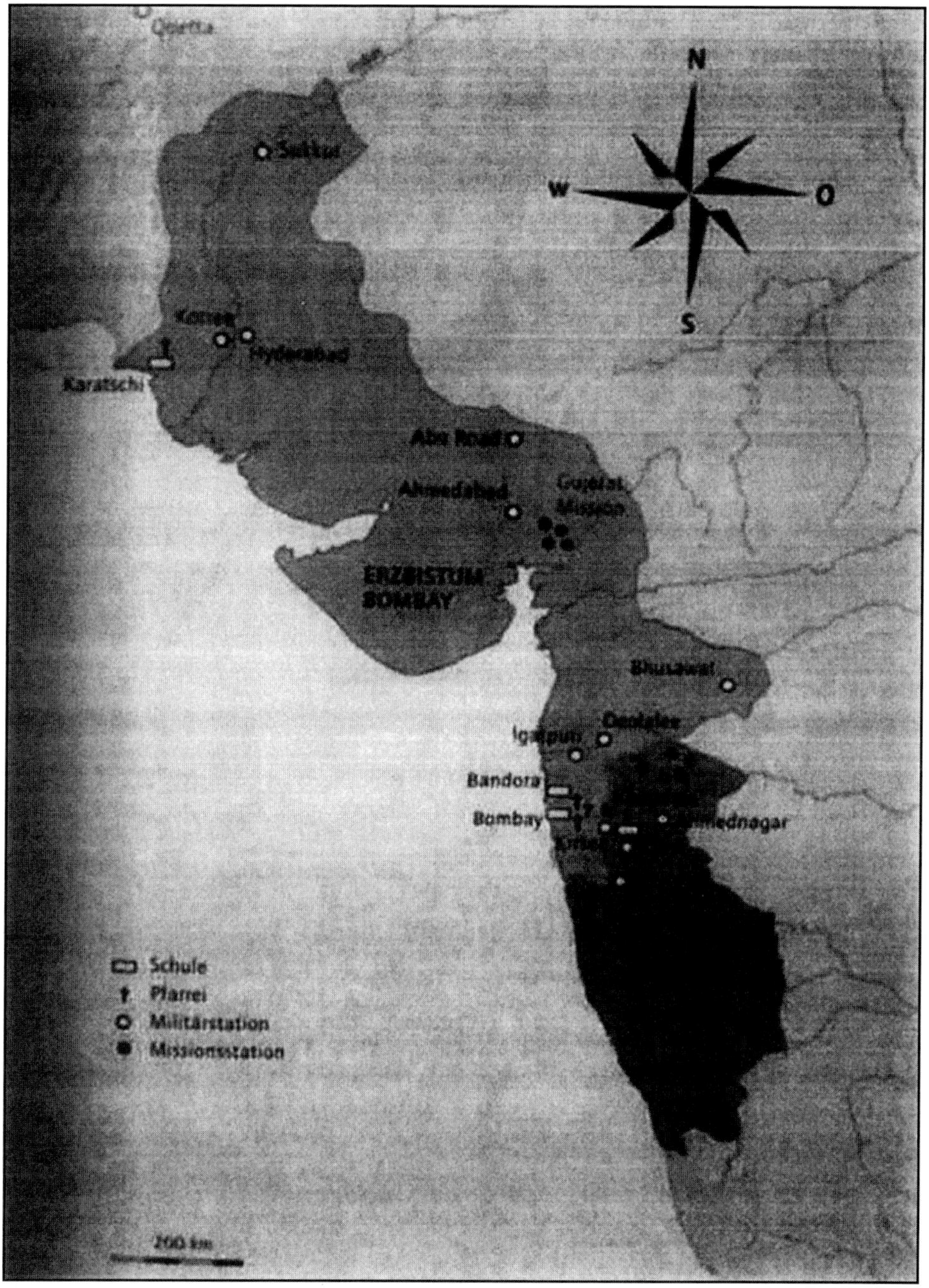

Source: Klaus Schatz. *Geschichle tier deutschen Jesuiten, Vol. II 1X72-1917* (Minister: Aschendorf, 2013), 233.

6. Map of Poona Mission (1920)

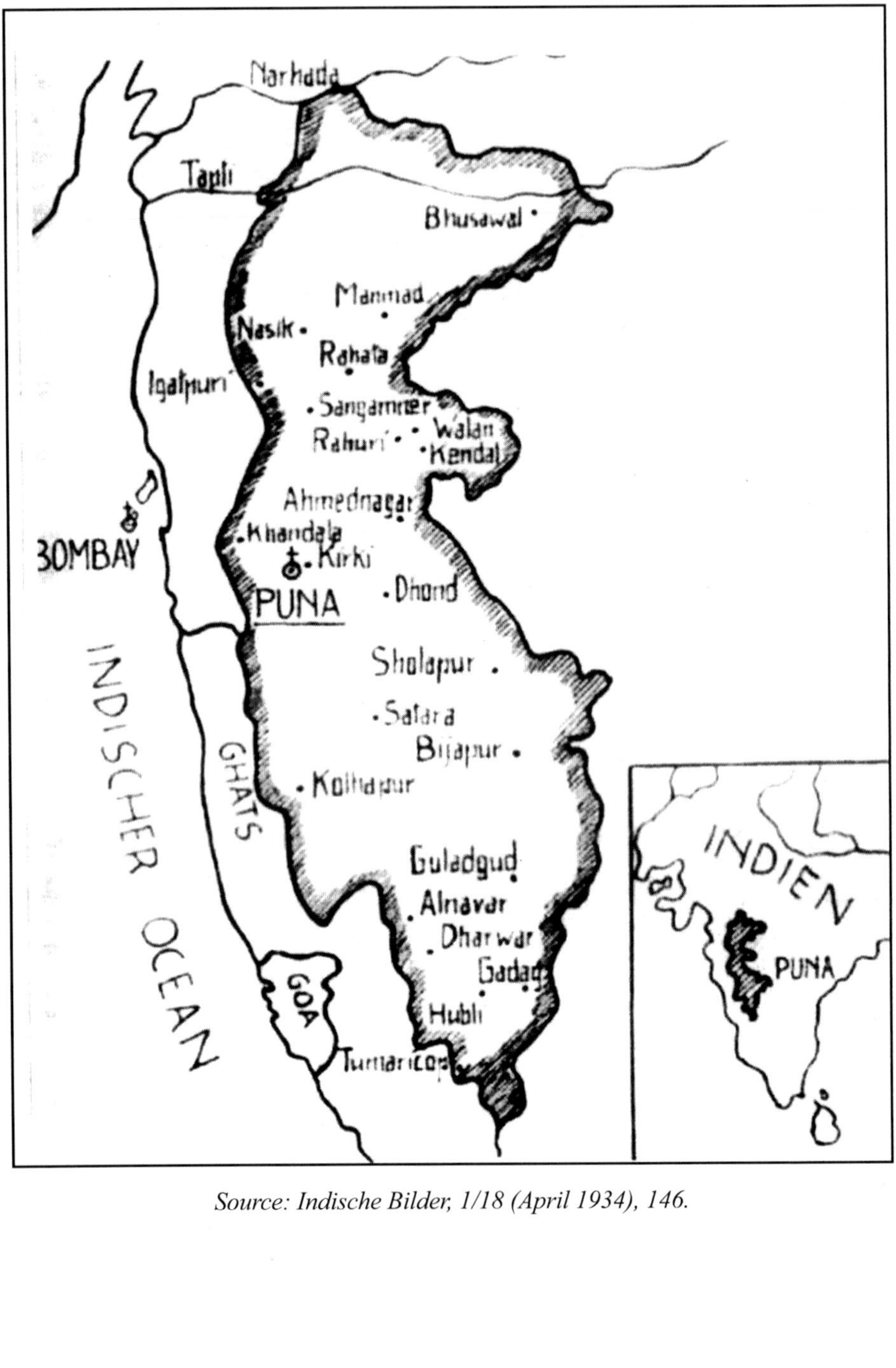

Source: Indische Bilder, 1/18 (April 1934), 146.

7. Map of Poona Mission (1951)

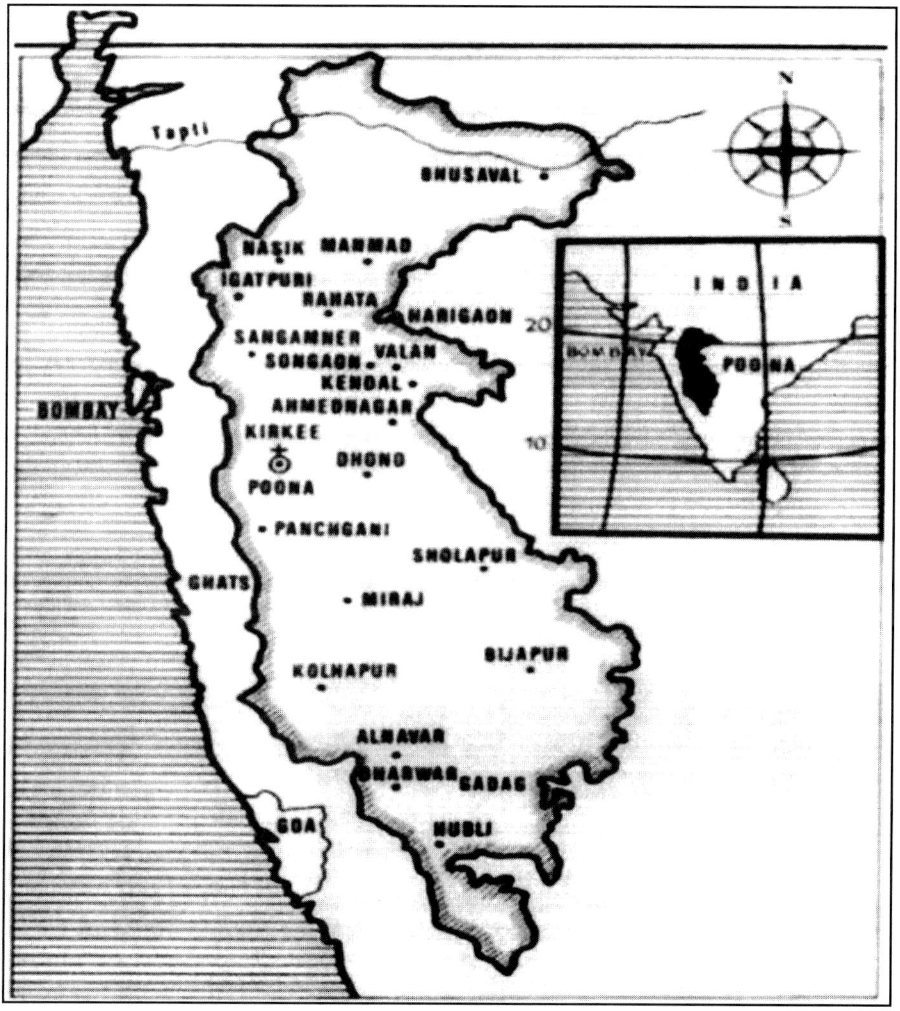

Source: Indische Bilder, 1 (January/February 1951): 7. The same map was maintained till the erection of the Vice-Province of Belgaum-Poona in 1956.

8. Map of Belgaum-Poona Vice-Province (1956)

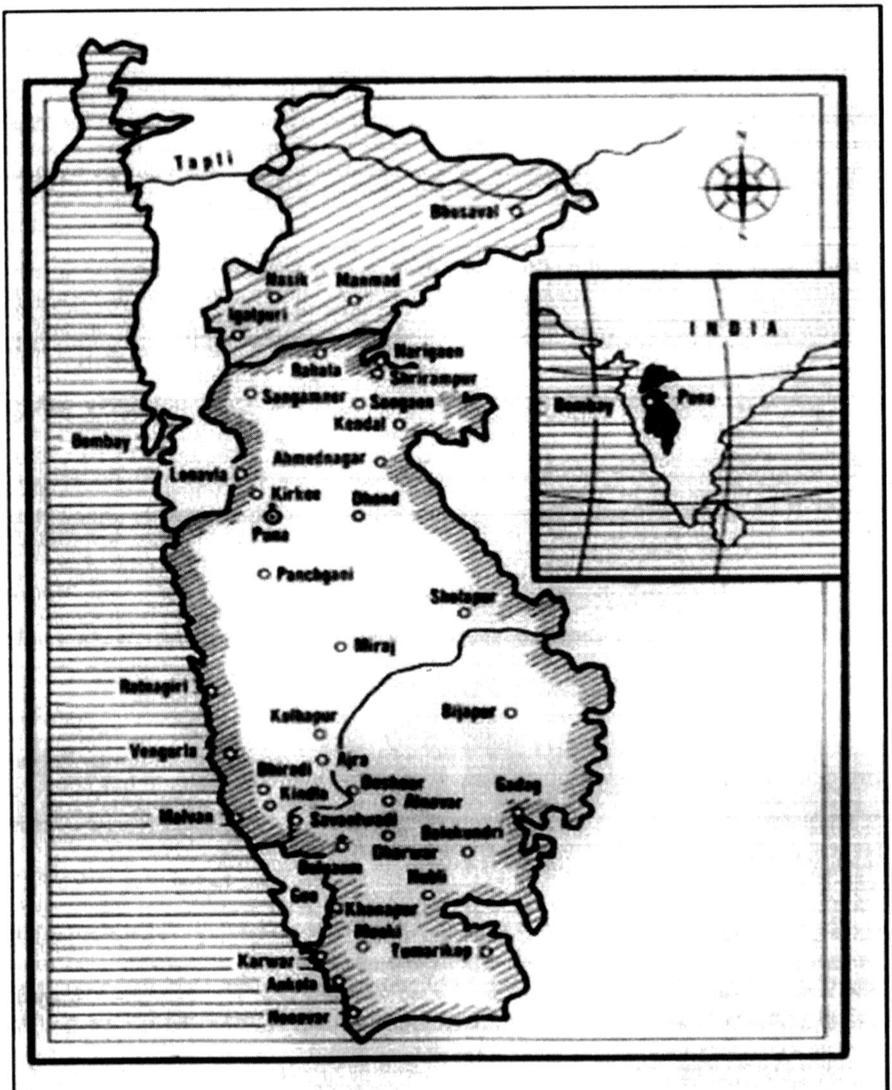

Source: "Summary Report of the General Sociological Survey Goa-Poona Vice-Province," *ARSI, Historia 2001-Poona.*

Introduction

Christian Missions in India
An Overview of Jesuit Missions

*Jose Kalapura**

0.1. Introduction

Early writings on Christian missions in India have been mostly in the form of mission reports, travelogues, apologetics, chronicles, etc., generally by missionaries themselves or travelers. However, a new genre of studies have emerged in the past fifty years, thanks to the interest by modern scholars. These scholars tend to view Christian mission from a non-passionate, objective perseptive.[1] They approach the subject from a multi-disciplinary perspective and tend to show that Christian mission is not just an agent of Christian expansion, but an agent of service, social transformation and development, making deep impact on target communities.[2]

This book entitled, *Christian Missions and Service: Contribution of Bombay-Poona Mission (1914-1962)*, by Cornelius Ekka is a significant contribution in this category of Christian studies. As the title indicates, the topic is limited to one Jesuit Mission, in one area (western India), and the time period is about 50 years of the 20th century. No doubt this is an in-depth study giving an ant's eye-view of the subject matter.

* Dr. **Jose Kalapura,** Patna Jesuit, did his M. Phil and Ph. D in Christian History from Jawaharlal Nehru University (New Delhi), and has taught Church History and Jesuit History in several institutes. He has authored/co-authored/edited 19 books and has 85 research papers to his credit. He is a member of the 'Indian History Congress' and 'Church History Association of India'. He has been the Executive Editor of the *Indian Church History Review* since 2009. Currently he is the Director of Xavier Institute of Social Research, Patna, India.

There are at present 21 Jesuit Mission organizations in South Asia. This special introduction is an attempt to give the general readers and scholars a wider perspective of the Christian missions undertaken by the Jesuits in South Asia since the 16th century. It is envisaged that this book, when located on a wider canvas, would give a bird's eye-view of the entire Jesuit missionary enterprises in South Asia.

This essay has three parts: 1) a brief note on Christian missions in ancient and medieval periods, in south India and western India. Also included in this part a small section on the 19th -20th century Protestant missions in western India as to show that the Bombay-Poona Mission of the Jesuits was one player among many in western India; 2) a brief narrative on the Jesuit mission in South Asia from 16th to late 18th century, when the Jesuit Society was suppressed, and 3) the second beginning of Jesuit missions in South Asia, in mid-19th century, their growth and areas of service to society, since then.

I

0.2. Ancient Christian Missions in India: Malabar

Christian Missions in India is as old as Christianity itself. According to tradition, the first Christian mission to India was by St. Thomas, one of the apostles of Jesus Christ, who, after preaching to the inhabitants of Socatra, Parthia and in the Kingdom of Gondophares, North-Western India, landed at the ancient port of Cranganore, in Malabar (Kerala) in 52 A.D.[3] Recent studies point out that Apostle Thomas was only trailing the Jewish migrants' path to India that existed before the Christian era.[4] He preached the Gospel and established seven churches on the Malabar Coast. The community grew naturally, through conversions, intermarriages and in-migration. The Christian community emerged from his ministry calls itself St. Thomas Christians (also known as Syrian Christians[5]). From Malabar the saint proceeded to Mylapore, on the Coromandal Coast,[6] where he died as a martyr for the faith at a place near Chennai known as San Thome.[7]

Much controversy was raked up by European scholars on the claim of St. Thomas Christians of the apostolic origin of their Church.[8] But scholars are less skeptical of it at present than they were fifty years ago.[9] Further, in recent times oral histories are taken seriously by historians.[10]

The community has a very strong oral history tradition which highlights their living faith in the past 20 centuries.

Historical records point out evidence of further overseas missions to India. In 345 AD a group of Christians led by Thomas of Cana sent from Edessa, Persia, came and settled in Kerala.[11] In the last quarter of the fifth century, Nestorian missionaries were said to have made attempts to persuade the Indian Christians to accept their doctrines, but failed. The historical evidence regarding the existence of a Church in Kerala can be found in a book written by an Alexandrian merchant Cosmas Indicopleustes (*The Voyage to India), who visited India in the second quarter of the sixth century AD.*[12]

The Venetian traveller Marco Polo (1293), has testified to the missions of John of Monte Corvino, a Franciscan friar (1292-93), Friar Jordan of Toulouse, a Dominican (1302), and John de Marignolli (1348). From the evidence that is available, we may infer that, during this period, the Christians on the Malabar coast established themselves as good traders as well as patriotic soldiers and administrators,[13] and continue to survive till today. The Thomas Christians today comprise the largest segment of the Christian communities in Kerala and India and are presently divided into several denominations (Catholic, Orthodox and Protestant).

0.3. Ancient Christian Missions in Western India

Ancient Christian missions also reached western India. On the Konkan coast the Apostle Bartholomew might have landed in Kalyan, Maharashtra, in about 55 A.D.[14] He preached by word of mouth and by example. News of this Christianity was communicated to the west by the Dominican priest Jourdain (Jordanus) Catalani de Severac in the year 1321.[15] He was the first Latin missionary to arrive in North Konkan.[16] He had reached the shores of India from Persia in the company of four Franciscan Friars, three priests, Frey Thomas of Tolentine, Frey James of Padua, Frey Peter of Sienna and one lay brother Frey Demetrius of Tiflis. These four Franciscans landed in Thana (Thane) where they were martyred a few days later. In the meantime Fr. Jourdain baptized thirty-two catechumens at Sopara,[17] where he found many Nestorian Christians and a church dedicated to St. Thomas, the Apostle. In the earlier periods Christianity was introduced by missionaries or traders belonging to the Eastern Church who did not lay claim to any political power. The inherent spiritual power appealed to the religious faith of the people.[18] However, due to some adverse factors, the contact with the main church was lost and the Christian communities in this area faded into oblivion.[19]

Historical evidences point to the presence of ancient Christianity in other regions in India such as south Konkan,[20] Goa,[21] Fishery Coast,[22] Mylapur, and in Sri Lanka.[23] Unfortunately, all these communities could not survive time, except in Kerala. The Christianity that exists in western India resulted from the modern missionary movement since the sixteenth century.

In early 18th century, a Protestant mission began to work in south India (Tranquenbar) in 1706), whereas in Bengal (Serampore) a mission was started by William Carey in 1793.[24] As for western India Protestant missions began only in early 19th century (1813). As this study focuses on western India, I make a digression here to give a brief overview of the Protestant missions in western India to have a broader view, after which I attempt to give an overview of the Catholic missions in western India and elsewhere in South Asia focusing on the lead role played by the Jesuits since sixteenth century.

0.4. Protestant Missions in Western India: 19th-20th Centuries

The arrival of William Carey in Bengal in 1793 opened a new chapter in the history of Protestant Christianity in India. With him begins, according to Latourette, "a new era in Protestant Missions not only in India, but also in the entire world."[25]

Once the Charter Act of 1813 opened the door for Western missionaries, the first to take advantage of it in western India was the American Board of Commissioners for Foreign Missions whose representatives Samuel Nott and Gorden Hall were already in Bombay in 1812 and were just about to be expelled by Sir Evan Napean, the Governor, when the news of the passing of the Chapter Act of 1813 reached Bombay. Thus the American missionaries were spared and they became pioneers in the introduction of Protestant Christianity in Western India.[26]

The American Mission, later known as the American Marathi Mission, is the oldest Protestant Mission in the Bombay Presidency. Its work started in Bombay in 1813, and one happy outcome was a large proportion of missionaries who were children of missionaries earlier in the field. This mission expanded and opened a centre at Ahmednagar in 1831. As the work at Ahmednagar assumed significance, it came to be divided, for convenience, into two – Bombay and Ahmednagar Missions. The Satara Mission came to be separated from Bombay in 1852. There were a few other missions too.[27]

The American Presbyterian Mission which started its work in Maharashtra at Kolhapur in 1870 under the leadership of R. G. Wilder covered Miraj, Sangli, Nipani, Kodoli, Panhala, Vengurla, Ratnagiri and many surrounding villages. The Methodist Episcopal Church in Maharashtra was founded by William Taylor in Bombay in 1872 which later spread to Poona, Puntamba and to other centres in Maharashtra.[28] The Church Missionary Society (CMS), started in London in 1799, began its work in Bombay in 1818. The Society for the Propagation of the Gospel (SPG) in foreign parts was started in 1701, but came to Bombay in 1827, but it was not until 1859 that a mission was established. The CMS and SPG missions worked at Bombay, Poona, Lonavala, Khandala, Panvel, Igatpuri, Nasik, Aurangabad, Ahmednagar and in the surrounding villages. Nasik, where the CMS established a separate Christian village called Sharanpur became the main centre of its activity in this region. The Church of Scotland Missionary Society, formed in 1796, sent its representative Donald Mitchell to Bombay in 1823, and three others, namely John Cooper, James Mitchell and Alenxder Crawford. The Scottish Mission began its work in Alibag, Thana, Pen, Panvel, Lonavala, Revadanda, Kalyan and Karjat in north Konkan. The mushrooming of missionary societies and religious congregations in Europe and US had its impact in Western India in 19th and 20th centuries.[29]

II

0.5. Christian Missions in India in Modern Times: the Portuguese Period

Christianity entered upon a second stage of its history with the coming of the Portuguese to India in the beginning of the sixteenth century. The Portuguese helped the spread of Catholic Christianity under state support in the Portuguese territories of Bassein, Bombay, Chaul and other places in the Konkan, and also in the coastal towns of south India.

From the beginning, the Portuguese rulers made it clear that they intended to promote Christianity in the territory they controlled. The use of compulsion or force for attaining, what they conceived to be the highest good of those who were outside the Church, was perceived as a mission mandate by the Western Church of those days. The Portuguese method of coercion and persecution which they resorted to for the purpose of winning adherents to the Christian Church form one of the darkest chapters in the history of Christianity in India.[30]

The Portuguese power began to decline by end 17th century. But the Portuguese period, especially from 1534 to 1600, saw the launching of great missionary enterprises. Under the Portuguese *Padroado*[31] (patronage) system several mission societies from Europe such as the Franciscans (arrived in 1500, at Cochin), Dominicans (arrived in 1503, at Cochin, Jesuits (arrived in 1542, in Goa, Augustinians (arrived in 1569 in Goa), etc., were established. Among these the Jesuits played the most prominent role.

0.6. Jesuit Missions, Phase-I (1542-1773)

St. Francis Xavier, the first Jesuit missionary came to India in 1542, at a time when Portuguese were at the zenith of political power. As noted above, by this time the Franciscans and Dominicans who had followed the Portuguese to Cochin came and set up missions in Goa. By 1540s the Franciscans founded residences and churches in Goa Bassein, Salsette, Bombay, Karanja and Chaul. Xavier visited Bassein three times, once in 1544 and twice in 1548, when the foundations of churches and residences were laid, besides a Seminary and a college. The Jesuits built the residence of St. Paul at Daman in 1567, a church in 1580 at Nirmol, a church and residence in 1580 at Chaul, where later there was a college, besides a college at Diu and on the island of Salsette, eight churches. The Jesuits were the first to begin work in Bandra about 1570, and by 1603 the whole place was Catholic.[32] Vigorous evangelisation was undertaken in Goa by the three resourceful missionary societies, the Franciscans, the Dominicans and the Jesuits. The Jesuits among the three were allotted larger areas within the Portuguese controlled areas of Goa.

Xavier and the succeeding Jesuits progressed so well and rapidly that in 1549 the mission was raised to the status of a Province, called Goa Province, with headquarter at Goa. The Jesuit missions outside

India such as of Mozambique, Monamotapa (Transval), Abyssynia, Ormuz, Ceylon, Assam, Pegu, Malaya, The Moluccas, China and Japan were all dependent on the Province of Goa.

In 1580 the Jesuits were invited by Emperor Akbar to his court. Though this mission was short lived, a permanent mission was founded in 1595. They were very well received by Akbar who gave them full liberty to preach the gospel within his empire. Though the main aim of the missionaries was not achieved, the missions did a lot of good in many other ways. Further, mission stations were established in Agra, Fatehpur Sikri, Sambhar, Delhi, Bikaner, Labore and Kabul. Later on they worked also in Jaipur, Marwar, Nagpur, Golconda and Bijapur. For a time there were small Christian communities in many of these parts. But most of these missions were short lived. Towards the end of the century Goa with its 41 establishments manned by 300 Jesuits became the biggest Province of the Society.

Xavier visited Cochin four after his arrival in Goa (1542) and established a mission at Cochin and later he and his successors started mission centres at Cranganur, Vaipincotta, Tanur, Calicut, Tellichery, Quilon, Trivandrum and in a few places on the Fishery Coast such as Vempar, Punnaikayal, Tuticorin, Mylapur, etc. Great conversion movement took place in many of these places such as around Cochin, Quilon, and in the Fishery Coast. The Jesuits had at Vaipincotta a printing press and a seminary; the latter was transferred in 1667 to Ambalakad and in 1731 had about 50 seminarians. There was also a high school at Cochin and another at Cranganore.

In Kerala, the Jesuits were always great friends of the Syrian Christians from the very beginning. The great admiration of St. Francis Xavier for the Syrian Bishop Mar Jacob is recorded in the Saint's own letters. Later on the Fathers of the Society worked incessantly in giving missions to the Syrians and instructing them in the dogmas of the Catholic Church from which they had never formally seceded.[33] However, the Portuguese colonial government-controlled hierarchy's hegemonization over this Eastern Church entailed conflicts and rite-based fissures.[34]

Besides the western and southern coastal regions, the Jesuits established missions in Sri Lanka, and in north east coast of India and beyond: at Hooghly, Dacca, Chittagaong and in lower Burma. The growth of the missions in south India was so much so that in 1602

Malabar was erected a Vice-province with Cochin as its headquarter and in 1605 the Vice-province was made a Province. By 1650, the Malabar Province had larger number of Jesuits and larger number of establishments in Kerala, Fishery Coast, Madurai, Carnatic Region, Bengal, besides Ceylon.

In the interior areas, they opened a Residence in 1599, at Chandragiri, Chitoor District, which was the court of the Emperor of Vijayanagara. This monarch favoured them with his friendship and royal patronage. Some years later when the court was transferred to Vellore, the Jesuits also shifted there. The residence of Chandragiri was the first Catholic mission in the Telugu country.[35] Later, in 1702 Fr. Bouchet, a great French Jesuit missionary, started the Carnatic Mission in the Telugu-speaking region which comprised Pondicherry, Arcot, Chingleput, Karikal, and south Kistna District. By 1750 in spite of the endless wars and famines there were thousands of converts from different castes.[36] The Madurai Mission, though started by Gonsalvo Fernandes in 1595, was revitalised during the first half of the 17th century, by the charismatic Fr. Robert De Nobili, known for his method of adaptation. The Mission became "the masterpiece of the Province of Malabar", under him and his successors.[37]

Jesuits from both Provinces attempted, though severally, to explore China, Tibet and Bhutan. For a quarter of a century some 25 Jesuits were engaged in expedition missions in various parts of South Asia.[38] The two Provinces remained till the Society was suppressed in 1773. Jesuit presence in India during this phase was noted not only for founding mission centres, evangelisation and pastoral service, but for making lasting contributions in scholarly and scientific fields.

0.6.1 Jesuit Contributions: Scholarly and Scientific Works

During this period of Mission history, some well-known Jesuit scholar-missionaries have left lasting contributions to Indian Christian literature, grammar, lexicon, travelogues, etc. The earliest one was Enriguqe Enriquez (1520-1600) who wrote apologetic treatises, a grammar and a lexicon in Tamil, Thomas Stephens (d. 1618) who wrote the classic Christian epic in Marathi-Konkini, *Kristupurana*, Giacome Fenicio (1558-1632), an Italian Jesuit of the Calicut Mission, whose account on Hindu religion and customs was the first ever written in a European language, Robert De Nobili (1577-1656), the first European Sanskrit scholar who could quote from Manusmriti and the Puranas. Henry Roth (1620-1668) who worked at Agra, and was a Sanskrit scholar who made the Western world acquainted with the *Devnagri* script, Manuel Martins (1697-1756) who wrote *Gnana Muthumalai* (The Spiritual Garland of Pearls) and Constantius Beschi who wrote the classic in Tamil, *Thembavani*. There were others: Earnest Hanxlenden (1689-1732), a pundit in Sanskrit and Malayalam, who composed bilingual dictionaries and a grammar and some 12 books, including the famous *Puthenpana* (New Ballad), the equivalent of the *Lamentations* in Malayalam, Peter Lalane (1669-1748) who compiled a good grammar and a lexicon in Telugu, Leonardo Cinnami (1609-1676) who composed a dictionary and grammar in Kannada, Miguel D' Almeida who contributed to Konkani, Archbishop Francis Roz who wrote extensively in Syriac, and Henry Roth who worked at Akbar's Mogul court and wrote in Persian, Arabic, Urdu and Hindustani.[39]

Jesuits of this period also contributed to science, especially astronomy and geography. Their fame was such that King Jai Singh II of Jaipur, the royal astronomer, requested the Superior General of the Jesuits to send some scientist-priests to work in his observatory. Fathers Claude Boudier and John Baptist Pons were sent to the royal court. Boudier's astronomical observations were published in *Observations Mathematiques,* edited in Paris. Later Fathers Gabelsberger and Strobel succeeded Boudier and Pons as directors of the observatories of Jaipur and Delhi.[40] Among the geographers were Father Bouchet who drew up maps and gave descriptions of Madurai and its neighbouring kingdoms and also of Cape Comorin. Similarly, Fr. Thomas Stephens drew the map of Cranganore, Cochin and Goa and Fr. Noel, those of Calicut, Tuticorin and Goa.[41]

The most outstanding Jesuit scientist in North India in the 18th century was Fr. Joseph Tieffenthaller (1710-1785) from Austria. He was a genius and an all-round scholar; for, besides being well versed in such languages as German, Italian, Spanish, French, Latin, Greek and Persian, he was learned in Astronomy, Mathematics, Geography, Natural Sciences and Philosophy. His greatest work is *Historical Geographical Description of India* 2007.[42]

The first modern printing presses were brought to India from Europe by the Jesuits in 1550, and they printed Christian literature in Indian languages since 1556.[43] The Jesuits also maintained some 22 educational institutions in India where students from all over Asia were trained in language, civil and ecclesiastical knowledge.[44] However, all the Jesuit missionary enterprises collapsed with the Suppression of the Society of Jesus in 1773.

0.7. Suppression of the Jesuit Society and Collapse of the Missions

Jesuits were known as 'educators of Europe'. The Society produced great scientists, theologians, thinkers, writers, scholars, linguists, poets, astronomers, geographers, explorers, confessors, advisers to kings, ambassadors of popes, liberators of the oppressed peoples, and thousands of pastors in five continents. Its membership increased rapidly: in 100 years (1640) it had 16,000 members, in 200 years (1740) 22500, and at Suppression (1773) it had 23,000 members. The Society was suppressed on July 21, 1773. This meant the collapse of some 3000 mission centres across the globe, where they were pastorally caring for millions of people; handing over of thousands of Jesuit institutions (universities, colleges, schools and other institutions) to governments or church authorities; and loss of Jesuit identity of 23000 members of whom 12,000 were priests. They ceased to be called Jesuits, but continued to work as non-religious priests in different areas; some left clerical life, some joined other religious societies and so on.[45]

Why was the Jesuit Society suppressed? Among the many unjustified reasons for suppression, the opposition of the Catholic colonizing nations was the most vicious. Though the Jesuits operated under the *Padroado* system supported by the Catholic colonizing countries, they stood up against the colonizers who exploited the native peoples, and defended them in the colonized regions. Spain and Portugal, two Catholic empires which gave patronage to the Jesuits, accused them of encouraging revolutionary actions among the natives in Latin America. Jesuits and Dominicans were leaders in protecting the rights of the natives since the 16th century. Since the mission policy of the Jesuits went against the interest of the colonizing nations, they pressurized the pope to suppress the Society.

When the Society was suppressed the Jesuit establishments were taken over by dioceses or handed over to other religious societies[46] For instance, the mission centres and institutes in the Malabar Province were handed over to the Franciscans who shouldered the additional responsibility for the former Jesuit Missions in Travancore, Calicut,

Fishery Coast, Marava country, Mysore, Raichur and parts of the Carnatic Mission in spite of inadequate personnel.[47] Eventually, when the Franciscans suffered acute personnel crunch, these Missions suffered much. Similarly, the former mission areas of the Jesuits in the Dioceses of Cochin and Cranganur were given to other Religious Orders: Mysore was given to the Oratorians and the Seculars; Raichur Mission was given to the Dominicans; and the Augustinians were given the former Jesuit centres in Diu and Daman.[48]

According to Coreia-Affonso, a great tragedy of the Society was that it overly depended on European members. Hence when the ties with Europe was broken, no solid structure was left standing on the foundations of native rock. The failure to implant and establish the Church, the Hierarchy and the Society, through sons of the soil, cannot be explained away, and is to be greatly regretted. If this was the principal unsuccess of the Jesuits in India, there were also others. These include the inability to reconcile the Thomas Christians firmly to the Roman Catholic Church, the perpetuation of the caste system within the same, and the lack of overall planning and concerted effort.[49]

Teotonio de Souza remarks that "whatever may have been the compulsion of history, the Society of Jesus has played a prominent role in helping many in India, as elsewhere, to rise and face more adequately the oppressions and challenges of history, through their pastoral and educational activities."[50]

At the close of the 18th century, Roman Catholic Christianity was in decay and the outlook was very grim, partly because of the orphaning of the Missions after the Suppression of the Jesuits and partly because of the declining power of the Portuguese.[51] But Jesuits were not finished yet. They were back in India in 1834, dawn of their Second Spring.

On the other hand, the period saw the entry of European Protestant missionaries into the Mission field. Overall, while the 16-18th centuries saw vigorous Catholic missionary movements, the 19th and 20th centuries saw vibrant Protestant missionary ventures in India.

III

0.8. Jesuit Missions: Phase-II, Re-entry of Jesuits since mid 19th Century

The Restoration of the Jesuit Society in 1814 and re-entry of the Jesuit Missions in South Asia in 1834 was characterized by more discontinuities than continuities. Continuity can be seen in its inheriting certain super-structures such as the basic spirit and charism of the Society, the directions of the Constitution of the Society and certain organizational arrangements. Discontinuities were more vivid as none of the pre-Suppression institutions, colonial patronage, territory of operation, etc., was restored to the Restored Society in South Asia.[52]

0.8.1. Factors that Triggered the Re-entry

There were many factors which triggered the Restoration of the Society in South Asia. First, the vigorously expanding restored Society in Europe wanted to work overseas and South Asia offered ample opportunities.[53] Secondly, the mandate and encouragement of Pope Gregory XVI helped missionary societies to found overseas missions. Thirdly, the critical pastoral situation in Tamil Nadu warranted the return of Jesuits in Madurai.[54] Similarly in Patna Mission, there was apparently a threat by the colonial Government to hand over to the Protestants, the Austrian Catholic Capuchin Mission in Bihar (the Austrian Capuchins were interned as enemy subjects by the British Government during World War I). This led the American Jesuits to shoulder the responsibility for Patna Mission.[55] Fourthly, the pleas of the laity for modern missionary educators (Calicut-Mangalore Mission,[56] Bombay, and Calcutta) were compelling reasons for opening Jesuit Missions in these regions. Fifthly, Jesuit missionaries were invited by Local Ordinaries to offset the domineering presence of the Protestants (Bombay Mission). Sixthly, some of the Local Ordinaries perceived that Jesuits could train the local clergy better.

Invariably, the neglected pastoral ministry after the Suppression cried for zealous pastors of the Jesuit Society. In many cases, there was a combination of compelling reasons: pastoral and educational. Similarly, replacement of mission personnel in some Missions by Jesuits from other Provinces was due to certain crisis situations as for instance, the internment of the Germans precipitated the coming of the Spanish Jesuits in Bombay Mission.[57] Lack of adequate personnel in one Province also made it to hand over a part of the mission area to some other Jesuit Provinces creating new Missions.

In South Asia, the Society was called to work in their former mission areas only in some cases but in most cases, in new mission areas. Those who were called to work in the old mission areas had to face jurisdictional conflicts created by the Padroado authorities as for instance, in the diocese of Calcutta, Mylapore and Bombay.[58] In Bengal, though invited by the local bishop, the Irish, English and French Jesuit pioneers who came in 1834 were caught in a conflict situation due to the Padroado Bishop of Calcutta. Unable to suffer public affronts, they closed down the Mission in 1846.[59] However, when the Belgian Jesuits came to work in Bengal (2nd Bengal Mission) in 1859, the Vicariate of Calcutta was handed over to them which made it easier for them to work and develop the second Bengal Mission.[60]

Similarly, after the Suppression, parts of the former Madurai Mission was handed over to the Pondicherry Mission of the Society of the Foreign Missions of Paris (called MEP) under whom the ex-Jesuits continued to work from 1777. The MEP was given authority over Madurai, Tanjore and Mysore Missions[61] of the pre-Suppression Society. There were objections to this from the Padroado authorities of Goa, Mylapore and Crangannur (Kodungallur, Kerala). The pre-Suppression Mission of Mysore was ecclesiastically under the Padroado Archdiocese of Crangannur, but the Jesuits of Goa Province had supplied the resources and personnel. So also, some parts of the Madurai Mission belonged to the Crangannur Archdiocese, whereas some parts belonged to Mylapore Diocese. Hence, when the French Jesuits came to work in 1838 in Madurai Mission, they were caught between the Propaganda and Padroado authorities.[62] Due to the opposition of the Padroado authorities of the Diocese of Mylapore, the MEP Mission Superior was not given the title of Vicar-Apostolic, but he functioned as Ecclesiastical Superior. And the Jesuits obediently and harmoniously worked under them hoping that eventually their former Madurai Mission would be restored. But it did not happen immediately. Independent areas were assigned to them only much later. In all the other Missions the Restored Society was assigned new areas such as in Mangalore-Calicut, Galle, Goa, Trincomalle, and Patna.

In Bombay, when the German Jesuits came to work in 1858, at the invitation of the Capuchin Bishop Anastasius Hartmann (formerly

Vicar Apostolic of Patna), the Padroado clergy and the laity harassed the Bishop and created problems.[63] But the Bishop patiently managed the situation and ensured that Bombay Vicariate along with Poona Vicariate should be handed over to the Jesuits. Hence the German Jesuits were able to begin the ministry of the Society in the newly founded Bombay-Poona Mission,[64] which later developed the Ahmedabad Mission.

However, when World War 1 broke out the German Fathers were interned and later repatriated. The Mission was now handed over to the Spanish Jesuits of the Aragon Province who devoted their attention to the promotion of vocations both to the diocesan clergy and the Society. As a result with the exception of a few stations still manned by the Jesuits, the Archdiocese is run by the diocesan clergy.[65]

When the Spanish mother Province was divided, the territory of Ahmedabad was handed over to the Fathers of the Province of East Castille while the Bombay Mission became the Bombay Province under the charge of the Tarragona Province.[66] Poona Mission was detached and handed over to the Upper German Province, after the German Jesuits were allowed to return to India, along with the Swiss Jesuits who were already in that area.[67] The entire narrative in this book is an in-depth study of the Poona Mission.

0.8.2. Eight Independent Mission Foundations

While the India Mission of the pre-Suppression period, founded by St. Francis Xavier in 1542, began as a single mission unit which developed into two Provinces, the post-Restoration missions in South Asia were established as extension missions of different Jesuit Provinces of Europe and were independent foundations.

As noted above, the Restored Society first began its operations in South Asia with the founding of the Bengal Mission in Calcutta in 1834, but was closed down in 1846.[68] Thereafter, eight Missions (Madurai (1838), Bombay (1858), 2nd Bengal (1859), Mangalore-Calicut (1878), Goa (1890), Galle (1893), Trincomallee (1895) and Patna (1919) were established in South Asia during the period from 1838-1919, a period of 80 years[69] These were established by different European Provinces: Madurai by French Toulouse Province, Bombay by Upper German Province, 2nd Bengal by Belgium Province, Calicut-Mangalore by Italian (Venice-Milan Province), Goa by the Portugal Province, Galle (Sri

Lanka) by Belgian Province and Trincomalle (Sri Lanka) by Champagne (French) Province, and Patna, by Missouri (USA) Province.[70]

As ministries expanded geographically which covered more communities, parts of some of the eight original Missions were handed over to volunteering Provinces of Europe, America, Australia and Canada. Thus, the Santal Mission of the Bengal Mission was entrusted (1924) to the Maltese Jesuits of the Sicily Province,[71] the Singhbhum District of the same Mission was handed over (1947) to the American Jesuits of Maryland Province[72] and Darjeeling and Sikkim were handed over to the Canadian Jesuits (1950).[73] The Palamau District area was given over (1952) to the Australian Jesuits[74] by the Ranchi Mission which itself had emerged as an independent Mission from Bengal Mission in 1935.[75] Some Yogoslavian Jesuits helped out (1927) in the 24 Parganas District of the Bengal Mission.[76] Some more European Provinces came to supplement personnel or take charge of the missions. For instance, in Sri Lanka, while the New Orleans Jesuits came (1924) to help out in Galle, Neapolitan Jesuits came (1933) to help out in Trincomalle.[77] Eventually the latter shouldered the full responsibility (1939) of the combined Sri Lanka Mission.

Overall, Jesuits belonging to some 15 foreign nationalities along with native Jesuits had worked to develop the Society in South Asia. The present-day 21 Province/Region units of the Society in South Asia have emerged and expanded from the original eight Missions.

It may be noted that unlike in the pre-Suppression period when the Catholic Missions in South Asia were supported and controlled by the Portuguese Padroado, the Restored Jesuit Missions were under the authority of the *Propaganda Fide*[78] of the Vatican.

0.8.3. Further Expansion of the Missions

Gradually, after the 1950s, the South Asian Missions expanded to include further areas in the sub-continent for their missionary outreach. The Karnataka Province opened a Mission in Nagaland in 1970, which has developed to become the Kohima Region.[79] The Kerala Province opened a Mission in Mizoram (Lunglei, which was later incorporated into the local diocese), the Madurai Province expanded to Andhra Pradesh (1953) which developed as the Andhra Province.[80] The Bombay-Poona Mission developed the Ahmedabad Mission (1893) which eventually became the Gujarat Mission (1934) and Province.[81]

The Ranchi Mission further expanded missions in Chattisgarh (begun in 1907), formerly part of Madhya Pradesh State. As mission centres and ministries expanded, this mission developed into a separate Madhya Pradesh Province in 1992.[82] The Ranchi Jesuits are trailing the paths of the pre-Suppression Jesuit pioneers in the Andaman and Nicobar Islands,[83] and have established several mission centres in Assam,[84] Darjeeling Region expanded its ministry to Bhutan,[85] Calcutta Province did so to Bangladesh and Sri Lanka to Pakistan in recent years. Patna Mission opened two extensions within India--a school at Jaipur (1942) and another in Delhi (1959), a third extension outside India, at Godavari, Nepal (1951). The Nepal Mission eventually became an independent Nepal Region,[86] and the Jaipur and Delhi Jesuit communities were incorporated into the North-West Project of the South Asian Assistancy to became Delhi Region (1988) and later the Delhi Province (2005).[87] Besides, some Provinces sent missionaries to a few missions in Africa, Americas and other parts of Asia. The South Asian Conference itself has shouldered the responsibility to expand its ministry to Afghanistan.

0.8.4. Ministries of the Restored Society

The Jesuits in the Restored Society engaged in various ministries some of which were in response to particular contexts. They engaged in pastoral works including parish/mission station management, taking care of the pastoral needs of the Catholics through preaching, Sodality of Mother Mary, devotion to the Sacred Heart, Apostleship of Prayer, Eucharistic Crusade, retreat preaching, and preaching to non-Christians, etc. Jesuit work among the marginalised groups (Dalits and Tribals) saw mass conversion movements particularly in the Missions of Ranchi (including Madhya Pradesh/Chattisgarh), Gujarat, Patna, Dumka, and Hazaribagh.[88] Certain marginalized communities responded through group conversions in Bombay Mission (Katkari, Zaroli and Talassari missions), Pune Mission (Sangamner and Ahmednagar centres), Madurai Mission, Calicut Mission (Chirackal Mission),[89] etc.

In the educational field, from the beginning, they engaged in school education at all levels, besides in technical and higher education. Today nearly 81 institutions of higher education (2 universities, 14 autonomous colleges, 25 colleges, 11 management institutes, 11 colleges of education, 4 engineering colleges, 3 law colleges and 11 research institutes), besides 380 schools, are run by the South Asian Jesuits. They are engaged in traditional charitable and social works, which, in the past three decades, have been re-oriented strategically and structurally into social action service with more focus on conscientisation, campaign, capacity building, advocacy and community development. This ministry received much impetus since mid 1970s after the 32nd General Congregation (the apex decision-making assembly of the Society) which focused on "option for the poor".

In the ministry of the Word they have produced substantial amount of Christian literature through printing and publishing books, booklets, scholarly journals, popular and devotional magazines, etc. In late 19th and early 20th centuries, tremendous amount of Catholic literature was produced.

The Jesuits in the modern phase also have contributed substantially in scholarly writings in various disciplines.[90] Some of these are: Richard De Smet, Pierre Johanns, Pierre Fallon, Robert Antoine, Dandoy, Bayart, William Wallace, Georg Gispert-Sauch, Ignatius Puthiadam, Noel Sheth, Anand Amaladass, Ishanand Vempany, John Feys, John Vattanky (indology/Sanskrit);[91] Vito Pemiola (Pali), Camille Bulcke (Hindi), Carlos Valles (Gujarati), Caridade Drago, Christopher Shelke (Marathi), Abraham Adappur (Malayalam), Mathew Almeida, Pratap Naik (Konkini),[92] Mathew Lederle (Indian Christian Art); et al. They have also contributed eminently in science: Louis Anglade, Alfred Rapinat, Leo D'Souza, Hermegild Santapau, Cecil Saldhanha, K. M. Mathew, V. S. Manickam, Lourdu Yeddenapalli, Ignacimuthu, et al.[93]

Another significant contribution has been training of native clergy and Church leaders through ecclesiastical institutes, major seminaries, apostolic schools, novitiates, philosophates, theologates, catechist training centres, pastoral institutes, etc., some of which have been handed over to the diocesan authorities in recent years. They engaged in humanitarian works such as running orphanages, providing relief and organizing rehabilitation of the affected people during natural calamities. The Jesuits collaborated with women congregations to manage health care ministry and ministry to women, and with the laity in diverse ministries.[94]

0.9. Conclusion: Re-structuring and Re-orienting for 21st Century

The Jesuit Society in South Asia presently consisting of 21 Provinces/ Regions, is organisationally structured as one continental unit

(Assistancy) called Jesuit Conference of South Asia (JCSA), which is one of the twelve Assistances into which the world-wide Society of Jesus is divided for purposes of administration. The largest Assistancy having over 4000 member Jesuits, it was established in 1976, with headquarters in New Delhi, with a Major Superior as President. The President of JCSA is entrusted with the care of the Common Works (presently 11 institutes), mostly for religious formation and intellectual and social ministry.

One can discern discontinuities of certain policies and practices and new orientations in the Jesuit Society. The first missionaries of the original eight missions came from Europe and America. Further missionaries came from Europe, America, Canada and Australia. Over the years native members were recruited from India and other countries in South Asia. This policy helped increase the number of Jesuits in each Mission/Province which enabled them to expand the ministries to newer and larger areas. However, some Missions began to actively foster native vocations only after Indian Independence as the continued arrival of foreign missionaries to India was restricted by the Government of India. In the same manner handing over administrative responsibilities to native Jesuits largely began only after the Independence and not without much hesitation. In planting the Society locally and making it self-sufficient by recruiting natives, the foreign Jesuits of the 19th century, with one exception, seem to have learnt the bitter lesson from the pre-Suppression Society which never fostered native vocations in South Asia.[95]

The structure of operation in the 21st century has been changing: inter-provincial networking in advocacy and action programmes on issues of national and global concerns ranging from human rights, especially of marginalized sections of society with a mission project among the refugees in Afghanistan, and of eco-rights of planet Earth. With the fast declining membership in European Jesuit Society, the Jesuits of South Asia are being recognised and challenged to shoulder global responsibility.

To attain the goals of the Society in the 21st century, it seems certain new orientations have been initiated. Education was not only to raise the moral standards of the people, but was employed as a tool of empowerment of the poor. In the post-1980 period, thanks to the 32nd General Congregation, the Society underwent a radical re-orientation in its understanding of the world reality of inequality and injustice, its approach and style of functioning and scope of ministries, in order to re-focus itself to live its ideals. Thanks to the heroic leadership of Pedro Arrupe, Superior General of the Society (1965-83), the new Society took lead roles in networking with global non-governmental organizations for humanitarian action such as the world-wide Jesuit Refugee Service and to create an eco-friendly earth. Scores of social action centres were established to translate the ideals of the General Congregation, namely 'service of faith and promotion of justice' to create a more humane and just society.

Endnotes and References

1 For instance, see Samuel H. Moffett. *A History of Christianity in Asia, Vol.I & II* (San Francisco: Harper Collins, 1992); Robert E. Frykenberg, *Christianity in India: From Beginnings to the Present* (New York: Oxford University Press, 2008).

2 To cite as examples, Dick Kooiman, *Conversion and Social Equality in India: The London Missionary Society in South Travancore in the 19th Century* (New Delhi: Manohar Publishers, 1989); G. A. Oddie (ed), *Religion in South Asia: Religious Conversion and Revival Movements in South Asia in Medieval and Modern Times* (New Delhi: Manohar Publishers, 1991).

3 George Mark Moraes, *A History of Christianity in India from Early times to St. Francis Xavier: AD 52-1552* (Bombay: Manaktalas, 1964), 25.

4 It is well-known that some Jews from Palestine had migrated to India (Cochin) after the Roman occupation of Palestine in 63 BCE. Based on archaeological, anthropological and etymological evidences, Abraham Benhur says that some of the first converts in Kerala were Jews: See Abraham Benhur, *The Jewish Background of Indian People: a Historical Study* (Calicut: Jeevanist Books, 2011).

5 'St. Thomas Christians' was the name usually applied to these people who in modem times are known as Syrian Christians, on account of their connection with the Syriac-speaking Churches in the East, and the use of Syriac as their liturgical language.

6 A. C. Perumalil, *The Apostles in India* (Patna: Catholic Book Crusade, 1952), 71.

7 Arab merchant Suleiman mentioned this in 851 AD: C. E. Abraham, "The Rise and Growth of Christianity in India" in *Cultural-Religious Heritage-India,* Vol. 8, (ed.) Suresh K Sharma & Usha Sharma (New Delhi: Mittal Publications, 2004), 18.

8 Mathias Mundadan, C.M.I, *Indian Christians in Search for Identity & Struggle for Autonomy* (Bangalore: Dharmaram Publications, 1984).

9 Benedict Vadakkekara, *Origin of India's St.Thomas Christians, (A Historiographical Critique)* (New Delhi: Media House, 1995; George Nedungatt, SJ, *Quest for the Historical Thomas Apostle of India: A Re-reading of the Evidence* (Bangalore: Theological Publications in India, 2008).

10 For instance, many tribal or indigenous communities have only oral traditions. Can we deny that they existed on this earth for thousands of years before the historical periods? See Laurice Mercier & Madeline Buckendorf, *Using Oral History in Community History Projects* (New York: Oral History Association, Pamphlet Series, No. 4, 1992).

11 Perumalil, op. cit, 150.

12 Permalil, H. C. & E. R. Hambye, *Christianity in India: A History in Ecumenical Perspective* (Alleppey: Prakasam Publications, 1972).

13 Observations of John de Marignolli, who stayed at Quilon for over a year: see D. Ferroli, S. J. *The Jesuits in Malabar,* Vol. I, (Bangalore: The National Press, 1951), 66.

14 M. D. David, *Missions: Cross-Cultural Encounter and Change in Western India* (Delhi: ISPCK, 2001), 27.

15 Moraes, op. cit. 73, 92-102.

16 Aiyangar S., "History of The Syrian Church" *The Quarterly Journal of the Mythic Society* Vol. 3, No. 4, 1912: 138.

17 Sopara refers to present day NalaSopara in Mumbai.

18 Oomman Philip, "Christianity in India-Retrospect" *The Indian Review* Vol. 46. No. 2, February 1945: 76.

19 *Catholic Directory of the Archdiocese of Bombay*, 3rd Edition (Bombay: Ahura Printing Press, 1982), 1-2.

20 Elsie Baptista, *The East Indians: Catholic Community of Bombay, Salsette and Bassein, Bandra*, (Bombay: The Bombay East Indian Association, 1967).

21 Scholars have brought out evidences on the presence of ancient Christianity in Goa. But there has not been a continuous living tradition there.

22 Thomas, N. A., *Asiayile Marthoma Sabhakal* (Malayalam-*Mar Thoma Churches in Asia*), Vol. I & II (Trivandrum: Jaya Matha Bhawan, 1982 & 1985): a well-researched work showing archaeological proofs of Christian presence in Fishery Coast.

23 Recent research has shown that Syrian Christian presence was there in the principality of Anaradhapura, north Sri Lanka, which declined due to Buddhist onslaught around 500 AD.

24 Danish mission led by Ziegenbalg and Plutsch: Neeta M. Khandpekar, Dr., *The Christian Missionaries in Coastal Maharashtra* (New Delhi: Christian World Imprints, 2015), 27.

25 G. D. Bearce, *British Attitudes Towards India 1784-1858* (London: OUP, 1961), quoting Kenneth Scott Latourette *A History of the Expansion of Christianity*, Vol. VI, (London: Paternoster Press, 1940), 36.

26 M. D. David, op. cit., 41.

27 Khandpekar, op. cit., 81.

28 David, op. cit., 41-42.

29 Khandpekar, op. cit., 27.

30 Ibid., 10.

31 *Padroado* is the Portuguese term for patronage. Pope Paul III granted (1534) this right to the kings of Portugal as a reward for their sustained efforts in providing men and money to evangelize the countries of Africa and Asia. It implied the rights to nominate candidates to ecclesiastical offices as well as the duty to spread the Christian faith in the areas in question. For an exhaustive study on the Padroado in India, see Ernest R. Hull, SJ, *Bombay Mission History: with a Special Study on the Padroado Question, 1534-1858*, Vol. I & 1858-1890, Vol. II (Bombay: Examiner Press, 1927 & 1930).

32 Henry Heras, SJ, "The Jesuits in India before the Suppression of the Order", in *In Xavier's Footsteps* 1540-1940, *Souvenir of the 4th Centenary of the Society of Jesus* (hereafter, *Xavier's Footsteps*), Fr. A. M. Espasa (ed.), (Anand: Anand Press, 1940), 13-15.

33 Ibid., 18.

34 Jonas Thaliath, *The Synod of Diamper* (Roma: Pontifica Institute Orientalium Stuiorum, 1958).

35 Heras, op. cit., 20.

36 Joe Sebastian, SJ, *The Jesuit Carnatic Mission: A Foundation of Andhra Church* (Secunderabad: Jesuit Province Society, 2004).

37 Heras, op. cit., 19.

38 C. Wessels, S. J., *Early Jesuit Travellers in Central Asia, 1603-1721* (the Hague: Martinus Nijhoff, 1924), reprint New Delhi: Asian Educational Services, 1992).

39 Jose Kalapura, "Christian Contribution to Language and Literature, 16-19th Centuries", *Indian Church History Review* Vol. 51, No. 2, July 2017: 29-57.

40 Jose Kalapura, "Church and Science Mission: Jaipur King and Jesuit Astronomers, 18th Century", *Indian Church History Review* Vol. XLVII, No. 1, June 2013: 17-37.

41 Fr. Alex Ekka, "Jesuit Education in India: Struggles and Promises", *Jharkhand Journal of Development and Management Studies* Vol. 5, No. 3, July-Sept 2007: 2499.

42 Jose Kalapura, "The Mapping of Hindustan: A Forgotten Geographer of India, Joseph Tieffenthaler (1710-1785) (Bangalore: *Proceedings of the Indian History Congress*, 58th Session, Bangalore University, 1997): 400-410.

43 Jose Kalapura, "India Inscribed: Development of Printing Technology in India, 16-18th Centuries," (Delhi: *Proceedings of the Indian History Congress, 68th Session,* Delhi University, 2007): 436-463.

44 Chacko Marattukalam, SJ, "The Jesuits and Education in India," in *Catholic and Indian Education,* St. Ignatius Loyola, 4th Centenary Death Jubilee (Thrichinopoly: St. Joseph's Industrial Press, 1956), 158-172.

45 Much of the gains in India had been lost since the Suppression. Despite the efforts of the Foreign Mission Society of Paris to replace the exiled Jesuits, the chaotic and disturbed conditions in France blocked the way. Between 1777 and 1792 they sent only three priests to India; between 1792 and 1820 not one: see Jose Kalapura, S.J, "Suppression and Restoration of the Jesuit Society in South Asia: An Historical overview," (hereafter, *Suppression-Jesuits), Indian Church History Review* Vol. 53, No. 2, July 2019): 60.

46 Ibid: 63.

47 Achilles Meersman, OFM, *The Ancient Franciscan Provinces in India* (Bangalore: Christian Literature Society Press, 1971), 485-550; Archilles Meersman, OFM, "The Mysore Mission During the Period Subsequent to the Suppression Decree of 1759", *Indian Church History Review*, Vol. IX No. 2, (Dec 1975): 147-159.

48 Meersman, OFM, *The Ancient Franciscan Provinces,* op. cit., 536-541.

49 John Correia-Afonso, S.J., *The Jesuits in India 1542-1773* (Anand: Gujarat Sahitya Prakash, 1997), 270.

50 quoted in Ibid., 271.

51 Jose Kalapura (ed), *Christian Missions in Bihar and Jharkhand* till 1947: A Study by P. C. Horo (Delhi: Christian World Imprints & Ranchi: Gossner Theological College, 2014), xxxii.

52 Kalapura, *Suppression-Jesuits*, op. cit, 65.

53 Ibid., 67.

54 There were instances of Catholics leaving their Church and joining Protestant groups: see Thomas Anchukandam, SDB, "The Return of the Jesuits to India and the Establishment

of the Vicariate Apostolic of Madurai – the MEP Factor (1837-1847)," *Indian Church History Review* Vol. XLVI, No. 1, (June 2012): 27-52.

55 Henry Pascual Oiz, S. J., *Blessed by the Lord; A History of the Patna Jesuits* (Patna: St. Xavier's, 1991).

56 *Karnataka Jesuit Centenary, Souvenir* (Bangalore: Loyola Mandir, 1978).

57 Kalapura, *Suppression-Jesuits*, op. cit, 68.

58 Ibid., 66.

59 Udayan Namboodiry, *St. Xavier's: The Making of a Calcutta Institution* (New Delhi: Viking/Penguin India, 1995), 1-23; Henri Josson, SJ, *Bengal Mission, 16th century to 1858* (hereafter, *Bengal Mission-I)*, (tr) Albert Huart, SJ (Kolkata: Calcutta Province of the Society of Jesus, 2014).

60 Henri Josson, SJ, *History of the 'Bengal' Mission: 1858 to 1920* (hereafter, *Bengal Mission-II*), (tr) Huart SJ and L. Clarysse, SJ (Anand: Gujarat Sahitya Prakash, 2009).

61 Lourdu Prasad Joseph, "The Jesuit Mission in Mysore between Expulsion 1759 and Suppression 1773," in *Studies on the History of Church in India,* ed. Joy Kaipan, SDB (Bangalore: Kristu Jyoti Publications, 2011), 54-76.

62 Kalapura, *Suppression-Jesuits,* op. cit, 67; Anchukandam, op. cit.

63 Jose Kalapura, "Heroic Church Leadership: Bishop Hartmann of Patna, Bombay and Poona," *Indian Church History Review* Vol. XLVI, No. 1, (June 2012): 53-68.

64 Joseph Velinkar, SJ, *German Jesuits on the West Coast of India* (Pune: Pune Jesuit Society, 2004).

65 *Karnataka Jesuit Centenary,* op. cit., 117.

66 Ibid.

67 Velinkar, op. cit., 64-77; *Reise*: *The 150-year Journey of the Jesuits of the German and Swiss Provinces in India* (Pune: Pune Jesuit Province, 2004).

68 There is very little data about this Bengal Mission as it was wound up after 12 years. One gets a brief description about this mission in Namboodiry, op. cit. Another source is Henri Josson, *Bengal Mission-I*, op. cit.

69 See *Xavier's Footsteps,* op. cit.

70 Kalapura, *Suppression-Jesuits*, op. cit, 66.

71 Jos M. Gauci Sacco, SJ, ed., *The Santal Mission, 1925-2009: Origins, Profiles and Highlight,* (Dumka: Dumka Jesuit Society, 2010).

72 James V. Keogh, SJ, *Surprised by Grace: A History of the Jamshedpur Province,* Vol. I (1948-88), Jubilee Publication (Jamshedpur: Jamshedpur Jesuit Society, 1998).

73 Yves de Steenhault, S. J. *History of the Jesuits in West Bengal* (hereafter, *Jesuits-Bengal*) Part II (Ranchi: Catholic Press, (n. d)), 51-54, 159-175; Josson, SJ, *Bengal Mission-II,* op. cit. 123-147.

74 Kevin Cronin, SJ, *In Ever-increasing Measure: Hazaribagh Jesuits 1951-2001, A Celebratory History* (Ranchi: Catholic Press, 2001).

75 Henri Josson, SJ, *The Mission of West Bengal or The Archdiocese of Calcutta: Belgian Province of the Society of Jesus* (Ranchi: Catholic Press, 1993); Josson, SJ, *Bengal Mission-II,* op. cit., 101-121, 277-339; T. Van Der Schueren, SJ, *The Belgian Mission of Bengal Part-I, II, III* (Calcutta: Thacker, Spink & Co., 1922).

76 Yves de Steenhault, SJ, *Jesuits-Bengal,* Part I (Ranchi: Catholic Press, (n.d)), 58-65; Also, Steenhault, SJ, *Jesuits-Bengal* Part II, op. cit., 176-199.

77 Father S. G. Pereira, SJ, *The Jesuits of Ceylon*, (2nd edn) (Ontario: Humanics Universal Inc, 2006).

78 *Congregation de Fide Propaganda* (in short, *Propaganda Fide*): Sacred Congregation for Propagation of Faith, established in 1622 by Pope Gregory XV, is the department of the pontifical administration charged with the spread of Catholicism and with the regulation of ecclesiastical affairs in non-Catholic countries.

79 S. Coelho, SJ, *Even to the North-East: The Story of the Jesuits in Nagaland* (Kohima: Jesuits in Nagaland, 1984).

80 Fr. Gordon, "The Jesuit Presence in Andhra Pradesh," in *Recall, Renew, Respond: 150 Years of Jesuit Presence in Madurai Mission* (Madurai: Provincial House, 1988), 46-53.

81 Carlos Suria, SJ, *History of the Catholic Church in Gujarat* (Anand: Gujarat Sahitya Prakash, 1990), 57-68, 89-104.

82 Agapit Tirkey, Antony Parappullil, Stany Tirkey, Vincent Ekka, and Isaac Kujur, *History of the Madhya Pradesh Jesuit Province, 1905-2014* (Bilaspur: Madhya Pradesh Province of the Society of Jesus, 2014).

83 Jesuits had visited Andamans in the pre-Suppression period too. See *Silver Jubilee Souvenir of Stella Maris Cathedral, 1987-2012* (Port Blair: Stella Maris Cathedral, 2012).

84 Xavier Lakra, SJ, "The Assam Mission," in *Ranchi Jesuits Year Book 2015* (Ranchi: Ranchi Jesuit Society, 2015), 88-91.

85 Steenhault, *Jesuits-Bengal,* Part II, op. cit, 51-54, 159-175; Josson, *Bengal Mission-II*, op. cit. 123-147.

86 Roy Sebastian (ed), *Placed with the Son in Nepal: 50 years, Golden Jubilee Souvenir* (Kathmandu: Nepal Jesuit Society, 2001).

87 Augustine Perumalil (ed), *Aflame with Love, Eager to Serve: A Short History of the Delhi Province* (Jaipur: St. Xavier's College, 2013).

88 See *Xavier's Footsteps,* op. cit.

89 Kalapura, *Suppression-Jesuits*, op. cit, 72.

90 Jesuit theologians started the famous journal *Light of the East*, from St. Mary's College, Kurseong, to articulate their appreciation of Indian traditions in Christian theology. Jesuits contributed much to indological studies and study of Sanskrit thanks to the 'Calcutta School of Indologists': see Anand Amaladass, "Jesuits and Sanskrit Studies," in *Jesuits in India: in Historical Perspective* (hereafter, *Jesuits-Historical Perspective*) eds. Teotonio R. de Souza & Charles J. Borges (Macau: Instituto Cultural de Macau & Goa: Xavier Centre of Historical Research, 1992), 226-227.

91 Ibid, 227-232.

92 Mathew Almeida, "Jesuit Contribution to Indian Languages", in *Jesuits-Historical Perspective*, ibid., 197-207.

93 Job Kozhamthadam, "Jesuit Contribution to Science in India", *Vidyajyoti Journal of Theological Reflection*, Vol. 68, No. 12, 2004: 892-916.

94 Ulahannan, S. J. (ed), *Jesuit Survey: Report on the Indian Assistancy* (New Delhi: Indian Social Institute, 1969).

95 Kalapura, *Suppression-Jesuits*, op. cit, 76.

Chapter-1

Tracing the History of Bombay-Poona Mission

1.1. Introduction

The Jesuit missionary project known as the Bombay-Poona Mission (B-PM), launched by German and Swiss Jesuits, began in mid-19th century, in the year 1854 to be precise. The specific aim of the Mission, as indicated by the inviting Bishop Anastasius Hartmann of Bombay, was to give modern education to the Catholics and others in Bombay. The development of an educational system in order to achieve the purpose of uplifting the socio-economic status of the Catholic community formed one of the primary concerns of the Mission.[1] Till World War I (1914), the basic engagement of the Mission was educational and pastoral service mostly among the urban population in Bombay and Poona. However, in the last decades of the 19th century mission works in rural areas also started. In terms of geographical expansion as well as consolidation of works, the Mission had achieved considerable growth within the first fifty years, notwithstanding numerous challenges. But World War I (1914-19) dealt a heavy blow to the same. A number of German missionaries were either interned in the camps as prisoners of war or repatriated to their homeland. This crippled the missionary work severely because of which a large number of the Jesuits in the Mission began to nurture a

1 See Alfons Vath, Die deutschen Jesuiten in Indien: Geschichte der Mission von Bombay:-Puna (1854-1920) (Regensburg: Jos. Kosel & Friedrich Pustet, 1920), 58-60; Ernest R. Hull, Bombay Mission History: With a Special Study of the Padroado Question (Bombay: Examiner Press, 1927), 476; Gense, The Church at the Gateway of India, 1720-1960 (Bombay: St. Xavier's College, 1960), 165-181.

strong sense of pessimism about their future. The Mission, thanks to the unflinching courage of some of the remaining Jesuits, was saved in spite of the formidable hardships on the road. The Swiss Jesuits played a significant role in this regard, but there were Jesuits from other neutral nations too. Were it not for these courageous and untiring Jesuits who worked with unparalleled enthusiasm and energy, the Mission would probably have taken an entirely different course or even would have got lost. This claim is true to a greater degree in the context of World War I, although the German Jesuits in the Mission had to suffer internment again during World War II.

In the history of B-P M, the decade immediately subsequent to World War I (i.e., 1920s) was noted as a decade of survival and sustenance with limited number of missionaries. However, the second decade (i.e., 1930s) can be considered as a decade of consolidation and expansion, although not many new stations and institutions were established during this period. Apparently the problem of lack of personnel still persisted in spite of the fact that the Jesuits continued to return to the mission field in small groups by 1920s. Notwithstanding the hardships, a considerable amount of work was done towards consolidation of the Mission. Hardly had the Mission emerged out of the shock of World War I, World War II (1939) broke out giving a second blow to it. However, the latter shock seems to have been relatively less severe as compared to the former one, for none of the Jesuit missionaries were repatriated to their homelands as had been the case during World War I. Instead, a good majority of them were taken into internment camps and that too for a much lesser span of time. However, some negative impacts had taken place.

By 1940s, i.e., by the time World War II was over, a number of new developments were witnessed both in the Indian political scenario as well as in the history of the mother Province in Germany. The Poona Mission, though bifurcated from B-PM in 1929, was directly under the Southern German Province and had to face new challenges. It may be noted that in the year when India gained freedom from the British rule (1947), the Swiss Jesuit Mission back home was erected as Swiss Jesuit Vice-Province. This meant not only the challenges of developing an independent Province but also continuing the development of Poona Mission entrusted to it. The future security, method of work, etc., were uncertain to the foreign missionaries working in independent India. New approaches and strategies had to be adopted. It was during this phase that the members of the Swiss Vice-Province often entertained the idea whether Poona Mission could be entirely entrusted to them alone. This apparently never materialized. In fact, the Swiss Vice-Province as well as Poona Mission continued to remain as part of the Southern German Province.

Given the specific nature of the circumstances in the Indian national scenario as well as the reality of personnel crunch in the Mission, the contributions at the service of India and achievements made by the Mission must be evaluated with objectivity and magnanimity. Within this framework of consideration, therefore, the success in saving the Mission itself may be considered a significant achievement. Among other achievements, the initiatives to start a national Theologate and a Seminary, i.e., De Nobili College and Papal Seminary respectively at Poona for training native seminarians and Jesuits were the two most significant contributions of this period. These initiatives had far-reaching consequences and positive bearing not only on the future of all the Jesuit missions, but also on the entire Indian Church. Paradoxically, a mission which faced the criticism of not having a single native recruit until mid 1930s took a lead in taking this significant initiative. Besides, the thrust on education service was further strengthened. Health-care and social service sectors were two other major areas of thrust that deserve a special treatment in the present work.

A comprehensive view of all the mission undertakings, initiatives, course of development, their impact, etc, have been dealt with in the coming chapters. However, a few preliminary aspects of this study, namely its aims, rationale, sources, method, scope, etc, are in order, in this chapter.

1.2. Selection of the Topic of the Study and Title of the Book

Stephen Neill, a Protestant Bishop and famous historian of Christian missions in India wrote: "Most of the work of the Roman [Catholic] missions in India was of that quiet, patient, pastoral kind which in the end builds up a strong, coherent and self-conscious Christian community, but in which there is little that is striking or outstanding to record."[2] But the B-PM seems to have proved this statement wrong. It was a unique Mission which underwent two major crises in a period of fifty

2 Stephen Neill, A History of Christian Missions (Middlesex/New York/Victoria/Auckland: Penguin Books, 1964), 404.

years during the first half of the 20th century, but came out successfully. Besides, several unique mission ventures are noted in the history of B-PM.

This study is a reconstruction of the history of service to the nation by the B-PM. Thye study was originally brought out in the form of a dissertation entitled, The German-Swiss Jesuits in India (1914-1962): A Historico-Missiological Study. Though the title tends to indicate a biographical history of the German and Swiss Jesuit missionaries in B-PM, the orientation of the entire narrative is pre-dominantly on the Mission and its works of service to the beneficiaries and not on missionaries per se. That is to say, this is not a missionary- focused history, but a Mission-focused history.

Therefore, unlike the title of the thesis, this book has a straight forward title, *Christian Mission and Service in Western Indian: Contribution of the Bombay-Poona Jesuit Mission, 1914-1962,* justifying the actual content and focus of this study, namely the mission as a service organization, rather than individual missionaries from Germany and Switzerland. Mission histories seldom focus on the national or ethnic identities of the missionaries who come to serve a mission from elsewhere, but on the mission area. For instance, the mission founded in Bengal by the Belgians is known as 'Bengal Mission', by the French in Madurai, as 'Madurai Mission', by the American in Patna, as 'Patna Mission', and so on. The focus is on mission as an organization of the Church, rather than on hagiographical account of missionaries. Of course, the narrative does include aspects on the biographies, nature, commitment and charisma of the missionaries and their contributions in the mission.

The term 'Bombay-Poona Mission' in the title implies the following: it was a missionary undertaking of the Southern German Province of the Society of Jesus in western India, in 1854. The Jesuit missionaries--priests and brothers--who came to work in this Mission belonged mostly to Germany, Austria and Switzerland, but there were a few others from other nationalities of Europe such as Netherlands, Luxemburg, Italy, Ireland and Britain.

Till the beginning of World War I, German Jesuits who were numerically larger, played a larger role in the Mission, but due to their internment and departure since the war, the Swiss Jesuits eminently carried forward the Mission. Besides, in 1921/1929, the Bombay region of the former B-PM was handed over to the Spanish Jesuits due to want of missionaries. And so the role and contribution of the Swiss Jesuits in the bifurcated Mission in the Poona Region were undeniably crucial. Besides, were it not for them, the history of the erstwhile Bombay-Poona Mission possibly might have been entirely different after World War I. In fact the Mission was saved from a possible ruin, thanks to their active role.

Having said that, the title 'Bombay-Poona Mission', strictly speaking did not hold true after the official bifurcation of the Mission in 1929. In this study, therefore, an attempt has been made to have a functional and practical demarcation of historical events and issues under this study. Events and issues pertaining to the period prior to year 1929 have been brought under the 'Bombay-Poona Mission' indicating the undivided status of the Mission, in spite of the fact that the Bombay area of B-PM was technically entrusted to the Spanish Jesuits already in 1921, but formally only in 1929. In sum, therefore, the Mission has been studied from the perspective of 'Bombay-Poona Mission' until 1929, and not as 'Poona Mission' from the end of World War I.

Also, when the separate Swiss Mission was created in Europe out of the Southern German Province and was elevated to the rank of a Vice-Province in 1947, it was still under the Southern German Province. After the Vice-Province was created, the responsibility for their Indian mission, now called Poona Mission, was vested with the Swiss Jesuits, who continued to belong to the Southern German Province.

As for the use of the names of the two cities, namely *Bombay* and *Poona* we retain their older nominal identities, in spite of the fact that the present names of the same are *Mumbai* and *Pune* respectively. This justification is in order to maintain uniformity in their use. Moreover, they correspond to the names used in the original sources. Similarly, with a clear view to respecting the present sensibilities of people of different religious faiths, we have deliberately used *'non-Christians'* instead of *'pagan' or 'heathen', unlike the occurrence of such usages in* the original sources. Lastly, it may be mentioned that the names of the castes of people or the words transliterated from native languages have been italicized as for examples, *Mahar, Dalit,* etc.

Perhaps certain readers might be put off by the limited scope of the theme of this study, namely only on one Jesuit Mission, limited to the geographical region of Bombay-Poona Mission, in western India.

However, I am quite certain that this reconstruction of the story of a heroic missionary venture by the Jesuits of Bombay-Poona will not disappoint them, because of its incisive, in-depth analysis of events, focus on certain trend-setting missionaries, and more importantly the analysis of the services it rendered and the impact of this Mission on the people groups it worked for, for over a century. It is a re-telling of the story of Christian service and mediation in social transformation toward nation building in India. It is intended that this historical narrative will enable the reader to re-live the events of missionary-people interaction of a bygone era and learn lessons from it.

1.3. A Brief Review of Literature

The literatures, especially publications directly and exclusively dealing with the present topic, are scarce. A book by Alfons Vath, namely *Die deutschen Jesuiten in Indien (1854-1920)* (Regensburg, 1920) is the only publication that exclusively deals with the history of the German Jesuit Mission of Bombay-Poona till date. On account of the sources it draws from various archives besides personal experiences of the author himself as being a part of the Mission, the work of Vath rightfully deserves to be ranked as the most significant one. It places the history of the Mission within the larger frame-work of both Indian Church History as well as Jesuit Mission History in India. The basic aim of the book is to give a narrative of the German Jesuit Mission endeavours until the end of World War I. It traces the beginning and development of B-PM highlighting its major focus,[3] achievements, contributions and challenges. However, in spite of the meticulous approach in dealing with archival data, the book occasionally tends to be quite subjective, especially in assessing the nature of the encounter of the British Government vis-a-vis the German Jesuit missionaries in India. In most likelihood this was due to his personal experiences of the war times. Secondly, the perspective is almost entirely that of the missionaries. In spite of these shortcomings, it is an excellent source of information on the beginning and expansion of B-PM.

3 For example, development of education system, mission among the outcastes and the marginalized, the migrant workers and among the European elite section of the society. See Alfons Vath, Die deutschen Jesuiten in Indien (1854-1920) (Regensburg: Jos. Kosel & Friedrich Pustet, 1920), 58-67;

The next in series are the books by Ernest R. Hull,[4] James H. Gense,[5] and Carlos Suria[6] which partially deal with the German Jesuit Mission history. The merit of Hull's work comprises in the fact that it draws on a huge corpus of primary literature. Although from the style of presentation it is lengthy and occasionally monotonous, it is a very valuable source of information. Gense, on the other hand, draws largely from Hull. His work may be termed as a more organized presentation of the book by Hull with a purpose of making it accessible to a larger readership. It cannot be denied, however, that he had his own corpus of primary sources, which has enriched the story of the history of the Church in Bombay. Its merit lies in the simplicity of presentation. As far as the question of issues like the internment of the German Jesuits is concerned, Gense too seems to be greatly prejudiced in favour of the Jesuits.

Carlos Suria's book deals with the history of the Catholic Church in Gujarat. It must be recalled that the Catholic Church in Gujarat is an off-shoot of the German Jesuit Mission of Bombay-Poona. Until Bombay Region was entrusted to the Spanish Jesuits of Aragon Province in 1921 (strictly speaking in 1929 when a formal division took place), Ahmadabad Mission (also known as Gujarat Mission) was part of the B-PM. Hence the book devotes substantial space on the role of the German Jesuits in the expansion of the Catholic Mission in Gujarat. Aimed at a wider readership, the style of presentation is chronological, and has been a precious source of information for this study.

All the three books are much broader in scope as they deal also with the general history of the old Bombay Archdiocese, which was later bifurcated into Bombay, Ahmedabad and Karachi Missions.[7] All these may be categorized under the popular history of missions. The most

---

4 Ernest R. Hull, op. cit.

5 James H. Gense, op. cit.

6 Carlos Suria, History of the Catholic Church in Gujarat (Anand: Gujarat Sahitya Prakash, 1990).

7 Ever since its erection (1637), known as Vicariate Apostolic of Idalcan / Deccan / Bijapur at the time, the Archdiocese of Bombay has had a chequered history. It goes back to the time of Portuguese dominion in Church's mission works in India. The extent of the jurisdictional expansion may be imagined from the fact that until 1948 Karachi (Pakistan), and until 1966 the two present dioceses in Gujarat state (India) namely Ahmedabad and Baroda besides the dioceses of Vasai and Kalyan in the suburbs of Bombay, formed part of the same Archdiocese. See Ernest R. Hull, op. cit., 45-56, 175-204.

important merit is their originality of presentation and use of primary literature.[8] It would not be wrong to claim that the perspectives that one comes across in the first two books were substantially prejudiced in favour of the Propaganda Fide (the mission department of the Holy See).

Besides the above books, a very recent five-volume work by Klaus Schatz on the general history of the German Jesuits[9] is a commendable source of information. Sadly, Schatz devotes only a few pages on the Bombay-Poona Mission or Poona Mission, although these were also concerns of the German Jesuits. But he presents here an excellent summary of the development of the Mission. The book is valuable for the sources it has drawn information from.

A recent work that is closely related to this study is a book by Benny Aguiar.[10] It draws mostly from two authors mentioned above, namely Ernest R. Hull and James H. Gense. One of the most serious drawbacks of this book is the complete absence of a bibliography, whereas one can clearly mark that the information contained in the work was undoubtedly borrowed from Gense and Hull.

Another book that was published very recently is by Jeewendra Jadhav[11] on evangelization in Ahmednagar District of Maharashtra which was within the mission territory of Poona Mission. The book deals precisely with the German-Swiss Jesuit mission in the area. Its approach is systematic and pastoral, and is a significant contribution by an insider, to the local community. A mention may also be made of a book by Ajit Lokhande.[12] This is basically a collection of the short life-sketches of the Jesuits who worked in the Bombay-Poona Mission, mostly belonging to the 20th century. The merit of this book lies in the fact that it draws information from personal interviews and some archival sources from Pune Jesuit Province Archive.

---

8 Takao Abe, The Jesuit Mission to New France: A New Interpretation in the Light of the Earlier Jesuit Experience in Japan (The Netherlands: Koninklijke Brill, 2011), 17.

9 Klaus Schatz, Geschichte der deutschen Jesuiten, Vols., I-V, (Minister: Aschendorf, 2013).

10 Benny Aguiar, Making of Mumbai: A History of Metropolis and its Catholic Past (Mumbai: St. Paul's Publication, 2012).

11 Jeewendra Jadhav, Evangelization as Community Building (Ahmednagar: Social Centre, 2006).

12 Ajit Lokhande, Mission, Missionaries & Me (Poona: Pune Jesuit Society, 2014).

Finally, a book of a general introductory nature may be mentioned here, by Felix A. Plattner.[13] It touches upon only the general points pertaining to the German-Swiss Jesuits while dealing with the historical sketch of the Catholic Church in India. Similarly H. C. Perumalil and Edward R. Hambye in their co-authored book[14] also make a reference to the subject under review, but only in the context of the impact of World War I on missionary endeavours.

Some authors contributing to the general knowledge of Jesuit mission histories as well as general history of the Church in India are: Stephen Neill,[15] Yves de Steenhault,[16] Henry Josson,[17] Peter Tete,[18] John Correia-Afonso,[19] Devadatta Kamath,[20] Anand Amaladass,[21] Hedwig

---

13 Felix A. Plattner, Catholic India: Yesterday and Today (Allahabad: St. Paul Publication, 1964). The German version of the same book is titled: Indien (Mainz: Mathias-Griinewald, 1963).

14 H. C. Perumalil and Edward R. Hambye, Christianity in India: A History in Ecumenical Perspective (Alleppey: *Prakasam Publications*, 1972).

15 Stephen Neill, A History of Christianity in India: From the Beginnings to 1707 (Cambridge: Cambridge University Press, 1984). See also by the same author, A History of Christianity in India: 1707-1858 (Cambridge: Cambridge University Press, 1985); *A History of Christian Missions (Middlesex/New York/Victoria: Penguin Books, 1964, reprint 1982).*

16 Yves de Steenhault, *History of the Jesuits in West Bengal Part I: 1921-1947* (Ranchi: Catholic Press, n. d.); *History of the Jesuits in West Bengal,* Part II: 1948-1985 (Ranchi: Catholic Press, n.d).

17 Henry Josson, History of the Bengal Mission: 1859 to 1920, trans. Albert Huart and Lucien Clarysse (Anand: Gujarat Sahitya Prakash, 2009).

18 Peter Tete, A Short History of the Expansion of the Catholic Missions in North India (Ranchi: St. Albert's College, 1997).

19 John Correia-Afonso, The Jesuits in India: 1542-1773 (Anand: Gujarat Sahitya Prakash, 1997).

20 Devadatta Kamath, The Burning Bush: The History of Karnataka Jesuits Province, Vols. I-II (Bangalore: Loyola Mandir, 2006).

21 Anand Amaldass, ed., Jesuit Presence in Indian History (Anand: Gujarat Sahitya Prakash, 1988).

Lewis,[22] Delio de Mendonca,[23] Charles J. Borges,[24] Jose Kalapura,[25] Agapit Tirkey, et al.,[26] Francis Minj & Alexius Ekka,[27] et al. Besides these book sources, we have a few articles, which although only partially touch upon the area of our study, are valuable sources of information. Among the authors of articles are Alfons Vath, Felix A. Plattner, Henry Doring, Christopher Shelke, Joseph Neuner, George Winiger, et al. Also, some other authors who have contributed towards understanding various approaches of missionary undertakings are Jeffrey L. Klaiber,[28] Ross Enochs[29] and Edward P. Murphy.[30] All these sources have contributed towards articulating the topic of this study.

1.4. Archival Sources

The primary sources for this study have been drawn mostly from six archives, namely *Pune Jesuit Province Archives, Pune* (PJPA), *Archiv und Bibliothek der Schweizer Provinz der Gesellschaft Jesu, Zurich* (ABSPGJ), *Archiv der Missionsprokur der Schweizer Jesuiten, Zurich* (AMPSJ), *Archiv der deutschen Provinz SJ, Munchen* (ADPSJ), besides the two major archives in Rome, namely *Archivum Romanum Societatis Iesu* (ARSI) and *Archivio Storico de Propaganda Fide* (ASDPF). A small quantity of material was also acquired from the *Heras Institute of History and Culture, Bombay* (HIIHC) and *Xavier Centre of Historical*

22 Hedwig Lewis, The Catholic Church in Gujarat: A Historical Survey 1934-1973 (Anand: Gujarat Sahitya Prakash, 2006).

23 See Delio de Mendonca, ed., Jesuits in India: Vision and Challenges (Anand: Gujarat Sahitya Prakash & Goa: Xavier Centre of Historical Research, 2003); Delio de Mendonca, Jesuits in India: History and Culture (Anand: Gujarat Sahitya Prakash & Goa: Xavier Centre of Historical Research, 2007).

24 See Charles J. Borges, The Economics of the Goa Jesuits (New Delhi: Concept Publishing Co., 1994).

25 Jose Kalapura, ed. *Christian Missions in Bihar and Jharkhand till 1947* (Ranchi: Gossner Theological College & Delhi: Christian World Imprints, 2014).

26 Agapit Tirkey, et. al, *History of the Madhya Pradesh Jesuit Province, 1905-2014* (Ranchi: Catholic Press, 2014).

27 Francis Minj & Alexius Ekka, *Jesuit Mission Among the Adivasis of Chotanagpur* (Ranchi: Xavier Publications, 2014).

28 Jeffrey L. Klaiber, The Jesuits in Latin America: 450 Years of Inculturation, Defense of Human rights and Prophetic Witness (St. Loius: The Institute of Jesuit Sources, 2009).

29 Rose Enochs, The Jesuit Mission to the Lakota Sioux: A Study of Pastoral Ministry, 1886-1945 (Cansas City: Sheed & Ward, 1996).

30 Edward P. Murphy, ed., A History of the Jesuits in Zambia: A Mission becomes a Province (Nairobi: Pauline Publications Africa, 2003).

Research, Goa (XCHR). However, the sources collected from the latter two institutes are largely secondary in nature.

Undoubtedly these archives as a whole contain a huge corpus of primary sources, both handwritten and printed. It must be underlined that the central archive of the world-wide Jesuits, namely ARSI (Rome) has been the main source of information for our purpose. According to Dr. Clemens Brodkorb, the archivist at the German Province Archive, Munich (ADPSJ), a considerable amount of documents, especially letters and reports from the missionaries belonging to the Southern German Province and working during the interwar years (1914-1939) in India, went missing in the process of transferring them back from Valkenburg (Netherlands) to Munich (Germany) after World War II. Hence there is a "vacuum of data"[31] especially in Munich for the period between the two World Wars. Hence, what one finds there today are mainly the official communications between the Provincials and Superior Generals, besides the Province Consult protocols, Acts of the Province Congregations and a few literary products of some of the missionaries who had worked in India. In normal conditions, the archives of the Southern German Province in Munich (ADPSJ) should have been the principal source of information, besides ARSI (Rome). While the ground experiences of the missionaries revealed through their personal letters addressed either to their Jesuit friends or relatives, besides the official reports, i.e. the annual letters *(litterae annuae)* are missing, it is often a formidable challenge to establish a better picture of the Mission on a substantial number of issues. Such challenges are partially overcome, thanks to ARSI (Rome).

For the period, especially after the mid-1930s, an additional and important source of information is the archive and library of the Swiss Province (ABSPGJ) and more especially the archive of the Jesuit Mission Procurator's Office (AMPSJ), both situated in Zurich. The latter, thanks to the foresight and efforts of Felix A. Plattner (one of the former Mission Procurators), who happened to be a prolific writer too, has a good quantity of letters and other correspondences. From the composition and variety of materials (i.e., letters, reports and other correspondences), it deserves to be called a valuable source of information. Unfortunately, the materials are not yet organized, except for the general titles of the

31 Prabhu Bapu, Hindu Mahasabha in Colonial North India, 1915-1930: Constructing Nation and History (Abingdon/New York: Routledge, 2013), ix.

files. A positive aspect, however, is that it is almost entirely unexploited until now. In recent times, only two Jesuits namely Klaus Schatz and Christopher Shelke did some amount of research on these materials. Lastly it must also be noted that it is impossible to consult and analyze all the materials available in the archives as the corpus of the same is too big to get possession of.

1.5. A Note on the Citation of the Archival Sources

As is normally followed for citations pertaining to archival sources, we have used abbreviations to indicate the corresponding archive. While the citation of the materials taken from ARSI, ASDPF and ADPSJ are more convenient to cite due to the thematic or periodical arrangements of the same, the citations of the materials acquired from five other archives, namely AMPSJ, ABSPGJ, PJPA, HIIHC and XCHR are complicated. Thanks to the management of ARSI (Rome), most of the sources are well-arranged. Yet, for reasons unknown, some of the files still remain un-paginated. In such cases we have adopted the following order of specifications in the citations: *Name of the Archive, Name of the File (Place, Date and Year).*

Similarly, the materials at AMPSJ, ABSPGJ, PJPA, HIIHC and XCHR are still largely unorganized, except for certain broader categorization. Consequently, it is not easy to locate a particular source of information without carefully paying attention to the place, date and year of the letters and reports, besides also noting the addressees and the addressed. In order to identify a particular source, therefore, the most reliable way seems to be identification of all the specifications noted above. For example, we cite a letter of Jerome Sanders to Pius Geisel addressed from Poona on the 20th March 1950 and preserved in ARSI (Rome) in the following order: *Name of the letter Writer, Name of the Recipient (Place, Date, Year), Name of the Archive, Title of the File/Collection, Serial Number of the Letter/Document* (page, if any). Here is a sample: Jerome Sanders to Pius Geisel (Poona, 20th March 1950), ARSI, *Poona. 1004-XIX,* 15 (1). For the subsequent references to this same letter/document after intervals we shall use only the second names (surnames) but retain the rest of the details intact except for the change of corresponding page numbers, if any, as shown here: Sanders to Geisel (Poona, 20th March 1950), ARSI, *Poona. 1004-XIX,* 15 (3). The same is followed for an article or report. Without following this method, it would be very tedious if not impossible to locate the items cited in the work.

Besides the difficulties described above, practically all the letters and reports have no uniformity in writing the dates. For example, some of the letters contain the following format of the dates: 1.1.1941. Others contain 1st January 1941. For the sake of uniformity in the citations, therefore, we have adopted the second method in this study, in spite of the fact that in the original sources, there are a number of items with the first category of format of the dates (i.e., 1.1.1941). Occasionally we have also added the page in the letters and reports if they contain more than two pages.

1.6. Delimitation of the Time Period of this Study

For a work of this nature it is necessary to delimit the time period and also the spatial aspects of the subject of study. A number of considerations therefore, were made in this regard in consultation with a few experts in the field. Based on their opinions and having come to a personal realization, it has been decided to demarcate the time period for the study as 1914-1962. Two reasons for this are:

i. Alfons Vath in his book, *Die deutschen Jesuiten in Indien: Geschichte der Mission von Bombay-Poona (1854-1920)* has dealt at length with the initial developments of the Mission until 1920. He has addressed practically all the issues emerging during this period. Klaus Schatz, on the other hand, has covered the period subsequent to it, namely from 1917-1983 in three volumes (i.e., Vol, II-IV) of his five volume work noted above. His presentation for obvious reasons[32] is very short but succinct. Then why did I choose 1914 as the beginning of the period of this study rather than 1920? Two important factors were, a) the discovery of a few documents and correspondences that helped me arrive at an alternative view, and b) my own intention to give a more objective view on the issues like internment and repatriation of the German Jesuits. These, in some measure, offered me more insights into a subject that was hitherto dealt with very subjectively.

32 He has dealt with this period of the history of this mission within the larger framework of the history of the German Jesuits and not as an independent history of this mission alone.

ii. Most of the mission issues that emerged in the intervening period between the two World Wars appear to have been addressed only after World War II. In addition, the time period demarcated for the study comprises of certain important departures in the history of this Mission.

An additional clarification may be added here. After the formal division of the Mission in 1929, the Mission undertaken by the Southern German Province began to be known exclusively as Poona Mission in the official records. Technically speaking this designation held true only till 1956, when the Mission was raised to the status of a Vice-Province, namely Belgaum-Poona Vice-Province.[33] Theoretically, therefore, the closing limit of the period of study should have been 1956. This would have been rather too abrupt a stop. It would be difficult to present a fuller picture of the progress of the Mission, for many of the new ventures that were initiated in early 1950s were incomplete in 1956. Similarly, Vatican Council II has been a decisive event for the world-wide Church. Considering these factors, therefore, the beginning of Vatican Council II has been chosen as the closing limit of the time period of this study. Thus it gives a clear demarcation even from the perspective of the general Church History. As we have remarked above, this demarcation may be termed as arbitrary all the same. Yet the justifications supplied in favour of our decision do seem to be important for the reasons what Vatican Council II implies in general to the entire Church.

1.7. Aims and Objectives

The aims of this study may be put as follows:

i. To record and appreciate the major contributions of B-PM at the service of the nation through education, health-care, social

33 "It is the set of houses or communities, canonically erected by the legitimate authority, which forms a part of the religious institute under an immediate superior major, which in turn depends on a provincial. The vice-provincial lacks some of the faculties proper to the provincials ... The 33rd General Congregation of the Society of Jesus gave to 23 vice-provinces the rank of province that depended directly on the General (independent vice-provinces ...)." Charles E. O'Neill & Joaquin M., Dominguez, eds., Diccionario Historico de La Compania de Jesus: Biogrdfico-Temdtico, Vol. IV (Roma: Institutum Historicum S.I./Madrid: Universidad Pontificia Comillas, 2001), 3783. In effect, this signifies the growth of a mission into an independent unit of administration, with its own head, namely the vice-provincial who in most cases is directly answerable to the Superior General.

welfare, humanitarian services and so on particularly to the Mahar community in Western India.

ii. To identify the missionary methods, strategies, priorities, options and challenges and to make a critical assessment of the same in the light of the contemporary papal encyclicals and theologies of mission. Stated differently, the study indirectly aims at identifying patterns of a Theology of Mission operative among the Jesuit missionaries.

iii. To make a critical analysis of some of the moot-points in the history of this Mission.

iv. To make a critical assessment and evaluation of the available sources, both primary as well as secondary, in order to trace a historical outline of the Bombay-Poona Jesuit Mission in India for the selected period, underlining thereby major turning points and events of larger significance.

v. As a corollary to the first objective, it is also intended to make an attempt at re-reading of certain issues such as the encounter between German Jesuit missionaries and the British authorities, in the light of some newly discovered primary sources. This is necessitated by the fact that the majority of the secondary sources in hand seem to be largely biased in favour of the German Jesuits, especially in the context of the internment and repatriation of the German missionaries in the wake of the two World Wars.

vi. To underscore some of the unique characteristics of this Mission and their relevance and significance to the 21st century India.

It is hoped that this work would make a modest contribution towards the growth of knowledge about Jesuit Missions in general, and about the Bombay-Poona Jesuit Mission in India, in particular. The attempt gains an even greater significance given the apparent historical apathy of scholars, including Jesuit scholars, towards Indian Jesuit historiography.

According to Zupanov, "Jesuit historiography of the Indian missions is one of the most neglected fields in Jesuit studies. In spite of intersecting in a significant way with the historiographies of early modern Europe and modern Indian history, it was never considered a fashionable line of research."[34] I hope that this work will not only rectify the apathy and neglect toward Jesuit history, but also contribute to the body of valuable existing literature on Jesuit Missions in India.

1.8. Methodology and Approach

In search of a suitable method and approach that facilitate a realistic assessment of the contributions of this Mission, we come across various theoretical concepts and frameworks. For example, we need to consider the world-views, politics, economy and religio-socio-cultural contexts of particular groups of people who are the immediate target of a missionary enterprise. Therefore, a research on the history of a Christian mission in India could rightfully claim to have identified the dynamics operative therein only when the missionary enterprise in focus is analyzed within the context of its multi-cultural and multi-religious identity alongside its socio-political characteristics, because a missionary enterprise does not take place in a vacuum; rather within a concrete framework of politico-economic and religio-socio-cultural contexts. By its nature, therefore, the study of this theme touches upon various theological, historical and sociological disciplines, i.e., Missiology, Church History, Socio-cultural History, Anthropology, Social Sciences, etc.

It must be underlined, however, that we have not adopted what is today called an interdisciplinary method in its classical sense. What is attempted here is incorporating to a greater or lesser degree, the insights from these fields in order to achieve the objectives stated above.[35] The method used here may loosely be categorized under the deductive method. And the conclusions are based on analysis of substantially large corpus of materials from various sources. The work itself may be termed as a historico-missiological study of one of the missions in India. As a viable and meaningful approach, an attempt is made here to critically analyse the more significant and relevant aspects, in preference to mere chronological presentation of events.[36] Besides, effort has been made at interpreting the mission history with a conscious endeavour to avoid

34 Ines G. Zupanov, Missionary Tropics: The Catholic Frontier in India (16lh -17lh Centuries) (Ann Arbor: The University of Michigan Press, 2005), 4.

35 See Julia Lederle, Mission und Okonomie der Jesuiten in Indien: Intermedidres Handeln am Beispiel der Malabar-Provinz 18. Jahrhundert (Wiesbaden: Harrassowitz Verlag, 2009), 45.

36 A popular presentation of a missionary history, intended at a general readership normally takes this approach.

any overt Eurocentrism and paternalism. In other words, the study is an attempt, as far as possible, at incorporating a certain amount of *native* perspective, at least by consciously avoiding the issues that overtly tended to represent such positions. These are partly achieved by highlighting some aspects of cross-cultural communications between the two parties: the missionaries and the natives.[37]

1.9. Scope and Limits

This study is neither intended to be comprehensive nor a textbook history of B-PM. Hence, one has to accept the limitedness of the source materials. The other significant limit of the work is the use of the corpus of information in multiple languages. The sources of information mostly consist of materials in three languages: English, German and to a lesser degree also Latin, besides Marathi. This implies that a substantial quantity of relevant materials are bound to be omitted that are in other European languages. Similarly, in the course of our research it was found to be a herculean task to form a fuller picture of a particular sub-topic on account of the ample availability of the materials in the archives. On the other hand, a serious limit was lack of literature from the native people. Hence, overcoming an overt Eurocentric presentation was a serious challenge. I believe that there is ample scope for further research and incorporation of other data to present a more comprehensive history of this Mission. Borrowing from John 21:25, at the end it may be said that "many more things could be said and written" on this topic. We need to bring to conclusion the journey we have begun as no topic can be dealt with exhaustively within a given frame of time.

1.10. Major Arguments of the Study

No other Jesuit mission in India (or for that matter in the entire world) had witnessed such a circumstance in the wake of the two World Wars wherein a majority of the missionaries had to leave their work and were

---

37 See Julia Lederle, Mission und Okonomie, 47-55. See also Michelle Marie Lorimer, Reconstructing the Past: Historical Interpretations and Native Experiences at Contemporary California Missions (PhD diss., University of California, 2013), 1-19. For an extensive treatment of the topic on the cross-cultural communications in Christian missions in Indian context, see Robert E. Frykenberg, ed., Christians and Missionaries in India: Cross-Cultural Communications since 1500 (Grand Rapids/ Cambridge: William B. Eerdmans, 2003. For a general treatment of the subject see Robert E. Frykenberg, Christianity in India: From Beginnings to the Present (Oxford: Oxford University Press, 2008).

sent to internment camps or repatriated to their homelands. Thus, due to the vacuum created by the lack of missionaries, the Mission was faced with numerous challenges. The challenges of maintaining, consolidating and expanding the Mission took place in a context of socio-political movements such as the rise of national consciousness, freedom movements and emergence of Hindu Renaissance in Maharashtra. Also, Bhimrao Ambedkar's Movement among the former 'Untouchables' (*Dalits)* who were the main beneficiaries of evangelization too posed not a less formidable challenge.

Given such challenges, the missionary enterprise of the German-Swiss Jesuits of Bombay-Poona Mission, later only of Poona Mission (1929ff), was significant because of various missionary initiatives, especially community development through education and empowerment programmes among the marginalized sections of people, especially the *Mahars* and other such 'outcastes'. The missionaries through their educational, pastoral, social and humanitarian works set in motion a great process of social, cultural, religious and economic transformation among these people.

As for the strategies, options and priorities, it is argued that even after B-PM was limited only to the region of Poona under Poona Mission, there were continuities as well as changes. Also, this Mission shared a number of common aspects with the other Jesuit missions in India. Precisely for these reasons the study of B-PM is significant for scholars, historians, missiologists, theologians and missionaries in the 21st century.

1.11. Significance of the Study

Ever since its founding, the Society of Jesus has been engaged in strategic, goal-oriented and substantial amount of works towards the spread of practical Christianity in India. However, there has not been many publications on their work and its impact on the people, except for a few volumes dealing with their contributions in various fields. In recent times some Jesuit Provinces have brought out works on the history of their respective missions. But they seem to fall more under the category of popular presentations of mission stories, histories, mostly aimed at a general readership. Most of these give a lot of knowledge about the missions, but do not present an assessment of the impact of their works for the target people. The same is the case with the mission history of

B-PM. In the period after World War I, the history of B-PM and the roles of German-Swiss Jesuits have not received enough attention, at least it has not been consigned to writing. Hence, a systematic study of its history after World War I has been a felt need of the time. This study is a modest effort to bring to light a few important aspects of this phase of the history of B-PM. It is hoped that this study will make a modest contribution towards the growth of knowledge of B-PM in particular, and Jesuit Missions, in general.

1.12. Chapter Outline

This book is divided into the following chapters.

The First Chapter, as already noted above, discusses the main aspect of the topic, besides giving a review of literature, note on sources and archives, discussion on the rationale behind choosing the period of this study, description of the aims and objectives, of the methodology, scope and limits, certain clarification of terms and significance of the study.

The Second Chapter is a brief historical sketch of the major events between the two World Wars in the first half of the 20th century.

The Third Chapter is a systematic treatment of the missionary strategies, methods, priorities, options and challenges involved.

The Fourth Chapter discusses the role of the co-workers and helpers in the growth of the Poona Mission.

The Fifth Chapter takes a look at some of the major obstacles and challenges in the Poona Mission.

The Sixth Chapter underlines new departures, milestones and achievements of this Mission.

The Seventh Chapter focuses on the contribution of Poona Jesuits to all-India service, especially founding ecclesiastical training institutes and a national social institute.

The Eighth Chapter takes a brief look at some of the most significant moot-points. These points are deemed as having a larger significance not only for the Jesuit missions, but also for the Church in India as a whole.

The Ninth Chapter is a critical evaluation of some of the larger issues in the context of this Mission History in the light of the prevalent mission theology.

The Tenth Chapter is an epilogue which attempts to look at the history of this Mission within the larger framework of the evolving theology of mission in the Church, with a special emphasis on the articulation of the same in the General Congregations 32 and 34 of the Society of Jesus.

Chapter-2

The Travails of a Mission during Two World Wars An Overview

2.1. Introduction

This chapter aims at giving an overview of the travails and turning points of the Bombay-Poona Jesuit Mission during the period of this study. Given the scope of the work, however, it is not possible to deal with each event in detail. Yet, given the extent of their impacts, the two World Wars receive comparatively a greater space in the entire narrative. This is rightly so for the simple reason that the two wars played a decisive role in many ways to adapt to newer orientations and thrusts in the wake of the ensuing situations. As a method of presentation of the historical sketch, we have adopted a chronological narrative here. A clear advantage of the same is that it allows us to have a bird's eye view both on the trajectory of the growth of the Mission and the turning points through which it advanced in various phases with the unfolding of the missionary as well as secular historical events.

2.2. Mission Prior to World War I: An Overview

At the very outset, the purpose of taking an overview of this Mission prior to World War I may be pointed out. It is also to show the continuity of the missionary strategies and methods showing an organic growth of the Mission from its beginning. This would give us a better view of the broader picture of the same, besides allowing us to appreciate the missionary endeavour in its totality and with more objectivity.

It may be noted that the beginning of the Mission is to be ascribed to Pope Pius IX calling the Capuchin Bishop Anastasius Hartmann, the then Vicar Apostolic of Patna, to Bombay in 1849 to help out the beleaguered Mission torn apart by the jurisdictional conflict, generally known as Goan Schism[38] or Padroado-Propaganda Controversy in the Church in western India. *Padroado* is the Portuguese term for patronage. Pope Paul III granted (1534) this right to the kings of Portugal as a reward for their sustained efforts in providing men and money to evangelize the countries of Africa and Asia. It implied the rights to nominate candidates to ecclesiastical offices as well as the duty to spread the Christian faith in the areas in question.[39] As long as Portugal retained her colonial power, the missions in her dominions flourished. When, however, the English and Dutch gained the supremacy in the Indian Ocean and the countries bordering on it, the influence of the Portuguese began to dwindle. In Church matters, however, the Portuguese were not ready to give up their influence over all those vast mission lands. Neither were they able to support and expand mission work in the areas under their control.

In order to prevent stagnation, Popes sent Vicars Apostolic to India, under their Department for missions, the *Congregation de Fide Propaganda* (*Propaganda* in short, established in 1622), who were not to be dependent on the Goan (*Padroado*) Church authorities. Missionaries of various nationalities and different religious societies were enlisted and sent to the East under Vicars Apostolic.[40]

"This ecclesiastical anomaly had resulted from two compromise concordats in the nineteenth century, and left a constant lack of understanding which undermined the unity of the Catholic community at an important period in its history."[41] In simple terms it was the conflict resulting from the double ecclesiastical jurisdiction of the Portuguese

38 Goan Schism is also known as the Indo-Lusitanorum Schisma. See G.T. McKenzie, "The Royal Patronage in India: A brief History of the Portuguese Indian Empire," TDR 112 (1893): 32.

39 See Ernest R. Hull, SJ, *Bombay Mission-History: with a Special Study on the Padroado Question, 1534-1858,* Vol. I, (Bombay: Examiner Press, 1927).

40 Jose Kalapura, SJ, "Heroic Church Leadership in India: Capuchin Bishop Anastasius Hartmann 1803-1866)" in *zmr (Zeitschrift fur Missionswissenschaft und Religionswissenschaft,* (Heft 3-4, 101. Jahrgang, 2017): 226-227.

41 Thomas Reddy, "The East Indian Catholics' Perseverance Bears Fruit: Tracking the Protagonists in the Double Jurisdiction Controversy in the Bombay Archdiocese through ARSI: 'Bombay de Patronatus 1921-1928," (Ph.D. diss., Pontificia Universitas Gregoriana, 2004), 1.

Padroado Diocese of Damaun and the Congregation of Propaganda Fide Dioceses of Bombay on account of the interpretation of the Right to patronage, namely *Padroado* or *Padroado Real*[42] *(Royal Patronage)* by the Portuguese Crown.[43]

Portugal took umbrage at the presence of *Propaganda* missionaries, and a long and bitter struggle began. The Portuguese court and the Goan clergy who were deeply devoted to it, did all in their power to embitter the lives of all Vicars Apostolic nominated by Rome, insulting them as "wolves", "propagandists", "invaders", even "anti-Christs". The Vicars Apostolic were harassed in every way. Clashes for power arose between the *Padroado* clergy and Catholics and those under *Propaganda.* This problem was very acute in Bombay. In effect the parishioners with a majority vote could pass on from one jurisdiction to the other and thus all canonical discipline was undermined. This was a major lacuna in the ecclesiastical administration. Bishop Hartmann met with stubborn resistance from the clergy who were very sympathetic towards *Padroado*. He had to confront diverse pastoral challenges arising from jurisdictional conflicts.[44] On this topic a number of studies have been made. One of the most recent ones, showing the role of the Jesuits towards devising ways towards its resolution is the unpublished work of Thomas Reddy.[45]

---

42 In the words of Robert E. Frykenberg: "The Padroado Real granted by the Church of Rome to the Portuguese Crown, gave it exclusive authority to fill clerical positions within its overseas domains. Resting on a series of papal letters and bulls stretching back to 1418 and 1443, this was increased when the papal bulls of Pope Nicholas V in 1452, entitled Dum diversus and Divino amore, authorized the Portuguese Monarch to invade, conquer, subdue, and subject all kingdoms and territories of unbelievers and confirmed the Crown's spiritual authority over all countries from 'Cape Bojador to the Indies' and when the bull of 1455 authorized the Portuguese Crown to establish churches, monasteries, and other places of pious usage in all countries yet to be conquered. The exact meanings of all previous bulls were further spelled out in Inter caetera, of 13 March 1456. This gave authority to pronounce excommunication. The whole of such jurisdiction was transferred to the military Order of Christ, an institution that was itself held by the Crown." Frykenberg, Christianity in India, 127.

43 See H. Comes, "Bombay Mission," in Xavier's Footsteps 1540-1940: Jubilee Souvenir of the Centenary of the Society of Jesus (Anand: Anand Press, 1940), 39. The Anand Press has been renamed as Gujarat Sahitya Prakash now.

44 Jose Kalapura, "Heroic Church Leadership in India: Capuchin Bishop Anastasius Hartmann 1803-1866)" op. cit., 226-227.

45 Reddy, "The East Indian Catholics' Perseverance," 1.

In the initial stage of arrival of the German-Swiss Jesuits, the process of resolution of this conflict cost a lot of time and energy. Here we shall sketch a brief history of the events leading to the invitation to the Jesuits, their arrival in Bombay and the first interruption of the missionary work as a result of the breaking out of World War I.

Amidst this controversy, the *Propaganda Fide* sent the first request to John Philip Roothaan, the 21st Superior General of the Society of Jesus (1829-1853) to send Jesuits to Bombay. The request could not be fulfilled immediately due to the lack of personnel. A little later, however, two Irish Jesuits namely Alexander Kyan and Patrick Sheehan arrived in Bombay in 1848. Unfortunately, within two years (i.e., in 1850) Kyan was recalled back to Ireland and Sheehan died.[46]

To resolve the jurisdictional conflict, Bishop Hartmann was appointed Vicar of the Bombay Vicariate. Hartmann arrived in Bombay on March 28th, 1850.[47] Immediately realizing the pathetic state of affairs especially with regard to the education of the Catholics he set out on his plan of action. He wrote a letter to the *Propaganda* Fide on September 27, 1851 with the request that the Jesuits could take up the responsibility of bettering the educational apostolate in Bombay, which was in a very poor state. In fact already from the end of 1850 he was insistent that the Jesuits could take over at least the southern part of the Vicariate with Poona as its centre so that they could open a school there. In his opinion, Poona offered the advantage of being outside the *Padroado-Propaganda* controversy as there were no members belonging to the Padroado group in Poona.[48]

Under the new arrangement, the first Jesuit to arrive in Bombay was Walter Steins, a Hollander, belonging to the Belgian Province of the Society of Jesus. He landed in Bombay on 5th January 1853. His decision to opt for Indian missions goes back to his meeting with Alexis Canoz, Bishop of Madura[49] Mission (1846-1888), Tamil Nadu, who was on a tour to Europe. Bishop Canoz, meanwhile, visited the Jesuit School at Katwyk (Netherlands), where Walter Steins was the Rector.

46 See Gense, Church at the Gateway, 165. See also Klaus Schatz, Geschichte der deutschen Jesuiten, Vol. I, 1814-1872 (Milnster: Aschendorf, 2013), 243.

47 See Gense, Church at the Gateway, 157.

48 See Schatz, Geschichte, Vol. II, 243; Gense, Church at the Gateway, 175-179.

49 He was also made the Administrator Apostolic of the Bombay-Poona Vicariate from 1858 to 1861. See Gense, Church at the Gateway, 247-253.

Bishop Canoz's zeal for missions left such a great impact on Steins that he decided immediately to opt for the Indian missions and consequently arrived in India (1853) with the desire to work in the Madura Mission. Given the constant requests from Bishop Hartmann, the *Propaganda Fide* directed Bishop Canoz to send some members to Bombay. Thus Steins landed there.

In the same year (1853), on 19th May two Goan-born Jesuits arrived in Bombay namely Anthony Pereira and Anthony Jacques belonging again to the Madura Mission. Later on 24th November came Jacob (James) Peniston from the English Province. The fifth member of the first group of Jesuits was William Strickland, a British native also belonging to the Madura Mission since 1847.[50]

Thus the first arrivals mentioned above were all members of the Madura Mission and non-Germans by nationality. They were sent to Bombay Mission for two reasons. Firstly, because Bishop Hartmann was insistent on having the Jesuits at the earliest; and secondly, there was a delay in the arrival of the German-Swiss Jesuits. It may be mentioned at this juncture that at the time when the Jesuits took over the Mission, the geographical territory of the Vicariate of Bombay was immense. In order to have an idea of the same we may refer to the map (# 1). One may imagine the vastness of the mission field in terms of its geographical expanse from the distance between Quetta (Pakistan) and Coorg in southern India. These two places were separated by a distance of nearly 3000 kilometres. The challenges of administration of the same may not be hard to guess.

In 1854, therefore, Pope Pius IX bifurcated the Vicariate into northern and southern Vicariates. It may be worthwhile to mention here that from 1720 to 1854 the so-called Vicariate of the Great Mogul (roughly coinciding with the Empire of Emperor Akbar) was under the Italian Carmelites. The limits of the Vicariate remained invariably vague, as there was no way to delimit the same. In 1854, the Holy See made a kind of a demarcation of the Bombay-Poona Mission territory. It is here that the above-mentioned division into two Vicariates, namely Bombay Vicariate with Bombay as its centre and Deccan Vicariate (later known as the Vicariate of Poona) with Poona as its centre respectively took place. On 13th August 1854 the northern Vicariate, namely Bombay was

50 See "Vor hundert Jahren," IB 1-2 (1954): 10; "Schweizer Jesuiten und Weltmission," AMPSJ, Belege 1930-1940.

entrusted to the Capuchin Order while the southern Vicariate comprising Poona and the surrounding areas, to the German-Swiss Jesuits. Bishop Hartmann was appointed Vicar Apostolic of Bombay and Administrator Apostolic of Poona.

The Provincial of the Southern German Province, Otto Faller immediately accepted the proposal to govern the Southern Vicariate. Once the Mission was entrusted to the German-Swiss Jesuits (1854), many more Jesuits from Europe began to come, who initially were mostly Swiss by nationality. They were those, who after their expulsion from Switzerland (1847) had been residing in various Jesuit Provinces of the United States of America.[51] Thus, on 21st January 1855, the following Swiss Jesuits in Bombay arrived: John Esseiva, Francis Serasset, and Ludwig Gard along with a Coadjutor Brother Wendt (the first name unknown). A few months later on 20th August came Kasper Midler and Henry Charmillot. A year later, on 5th July 1856 arrived Basil Hafely and Edward Iten.[52] Finally on 20th April 1857 came Joseph Brunner and Joseph Weber. Except Br. Wendt, who was a German, all others were Swiss nationals. Immediately after their arrival, they began to devote their time in learning Marathi, the local language. Within a few months, thereafter, all were dispersed to various military chaplaincies, schools, mission stations or other ministries, including work at the seminary.[53]

With the passage of time, the Franciscan Capuchins resigned from the charge of Bombay Vicariate in 1858. Subsequently, this Vicariate too was entrusted to the Jesuits, while the two Vicariates remained as distinct entities under one mission field of the Jesuits. Initially the administration of the Poona Vicariate was under the charge of the Vicar Apostolic of Bombay until the Indian Church Hierarchy was created in 1886. Bernhard Beider-Linden became its first Bishop (1886). Gense

51 See Schatz, Geschichte, Vol. I, 244.

52 See "Wie die deutschen Jesuiten zum ersten Mai nach Bombay-Puna Kamen," IB 1/3 (July 1930): 1; "Vor hundert Jahren," IB 1-2 (1954): 10; "Schweizer Jesuiten und Weltmission," AMPSJ, Belege 1930-1940. There are conflicting accounts on the first group of the Jesuits to arrive in Bombay. Ernest R. Hull, for example, writes: "The few Jesuits who are found in the Bombay and Poona Vicariate prior to 1854 were not Germans but Irish, French, Italians and Dutch. In the Catalogue of the German province the first entry occurs thus under the year 1855: 'In via ad Missionem Bombayensem in Indiis Orientalibus, P. Joannes Baptista Esseiva, Superior; P. Franciscus Serasset; P. Lodvicus Gard; et Joannes Wendt, Coadjutor." CPGSSI (1885)

53 See Vath, Die deutschen Jesuiten, 68-69; "Vor hundert Jahren," IB 1-2 (1954): 10; "Schweizer Jesuiten und Weltmission," AMPSJ, Belege 1930-1940.

mentions that the bifurcation and consequent allotment of the northern and southern parts of the Vicariate to the Capuchins and the Jesuits respectively was a cause of much disaffection. One of the reasons for the same was that the Italian Carmelites who had served the Vicariate for more than a century had to leave the same without much ado. Similarly the Jesuits who were insistent on taking over the northern part along with Bombay were entrusted with the southern part with Poona as its centre.[54]

As for the year of the actual beginning of the German Jesuit Mission of Bombay-Poona, it must be stated that since Walter Steins did not belong to the German Province, the year 1854 must be considered the actual landmark, although he arrived in 1853. John Peter Beckx, the 22nd Superior General of the Society of Jesus (1853-1887) wrote a letter to Bishop Hartmann on 15th September 1854, officially approving the plan of sending the Jesuits to Bombay-Poona Mission.[55] To this effect he wrote in the letter:

> After a careful survey of the Society in Europe, I have come to the conclusion that no Province will do better [in Poona] than the one which was formerly in Switzerland and now in Germany; it has many members, quite a fair number of novices, and no mission field outside Europe. I have, therefore, committed the care of the Indian Mission to the German Provincial [Father Clement Faller]. He himself and his subjects have accepted this decision not only in a spirit of prompt obedience but with manifestations of great joy. I already sent orders [Father Faller] to pick a chosen band from those offering themselves of their own accord for this enterprise; and the news of their departure may reach me any day.[56]

Clearly the criteria revealed in the above letter may not be sufficient to satisfy the curiosity of the reader. Yet it is significant to note that German Jesuits, and not the Jesuits of any other Province were chosen for this mission. Looking retrospectively, therefore, one feels without malice towards any other European Jesuit Provinces, that it was the best choice. The spirit of determination and adventure that the Germans in general were known for, seem to have added to their suitability for this mission. These details apart, given the fact that Walter Steins was the

---

54 See Gense, Church at the Gateway, 179-181.

55 Ibid., 250.

56 Ibid., 250-251. The editorial changes are that of the author himself.

first one to arrive in Bombay (1853), he may rightfully be considered as the founder of the German Jesuit Mission of Bombay-Poona, although as we have noted above, he did not originally belong to the German Province.

The argument is supported also from the fact that for the first fourteen years he was the one to shoulder the mission as the Superior of the Bombay-Poona Mission (1853-1861), and later as the Vicar Apostolic of Bombay (1861-1867).[57] Among the important decisions made by Steins, it may be mentioned that he was instrumental in making a decision in favour of the present location, rather than Poona or later Bandra, for St. Xavier's College, Bombay. The first choice of Bishop Hartmann for the purpose was Poona. The next was Bandra, on the outskirts of Bombay. Walter Steins opposed both these plans and prevailed upon him so that the decision was finally made in favour of the present location. This in the long run proved a blessing on account of its central location and many other considerations.[58]

By 1857, the question of founding of a university college needed to be addressed urgently and a prompt decision was needed to be made. This, in the opinion of Walter Steins, was possible only in Bombay. As for the Carmelites, the personnel were very few and Franciscans had neither the personnel nor the resources for this purpose.

Bishop Hartmann, while in Poona, received an urgent summons to return to Rome in 1857. Complicated negotiations regarding the Bombay-Poona Mission with the representatives of the Jesuits and the Secretary of the *Congregation de Fide Propaganda*, occupied the better part of four months. In 1858, the Capuchin Superior General, to steer clear of the never-ending disputes, preferred to hand over Bombay and Poona to the Jesuits. The Capuchin missionaries either went to North India or back home. Hartmann was accused of being the cause of the loss of the mission to his Order and even the word 'treason' was used to discredit him. In a selfless gesture Bishop Hartmann resigned from his office as Vicar-Apostolic of Bombay-Poona, and the whole Mission was handed over to the Jesuits.[59] This was the reason that ultimately led to the decision in 1858 to entrust both the Vicariates, namely Poona and

57 See Vath, Die deutschen Jesuiten, 80-83.

58 See Gense, Church at the Gateway, 17

59 For a detailed biography on Hartmann, see Fulgentius Vannini, OFM Cap, *Bishop Hartmann* (Allahabad: St. Paul Publications, 1966), 247-280.

Bombay (known at this point of time as Bombay-Poona Vicariate), to the Jesuits.[60]

Overall, when Bishop Hartmann left Bombay in 1858, he had started no less than seven educational establishments, in addition to five or six parochial schools, either revived or newly begun by him. He had firmly laid the foundation of educational and charitable enterprises, paving the way for rapid development in the near future. Bishop Hartmann truly deserves to be called the pioneer of Catholic education in the Bombay Vicariate.[61]

As for the Jesuit mission, a period of rapid growth began. Already by the end of 1859, the total number of the Jesuits rose to 27 in the Mission. The important mission stations and other institutions of the time came under their care.[62]

Before Walter Steins took over as the Vicar Apostolic of Bombay and Administrator of Poona (1861-1867), while simultaneously shouldering the responsibility as Mission Superior, Earlier, Bishop Alexis Canoz of Madura had taken charge of the Vicariate of Bombay for a period of two years (1858-1861). The tenure of Bishop Steins may be termed as the period of initial foundations. The number of the Jesuits began to rise gradually. By the end of his tenure there were 58 priests (42 regulars and 16 diocesans), 5 Jesuit Scholastics and 13 Coadjutor Brothers. Besides,

60 See P. W. Kaesen, Die Puna-Mission in Vorderindien (Booklet for Private Circulation only), AMPSJ, Belege 1930-1940. See further in the same file Felix A. Plattner, "80 Jahre Mission in 'indischen Hungersgebiet," WMKK (January 1935). The decree to this effect ran as follows: "The Minister General of the Order of Minors (Capuchins) has explained to the Sacred Congregation how, on account of the needs of other missions and the scarcity of men, and specially on account of the damage which has been done to the mission of Agra and Patna by the recent civil disturbances (and the Mutiny of 1857) it is hardly possible to bear the burden of the Bombay Mission lately placed upon them, and has earnestly offered to resign from the same; suggesting that the Jesuit Fathers, who have been already working in the Bombay Mission could easily take charge of both the districts. In view of this representation of the Sacred Congregation, after discussing the matter with the General of the Society of Jesus, he thought well to ask His Holiness to accede to the request of the Capuchins and to give both portions over to the Jesuits, retaining however the division already made between the northern and the southern vicariates. Having thus exposed the matter, his Holiness has ratified and confirmed the proposal and ordered a decree to be published accordingly." Hull, Bombay Mission History, 488. For greater details on the call of the Jesuits to the Bombay mission see Gense, Church at the Gateway, 165 - 173.

61 Vannini, Bishop Hartmann, op. cit, 137.

62 See Felix A. Plattner, "Achtzig Jahre deutsche Jesuiten Mission in Indien," KM621% (August 1934): 209.

the Sisters of Jesus and Mary (who came in 1856) and Daughters of the Cross were active in the mission. One of the major works of his tenure was revival of the Diocesan Seminary. The foundations of the mission stations during his time may be seen from the conspectus given at the end of this sub-topic.[63]

In terms of innovative methods of evangelization (i.e., dialogue and debate)[64] and the beginning of direct evangelization among non-Christians (especially the *Mahars)* began during the tenure of the succeeding Bishop Leo Gabriel Meurin (1867-1886).[65] He holds an important place in the history of this Mission. As for the new foundations, his main initiatives included the foundation of St. Xavier's College (Bombay) in 1869, efforts to run a Jesuit novitiate[66] and further development of St. Mary's School, Bombay. With a clear view to reach out to the elites and educated classes, he also started (1874), a weekly newspaper in Portuguese i.e., *A India Catholica,* which continued to exist until 1885. The *Bombay Pastoral Gazette* for the clergy was started by him in 1872 which ceased in 1904. On account of his zeal for missions among non-Christians and a rather controversial personal style of functioning he often came into conflict with his own Religious brothers and Superiors of the mission stations. One of the reasons for the same was the shouldering of two important responsibilities in himself: Meurin was both the Bishop of the Vicariate as well as the Superior of the Mission from 1867 until 1876. Finally in 1888 he was recalled to Rome.[67]

At the time of his departure from the Vicariate (1886), three important events took place in the Church: a new concordat was signed between the Portuguese Government and the Holy See,[68] an independent

63 See Gense, Church at the Gateway, 269-275; Benny Aguiar, 77je Making of Mumbai (Mumbai: St. Pauls, 2012), 176-178.

64 See Schatz, Geschichte, Vol. II, 232.

65 Ibid.

66 For the discussion on its failure, see Chapter six (i.e., # 6.3.5).

67 The Mission Superiors whose tenure coincided with that of Leo Meurin as Bishop of Bombay-Poona were: Henry Daling (1876-1881), Eduard de Vos (1881-1882), Bernhard Beider-Linden (1882-1885) and Joseph Willy (1885-1888). See Schatz, Geschichte, Vol. V, 76.

68 Accordingly, the Archbishop of Goa was granted an honorary title of a Patriarch. However, the situation did not improve significantly until the new Accord of 15th April 1928, which limited "the Padroado jurisdiction to territories under direct Portuguese political control and to Cochin and Mylapore, and maintaining a double jurisdiction over Bombay,

Indian Church Hierarchy was established in India through Leo XIII's Bull *Humanae Salutis* and Poona was elevated to the status of a new diocese, while the Vicariate of Bombay was elevated to the status of an Archdiocese.[69]

The creation of the Indian Church Hierarchy was a result of the Concordat signed between the Holy See and Portugal in 1886.[70] The long standing conflicts between the Padroado and Propaganda parties were gradually losing their sharpness. Moreover, this was the time when Propaganda Fide began to lay special emphasis on the formation of native clergy in the missions.[71] Besides, it may be mentioned that this phase in the history of the B-PM signaled the beginning of the third-frontier in missionary efforts, namely the *Dharwar Mission.*[72] This began with the establishment of mission stations in the southern part of the diocese of Poona namely at Dharwar and Bijapur Districts (in today's Karnataka State). Initially an exclusive effort was made in these districts to concentrate on the evangelization of higher caste Hindus. However, the number of conversions in these districts was much less

---

Mangalore and Quilon and Trichinopoly. The conflicts that resulted from the double jurisdiction were solved by a new concordat of May 1940. Following the independence of India, yet another accord was signed on 18 July 1950, whereby Portugal renounced its Padroado rights in all territories in independent India." Teotonio R. de Souza, "D. Jose Costa Nunes - a Patriarch who cared for more than Souls," in Mission und Macht im Wandel politischer Orientierung: Europdische Missionsgesellschaften in politischen Spannungsfeldern in Afrika und Asien zwischen 1800 und 1945, pub., Ulrich van der Heyden & Holger Stoecker (Wiesbaden: Franz Steiner Verlag, 2005), 246.

69 See Gense, Church at the Gateway, 283-286; 333-334.

70 See Arnulf Camps, Studies in Asian Mission History: 1956 - 1998 (Leiden/Boston/Koln: Brill, 2000), 149. According to the agreement, the Archbishop of Goa was granted an honorary title of Patriarch. However, the situation did not improve significantly until the new Accord of 15th April 1928, which limited "the Padroado jurisdiction to territories under direct Portuguese political control and to Cochin and Mylapore, and maintaining a double jurisdiction over Bombay, Mangalore and Quilon and Trichinopoly. The conflicts that resulted from the double jurisdiction were solved by a new concordat of May 1940. Following the independence of India, yet another accord was signed on 18 July 1950, whereby Portugal renounced to its Padroado rights in all territories in independent India." Teotonio R. de Souza, "D. Jose Costa Nunes - a Patriarch who cared for more than Souls," in Mission und Macht im Wandel politischer Orientierung: Europdische Missionsgesellschaften in politischen Spannungsfeldern in Afrika und Asien zwischen 1800 und 1945, pub., Ulrich van der Heyden & Holger Stoecker, (Wiesbaden: Franz Steiner Verlag, 2005), 246.

71 See Schatz, Geschichte, Vol. II, 220.

72 The mission undertaken in the southern parts of Poona, mostly in the adjoining districts in the present State of Karnataka is known as Dharwar mission.

in comparison with Ahmednagar District where greater concentration was made to evangelise the *Depressed /Backward* Classes among the Hindus.[73]

In 1878 the first mission station at Kendal was established, followed by mission stations at Valan and Sangamner in 1889 and 1892 respectively. The foundation of the Sangamner mission station posed extraordinarily difficult challenges. In spite of these the mission station grew to such a stature that by 1907 it could count 6 Fathers, 80 catechists and more than 6000 Catholics under its jurisdiction. Each of these mission stations had a residence for the Jesuits, a chapel, a parochial school and a catechist training school. Besides, practically all the villages had a school with a catechist-cum-teacher. At Kendal a training school for weaving too was founded. Meanwhile, Poona was elevated to the status of an independent diocese in 1886. Bernhard Beider-Linden, from Westphalia (Germany) was appointed as its first Bishop.[74]

The general atmosphere with regard to the internal conflicts of the Church seems to have been resolved considerably from the beginning of the tenure of Archbishop Theodore Dalhoff (1891-1906).[75] His main contributions included calling of a Provincial Council of Bombay (1893), which was a decisive council to decide on questions like native clergy and other missionary strategies based on the new developments. The second important contribution was starting of the *Gujarat Mission* (also known as *Anand Mission).*[76] Besides, he established a few

73 See Plattner, "80 Jahre Mission," WMKK (January 1935) in AMPSJ, Belege 1930-1940. See also Schatz, Geschichte, Vol. II, 238-39.

74 See Planner, "80 Jahre Mission," WMKK (January 1935) in AMPSJ, Belege 1930-1940.

75 His predecessor George Porter, the first Archbishop of Bombay remained in the office less than three years (1886-1889). After taking over the office, he got two severe attacks of Malaria (i.e., in 1888 and 1889) and died subsequently on 28th September 1889. Consequently he could not make any mark. See Hull, Bombay Mission History, Vol. II, 239.

76 This mission was started in 1895 as an immediate resolution taken at the Provincial Council of Bombay (1893). It began at a place called Anand (hence also known as Anand Mission) between Ahmedabad and Baroda in the present State of Gujarat. The main target group of evangelization in the context of this mission was a caste group known as Dher. The social status of this group is no better than the Mahars in Maratha mission. In comparison with them, however, the Dhers seems to have had a slightly better position in the society. See Schatz, Geschichte, Vol. II, 239.

churches, convents, orphanages and other institutions.[77] The Mission began to make good progress within a decade of its beginning.[78] After the death of Archbishop Dalhoff (1906), due to the growing tension between Germany and England, an influential group of British and Irish Catholics were in favour of having an English citizen as the successor to Archbishop Dalhoff.[79] However, after much consideration Hermann Jurgens, a German (rather than an English) was appointed Archbishop of Bombay (1907-1916).

Meanwhile, Henry Doring was appointed Bishop of Poona (1907-1914). Since he will be figuring frequently in our discussions, let it be noted here that in May 1914 he set out for Rome for his *ad limina* visit. While he was still in Europe, World War I broke out hindering his immediate return to Poona. He resigned from the See of Poona, in 1921. In 1923 he was raised to the dignity of a titular Archbishop of Madytus and was appointed as the Vicar Apostolic of Hiroshima in Japan. On 14th July 1927 he was appointed once again as the Bishop of Poona. It is because of this titular honour that subsequently he was addressed as Archbishop till the end of his tenure, in spite of the fact that Poona was never raised to the status of an Archdiocese.[80]

The tenures of Archbishop Jurgens and Bishop Doring in the Archdiocese of Bombay and the Diocese of Poona respectively prior to the breaking out of World War I may be termed as the period of expansion and consolidation of the Mission. Archbishop Jurgens worked for the expansion of the *Gujarat Mission,* establishing new institutions. Similarly Bishop Doring concentrated on the expansion of the *Maratha Mission,* opening a school for girls at Hubli (in the State of Karnataka) and establishing a preparatory Seminary for the Canarese boys. About this Seminary we shall discuss in greater detail in *Chapter Six* (i.e., # 6.3.5).[81]

---

77 See Archbishop Theodore Dalhoff to the Superior General (Bombay, 3rd August 1901) ARSI, Bombay. 1003-1, 2; Hull, Bombay Mission History, Vol. II, 241-42.

78 See Archbishop Theodore Dalhoff to the Superior General (Bombay, 11th August 1900), ARSI, Bombay. 1003-I, 1. See in the same file Henry Bose to the Superior General (Bombay, 22nd August 1914).

79 See P.A. Baptista to Pope Pius XI (Bombay, 6th October), ARSI, Bombay. 1003-1, 11, Annexure. It is a copy of the original memorandum.

80 See CVAB (1917), 34; Gense, Church at the Gateway, 375-376; Hull, Bombay Mission History, Vol. II, 243- 44.

81 See Hull, Bombay Mission History, Vol. II, 243-44.

Finally a new mission field was explored in 1900 as Br. Leonhard Zimmer began to evangelize the *Kathkaris,* a wandering tribe mostly inhabiting in small pockets in the jungles of Khandala hill ranges on the Bombay-Poona highway. Their main occupation included hunting, fishing and burglary, the latter occupation being considered as their traditional profession. At Khandala, the Jesuits had established a summer villa house. In a place called Kune nearby Khandala, the Jesuits settled 30 families of the *Kathkaris* in an attempt to make them permanent settlers to tame their wandering nature. They were taught some handiworks under the supervision of Br. Leonhard Zimmer. A school for their children too was opened there. All these works were not easy or simple: these involved huge effort and finance. It was a hard task 'to domesticate' the Kathkaris. On the other side, the *Kathkaris* found it extremely hard to adapt to the new conditions and norms of Christian life demanded by the missionaries. It took more than a decade to overcome the initial challenges in this regard. Thereafter, however, the Kathkari Mission seems to have made a slow yet steady progress.[82]

One of the major contributions of B-PM prior to the breaking out of World War I was in the area of education. Around mid-19th century, a certain competitive spirit seems to have prevailed in founding of schools and colleges. The British Government was especially keen on higher education. Therefore, only those missionaries who possessed a graduation certificate, were issued permission to work in India. One of the first Jesuits who was well qualified for the management of schools was Joseph Anthony Willy, a Swiss national. He wrote in 1858:

> In the entire Bombay and Poona area there was only one miserable Catholic school. A direct consequence of the same was that all those who wished to learn English went to the Protestant schools and thus lost the chance of being catechized in their faith and religion. We have to concentrate on this generation. We must have schools and more schools. We need more personnel, especially one man who can direct the project and bring vibrancy to the entire system.[83]

Unwittingly, such a figure was found in the person of Joseph A. Willy himself. He may rightfully be called as the founder of the school system in the B-PM, which began with his tenure as the Superior of the

82 See Schatz, Geschichte, Vol. II, 239; "Aus der Heimat," IB 1/25 (January 1936): 207-08;

83 As quoted in Planner, "80 Jahre Mission," WMKK(January 1935), AMPSJ, Belege 1930-1940.

school and orphanage at Mazagaon (Bombay), which later became St. Mary's Institution. Unfortunately, sometime later he was transferred to Karachi (Pakistan), where he worked until 1867. Once he was recalled to Bombay, he became once again the Superior, Prefect of Studies and teacher at St. Mary's Institution. One of his biographers writes: "With this appointment began for Fr. Willy a period during which he established for himself a high reputation as an educationist, most probably second to none of those days except Dr. Wilson of the Scotch College."[84] He contributed his expertise in education not only in Bombay, but also in St. Vincent's High School, Poona and in the Mangalore Mission of the Italian Jesuits.[85] One of his biggest achievements lies in the contributions he made towards the establishment of the present St. Xavier's College, Bombay along with stalwarts like Bishop Meurin and Bishop Steins, *et al.* The construction of the building was completed in 1869. This work eventually "came to be known among the Jesuits as the monumental establishment of the German Jesuits outside Germany in the period prior to World War I."[86]

Besides these, many other educational institutions were opened. The British authorities never hesitated to acknowledge their merit by naming them as ranking among the best educational institutions. Thus the dream of Bishop Hartmann was already being realized within a period of less than two decades of the beginning of the Mission. The Catholic Church once in oblivion began to be projected in a positive light as a promoter of education among the non-Christians. A few individual Jesuits played very influential roles in the education programme of the Government.[87] We get a good summary of their achievements in the area of education from the following account:

> Before ten years had elapsed [afte4r officially being entrusted with Bombay-Poona Vicariate in 1858], every important station had its own parish school; male and female orphanages for European and Indian children were securely established, St. Xavier's and St. Mary's in Bombay, St. Stanislaus in Bandra, St. Vincent's in Poona and St. Patrick's in Karachi were well on the way to become the

84 S., "Father Willy: The First Principal of St. Xavier's College," SXCMM2 (September 1908): 57. Unfortunately the name of the author is abbreviated as 'S.' in the magazine.

85 Ibid., 57-61.

86 Planner, "80 Jahre Mission," WMKK (January 1935), AMPSJ, Belege 1930-1940.

87 Ibid.

present great educational institutions, which have done so much for the Catholic youth and given so much credibility to the Church.[88]

In general, the decade prior to the breaking of World War I saw pretty good growth of the mission: "No less than 14 churches and chapels, some of them the legitimate prides of their parishes have been erected. Flourishing Pagan Mission stations have been established .. ."[89] H. Comes summarizes these developments well:

> Mission work, so long uninterrupted, sprang up like a sacred fire in many places. As early as 1859 foundations of the Dharwar Mission in the South were laid; from 1877 the vast Maratha Mission to the North of Poona began to grow; from 1890 the rich plains of Gujarat were explored and planned out of conquest; and by 1900 the heroic adventure of Br. Leonard Zimmer among the Kathkaris had begun. The Padroado, too, opened a number of very fine High Schools, built monumental churches and produced many eminent Ecclesiastics and Educationists. An era of progress had gradually set in.[90]

It may also be mentioned that there were some problems that had direct implications for the Jesuits as well was the Padroado-Propaganda controversy. In many and varied ways, these affected the mission of the Jesuits. As for the natural calamities, according to Alfons Vath, the epidemics that repeatedly occurred between 1896 and 1903 were among the biggest sources of anxiety. According to an estimate these epidemics claimed not less than 100,000 victims in the city of Bombay and its suburbs.[91] In fact two Jesuits, namely Leo Perrig and Gerhard Kipp also lost their lives amidst these epidemics.[92]

Given the specific nature of the challenges, Klaus Schatz mentions that in some manner or the other the Bombay-Poona Mission had acquired the label as a 'child of sorrow' in the home Province in Germany, for various reasons. According to him, many of the younger generation of Jesuits, even those nurturing high zeal for missions, did not seem

---

88 Comes, "Bombay Mission," 39.

89 Pastoral Letter of Archbishop Herman Jurgens (Bombay, 12th December 1908). A copy to the Superior General may be found in ARSI, Bombay. 1004-1 16, Annexure.

90 Comes, "Bombay Mission," 39-40.

91 See Vath, Die deutschen Jesuiten, 162-164. See also Christopher Shelke, "Gerhard Kipp (1862-1903): Ein Apostel der Maharashtria Kirche," SM 54 (2005): 128.

92 See Shelke, "Gerhard Kipp," 129-32.

to be inclined to come to Bombay-Poona. Citing an opinion of Mgr. Ladislaus Michael Zaleski (Apostolic Delegate to East Indies, 1892-1916), Schatz argues that one of the reasons behind this Mission being less popular was a lesser emphasis on mission among non-Christians *(pagans)*. While mentioning an incident he writes: "When, some time ago, he [Mgr. Zaleski] had spoken to the Scholastics at the invitation of the German Provincial, he had found a great enthusiasm for the mission among them. But no one wanted to go to India, since it was said that the Bombay-Poona Mission did not work for the conversion of the heathens. Thus, of course, one does not get out of the vicious circle."[93] Probably this was the reason why in regard to the number of the Jesuits the B-PM was the smallest among the three erstwhile overseas missions of the German Province (the other two being Sioux-Mission in South Dakota and Japan Mission). Together with these aspects, Schatz also mentions about the slow progress of native vocations (about which we shall discuss at length in chapter six, # 6.3) as one of the major shortcomings of the period. But he underlines that the literary contribution of the Jesuits of this era was worthy of acknowledgement.[94]

2.2.1. A Summary Overview of the Mission (1854-1913)[95]

As far as the number of mission stations are to be taken as a parameter of the progress of a mission, here is a brief conspectus of the same. Ever since the Jesuits took over the charge of the mission of Bombay-Poona, the first few decades marked a considerably fast pace of expansion.

---

93 [93] Schatz, Geschichte, Vol. II, 242.

94 [94] Ibid., 243-48.

95 The summary adapted from Hull, Bombay Mission History, Vol. II, 245-247. The correct names of the places have been given in brackets. Instead of the term 'Pagan' I have used a more acceptable term, namely, 'non-Christians' in the list. About the veracity of the dates the author himself admits that they "are irregular; some represent earliest visits, others the building of chapels, still others the first residence of priests, it being difficult to observe uniformity in this matter." But clearly the list facilitates an overview of the gradual addition of places after the take-over by the Jesuits, showing thereby the progress of the mission. Hull, Bombay Mission History, Vol. II, 245.

Table 2.1: Konkan Area (Bombay Vicariate)

Place	Present State	Estd.	Status
Rajkot	Gujarat	1854	Military station till 1857; later civil station
Maney	Maharashtra	1856	Cessation from Padroado; rural congregation.
Culvem	Maharashtra	1856	Cessation from Padroado; rural congregation.
Kandivli	Maharashtra	1861	Cessation from Padroado; rural congregation.
Kotri	Maharashtra	1861	Became Railway centre only.
Mount Abu	Rajasthan	1869	Military Sanatorium. Transferred to Ajmer 1924.
Jamnagar	Gujarat	1872	Civil centre; visited from Rajkot.
Orlem	Maharashtra	1880	Private Chapel made parochial in 1916.
Quetta	Pakistan	1880	Military Chapel. First Jesuit chaplain in 1882.
Bhavnagar	Gujarat	1881	Civil (court Centre).
Abu Road	Rajasthan	1891	Railway centre. Transferred to Ajmer in 1924.
Anand	Gujarat	1895	Mission among no-Christians in Gujarat begins.
Vadtal	Gujarat	1897	Second centre of mission among non-Christians in Gujarat.
Karamsad	Gujarat	1905	Third centre of mission among non-Christians in Gujarat.
Nadiad	Gujarat	1911	Fourth centre of mission among non-Christians in Gujarat.
Amod	Gujarat	1912	Fifth centre of mission among non-Christians in Gujarat.
Porbander	Gujarat	1922	Chapel donated by the king. Only visited.
Broach [Bharuch]	Gujarat	1923	Mission among the non-Christians begins.

Table 2.2: Deccan Area (Poona Vicariate)

Place	State	Estd.	Status
Kaladgi	Maharashtra	1861	Military Chaplain for two years, then deserted.
Khandala	Maharashtra	1861	Military Sanatorium; also civil centre.
Satara	Maharashtra	1863	Military chaplaincy. Double Jurisdiction till 1887.
Purandhar	Maharashtra	1865	Military Sanatorium.
Igatpuri	Maharashtra	1865	Railway Centre.
Bhusawal	Maharashtra	1867	Railway Centre.
Lanovla [Lonavla]	Maharashtra	1867	Railway Centre.
Deolali	Maharashtra	1868	Military Chaplaincy. Nasik added in 1896.
Gooledgood	Karnataka	1870	First Canarese mission centre among non-Christians.
Padatgal	Maharashtra	1870	Second Canarese mission centre among non-Christians.
Kendel [Kendal]	Maharashtra	1878	First Marathi mission centre among non-Christians.
Hubli	Karnataka	1885	Railway Centre.
Gadag	Maharashtra	1885	Railway Centre.
Mahabaleshwar	Maharashtra	1887	Received from Padroado (Govt. Hill Station).
Valan	Maharashtra	1889	Second Marathi mission centre among non-Christians.
Alnavar	Karnataka	1890	Received from Padroado; rural congregation.
Sangamner	Maharashtra	1894	Second Marathi mission centre among non-Christians.
Panchgani	Maharashtra	1895	Received from Padroado, civil station
Dhond	Maharashtra	1896	Railway Centre (visited only).
Miraj	Maharashtra	1900	Railway centre (resident priest).
Manmad	Maharashtra	1900	Railway centre (resident priest from 1911).
Assangi	Karnataka	1903	Third Canarese mission centre among non-Christians.
Kune	Maharashtra	1905	Kathkari Settlement (first at Sibi).
Rahata	Maharashtra	1912	Fourth Marathi mission centre among non-Christians.

2.3. The Mission amidst World War I (1914-1919)

In 1914 as the world was witnessing one of the most devastating events of the century, the Society of Jesus was celebrating the centenary of its Restoration (7th August 1914). This jubilation, however, was going to be short-lived. The onslaught of World War I was going to change the future course of the Society of Jesus too in many parts of the world, Bombay-Poona being one of them. In the initial months of breaking out of the war, however, namely "until December 1914 the German Fathers of Bombay and Poona Mission were not disturbed at all."[96] Indeed there was no real reason either to have a worry for the future as nearly six decades had passed ever since the Jesuits had begun their work in the Bombay-Poona mission. In spite of numerous odds, they had established the mission on a firm ground. It would not be an exaggeration to say that they had rendered a yeomen service to the spread of the Catholic faith in India. Moreover, speaking of their personal commitment and disposition, it would not be wrong to state that they had taken India as their second home and grown in close union with the land and its people. Their contact with practically every section of the society was doubtlessly extraordinary. On numerous occasions, the people in highest positions had acknowledged their integrity, honesty and loyalty. The institutions run by them were looked up to as models to be imitated. Thousands of students, who had passed out of these institutions looked up to them as the years of great formative values that had played a crucial role in shaping their future. The Christian community that was deeply sunk in backwardness and ignorance because of the lack of Catholic educational institutions, all the more, looked up to the lives of the Jesuits as examples of good Christian living. In the military chaplaincies too, there was a strong bond of trust between the Jesuit military chaplains and British officials. Not seldom had the Jesuit missionaries been instrumental in restoring the moral integrity among various ranks of officers. Such had been the past of the Jesuit missionaries in British India prior to World War I.[97]

---

96 Henry Bose to the Superior General (Bombay, 8* March 1915), ARSI, Bombay. 1003-III, 34.

97 See Vath, Die deutschen Jesuiten, 221. See further Alfons Vath, "Die Ereignisse der deutschen Jesuitenmissionare in Indien wahrend des Krieges," KM 45 (1916/1917): 9; Ernest R. Hull, The German Jesuit Fathers ofBombay: By an Englishman who knows Them (Bombay: Examiner Press, 1915), 55-72; Gense, Church at the Gateway, 387.

It was a natural expectation, therefore, that the Jesuit Mission would not be interfered with in the event of the war. True to such an expectation, the initial months seemed to be passing without any sign of troubles facing the Mission. The heaviness of the atmosphere was lightened when the then Governor of Bombay passed an information to Archbishop Hermann Jiirgens that the Jesuit missionaries had nothing to fear about, in spite of a general order from England to take a special note of all the German nationals residing in British territories. But the situation soon changed entirely against the expectation of the Jesuits as another "general order was issued on 17th August 1914 whereby every German national [the Jesuits included] was expected to report to the local police station in order to obtain a parole."[98] Moreover, with immediate effect, "all the mission personnel of German-Austrian origin were designated as members of enemy nations."[99]

A good number of Jesuits were taken into Internment camps as citizens of the enemy nations; others faced the prospect of being repatriated to their homelands. Thus the entire situation seemed to take a dramatic turn. The number of personnel in the mission field was soon going to be reduced almost to a half. The implications of the same may be imagined from the fact that already in the peaceful days the number of missionaries was insufficient in many cases. In other cases it was just sufficient to run the institutions and mission stations. As a result of either the internment or repatriation of a substantial number of Jesuits, there was a massive problem to maintain the existing Mission.

In their regular correspondences with the Superior General or with the Provincials (Germany), the Mission Superiors regularly updated them with the existing situation. In a substantial number of correspondences, among other things, the tone of anxiety and uncertainty is a common feature, often bordering on disappointment and discouragement. In the beginning of 1915 Henry Bose,[100] for example, wrote to the Superior General: "At the outset I wish to share that the situation has become worse over the months and the future of the mission seems apparently bleak."[101] Similarly in a letter addressed to the Provincial he wrote: "I am

98 Vath, "Die Ereignisse der deutschen Jesuitenmissionare," 8.

99 Vath, Die deutschen Jesuiten, 387.

100 Henry Bose was the Mission Superior of Bombay Mission from 1907-1915.

101 Henry Bose to the Superior General (Bombay, 9th March 1915), ARSI, Bombay. 1003-111, 35.

very sorry to say that the Bombay Mission will in these sad times cause to Your Reverence a good deal of anxiety. I wrote already a short time ago to your predecessor about the danger by which we are threatened at present."[102]

The prospect of internment was a real anxiety that preoccupied the thoughts of the missionaries in general: "For the present the situation here is more or less the same as described in my previous letter. Forty seven German Fathers and six Brothers are still able to discharge their duties, but must be prepared for internment at Ahmednagar at an earlier or later date."[103]

In spite of all these upheavals, a silver lining characterized this Mission quite consistently. A normal logic would lead to the conclusion that a mission under these conditions would have invariably reached a point of extinction. Other possibility would have been that the Mission would have been entrusted to some other Religious Order as an alternative way of saving it. But it survived till the end of the war and that too in substantially good condition. Indeed, at times, one wonders how it was kept still alive. A letter of Frederick Schaefer, then Rector of St. Xavier's College, Bombay,[104] described the situation as follows:

> Your Paternity will be pleased to hear the status of our mission as to the efficiency and all round progress has been pretty well maintained, so much so that even our opponents cannot help admiring it. All our schools kept up the number of pupils as in older times, and the results of the public examinations are as gratifying as ever. St. Xavier's College counts 1000 students, St. Xavier's High School 1200 and St. Mary's is crowded and filled to its utmost capacity. The news from the districts are also quite satisfactory and consoling; the work of former years is not only maintained but further expanded, and conversions continue as in former times. Great efforts are made to relieve the misery in the famine-stricken parts and help comes in for the purpose from many sources.[105]

---

102 Henry Bose to the Provincial [Ludwig Kosters] (Bombay, 1st July 1915), ARSI, Bombay. 1003-111, 38.

103 Henry Bose to the Provincial [Ludwig Kosters] (Bombay, 21sl July 1915), ARSI, Bombay. 1003-111, 40.

104 See, CABEP, 28.

105 Frederick Schaefer to the Superior General (Bombay, 6th September 1919), ARSI, Bombay. 1003-X, 3.

The same sentiment is substantiated by a report of J. Bressers, the Jesuit Visitor to the mission (19th August - 15th November 1920):

Figure 2.1: The Jesuits at the Internment Camp at Ahmednagar (1915).
Source: Alfons Vath, "Die Ereignisse der deutschen Jesuitenmissionare in Indien wahrend des Krieges," *KM 45* (1916/1917): 9.

Now that the visitation of the mission has come to an end, I wish to thank and to congratulate you, to thank you in the name of the Very Reverend Father General for the confidence and charity each of you has shown to his representative; - to congratulate you for the supernatural courage with which, notwithstanding an ever decreasing crew, you not only kept the mission afloat, but kept it sailing calmly and advancing steadily on the rough sea of this troubled time.[106]

In general, the phase depicts a story of heroic efforts to keep the Mission going on, on the one hand and daunting challenges which seemingly offered no options than to give up on the other. In sum, it may be said that there was something quite extraordinary in this phase of history, which must be acknowledged with a sense of objectivity.

106 Memoriale of J. Bressers to the Fathers and Brothers of Bombay Mission (Mangalore, 27th November 1920), ARSI, Bombay. 1003-XI, 1.

2.3.1. Internment and Repatriation during World War I

From the above discussion it is amply clear that a direct consequence of the war in the context of this mission was internment and repatriation of a substantial number of Jesuits of German-Austrian origin. It must be stated at the outset, however, that the sources on the issue do not present a unanimous opinion on the number of Jesuits subjected to this arrangement, seemingly to avert a possible situation of polarization of Indian masses against the British colonial rule in India. A simple logic that seems to have played a role in the entire episode may be put in the following Arabic proverb: 'the enemy of my enemy is my friend.' Britain being the opponent of Germany in World War I did not want to leave any chance for the polarization of ideas, even in its colonial territories. India being in the process of claiming its independence gave a sufficient ground for the authorities back in the London War Office to take every precaution, lest a chance of polarization of the masses arose. These conclusions would be further clarified under the subtitle: *Internment and repatriation: An attempt at an objective rereading.*

In the initial months, however, the Jesuits were not much worried about all these happenings. But the situation seemed to change as the Government issued an order that Principals of schools must obtain citizenship for their subsidiaries. The same was applicable to the Mission Superiors for the missionaries working in various parishes and mission stations, so much so that they required a pass from the government to travel outside Bombay. By the end of August 1914, the missionaries of Austrian-German nationality, though innocent, faced the prospects of internment or repatriation.[107] A letter of Henry Bose substantiates the aforementioned information: "I was since informed by the Bombay Government that the Viceroy's Government has already issued an order according to which all the Germans, also the Missionaries are to be interned except perhaps 'the old men' that were 30 or 40 years in the country. Later on the term may perhaps be defined more exactly."[108]

It may not be out of place to mention here that Ernest R. Hull, a Jesuit and a British by nationality was an important figure in the mission

---

107 See TEX 66/30 (1915): 312-315. See also Remigius Raw, "Poona Mission," in In Xavier's Footsteps J540 -1940, 97; Missions Entrusted to the Society of Jesus among the Heathen: Statistics and Information (Rome: Grafia, 1925), 37-39.

108 Bose to the Provincial [Ludwig Kosters] (Bombay, 1st July 1915), ARSI, Bombay. 1003-111, 38.

at this point of time. He arrived in Bombay on 19th October 1902 and soon assumed the editorship of *The Examiner,* a weekly magazine started by Bishop Anastasius Hartmann half a century earlier (1850). Under the leadership of Hull, the journal excelled among the Catholic publications in India. In the wake of the general order of internment of the German citizens, Hull put up a strong defense of the German Jesuits through a series of articles published in his magazine, highlighting the immense contribution they had made especially through their outstanding educational institutions. These institutions had benefitted not only the Catholics of Bombay, but also the larger society in general. The articles were later compiled by him and published in the form of a booklet.[109] But his efforts did not seem to bear sufficient fruit. On the contrary, despite his stout defense and a representation made by the Catholic Bishops, a number of German-Austrian Jesuits were taken into internment camps. Only a few exceptions were made in the case of those personnel who were absolutely needed for the maintenance of the educational institutions and other establishments. For example, the Rectors, Ministers of the Houses and Principals of High Schools and Colleges were accepted as indispensable members. Besides them, two lecturers and professors each of colleges and schools were allowed to stay. Outside the schools, the Archbishop, the Superior Regular of the mission and a few clergy brought up the list of thirteen members for exemptions. The rest--Priests, Scholastics and Brothers--were all listed for internment and the date of their departure was ultimately fixed for 29th December of the same year (1914).[110] A mission established and nurtured over the decades seemed to face a danger of standing still or even facing extinction. A letter of Henry Bose summarizes the situation well:

> Only a few days later we were informed that all of us below 45 years of age should be prepared to go for internment to Ahmednagar as prisoners of war on parole, i.e., they would be allowed to take walks outside the camp. Later on I learned through private sources that orders were issued from London War Office to the office in Delhi to take into internment camps all the German citizens in India, many of

109 The booklet was titled German Jesuit Fathers of Bombay: By an Englishman who knows them (Bombay: Examiner Press, 1915).

110 See Carlos Suria, "The German-Swiss Pioneers: 1894-1923," NJ(1979): 39-80. See also Gense, Church at the Gateway, 383.

> whom had been left free up to that time, and also the Missionaries. ... Government made this concession only reluctantly when it was told that we could not maintain an orphanage and boarding house without a number of prefects and would rather leave the care of the orphans to the Government. Naturally, for this they were not prepared and finally allowed the internment of these 10 Fathers and Brothers at Khandala. It is, however, a nominal internment, all facilities being given for the management of the establishment and looking after inmates numbering 150 boys. I urged repeatedly to allow also the younger Fathers, Scholastics and Brothers to live under the supervision at Khandala where accommodation is available for all. But this was not allowed and these 25 had to go as prisoners of war at Ahmednagar.[111]

As far as the sources in possession are concerned, it seems to be a daunting task to form a fuller picture of the total number of personnel either interned or repatriated. In an issue of *The Examiner* for example we find the following details: "By August 5th [1914] morning 100 German Jesuit Fathers, Scholastics and a Brother, besides two diocesan priests along with an Austrian Jesuit and nearly 40 Sisters were designated as 'enemies' of England."[112] Similarly in a letter we find: "In spite of all our endeavours to avert the blow and to save from internment as many as possible, 6 Fathers, 14 Scholastics and 5 Brothers of St. Xavier's College and High School and of St. Mary's High School had to leave for Ahmednagar on the 30th of December [1914]. Ten Fathers and Brothers, more advanced in age, were sent to our country place at Khandala in charge of the European orphans and boarders of St. Mary's."[113] Still another source says that on 3 0th December 1914, 25 Jesuits under 45 years of age were interned at Ahmednagar, near Poona, as Prisoners of War (POWs): 6 priests, 14 scholastics and 5 Brothers. Ten others--Priests and Brothers--instead of being sent to Ahmednagar, were interned at

111 Henry Bose to the Superior General (Bombay, 8th February 1915), ARSI, Bombay. 1003-III, 34. The Jesuits were divided into two groups in the camps as civil prisoners and prisoners of war respectively based on the judgement of the British authorities.

112 KM 45 (1916): 35-39; 56-60. See also Vath, Die deutschen Jesuiten, 229. It may be added, however, that the word 'enemy' does not carry here the conventional meaning. Since these Jesuits and others working in India incidentally happened to be coming from Germany and Austria, the opponent countries during World War I, they were designated as such. This may be the personal opinion of the author as well.

113 Bose to the Superior General (Bombay, 8th February 1915), ARSI, Bombay. 1003-III, 34.

Khandala, on the present Bombay-Poona highway.[114] The catalogue of the Bombay Mission (1917) gives the following figures: 12 Fathers, 15 Bothers (7 interned and 8 imprisoned). For the period from August 1914 to February, however, the catalogue shows the total number of Jesuits as 91 who were interned and 65 as of those who were repatriated during this period.[115]

It may be noted, however, that in certain cases the implementation of the order for internment was much milder. They took the form of parole. For example, the parishes in Bombay, the schools at Karachi, Poona and Bandra were treated much mildly. In these cases the Fathers were put only under minimal supervisions with restrictions on free movements outside the towns and cities.[116] In sum, what we constantly come across during this phase is the fact that in spite of all these rather unpleasant developments, there was something positive about the entire period, i.e., the British government was disposed to make certain concessions in spite of the general order being issued from London War Office.

As regards the question of repatriation, to some extent it was left to the discretion of the local governments to grant exemption in individual cases. The conditions that applied in this regard can be known from a letter of Archbishop Hermann Jurgens:

> Our position here is now very much upset. All the Fathers above 45 years of age, except some very old and infirm ones, must prepare for their repatriation. I can remain here, if I like and I will remain. Only Fr. [Martin] Durach [the oldest Jesuit Father in the region, who is] the chaplain of Panchgani [near Poona] remains in his place. All other German Fathers above 45 are to be sent back to Germany or Netherlands. Those not engaged in educational work may be sent soon, within a month's time... The fate of those below 45 is not yet decided. It was said that they also would be sent at once but the Superintendent of the Camp at Ahmednagar believes this to be an error.[117]

---

114 Ibid. See also Carlos Suria, "The German-Swiss Pioneers: 1894-1923," NJ (1979): 39-80; Gense, Church at the Gateway, 383.

115 See CABEP, 16-50.

116 See Bose to the Superior General (Bombay, 8th February 1915), ARSI, Bombay. 1003-III, 34. See further in the same file Henry Bose to the Superior General (Bombay, 9th February 1915).

117 Archbishop Hermann Jurgens to the Superior General (Bombay, 27th August 1915) ARSI, Bombay. 1003-111, 43.

In other words, an exception could be made in favour of those Jesuits who were elderly and infirm, to whom removal from the country would involve a serious hardship. Secondly, the priests of military age (below 45 years) were to be interned instead of being repatriated. Here again the following exceptions were made: Archbishop Hermann Jilrgens was allowed to stay in Bombay. Besides, as noted above, Martin Durach was permitted to stay at Panchgani. We come across a more unambiguous information in a letter of Henry Bose to the Superior General as to how many Jesuits were to be repatriated: "51 Fathers, 14 Scholastics and 12 Brothers have now been informed by the government that they must prepare themselves for repatriation at an earlier or a later date, probably during October or November [1915]."[118]

Towards the end of 1915, a ship named, Golconda steamed out of Calcutta with a number of Germans and Austrians on board, who were being repatriated. Among them were 10 Catholic nuns (of the Institute of the Blessed Virgin Mary-IBMV) from the Allahabad diocese, 4 German Jesuits working in the Calcutta region, one priest from Dhaka (in present-day Bangladesh), and four others from the Bettiah region (present-day Bihar). On 30th March 1916 the Golconda steamed out of Bombay taking the second batch of repatriates that included 40 German Jesuit priests, 2 secular priests, 14 scholastics, 1 Brother from the Bombay-Poona region, besides a number of Fathers, Scholastics and Brothers from other missions. According to Alfons Vath there were 69 Jesuits among the repatriates, 65 belonging to the Bombay-Poona region and 4 scholastics coming from Madura mission.[119] On all these developments, Hull comments tersely: 'His Grace the Archbishop, the editor of the Examiner and a few other Fathers managed to take a silent farewell from a distance, feeling the pathos of it all but unable to do more.'[120]

2.3.2. World War I Travails

The question of internment and repatriation of the Jesuits was certainly an ambiguous issue, at least at the moment, as far as it is considered from the perspective of the immediately affected Jesuits. In what way

118 Henry Bose to the Superior General (Bombay, 1st October 1915), ARSI, Bombay. 1003-111, 45.

119 See Schatz, Geschichte, Vol. II, 249.

120 Hull, German Jesuit Fathers, 102.

did they pose a challenge to the British Empire so as to be repatriated or taken into internment camps was unclear so far as it appeared from the way the officials chose to remain silent when an explanation was sought. Ernest R. Hull and Alfons Vath, who were observers of the entire event as well as enjoyed the privilege of getting first-hand information from the Jesuit companions interned in the camps, choose a tone of virtual condemnation against the British authorities.[121] However, it may be a matter of discretion to weigh pros and cons of the entire situation. A few descriptions help to understand the situation better.

In January 1915, for example, the Superior Regular of the mission was allowed to visit his subjects in the internment camp and represent to the Government the undesirability of their surroundings. Early in February of the same year the Government of India issued the concession that the Jesuit Fathers, who had been confined in the military camps up to that point of time, should be transferred to the civil camp, known as C camp and supervised with much leniency as compared to the previous one. The same was to be done in cases of further internments.[122]

Again in March 1915 the then Mission Superior, Henry Bose was permitted to visit his subjects at the camp in Ahmednagar. He describes the atmosphere in the barracks vividly:

> With special permission of the Government I visited last week our prisoners of war for several days. I found them on the whole well, although they have to suffer many discomforts and hardships. The food is often insufficient, often badly prepared and does not suit the stomachs at least of the weaker ones. But we are allowed to send them money and provisions from here. I found 22 staying in 3 tents each of the size of one of our rooms, so that there is scarcely space for moving about and the inconvenience caused to them by this over-crowding is rather great. Besides, they begin now to suffer from the heat which is already being felt very much about noon. They were promised accommodation in barracks which are substantial buildings, but this promise was not yet fulfilled as the barracks are filled-up by the prisoners who arrived before our Fathers. Another cause of complaint is that they have to live together with the people of the most various descriptions, also with sailors of German vessels, waiters, cooks, mechanics, etc., many

121 See Gense, Church at the Gateway, 380-390; Vath, Die deutschen Jesuiten, 229-240; Hull, German Jesuit Fathers, 73-94.

122 See Gense, Church at the Gateway, 383.

> of whom are used to a language which the Religious should not hear; also of the more cultured inmates some indulge in jokes and remarks that are unbecoming and even indecent. Ours cannot help them hearing in certain places where many prisoners meet.[123]

One notes a unique style of reporting by a Jesuit who is a typical product of the times. For modern readers some of the points in the above report might sound obsolete, probably even ridiculous. But they still stand valid while the text of a particular time must be read within its own contextual framework.

Alfons Vath has a still stronger negative tone in the description of the event. He mentions that the twenty-five imprisoned Jesuits were made to feel that they were 'disliked' missionaries, so to speak. The objective of the description clearly seems to be generating sympathy for the concerned characters. He goes on to the extent of narrating that they were lodged in batches of eight, in small-sized huts standing unpleasantly close to the toilettes. He believed that such an arrangement was a deliberate one on the part of the British authorities. In his opinion, therefore, there was no need for this, for there were empty barracks available. But the commandant, a certain Colonel, seems to have treated the internees as convicts, besides appearing strongly prejudiced against the missionaries.[124] Vath continues to narrate the experiences of the Jesuits in the camps as he writes:

> The twenty-five Jesuit prisoners thus spent twelve miserable weeks and received hardly enough to eat. One of the scholastics [Peter Aneder] contracted the germs of a fatal disease. In the following month of April he was allowed to sail for Europe, where he died of pulmonary Tuberculosis two years later. Of the other Jesuit prisoners, five or six were as a rule hospitalized in the camp. So when the summer season set in and life in the huts became unbearable, their transfer to the civil camp was a pleasant change indeed... But, even there the accommodation left much to be desired. The prisoners were housed in barracks built for native troops, structures made of clay walls, with mud floors and small windows.[125]

---

123 Bose to the Superior General (Bombay, 8th March 1915), ARSI, Bombay. 1003-III, 34. See also a subsequent letter of the same author (Bombay, 2nd May 1915), ARSI, Bombay. 1003-111, 36.

124 See Vath, Die deutschen Jesuiten, 230-231.

125 Ibid., 231-232.

On regular representations to the authorities, steps began to be taken to render the accommodations fit for habitation and the camp-superintendent, a certain Mr. Garret, did his best to address the concerns of the interned Jesuits. Life became bearable, all were given sufficient food, and they also enjoyed greater freedom of movement with less restrictions. The Jesuits reacted at once to their changed surroundings under more humane conditions, and they became more contented lot, if not more happy, so much so that they began to entertain hopes that their trial would not be unduly prolonged and that before long they would be allowed to take up their interrupted tasks again. But such a hope did not materialize as expected. On the contrary new incumbents began to come. For example, in April 1915 came the unexpected news of the arrival of Fr. Otto Richter, in their midst. He was an energetic priest working very successfully in the *Dharwar* District of Karnataka where he was organizing a new settlement for a criminal tribe known as *Lambadi*. The local British authorities, who held him in high esteem, pleaded that his internment be put off on account of the useful work he was engaged in. But he was under 45, and so no exceptions were made even in his case. Shortly afterwards three more Jesuits arrived. Moreover, without a prior notice all German members of St. Stanislaus' School, Bandra and chapel community were booked for internment.[126]

Thus we get an impression that the contemporary Jesuit authors we have mentioned often seem to be inclined to present the event with more subjective perspectives. To a large extent they cannot be blamed for the presentation of the events. Their presentation of the events were typical of the kind of narratives of the insiders who were deeply affected by the unfolding of the events. An example might throw some more light on the same. Alfons Vath, narrating the general order of internment and repatriation applicable to all German and Austrian nationals, irrespective of their professions has the following account:

> The Jesuit missionaries from Germany had left their homeland and accepted India as their second home. They had grown in close union with the land and its people. Their relationship with all sections of the society was excellent. The highest authorities had thanked and praised them on a number of occasions for their selfless, dedicated and fruitful lives. The Jesuit institutions were depicted as examples

126 See J. B. Bartholome to W. Wasskuhler (Bombay, 18lh April 1915) MDP, 6 (1912-14), 99-100. See also Vath, Die deutschen Jesuiten, 232-233.

> of perfection and high standard. In them the most loyal citizens were formed ... Thousands of Christians and non-Christians, who were educated in the Jesuit schools would represent their 'fathers,' as one mind and one heart. It was expected that the Catholic community that had acquired a higher social status through the selfless service of the Jesuits would be standing by them. Similarly, there existed a wonderful relationship between the Military Chaplains and the Officers and their Troupes. Numerous examples may be added whereby the entire Regiments were morally uplifted quite visibly by the efforts of the Jesuit Chaplains. The soldiers were united with their Chaplains with respect and love. The highest Officers, like Lord Roberts, had expressed his deep sense of gratitude for the good work done to the British Troupes. How can the British, known for their pragmatism, rationality and integrity of judgment and more especially given such a wonderful history of good relationships, could treat the Jesuit missionaries in such a manner? So thought one. The things, however, turned out to be entirely different.[127]

There is no need of elaborating on the issue any further. One aspect that becomes pretty clear and supports our argument is the fact that authors like Alfons Vath, Ernest R. Hull and James H. Gense do seem to have fallen prey to over-subjective interpretation of the entire episode. In the following paragraphs we shall make an attempt at the re-reading of the episode with greater objectivity.

2.3.3. An Attempt at Re-reading World War Travails

The episode of internment and repatriation of the Jesuits may be interpreted differently by different readers. It is a known fact that the sight of objectivity often tends to be lost when an incident is observed as an insider, for the personal experiences often tend to shape the expressions and articulations of an author. This seems to have happened to a certain degree with the Jesuit writers mentioned above. As indicated elsewhere, one often notices, a tone of outright condemnation of the British authorities of the time. Probably quite unintentionally of course, certain silver linings in the entire episode seem to have been missed. In other words, the fact that the British authorities were under obedience to their higher authorities is normally missed in many of the presentations of the episode. In order to arrive at an objective conclusion we need to see the entire episode basically from two perspectives: from the perspective of

127 Vath, Die deutschen Jesuiten, 229.

the constraints of the British officials and that of the Jesuits interpreting the same in the light of their own experiences. For the purpose we shall supply a few examples mostly taken from the letters of Henry Bose as the head the mission at the time of these events. Firstly we shall see what the positive sides of the episode were.

Alfons Vath, although often appears rather critical about the role of the British officials, himself testifies to the fact that generally they were positively disposed towards the Jesuits:

> In order to continue the works of the mission further, the Government was ready to make a few exceptions. Thus the Archbishop and thirteen Fathers were spared [from being either sent to internment camps or repatriated] ... The officers gave still further proofs of their goodwill and positive disposition towards the Jesuits. The Government grant to the schools and the extra expenses in paying out to the teachers from outside were further continued. The Superiors of the mission were assured as always that nothing unpleasant would befall the Jesuits. No further steps were foreseen against the mission.[128]

Another positive aspect of the phase included the confidence of the parents of the English children who seem to have shown full trust on the loyalty of the Jesuits. This is proved by the fact that the number of children consistently increased in the school at Khandala. Besides, the British Government continued to pay the salaries of the lay teachers who were employed by the Jesuits as part of the temporary arrangements to fill-up the gap created as a result of the Jesuits taken to the internment camps. The Government also bore all the extra expenses incurred in the schools and granted a higher grant for the European orphans lodged at Khandala, as it was believed to be more expensive than Bombay while it was a hill station.[129]

Similarly a majority of the parishes in Bombay, the schools at Karachi, Poona and Bandra (Bombay) were given considerable concessions by allowing some of the Jesuits to continue their ministries. In these cases the Jesuits were put only on parole with the restriction that they could not travel to other places without a special permission. In some cases the highest civil authorities too came forward to assure

128 Alfons Vath, "Die Erlebnisse der Jesuitenmissionare," KM4571 (1916/1917): 3.

129 Ibid.

the Jesuits that there would not be any interference on the part of the Government. The benevolence on the part of the British officials is revealed also from the fact that the Mission Superiors and the Rectors of the schools were instructed to obtain Residence Permits for the members under their care, so that in future the same could be utilized as a legal safeguard for them. As for the internment camps, the Jesuits were allowed to form a small community under a Superior, where some Scholastics were allowed to study Theology and others were given permission to undertake the study of languages. It is further revealed that the condition of the Jesuits there was much better than in the case of many others of German-Austrian nationality.[130] From a letter of Henry Bose we get the following information:

> I also very earnestly recommend to the Holy See the condition of 5 Hill Mill Fathers from Madras, mostly Austrians, 1 Salesian Father of Vizagapatam and 1 Father of the Congregation of the Holy Spirit from British East Africa, who are kept already for 4-5 months in a much stricter internment at Ahmednagar than our Fathers. They are in the 'A Camp' and never allowed to leave the enclosure to which they have been confined for reasons unknown to them. I informed their Prelates of their condition suggesting means how perhaps a transfer to the 'B Camp' might be obtained and shall see how I can help them. Their condition is in many regards much worse than that of our prisoners of war.[131]

Having indicated some of these acts of 'benevolence' on the part of the British officials, we may also cite a few examples to show that they were often under constraints of executing the orders received from the London War Office. From some of the documents it becomes clear that the Jesuits, at least those in the positions of responsibilities (i.e., Archbishops and Mission Superiors, etc.,) were aware of these constraints. For example we have the following text that implies the same:

> After my return to Bombay I communicated my observations to one of the highest Government officials with whom I had to deal since the question of internment arose. He promised redress but rejected

130 Ibid.

131 Henry Bose to the Superior General (Bombay, 9th March 1915), ARSI, Bombay. 1003-111, 34.

> again my suggestion to transfer the Fathers from Ahmednagar to Khandala on the pretext that they could not be sufficiently controlled there... .Considered in the light of this fact the internment at Ahmednagar appears to be a mere farce which must be enacted because somebody wants it.[132]

This is further revealed in a letter of Alban Goodier, later Archbishop of Bombay (15th December 1919 - 1st October 1926):

> Last May Government told me that no further proceedings were intended on their part against the German Fathers ... But scarcely had the term begun when the political secretary to Government let me know that new troubles were brewing. He said that a general order from internment had come out including women as well as men and not excluding nuns. He added that the Bombay Government was trying to delay the sentence but that of its ultimate fulfillment there could be no doubt... I don't think that the government wants to hurt the Church or to take the colleges from us, but the Secretary said that if the right staffs were not available, they would take the institutions over, staff them themselves and henceforth use them as their own.[133]

The argument in favour of the benevolence or for that matter at least the neutrality on the part of the British officials is supported through certain indirect helps rendered to the Jesuits as well. Henry Bose has the following example for the same:

> I was also urged by the Government to do my very best to get out from Europe or America a number of other Fathers of British or Neutral nationality, who might step in for them that are still to be interned and thus keep our institutions and parishes going. Government have all along been trying to save the institutions though they could, on account of the pressure from home, not save the Fathers from internment. We shall also now get the time that is required for the changes, 3 or 4 months, if necessary, in certain cases also more.[134]

---

132 Bose to the Superior General (Bombay, 8th February 1915), ARSI, Bombay. 1003-111, 34.

133 Extract of the letter of Alban Goodier (Bombay, 16th July 1915), ARSI, Bombay. 1003-III, 39.

134 Bose to the Provincial (Bombay, 1st July 1915), ARSI, Bombay. 1003-III, 38.

The above citations throw considerable light on the positive side of the entire episode. A fact that becomes quite clear here is: one finds no evidence of the prejudice either of personal or collective prejudice against the Jesuits. Hence, it may be concluded without a doubt that there was no attempt at disrupting the missionary endeavour carried out by the German Jesuits, only on the ground that they happened to come from an 'enemy' nation. On the contrary, the compulsion of the British officials to implement the orders received from London becomes quite clear. Hence the condemnations that "the gentlemen of the company [British East India Company] have never had sympathy and apparently availed no help whatsoever, were bitterly antipathetic as was the case with England of the time"[135] not only seem to be uncharitable and one-sided but also an exaggeration. As stated above, at least some of such conclusions may be taken as individual impressions based on a concrete situation. A generalization, therefore, would be unjustifiable.

Besides these aspects, a few other justifications may be supplied in favour of the foregoing arguments. Accordingly, the fact must be underlined that the British colonial power had no missionary objective right from the beginning, in spite of the fact that on some occasions it did show a certain preferential option for the Anglican Church. It must be recalled that the British colonial power had purely political and economic interest in India. Consolidation and expansion of the empire were among its priorities. Hence, it must be taken as a matter of fact that the officials took a neutral approach to matters of religions and morality. Moreover, given the volatile atmosphere in India in the wake of movements for freedom, the decision taken back at home in London had a greater value than to leave a group of German nationals, who coincidentally happened to be Jesuits, untouched.

Another possible reason for not leaving even the missionaries, especially the Jesuits, may have been their influence in the public life. Through their educational institutions and mission stations they had gained good reputation among leaders. In the opinion of the British authorities, the stature of the Jesuits in the public life would have easily played a catalytic role. Hence the precaution may have been taken.

On the other hand, seen from the perspective of the Jesuits, a few facts must be kept in mind. Firstly, it must be recalled that during the

---

135 E[mil] K[aufmann], "Die britische Macht und die katholische Mission in Indien," IB 3 (1947): 43.

pre-war decades there was a general atmosphere of amity and mutual trust between the British officers and the German Jesuits, especially the military chaplains. Hence, Jesuits, all in good faith, may never have imagined that one fine morning they would be regarded as 'enemies' of England. Therefore the articulations of the experiences of certain Jesuits of the time in a rather bitter tone is understandable.

Having weighed the compulsions of the British authorities on one hand and the real situation of helplessness of the Jesuits on the other, it may be stated that the entire event of the internment and repatriation of the Jesuits was apparently a bitter shock to the Jesuits. Yet an objective reading in the light of available documents does not justify, especially the outright condemnation of the British colonial power. Of course such a position opens a plethora of questions to answer. However, at this juncture, it suffices to conclude that at the end of the day there still was some opening for the survival of the Mission. A historian must never fall prey to sentimental judgements. Yet, we may underline the fact that something extraordinary happened during the entire phase. The words of appreciation of J. Bressers, the Visitor who toured the mission once the war had ended are fitting here: "After having carefully examined each of your numerous institutions, I may say that I admire not only your and your predecessors' work, but the way in which...you saved that work from destruction by your unflinching tenacity."[136]

2.4. The Transfer of Bombay Region to Spanish Jesuits

In 1919 Alfons Vath concluded his book, *Die deutschen Jesuiten in Indien* (1854-1920) with the following words:

> Thus in the beginning of the 1920s, as we conclude the history of the German Jesuits, the future of the mission of Bombay-Poona is wrapped still in darkness. The German Jesuits would be forbidden to re-enter India for some five years. Could they return and freely continue their work again? Would the Jesuits until then be assigned to a different, more grateful mission field? Who will take their place? Or would England soon judge it right and just; and shorten the five-year period? Would the mission of the German province still remain?[137]

136 Memoriale of J. Bressers to the Fathers and Brothers of the Mission of Bombay (Mangalore, 27th November 1920), ARSI, Bombay. 1003-XI, 1.

137 Vath, Die deutschen Jesuiten, 239.

The anguish and anxiety of foregoing a mission so dearly established may clearly be noted from this account. The missionaries, quite naturally, were bound to be attached to the Mission they had established virtually at the cost of their sweat and blood. The internment and repatriation of a sizeable number of German-Austrian Jesuits from Bombay-Poona in the event of World War I, however, was bound to change the future course of their mission in India. Apparently, as expressed in the foregoing citation from Vath's book, the chance of immediate return of the German Jesuits to Bombay-Poona seemed either a distant future or almost impossible. The *uncertainty* was the only thing that was *certain* in anyway. The history was soon to change. With the limited man-power in the Mission it was virtually impossible to carry forward the apostolate. The Society of Jesus could not risk losing the Mission established at the cost of much effort. Hence the Superior General of the Society of Jesus, Fr. Wlodimir Ledochowski decided to hand-over the Bombay mission to the Aragon Province, Spain.[138]

This was done in 1922. The Bombay area of the Mission was handed over to the Aragon Province, while the remaining part, namely the diocese of Poona, which in 1924 gained its independent identity, was retained by the Southern German Province.[139] As for the personnel, a cursory view on this period reveals that in 1914 Poona Mission was staffed with 38 Priests and 2 Jesuit Brothers. Among the Priests 25 were Jesuits and the rest diocesans. By 1922-23 this proportion of the Jesuit and non-Jesuit personnel in the mission had changed. By then the total number of the priests in the mission was 32 (14 Jesuits and 18 diocesan clergy) and that of the Brothers remained constant at 2. Among these more than half were brought in from other dioceses and missions. One of the major difficulties that this group of the missionaries faced was lack of knowledge of local conditions and even of the local vernacular. Among the older missionaries there were only two missionaries left to carry out the work. They were Francis Xavier Schubiger and R. Gonsalves, a diocesan priest from the Poona Diocese.[140]

138 See "Die Ubertragung der Puna-Mission an die oberdeutsche Provinz der Gesellschaft Jesu," IB 1 (1930): 1. See also Schatz, Geschichte, Vol. Ill, 314.

139 See Maximilian Riklin to the Provincial (Poona, 27"' December 1926), AMPSJ, Pune Alt. Maximilian Riklin was the Apostolic Administrator of the Diocese of Poona during this time.

140 Maximilian Riklin, "State of the Poona Diocese before the Arrival of Dr. Doring," (Poona, 7th Oct. 1959), AMPSJ, Pune Alt. First name of the priest is unknown

2.4.1. Rescuing the Mission (1917-1921)

The latter half of the 1910s was not only significant for the German history in general, but also for the Society of Jesus in Germany as well. In the history of the new Society, this period is marked by the dynamic leadership of Fr. Wlodimir Ledochowski as its Superior General. Besides his predecessor and his successor,[141] probably there has been no other Superior General in the new Society who made his presence felt in the Society so strongly. He was gifted with tackling complex issues. Often he did not leave the matter until every single aspect was put in proper perspective. Such was applicable in his dealing with the problems and crisis faced by the Missions.[142]

As a first step towards saving the Mission, Father Wlodimir Ledochowski requested the British authorities for permission for the re-entry of the German Jesuits in their respective mission fields. But the latter did not oblige. Indeed the grant of permission was right-away refused as "the Foreign Office, London, decreed that no German or Austrian National will tread British soil around the world within five years."[143] The hope of Father Ledochowski of making immediate arrangements to save the Mission was shattered. This was a severe blow to his entire plan. It was apparent that the refusal for permission by the British authorities was going to cause a serious harm to the mission of Bombay-Poona in the following years and eventually it did do so to a large extent.[144] Hence other contingency plans were needed to be devised. But, there was no other Province in view that seemed to be capable of sparing personnel to be sent to Bombay-Poona Mission.

In the midst of these uncertainties, Father Ledochowski decided upon the Jesuits of Maryland and New York Province as the most suitable choice given the urgency of the situation. He believed that the British authorities would have no problem with granting permission to the American Jesuits to enter India to take charge of the Bombay-Poona mission. However, while he was still pondering over the decision to handover the mission to the afore-said Province, he was unaware of the possible obstacle on the way. One of the compelling reasons for the same

141 His predecessor was John Roothaan and the successor Pedro Arrupe.

142 See Schatz, Geschichte, Vol. Ill, 1.

143 Suria, History of the Catholic Church in Gujarat, 215.

144 See Suria, "The German-Swiss Pioneers," 215. See also K[aufmann], "Die britische Macht," IB 3 (1947): 43.

may have been his perception of the mutual relation and cooperation between Britain and America in the event of the war. It is a known fact that Germany-Austria and Britain-France were at the helm of the war. Whatever the pretext may have been the immediate cause of breaking-out of World War I, it was the war of supremacy in Europe in the final analysis. Britain-France wanted to maintain their respective realms of supremacy at all costs, even if it meant turning against their own allies. It was clear that Britain-France and their allies would not have won the war unless the Americans had joined them. Therefore the expectation of Father Ledochowski, that Britain would have a friendly approach towards the American citizens subsequent to the war, was quite natural. But it was not the case, at least on some issues.[145] After the armistice the approach of Britain towards American citizens did seem rather peculiar. This was manifested in a concrete incident of refusal to issue visas to ten American Jesuits.[146]

This occurred when Father Ledochowski, after an intense deliberation with the Provincial of Maryland and New York Province decided to supply at least ten Jesuit personnel to Bombay-Poona as an immediate measure towards a rescue operation of the Mission. It did appear as though Britain had acted quite deliberately contrary to the expectations. Once again the hope of immediate arrangement of personnel for Bombay-Poona Mission failed. This is the time when two Jesuits - Frs. Joseph Duhr and Joseph Fell - of Luxemburg origin were sent to Bombay-Poona.[147] Both of them were studying theology in Kurseong, near Darjeeling in West Bengal.

While the efforts were still continuing, time was elapsing with its own pace. As it is clear, a substantial period of time had already elapsed before any concrete plan could be realized. It is here that it may at times give a space to the critics saying that a contingency plan to save the

145 See G.R. B. Holle, pub., Holle Universal Geschichte (Erlangen: Karl Mttller, 1988), 569-576.

146 Suria underlines a reason behind such a move of the British authorities. He writes that "fifty years later it was discovered that the ten Jesuits bore Irish and German surnames: Kelly, Murphy, Preuss, Donnelly. Ireland was in political ferment demanding independence. The British feared trouble from those to-be-Missionaries in India." Suria, "The German-Swiss Pioneers," 215.

147 See Hans Staffher, "Fr. Joseph Fell," in Deceased Members of the Western Region of the South Asian Assistancy of the Society of Jesus (Pune: Sanjeevan Niwas, 2008), 44-45, 50. See also Velinkar, German Jesuits on the West Coast of India, 68.

Mission came rather late. But the fact is Fr. Ledochowski was all along watchful and keenly interested in saving the Mission even in the event of the war. He tried to explore every possibility that would suitably make up for the harm caused by the lack of personnel. Finally he wrote a letter to Fr. Rembert Richard, the vice-Provincial of Southern German Region *(Regio Meridionalis)*[148] requesting him to make a selection of the Swiss Jesuits who could immediately be sent to Bombay-Poona Mission to carry on the work of the mission. At this point of time, there is also an indication that Fr. Ledochowski was pondering over a possibility of constituting Swiss Jesuits as a separate missionary entity, i.e., Mission, in order to entrust to them with the Poona Mission. Such is evident from the following letter:

> I ask you Reverend Father, to please give me the names of Jesuits of Swiss origin, fit for missions, and who could be sent to Poona Mission as soon as possible. As for the required permission from the Sacred Congregation for the Propagation of the Faith, it will be taken care of in the suitable time. The problems arising on the part of the civil authorities, if any, shall be dealt with. The Poona mission once so flourishing and well-organized, is now at the point of disaster. All of us must, therefore, come forward with diligence and care for the help of the mission. This affair must be binding on us as a mandate. Taking into consideration the opinion of the Fathers of the Mission and that of the experts as well as with the full approval of the Sacred Congregation for the Propagation of the Faith, I would like to join the Swiss Fathers of the Poona Mission, so as to constitute it into a separate mission from that of the Bombay mission. Things are still a secret. The obstacles arising on the part of the British Government need to be first tackled. But Reverend Father, this is the purpose of communicating with you with utmost urgency.[149]

---

148 This Region comprised of Bavaria, Wiirttemberg, Baden, Hohenzollern-Sigmaringen, Hessen except Upper Ffessen, Switzerland and Vorarlberg. See Schatz, Geschichte, vol. Ill, 16.

149 Wlodimir Ledochowski, Superior General to Rembert Richard (21st November 1919). "Rogo RVam, ut mihi nomina dare velit Patrum origine Helvetica qui apti ad vitam Missionum quam primum in Poonensem Missionem mitti possint. Per S. Congregationem de Propaganda Fide curabo, ut dificultates, si quae sint ex parte auctoritatum civilium, removeantur. Missio Poonensis, tam florens quondam ac bene ordinata, nunc vero tot tantisque obruta calamitatibus, omnio a nobis iuvari debet ideoque curae diligentiaeque RVae. hoc negotium mandans commendo. Re cum gravibus Patribus rerum Missionis

Although a number of Jesuits of Swiss and Luxemburg origin were working in Bombay-Poona right from the beginning of the mission, they did not form a separate entity. They were members of the united German Province. At this point, however, the consideration of the Swiss Jesuits as a possible choice for replacement in Bombay-Poona seems to spring from two major factors: firstly Switzerland and Luxemburg were neutral nations and secondly a number of the Swiss Jesuits were already working in the mission, having thus gained a good experience of the ground reality. The neutrality of Switzerland and Luxemburg would save from lot of inconveniences on the way.[150] But the plan was aborted for reasons best known to the curia of the General.

During this period the German Province itself, after the period of its exile,[151] was in the process of reorganization and division into two distinct entities. By the end of 1920 the final decision was made to the effect that the larger German province was divided into two independent provinces.[152] Apparently this process had already started in 1917 while World War I was still causing havocs in various parts of Europe. The reasons for the same were many and varied. One of the most compelling one was the big number of the Jesuits in the Province. The division of the German Province was effected by the decree of Fr. Ledochowski, published on 6th January 1921.

Meanwhile the consideration about the possible personnel for the takeover of the mission continued both in Rome as well as in Munich. The Province Congregation of the German Province held in 1920 took up the issue for further consideration. It came to the conclusion that the

---

peritis collata et cum plena approbatione S. Congregationis de Propaganda Fide velim Missionem Poonensem Patribus Helvetis committere, ita ut separatam a Missione Bombayensi Missionem constituant. Res adhuc es secreta eo magis, quod nondum omnes difficultates ex parte gubernii anglici remotae sint, sed R.V. hoc consilium communicandum esse censui, ut quid de eo sentiret mihi aperte diceret." ADPSJ, 45B-221 (1919), Nr. 1381, 6.

150 See "Acta Congregationis Provincialis Germaniae," ADPSJ, 45B-244 (1920), 1724; Joseph Guentensperger to Felix A. Planner (Poona, 28th August 1920), AMPSJ, Pune Alt.

151 See Schatz, Geschichte, Vol. II, 24.

152 See Wlodimir Ledochowski, Superior General to Rembert Richard (16th December 1920): "Cum mos sit in Societate, ut gravioribus in negotiis, quibus certe diviso Provinciarum est, singulorum quoque Superiorum et Consultorum audiantur vota, velit RVa. quamprimum separatis litteris nos certiores reddere, quidnam sentiat de rebus, quae in ultimis Consultationibus unanimus votis fuerint decisae, praesertim de territorio, de sociis, de rebus temporalibus." ADPSJ, 45B-221 (1920), Nr. 1382, 11.

Province as a whole was prepared to accept the final decision of the Superior General in the matter. It was apparent that the General was considering the Spanish Jesuits as a possible option.[153]

2.4.2. The Choice Falls on the Aragon Province

When the plan of entrusting the Bombay mission to the American Jesuits could not be realized, the final choice fell on the Aragon Province. It was a hard decision, for it implied that the Aragon Jesuits had to leave their Mission of the Philippines and move to Bombay Mission. It was not only a matter of emotional attachment. Rather the implementation of General's decision also implied setting their foot once again in a new milieu, with entirely new geographical, sociopolitical and cultural background. Yet the larger aim of the Society of Jesus was to be kept upper most. The process that followed does attract our attention.

2.4.3. The Philippine's Loss was Bombay-Poona's Gain

As briefly mentioned above, Fr. Ledochowski had intended to hand over Bombay Mission to the Jesuits of the Maryland and New York Provinces. He had hardly any inkling, however, that the British authorities would be proving hurdles on the road ahead. Eventually the British authorities refused to issue the required passports to the American Jesuits and the plan to send the American Jesuits to Bombay was aborted. The Superior General had to look for other possibilities. His sight fell on the Jesuits of Aragon Province.

The Jesuits of Aragon Province were working in the Philippines for a number of decades, in fact centuries and by the time the war broke out they had established the mission on a solid ground. Their firm position in the Philippines mission is well revealed from the following account:

> They were proud of their Ateneo, where instruction was imparted to 1,123 students in 1914. They were in charge of the Inter-diocesan Seminary, and held in high esteem by the ecclesiastical authorities. Their observatory had made a name for itself throughout the eastern typhoon-infested seas. In the mission field they had a hundred schools, chapels and churches; they loved the Philippines, and were loved by them.[154]

153 See "Acta Congregationis Provincialis Germaniae," ADPSJ, 45B-244 (1920), Nr. 1724: "Missio Bombayensi nobis dempta et advocatis Patribus Hispanis immediate Pi Generali subiecta est."

154 Ibid., 400.

The Spanish Jesuit presence in the Philippines was almost as old as the Society of Jesus itself. Indeed the Jesuit presence in the Philippines is recorded in 1581.[155] This was around the same time when the mission to China was started. As the Society of Jesus was suppressed in the Philippines (1769), as many as 158 Jesuits were expelled from there.[156] Apparently the mission could be resumed only from 1859 again, when the Spanish Jesuits landed in Manila once again.[157]

In 1914 when World War I broke out, the Spanish Jesuits were doing a yeomen service in the Philippines. Their cumulative presence by this time was nearly 350 years. Undoubtedly, therefore, the mission was well consolidated which was much weakened in the formal period of suppression (1773-1814) and the decades following the restoration (1814) of the Society of Jesus. However, the time had come to hand over the mission so dearly loved and established with much hardship and labour. Humanly speaking it was bound to be painful. Yet such was the demand of the Jesuit obedience. "In 1921 the Spanish Jesuits in the Philippines were ordered to hand over the Philippines to American Jesuits and to undertake instead the Mission of Bombay."[158]

The situation created by the letter of the Superior General to this effect may be well imagined, all the more while it was completely unexpected. The urgency of the situation to save Bombay mission, however, was of paramount importance. This phase of history, when official exchange of letters between the Provincial of Aragon Province and the General of the Society of Jesus continued, was surcharged with emotions. On the one hand there was a pressing need of immediate rescue of the Bombay mission, while on the other there was a natural human tendency of attachment to centuries-long mission of the Philippines. That Fr. Ledochowski himself may have found the moment difficult is evident from his letter to the Provincial of Aragon Province, Fr. Juan Guim:

> I am fully aware, Reverend Father, that I am asking a difficult and heart-breaking thing by thus ordering our Fathers in the Philippines

155 See William V. Bangert, *A History of the Society of Jesus,* 236-251. See also C. Suria, *History of the Catholic Church in Gujarat,* 217; Christopher Hollis, *Die Jesuiten,* 48-49.

156 See Suria, *History of the Catholic Church in Gujarat,* 220.

157 See Baengert, *A History of the Society of Jesus,* 471-472. See also Gense, *Church at the Gateway,* 400.

158 Gense, Church at the Gateway, *400.*

> to give up, for the good of others, their Mission which is so dear to them, and where they have labored for so many long years, with such great apostolic zeal and in a most exemplary and noble manner and this thought has greatly exercised my mind. But after long and mature deliberation, after having often and earnestly prayed to God, I saw no way other than this to save the mission of Bombay, which is in such a parlous state; and I feel confident that in all this I am but doing God's Holy Will.[159]

That the Spanish Jesuits in the Philippines found it hard to believe their own ears as the news was made known them, is made apparent from the personal diaries of two Spanish Jesuits, who were eye-witnesses to the emotionally surcharged moment of the letters of Fr. General being read in Manila on 11th May 1921. Yet they accepted the decision of Fr. General with exemplary humility and generosity.[160] In spite of heavy hearts, ten Jesuits volunteered for the new mission within a few days of arrival of this news.

2.4.4. Bifurcation of the Mission (1929)

At the time of the transfer of the Mission to the Upper German Province (10.10.1929), the Poona Mission was coincidental with the Diocese of Poona where Bishop Henry Doring after a gap of about 12 years was back again in 1927. Poona, at the time, was a huge geographical area of about 150000 square kilometers with 10.5 million inhabitants; of which 27000 were Catholics. Besides, the separation of Christian communities by vast distances, poor means of transportation, the many new Christians who do not have a school with a catechist in the area, the non-Christian surroundings etc., were daunting challenges. In such circumstances, not less than 40 missionaries were required to attend to the pastoral care of the converts and for further expansion of the work. The number of existing missionaries could hardly suffice to preserve the mission from decay. But only a few missionaries were left there. Among them too some could be considered virtually numbers, i.e., Francis X. Trenkamp, and others, as they could assist only in hearing confessions. Besides financial crunch, the severe crunch of missionaries forced the number of catechists and their respective stations to be reduced to a

159 Ibid., 401-302.

160 See Suria, History of the Catholic Church in Gujarat, 218-219. These two Jesuits were Fr. Thomas Molina and Br. Vincent Bou. See Gense, Church the Gateway, 400-406.

minimum. The missionaries could hardly afford half a dozen times in a year to visit the villages. What would become of the new Christians under such circumstances, especially the many small stations without catechists, was probably self-evident.[161]

One the positive side, however, during this entire phase of history there were 18 native priests active in Poona Mission by 1929. But the sad part of the story was that none of these native priests were products of the German Jesuit Mission. The native priests were products of the Archdiocese of Goa or other Jesuit Missions, who had volunteered to work in Poona Misison.[162]

2.5. The Second World War: A Second Interruption[163]

From a few sources of information a point becomes amply clear that the Jesuits, although not free from apprehensions about the possible gravity of situation, were slightly more prepared to face the situation in the wake of the breaking out of World War II in comparison with the previous war, for "a general apprehension among the Jesuits was that they would be treated in the same manner as was the case during the previous war."[164]

As a precautionary measure, therefore, one of the first steps that they had taken was to apply for obtaining a status as British subjects, for which they had to fulfill a few requirements. It would not be wrong to say that they had learnt lessons from the previous experiences. In the case of a general order of internment and repatriation, this step would save at least some Jesuits in the mission field. These aspects are clearly underlined in a letter of Remigius Rauw (Mission Superior):

> At present, our attention is focused on the international situation. We expect the outbreak of war at any moment. This would again be a great misfortune for the mission, but not as badly as 25 years

161 See Francis X. Schubiger to Joseph Tschudi (Sangamner, 05th Feburaryl932), AMPSJ, Pune Alt.

162 See "Annual Report of Bishop Henry Doring for the Year 1929," AMPSJ, Pune Alt. See also Gense, Church at the Gateway, 392.

163 Under this sub-topic we shall mention only those aspects that are more general in nature having an implication for the entire mission. Other aspects directly pertaining to a certain particular issues, i.e., internment of Professors and challenges of running the De Nobili College, etc. will be discussed in chapter five (i.e., # 5.2.2.1).

164 Felix A. Plattner, "Die Mission im neuen Weltkrieg: Indien," M/MS(1940): 37 in AMPSJ, Belege 1941-1949.

> ago. For all the Germans who were able to do so under the law have acquired British citizenship. Besides the 2 Italians, the Germans who are at the risk [of being taken to internment camps] are [Francis] Benz, [Emmeran] Sturm, [Francis X.] Daschner, [Paul] Hormann and [Maximilian] Zinser and [Joseph] Neuner, [Felix zu] Lowenstein as well as Scholastics [Rupert] Schweigert, [Joseph] Braunger, [Guido] Martini and [John] Roder besides Brothers [Joseph] Neukamm and [Bernhard] Tretter. Over and above that, the 3 whom we still await cannot come [from Germany] anymore.[165]

This apprehension finally did come to be true. Even the steps taken in precaution could not save some of the Jesuits from being taken to the internment camps. This is revealed in another letter by Remigius Rauw addressed to the Superior General:

> I know Your Paternity will be anxious about the state of our Mission in these troubled times ... The third of September did not find us quite unprepared ... Fifteen younger members, however, were interned at once at the outbreak of the war. Of de Nobili College three Professors: Frs. [Joseph] Neuner, [Felix] zu Lowenstein and [Maximilian] Zinser, and 2 Scholastics [Joseph] Braunger and [Rupert] Schweigert were taken, of St. Vincent's High School 2 Priests (Fathers [Paul] Hormann and [Francis X.] Daschner) and 2 Scholastics ([John] Roder and [John Baptist] Thiel) and Br. [Joseph] Neukamm and Fr. [Rudolph] Schtitz, General Director of the Students' Missionary League. Thus this house lost 11 members. Hubli High School lost Schol. [Guido] Martini. Fr. [Emmeran] Sturm was taken from his Parish at Deolali, Fr. [Francis] Benz from the Mission Station of Kendal and Br. [Bernhard] Tretter from Sangamner.[166]

As far as their treatment in the camps is concerned, it appears to have been comparatively better in many respects than with the previous war. A report of two Steyler missionaries, i.e., certain Haberl and Golomb, who

---

165 Remigius Rauw to John B. Villiger (Poona, 25th August 1939), AMPSJ, Pune Alte-II. Villiger was the Superior of the Jesuit community at Schonbrunn (Switzerland) from 1937-1941.

166 Remigius Rauw to the Superior General (Poona, 11th October 1939), ARSI, Poona. 1004-XII, 9. See also Remigius Rauw to John B. Villiger (Poona, 25th August 1939), AMPSJ, Pune Alte-II; Augustine Rosch to the Parents and Relatives of the Missionaries in Poona (Munich, End of November 1939), AMPSJ, Pune Alte-ll; Schatz, Geschichte, Vol. Ill, 320.

had worked in Chinese Turkestan, after their arrest in India on their way to Rome and three week internment at Ahmednagar camp confirms this claim. On signing an affidavit that they did not desire to return to India or China, they were released from the camp and subsequently could travel back to Europe. Sharing their personal experiences they revealed that the inmates of the camps were treated reasonably well provided they observed the rules of the camp and shared in the works of the same. According to them, the Jesuit Fathers (as well as others) were permitted to celebrate the Holy Eucharist regularly. It must be clarified, however, that for a chapel the missionaries had to virtually fight against the camp authorities. In any case, after almost a year, the request was granted.[167] The meals were normally satisfactory. In case they wished, they could also do some physical exercises. Visitors, however, were not permitted. It would, however, certainly be a simplistic presentation of the entire situation if we maintain that the interned Jesuits and others did not have to face inconveniences. Indeed, there were inconveniences. Some of the Jesuits along with others were interned for the entire period of war. Among the Jesuits of Poona mission Joseph Neuner along with Felix zu Lowenstein, Paul Hormann and Rudolph Schiitz was interned for the longest period of time namely till the end of the war. Rudolph Schiitz was once released in between and later taken to the camp at Purandhar, which seems to have been much more lenient in every respect. He was permitted to make occasional pastoral visits to the sick of the families of the interned members.[168]

The period of internment also offered some chances of interaction and sharing with other missionary bodies. The questions that such interactions gave rise to were basically pertaining to the adaptation and challenges to evangelization in the emerging political scenario. In any case, a majority of the missionaries made use of the period of their stay in many creative activities like study of theology,[169] learning new languages, teaching and composing hymns, etc. It may not be directly relevant to our discussion but it may be mentioned all the same that a few Steyler missionaries were ordained to priesthood during their stay

---

167 Joseph Peters, "Kriegsschicksale unserer deutschen Missionare," .KM (1947): 5.

168 Ibid., 4-5.

169 This aspect will be dealt with in a greater detail in chapter five (Cf. # 5.2.2.1).

in the camps by Bishop Sinyangchow of China.[170] Felix A. Plattner summarizes these points in the following words:

> The treatment of the inmates in the camps, by and large, was good, so that the younger Jesuit Scholastics could continue their studies, while other Jesuits were not hindered from practicing their Religious obligations. This became more relaxed once they were transferred from Ahmednagar to the camp in Dehra Dun in north India. The climate of the place too was beneficial to the inmates.[171]

In a majority of the cases, the condition in Dehra Dun camp was much better as compared with the one in Ahmednagar. In Dehra Dun the internment was a kind of parole-camps where the rules and regulations were much relaxed in comparison with the other forms of internment, i.e., camp A or B at Ahmednagar meant for prisoners of war and civil prisoners respectively. Some of the missionaries who had acquired British citizenship, were also taken once again in the camp here in the wake of an intelligence report. The total number of the interned members never rose above 50 here. By the beginning of 1947 all the members were released.[172]

The main concern, however, was to facilitate a speedy acquittal of the Jesuits. Based on their experiences, the two Steyler missionaries mentioned-above proposed the idea that if the Jesuits wished to achieve the objective at the earliest possible time, they would require to sign an affidavit with an assurance that they do not wish to return to India anymore. This condition, be as it may, was rather intricate, especially in relation to the Jesuit mission. Hence, a dilemma prevailed among the authorities - the Archbishops of Bombay and Poona as well as the Mission Superior of Poona.[173] Consequently, an attempt was made to explore an alternative possibility for the release of the Jesuits along with other missionaries of German nationality (nearly 100 in all),[174] whereby the intervention of Archbishop Thomas Roberts of Bombay was sought. He

---

170 See Peters, "Kriegsschicksale," op. cit, 4-5.

171 Plattner, "Die Mission im neuen Weltkrieg: Indien," MJBKS (1940): 37 in AMPSJ, Belege 1941- 1949. See also Peters, "Kriegsschicksale," op. cit., 5.

172 See Peters, "Kriegsschicksale," op. cit., 4.

173 See Karl Brust to the Superior General (Rome, 22nd October 1939), ARSI, Poona. 1004-X11, 10.

174 See Archbishop Thomas Roberts to the Cardinal Prefect of the Propaganda Fidei (Bombay, 26th November 1939) (Copy), ARSI, Poona. 1004-X1I, 13.

was in an advantageous position because of his being a British national. He took a personal interest in intermediating the process and to that effect he undertook an interview in his capacity with Sir Roger Lumley, the then Governor of Bombay Presidency. He was able to win "the confidence of the Government and of the Investigating Commission"[175] and thus was able to establish a good rapport with the British officers. Reporting on 26th November 1939, in his three-page typed letter he brought to the notice of the Cardinal Prefect of the Propaganda Fide the general disposition of the British Administration as well as certain technical issues on the way to the release of the interned members. In his opinion, Sir Roger Lumley, the Governor of Bombay Presidency as well as Sir Malcolm Darling (Chairman of the Commission of Inquiry about the allegations against individuals) were positively disposed towards the missionaries in general. However, under the general order of the Government they were helpless to act in favour of the missionaries. One of his letters reveals an important aspect with regard to the hurdles on the way to the release of missionaries. In his own words:

> A commission under Sir Malcolm Darling had already been investigating the cases of refugee German Jews in the camp and most of these had been released. Reports from the camp, however, declared that the Commission had no authority to examine missionaries (I learnt later that some influential persons in the Army and Intelligence departments were opposing the release of the missionaries).[176]

In another letter he wrote about the issue in more unambiguous terms:

> Individually and collectively the members of the Commission were most reasonable and considerate. Sir Malcolm Darling who had invited me to stay with him made it clear that there were influential people both in the Government and police opposed to the release of missionaries, and these had to be taken into account by the Commission which itself had power only to recommend release.[177]

---

175 Remigius Rauw to the Superior General (Poona, 12th October 1940), ARSI, Poona. 1004-XIII, 5.

176 Archbishop Thomas Roberts to the Cardinal Prefect of the Propaganda Fidei (Bombay, 26th November 1939) (Copy), ARSI, Poona. 1004-XII, 13.

177 Archbishop Thomas Roberts to the Governor of Bombay Presidency (Bombay, 26th November 1939) (Copy), ARSI, Poona. 1004-XII, 13 (Annexure).

The main terms and conditions in the demand by the Government in processing the request for the release was basically a demand of pledge of loyalty to the British Government from all the interned members and more especially from the missionaries. The Commission of Inquiry headed by Sir Malcolm Darling was insistent upon one single point in order to justify the cases of individuals before the British Government: that the missionaries in no manner depicted an allegiance to the Nazi ideology. This was done in view of certain indiscretion occasionally shown by the missionaries themselves. From the sources of information it is rather ambiguous to point out as to which Religious Order or which group of missionaries had indulged in a kind of Nazi plot in the camp. Yet it is clear that some kind of attempt did seem to have taken place, which eventually became an obstacle on the road to instant order of general release of the inmates of the camps. A Letter by Edward Goulet (Secretary for the Missions of the Society of Jesus), which quotes Archbishop Roberts reveals the same:

> There is a severe paragraph in the undertaking to be signed by the Superiors: this was put in by the commission in the knowledge of strong opposition to any release at all. The Government of India has been forced to be more severe than in any other part of the English Empire owing to the discovery of a Nazi plot which would have embarrassed England very much; there also the very critical political situation, and no one can be surprised that Government does not want higher education to be directed against England. There is no more than a veiled hint of these things in my letter to Propaganda, but it would be very much to the interest of the Church and Society that these things should be clearly understood.[178]

It is not clear as to what the nature of the above-mentioned plot with regard to Nazi ideology allegedly discovered in the camps. Yet the burden of proving the contrary was laid on the Religious Orders. To achieve this purpose, Archbishop Roberts, on behalf of the Superiors of Religious Congregations, submitted the missionary programme of each congregation in detail, which included "the instructions from the Holy See and the Constitutions of the various Orders concerning exclusion of politics and censorship of letters."[179] This proved a great safeguard for many congregations, which eventually expedited the process of

178 Edward Goulet, "Ad Notitiam," (Rome, 9th December 1939), ARSI, Poona. 1004-XII, 16.

179 Ibid.

release of the missionaries later. The Steyler missionaries were the first beneficiaries of this arrangement. On account of their clear presentation of their missionary program, rules and regulations, a maximum number of them were released first. The Jesuits too, in a majority of cases, were eventually the beneficiaries of this arrangement. The Protestant missionaries, on the other hand, were on the receiving end on account of their failure to submit the same.[180] Most likely, this may have been the reason why the story of this phase of history seems to come in darker shades from the perspective of the Protestant missionaries as compared to the Catholic point of view. What appears, all the same, to be a common denominator in the experiences of the Christian missionaries-- both Catholic and Protestant--in general is that the entire episode of internment was generally interpreted as "an exaggerated process, particularly since the Central Intelligence Department had a fairly clear knowledge concerning the German missionary families [as well as missionary bodies]."[181]

Although the period of internment was much shorter than the previous case, we get an impression that the process may still have been expedited, if a few things had been taken into consideration. According to Archbishop Roberts, one of the major reasons for the delay in releasing the missionaries seems to have been a sort of occasional lack of tactical approach on the part of the missionaries in general in framing the letters addressed to the Government.[182] In spite of such initial obstacles the process of releasing the interned members began within a few months as we read in a letter of Archbishop Doring: "We have good hopes that the interned Fathers and Scholastics will be released. As a matter of fact, 2 Scholastics and 2 lay brothers have already been allowed to return to their work. We are to be very grateful to the Government for their helpful attitude towards us, you need not have any anxiety."[183]

These incidents apart, a few Jesuits themselves seem to have been partially responsible for the delay in their release. The cases of Felix zu

---

180 Ibid.

181 Paul von Tucher, Nationalism: Case and Crisis in Missions: German Missions in British India 1939-1946. (Erlangen: Selbstverlag Paul von Tucher, 1980), 503.

182 See Archbishop Thomas Roberts to the Cardinal Prefect of the Propaganda Fidei (Bombay, 26th November 1939) (Copy), ARSI, Poona. 1004-XII, 13.

183 Archbishop Henry Doring to the General (Poona, 10th December 1939), ARSI, Poona-XII, 14.

Lowenstein and Paul Hormann tend to come more often in the available correspondences as being rather peculiar in nature. Though the identity is not revealed, a letter of Pius Geisel gives an indication to the fact that some of the Jesuits did show some amount of lack of discretion on their part in dealing with some of the sensitive issues of the time. The letter reads: "The Fathers who are interned will be sent back. But they are themselves responsible for their fault. How can they do such foolishness and celebrate the Holy Mass for the departed Hitler, etc.? I really cannot understand such things."[184] Similarly Archbishop Roberts mentioned about the peculiar case of Felix zu Lowenstein and Paul Hormann. About the latter he wrote: "Concerning Fr. Hormann, it was again the unanimous verdict of the Commission that Fr. Hormann was 'fanatical'; I myself do not know him at all, but the belief of the Commission is frankly shared by at least two of his brethren who have spoken to me on the subject."[185] These are a few instances that suggest that in some cases the obstacles were created from among the Jesuits and other missionaries themselves.

After the outbreak of the war, apparently the exchange of information and news between Europe and the mission field was not easy. The correspondence was not prohibited as such, but certainly restricted and consequently became irregular. The letters took nearly 4-5 months to reach Europe and usually had to go through three different stages of censorship. The missionaries, therefore, wrote shorter letters and refrained from mentioning what was more than personal or local. What was responsible for the partial picture of the reality in the mission field, according to Felix A. Plattner, was the deliberate control of press as a precaution to restrain from giving a realistic picture, which might have fueled the animosity between nations and in international relations may not be affected.[186]

In Germany too, the news reached only through friends and Jesuits in Switzerland.[187] Therefore, it is certainly not possible to form an idea

184 Pius Geisel to Francis Hayler, Provincial of Southern German Province (Rahata, 25th October 1945), AMPSJ, IB. Rahata Briefe.

185 Archbishop Thomas Roberts to the Superior General (Bombay, 12th March 1940), ARSI, Poona. 1004-XIII, 5.

186 Felix A. Plattner, "Die Mission im neuen Weltkrieg: Indien," MJBKS(1940): 36 in AMPSJ, Belege 1941-1949.

187 Augustine Rosch to the Parents and Relatives of the Missionaries in Poona (Munich, End of November 1939), AMPSJ, Pune Alte-H. Rosch was the Provincial of Southern German Province from 1935 to 1945.

into the exact details of the events unfolding during this time. Yet, through the sources we have, we may form a fairly good opinion that by and large the missionary endeavour was not so much affected as was the case during World War I. We have some testimonies to support this. For example, Archbishop Doring wrote: "Even in these evil days we have to thank God for many things. Most of our Fathers are working at their stations without any molestation and there is good hope that the others will soon return to their work. Elsewhere heavy trials and persecutions threaten your children, but we have learnt to see in all this hidden benefits."[188] The Mission Superior, Remigius Rauw described the situation as follows: "The work in our Mission is going on without difficulty in usual way, especially all Fathers, except four, have returned to their work."[189] Giving a general picture of the Jesuit missions in India during this period, John B. Moyersoen too wrote: "Work continues in all our missions, almost as if there was no war. Here and there some restrictions are there ... Seven Fathers from Poona, three from Calicut ... and one Scholastic from this Mission, are at Ahmednagar."[190] Towards the end of the war, Remigius Rauw gives a positive picture: "By this I wish to give the annual account of our Poona Mission. Not much, however, is to be said about it, which is a good sign that things here take their usual course. We are very thankful to [the] Divine Providence who has watched over us."[191] Finally, a short article captures these developments fittingly thus:

> Thus the Puna mission, despite war and consequent internment of some of the missionaries courageously and unbrokenly enters the last decade of the first century of its existence in India. Everything that had been created in this stony vineyard by the Swiss Jesuits and their German confreres with the grace of God would not have been possible without the support of the friends in the homeland.[192]

---

188 Archbishop Henry Doring to the Superior General (Poona, 24* November 1939), ARSI, Poona. 1004-XII, 12.

189 Remigius Rauw to the Superior General (Poona, 31st December 1939), ARSI, Poona. 1004-XII, 18.

190 "Ex Litteris R. P. J[ohn] B. Moyersoen, Sup. Miss. Calc, 15 Novembris 1940," ARSI, Poona. 1004-XIII, 8. John B. Moyersoen was the Superior of the Bengal Jesuit Mission who was entrusted with an additional responsibility of the Visitor to the Jesuit Missions in central and northern India during the period of World War II.

191 Remigius Rauw to the Visitor (Poona, 15th February 1944), ARSI, Poona. 1004-XIV, 20.

192 "Puna heute: Der Missionsobere meldet," IB 13 (March 1944): 16.

Felix A. Plattner, recapitulating the situation subsequent to the breaking out of World War II made the following observation:

> But Archbishop Doring, on the whole, was right about the events. When the Second World War broke out in 1939 and again brought the internment of a number of German missionaries, the mission was so consolidated that the remaining missionaries could keep all the stations and works through the long years of war without having to give up a single one of them.[193]

All these instances are substantial evidences to justify the claim that the impact of the war was not as devastating as the case was during World War I. A related point that is not too uncommon to maintain was that the British officers nurtured certain bias towards the Catholic Church. Felix A. Plattner too vouches for the same with a claim that there existed documentary evidences to prove that occasionally such cases did surface. In spite of these occasional instances what comes rather more emphatically is the fact that the British officers were generally impartial in dealing with all the missionaries. Citing a concrete example from the context of the internment he writes:

> In the internment camps it was often explained that the Government was not against the Jesuit mission in particular and the Catholic Church in general as such. But the Jesuits were victims of a general politics and hence their internment was a precautionary measure. A Swiss Jesuit even questioned the Governor: "What do you think of the internment of the Jesuits?" The frank response to the same was: "That was a virtual folly."[194]

This, in some measure, suggests a corrective course to the understanding that the British officers were either prejudiced or at least indifferent towards the Jesuits. We may cite a few more examples to support this claim. About his encounter with various ranks of authorities in the British Government, Archbishop Roberts wrote:

> Having seen the difficulties of the Government from within and noted with real edification the very reasonable and considerate attitude of the Commission, I may perhaps be allowed to advance the suggestion that a word of appreciation from the Holy Father to

193 "Erzbischof Doring Gestorben," IB 1 (January/ February 1952): 52.

194 Plattner, "Die Mission im neuen Weltkrieg: Indien," op. cit.

> the Government of India through the ordinary channels would be appreciated.[195]

Archbishop Doring too reiterated the same opinion in his letter to the Superior General saying: "We are to be very grateful to the Government for their helpful attitude towards us."[196] While making incessant efforts to acquire the release of two Jesuits namely Felix zu Lowenstein and Paul Hormann, Archbishop Roberts stressed the point once again emphatically about the impartiality and positive disposition of the British authorities:

> However, the members of the Commission have the same right as anyone else to their reputation, and since I know that their attitude has been most unfairly represented, I feel it my duty to point out: 1. That it is a priori most unlikely that a Commission which has treated all the other missionaries not only with fairness but with utmost consideration should single out two fathers for something like persecution ... I may add that nearly all of the one hundred Catholic missionaries released have testified to Sir Malcolm Darling or to me how deeply impressed they were with the Christian and humane attitude of the Commission.[197]

Pius Geisel reiterates the benevolence of the British Government: "Thanks to the fact that many of the priests of Poona Mission are British citizens or neutrals and thanks to the enlightened and generous policy of the British Government, which released so far nearly all German priests, all works of the Mission could be carried on."[198]

These points apart, the difference in the approach of the British authorities in dealing with the Jesuits in the camps was that they were treated on the basis of their individuality and not as a group. Most likely the reason for the same was the fact that the influence of the Church of England both in the British Parliament as well as in the Government became much less as compared with the years between 1914 and 1918.[199]

---

195 Archbishop Thomas Roberts to the Cardinal Prefect of the Propaganda Fidei (Bombay, 26th November 1939) (Copy), ARSI, Poona. 1004-XII, 13.

196 Archbishop Henry Doring to the Superior General (Poona, 10th December 1939), ARSI, Poona. 1004-XII, 14.

197 Archbishop Thomas Roberts to the Superior General (Bombay, 12th March 1939), ARSI, Poona. I004-XIII, 5.

198 Pius Geisel to the General (Poona, 28,h December 1939), ARSI, Poona 1004-XII, 17.

199 See Plattner, "Die Mission im neuen Weltkrieg: Indien," op. cit.

All these go on to prove that the British authorities, by and large, were impartial if not positively disposed towards the missionaries in general. Moreover, the survey also reveals that the mission was not so much affected as in the case of the previous war. The following remark by Joseph Peters pertains to the context of the German missionaries in general working in various mission fields, gives a good summary of the entire period:

> In summary, when looking back at the first part of the war, it can be said that the German missions in countries of the Allies, in comparison to the First World War, where about 940 missionaries were interned for a long time and then expelled, and still after the Treaty of Versailles had to leave the missions, the situation this time is much better. The percentage of the interned remains low. The overwhelming majority of the internees were at liberty at the end of the war.[200]

2.6. The Mission after the Independence of India (1947)

The independence of India on the 15th August 1947 was not only the beginning of a new era for the Indians in general but also for the Church in India. The Catholic Church in India, in spite of facing challenges of various descriptions had made a visible progress over the last decades. Undoubtedly such a growth was possible on account of the British policy of religious freedom and legal safeguard even if it did not mean a direct support from the Government.[201] The Jesuits and many other Religious Orders had established a good rapport with the English officials. This was the reason that often certain nationalist Hindus were hopeful that along with the British, the European missionaries would depart from India. No wonder, they were astonished when their expectations, at least in relation to the Catholic priests, were not fulfilled. What seems to have helped the Catholic missions at the most at this juncture was the clear separation of mission and colonial power. In spite of the good rapport with the British authorities, the Catholic missionaries refrained from taking an active part in politics. That separation meant a great advantage for the Church. Fortunately, under the leadership of Jawaharlal Nehru, the Indian Government adopted a Constitution that accorded equal

200 Peters, "Kriegsschicksale," op.cit., 4.

201 See Emil Kaufmann, "Die britische Macht und die katholische Mission in Indien," IB 3 (May/June 1947): 4.

rights to all the citizens and freedom to practice and propagate their own religion. The clear implication for the Church, thereby, was that the profound change in the political realm did not shatter or endanger the church organization.[202]

Concerning the mission proper, the year 1948 may be recognized, in the words of Felix Plattner as a year of transition and growth. He uses the imagery of an incomplete building to symbolize the Poona mission at this stage. In his own words:

> Somewhere during my last journey in India I saw an incomplete building. The foundation of the same was strongly laid down and the walls were built solidly with stones. But it suddenly collapsed ... The incomplete building should be an image and a reminder for us at the beginning of the New Year. That reminds me of the Poona mission in various ways. The solidly built walls are symbolic of what has been firmly achieved in ninety years. The arch symbolizes the plans and projects that have taken a concrete form und now stand as a sign of hope for the future. But one of them does not suit our construction plan: that the labourers leave the work and give in to complacence thinking that they have built a tower of Babylon ... Via remote communications with the Superior of the Mission I testify that 1948 was a year of transition and growth for Puna. For example a few important decisions were taken for the reorganization of the mission, a Major Superior visited the whole mission, the first supply of young Swiss personnel arrived in India, and a few capable persons were sent to Rome for higher education. The new building of the De Nobili College was opened again for the Scholastics. The Marathi Middle School was constructed and inaugurated. The indigenous vocations from the better off families grew up further. The rest of the work could be continued despite some anxiety and the price-hike for the consumer articles.[203]

This imagery was certainly meaningful in more ways than one. Meanwhile it also reveals some amount of anxiety and apprehension in the mind of the missionaries. Although Felix Plattner had never worked as a missionary in India, he possessed a deep understanding of what it meant to a missionary. His book on India, namely *The Catholic India:*

---

202 See Felix A. Plattner, "Zeitenwende in Indien: Zur Weihe des indischen Bischofs in der Puna-Mission," AMPS J, Belege 1941-1949. See also Felix A. Plattner, "Republik Indien," IB 1 (January/February 1950): 179.

203 Felix A. Plattner, "Das unvollendete Haus,"/£ 1 (January/February 1949): 128.

Yesterday and Today, is an articulation of his personal interest in matters that were significant for a missionary body working in India.

One of the more remarkable areas of achievement was that the considerable progress made in the promotion of indigenous vocations, apparently with no significant results till then.[204] All these were possible because of the wise guidance of the past Popes. Already Leo XIII had stressed the need for the indigenous clergy for India. Pius XI initiated the practical implementation of this program, who consecrated an Indian priest as the first native Bishop of the Latin rite. His successor went a step further. He appointed an indigenous Bishop to a North-Indian diocese, which was by no means far advanced. Thus, for example, Allahabad received an Indian bishop and Calcutta a coadjutor. The new diocese of Ahmedabad was placed under the care of a local Jesuit bishop. In the same year, Archbishop Doring too consecrated his successor, Mgr. Andrew D'Souza, who came from an old Christian family of Goa.[205]

This ideal began to be pursued more earnestly from around this time on. The foundation of the De Nobili College may be taken as a symbol of the commitment of the Jesuits in this direction. But there were areas that needed to be given a greater focus. Although Swiss and German Jesuits have been working for more than ninety years in the mission, the Jesuits had not yet succeeded in affording a sufficient pastoral care to approximately thirty parishes and mission stations that they had founded. The diocesan priests, who worked in collaboration with the Jesuits, belonged mostly to the neighboring Archdiocese of Goa. Even until this point of time, the mission had not been able to found further new mission stations and parishes, so that the entire mission could be handed over as an independent diocese to the indigenous clergy, which eventually is the highest ideal of a missionary body. Therefore, the burden of responsibility and work laid still on the Society of Jesus. It may be counted as an achievement, albeit, a bit late though, that for the first time in its history, the Bombay Mission had entrusted the ecclesiastical leadership to Andrew D'Souza as its first indigenous bishop.[206] On 4th December 1950, Valerian Gracias, a former student of the Jesuits was

204 We shall discuss the point more elaborately in chapter six (i.e., # 6.2).

205 See Felix A. Plattner, "Zeitenwende in Indien: Zur Weihe des indischen Bischofs in der Puna-Mission," AMPSJ, Belege 1941-1949. See also "Ecce Sacerdotus Magnus," IB 6 (Dezember 1949): 168.

206 Ibid.

appointed as the Archbishop of Bombay, who later was elevated as the first Indian Cardinal.[207]

As for the city of Poona and its suburbs, it must be mentioned that it was doubtlessly a key point of the Catholic mission, not only from the perspective of the Jesuit Mission but also from that of the Church in Western India. Although the beginning of the Catholic Church went back to no less than two centuries and the German-Swiss Jesuits had been active there for not less than ninety years, the church had not been able to establish itself beyond what may be called the foundation. This is verified from the fact that the city of Poona had just three parishes, three middle schools for boys and girls and a few budding associations. When one travelled in the outskirts of Poona, he could not see a Catholic Church for hours. In other words, the vast distances were still untouched by the Mission even after nearly hundred years of dedicated work in the area.[208] Yet, it cannot be denied that the Mission was making a slow yet a steady progress. Apparently its geographical vastness was a matter which cannot be ignored.

Amidst these developments, in 1956 the mission was elevated to the status of a Vice-Province with the name Belgaum-Poona Vice Province, about which we shall mention a few facts shortly. Underneath we make a mention of one of the major implications of the independence of India for the mission in particular and the Church in India in general. It pertains to the sense of uncertainty that the Jesuits along with other Religious Orders began to feel in the wake of the political power coming to the Indian masses represented by the Congress Party.[209] Such apprehensions were already surfacing among the Jesuits, which is revealed by Felix A. Plattner:

> The missionary enterprise now appears to be disturbed in India, but luckily it is not interrupted or even vengeful. The damage could probably be compensated in a comparatively shorter time. Much more lasting consequences are likely to arise from the general political situation. In its external development, the visible church is dependent on the play of economic, cultural and state forces. But

207 See "100 Jahre Puna Mission," IB 4/5 (1954): 1.

208 "puna. urisere Aufgabe heute," *Allen Alles: MICA-Sondemummerder,,IndischenBilder"*(September 1947): 13.

209 We shall discuss the issue in a greater detail in chapter four (i.e., # 4.4.2.2).

> today India is in the midst of a dramatic struggle and perhaps the turning point of its history.[210]

A positive side of the story was the safeguard received in the Constitution of India. But even prior to that the secular credentials of Jawaharlal Nehru, the first Prime Minister of India were even more assuring. His statement noted by Felix Plattner gives an idea that the missionaries in general might have felt a sense of relief:

> At a time when the Church is persecuted in so many countries, and every religion is at all opposed, it is a joy to be able to register two statements by Indian statesmen, which bear witness to a very different conviction. For the friends of the Indian missions, the following words are all the more important since they should be a guarantee statement for a peaceful and secure development of the Church of India. The first explanation comes from the Indian Prime Minister, Pandit Nehru, who, as is well known, paid a visit to our homeland [Switzerland] at the beginning of May [1949]. When, at the end of a press conference, the journalists were given the opportunity to ask questions to the leading statesman of India, a Catholic journalist inquired about the future of the church in free India. According to the "Press Information" of the Indian Embassy in Berne ... Nehru replied: "India is perfectly secular - it offers absolute freedom of religion. We do not grant any privileges to religion, although the overwhelming majority of the people adhere to the Hindu religion. It must not be forgotten that in India, although it has been divided, and unfortunately on a rather religious basis, there are still about 35 million Muslims. Moreover, a large number of Christians and Buddhists live in India, and the number of Catholics in India is as great as that in Switzerland."[211]

The official stand of the leaders of the stature of Nehru apart, the experience of the sense of insecurity among the Church leaders in free India was a realistic issue. The sporadic incidents of hostility towards Christian missionaries on various occasions were not lacking. Consequently, the skepticism was often reinforced. This kind of apprehensions are verified from other correspondences too. In his memoriale of Visitation, for example, Pius Geisel underlined the ensuing situation of uncertainty. He wrote: "The future of the mission may look

210 Plattner, "Die Mission im neuen Weltkrieg: Indien," op. cit.

211 Felix A. Plattner, "Indiens Stellung zur Kirche," IB 4/5 (September 1949):155-56.

dark, but it lies in God's hands."[212] Although a succinct statement, it gives a glimpse into the sense of anxiety not seldom experienced by the Jesuits and other missionaries. In any case, as far as the general growth of the mission is concerned, as noted above, there is no doubt that the mission made a good progress in every sense of the term. Apparently, a few points did need to be emphasized further.

2.7. Creation of the Belgaum-Poona Vice Province (1956)[213]

Foundation of an independent native Church is the highest goal of a missionary endeavour. A visible expression of the achievement of this goal is the handing over of a mission field to the indigenous clergy under a local bishop. This decisive step took place in the Poona Mission in 1949, just four years before the hundred-year jubilee of the German-Swiss Jesuits in India (1954). The Society of Jesus in general too had by this time achieved a considerable growth in India. Therefore it needed to adapt its own organization and restructure the same according to the new situation. On 12th March 1956, the Superior General through a decree elevated the Poona Mission into an independent Vice-Province of the Order.[214]

In fact, the early 1950s witnessed rapid political changes in India. According to the previous arrangement, Goa proper became the Goa section of the Portuguese Province of the Society of Jesus. Belgaum became a separate Jesuit mission, coextensive with the new Diocese of Belgaum, comprising the Districts of Belgaum and North Kanara in the present State of Karnataka. Until this point of time, they were parts of the Goa Archdiocese. On the other hand the districts of Bijapur and Dharwar in Karnataka were parts of the Diocese of Poona. According to the new reorganization, the district of Ratnagiri was brought under the diocese of Poona on the 20th October 1953 and thus was included under the jurisdiction of the Poona Mission. On 12th March 1956 the Poona Mission which until then was under Southern German Province and from 1947 onwards simultaneously under the Swiss Vice-Province

212 Pius Geisel, "Memoriale Visitationis, November 1950," ARSI, Poona. 1004-XIX, 36.

213 For a copy of the Decree of Erection of the Vice-Province of Belgaum-Poona, see ARSI, Belgaum-Poona. 1007-1 5.

214 See Felix A. Plattner, "In Puna-Belgaum," IB 4/5 (1956): 2.

as well.[215] The Belgaum mission was combined to form an independent unit named Belgaum-Poona Vice-province. Although it may not be relevant for the immediate purpose, yet it may be mentioned that on 19th March 1963, three months after the merger of Goa into the Indian Union, the Goa Section and the Belgaum-Poona Vice-Province were once again combined to form Goa-Poona Vice-Province. As the Districts of Dhulia, Jalgaon and Nasik had been handed over to the Bombay Province, the Goa-Poona Vice-Province included seven Districts of Maharashtra (Poona, Ahmednagar, Ratnagiri, Satara, Sangli, Kolhapur and Sholapur), four Districts of Karnataka (Belgaum, Bijapur, Dharwar and North Kanara), and the Union Territory of Goa. However the major work was mostly carried out in the districts of Poona, Ahmednagar, Satara, Kolhapur, Belgaum and Goa. Later on 14th November 1983, Goa-Poona Province was established as the 33rd General Congregation of the Society of Jesus suppressed the distinction between Province and an independent Vice-Province. Finally on 15th August 1992 the Pune Province was established.[216]

The implication of the new status as the Vice-province was that the Jesuits in Poona were no longer members of their European mother province. The Vice-Provincial was no longer under the direct instructions of the Provincial in Europe. He became directly answerable to the Superior General. He took the full charge of the personnel and other aspects of management. In a sense the Mission thus became mature. Moreover, it began to be seen technically as a part of the indigenous, Indian Church. At the moment of its new status as the new Vice-province there were 130 members, among whom 60 were Priests, 52 Scholastics and 18 Brothers.[217] Until 1958, Pius Geisel who was the Superior Regular of the Mission before its erection into a Vice-province, was the first Vice-Provincial. Gerhard Baader became his successor in 1958 and continued until the end of the period of this study (1962).[218]

215 In 1947 Switzerland was erected into an independent Vice-Province, prior to which it was part of the Southern German Province. See ARSI, Data Chronologica: Originis et Evolutionis - Regionum, Provinciarum, 1997.

216 See "Summary Report of the General sociological survey Goa-Poona Vice-Province," ARSI, Historia 2001-Poona, 5.

217 See Plattner, "In Puna-Belgaum," op.cit, 3.

218 See "Der neue Obere in Puna " IB 213 (1958): 2.

2.8. Conclusion

The survey undertaken, in spite of some discrepancies, due to the lack of primary literature reveals fairly good idea of the progress of the mission. Since we shall be dealing with the challenges and obstacles in a separate chapter (i.e., four) we have avoided from going in detail on those points. Besides making an attempt at tracing the events unfolding at important junctures of the history, what I consider an important discovery in the course of the survey is the stand of the British authorities vis-a-vis the Jesuits in relation to the issues like internment and repatriation. Without any hesitation I can assert that I was able to make a little more objective reading based on certain new documents that I have frequently cited. The trajectory of the growth of the Mission reveals that it virtually went through numerous ups and downs.

Chapter-3

Methods, Strategies, Priorities and Options of the Mission

3.1. Introduction

A systematic study of the Bombay-Poona Mission (B-PM), as a service organization involves a survey of the strategies, priorities and options. In the context of the history of the Church, the first figure who invariably crosses our imagination is undoubtedly St. Paul. He is considered the first cross-cultural missionary who went beyond the boundaries of Judaism to preach the Gospel of Jesus Christ. The Pauline missionary strategy is epitomised in Acts 13-28. The mention of this must be made here because one comes across here the fundamental principles that all the missionaries of every era have employed in some form or the other in their missionary enterprises.[219]

Jesuit missions are not exceptions. And the Bombay-Poona Mission (B-PM) may not be considered an exceptional and extraordinary Jesuit mission in India. Yet, the socio-political and cultural specificities of the mission field do render the mission unique among all other Jesuit missions in India. The Jesuits adopted unique missionary methods and strategies in order to be able to render relevant and meaningful service to the people. Moreover, according to the signs of the times, they also prioritized their missionary thrust. A corollary to the same was that they

---

219 Hoo-Soo Jose Nam, Missions Strategies of Korean Presbyterian Missionaries in Central and Southern Philippines: In Light of 'Paul's Missions Strategies (Scotland: Hermit Kingdom, 2006), 2.

adopted at a given time the most urgent options among many that were placed on them,. All these were organically linked with each other. This chapter takes a cursory survey of these aspects.

3.2. Missionary Methods and Strategies

"Strategy is indispensable to the doing of any task... [In the context of mission studies it] is defined as the practical working out of the will of God within a cultural context."[220] Carrying out an enterprise without a proper strategy fails to yield an expected result. Stated differently, "the objectives and methods of the work are intimately related."[221] Hence, every missionary body devises certain general strategies to achieve the objectives before it. The missionaries themselves, being sent into a particular cultural milieu, must devise concrete strategies suitable to the cultural and political situation of the place. Copying a model from one context and trying to implement in some other would invariably meet with failure and disappointment. A simple analogy of trying to interchange parts of machines from two different companies explains the case as they are bound to mismatch. One of the most important characteristics to take note of is the uniqueness of human beings and their cultures, which necessitate that they be treated uniquely and be approached with unique strategies. "People and cultures are not like standardized machines that have interchangeable parts. We cannot simply use an evangelism approach that has worked in one context in another and expect the same results. Strategies must be as unique as the peoples to whom they apply."[222]

Often one does not come across "a deliberate, well-formulated, duly executed plan of action,"[223] which may be termed as a codified handbook on methods and strategies in all the missionary enterprises. In fact, they are mostly drawn from the general principles underlying the charism of a particular missionary body. Moreover, they are often identifiable in

220 Gailyn Van Rheenen, Missions: Biblical Foundations and Contemporary Strategies (Michigan: Zondervan Publishing House, 1996), 139-40.

221 Noelline Pinto, "Human Organization for Pioneering in Education: An Attempt in Community Building and Functional Education," (Typed Material), PJPA, Varia.

222 Edward R. Dayton and David Allen Fraser, Planning Strategies for World Evangelization (Michigan: Grand Rapids, 1980), 38; as quoted in Van Rheenen, Missions: Biblical Foundations and Contemporary Strategies, op. cit. 145.

223 Herbert Kane, Christian Mission in Biblical Perspective (Grand Rapids, MI: Baker Book House, 1976), 73.

particular activities and initiatives undertaken by individuals or a group of missionaries. In the case of the B-PM too, we encounter a similar situation. In order to identify these aspects, we need to investigate the letters and reports of the Jesuits whereby often we may need to focus on some important or representative figures by virtue of their position of responsibilities in the mission. The objective of this section is to explore and identify some of the more important missionary methods adopted by the Jesuits in the context of Bombay-Poona area.[224]

Before proceeding further, we may make a short note on the procedure and the period in consideration. Though the period of this study is from the First World War (World War I hereafter), it would be useful to see whether there was any continuity of the mission strategies and options that were adopted by the Jesuits from the beginning of the B-PM (1854). Two reasons may be supplied in favour of doing the same. Firstly, in spite of being entrusted with a new field of operation[225] in the wake of the ensuing situation of crisis during the post-World War I years, the Jesuits essentially were the same in the Mission.[226] However, the new area of operation did necessitate certain new methods and strategies. Secondly, the mission field did not alter substantially from the previous larger mission field in terms of socio-cultural specificities.[227] Besides, both areas belonged to the former Bombay Presidency in western India.

3.3. Education as the Key Service

By 'education', we imply both forms, namely formal as well as informal, from the elementary to the university levels. It goes without saying that education has been "a true ministry of the Order [Society of Jesus],

224 Leonardo Cohen, The Missionary Strategies of the Jesuits in Ethiopia (1555-1632) (Wiesbaden: Harrassowitz, 2009), 4.

225 It would be incorrect to say that Poona area was completely new. Yet the term 'new' may still be used given the fact that the mission-field was fully entrusted to the Southern German Province in 1929. The former Bombay-Poona Mission was much bigger in terms of geographical spread, namely from Karachi in Sindh to Ahmedabad in Gujarat. Similarly in western India it comprised Bombay and surrounding areas, Ahmednagar in Deccan region and further in the south it went down to Hubli in Karnataka. See "Hundert Jahre, *Puna-Mission 1854...*

226 They were German, Austrian, Swiss and Luxemburg nationals who belonged to the Southern German Province of the Society of Jesus.

227 After World War I once the Bombay-Poona Mission was bifurcated, the Poona area was entrusted to the Southern German Province of the Society of Jesus (1929), whereas the rest of the areas were entrusted to the Spanish Jesuits of the Aragon Province. This is implied when mentioning about the previous and latter mission fields respectively.

indeed its primary ministry.. .No group in the church, or in society at large, had ever undertaken an enterprise on such a grand scale ... [Indeed, therefore, the Society of Jesus has a pride of place of being] the first teaching order within the Catholic Church."[228] While making a mention of these aspects, it would not be out of place also to note that this ministry eventually became the most compelling factor for the restoration of the Society of Jesus as "Pope Pius VII, resurrecting the Society in 1814 from its suppressed state, had given the service of education as his main reason for restoring it to life."[229] Pius VII said that he did so in order "that the Catholic Church could have, once again, the benefit of their [the Jesuits] educational experience."[230] Indeed, therefore, the "Jesuits still believe that 'of great importance among the ministries of the Society are the educational and intellectual apostolates."[231] Precisely within this framework of reflection that the Jesuits have been the fore-runners in the field of Catholic education right from the beginning of their history in India.[232]

Within the general framework of the understanding of Catholic education in India, Rudolph C. Heredia, in an insightful article, captures three-fold goal of Christian education. This reflects also the Jesuit understanding of the same.

> First, education of Christians themselves in a Christian atmosphere so that they could be good members of their church and occupy important positions in secular society; secondly, to render service to Indian youth at large; thirdly, to build evangelical bridges towards the country's intelligentsia and thus pave the way for an acceptance of the faith.[233]

228 Vincent J. Duminuco, ed., The Jesuit Ratio Studiorum: 400th Anniversary Perspectives (New York: Fordham University Press, 2000), 57.

229 Paul Andrews, "The Jesuits and Education," SIQR 80/317 (Spring 1991): 22. See also Thomas M. McCoog, ed., Promising Hope: Essays on the Suppression and Restoration of the English Province of the Society of Jesus (Rome: Institutum Historicum Societatis Iesu, 2003), 328.

230 Quoted in Roger C. Bergman, Catholic Social Learning: Educating the Faith that does Justice (New York: Fordham University Press, 2011), 21.

231 Gregory Naik, ed., Jesuit Education in India (Anand: Gujarat Sahitya Prakash, 1987), vii. See also Andrews, "The Jesuits and Education," op. cit., 25.

232 C. Marattukalam, "The Jesuits and Education in India," in Catholic and Indian Education (Trichinopoly: St. Joseph's Industrial School Press, n.d.), 158.

233 Rudolph C. Heredia, "Education and Mission: School as Agent of Evangelization," EPW 30/37 (September 16, 1995): 2337.

Heredia further mentions that all these three objectives have been present in missionary-education endeavours in India in varying degrees at varying times among Christian denominations. The Catholics, for example, during the British colonial period seemed to be more in line with the first objective, whereas the Protestants with the third one.[234] While anticipating some of the arguments, it may be said that these strands of thinking did get transformed or even got revised with the passage of time. But the basic import of the same has remained largely unaltered, often becoming more complex to articulate in distinct terms. For example, if we take the outbreak of World War I as the closing of an era in Indian history, we may be able to identify the strands of such patterns of understanding more easily. Prior to this era, the missionaries could articulate in unambiguous terms that the school system was meant to achieve the above-mentioned objectives. Such a clear-cut articulation of the same got blurred and became more complex when the missionary endeavours were faced with the rise of nationalist movements on the one hand and crisis of colonial power on the other. In the articulation of the objectives more caution began to be applied so as not to give occasions for misinterpretation and consequent skirmishes.

In the context of this mission too, a special emphasis was laid on the need of opening schools. From some of the statistical figures this becomes even more explicit. For example, by the end of World War I (1919), there were 70 elementary schools with 6958 pupils in Bombay Diocese alone.[235] The administrative unit namely Bombay Presidency, with much bigger geographical area, included even greater number of schools and other educational institutions that came directly or indirectly under the management of the Jesuits. More than 50% of the Jesuit personnel were directly involved with educational apostolate until this period. Thus, "during the period spanning three quarters of a century approximately 400 Fathers worked under the mission. At least 250 Fathers were directly involved in educational work."[236] It would not be surprising, therefore, that the most tangible fruit of the mission,

234 Ibid., 2338.

235 See the Report of Anthony Bruder to G. M. Cardinal van Rossum, Prefect of Propaganda Fide, "Ex Diocesi Bombayensi" (Bombay, 1st December, 1919), ARSI, Bombay. 1004-1, *1: Ernest R. Hull records the total number of schools at a much higher figure, i.e., 154. See Hull,* German Jesuit Fathers, 23.

236 H. T. Punjabi, "A Critical Study of the Contribution of the German Jesuit Mission to Education in Bombay," (PhD diss., University of Bombay, 1984), 368.

i.e., establishing contact with others could be experienced precisely from this apostolate. The impacts effected by St. Xavier's College and High School, St. Mary's High School, St. Stanislaus School (all in Bombay) and St. Vincent's High School (later also St. Vincent's Day & Night College), Pune and St. Patrick's School, Karachi to name a few--all established in the first two decades of the arrival of the Jesuits in Bombay--stand as testimonies to this claim.[237]

3.3.1. The Objectives of the Schools and Colleges[238]

As we focus our study of the B-PM, we clearly notice that it followed the tradition of the Society of Jesus faithfully and adopted education through schools and colleges as an important apostolic instrument. After the pattern of western Catholic education system, however, "schools were wanted for Catholics, so schools were opened,"[239] as E. R. Hull pithily stated in one of his articles. In the words of H. C. Perumalil, they "were meant in the first place to cater to the needs of the Catholics ... [and] the imparting of a good education in all its aspects was the direct aim of these centres of learning, [yet at the same time] it was hoped [that] it would also lead to an acceptance of Christ by at least a number of students."[240] There is hardly any need to elaborate on these perceptions. However, what we eventually mark in the period under review is that the Jesuits have gradually moved from a traditional to a more accommodative understanding of the purpose of the schools and colleges. We shall discuss a little more under the subsequent sub-topics. In other words, the understanding as a means of evangelization (i.e., a means of conversion to Catholicism) was slowly transformed into a means of preparation for evangelization, building a better human society and a means of an integral human formation, etc. Let it be noted, however, that these developments in the understanding did not replace or discard the earlier understanding. On the contrary, in spite of the

237 See Hull, German Jesuit Fathers, 22.

238 Some important points related especially to the debates pertaining to the primary objectives of schools and colleges would be discussed in chapter six (# 6.4). Here we shall be mentioning some of the points just in passing.

239 E. R. Hull, "Some Moot-Points in the Indian Missions: With Special Relation to Bombay," TE (May 1926) (offprint for private circulation only), 4. A related aspect of admission to the non-Catholic and non-Christian students will be dealt with in Chapter Six (#6.4.1).

240 H. C. Perumalil & F..R. Hambye, eds., Christianity in India: A History in Ecumenical Perspective, 259.

wider understanding gaining currency, the earlier understanding of the objective remained ever prevalent alongside the latter ones.

*3.3.2. **The Schools as the First Entry Point***

It would not be wrong to say that the schools, especially the elementary ones in the rural setup, often acted as a first point of entry to a particular new place. There are ample examples to substantiate the argument that the early Jesuit missionaries mostly used this method. Without elaborating on the point any further we may state that such an approach was adopted with an unmixed hope that the schools would open up further possibilities of establishing a contact with the non-Christians. In Sangamner, for example, seeing no other possibilities of establishing a contact with the Hindus and Muslims, Otto Weishaupt started a village school in a small hut, which comprised of three rooms - one each for himself, for the family of the teacher and for the class room respectively.[241] Initially such "schools at the mission stations ... [were meant to] train boys to become teachers and catechists,"[242] besides imparting a general education to all. In other cases, the village schools were perceived as platforms of general religious instruction, while also serving as a means of establishing further contacts. Albert Huber implies the same:

> In a new mission field one needs to begin everything anew. This consists in bringing in a number of young boys to the mission station, so that they can grow in a Catholic atmosphere. This is not possible in an outer station, while they get to attend the Holy Mass and listen to the homilies only once in a month at the most, if everything goes well.[243]

Precisely due to this special significance of the schools and colleges in imparting catechism and religious instruction that the Jesuits began to grow anxious in the wake of growing cultural nationalism in the country. In the words of Schubiger: "The chief problem now is: how to get religious instruction across to the children, who are no more in our schools. Then the question arises how to spread the gospel to new

---

241 See John B. Winiger, "Die Missionsstation Sangamner: Ihre Grilndung und Entwicklung," ADPSJ, Abt. 45B-26, Nr. 1509.

242 Hubert Sixt, "The Ahmednagar District Mission: 1878 - 1983," PJPA, *Varia.*

243 Albert Huber, "Beiblatt zu Project Nr. 106.1 [21st March 1961]," AMPSJ, Projekte der Puna-Mission.

places without the means of schools."[244] Thus the role of the schools was perceived not only as the first entry point but also as essential for imparting catechism and general religious and moral instruction.

3.3.3. Schools as a Means of Evangelization

It has already been pointed out that the Jesuits initially did understand the purpose of schools and colleges as one of the potent means of leading people to conversion to Catholicism. Having said that, it must also be stated that it often becomes quite difficult to establish a clear demarcation between two strands of thoughts. The first reason for the same is that we come across quite conflicting accounts on this point. Some of the sources strongly seem to suggest that the primary purpose of opening schools and colleges was to win over converts to Catholicism. Others seem to suggest that they were only indirect means of evangelization or rather a preparation for evangelization. Some of the examples might serve the purpose of clarifying the point. Still others include both as complementing each other.

Fr. Willekens, the Jesuit Visitor to Madura mission, for example, in a conference of the Jesuit educationists held at Loyola College, Madras (now Chennai) in 1930 expressed his opinion in the following words: "We should frequently recall to our minds the end of our [schools and] Colleges. The sole reason for our coming to India is the promotion of the religion of Christ."[245] In the context of the emerging post-Vatican Council II theology of mission, it is certainly untenable to maintain such a position today. This goes on to prove the fact that the Jesuits often found themselves within the confines of narrow denominationalist understanding of mission, which by implication placed a serious challenge before them to evolve a more inclusive understanding of the same.

Other groups of the Jesuits seem closer to the view that represents the opinion that education through schools and colleges was an *indirect means of evangelization.* Indeed, thus the same was seen as a means of preparation for evangelization. It may be noted here, however, that the scenario of the changing political atmosphere and heightening religio-

244 Francis X. Schubiger to the Superior General (Sangamner, 3rd July 1936) ARSI, Poona. 1004-IX, 15.

245 "Minutes of the Educational Conference Held at Loyola College, Madras. 27-30th Dec. 1930," ARSI, Prov. Bombay-Poona. 1404- De Collegiis in India: 1927-1930. 2.

cultural fundamentalism may be said to be among the main external factors for the same, while the changing self-awareness of the Church as the servant of the faith along with the emerging theology of mission is doubtlessly among the most important internal factors for the same. Why do we say this? It is simply because initially the understanding of the Jesuits on the question seems to have been generally in the line of the view expressed by Willekens above. But once the experiences began to show that the number of conversions resulting from schools and colleges were barely corresponding to the investment in terms of personnel and finances, the understanding of the objectives seem to have been more in the line of indirect method of evangelization.[246]

Within this framework of discussion as we briefly go back once again to discuss the B-PM in the aftermath of World War I, we notice that it was necessitated by the understanding that the initiation of evangelization must begin by educating the children. This is well underlined in a report:

> This method[247] has now become impossible. First financial difficulties arising from the effects of war forced us to reduce the number of teachers (Rahata for example had 45 before the war, now only 25). Secondly the introduction of compulsory primary education makes it impossible to open new schools, even the old ones are endangered, as neither the number of children is sufficient to comply with government regulations, nor [is] our staff sufficiently qualified ... This method was undoubtedly a solid one, but costly, as it meant a school and salaried teacher in every new village. It had the disadvantage that the children found in their homes pagan atmosphere as their elders were unconverted and practically left alone.[248]

An opinion of Hubert Sixt is even more explicit:

> In this part of the country the only chance of missionary success seems to lie in first opening a school for the children, who, without being forced, are instructed in Christian doctrine and later on, where there appears no obstacle, baptised. A good influence is secured

246 For further details, see Chapter Six.

247 Opening an elementary school alongside a mission station was a common practice among the missionaries.

248 Anonymous, "Report on the Missio ad Paganos (n.d.)," AMPSJ, Pune Alt. As for the date of the letter it becomes clear from the rest of the report that pertains to the 1940s.

> over the minds of the adults and some efforts made to bring them to conversion... Thus real hope lies in the rising generation who, as they grow up, develop into a fairly well trained adult Christian population.[249]

The above text may be taken as representative of a widely accepted view among the Jesuits of the time whereby education was considered an "indispensable means to the end of establishing churches that would be self-governing, self-supporting and self-propagating."[250] Doubtlessly this was true with regard to the B-PM as well. We may identify here a few pertinent points that are inherent in the citation. Firstly, the view expressed above represents a Jesuit whose immediate as well as ultimate concern was the growth of the Church, mostly in the numerical sense. Therefore, one notices almost a clearly defined target group and objective of education, namely children and through them exerting 'influence over the minds of the adults' in order to lead them to the conversion to Christianity. Secondly, there is an unambiguous implication that the remote target of the missionary enterprise was to achieve 'a fairly well trained adult Christian population'. We may see, thus, that education was not perceived purely as a means of enriching the quality of human life in an altruistic sense; rather it was "considered as a means, direct or indirect, towards the end of making Christian disciples"[251] in the immediate circumstance.

As for the number of converts coming from the schools and colleges as a result of receiving education, we do not have statistical data. Yet it is absolutely undeniable that the schools and colleges have always been considered as "indirect help for the conversion of Hindus [and others]"[252] by projecting the image of Catholicism in a positive light by dispelling the doubts about the same.[253]

What seems to be quite unambiguous with regard to the gradual transformation in the understanding of the schools and institutions is the fact that with the passing decades, the understanding seems to have

249 Hubert Sixt, "The Marathi Mission at Ahmednagar," PJPA, Varia, 3.

250 Brian Stanley, The World Missionary Conference 1910 (Grand Rapids/Cambridge: Wm. B. Eerdmans, 2009), 182.

251 Ibid., 177.

252 "Educational Conference [1930] [Fr. Mahe]," op. cit, 9. This is more verifiable in the case of Protestant missions.

253 Ibid.

taken the second line of thought (i.e., as a means of preparation for or an indirect means of evangelization) more concretely. While not replacing the first goal of gaining converts to Catholicism even if it meant long years of patient waiting, the Jesuits moved along this trajectory to accommodate wider dimensions of the purpose of schools and colleges. This is well expressed in a Report of George Kester, Jesuit Visitor to the Indian Missions (1963):

> No doubt the apostolate in the high schools is a very excellent one. We educate Catholic boys, we establish contact with Hindu families. It prepares the mind of the coming generation towards the Church. It gives the Church standing and authority in the eyes of the non-Catholics, v.g. the position of the Church in Poona city and Belgaum city without our high schools would be quite different. I believe it was especially the excellent work done in our high schools and colleges which saved the direct missionary effort during some critical periods within the last 10 years. Mr. [Jawahar Lai] Nehru himself has a very high opinion of our educational institutions. We should never forget the very positive elements of this form of apostolate.[254]

Leaving aside other dimensions, if we see the purpose of the schools and colleges in terms of being direct or indirect means of evangelization, it may be said that they were primarily meant for the Catholics on the one hand and for the preparation of other students for acceptance of Christianity on the other. In the words of John Misquitta, the two-pronged objective of the schools and colleges were "to uplift the Catholic community and to expose non-Christians to Christianity."[255]

3.3.4. Schools and Faith Formation

Another dimension of the missionary understanding of the schools and institutions was: they were perceived as means of faith formation. To substantiate this argument we need to underline one of the primary concerns of Bishop Hartmann as he landed in Bombay. He wanted to establish schools in order to save the Catholic children from being forced to go to the Protestant schools due the lack of the Catholic schools. He

254 George Kester, "Goa-Poona: Visitor's Report (1963)," ARSI, Poona. 1501-Litterae Annuae (1963), 17-18.

255 John Misquitta, The Identity of the Catholic Colleges in India (Bombay: St. Xavier's College, 1989), 8.

often lamented the same: "As regards the state of Catholic education, no mission field in India has been so badly served as Bombay. The new existing schools are of poor standard, and Catholic parents have no alternative other than to send their children to Protestant schools, where, year after year, a number of them turn Protestants."[256] Thus the vexing question of the Catholic students being obliged to attend the Protestant schools thereby being deprived of the opportunity of growing in their Catholic faith always perturbed him. Hence his primary intention was to save the Catholic children from drifting away from the Catholic community, while also hoping that other students too would be attracted to the Catholic faith with the passage of time.[257]

Although the preoccupation with the concern for saving the Catholic children from being sent to Protestant schools became much less with the passing decades, it may not be denied that the very purpose of opening more and more schools even in the later decades included inherently the dimension of faith formation. Apparently, as the number of schools increased, this preoccupation began to lose its negative connotation of fear and anxiety of losing the Catholic children to Protestantism or other faiths. But certainly the original charism of the Jesuits, namely 'defence and propagation of the faith' *{Formula of the Institute)* remained (rather remains) as a constitutive element of their understanding even later. As opposed to a section of the Jesuits who interpreted the primary purpose of the schools and colleges in terms of being a means of conversion to Catholicism, there was a section of the Jesuits who understood the same in terms of defence of the faith. This is represented in the view of Medard Vermeire, a member of the Ranchi Mission, expressed in the Conference of the Jesuit Educationists (1930) mentioned above: "Their [Jesuits] primary object was not the conversion of pagans as was the case with the Protestant [schools and] Colleges, [as may be expected in the case of direct evangelization]"[258] but "to defend the faith of the Catholics,"[259] in accordance with the Ignatian vision of education. Willekens who in another context had maintained that the primary objective of the missionary endeavour through schools and

256 As quoted in Gense, Church at the Gateway, 198.

257 See Herman Castelino, "The Contribution of Jesuit Schools of the Bombay Province in the last Hundred Years, (For Private Circulation only), PJPA, Varia.

258 "Educational Conference [1930] [Fr. Vermeire]," 8.

259 Ibid. [Fr. Mahe], 9.

colleges was to win over converts, underlined the defence of the faith integral to the missionary purpose of schools and colleges.

> The ecclesiastical history of India tells us ... that the Colleges were founded first of all, because the bishops realized, that, owing to the lack of Catholic higher educational institutions, the Catholic students were losing their faith in non-Catholic Colleges and the Catholic community was becoming in an increasing degree the most despised of communities in the land.[260]

It may not be out of place to note here that in several parts of India, as also in the area of B-PM, the Protestants were often the strongest competitors to the Catholics. One of the biggest hurdles they created all over, according to Fr. J. Mahe, was imparting of the distorted views of Christianity. Worse still, the non-Christians often derived the knowledge of Christianity from them.[261] Willekens, therefore, remarked while speaking on the role of the Catholic Colleges, particularly with regard to safeguarding of the Catholic faith:

> If there had been no Catholic Colleges, for the past 70 years, the better part of the Catholic young men in India and the families formed by them would have been lost to Protestantism, or rather to unbelief, or they would have swelled the ranks of the so-called liberal-Catholics, who are the natural products of neutral education. The Catholic community would still be as despised as before, i.e., in a state of dejection so deep, that it caused the despair of a Bishop Hartmann and others.[262]

This thrust was more explicit in the schools and colleges in the urban set-up. Moreover, it was more conspicuous in the case of the secondary schools and colleges where there were greater chances of Catholic students going to Protestant institutions, while also being exposed to the influences of many other religions.

3.3.5. School for Forming a Better Society

In order to put this understanding in a proper perspective, it would be helpful to recapitulate briefly the circumstances of the past. In the

---

260 Ibid., 2-3.

261 "Educational Conference [1939] [Fr. J. Mahe]," op. cit, 9. J. Mahe was the Superior of Madura mission and took part in the Educational Conference of the Jesuit educationists in Madras (1930).

262 "Educational Conference [1930] [Fr. Willekens]," op. cit., 3. We shall discuss some aspects related to this sub-topic in Chapter Six (i.e., #6.7).

preceding paragraphs, we have noted that Bishop Hartmann's primary objective behind inviting the Jesuits was to introduce Catholic education for the betterment of the Catholic community as he was painfully aware of its pitiful condition. He realized that education of the youth was essential for the growth of the Catholics into a self-reliant community, having a social standing of their own. But the fruits of Jesuit education began to be visible only in the later decades. Indeed, it impacted a very tangible transformation in the Christian community, as Herman Castelino states: "That the system of Jesuit education bore remarkable fruit is evident from the well-educated Christian community that now exists in Mumbai and its environs, in Mangalore and elsewhere."[263]

Prior to the arrival of the Jesuits, a small number of wealthy Christians in Bombay, did enjoy a place of honour in private as well as in public circles. Such was not the case with the majority of them who were untouched by the benefits of education. They were mostly rural populations residing in small hamlets. Consequently they were considered low in the social ladder. Over the years this situation changed quite tangibly once the Catholic community had educational institutions like St. Xavier's High School and College, Bombay and St. Vincent's High School, Poona including many other schools in the rural areas. The chances of educational facilities that were considered once the prerogative of the rich and the elite were made available to the humble sections of the society too. But this kind of impact was not restricted to the Catholic community alone; rather it went beyond to the larger Indian society as well. This is evident in the following account:

> But St. Xavier's - both school and college - under the disciplining influence of the German Jesuits became the nursery of many persons belonging to all creeds and communities who attained the highest honours and eminence in every walk of life, be it medicine, politics, education, law, art or business.[264]

263 Herman Castelino, "The Educational Enterprise of the German Jesuit Mission" (Paper presented at a Workshop on Mission on the occasion of the Sesquicentennial Anniversary of the Arrival of the Jesuits of the Garman- Swiss Provinces in India, Ishvani Kendra, Pune, December 27th - 29th, 2004). See also Punjabi, "A Critical Study of the Contribution to Education," 369.

264 Teresa Albuquerque, To Love is to Serve: Catholics of Bombay (Bombay: Heras Institute of Indian History and Culture, 1986), 10-11.

The foregoing discussion, thus, shows us how this strategy always remained a favoured one in this mission, in spite of the fact that the cases of conversions directly resulting from the schools were meagre. We have stressed above that the major objective of education was not to prepare a ground for conversion but to contribute towards forming a better society, which was an intrinsic characteristic of Jesuit education.[265]

3.3.6. Management of the Schools and Colleges

A final point that may be discussed here pertains to the management of the schools and colleges. The question we need to address here is: How did the Jesuits manage the schools and colleges? This question gains significance for the simple reason that a majority of the Catholics of the mission field were "in bulk poor people."[266] The poor people were not capable of paying the school fees. As far as the village schools were concerned, the majority of the school children were "kept in the boarding homes attached to the schools and needed to be supported entirely - their food, clothing, books, school fees and first medical aid, etc."[267] Thus the Jesuits were not only the care-takers of the school children, they were their virtual 'parents' as well.

As for the university students coming from poor Catholic families, there were many cases for whom large concessions in the fees were made to facilitate their studies. A caution expressed in the meeting of the Jesuit educationists (1930), leads us to the conclusion that such benevolence was often a heavy burden on the colleges as a majority of the students could never repay the loans given out to them. The consequence of the same went to the extent of often crippling the already poor financial status of the schools and colleges.[268]

Amidst such a situation, the herculean task of making arrangements for everything for the students was a real challenge especially in the years subsequent to World War I, when neither personnel nor material help was sufficiently available for a considerable period of time. Yet it is clear that certain constructive efforts were made to rectify the

265 See Henry Heras, "On the Mission Methods in India: A Report Submitted to the Most Rev. John B. Janssens, S.J., General of the Society of Jesus - 1947," ARSI, Bombay. 2010-Varia Historica, 81-84.

266 Hull, "Some Moot-Points," 6.

267 "Die Fahrt ins Missionsland,'7B 1/17 (January 1934): 138. See also Joseph Giintensperger, "Die Schulen der Puna-Mission," IB 1/17 (January 1935): 167.

268 See "Educational Conference [1930]," op. cit., 26.

situation, which continued even until the 1950s and later. As a concrete example, we may refer to Emmeran Sturm's[269] initiative whereby he raised small funds from his friends and relatives in Europe to help out the poor children to continue their schooling. His sheer commitment to the cause may be imagined from the fact that at his death (1969), nearly 800 envelopes with full addresses typed on them were discovered at his writing table. Since the purpose of those envelopes was known to all, letters were written to the respective addresses to continue the help to the poor children. This is how a small foundation, later known was Sturm Foundation was established. Eventually other Jesuits too joined in the venture contributing funds from their relatives and friends. With the realization that quite a substantial amount of welfare was being effected by the venture, Hermann Bacher (the District Mission Superior at the time) declared it as a common project of the Jesuits of the vice-Province. A good number of Catholic students coming from poor families were helped in their pursuit of higher studies.[270]

To give an idea into this kind of efforts, the statistics for the year 1926/27 might be furnished here. The table below clearly shows that 1,853 students were admitted in the schools for a reduced fee while 856 were given admission free of cost. The total number of such students, thus totals to 2,709, which almost comes to 50% of the total number of Catholic students (5,643). The example of Emmeran Sturm's initiatives shows that such efforts were continued even in the later decades. Unfortunately we lack documents to prove to what extent it was possible in spite of two main factors - consistent problem of finances and gradual growth in the number of the students.

---

269 Born on 31st August 1905 at Seeborn Huy in Germany, Emmeran Sturm came to India in 1938. From 1946 to 1963 he was in-charge of the mission station at Kendal in Ahmednagar District. He died in 1969 at Rahata. During his missionary carrier of three decades in India, he dedicated a major part of his services to pastoral work. Yet he was keenly interested in the education of the boys and girls alike. It was during his stay at Kendal that he realized that Catholic boys would not be able to pursue their higher studies without the financial help by the mission. Hence he established a foundation for helping them. See "Fr. Emmeran Sturm," in Deceased Members, 64-65; "An Attempt at Formulating an Overall Plan for the Ahmednagar D[istric]t," AMPSJ, Pune Alt.

270 See "An Attempt at Formulating an Overall Plan," ibid. See also Hermann Bacher, "Kinderhilfe fur Indien: Information iiber die Pater-Sturm-Stiftung," AMPSJ, Varia/Felix A. Plattner

Table 3.1: Number of Children Studying with Reduced School-Fee

Institutions	Total	Boarders		Day-Scholars		Non-Catholics paying full Fee
		Reduced Fee	Free	Reduced Fee	Free	
University	207			227	3	727
St. Xavier's, Bombay	453		02	250	23	851
St. Mary's, Bombay	460	50	80	71	13	62
St. Stanislaus, Bombay	710	50	55	118	14	67
St. Patrick's, Karachi	528			200	20	177
St. Vincent's, Poona	221	18	02			156
Total Boys' Institutions	2,579	118	139	866	73	2,040
13 Convent Girls' Schools	3,064	425	350	444	294	1,033
Grand Total. Higher Education	5,643	543	489	1,310	367	3,073

Source: Adapted from ARSI, *Prov. Bombay-Poona 1404-De Collegiis in India (1927-1930)*, 6.

Finally, it may be stated here that the approach of education being an apostolic instrument was, by no means, a unique feature of B-PM. In fact, it was one of the principal approaches of practically all the Jesuit missions in India. Yet, taking a retrospective view of this Mission, it may be claimed that the emphasis laid by this Mission on education was unique in more than one sense. This tradition of imparting education to the Christian and non-Christian children alike continued in the 'Poona Mission' too, except for the fact that the schools began to have more of a rural character. This was necessitated by the fact that 'Poona Mission' largely embraced the rural population as opposed to the 'Bombay-Poona Mission' that was largely concentrated in the urban set-up.[271]

In view of achieving a wider impact that the schools and colleges could effect on the larger society, the strong emphasis on the establishment of the school system remained even in the later period,

271 See Klaus Schatz, "Optionen und missionarische Prioritaten in der Bombay-Mission der deutschen Jesuiten (1858-1916)," SM 60 (2011): 392. See also Vath, Die deutschen Jesuiten, 102-106; Schatz, Geschichte, Vol. Ill, 315; Gense, Church at the Gateway, 157-159.

which becomes clear from the statistical data borrowed from the annual report of Poona Mission by Archbishop Henry Doring in 1929: 114 Elementary/Vernacular and 16 Inter Schools with 2300 and 1218 pupils respectively; besides 5 High Schools (1 for boys and 4 for girls) with 420 and 968 pupils respectively. During the same period there were only 18 parishes with 8 affiliated mission stations. The figures, therefore, show 16 vernacular schools, practically one school under each parish on an average.[272]

To summarise the discussion, we may ask a question as to why school education was considered as one of the most potent strategies. It was for the simple reason that education is vital for shaping of the young minds.[273] The 33rd General Congregation of the Society of Jesus recognized it well when it acknowledged that "those who work in schools of whatever kind or level or who are engaged in non-formal or popular education can exercise a deep and lasting influence on individuals and on society" (GC 44). Human psychology holds that new ideologies are best grasped by young minds as they are devoid of prejudices and presuppositions. This simple truth is one of the fundamental ideas behind introducing elementary schools as well.[274]

3.4. Evangelization of Groups and Communities

In modern missionary discourses we come across with two terms, namely 'evangelization' and 'evangelism' often being used interchangeably. Yet, some authors do tend to differentiate between them with nuances added to their meanings. In the end analysis, however, both of them share the same meaning of communicating the gospel and offering a valid opportunity to accept Christ, albeit in different degrees.[275] There

---

272 See Archbishop Henry Doring, "Annual Report, Poona Mission" (Poona, 30th June, 1929), ASCPF, Nova Series 1251, 403. See also Francis X. Schubiger, "Memorandum von F. Schubiger S.J. Konsultor der Poona Mission an A.R.P. General uber die Guterverteilung der friiheren Bombay-Poona Mission," (Memorandum) (Poona, 3rd January, 1930), ARSI, Poona. 1004-111, 2; "Prospectus Status Missionis" (Poona, 30th June 1936 and Poona, 30th June 1937), ASCPF, Nova Series 1251, 691C; 705C.

273 Teotonio R. De Souza, Discoveries, Missionary Expansion and Asian Cultures (Goa: Xavier Centre of Historical Research, 1994), 111.

274 See William Cooney, et al., From Plato to Piaget: The Greatest Educational Theorists from Across the Centuries and Around the World (Lanham/London: University Press of America, 1993), 49.

275 See Jonathan Lewis, ed., World Mission: An Analysis of the World Christian Movement (Pasadena: William Carrey Library, 1987), 6-7.

are numerous definitions of these key terms, probably as many as the number of authors in this area of study, whereby each author tends to add nuances to the same in order to highlight the focus and orientation of the topic under consideration. Dayton and Fraser, for example, define the terms in the following words: "Evangelization is the total process of announcing the gospel and bringing people into discipleship...In contrast, evangelism refers to specific actions or methods associated with the process of evangelization."[276] Another author employs a further nuance as he writes: "Evangelism is understood as the proclamation of the gospel to the 'unchurched' within a culture."[277] The cultural milieu of a people is an important consideration here. From a Catholic point of view Avery Dulles gives a definition of evangelization that seems to be more comprehensive in its content but more general in nature:

> ...the word evangelization originally meant the proclamation of the good news that the day had arrived...Evangelization, accordingly, has two senses. In the narrow sense, it means announcement of the global Christian message to those who do not believe, that is to say, primary evangelization. But in a broad sense it means everything that brings human life and the world under the sway of God's word. In this second sense, evangelization practically coincides with the total mission of the Church.[278]

In the magisterial documents, however, we come across probably the best definition of evangelization in *Evangelii Nuntiandi* by Pope Paul VI as he writes:

> If it had to be expressed in one sentence the best way of stating it would be to say that the Church evangelizes when she seeks to convert, solely through the divine power of the message she proclaims, both the personal and collective consciences of people, the activities in which they engage, and the lives and concrete milieu which are theirs (EN 18).

Taking into account all these definitions we may underline a few aspects that seem to be common to all. Nuances apart, the contents of the

276 Dayton and Fraser, Planning Strategies for World Evangelization, 55.

277 Michael A. Hayes, ed., Mission and Evangelisation (London: Burns & Oates, 2004), xiii.

278 Avery Dulles, Evangelization for the Third Millennium (New Jersey: Paulist Press, 2009), 5. See also Stephen Neill, "Evangelisation," in Lexikon zur Weltmission, eds. Stephen Neill et al. (Wuppertal/Erlangen: Theologischer Verlag R. Brockhaus/Verlag der Evang.-Luth. Mission, 1975), 141-142.

definitions seem to boil down to certain basic affirmations. They may be summarised in terms of bringing the non-Christians to the Christian faith in the first place. That is apparently the primary level of understanding. But evangelization today would mean much beyond to include not only the activities of the Church from converting non-Christians to Christian faith but also consolidating and nurturing their lives as members of the Church as a community of the faithful.

Having made the above preliminary remarks in order to situate the sub-topic in a proper perspective as we turn to the Mission under review, we discover that evangelization of groups may be identified as an accepted missionary method during the period of this study. Success in getting a large group of people to convert to Christianity, was invariably considered laudable. In fact such a method of evangelization was well in keeping with the magisterial teaching of the time (Cf. *M* 1 1).[279] Such a claim may be verified with a few examples. As we a take a brief retrospective view on the beginnings of the *Maratha Mission,* for example, we identify two distinct phases. In each of them, the objective of the missionary endeavour as evangelization of groups is implicitly implied. In the first phase, which apparently proved an utter failure, such an import is identifiable. Based on the accounts in our possession, we may conclude that the missionaries became victims of selfishness and greed of those individuals who converted for their personal gains. Yet the motivation that seems to have driven the Jesuits concerned, namely George Winiger and Bishop Leo Meurin, was to indulge in such a step was undoubtedly a desire to accomplish a group conversion of the *Mahars* at the shortest span of time possible. In the words of Gense:

> This is what happened. In the beginning of 1878, Father [George] Winiger, military chaplain at Ahmednagar, was badly taken in by two Mahar swindlers. Shivarao [Sevakrao] and Tatiaramji [Tatyaramji], had been dismissed for good reasons by the American Protestant Mission and the S.P.G. Protestant Mission. Without inquiring into their dubious past, he [Bishop Leo Meurin] believed their story that a number of Protestant Mahars and many more non-Christians were ready to become Catholics... The Jesuits in Bombay were likewise taken in, and wrote the most enthusiastic letters about the 'Pentecostal' conversions among the Mahars. Bishop Meurin was

279 See Thomas J. M. Burke, ed., "Maximum illud," in Catholic Missions: Four Great Encyclicals, (New York: Fordham University Press, 1957), 12.

> not the only person hoaxed. The movement developed as a mixed but totally bogus-affair, and it ultimately yielded good results.[280]

The above incident clearly underlines the fact that the missionaries were taken up by the promise of gaining a large number of converts, for such a pattern of evangelization had invariably proved rewarding right from the beginning of Christian missions. A majority of followers of a leader of a particular group would become Christians after the example of their leader.[281] This pattern may be noticed within the general framework of other Jesuit missions in India too right from the beginning.[282] In the new Society some Jesuit missions in India had even more tangible experiences in this regard. The Bengal Mission of the Belgian Province begun around the same time, for example, stands as a testimony to this claim. As of the status of the mission recorded in 1920 there were 159,743 baptized Christians besides 47,402 Catechumens. Within a span of some four decades of the beginnings that Mission, the numerical strength of the Catholics does substantiate the application of this strategy.[283]

The example above, although coming from a much earlier period than the time period under review, has been cited here with an underlying assumption that such an approach to the growth of the mission did not take a radical departure until the end of the time-frame of this research. Besides, there was no substantial change either in the constitution of the group of missionaries, except for the change of the field of operation. Therefore, it may be stated that this method of evangelization was largely adopted by the Jesuits of Poona Mission even in the later decades. Apparently, the results of conversion of groups under this Mission would be meaningless to be compared with those under the Bengal Mission of the Belgian Jesuits.[284] Yet, the currency and acceptability

280 Hubert Sixt, "The Marathi Mission at Ahmednagar: Fr. Marcel De Souza's Account," ASJZ, Pune Alt, 1-2. Emphasis in the text mine.

281 See Julian Saldanha, Patterns of Evangelization in Mission History (Bombay: St. Paul Publications, 1988), 17.

282 See Richard Fox Young (ed.), India and Indianness of Christianity (Grand Rapids: Wm. B. Eerdmans, 2009), 41; See also Neill, A History of Christianity in India: The Beginnings to 1707, 141.

283 See Yves de Steenhault, History of the Jesuits in West Bengal (1921-1985): Part I: 1921-1947 (Ranchi: Catholic Press, n.d.), 8.

284 The underlying factors for such a difference will be discussed in one of the following chapters.

of this approach in the period in consideration is beyond doubt. We must hasten to add, however, that due to various factors appearing in the wake of the rise of nationalist consciousness among Hindus as well as the movement of Bhimrao Ambedkar among the *Dalits,*[285] the results of conversion of groups were less tangible and less sensational, to use a modern media jargon. The same becomes apparent from the fact that a rather exponential rise in the number of converts witnessed in the first six-seven decades of the Mission (1860s-1920s) seems to have slowed down by 1930s. A cursory glimpse on the relevant figures would justify the claim. One point, however, must be made clear at this juncture that the fluctuations in the number of converts noted in the table below are the consequences of various other factors besides the ones mentioned above. The other reasons for the same were migration of the Catholics in search of jobs, deaths and lapse in the faith.[286]

Table 3.2: Conspectus of the Number of Christians

Year	Catholics			Total
	Indigenous	Europeans	Others	
1929	26,693			26,693
1930	24,044	3025		27,069
1931	24,654	3055		27,709
1932	25,283	3544		28,827
1933	29,951			29,951
1934	17,217	3700		20917
1935	30601			30601
1936	28876	3504		32380
1937	30,577	3509		34086

The Annual Letters of Bishop Henry Doring from 1930 to 1937 mention these factors. See Henry Doring, "Prospectus Status Missionis," ASCPF, *Nova Series 992, 402; 437(C); 465 (C); Nova Series* 1123, 374; 461; *Nova Series* 1251, 691 (B)

285 Literally the term Dalit means 'trampled underfoot.' There are a number of definitions of the same. A working definition may be taken from the Encyclopaedia of Dalits in India: "... Dalit is not a caste. He is a man exploited by the social and economic traditions of his country." See Sanjay Paswan and Paramanshi Jaideva, eds., Encyclopaedia of Dalits in India (Delhi: Kalpaz Publications, 2002), 14.

286 The Annual Letters of Bishop Henry Doring from 1930 to 1937 mention these factors. See Henry Doring, "Prospectus Status Missionis," ASCPF, Nova Series 992, 402; 437(C); 465 (C); Nova Series 1123, 374; 461; Nova Series 1251,691 (B).

This short discussion proves that there was no fundamental departure in the missionary method, except the fact that the conversion of groups became more difficult in the later decades. Moreover, the results were mostly constrained by the external factors. From the disposition of the Jesuits, it is clear that they were open to such possibilities.

3.4.1. Regular Contact with the Target Groups

To a reader with a background of other classical disciplines in theology, i.e., Biblical studies and Systematic Theology, etc., the terms like socio-pastoral care may be rather obsolete, nay hardly deserving any consideration. But this practice has proven invariably an effective means of winning over Christians as well as of consolidating the groups already won-over to Christianity. At a very basic level it may be pointed out that such an effect is achieved through regular contact which paves a way to establish a bond of trust and confidence between the missionary and the target groups. At the deeper level it becomes imperative in a mission as it derives its origin from the basic call of humankind to relationship and *relationality.* The same may be articulated in the words of Patton:

> The ministry of pastoral care is theologically based on the Christian affirmation that God created humankind for relationship with God and with God's other creatures. God continues in relationship with humankind by remembering and hearing us. Our human caring is based in God's care; we care for each other because God cares for us.[287]

Establishing a regular contact with the target groups formed an integral part of the socio-pastoral care of the faithful. Indeed the Jesuits attached a vital importance to this practice. To trace this as a viable method of consolidating the Christian communities we illustrate the cases of a few missionaries from this Mission. John Baptist Eichhorn, who worked for a substantial number of years in Rahata, one of the first *Maratha* mission stations underlined the importance of visiting the villages in the following words:

> It is of utmost significance that the missionary visits the villages under his care as often as possible, in order to assess the situation well, to remain in touch with the people, to administer baptism to the children, to administer last sacrament to the old and the sick

287 John Patton, Pastoral Care; An Essential Guide (Nashville: Abingdon Press, 2005), ii.

> and to prepare those in deathbed for a worthy death. The Christians would be always thankful to him for the same because they know what a sacrifice it costs and God does reward him for the sacrifice ... To these is included also a substantially good health in order to stand the strong heat from morning till evening while visiting the villages giving particular care to specific needs of every village.[288]

One notices practically all the significant elements of a good pastoral care in the above citation. Apparently, they are very basic in nature, i.e. assessing the situation, administering sacraments etc. The profound impact that was evident as a result of a consistent following of the method was conspicuous in the approaches of many other missionaries as well. Henry Doring, for example, before being appointed the Bishop of Poona typically embodied this approach as he regularly undertook pastoral visits. The erstwhile catalogue too designated "visit to villages" as one of his primary apostolates.[289] Francis Xavier Schubiger,[290] is described as enthusiastically carrying forward this tradition. His zeal for establishing personal contacts with the people in their own villages may be judged from the fact that "on the day of visit to a particular village he would normally get up at three o'clock in the morning. After the Holy Mass and breakfast he would pack some loaves of wheat bread and immediately set out for the village. Around 7.00 o'clock he would reach a village."[291]

No wonder this method bore abundant fruit in consolidating the Mission, if not winning new converts in bigger numbers. We are told that through these visits and missionary tours to the villages, he was able to establish himself as one of the most endearing missionaries among the *Mahar* Christians. He was popularly known among them as *Mothe Saheb* (Big Master/gentleman). Such an achievement does not come without

288 John B. Eichhorn, "Rahata," IB 1/9 (January 1932): 59. See also Ludwig Hassle to Joseph M. Wiget (Songaon, 27th March 1942), AMPSJ, IB. Songaon-Briefe. Further in the same file see Ludwig Hassle to Felix A. Plattner (Songaon, 17th May 1942); Ludwig Hassle to Felix A. Plattner (Songaon, 6th July 1945); Ludwig Hassle to the Benefactors (Songaon, 6th July 1945); R. Wasserer to Felix A. Plattner (Valan, 7th September 1945), AMPSJ, LB. Valan-Briefe.

289 For example see CPGSSI(1935), 34; (1937), 37.

290 One of the key figures of the Mission, Francis Xavier Schubiger was a Swiss native. He played a very vital role in saving the mission especially during the crucial period subsequent to post World War I. More about him will be discussed later on.

291 "Eine Schulstunde in der Heidenmission," IB 1/3 (January 1930): 15.

a price. This acknowledgement of the trust and confidence that he had won among the people comes from one of his own contemporaries in the Mission:

> Our Mothe Saheb (big master, the parish priest, Fr. Schubiger in contrast with smaller masters, the chaplains) enjoys by far much greater confidence of people because of his healing. The mothers, especially, hold him as someone who can do everything for them. With good counselling and harmless medicines he helps them keep their children safe from diseases. Hence they are thankful to him all the more, while on the one hand the infant mortality rate is extremely high; on the other they are expected to bear more children.[292]

Often the missionaries would undertake the plans of visits to the villages for a week or more at a stretch, so as to be able to visit a maximum number of villages. Maximilian Maier was fond of undertaking such a pattern of pastoral visits, whereby he regularly undertook pastoral visits "from one village to another, up to six days in a row."[293] This helped him establish a regular contact with the maximum number of villages. Similarly, Otto Weishaupt, one of the founders of the *Maratha* mission precisely followed this pattern even before the mission stations were established, while he was still living in a small mud house in Sangamner: "From one village to another did he travel"[294] to establish contacts and explore possibilities for establishing mission stations.

Figure 3.1: Bullock-cart of the missionaries at Sangamner.
Source: *DS* 5 (1930): 99 in AMPSJ, *Belege 1930-1940*: Felix A. Plattner, "Achtzig Jahre deutsche Jesuitenmission in Indien," *KM62/8* (1943): 211.

292 Joseph Stark, "Wie wir an die Heiden Herankommen," IB 1/10 (April 1932): 64.

293 Maximilian Maier, "Deolali bei Nasik," IB 1/13 (January 1933): 95.

294 Winiger, "Die Missionsstation Sangamner," ADPSJ, Abt. 45B-26, Nr. 1509.

It would be an incomplete picture, if we omit to make a comment on the decades especially after World War II. It is true that Poona Mission began to face changed situations and newer challenges. In no way the value of this approach at least in principle suffered any loss. The fact, however, was that a certain section of the Jesuits seem to have lost sight of its significance in the consolidation of the Mission. While lamenting the situation, George Kester as Visitor of the Mission underlines its value and holds the lack of the same among a section of the Jesuits as a factor responsible for the failure of holding a group of *Mahars* deserting the Catholic Faith. In his own words:

> Many Fathers devote quite a lot of their time in meeting their Catholics in the villages. In Rahata and Sangamner but also in other stations the Fathers make many visits in the villages, but they go there, hear confessions, say Mass and return after two hours again to the station. They hardly speak with the people. The Fathers should take more time to talk and discuss with their people, staying a little, visit their houses and stay in the villages during the night. Only in this way the Fathers will establish personal contacts with their people. In times of crisis for these people everything depends on this personal contact: their priest is their religion. If too many have dropped away into Buddhism, at least nominally, I think this is the root of the trouble. Some Fathers got too much involved in the welfare schemes and administrative arrangements. The Fathers in Harigaon and [Ahmed]Nagar made a happy exception and see clearly the point at issue. The Catholics who dropped away into Buddhism, will return, if we do not write them off and keep at visiting them regularly and patiently.[295]

That pastoral visits and establishing regular contacts with the Catholics occupied a central place in the Jesuit approaches of evangelization is well underlined in the text above. An additional aspect that is evident in the text is that only through regular contacts can a lively relationship of trust can be established, which in turn is essential for a Christian community especially in its infancy. The conclusion of the analysis of the situation expressed in the above report on certain members of the Catholic community deserting the fold may be disputed, for the issue seems to have been other than religious ones. A few aspects on this will be discussed in the chapter dealing with the moot-points

295 George Kester, "Goa-Poona: Visitor's Report," op. cit., 74-75.

in the history of this Mission. Yet the veracity of the argument is not wholly unfounded.

3.4.2. Works of Charity and Humanitarian Concerns

In the history of Christian missions, works of charity and various forms of humanitarian concerns have invariably functioned as effective means of evangelization. Hence "caring for orphans and widows, for the sick and the aged"[296] has been among the primary charisms of the Church. In other words, performing works of charity and undertaking various forms of humanitarian works formed one of the principle aspects of the Church's threefold mission, the other two being proclaiming the Word and celebrating the sacraments.[297] In a broader sense of the term, it may mean various other things as well, i.e., establishing schools, orphanages and health care centres; organizing relief programmes and extending various forms of material as well as spiritual aids, etc. In recent times, the charism of St. Theresa of Kolkata (erstwhile Mother Theresa of Calcutta) seems to have captured the imagination of common people, whereby the meaning of works of charity seem to be confined to such works as those undertaken by her. But as indicated above, it is much more comprehensive in meaning to include every humane act that is undertaken in order to restore the dignity of a person living under any form of deprivation.

We have already discussed on education through schools as an apostolic instrument. Therefore, we shall focus our discussion here on other aspects, such as taking care of the orphans and widows, the aged and the sick, organizing welfare schemes, undertaking humanitarian concerns, creating job opportunities, etc. , which were also perceived as apostolic instruments. Yet before dealing with this sub-topic in detail, it may not be out of place to see whether these instruments were entirely new and unique in this Mission. Seen in retrospect we discover that these methods were not new in Jesuit missions. Indeed these have occupied an important place among all the strategies adopted in Jesuit missions elsewhere in India right from the beginning. During Francis Xavier's time, for example, one notices a typical missionary method wherein

296 Avery Dulles, Evangelization for the Third Millenium (New Jersey: Paulist Press, 2009), 98.

297 See Benedict XVI, Deus Caritas est, nos. 19-25. See also J. Brian Benestad, Church, State, and Society: An Introduction to Catholic Social Doctrine (Washington: The Catholic University of America Press, 2011), 449.

he visualised works of charity to non-Christians as potential attraction to Christianity. His vision is summarised in a phrase: "attracting the non-Christians through good works [and thus] to orient them to come under the yoke of the Gospel."[298] In other words, through the works of Christian mercy and charity the non-believers would be led to learn in reality about Christianity, its excellence, its core teaching and thus may be disposed to embrace Christianity.[299]

In the Bombay-Poona Mission too it is conspicuous in various phases of its history. Why was it necessary to adopt this method? It was because the task of penetrating the non-Christian society was no easy, given the stiff opposition from various quarters. The story of the beginning and development of the mission at Sangamner, the third station of *Maratha* mission, exemplifies the case well, which contains elements of typical missionary stereotype of the older times, namely hardships and adventures that one often comes across in the stories of the older missionary enterprises. Traditionally the town (Sangamner) was a strong Brahmin dominated centre, besides a substantial percentage of Muslims being the residents of the place. The opposition mainly came from the Brahmins. They were determined to resist the entry of the Christian missionaries in the area. To achieve the objective, they employed occasionally physical harassments too.[300] This was not an isolated case. The missionaries did experience, often in subtle forms, many other occasions of opposition from Hindus.[301] Given such circumstances, there was virtually no possibility of direct evangelization. Even normal interaction with people was bound to create suspicions against the Christian missionaries.[302]

---

298 As quoted in Josef Schmidlin, Katholische Missionslehre im Grundriss (Miinster: Aschendorffschen Verlagsbuchhandlung, 1919), 428.

299 Ibid.

300 See Winiger, "Die Missionsstation Sangamner," ADPSJ, Abt. 45B-26, Nr. 1509, 2. See also F.X. Schubiger, "Aus Sangamner," IB 1/3 (July 1930): 14-15.

301 See F. X. Schubiger, "Aus der Bewegung unter den AusgestoBenen," IB 1/26 (April 1936): 215; L. HaBle, "Der Bose fangt an, sich zu argern," ," IB 1/29 (January 1937): 250. In the first case the local Hindus demanded a space for the road through the mission property in order to harass the missionary. In the second case they beat a widow who was working at the church building site in order to earn a livelihood.

302 Some of the rumours spread against the missionaries were the following: "he [Otto Weishaupt] and his catechists are agents of slave-traders, child-robbers, the liquid that the *'Saheb '* [Gentleman] uses for the baptism is the urine of the swine (the worst that a

Hence there was a need to employ other methods of evangelization. With patience and perseverance as the missionaries gradually began to have contacts with the people, they realized that the first contacts with people were possible through opening up schools. But winning the people for Catholicism was still a far-fetched dream. The crux of the situation may be summarised in the words of Hubert Sixt: "But unless induced by worldly interests very few are willing, and fewer still show the necessary good dispositions to make baptism advisable, except when they come to die."[303] We must hasten to add that the account of Hubert Sixt may not be unduly generalized. But the fact remains that the works of charity of any form was certainly helpful in attracting the people to Catholicism. Hence this strategy began to be adopted alongside others. The works of charity took various forms, i.e., caring for orphans and widows, availing certain first aid medicines, job creation for the Christians in the wake of famines that hit the mission field quite regularly, especially in 1918-1919, 1927 and again in 1835-1936; supporting education of children free of cost, occasionally lending money with nominal interest, etc.[304]

To begin with, opening a widows-home was a very tangible sign for the local people to perceive what Christianity is all about. In his long years (18) of committed engagement with evangelization of the local people, Francis Xavier Schubiger, who was based in Sangamner realized that this initiative must be a natural consequence of spreading the Catholic Faith. Hence in the wake of the severe famine of 1918-1919 the first step he took was to open a home for the widows, many of whom were widowed during the outbreak of pest following the famine. There was no restriction on the admission of the widows in the home on the basis of their religion, although certain amount of preference for the Christian widows did exist. The reason behind was an unmixed motive: the missionaries took it as their primary duty to take care of their own flock.[305]

caste Hindu may imagine) and many such things." See Winiger, "Die Missionsstation Sangamner," 3.

303 Hubert Sixt, "The Marathi Mission at Ahmednagar," 3. See also Staffner, "Die katholische Mission in Ahmednagar-Distrikt in Indien," AMPSJ, Ahmednagar, 6.

304 Pius Geisel, "Hungersnot," IB 1/28 (October 1936): 235-238.

305 See Winiger, "Die Missionsstation Sangamner," 23. See also F. X. Schubiger, "Wie es auf einer Missionsstation aussieht," IB 1/14 (April 1933): 104; "Die Fahrt ins Missionsland," IB 1/17 (January 1934): 138.

Although this initiative could not be implemented in all the mission stations because of the practical difficulty of space and resources, the willingness on the part of the missionaries to take care of the orphans and the widows given their own concrete local possibilities and constraints always remained with them. Precisely for this reason the religious Sisters were invited to continue the work more efficiently and with greater dedication. The Sisters who first came were St. Anne's Sisters working in those days in Hyderabad area of western India. They had a good experience of looking after the orphans and the widows. However, once Poona Mission was re-entrusted to the Southern German Province of the Jesuits, the consideration changed in favour of the Franciscan Sisters of Erlenbad in Baden, Germany, who arrived in Rahata on 16th December 1936. Initially their work consisted of taking care of the orphans and the widows, besides helping out at the mission stations.[306] Beginning from mid 1930s, they were entrusted with running the dispensaries too. They started good hospitals "at *Shrirampur, Shevgaon, Songaon* and *Ghodegaon.* There are small dispensaries at most of the mission stations with mobile units."[307] Such a care had a noticeable impact upon the people, which inspired them even to convert to Catholicism.[308] Later of course, they began to run schools for girls as well.[309]

The other aspects of the works of charity and humanitarian concerns included, as noted above, supporting the education of children free of cost[310] and extending financial help to the helpless and the needy. However, the initiative undertaken in the wake of repeated occurrences

---

306 See "Ersehnte Hilfe," IB 1/30 (April 1937): 251-252; "Zwei Waisenkinder aus Sangamner," IB 1/25 (January 1925): 217. We shall discuss some more aspects with regard to the Sisters later below.

307 J. Jadhav, Evangelization as Community Building (Ahmednagar: Social Centre, 2006), 126. The emphasis in the original text. We shall discuss more about the health-care apostolate in the chapter on the new ventures.

308 See F. X. Schubiger, "Unser kleiner Guido," IB 1/21 (January 1935): 169-171.

309 See Sr. M. Helmtrudis, "Unsere neue Madschenschule," IB 1/31 (July 1937): 272; "P. Eichhorn berichtet erganzend," IB 1/30 (April 1937): 254; J. Stark, "Altes undNeues aus Kendal," IB 1/26 (April 1936): 220.

310 See "Die Fahrt ins Missionsland," IB 1/17 (January 1934): 137-138; "Wie es auf einer Missionsstation aussieht," IB 1/14 (April 1933): 104; J. B. Eichhorn, "Eine Schwere Sorge," IB 1/20 (October 1934): 157-158; J. Stark, "Altes und Neues aus Kendal," 217; J. B. Eichhorn, "Eins urns andere," IB 1/28 (October 1936): 233; "Valan," IB 1/29 (January 1937): 247; P. Geisel, "Mariaschein - ein Kollege der Leistung," IB 1/32 (October 1937): 275.

of famines in the area are by far more commendable and deserve to be dealt with in greater detail. This initiative was started initially by Henry Doring, later Archbishop of Poona, who worked as a missionary in Valan for about a decade.[311] His purpose to start it originated from a basic question: "How can we make our newly converted Christians and their families financially self-sufficient?"[312] Later, in the years subsequent to World War I, under the leadership of two committed and trained Coadjutor Brothers namely Moritz Emmenecker and Maximilian Demmeler, the Weaving Training Unit became further organized touching new heights of growth and consolidation.[313] This initiative was capable of generating a new hope among a substantial number of Christians, in spite of the fact that on many occasions the Weaving Training School itself faced a number of difficulties, i.e., sudden fall in the demand for the carpet, obstacles inacquiring raw materials, complications with contract deals, inflation, etc. These facts apart, it was a noble effort towards making the Christians into a self-reliant community. It is evident from the fact that in an ideal situation, at least 100 workers were employed at a time, which in turn meant a reasonably good standard of livelihood for an equal number of families.[314] The initiative gains further significance, for the sheer fact that it began during one of the most difficult periods for the local people, i.e. famine of 1899/1900.

Although, the initiative was primarily intended to support the newly converted Christians, it often acted in favour of the conversion movement towards Christianity, especially among the poor sections of the society. But the natural question is how it happened. Taking a very concrete example of the Christians employed at the Weaving School, it may be stated that their improved status of life was a primary attraction to others as well. Similarly a very tangible expression of Catholicism was experienced by the people as they began to receive the basic medical aids by the missionaries.

Still another aspect of the humanitarian concerns that seem to have played a significant impact on the local people was availing of basic

311 See J. van Aken, "Erzbischof Heinrich Doring," UB (January-February 1952): 27-28. See also Anonymous "Doppelfest der altesten Deutschen Heidenmission," PJPA, Varia.

312 Moritz Emmenecker, "Die Teppichweberei in Kendal," IB 1/24 (October 1935): 193.

313 Ibid.

314 See M. Demmeler, "Aus Kendal," IB 1/17 (January 1934): 136-137; Stark, "Altes und Neues aus Kendal," 219.

medical aids. In the absence of health-care facilities, people mostly relied upon local sorcerers and witch-doctors besides a few indigenous means of healing. The recourse to the sorcerers and witch-doctors had serious implications, which included endangering one's own health as the witch-doctors and sorcerers were hardly qualified to understand the functioning of the human body. Besides they suffered loss of resources in the hands of manipulative witch-doctors, who took delight in extracting maximum amount of money from these poor folks.[315]

The Jesuits, within their own capacities, tried to do what they could with the help of medicines available from Europe. However, the two missionaries who seem to have excelled in this area were Francis Xavier Schubiger and Pius Geisel, who also happened to be the Consulter and the Superior of the Mission, respectively. As far as the evidence goes, they had no formal training in medical assistance.[316] Yet, they learnt the basics of some common medicines and their effects. This knowledge helped them to reach out to a good number of people, especially in the wake of the outbreak of epidemics and pests. During their pastoral visits they always carried a kit of some common medicines, besides oils for anointment and communion for the sick. Often the stock of medicines ran out even before the sacraments to the sick were administered.[317] For example, Francis Schubiger spent a whole day at times distributing medicines at his mission station. He noted, "Often in the evenings I do not know where my head is lying; for I am so much pressed by urgency. Besides, the whole day the sick and the hungry keep on knocking at my door."[318] Similar efforts were made by other missionaries as well, of course with lesser success as compared to these two. But the dedication and commitment to this work on their part was beyond doubt.[319]

315 See J. B. Winiger, "Die Choleragottin," IB 1/29 (January 1937): 248; F. X. Schubiger, "Indische Feuerprobe und ihr Ausgang," op. cit, 248-249.

316 The only sources of information, namely their necrologies found in various sources as well as in O'Neill & Dominguez (eds.), Diccinario Historico de la Compahia de Jesus do not mention this detail.

317 "Hungersnot," IB 1/28 (October 1936): 236.

318 See "Valan," IB 1/29 (January 1937): 247.

319 See Francis X. Schubiger & J. Stark, "P. Franz X. Trenkamp," AMPSJ, MDP 13/102 (1934): 211.

Consequently, in the wake of breaking out of the plagues and epidemics, some of them got infected with the sickness and lost their lives.[320]

As a consequence, of these works of charity and humanitarian concerns, the conversion movement, by and large, never remained stagnant even during the years subsequent to wars, famines and plagues, etc. No wonder that the missionaries reported often about their satisfaction with the numerical as well as overall growth of the Catholic community. Even amidst the famine situation, a missionary reported for example, "Mission as such is going on well."[321] From another station John Baptist Eichhorn reported: "The work here is progressing well."[322] And the third report has the same import, in fact underlining even a better situation: "The work everywhere is going on so well, like never before."[323]

Although a few more remarks will be in place under chapter six (i.e., Some Moot-Points and Contemporary Contentious Issues), it is apt to make a comment right here. Often the conversions following as a result of certain charitable works and humanitarian concerns have come under heavy criticism from various quarters. The motive behind the conversion of local people to Christianity seems to have been their perception and hope for a better prospect of life.[324]

Seen from the perspective of other missionary religions, the initiatives might be branded as pure allurement. In recent years against the background of the growing nationalist consciousness among people of other religions, especially Hindus these initiatives have come under severe criticism from various quarters. But this criticism is not a very recent development. Mahatma Gandhi, for example, saw charitable works as mere preparation for something more. A citation from a Hindu critic gives a glimpse into this side of the story:

> But there was an even deeper problem with these services, and [Mahatma] Gandhiji drew attention to it again and again. The services were incidental. They were the means. The objectives

320 See H. Sixt, ed., "Historical Notes on the Ahmednagar Mission," PJPA, Valan Diary IV, (n.d.), 12-13.

321 Ludwig HaBle, "Dies und Das," IB Mil (July 1936): 230.

322 J.B. Eichhorn, "Eins urns andere," IB 1/28 (October 1936): 233.

323 "Ein gesegnetes neues Jahr gebe Gott alien Freunden und Wohltatern der Punamission," IB 1/29 (January 1937): 244.

324 This aspect will be dealt with in greater detail in chapter 8 (# 8.2.1).

was to convert the natives to Christianity. The Collected Works contain several accounts as do Mahadev Desai's Diaries in which missionaries acknowledge to Gandhiji that the institutions and services are indeed incidental, that the aim is to gather a fuller harvest of coverts for the Church.[325]

Apologetics apart, Christian religion has always perceived works of charity undertaken with an unselfish motive to contribute towards bringing a dignified standard of life to people who in any manner are deprived of such a state of things as noble and desirable, nay belonging to the very core of Christian life and message. So far it is seen with an objectivity, the strategy served a great deal of good towards the growth of the Catholic community. The essence of Christianity that was imparted to local people through these acts could by no means be ignored.

3.4.3. Collaboration with those in Positions of Influence and Power

The Jesuits world-wide, right from the beginning of their Order, have shown an inclination to keep contact with those in positions of power in order to facilitate a smoother process of conversion of the natives.[326] A model described as 'from the top down' by Nicolas Standaert has been, thus, a tested and trusted strategy of evangelization among the Jesuits.[327] A brief analysis would reveal that such a model was operative in some form or the other in this Mission too. However, such an option was not always deliberately chosen. Rather in the process of exploring and establishing contacts in the initial stages of starting a new mission station they invariably came into contact with one or the other person in positions of power and influence. Often such people were no authorities in the conventional sense of the term, although the contrary was true as well. They were people who had occupied a place of influence in their communities and societies, because of their natural talents, leadership qualities, higher position in the caste hierarchy or better financial position as compared to the majority of their classes of people. Regular contact and alliances with such people often facilitated the smoother

325 Arun Shourie, "Missionaries in India," in *Paths of Mission in India Today,* ed. Augustine Kanjamala (Bombay: St. Pauls, 1997), 69.

326 John W. O'Malley, et al, *The Jesuits: Cutlures, Sciences and the Arts 1540-1773* (Toronto/Buffalo/London: University of Toronto Press, 1999), 352-353.

327 See Catherine Pagani, "Clockwork and the Jesuit Mission in China," in *The Jesuits II: Cultures, Sciences and the Arts, 1540-1773,* eds. John W. O'Malley, et al. (Toronto/Buffalo/London: University of Toronto Press, 2006), 671.

process of starting a mission station and eventually the growth of the mission in the long run.

In this perspective the elements of such an approach in this Mission are identifiable in a substantial number of cases. The story of the beginning of Sangamner Mission exemplifies the case once again. In July 1892 Otto Weishaupt reached Sangamner where he settled in a rented mud house in the town, rented another house for teachers and boarders, whom he had brought along and got permission to use the municipal *dharamsala* (travellers' inn) as a school. The size of his room was so small that even one bed could not be accommodated properly therein. No wonder he had to sleep on the floor as long as he stayed there. Yet, he was thankful for having a roof over his head. For, the process of acquiring even these mud-houses were not easy and probably would have been almost beyond his reach as well, had the highest authority of the place (Mamlatdar in local parlance) not mediated in the entire deal. This gentleman, a Brahmin by birth, had studied in a Jesuit school in Bombay and desired to express his gratitude for the education and training he had received, by mediating in the process of acquiring the rooms for a rent.[328] This contact, it appears, gave a base and an opening for Otto Weishaupt for further penetration in the area.

Going a step further, in spite of the fact that some of the authors dealing with the history of this Mission have adopted a tone of condemnation towards the British authorities,[329] generally it appears that the missionaries by and large had a good rapport with the British authorities. There is no denying of the fact that in the years subsequent to the breaking of World War I certain stringent policies were adopted by the British towards the German nationals working in India. Moreover, the missionaries did testify occasionally to a certain amount of bias towards the Protestant and Anglican missions in India. But, if we take the period of the two World Wars as an exception, it may safely be concluded that the relationship by and large was cordial especially at the official levels of dealing. No wonder, such a rapport with British

328 See Winiger, "Die Missionsstation Sangamner," 3; Staffher, "Die katholische Mission in Ahmednagar-Distrikt in Indien," AMPSJ, Ahmednagar; "Wie Pater Weishaupt die Sangamnermission griindete," IB 1/ 2 (March 1930): 5.

329 E. R. Hull, J. H. Gense and Alfons Vath dealing with the history of the Mission seem to have occasionally given in to this inclination. See Hull, *The German Jesuit Fathers,* 107-108; 121-122; Gense, *Church at the Gateway,* 380-386; Vath, *Die deutsche Jesuiten,* 236-237.

officers was immensely helpful in consolidation and expansion of the mMssion. This aspect was especially noticeable in the circumstances when native Christians faced some legal problems. The unbiased judgement they received in such cases was ultimately the result of a fair policy of the British officers, on the one hand, and a good relationship of the missionaries with them, on the other.

To illustrate the point we may take an example from the life of Francis Xavier Schubiger. In 1936 in a place called Nandur-Shingote, some 20 kms from the main mission station, i.e., Sangamner, there was a conflict between the upper caste Hindus and the poor Mahars. The conflict consisted basically of the upper caste Hindu harassment of the Mahars; because the latter were being influenced by a famous movement among the untouchables of Maharashtra that was spearheaded by Bhimrao Ambedkar,[330] about which we shall discuss in greater detail elsewhere. Consequently the upper caste hegemony was at danger. The ugliness of the incident may be imagined from the fact that the upper caste Hindus set free their oxen and other domestic animals to graze in the cultivated fields of the Mahars. The fields were the only means of livelihood of the poor Mahars, who sought the help of the missionary, i.e., Francis Xavier Schubiger. The latter prepared a detailed account of the incident along with the estimate of the loss incurred and sent it to the District Collector, who acted promptly on the case and consequently a peaceful settlement of the case was arrived at. The Mahars received compensation for the loss. No wonder the Collector was among the good acquaintances of the missionary.[331]

---

330 Bhimrao Ambedkar, born on 14th April 1891 was himself an untouchable. When he was in school he already began to feel the sting of untouchability as he was not permitted to sit with other students of his class. He could drink water only when other students of higher caste poured it for him. Stung by such experiences right from his childhood, he decided to fight against such discrimination. He raised himself from the lowest rung of the society to an enviable position in Indian political life by his sheer hard work and will-power. Later he led a heroic struggle for the liberation of the suppressed people in India. As he was a contemporary of Mahatma Gandhi, he came into confrontation with him too on these and related issues. He is considered one of the architects of modern India as he was appointed the Chairperson of the Drafting Committee of Indian Constitution. Indeed he epitomizes the rebellion against caste hierarchy in Hindu society. See Dhananjay Keer, *Dr. Ambedkar: Life and Mission* (Mumbai: Popular Prakashan, 1999).

331 See Francis X. Schubiger, "Aus der Bewegung unter den AusgestoBenen," IB 1/26 (April 1936): 214-216.

The cordial contact with the British officers seems to have born even more tangible and positive results during the time of the two World Wars when the German Fathers were interned in the camps. The incident seems to have generated bitterness in the mind of the German Fathers against the British officers. But an objective reading of the entire episode reveals that the British officers were not as ill-intentioned towards the German Fathers as the latter had perceived. Writing as the Vicar Foraine of the Mission, Francis Xavier Schubiger acknowledges that "there is no problem from the British Raj [British Government].On the contrary there is a helpful attitude towards the missionaries."[332] Similar positive experience is expressed in the letters of Archbishop Thomas Roberts to the Superior General in the event of the Second World War (World War II). Describing the events leading to the internment of the German Fathers at the outbreak of World War II, he writes:

> Last July, he [Sir Roger Lumley, Governor of Bombay] told me that no restriction at all would apply to Spanish Fathers and that he hoped not to intern even the German missionaries in case of war. On the outbreak war, Sir Roger Lumley at once returned to Bombay and I visited him on the evening of his arrival. He told me that the Central Government had already interned all Germans on its own authority and that his power was limited to investigation and recommendation for individuals. I left with him a memorandum ... This document his Excellency promised to forward to Delhi at once with his own endorsement, and to intercede with the Viceroy.[333]

After a few months, reporting about the release of a majority of the missionaries from the internment camps, Archbishop Roberts writes: "I may add that nearly all of the one hundred Catholic missionaries released have testified to Sir Malcolm Darling or to me how deeply impressed they were with the Christian and humane attitude of the Commission."[334]

---

332 Francis X. Schubiger to the Superior General (23rd January 1924) ARSI, Bombay. 1004-IX, 5.

333 Archbishop Thomas Roberts to the Cardinal Prefect of Propaganda Fide (Bombay, 26th November 1939), ARSI, Poona. 1004-XII, 13.

334 Archbishop Thomas Roberts to the Superior General (Bombay, 12th March 1940) ARSI, Poona. 1004-VIII, 5.

Let it be noted that besides the basic principle of holding to fair judgement in matters of justice, the British officers were also influenced by some of the missionaries, thanks to their personal contacts. Archbishop Thomas Roberts, for example, had a very good personal rapport with the high officials in the British government, to the extent that he considered the then Governor of Bombay as a close friend. In this regard, therefore, the consequences of good relations with the people in positions of power and influence must not be seen only in the aspect of expansion of the mission and the numerical increase of the converts; rather they must also be seen in terms of creating positive atmosphere for peaceful work among the people. The latter aspect is what is implied here while discussing about the relations with the British officers.

In the later decades too, the collaboration with people having positions of influence came as a great help in the Mission. In connection with the foundation of Dnyanamata Vidyalaya at Sangamner, for example, Rudolph Schoch narrates of his personal experience with a Brahmin of the place. His name was Raobahadur Parasharami.[335] A big credit goes to his influence and efforts thanks to which the school was founded in Sangamner. In the words of Schoch:

> Mr. Parasharami has been very committed to our school from the very beginning. He helped us to buy the beautiful place, he obtained the necessary permission in a record time, he promoted the school among his friends and in a most selfless manner had done all that was in his power to make it possible ... Mr. Parasharami is perhaps the most influential person in Sangamner.[336]

3.4.4. Theatre and Plays as Means of Evangelization

An important means of evangelization, more especially prior to the 1940s, was the use of nativity and passion plays and theatre as means of evangelization. The plays were presented mostly on festive occasions.

335 In fact the Jesuits, at least some of them like Rudolph Schoch and others, made best of efforts to establish a good contact with the people of higher stature and influence in the society. Besides Mr. Parasharami, we come across mention of persons like Dr. Date who was the publisher of Marathi Lexicon, President of the Literature Society of Poona and no wonder an authority in Marathi. See Rudolph Schoch, "Dnyanamata," IB 3 (May/June 1948): 2.

336 Rudolph Schoch, "Dnyanamata," IB 3 (May/June 1948): 2. See also "Dnyanamata Vidyalaya," IB 2 (1948): 10.

In an era when the conventional means of entertainment, i.e. cinema, orchestra or sports, etc., were rare and mostly out of reach for the common people, plays and theatre offered a great attraction among them. Precisely, the importance of this art was recognized by the Jesuits because of this innate attraction that the native people depicted towards these forms of arts. One missionary has recorded:

> In our mission, besides the Feast of the Sacred Heart of Jesus, Corpus Christi and Christmas have gained a special importance, thanks to the Christmas plays or religious theatre. In the same manner as they have a special importance in our schools and colleges [in Europe] for the ducation of boys, so also in the mission they play an important role in deepening and spreading the faith life. Why is this? [Because] the Indians passionately love theatrical performances, singing and music.[337]

They were incentives to gather people from far off places. Otherwise fewer number of people would have gathered on occasions like Christmas for the midnight Masses under the open sky amidst biting cold. Hence, a theatre play on some biblical themes were prepared and presented before the Holy Mass began. For example, at the Sangamner mission station the title of the passion play in the year 1936 was: "A Sacrifice of the Mystery of Confession" (Ein Opfer des Beichtgeheimnisses). The original writer of the play was P. Spillmann. Francis Schubiger translated, edited and adapted the same to the context of the place.[338] Similarly, during the Christmas Vigil Mass at Songaon, the title of the play was "Theresa of Child Jesus."[339]

Occasionally the Jesuits themselves acted in the plays when the nature of characters so demanded. This underlines the fact that the Jesuits considered the plays[340] much more effective than as means of entertainment. Indeed they proved to be powerful means of communicating deeper truths of Christianity to simple people. In most likelihood the people may not have grasped what Christianity is all about, had they been communicated through the means of elegant sermons and tracts. In this regard the effectiveness of the method is best captured in

337 Weihnachten in Indien," MB (December 1929): 1.

338 Pius Geisel, „Sangamner," IB, 1/30 (April 1937): 257.

339 Ludwig Hassle, "Songaon: II. Weihnachtsbericht 25. 12. 39," IB 2/10 (April 1940): 112.

340 See "Diary of the Kendal-Mission: April 1939-May 1981," PJPA, Kendal.

the words of Pius Geisel as he writes: "I can assure you that it [Theatre Play] works like a very good sermon. It was already experienced during the rehearsals."[341]

What was the mode of presentation of the theatre plays? Apparently the normal dialogical delivery of the message through the means of characters playing various roles would have been rather eclectic in nature. Hence, "according to the taste of the local people, they [theatre plays] are presented mostly by melodious recital of the dialogues."[342] They were formulated in simple languages that were well understood by people. Basically they were works of some well-known authors and play-writes. They were translated and adapted to the local circumstances by the missionaries. It may be easily imagined how much of work and time of the missionaries they may have consumed. For a westerner it would have been much easier to do a literal translation. But here they needed to do much more: to enter into the cultural milieu of the people and adapt the messages in local languages. Yet, the difficulties did not end here. The Jesuits needed to get accustomed to the so-called local music. This is revealed by Ludwig HaBle, a Jesuit keenly involved in these activities: "The melodies sound very alien and strange, and with no particular [musical] scales and are of a rather peculiar rhythm. The accompaniment here consists of a small harmonium, kettle drum and a certain indigenous blowing instruments (pipes)."[343] This effort drew a substantial number of people as audience, not only the new Christians but also others. The seeds of faith were, thus, sown indirectly among the non-Christian audience.

3.4.5. Acquaintance with Native Language

The study and knowledge of native language and culture is of paramount importance in missionary enterprises. For language, as it were, is an opening into the world of a people: without the knowledge of which it is not possible to appreciate the richness and the beauty of the world-view, rituals and their meaning systems. One can only access the exterior aspects of the culture of a people.[344] Since the linguistic and cultural

341 Pius Geisel, "Von Freud und Leid der Missionare: Sangamner," IB 1/ 30 (April 1937): 257.

342 L. HaBle, "Weihnachten in Songaon," IB 1/18 (April 1934): 141.

343 Ibid.

344 Achiel Peelman, *Christ is a Native American* (Ontario: Wipf and Stock, 1995), 116.

milieu of a people is a dynamic and not a static reality, it demands a personal engagement in order to attain an experiential knowledge of the same from all those who desire to enter into such a milieu. An unambiguous implication, therefore, is to engage in learning the language of the native people as a living and not as some static reality; for it belongs to the living societies and living peoples. Besides, for the Gospel to be meaningful and truly to be the 'Good News' to the native people it is an imperative that it is preached in their own languages. Such has been a basic mission principle already from the New Testament era.

Without a sound knowledge of the native languages, the missionaries stand at a danger of indiscriminately condemning some rites, habits and customs of the local people even if they may not be fundamentally opposed to religion and good morals. Moreover, they stand in danger of introducing their own pet ideas and world-views.[345] The emphasis on learning native languages becomes even more evident as we take a look at the papal Bulls and Encyclicals of the 20th century. In this regard, Benedict XV's encyclical, *Maximum Mud* (1919) may be said to contain a representative idea:

> Among the attainments necessary for the life of a missionary, a place of paramount importance must obviously be given to the language of the people to whose salvation he will devote himself. He should not be content with the smattering of the language, but he should be able to speak it readily and competently. For in this respect he is under an obligation to all those he deals with, the learned and ignorant alike, and he will soon realize the advantage a command of their language gives him in the task of winning the confidence and sympathy [MI #24].[346]

In Jesuit tradition the importance of learning local language and culture may be traced back to its very origin. Indeed, Ignatius of Loyola himself considered the "knowledge of the local culture and proficiency in the local language [as] directly correlated to the success of a mission. The importance Ignatius attached to the learning of native languages, to complement the missionary task, can be traced to the Constitutions of

345 Augustine S. O. Okwu, *Igbo Culture and the Christian Missions 1857-1957: Conversion in Theory and Practice* (Maryland: University Press of America, 2010), 238.

346 Benedict XV, "Maximum illud," in *Catholic Missions, 17.*

the Society of Jesus."[347] His 25th successor and the 26th General of the Society of Jesus namely Wlodimir Ledochowski, who happened to be a contemporary of Benedict XV closely shared the above views. His keen interest on missions is reflected through his regular addressing of the issue in his letters and exhortations. This may be seen also from the fact that the total number of Jesuits sent on mission world-wide grew to 3,902 in 1940 from a mere 1,971 in 1915 when he became the Superior General.[348] His contribution and achievements in the expansion of the Catholic missions worldwide are well summarized in the following text:

> Missions to the pagan world, to the nations which are rapidly emerging from tutelage and are perhaps destined within another hundred years to overshadow if not to dominate the present leading powers was another ministry pushed on by the far-sighted energy of our General [Vladimir Ledochowski]. The recovery of our ancient position in the forefront of missionary work is one of the most amazing achievements of the restored Society ... To what extent this accomplishment is due to the inspiration of Father Ledochowski is evident in the fact that during his term of office the personnel of Jesuit missions increased nearly 100 per cent. At the outbreak of the Second World War the Society had a fifth of the pagan world within its mission territories. It had nearly 4000 missionaries working in 48 missions. Among its institutions for the betterment of the people it numbered 41 hospitals, 11 leper stations, 107 orphanages, 133 dispensaries. Education was carried on in 11 universities, about 60 secondary schools and colleges and many primary schools. The work was not only extended under Father Ledochowski but the organization of the work of recruiting man power and collecting means for the support of the missions was perfected by him. Only

347 Cohen, *The Missionary Strategies,* 97. In section 447, there is an explicit mention of the important languages to the learned. In addition to Latin, Greek and Hebrew, the other languages mentioned are Arabic, Indian and Chaldean. The latter languages according to the Constitutions were needed to teach the others the knowledge, divine love, salvation of their souls, etc.

348 John W. Witek, "Ledochowski, Wlodimir," in *Biographical Dictionary of Christian Missions,* ed. Gerald H. Anderson (Grand Rapids, Michigan/London: Wm B. Eerdmans, 1998), 390. For similar content see Francis X. Schubiger, "On the Division of Bombay Presidency into various Ecclesiastical Dioceses or Prefectures Apostolic [13th June 1925]," ARSI, Bombay. 1004-X1V, 8.

the veterans who have served under both the old conditions and the new will be able to describe the improvement.[349]

Moreover, throughout his entire tenure as Superior General, he relentlessly addressed the need of laying down a specific time-frame for achieving this objective: "He [Ledochowski] stressed that all Jesuits sent to the missions were to study the native language for two years before embarking on apostolic work."[350] Seen from such a perspective, Ledochowski comes across as the Superior General who had gone a step further than to ensure that all the Jesuit missionaries made it a point to learn the language of the natives.

Although, it may seem too innocuous to make a link, yet it may be pointed out that Ledochowski may certainly have been reminded of the Chinese Rites' controversy created during the mission of the Jesuits to China beginning from 16th century due to conflicting and often contradicting interpretations of the Chinese Rites, as he issued directives and exhortations to the universal Society. Since the issue is a vast topic and has engaged lots of research and writings, it is entirely outside the purview of our discussion to engage with the topic here. It may conveniently be concluded, however, that there lay, among other factors, immense difficulties in objectively interpreting the meaning system centred on major Chinese rites and rituals and more especially expressing Christian ideas using Chinese concepts and terminologies. For, interpretation of the meaning system of a native people belongs largely to the sound knowledge of the corresponding language.[351]

In Bombay-Poona Mission it was, as though, an unwritten policy to take up the study of the native languages and vernaculars before embarking on an apostolic work for the success of the missionary enterprise. This policy was adopted undoubtedly with a sense of urgency.

---

349 John W. Witek, "Ledochowski, Wlodimir," in *Biographical Dictionary of Christian Missions,* ed. Gerald H. Anderson (Grand Rapids, Michigan/London: Wm B. Eerdmans, 1998), 390. For similar content see Francis X. Schubiger, "On the Division of Bombay Presidency into various Ecclesiastical Dioceses or Prefectures Apostolic [13th June 1925]," ARSI, Bombay. 1004-X1V, 8.

350 Witek, "Ledochowski, Wlodimir," 390.

351 See George H. Dunne, *Generation of Giants: The Story of the Jesuits in China in the last Decades of the Ming Dynasty* (Notre Dame, Indiana: University of Notre Dame Press, 1962), 282-301. See also Robert Entenmann, "The Problem of Chinese Rites in Eighteenth-Century Sichuan," in *China and Christianity: Burdened Past; Hopeful Future,* eds. Stephen Uhalley, Jr. & Xiaoxin Wu (New York: M.E. Sharpe, 2001), 129; 135-136.

However, since our present focus is mostly on the mission after World War I, we shall discuss how the urgency to study the native languages was perceived by them. In order to present a more comprehensive picture, we briefly indicate how this issue was approached by the missionaries prior to this period. Accordingly, there are two distinctive approaches identifiable. We shall term them here as a basic or pragmatic approach and a scholarly or literary approach for our convenience. By the basic or pragmatic approach it is meant here that the Jesuits took upon themselves the task of learning a native language as a mere pragmatic means of gaining accessibility to the indigenous people in order to be able to carry out the daily activities of a mission station. The scholarly or literary approach, on the other hand, implies a sound and thorough study of a native language, not only in order to be able to carry out the routine activities but also to be able to engage in scholarly use of the language, i.e. for the translation of the Bible and producing indigenous literature, etc. It must be noted that such a distinction was never a watertight compartmentalization of the two. Often, the same missionaries represented both the categories. Under this sub-topic we shall mostly focus on the first category of the Jesuits.[352]

One need not explain the fact that for a Jesuit as missionary in an alien land it was an absolute requirement to learn the language of the local people. It was as though the door opening up into the world of the indigenous people. One could not expect to continue the mission solely with the help of catechists and school teachers as intermediaries and interpreters.

The later generations of Jesuits too attached a special importance to learning the native languages. In spite of the fact that the need of learning the native language was constantly stressed upon,[353] however, a fact remains to be pointed out that a substantial number of the missionaries could not fulfil the expectation of learning the languages to the extent of utilizing the same for producing literature. We must hasten

352 We shall focus on the second category of the Jesuits under the following sub-topic, namely under 'Art and Literature as Means of Evangelization (# 3.4.7).

353 For example, the Reports of the Visitors to the Mission at various times make a point to underline the fact. See Joachim Villalonga, "Visita a la Mission de Poona: 2 Agosto a 1 Novembre 1930," ARSI, 1401-Poona Visitatio 1930; Adrian van Kalken, "Litterae Visitatoris Missionum Societatis Iesu in India et Ceylon (Ahmedabad, 8th Oct. 1936)," ARSI, 1402- Visitatio Miss. Poonensis 1935-1941, 4; George Kester, "Goa-Poona: Visitor's Report (1963)," op. cit, 15-16; 62.

to add here that it would be tantamount to stereotyping the character of a mission when we make a general conclusion that invariably all the missionaries are expected to produce literature in native languages. Indeed all the missionaries cannot be expected to do so. However, the point here is to identify as to how much of importance the missionaries attached to learning a native language so as to be able to become effective missionaries. In fact, most of the missionaries did not have sufficient time to devote exclusively for learning native languages. It is especially true of the missionaries who came to India in the intervening period between the two World Wars when there was a serious crunch of missionaries. As a result they needed to be sent to the mission stations often within a very short span of their arrival in India, without completing a full term language course.[354] In such circumstances, most of the missionaries needed to conduct normal affairs of the mission stations with bare minimum knowledge of native languages. Yet given the hard lessons learnt from the strategic failure[355] in the previous century, it was a constant reminder that native language must be learnt by all means if a mission endeavour is expected to meet with a desired success. Hence the veteran missionaries, i.e., Francis Xavier Schubiger, Maximilian Riklin, Pius Geisel and others, who had worked in the mission prior to the breaking out of World War I realized its significance more acutely and lamented the lack of the same among some of their companions. In fact Francis Xavier Schubiger considered this aspect as a key to the success of the mission. Conversely stated, he considered the lack of the same as a reason enough for failure of the missionary enterprise. He cites an example of the Spanish Jesuit, Tarago who seems to have failed to learn Marathi, nay "not a single word of Marathi after nearly a quarter of a year of stay in Ahmednagar."[356] Schubiger further mentions in the

354 The following names may be mentioned in this regard: Otto Futterer and John Fackler (arrived on 13th May 1932), Anthony Rehm, Albert Weber and Alois Schlegel (arrived on 25th August 1935), Francis Benz, Bernard Tretter, Joseph Braunger and Ivo Meyer (arrived in 1936), Joseph Neuner, Felix of Lowenstein, Joseph Benoit, Rudolf Schutz, Emmenecker Sturm, Francis Xavier Daschner, Rudolph Schoch, Guido Martini, Joseph Pfiffher, Paul Gachter, Basil Hafeli, John Baptist Thiel (arrived in 1938). See IB 1/11 (July 1932): 76; IB 1/24 (October 1935): 200; IB 1/26 (April 1936): 222; IB 1/28 (October 1937): 242; IB 2/5 (January 1939): 58-62.

355 See Hubert Sixt, "The Marathi Mission at Ahmednagar: Fr. Marcel De Souza's Account," AMPSJ, Pune Alt,1-2.

356 See F.X. Schubiger to the General from Sangamner (Sangamner, 8lh February 1924), ARSI, Bombay. 1004-IX,5/2.

same letter that Tarago could not succeed anywhere due to his handicap with Marathi.

In the concrete situation ensuing in the background of the discussions about the division of the Mission both in the Roman curia as well as in Bombay and Poona, Francis Schubiger goes even further to say that the Mission would face the danger of being doomed if the Maratha Mission would be handed over to the Aragon Jesuits. Among other reasons that he cites for the same is the initial difficulties of the Aragon Jesuits in learning Marathi language. A personal account of Francis Schubiger may be cited in order to justify the claim that he did imply the lack of the knowledge of the native language as a possible factor that might even cause a doom to the mission:

> The present Vice Superior of the Gujerath [Gujarat] Mission can even now, 4 years after his arrival in the mission, not yet fluently, much less correctly speak (I have this on absolutely reliable authority). Fr. Romany was for two years in Gujerath (Gujarat), now for nearly one year in the Maratha mission (Kune) and does not yet know [n] either the usual prayers, much less to speak, nor even to read in the native characters. On the recent consultation at Khandala I met him ... and thanked him for sending a Marathi Bible to Fr. Trenkamp. There he himself told me: I cannot read it, don't understand Marathi, so the book is useless to me ... Hence once more if Aragon is to be given charge of the Maratha Mission, then we are simply doomed and the sooner the curia realizes this the better.[357]

Realizing the immense importance of learning the native languages as a key to the fruitful missionary endeavour, the Jesuits of the Bombay Vice-Province proposed a guideline for themselves (which may be seen as a virtual policy to this effect) towards the end of the 1940s to encourage the Jesuits in formation to take up the cause. In effect this guideline was directly applicable to the Jesuits in Poona Mission too.

> As to the place and time for the study of the vernaculars for those who are beyond the stage of the Juniorate, it was agreed that as far as possible no one should be sent to the next stage of formation unless he had put in a full year of vernacular study and passed

357 Francis X. Schubiger to Albert Rembold (Sangamner, 18th June 1925), ARSI, Bombay. 1004-XIV, 10.

ordinary examination, in the ordinary Language School of Anand and Shembaganur respectively.[358]

Finally, we conclude by noting that the above-mentioned missionaries are not hand-picked arbitrarily in order to justify the claim. On the contrary, a general disposition towards this mission policy was a consciously accepted fact among the missionaries. In the later decades, the importance on the need to learn the language began to be emphasized even more. The Jesuits who arrived in India after World War II deeply understood its significance especially in view of establishing contacts with the Hindus through formal dialogues with them. Among these groups of Jesuits, Matthew Lederle's name deserves to be placed first as he mastered the language in a much shorter time.[359] For our purpose therefore it is sufficient to conclude with the remark that acquaintance with Marathi language formed an important aspect of the missionary strategy.

3.4.6. Native Literature as Means of Evangelization[360]

Undoubtedly, art and literature have played an important role in gaining access among the native literati and educated masses. The older Jesuit missions in India represent the use of these as means of gaining access to this section of the society. The mission to Emperor Akbar's court,[361] the missionary methods of Robert De Nobili and Joseph Constantine Beschi invariably implied the use of art and literature. Beschi, for example, wrote Christian literature in Tamil language to bring the truth of Christianity to the natives of Tamil Nadu.[362]

Generally speaking when one talks about evangelization through literature, it implies first and foremost the translation of the Bible in the native language. This understanding has dominated many of the Protestant missionary endeavours. The rationale behind the same has been the importance placed on the Bible in the context of

---

358 Joseph C. to the Superior General (Bombay, 14th August 1948), ARSI, Poona. 1004-XVII, 17.

359 See Lokhande, *Mission, Missionaries & Me*, 279.

360 This sub-topic organically belongs to the previous sub-topic. Yet for the sake of greater emphasis we discuss the same under a separate title.

361 See Gauvin Alexander Bailey, "The Truth Showing Mirror: Jesuit Catechism and the Art in Mughal India," in *The Jesuits II: Cultures, Sciences and the Arts, 1540-1773*, 380-381.

362 See Kanjamala, *Future of Christian Missions*, 190.

the Reformation theology with its popular slogan *sola fide* and sola scriptura, etc. Similarly the endeavour included the translation of the life of saints and other such literature related to faith and morality.[363] Often these translated publications were meant for free distribution among the potential converts.[364] In our discussion these aspects are inclusive here. Yet, what we basically wish to include here are the efforts made by the Jesuits (of whatever humbler descriptions) to communicate the Christian message to the native people.[365] In the developed countries in the west such efforts would loosely be termed as "Press Apostolate."[366]

Having made these preliminary remarks, it must be stated in unambiguous terms that in comparison with many other contemporary Jesuit missions, the Jesuits of this Mission could not produce indigenous literature and art that received wider recognition. Yet, it would be tantamount to minimizing the genuine efforts they made (although in a smaller scale), if we fail to make a mention of them. In order to show a broader picture we need to make a mention also of the efforts made prior to the period of this study.

We make a brief mention of the Jesuits who took upon themselves the responsibility of studying the native languages for a special purpose like teaching at the universities or producing native literature. Although the Jesuits under this category mostly belonged to the era prior to World War I, the brief discussion would help us situate the sub-topic in a proper perspective. This in turn would also show how much the Jesuits laid emphasis on the importance of learning the native languages. As examples, the contributions of a few Jesuits may be cited here, which may well be recognized as pioneering contributions not only towards the linguistic inculturation of the Church, but also towards the general growth of knowledge on various topics. We shall mention the contributions in this regard without making a distinction of areas, namely contribution to secular knowledge and for serving the catechetical purpose. The

363 See James Karanja, *The Missionary Movement in Colonial Kenya: The Foundation of Africa Inland Church* (Cuvilier: Gottingen, 2009), 118-19.

364 See for example Paul Barton, *Hispanic Methodists, Presbyterians, and Baptists in Texas* (Austin: University of Texas Press, 2006), 38-44.

365 See Haruko Nawata Ward, *Women Religious Leaders in Japan's Christian Century, 1549-1650* (Surrey, England: Ashgate Publishing Ltd., 2009), 40.

366 "Presse Apostolat," IB 3 (1957):5.

rationale is that they were ultimately aimed at serving the Indian society in general. They served also the evangelistic purpose of the mission.

To begin with, "Fr. Otto Weishaupt, a missionary in Maratha-mission, published in the beginning of [18]90s the Sunday and Feast Day Gospels and Readings in Marathi, Fr. Alois Gyr, as Superior in Anand [Gujarat] published the first Catholic book in Gujarati."[367] The other prominent name in this regard is that of Robert Zimmermann. A Swiss by birth he was already prior to his ordination to priesthood earmarked for the work in the Department of Sanskrit and Indology at St. Xavier's College, Bombay. In view of preparing himself for such an assignment he enrolled himself at the University of Berlin for a doctorate in *Upanishads*,[368] which he completed with a distinction. As soon as he landed in Bombay (3 rd January 1914) he took up the job of teaching Sanskrit and Indian Philosophy at St. Xavier's College and soon won the appreciation of both students and the staff alike. As recognition of his scholarship in Sanskrit and Indian Philosophy, he was nominated as a member of the Academic Senate of the University. To him goes the credit of founding the first Sanskrit seminar in the University of Bombay. Through a series of publications he emerged as an acknowledged scholar of Sanskrit. His better known publications included a selection from *Rigveda*, the oldest text of Hindu Scripture, which was acknowledged for its scholarly approach.[369] As a sequel to

---

367 Klaus Schatz, "Optionen und missionarische Prioriraten in der Bombay-Mission der deutschen Jesuiten (1854-1916)," SM60 (2011): 406. See also "P. Alois Gyr," MDP 8/67 (1919): 300-302.

368 To understand what *Upanishads* mean, one must first know what Vedas are. According to *Encyclopedia of New Age Beliefs:* "Hinduism originated from a body of conflicting and contradictory (1358) literature called the Vedas (ca. 1500 -1200 BC.) The four Vedas are the *Rigveda, Samaveda, Yajurveda* and the *Atharvaveda*. They are divided into two parts: the 'work' portion (basically polytheistic ritual) and the 'knowledge portion' (philosophical speculation). This latter portion comprises what is called the Upanishads or Vedanta: 'Since they brought to a close of each of the four Vedas, the Upanishads came to be spoken of often as the Vedanta - the anta or end of the Vedas' (1359:21)."John Ankerberg and John Weldon, *Encyclopedia of New Age Beliefs* (Oregon: Harvest House Publishers, 1996), 217. In the quotation cited above the numbers in brackets signify the following: 1358, for example refers to number 1358 in the bibliography. Similarly 1359:21 refers to number 1359 in the bibliography and page number 21 in that source.

369 See John Fackler, "P. Robert Zimmermann," MDP 13/101-103 (1932-1934): 176; Klaus Schatz, "Optionen und missionarische Prioritaten," 406.

the same he also annotated, edited and published, A Second Selection of Hymns from the Rigveda.[370]

In the same array of the Jesuits, mention may be made also of Henry Bochum. He had specialized in Zoroastrianism. He taught Philosophy and History and through his articles he earned a name in the literary circles. The last Jesuit who deserves to be mentioned in this regard is Charles Joppen who was a historian of repute and has the pride of publishing the first historical atlas of India with the title, *Historical Atlas of India*, for the use of High Schools, Colleges, and private students.[371] About the significance of this work Klaus Schatz makes the following comment: "In a land with a decidedly a-historical culture and without its own historical writings, a work of such a nature gains even more importance."[372]

The first category, as indicated above, consisted of the majority of the missionaries, nay all the missionaries at the primary level. It was as though to equip themselves with the necessary tools before embarking upon the missionary works. For a missionary without the knowledge of the native language may be likened to an artisan without tools.[373] Besides, it is also true that "it is precisely language that is the Church's basic tool in its task of proclaiming the gospel of salvation."[374] The Bombay-Poona Mission, like many other Indian Jesuit missions, was fraught with linguistic, cultural and social complexities. As for the linguistic considerations, the Mission comprised of more than one linguistic group of people. Therefore, it remained a major challenge to almost every single new missionary to acquaint himself with not only one native language, but often with four languages, almost simultaneously.[375] Only a few missionaries depicted such an extraordinary talent to learn so many languages and to the level of having a command over the same

370 See John Luis to Robert Zimmermann (Gandia, 4th May 1923), ADPSJ, Abt. 47, Nr. 781.

371 See Klaus Schatz, "Optionen und missionarische Prioritaten," 406. See also Charles Joppen, *Historical Atlas of India, for the Use of High Schools, Colleges, and Private Students* (London: Longmans, Green, 1907).

372 Schatz, "Optionen und missionarische Prioritaten," 405.

373 See Okwu Igbo, *Culture and the Christian Missions,* 238.

374 Welmers, "African Languages and Christian Missions," 545.

375 In former Bombay-Poona Mission, for example, a missionary destined to work at mission stations needed to learn Hindi, Marathi, Tamil and Gujarati almost simultaneously as the geographical spread of the mission included all these language groups. See Vath, Die deutschen Jesuiten, 94.

to read, write and preach fluently. Francis Xavier Trenkamp was one among them. He always wrote his sermons and other instructions. His ability to learn new languages and the consequent utilization of the same may be seen from the following testimony:

> Apparently no other missionary in India had so much written sermons in so many languages addressed to such a diverse audience to his credit. That was not enough. In his parish school there were also numerous non-Christian children. For them he wrote in English, A short Outline of Good Manners (Kurzen Abriss des guten Betragens), which in effect was a treatise on moral philosophy. The treatise was so excellent that someone got it printed with bare minimum changes without either his permission or mention of his name therein.[376]

Francis Xavier Trenkamp's linguistic ability was not restricted to this aspect. In fact he had a great desire to translate the entire New Testament into Marathi (the language spoken in Maharashtra, India). As he received a notice on 9th of December 1914 from the British Government that he needed to be interned in Khandala near Poona, he did not get disappointed. In spite of his advancing and almost a ripe age (he was 64 at this point) for lighter works, rest and relaxation, he decided to make use of the time in the camp for his favourite project, i.e., translation of the New Testament into Marathi, besides updating and revising what he had written earlier. He did begin the work of translation but the pace was rather slow for obvious reasons of lack of suitable atmosphere at the camp as well as his advancing age. Yet he carried forward the work. But once the peace-time signs began to appear, he was allowed to move to a mission station known as Kune, at some distance from the internment camp of Khandala on the Bombay-Pune highway. He was still under the close supervision of the British authorities. He could not undertake any mission work without the permission of the British authorities except for being spiritual guide or confessor at the mission station. He remained at this station from 1919 to 1924. Finally on 23rd January 1924 he received the news from the British Government that he was permitted to resume his mission works. He decided to move to Sangamner mission station and carry forward his pet projects, namely the translation of the New Testament and revision of his earlier

376 F. X. Schubiger, "Franz Xaver Trenkamp S.J.," IB 1/14 (1933): 108

works along with other engagements there. He realized, however, that the translation of the entire New Testament was beyond his present capabilities. Hence he decided to compile a collection of Biblical stories in Marathi, which he successfully completed. Unfortunately he could not see its publication as he lost his memory as well as his physical health almost entirely by 1927. It was published after his 79th birthday in 1930. It must be remarked here that his work was not a major work from any literary standard. But it does testify to the effort made by the Jesuits in this regard.[377]

Secondly, it may also be noted that Trenkamp had produced a few text books for lower standards for the Marathi medium schools besides compiling a prayer book in Marathi with the title: *Subhaktisar: Prarthana ani Bodh* (Gist of Devotion: Prayer and Religious Instructions)."[378] This book was among the initial publications of Francis Trenkamp and was acclaimed by both Catholics and non-Catholics. On the contents of the book, Ajit Lokhande writes: "It contained prayers of the Holy Mass, of the sacramental rituals, the usual prayers of piety (Andacht), explanations of the feasts and the corresponding prayers, litanies, religious instructions, etc. In short it was a book of prayers (prarthana) and of religious instruction (bodh)."[379] He also published a calendar in Marathi (1993) with the title, *Panchang*. About other publications, i.e., school textbooks, moral philosophy, etc., we come to know from the following conclusion of his necrologist, Francis Xavier Schubiger: "Thus indeed he had published all the important books for Marathi schools and now could proudly utter the words of Simeon: Lord, now

---

377 The account has been collated from the following sources: F. X. Schubiger, "Franz Xaver Trenkamp S.J.," IB 1/14 (January 1933): 105-108; IB 1/15 (April 1933), 115-116; Lokhande, *Mission, Missionaries and Me,* 75-80; Parkhe, *Contribution of Christian Missionaries,* 153-162; "Young at 82, *Reise: The 150-year Journey of the German and Swiss Provinces in India* (Poona: Pune Jesuit Province, 2004); F. X. Schubiger, "Deceased Members," 14-16.

378 See "Young at 82," op. cit., 15. See also Parkhe, Contribution of Christian Missionaries, 155. Most likely, for the purpose of imparting an idea of what a missionary in India needs to do, a German translation of the book was made with the title, "Katholisches Gebet-und Erbauungsbuch," for private circulation, mostly among the benefactors and friends. See Robert Streit & Johannes Dindinger (eds.), Bibliotheca Missionum: Missionsliteratur Indiens u. Indonesiens, 1800-1909 (Aachen: Internationalen Institut fur Missionswissenschaftliche Forschung, 1951), 610.

379 Lokhande, *Mission, Missionaries and Me,* 77.

let your servant depart in peace!"[380] He represents the missionaries of both periods - prior to and after World War I.

The next Jesuit who deserves a due mention, is Henry Doring, who later became Bishop (1907-1921) and Archbishop (1927-1949) respectively of Poona. He, like other German Jesuits, learnt the Marathi language to preach Christianity to the natives. His ardent desire to reach out to the natives as soon as possible aided his ability to learn the language in a very short period of time so well that shortly later he could take up almost an impossible task of editing and publishing a magazine in Marathi, about which we shall discuss shortly.[381] He went a step further in his effort to learn the local variation of Marathi, "the dialect of people from Ahmednagar district and also specific terms and concepts used in Hindu religious literature"[382] in order that he may be better understood by common masses, both in his personal addresses as well as in his writings. As he began to work at the mission stations at Kendal and Valan, he realized that there was hardly any Catholic literature in Marathi available as aids in teaching and catechizing the natives. In his own words:

> Except for a 'tiny book of catechism' consisting of 51 fully condensed pages, a small booklet of Biblical stories and 'Prayer and Teaching Book', probably the best among them, composed by P. [Francis Xavier] Trenkamp, there was nothing worth its name. There was also a relatively poor translation of the Sunday Readings and Gospels besides the controversial catechism booklet of Fr. Hall already being out-of-print; all being amateur in nature and very basic in Marathi. That was not enough in the long run.[383]

The publication of *Niropya* was a very concrete step taken by him to achieve the purpose stated in the text above. From these accounts, it can be surmised that the work of a missionary was multi-faceted in nature. It was not restricted to one particular area of activities. Such was the case in the days of Henry Doring as well. As a missionary he was supposed to preach every Sunday, year after year, besides teaching

380 "Pranz Xaver Trenkamp S. J.," op. cit., 115.

381 See Rainhold Schneider, "Erzbischof Heinrich Doring J.S.," UB 3/2 (1952): 27.; Felix Plattner, "Der alteste deutsche Missionsbischof gestorben," KM11I2 (1952): 52-53.

382 Parkhe, *Contribution of Christian Missionaries,* 157.

383 "Aus dem Leben des hohen Jubilars: Der Marathi Sendbote, *Niropya*," IB 1/12 (October 1932): 85-86

catechism and hearing confessions. Due to the scarcity of suitable literature, priests and catechists faced a realistic problem in preaching Christianity to the children and the adults.[384] The challenges did not end there. As a report says,

> In fact, the task of making Christian Dogma, Morality, Church History and Canon Law more intelligible and interpreting the Scripture in teaching and preaching in order to make it more easily comprehensible, yet theologically sound, were the real challenges. The above-mentioned sources and the abundance of Protestant writings obviously could not offer such an assistance. The situation of the catechists in the villages was even worse. The lack of such necessary literature not only left them shallow in knowledge but also hampered the opportunity of deepening the knowledge of those zealous ones among them who were willing to do their personal study. The monthly instructions were hardly sufficient to yield any lasting effect. And what should have the catechist offered to the adults, whom he, in place of the far away situated missionaries, needed to keep steadfast in Christian Faith? The same old stories narrated in the schools? On the long run it did not help![385]

Faced with such significant aspects of challenges in carrying forward the work of evangelization, Henry Doring strongly felt the need of doing something in this regard. He also noticed that with the progress of the work of evangelization, numerous 'Untouchables', i.e., Mahars, Mangs[386] and other similar groups, were getting converted to Christianity but the mere fact of conversion did not bring much transformation in their socio-economic conditions.[387] Besides, consolidation of the Christian community needed to be carried forward persistently through gradual instruction on the Christian Faith and morals. In other words a programme of education in Christian values and morals was the need of the hour. Hence, with his own simple assessment of the situation and a clear perception of the lights and shadows in the lives of the newly baptized Christians, Henry Doring came to the conclusion that the

---

384 See Parkhe, *Contribution of Christian Missionaries,* 156.

385 "Aus dem Leben des hohen Jubilars," op.cit, 86.

386 See M. D. David, "Christianity in Maharashtra," in *A Concise Encyclopaedia of Christianity in India,* ed. Errol D'Lima, et al. (Pune: Jnana-Deepa Vidyapeeth/Mumbai: St. Pauls, 2014), 229.

387 Parkhe, *Contribution of Christian Missionaries,* 155.

periodical publication of a magazine with sound theological basis could provide substantial solution to all the challenges mentioned above. He realized that one needs much more literary resources to carry forward the afore-mentioned tasks with tangible apostolic fruitfulness. Since Valan, his mission station, was consecrated to the Sacred Heart of Jesus, a thought occurred to him to bring the future magazine in association with the already published journal, Messengers of the Sacred Heart {Sendbote des gottlichen Herzens) uniting thereby the newly baptized Christians with the world-wide Christian community. Thus after due permission of the competent authorities and financed from the alms collected by Henry Doring there appeared in April 1903 the first issue of *Niropya* (Messenger) in Valan.[388] In 2003 this magazine celebrated 100 years of its existence. On its historical journey and significance, Camil Parkhe has the following comment:

> It is indeed creditable that a Marathi publication launched by a German Jesuit is among a handful of publications, which have managed to survive despite various problems faced by it ... Now it has become a mouthpiece of the Marathi-speaking Christians, a majority of whom was brought to the fold of Christianity by the missionaries during the last 110 years.[389]

The magazine, *Niropya* continues even now. The main thrust of the magazine has been education of the people in Christian life and message, besides functioning in some manner as a mouth piece of the people on matters pertaining to the communitarian and developmental issues. It also includes information and updates on some of the current issues faced by the universal Church. In sum, it is an organ of the Catholic community of the place.

As for the contents of the journal, it contained monthly intentions for prayer, edifying stories and simple responses to ordinary catechetical questions. The history of the Church was presented in the form of the lives of the patron saints for the month. Besides, a short chronicle was included to present the situation of the universal Church in order to

388 See "Doppelte Fest in der altesten deutschen Heidenmission," PJPA, Varia; "Aus dem Leben des hohen Jubilars," op. cit., 86; Jeevendra Jadhav, *Evangelisation as Community Building* (Ahmednagar: Social Centre, 2006), 127. See also Hubert Sixt, ed. "Historical Notes on the Ahmednagar Mission," PJPA, Valan Diary, VIII, 12; Jadhav, *Evangelization as Community Building,* 127.

389 Parkhe, *Contribution of Christian Missionaries,* 154.

broaden the views of the new Christians on the beauty and world-wide expansion of the same. Besides, the Pastoral Letters of the Bishops were made accessible to all Christians.[390] A translation of the Latin classic *Imitatio Christi* (Imitation of Christ) soon followed which was published serially under the title *Kristanuvartan* (Imitation of Christ) until the 17th chapter of the 3rd book.[391] "During his retirement 60 years later, he still worked at the completion of the Fourth Book."[392] In short, ever since its inception, *Niropya* endeavoured to offer a comprehensive programme of education in all aspects of Christian life. In fact, with the exception of a few years during the First World War, this magazine has been published regularly till date.[393]

The significance of the contribution of Henry Doring may be appreciated from the simple fact that he dared to publish a magazine in a language that he had newly learnt. It is not hard to imagine the initial hurdles in taking up such a challenging task while still being engaged full-time in other missionary activities of the place. The extent of the demand of time and energy, patience and perseverance that such an enterprise may have made on the missionary is not too hard to imagine, especially in a missionary field like Ahmednagar which was underdeveloped --the place lacked basic facilities like roads, housing, safe drinking water, electricity, etc. While reading an issue of *Niropya* a reader hardly had an idea as to how much of work had gone into, how many hours in the night in searching for the most suitable rendering of the complex expressions and statements were spent, etc. In normal circumstances it would suffice to have the knowledge of a few hundred words in dealing with ordinary uneducated people. But in order to publish a magazine it is barely sufficient. One requires a considerable degree of proficiency in that language to engage in such tasks.[394]

390 See "Aus dem Leben des hohen Jubilars," op. cit, 86; Parkhe, *Contribution of Christian Missionaries,* 158; Lokhande, *Mission, Missionaries and Me,* 87.

391 See Henry Doring to the Superior General (Poona, 27th October 1932), ARSI, Poona. 1004-V, 3a. See also "Aus dem Leben des hohen Jubilars," op. cit., 86.

392 "Archbishop Henry Doring (13th Sept. 1859 - 17 Dec. 1951), in "Deceased Members," 39.

393 See Parkhe, *Contribution of Christian Missionaries,* 156; Lokhande, *Mission, Missionaries and Me,* 87.

394 See Arnold Rickert, "Bocholt, Heimat der Bischofe Laurenz Boggering, Hermann Kunst, Heinrich Doring und Melchior von Diepenbrock," UB 19/1 (1968): 24-25. *Unser Bocholt* is a periodical published four times a year since 1950 from Bocholt in Germany. The main thrust of the periodical has been culture and native care.

It may also be noted here briefly that he wanted to forget Marathi deliberately in order to learn Japanese better when he was appointed the Titular Bishop of Madytus and Vicar Apostolic of Hiroshima in 1922.[395] He thought that he needed to commit himself entirely for the rest of his life to the Japanese Church with the same kind of dedication that he had shown in Poona.[396] But that was not to be. He was nominated the Archbishop of Poona in 1927.[397] As soon as he returned to Poona he revived once again his brainchild, *Niropya*. Apparently due to his absence of more than a decade from the Poona Mission (1914-1927) he had lost the fluency in Marathi. Yet he earnestly took upon himself the task of re-learning the language and soon regained fluency. On the request of the Christians, he once again took up the task of publishing the magazine. Thus it got its former perspective and touch once again back with the same level of elegance and proficiency. On the level of proficiency that Henry Doring had attained in Marathi and on the merits of his contribution towards instilling inspiration among his fellow missionaries and imparting Christian values, the following account pays an apt tribute:

> In order to appreciate his work [contribution] in a proper perspective, one needs only to take in hand a modern Marathi newspaper ... Under such circumstances, it is amazing to note how sophisticated a Marathi did a foreigner Fr. Doring use, how smooth interpretation for complex concepts did he render and how few English or Latin words did he transcribe into Marathi in his writings! Already the first issue of April 1903 demonstrated the proficiency of the [editor] -publisher, which eventually touched newer heights with the passing time. Initially the language was vivid and popular in style, which became clearer and richer with more philosophico-theological in content. In individual cases it may obviously be contended, but all must admit that Father Doring had the rare skill of avoiding too many Latin or English expressions in his writings and knew how

395 See Wilhelm Kosch et al., ed., , Deutsches Literaturlexikon. Das 20. Jahrhundert: Band 6: Deeg-Durrenfeld (Zurich/Munchen: K.G. Saur, 2004), 2000.

396 See "Aus dem Leben des hohen Jubilars," op. cit., 82; Henry Doring, "Die neue Mission Hiroshima in Japan," KM5Q (1921-22): 54-55.

397 See Henry Doring to the Superior General (Singapore, 4th October 1927), ARSI, Poona. 1004-11, 1; See Rickert, "Bocholt, Heimat der Bischofe …." op. cit., 25.

to avoid the danger of misinterpreting equally incomprehensible Sanskrit-Marathi expressions.[398]

Even as the Archbishop of Poona, Henry Doring was one of the chief contributors, in fact virtual editor and publisher of the magazine. Only during his absence, did he entrust the responsibility of editing and publishing the magazine to Francis Xavier Trenkamp (1909) and Anthony Wessendorf (1914) respectively. Nevertheless, he did so on both the occasions with the manuscripts almost ready for publication.[399]

In spite of the fact that the number of subscribers of the magazine did not exceed 400 during the life-time of Henry Doring, the decisive impact it created on the local Christian community is significant to underline. Since the villagers were too poor to afford single copies of the magazine for each family, the catechists were instructed to read the stories and articles published in the magazine to the villagers on Sundays and other occasions, which the villagers waited for with much enthusiasm. The magazine became a means of achieving the objective of catechizing and educating the people; which was realized to a substantial extent to the satisfaction of Henry Doring.[400] Eventually it turned out to be the mouth-piece of the Catholics of the place, besides being a source of inspiration for the new missionaries to learn the new language.[401] An additional dimension of the impact of *Niropya* was not only to inculcate reading habit among the Marathi-speaking Christians but also to provide a useful platform for the budding Catholic and Protestant writers of the place. Many of them later earned a name in Marathi literature.[402]

Besides the contributions made through *Niropya,* Henry Doring also tried to bring to the knowledge of the general public, as well as the Christians, an important work that is undoubtedly the first of its kind in the Jesuit history in India, namely British Jesuit Thomas Stephens' (1549-1619)[403] epic composition Khristapurana.[404] This epic was

398 "Aus dem Leben des hohen Jubilars, "op. cit, 86-87.

399 See Lokhande, *Mission, Missionaries and Me,* 88.

400 Ibid., 87; Plattner, "Der alteste deutsche Missionsbischof gestorben," op. cit., 53; "Aus dem Leben des hohen Jubilars," op. cit., 87.

401 Parkhe, *Contribution of Christian Missionaries,* 156.

402 Ibid., 157.

403 Thomas Stephens is considered the first grammarian of Marathi.

404 The *Puranas form* an important part of the ancient Hindu religious texts. The term *Purana* literally means something ancient. In the context of the Hindu religious texts, it symbolizes

completed in 1614. It is the first systematic work by a Jesuit towards indigenization of the Christian message. It is a classic in Marathi but rendered in Latin script, comprising some 11,000 verses, "a work setting forth the mysteries of the Catholic faith in poetic form."[405] Thomas Stephens adopted the form and style of Hindu religious literatures. Hence the language is of poetic beauty, the content deeply Christian and form fully Indian. The epic in essence is "an account of the Old and New Testaments in Marathi intended to reveal through comparison with Hindu Puranas the idolatrous and heathen nature of Hinduism."[406] It must be underlined, however, that his effort was ultimately aimed at indigenization by making the Christian message meaningful to the Hindus while also showing simultaneously the incongruities in their own religion. As for the older Christians it served both as a literary as well as catechetical masterpiece. Its popularity may be imagined from the fact that the Christians in Goa had a deep appreciation for the same, so that it was reproduced by them in their handwriting and in some of the families even recited or sang regularly.[407] Henry Doring was instrumental in his role as translator and commentator of this classic. He studied the epic, comprehended the significance of the literature and published some portions pertaining to the life of Jesus in the form of three booklets transcribing the text of Thomas Stephens into Devanagari script (the script used for Hindi and other Indian languages).[408]

Thus the contribution of Henry Doring, though not known to many, was no mean achievement, especially given the situation of his time. Besides, being full-time engaged with every aspect of ministry which a classical missionary would be expected to do, he achieved something remarkable, which many of his contemporaries would not have dreamt of. Hence, the most apt tribute to Henry Doring in this regard, may be

---

a record of the past events or an ancient tale/narrative. See Swami Parmeshwaranand, *Encyclopeadic Dictionary of Puranas,* Vol. 1 (New Delhi: Sarup & Sons, 2001), 190-91.

405 Charles J. Borges et al., eds., *Goa and Portugal: History and Development* (New Delhi: Concept Publishing Company, 2000), 262.

406 John Marriott, *The Other Empire: Metropolis, India and Progress in the Colonial Imagination* (Manchester, UK: Manchester University Press, 2003), 58. See also M. Stephen, *A Christian Theology in the Indian Context* (Delhi: ISPCK, 2001), 8.

407 "Ein katholischer Bestseller," IB 3 (1957):3.

408 See "Aus dem Leben des hohen Jubilars " op. cit., 87; Parkhe, *Contribution of Christian Missionaries,* 156. See also Edward Birrer, "Mahars Singen," IB 3 (June/July 1951): 28-29.

paid in the following words: "Thus Bishop Doring, besides Fr. Trenkamp, through his Niropya [and some other endeavours] undoubtedly did more service towards making Marathi Catholic Church indigenous than any other missionary of his time."[409]

We may also dwell briefly on the efforts of some other Jesuits to bring this classical work to the larger public domain. It may be said that a work of such a great significance was not known outside the Christian community. However, thanks to the efforts of Hans Staffner (26th Nov. 1909 - 27th July 1997)[410] this highly significant Christian epic became accessible to the Hindus in Maharashtra. Hans Staffner was aware of the interest of the Hindu intelligentsia on this work as well as of their desire to be able to read it in their own language, Marathi. Meanwhile, around 1953 he came to know about the efforts of a certain professor Dr. Bandelu, who had transcribed *Khristapurana* in Devanagari script. A Protestant, Dr. Bandelu was so enthusiastic about the poetical beauty of this Catholic masterpiece that he offered to donate the fruit of years of his tedious work free of charge to Hans Staffner. The latter wrote a brief explanation on the Catholic faith which was intended to facilitate the understanding of the Hindus. He provided short annotations, dogmatic remarks and notes on the bibliographies. But he was anxious as to where he could publish this work. Finally, he found in the person of Mr. Y. G. Joshi, the owner of the most important Marathi publishing house in Poona, an understanding and sympathetic publisher. A Hindu by religion, Mr. Y.G. Joshi assured Hans Staffner of making the best possible presentation of this classic.[411] Interestingly thus, a Hindu, a Protestant, and a Catholic priest worked together to finally publish the *Khristapurana* in a proper form nearly after 400 years after its original composition by Thomas Stephens.[412]

---

409 "Aus Jem Leben des hohen Jubilars," op.cit., 87.

410 Hans Staffner was an important figure in the development of De Nobili College in Poona. Born in Hofgarten in Tirol, Austria he came to India in 1934. His contribution to theological education in India may hardly be ignored. Through his publications, he always intended to integrate Indian cultural ethos in Christian theology and Philosophy. One of his important works is: *The Significance of Jesus Christ in India* (1985). See "Deceased Members," 164-65.

411 See "Ein katholischer Bestseller," op. cit., 4.

412 See Hans Staffner, "The Catholic Mission in Ahmednagar District," AMPSJ, Alte Nachrichten von Puna.

The book instantly became a best seller. Indeed its reception exceeded all expectations. The success of a book is often measured by its sale and market value. In the 1950s and 60s, for example, in Poona the publishers were greatly satisfied when about 600 copies of a novel written in Marathi could be sold out in the first year. If a hefty book on a religious theme, written in Marathi, would find some 800 buyers in the first month, it would be considered nothing less than phenomenal. That was precisely what happened with *Khristapurana*. On account of the splendid poetry of the work, many Hindus from the educated circles of Poona, perhaps for the first time came in possession of a Christian work, which was able to bring to their attention the beauty of Christian faith. What was even more interesting is that even in the villages the Christian peasants seem to have been enthusiastic about this work. In some villages they asked the teachers or catechists to chant the hymns for hours in the evening. Hans Staffner mentions that in Poona too, in the close vicinity of De Nobili College, some groups of Christian labourers gathered in the evenings during the Lenten season for what they called "Purana Evenings." In such prayer gatherings one of them presented and explained the hymns.

The significance of the work lies in the fact that this old Christian epic was made accessible to the Hindus, thanks to the efforts of Hans Staffner. It clearly shows that Catholic doctrine can be indigenous to Indian culture. And that is why we can call the courageous initiative of Hans Staffner as modern and contemporary missionary work. From the perspective of the missionary strategy too this work was significant as Pius Geisel attested:

> As direct mission work is now made more difficult we try to find another way through publications. Fr. Staffner has prepared the Christus Purana of our Fr. Stevenson and it will be printed soon. Many non-Catholics are interested, the Poona University was even prepared to have it printed under its auspices, however we decided to publish the book on our own for certain reasons.[413]

Around this time, with regard to the translation of the Bible, a humble milestone was achieved. Maximilian Zinser completed the translation of the Gospel of Mark in Marathi, though the finance for the

413 Pius Geisel, "Litterae Superioris Missionis," (Poona, January 1955), ARSI, Poona. 1005-IV, 20.

printing was still a hurdle to the realization of its objective. As for the importance of this work, a remark by Pius Geisel may be cited here:

> The Gospel of Mark has been translated and will soon be printed, if you could find a benefactor for the same. Apparently it would not be financially viable. The printing will cost us more than we could earn from the sale of the same. However, it is very important that the first part of the New Testament is published.[414]

Aside these, the efforts of Matthew Lederle too may be mentioned here. He was keenly interested in transmitting the Christian faith to the local people in their own language. The problem, however, was that there were no written texts to facilitate the same. He decided to produce something to this effect and wrote a short handbook on the History of the Church in Marathi and titled the same as *Khristamandalacha Sankshipt Itihaas* (A Short History of the Church). This he did in the very second year of his arrival in India, which goes on to prove his linguistic ability as well as his sheer interest in the local culture and commitment to his mission. In order to facilitate the production of a text that would be comprehensible to the common people of the place, he took the help of a Marathi language teacher. The latter helped him correct the manuscript to make it readable for the common masses. It greatly served as a textbook of catechism in schools.[415]

Another contribution of Matthew Lederle was the publication of a small monthly magazine, *Khrista Raja* (Christ the King), meant for the youth. The basic objective was to catechize the youth in the Christian faith and morals, besides exposing the youth to certain motivational and inspirational themes. Besides, a short presentation of the life of the saints also was a regular feature of the magazine. Under the *Ishvarividhyamala* series he published a number of Christian classics like The Inner Castle (Theresa of Avila) and the The Prayer of the Russian Pilgrim.[416] A necrology on him summarizes his literary contributions as follows:

---

414 Pius Geisel to Felix A. Plattner (Poona, 27th January 1954), AMPSJ, Superior Poona P. Geisel. See also Pius Geisel, "Litterae Superioris Missionis," (Poona, January 1955), ARSI, Poona. 1005-IV, 20.

415 See Lokhande, *Mission, Missionaries & Me,* 278; Pater Matthaus R. Lederle (13. Marz 1926 - 8. Juni 1986): Gedenkschrit zum 28. Todestag (A Booklet for Private Circulation, 2014), 8-9.

416 See Lokhande, *Mission, Missionaries & Me,* 280.

> Dr. [Matthew] Lederle was undoubtedly a scholar of great repute [and] a well-reputed Indologist ... He was a visiting editor for the 23 volume Marathi Encyclopedia called Vishvakosa [Global Dictionary]. He also edited a theological series called Ishvarividhyamala' [roughly *Divine* Knowledge Series]. Under the auspices of Marg Prakashan he encouraged the publication of books in Konkani [another local language].[417]

Lastly, mention may also be made of a simple yet meaningful initiative promoted by the Jesuits. Since there were no Catholic bookstores in Poona, the Jesuits in collaboration with the Men's Sodality started a unique initiative in the late 1960s. Every Sunday, after the Holy Mass, a bookstall was put up in front of the church. One could find there the Catholic weeklies, brochures and selected books, as well as rosaries, medals and other devotional items. Since many of the Catholics could not afford to buy them, an arrangement was made for the seating of the visiting readers so that some of them could spend a few hours to read them. In order to facilitate a better management of this initiative, some members of the Men's Sodality took turns on a voluntary basis to give guidance to the people, offering them the right advice and right stuff to read. Some of the students also sought during this time advices for the choice of their career, and other concerns. Humble as it was, the initiative made the Christian literature accessible to a greater number of Christians, especially those who could not afford to buy them.[418]

This survey throws a spotlight basically on two aspects. Firstly, it contends to some extent a common perception that the Jesuits in this mission failed to produce native literature, especially when their contribution is seen in comparison with many other contemporary Jesuit missions. However, their efforts, humble though, were certainly valuable. Our discussion, thus, serves as a corrective, at least in some measure, that in spite of the contingencies of the situation in the mission field, the Jesuits did make efforts towards achieving their purpose of communicating the message of the Gospel through indigenous literature. However, a critique that comes from the Jesuits themselves does seem to indicate a serious lacuna. In the words of Pius Geisel: "I often feel ashamed that even after 50 years of our missionary enterprise, no translation of the Bible has been taken up, not even of the N[ew]

417 “Deceased Members,” 116.

418 See "Presse Apostolat," op. cit, 5.

Testament and] other religious literature."[419] The remark, although made in 1939, stood valid until the end of the period of our study (i.e., 1962). In spite of the achievement in translating the Gospel of Mark, the task was still far from being accomplished. Stated differently, the translation of at least the entire New Testament was far from being realized. The second aspect that may be pointed out here was the financial viability of these publications. No doubt their publications were "a loss, [yet the same] was made up by their usefulness."[420] Finally what is to mark in a special manner is the nature of the entire literary contribution taken as a whole. They were of two categories: those directly serving as catechetical tools and the others contributing towards the general secular knowledge. As stated above, the magazines, books and booklets published by the Jesuits may not have been of great literary value in the secular world. Yet, the fact must be underlined that the significance of these works lie not solely on their scientific presentation of the subjects alone, but more so on their pioneering nature in creating local Marathi Christian literature.

3.4.7. Christian Art, Painting and Architecture as Mission Tools

Movies, paintings and various other forms of visual art have always served as powerful means of presenting abstract ideas and mysteries. By evoking imaginations and ideas, they lead the viewer to form an image of the mystery that is sought to be depicted. Recognizing the significance of art and paintings as mission tools,[421] the Jesuits through the centuries have used Christian paintings and other forms of iconography as tools of inculturation in order that they might be able to present the mysteries of the Christian faith to a cultural milieu they were placed in. In his attempt to inculturate the Christian faith to the local cultural milieu Matteo Ricci, for example, employed the incorporation of Christian elements in the indigenous paintings as one of the important methods of inculturation in China. He introduced Christian elements to the Chinese indigenous art.[422] Similarly the Jesuits in Portuguese Goa, on being

419 Pius Geisel to the Superior General (Valan, 2nd January 1939), ARSI, Poona. 1004-XII, 1.

420 "History of the Poona Mission 1952-1955," ARSI, Goa-Poonensis: Litterae Annuae -1501.

421 Gavin A. Bailey, *The Jesuits and the Grand Mogul: Renaissance Art at the Imperial Court of India, 1580-1630* (Washington, D.C.: Smithsonian Institution, 1982), 12.

422 See William A. Dyrness, *Christian Art in Asia* (Amsterdam: Editions Rodopi, 1979), 31.

invited by the Mughal Emperor Akbar at Fatehpur Sikri (near Agra in India), presented him as gifts a few "paintings and engravings ... [that] were neither mythological in their presentation of religious themes nor merely secular. The religious was shown in a human context, making the divine transparent in human form."[423] Alexander Valignano and companions did the same in Japan.[424] And the list can, thus, go on. How the early Jesuits perceived the power of images is well summarized by Gavin A. Bailey. Quoting Jeronimo Xavier (a grand-nephew of Francis Xavier who was one among the Jesuits sent as delegates to the court of Emperor Akbar) he writes: "He [Jeronimo Xavier] points out that pictures 'bring to life and renew in the memory those things which these pictures resemble,' an effect that is produced 'more quickly and pithily' than by speech, because the tongue is too long-winded."[425] Bailey quotes him further:

> The speech [of an image] is an abbreviated book and a brief worship. It is something that speaks without talking and is heard without the ear; something written that everyone understands; a letter that everyone can read; a book for the learned; an attribute that makes manifest things which are past and ancient. It is a mirror that reflects things held in trust [i.e., things that are not actually part of it] ... an assistant to the temperament, a teacher of the intellect; and it depicts intention.[426]

The text above may be cited as an example of how the Jesuits over the centuries have interpreted the potential of pictures and images. Precisely for these reasons they were keen on utilizing the same in their encounter with other cultures. Stated differently, art and paintings, along with many other media, i.e., theatre, music, architecture, etc., constituted as important means of communicating the Christian faith and mystery. They perceived the potential of art, paintings, icons, etc., and desired to make the mysteries of the

423 Matthew R. Lederle, *Christian Painting in India through the Centuries* (Bombay: Heras Institute of History and Culture/Anand: Gujarat Sahitya Prakash, 1987), 27. See also Tom Devonshire Jones, ed., *The Oxford Dictionary of Christian Art and Architecture,* Second Edition (Oxford: Oxford University Press, 2013), 278.

424 See Bailey, *The Jesuits and the Grand Mogul,* 12.

425 As quoted in Gavin A. Bailey, "The Truth showing Mirror: Jesuit Catechism and the Arts in Mughal India," in *The Jesuits: Cultures, Sciences, and the Arts 1540-1773,* eds. John W. O'Malley et al. (Toronto/Buffalo/Landon: University of Toronto Press, 1999), 388.

426 Ibid.

Christian faith comprehensible to the audience in order to draw them to the Christian fold. In plain terms, thus, it may be concluded that the paintings and art were employed as a means of evangelization or what Bailey calls 'mission tools'.[427]

While discussing this issue within the larger framework of this work, a few spontaneous questions that may come up here are: What was the nature and magnitude of the use of art and paintings as tools of inculturation for evangelization in this mission? What was the role of the Jesuits in applying this method? Were they themselves artists and painters? Let it be noted that the Jesuits of this Mission played only the role of discoverers and promoters of these media and not as creators of the same. Besides, the effort itself has not been on a large scale. Yet it deserves a mention here due to its novelty and pioneering approach. Moreover, it is one of the latest methods of evangelisation applied in this Mission. In order to appreciate the same, a brief mention of the background may be necessary here.

It is generally acknowledged that the cultural situation and artistic temper in India that were at their heights during the Mughal period[428] faced a total collapse with the arrival of the British East India Company (1600). Such a state of affairs continued until 1858, after which the British East India Company was abolished and India came under the direct control of the British Crown.[429] After this period one notices a decisive change of attitude in appreciation and recognition of Indian art in general. Meanwhile, from around the end of the 19th century, the cultural awakening in India began to be intensified with the rise of social reform movements and growth of national consciousness,[430] including the movement of Hindu revivalism and Hindu Renaissance, and movements aimed at attaining independence from the British rule. "Later on, in the beginning of [the] 20th c. with the awakening among the Indian intelligentsia, especially in Bengal, there was a new awakening and transformation on ideas about art and aesthetics and

427 See Bailey, *The Jesuits and the Grand Mogul,* 12.

428 The Mughal period in India was from 1526 to 1858. Its decline, however, began with the death of Emperor Aurangzeb in 1707. See Barbara D. Metcalf & Thomas R. Metcalf, *A Concise History of Modern India,* Third Edition (Cambridge: Cambridge University Press, 2012), xxix-xxxi.

429 Ibid. See also Lederle, "Interpreting Christ through Indian Art," TJT24/3-4 (July-Dec. 1974): 234.

430 Ibid.

literature also."[431] Consequently, an emphasis on such creative ways of expressions on religious themes gained once again prominence. There were changes within the Church: the realization of a greater need for inculturation in the Indian Church strongly began to be felt. This in turn acted as an impetus for the promotion of Indian Christian art. In the words of Paul M. Collins:

> The emergence in India of aspirations to independence and nation-hood, alongside the 'Renaissance' of Hindu spirituality and Indian art forms clearly provides a multi-layered background to the quest by Christians in India to discover ways and means by which to express the Christian tradition in Indian forms. The early advocates of indigenization, were undoubtedly influenced by their context... Their engagement with the task of inculturation was driven by the desire that Christianity should be able to be seen as an indigenous tradition and not simply as an adjunct of British imperial rule.[432]

In the B-PM, we may point out that Raymund Keel and Matthew Lederle[433] were the pioneers in promoting Indian Christian art. Born on 14th October 1917 in St. Gallen (Switzerland) Raymund Keel entered the Society of Jesus in 1946 and arrived in India in the autumn of 1949. Thereafter he began his theological studies. He always desired to work among the youth and students. Finally in 1956, he was allowed to begin his activities among university students, although he had already begun working informally ever since he arrived in India. It was during this time that he initiated his programme of promoting Indian Christian art among them.[434] Around the same time, he was also entrusted with the responsibility of constructing a new parish building at an outpost. Within a few months he fell sick there and died shortly thereafter in July 1956. Unfortunately we lack more information on the contribution of Raymund Keel aside the fact that

---

431 Loveneesh Sharma, "A Study of Visual Interpretations of Christian Faith in Indian Art," IJHSSS, Vol. II, Issue VI (May 2016): 302.

432 Paul M. Collins, *Context, Culture and Worship: The Quest for 'Indian-ness'* (Delhi: ISPCK, 2006), 184-85.

433 Matthew Lederle later became the Provincial of Goa-Pune Province in June 1985. Unfortunately he died due to heart infection on 8th June 1986, in Goa within a year of taking up this responsibility.

434 See "Wir stellen vor: zwei Neupriester: P. Raymund Keel SJ," IB 3 (1954):3; "Pater Raymund Keel S.J." IB 4 (1958): 16. See also Sixt, "The Ahmednagar District Mission," PJPA, Varia.

he began the initiative to promote the cause of inculturation through Indian Christian art. This he did through an art publication he founded, namely *Art India*, whereby

> He began with the printing of devotional pictures painted by Indian artists. Then followed the congratulatory Christmas and New Year cards, which eventually became very popular in India. Last year, he finally dared to publish larger images for Christian households. The first years were difficult, but now there seems to be a clear change in the attitude of the people. More and more new priests, for example, choose the souvenirs prepared by the Indian artists for their ordinations.[435]

We get a much broader picture of this initiative through the contributions made by Matthew Lederle as the immediate successor to Raymund Keel. In his approach he never departed from that of his compatriot and predecessor.[436] A question that arises here is: Did Raymund Keel and Matthew Lederle promote the Christian art purely for the sake of the love of art and architecture? No wonder the initial impetus for their appreciation of these forms of creative expressions came from their early days. But the vision behind promoting Christian art in the mission was driven by a more noble desire, namely to lead the missionary Church towards an indigenous Church. In their understanding, it was supposed to be a logical growth of missionary Church that it evolves into an indigenous Church. Its growth into an indigenous Church may be represented no more tangibly than through the medium of art in indigenous forms. The crux of the basic reasons for the initiative taken by Keel and pursued by Lederle is well captured in a short write-up:

> But where the Church is really rooted, the folk-art must also prosper. Often there may be periods of transition whereby the native artists face disappointments. For, their countrymen refuse to recognize their artistic expressions as they are still largely accustomed to the European models of representation. It is in such situations that the task of the missionaries becomes urgent to promote the nascent native art and to awaken their interest in them. In Poona,

435 "Ein Kunstverlag," IB 3 (1957): 4.

436 See Lokhande, *Mission, Missionaries & Me,* 280.

Fr. Raymund Keel adopted this apostolate and founded an art publication.[437]

This is the general background against which the initiative of promoting indigenous Christian art was taken. Before proceeding with the discussion, we need to mention another name here. For, indeed it would be unjust to omit the name of Felix zu Lowenstein[438] who was the first Jesuit of the period of this study who undertook "a journey to North India in order to make a research on the Christian art produced under the Mughal Emperor Akbar"[439] with a purpose to document it and bring to the notice of the general public. It is to be noted that his plan was duly sanctioned by Karl Brust, the German Assistant to the Superior General. This is an indication also of the fact that the Society of Jesus as a whole encouraged research projects that pertained to promotion of indigenous knowledge on Christian paintings and other forms of visual art. However, since the project undertaken by Lowenstein was more in the direction of contributing towards general archeological and anthropological knowledge rather than as a means of inculturation as done by Raymund Keel and Matthew Lederle, we deliberately attach here a greater importance to the works of the latter two. No doubt the research undertaken by Lowenstein, although not intended immediately as a means of inculturation, was a pioneering work. It is largely to his credit that the Christian paintings under Emperor Akbar have been brought to the knowledge of the general public. The findings of his research were published in 1958 with the title, *Christliche Bilder in altindischer Malerei.*[440] Lowenstein had begun his research on the subject already

437 "Ein Kunstverlag," op. cit., 4.

438 He was born on 6th April 1907 in Kleinheubach, Germany. After his ordination as a priest (1936), he arrived in India in 1938 and began teaching Church History in the same year at De Nobili College that was then housed at at St. Vincent's School, Poona. As a German national, he was taken to various Internment camps in India from 1939-47. After his release he returned to Germany (1947) and rendered his services in various capacities till the end of his life (21st October 1986). See Schatz, Geschichte, Vol. V, 267.

439 Felix Lowenstein to the Superior General (Poona, 5th June 1939), ARSI, Poona. 1004-XII, 6.

440 See Felix Lowenstein, *Christliche Bilder in altindischer Malerei* (Miinster: Aschendorff, 1958).

in 1939. This goes on to prove that he preceded the two Jesuits in the field.[441]

Coming back to Matthew Lederle, it must be noted that the fruits of engagement with the areas of his genuine interest namely Indian classical music, Christian art and dialogue with religions began to manifest themselves only in the later decades. As he arrived in India as a young Scholastic of 25 in 1951, he began to take a keen interest in the religions and cultures of the people. With the passing years his interest got further intensified and the search for more relevant ways of communicating the Christian faith continued during his days of formation. After his ordination as a priest in 1957, he began to show signs of innovative approaches to evangelization through inculturation and dialogue with religions, especially with Hinduism. He was deeply convinced of the potential of paintings and art in general. He was convinced that for the common masses, a large majority of whom were illiterates, visual presentation of Christian themes through paintings would be much easier to comprehend than plain talks.

Besides these pragmatic reasons, Lederle's inspiration for making use of Indian Christian art as mission tools originated basically from two concerns: the need of bringing out the knowledge of Christian art and architecture to the public domain and adopt the same as tools of inculturation. His objective thereby was to make the Christian faith relevant to Indian culture. For, on his arrival in India he soon realized that in India, although being rich in art and architecture, no sufficient space had been allotted to Christian art in literature. He lamented the same: in the words of Matthew Moozhyil,

> It is remarkable--and painful at the same time--to notice that when reading the many books on Indian Art one never comes across a single figure or mentioning of a Christian monument. You find Hindu temples and sculptors by the thousands, Budhhist Pagodas, mosques, towers of silence, Jain temples, etc., but Christianity seems as non-existing, or what would be still worse - unable to produce anything of the sort. Whatever the reasons, this remains a fact to be considered.[442]

441 See Lowenstein to the Superior General (Poona, 5th June 1939), op. cit.

442 Lederle, "Interpreting Christ through Indian Art," 232.

The necessity of gaining a rightful place for Indian Christian art and architecture in Indian literature apart, Lederle also perceived the need of promoting the same as an important, innovative and more so as a pioneering approach to inculturation. In his own words: "Interpreting Christ through Indian art is a pioneering work."[443] Rightly so, therefore, he is considered the pioneer of modern Indian Christian art.[444] In order to point out a few facts about it, we need to address first a few basic questions here. Firstly, how Lederle understood Christian art and paintings within the parameters of his mission in India? What were the ways and means that he utilized in order to promote the same? While addressing the first question it may be said that "he was not interested in art for art's sake, but rather in art as an expression of an Indian spirituality. He also felt that Indian Christian art could contribute to the wider field of emerging Indian Christian spirituality."[445] Moreover, Christian art for him unambiguously "meant the representation of the image of Jesus"[446] in and through Indian style of representation.

He was firm in his conviction that in order to make the Christian faith meaningful to the people in India, it must be presented in Indian forms and categories, for which he visualized art and paintings as among the most potential means. Since he was deeply influenced by the Christian ashram movement, he believed that the ashrams could provide a meeting-point for the Christian artists in order to draw inspiration from the deepest yearnings in other religions, especially Hinduism. Behind all these streams of his vision of Christian art, the idea of moving towards the foundation of an indigenous Indian Church was his ultimate objective. It must be remarked here that his efforts at promoting Christian art was the result of his deep interest and involvement with the Christian ashram movement and not the other way round. His regular contact with people of other faiths ever broadened his vision of the Catholic Church. He perceived all

443 Ibid.

444 See Solomon Raj, "Christliche Kunst in Indien," in *Die Bilder und das Wort: Zum Verstehen christlicher Kunst in Afrika und Asien,* eds., Theo Sundermeier & Volker Ktlster (Gottingen: Vandenhoeck & Ruprecht, 1999), 81. See also Schatz, *Geschichte,* Vol. V, 258.

445 See Lederle, *Christian Painting in India through the Centuries* (Bombay: Heras Institute of History and Culture/Anand: Gujarat Sahitya Prakash, 1987), 20.

446 Jyoti Sahi, "Foreword," in *Christian Painting in India through the Centuries*, 18.

peoples as belonging to the universal brotherhood.[447] To this it may be added that he understood the Church as a community of believers. Accordingly, he believed that any artistic expression that ultimately drew from the repertoire of Christian symbols and meaning systems must be placed at the service of the Church. While he always emphasized the communitarian aspect of artistic expression, he also believed that the individual freedom of the artists must be respected. However, the artists must also be aware that as Christians their artistic expressions must be aimed at the service of the Church. Besides, they need to bear in mind their faith and cultural heritage as well.[448] In his own words:

> In their effort to interpret Christ through Indian art, the Christian artists have to take upon themselves a task which is necessary and which among other people and cultures has been attempted through all the centuries of Christian history. The Christian artist in India has to master Indian forms and techniques. He has to develop his own style. His representations have to bear the stamp of his personality, his culture and his Faith.[449]

These discussions lead us to the conclusion that Lederle's attempts at promoting these media must be seen within the framework of his idea of inculturation of Christian faith in Indian culture. To substantiate we may quote Jyoti Sahi, one of the best known Christian artists in India. Sahi was strongly supported and deeply influenced by the commitment to the cause of Christian art shown by Matthew Lederle: "Fr. Lederle's concern with Indian Christian art must be seen within the context of his interest in the inculturation of the Church generally."[450] This inspiration in turn was prompted basically by the impact of his association with the Christian ashram movement.[451] It is important to point out, however, as to what was the nature of his involvement, contribution and role in the entire initiative. In order to describe the same we may refer to Jyoti Sahi, who wrote:

447 Ibid., 18-21.

448 Ibid., 7.

449 Lederle, "Interpreting Christ through Indian Art," 241.

450 Sahi, "Foreword," 17.

451 We shall discuss this point rather extensively in the sixth chapter, namely under the sub-topic The Jesuit Sanyasis /Swamis (i.e., # 6.4).

It is said that the Abbot Sugar of St. Denis in France did much to "create" Gothic art, through his deep understanding of a mysticism of light, and his vision of how Christian art should celebrate the mystery of light. This abbot was not an artist himself, though he was a patron of the arts. In the same way, there is much truth in the statement that Catholic art in India has been deeply influenced by the personal vision of Fr. Lederle. Further, what Fr. Lederle had to offer to the Church in India was his own personal appreciation and understanding of the work of Angelo da Fonseca.[452]

As for the ways and means he adopted to promote the cause, mention may be made of Art India and Marg Prakashan,[453] two art publications that functioned as organs for the promotion of young artists--both Christians and non-Christians--seeking to draw upon the Christian sources. An important aim of Lederle was to identify the talents among the youth. While doing so, he gave special emphasis on the 'local talent'. He wanted to encourage local people, both within the Church and outside of it, to work for the Church."[454] For, he was keen on promoting and encouraging the creative potentialities among them and strongly advocated the same by saying: "We have to encourage our artists, we have to give them tasks to be done."[455] True to his words, he

452 Sahi, "Foreword," 7. Angelo da Fonseca was one of the first Catholic artists whom Lederle greatly supported and promoted. In Lederle's words he was "the first important Christian artist of the new period." Matthew Lederle, "Interpreting Christ through Indian Art," 234. Matthew Lederle further mentions in this article the following names as some of the other known artists, among whom some have been contemporaries of Angelo da Fonseca: Angela Trindade (Bombay), Jyoti Sahi (Bangalore), Sr. Genevieve (Bangalore), Sr. Claire (Bangalore), Sr. Theresa (Ranchi), O. C. Rodrigues (Bombay), Joseph Pereira (Bombay), Desouza (Bombay), Everest Fernandes (Bombay) John G. Gonsalves (Bombay), Joachim Pastor (Panjim), Sr. V. Pereira (Bombay), Marie Pinto (Bombay), Julia Rodrigues (Pune), Sr. M. Silvestra (Madras), and W. Vandekerckhove (Ranchi). The mention of these artists is relevant here as they were all associated either with Art India or Marg Publication that was supported and promoted by Matthew Lederle. On this topic see further Friedrich Hobler, "Indisch-christliche Kunst: Gesprach mit Angelo da Fonseca," KM 6 (1955): 173-175; Gudrun Lowner, "Christian Art and Architecture in Asia," in *The Oxford Handbook of Christianity in Asia,* ed., Felix Wilfred (New York: Oxford University Press, 2014), 465-66.

453 As noted above, Art India was started by Raymund Keel. Later Matthew Lederle founded Marg Prakashan too for the promotion of the same cause. Unfortunately we have no information as to why Lederle needed to found another art publication. See Sahi, "Foreword," 20; Lokhande, *Mission, Missionaries & Me,* 280.

454 Sahi, "Foreword," 8.

455 Lederle, "Interpreting Christ through Indian Art," 241.

encouraged young artists who showed inclination and aptitude for art and painting. In order to provide an arena for the same he actively supported the foundation of a School of Art. Jyoti Sahi too played an active role there, who later functioned as its director. It was intended thereby that

Figure 3.2: *The Last Supper* by Angelo da Fonseca
Source: Matthew Lederle, *Christian Painting in India through the Centuries* (Bombay: Heras Institute of History and Culture/Anand: Gujarat Sahitya Prakash, 1987), 27.

the young artists would render their services to the Church in India through their artistic talents. Among the boys whom Lederle personally encouraged and supported financially as well for his training was a certain Arun Pardhe. Similarly Lucy D'Souza belonging to a secular institute, i.e., Christa Sevika (Servants of Christ) also was supported by him. These are only a few to name: Lederle had supported many more such talents.[456]

In the line of promoting Christian art, which although came much later (1980) and yet largely through the inspiration and encouragement of Lederle, was the foundation of an association called Indian Christian Art

456 Jyoti Sahi, "Homage to Pater Matthew Lederle," in Pater Matthaus Lederle S.J. (13. Mdrz 1926 - 8. Juni 1986): Gedenkschrift zum 28. Todestag (Pune: Association of Progressive Postgraduates, 2014), 61. This is a booklet originally published in Marathi for private circulation only. The Association of Progressive Postgraduates that published this booklet was founded by Matthew Lederle.

Association. The objective of this association was to present Christian themes through Christian art. Lederle became its first president. As a result of the general impact of these initiatives that began in the late 1950s, what came to be founded around the same time with that of Indian Christian Art Association is a centre known as National Biblical, Catechetical and Liturgical Centre (NBLCLC) in Bangalore. Through this centre too, the cause of Christian art has been largely promoted. Under its auspices the efforts of inculturation through catechetical and liturgical adaptation and renewal have flourished, wherein Indian Christian art has played an important role.[457] As the name suggests, the centre (i.e., NBLCLC) has a larger significance for the entire Indian Church that increasingly faces the challenge of indigenization.

One would appreciate these efforts more genuinely when they are seen vis-a-vis the historical context of the development of Indian Christian art in general. It is true that until the mid-1950s the attempts to represent anything in and through Indian ways was seen with suspicion and apprehension by conservative Churches. The image of Jesus, for example, was difficult to be accepted if it were presented in other forms than what had been the traditional way of presentation by European artists. The initial resistance to the reception of the attempts of Angelo da Fonseca is clearly a case in point. His initial paintings, i.e., Last Supper (see below figure 2.2) set in Indian context with clothing, sitting postures and background details entirely Indian, was not easy for the Indian artistic taste to accept.[458]

As may be noticed from the above image, the facial features have virtually been borrowed from the typical representations found in the Leonardo da Vinci's Last supper. Yet, as noted above, it was less enthusiastically received on account of the attempts at adaptation made by da Fonseca.[459] This is illustrative of the fact that the stereotyping with regard to the representation of the Christian images were so deep-seated in the Indian psyche, that it was not easy to be changed. It is here the significance of the contribution of Lederle emerges once again emphatically. Through his continual efforts in and through his engagement with Art India and Marg Prakashan, he achieved the

457 Ibid.

458 Matthew R. Lederle, 'Art India: Christian Paintings in Indian Style (Fxperiences of a Publisher)," II/9 (May/June 1972): 274-75. See also Sahi, "Foreword," 21.

459 See Sahi, "Foreword," 22.

objective of breaking down the stereotype, in the artistic expressions of Christian symbols to a considerable degree. What may be termed as another dimension of his pioneering contribution is his recognition of the contribution made by the non-Christians, as Jyoti Sahi would say: "Perhaps one of the most important contributions which Fr. [Matthew] Lederle made towards a realistic understanding of Indian art was to appreciate what non-Christians had contributed to this field, and recognize that the 'image of Jesus' had now become part of the heritage of India and not just the possession of the Christian community."[460] Summarizing the essence of the role undertaken and consequent contributions made in promoting Indian Christian art by Lederle, Sahi makes the following comment which may be taken as the most fitting tribute to the person of Lederle as a pioneer in this field:

> Finally, in trying to outline Fr. Lederle's personal contribution to the growth of Indian Christian art, I would like to mention that for many of us artists he was a "Father" in a very special way. Fr. Lederle's approach to art and artists has been essentially a pastoral one. His close friendship with artists like Angelo da Fonseca, Sr. Genevieve and Sr. Claire, has been a constant source of encouragement to these and many other artists, including myself. He was always willing to make himself available, to listen and share in our personal difficulties. I can say that I would never have been able to contribute my own creativity to the Church if it had not been for the constant care and guidance of Fr. Lederle. In this way he had not only many artists, but has also encouraged them to make a creative and fulfilling contribution to the life of the Church in India.[461]

Today Indian Christian art is largely accepted. It must be remembered, however, that the artists who worked in close collaboration with Lederle had to face considerable challenge to evolve an indigenous form of presentation of Indian Christian themes. If they borrowed much from Hindu mythologies, they risked the danger of syncretism; if not, their efforts would be seen as being trapped in the western Christian stereotype. The images given below may be cited as examples of initial efforts of the Indian artists. Clearly they are heavily influenced by Hindu symbols. Figure 3.2, for example, has been borrowed from a

460 Lederle, *Christian Painting in India,* 27.

461 Sahi, "Foreword," 22. For a similar note see also Sahi, "Homage an Pater Matthew Lederle," 60.

widely depicted image of goddess Saraswati (goddess of wisdom) in Hindu devotional practices. Figure 3.3 has been taken from the image the dancing Shiva (one of the three major gods of Hinduism). Figures 3.4 is reminiscent of Gopis (female cowherds) dancing with joy in the presence of lord Krishna (a popular Hindu god). Among these the figure 2.5 seems to represent an evolved form of adaptation, which depicts the Indian motherhood.

Figure 3.3: Jesus, the blood of Mary by Sr. Genevieve.

Figure 3.4: Madonna in Indian [Anonym.]
Source: IB 3 (1957): Cover Page.

Figure 3.5: **Nativity** by Sr. Claire

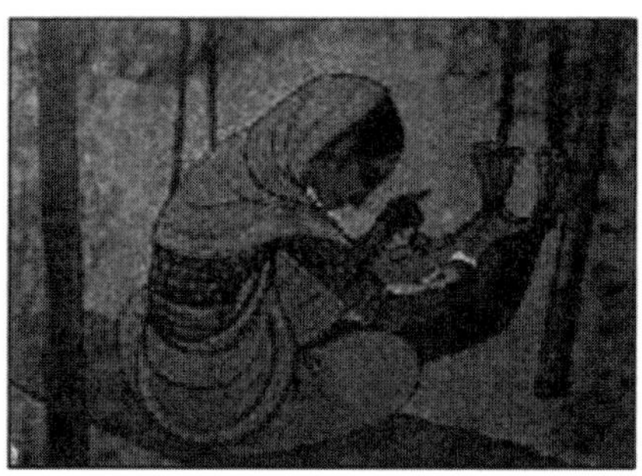

Figure 3.6: **Nativity** by Sr. Genevieve

Source: Matthew Lederle, *Christian Painting in India through the Centuries* (Bombay: Heras Institute of History and Culture/Anand: Gujarat Sahitya Prakash, 1987), 27, 67-68, 87.

The mention of these stages of evolution of the forms of representation of Christian symbols has been made to show how challenging the task of the artists initially must have been. Likewise it is also attributable to Lederle who was trying to pave a way for inculturation through promotion of Indian Christian art. The present state of acceptance of these forms are largely credited to him as we have tried to show in the preceding paragraphs. In the present context of growing demands for Indianization of the Church, his contribution is certainly worth taking note of.

Lastly a word may be said about the architectural adaptation in the Indian churches. The Portuguese brought European church architecture to India. The architecture was mostly baroque in style and was reminiscent of the 18th century understanding of religious symbols as reflecting victory and joyful faith. They were often copied in India too. Naturally the Indian Catholics accepted them as they had no other symbols to compare with. Moreover, because it corresponded to the richness and colour of the Indian soul, they found no hurdles in accepting the same. With the growing demands of inculturation after the independence of the country, however, Church leaders began to ponder upon church architectural styles too, which would resonate more closely with the Indian ethos. The Jesuits of this Mission came once again at the forefront, although until early 1960s they could not achieve much in this regard. But the process of reflection in this direction had already begun as may be concluded from the following text:

> Today ... the time has come to create Christian architectures that have their spiritual roots in the Indian cultural world. It is not a question of imitating Hindu temples or of adopting individual stylistic elements, but of making those fundamental principles tangible with which the Catholic Indian experiences God, Christ and his Church: His feeling of security and childlike trust in the omnipresent God, his knowledge of the warm humanity of Christ, and the community experience in the Church. Thus, great tasks await the native Christian artists to find a solution to these questions.[462]

The discussion above shows us that the Jesuits in the B-PM were keen on evolving new methods of making the Christian faith more relevant to the Indian masses. The merit of their efforts lie not

462 "Besinnung auf eine christlich-indische Kunst," IB 1 (1957): 7.

solely on their accomplishment, rather on their pioneering nature. As a concluding note it may be emphasized once again that all these efforts were ultimately aimed at winning more members for the Church.

3.5. Change of Options and Priorities

Besides the strategies, the priorities and options constitute the essential elements of a missionary endeavour. Within the general framework of the charism of a particular Order, the missionaries explore their own creative ways and means to actualize their vision. The fundamental priority of the Jesuits according to St. Ignatius, for example, is "ministry to the world ... by individual Jesuits ..."[463] Therefore this is the general framework within which the Jesuits seek "to be ever-creative and adaptive to the changing pastoral situations."[464]

Let it be noted, however, that often these aspects may not be found in a written document. Instead, they tend to be epitomized in the working style and method of a few or a majority of the missionaries who may be considered as representatives in a particular field of operation. Besides, it is also true that the priorities and options of a mission often tend to be shaped and forced to be changed when the missionaries are faced with the ground reality. Therefore, "instead of setting their own priorities, the priorities were [are] set for them."[465] In other words, the missionaries may not have the choice of implementing a pet programme of action, of whatever creative value, unless the ground reality is favourable to the same. For an example, if a target group is in acute need of pastoral care of a more basic level, they cannot afford to impose a plan of establishing an institution of higher technical education. The same is true of other circumstances.

Here, under this sub-topic, therefore, we shall discuss the priorities and options of the Poona Mission. The priorities and options in this Mission were largely a continuation of what were initiated in the former Bombay-Poona Mission. There was no radical departure from them as such, primarily in two senses: that the Mission continued to be oriented towards the marginalized groups and that the strengthening

463 Gerald A. Arbuckle, *From Chaos to Mission* (London: Geoffrey Chapman, 1996), 23. For further discussion see also John W. O'Malley, *The First Jesuits* (Cambridge, MA: Harvard University Press, 1993), 363.

464 Ibid.

465 Maryks Robert Aleksander and Wright Jonathan eds., *Jesuit Survival and Restoration: A Global History, 1773-1900* (Leiden: Koninklijke Brill, 2015), 306.

and expansion of the Mission continued as in the previous decades. A certain departure from the previous priority can be noted: There was a shift from the special focus on establishment and expansion of the urban school system to more rural school system. Geographically and demographically too the priority changed from mostly urban to rural set up. This in turn implied a greater focus on the marginalized sections of the society. We shall discuss this aspect further.

3.5.1. Mission among the Outcasts, the Untouchables and the Marginalized[466]

The mandate of 'preferential option for the poor' became a dominant theme in the social teaching of the Catholic Church since the late 1960s and especially after Vatican Council II to be more precise. The phrase was originally coined by Pedro Arrupe, the 28th Superior General of the Society of Jesus (1965-1983) and was first used in a letter addressed to the Jesuits in Latin America in 1968 in the context of his exhortation on the primary identity of the university run by them. The phrase gained much wider currency in theological discourses, thanks to the Latin American theologian Gustavo Gutierrez, often known as the Father of Liberation Theology,[467] subsequent to one of his most famous publications, i.e., *A Theology of Liberation* in 1973.[468] But the central content of the phrase as such was not so recent in its origin. In fact it is as old as the Christian tradition, nay the biblical tradition itself. For, in the biblical tradition,

> God ... is viewed as the God of the poor, a tender Creator moved by and caring for suffering innocent creatures. God is seen opting for the poor through the birth, passion, death and resurrection of Jesus and urging all of us in the Spirit to listen to the cry of the poor and thus to live in loving solidarity with the poor.[469]

In Jesuit missionary endeavours or for that matter in any other mission endeavours the option to work among the marginalized sections

466 Clearly the terms used in the subtitle are redundant. Yet, it is also true that each of these terms contain certain exclusive nuance with it. Hence the use of all the three.

467 See Frank K. Flinn, *Encyclopedia of Catholicism* (New York: Facts on File, 2007), 339. See also Deen K. Chatterjee (ed.), *Encyclopedia of Global Justice: A-J, Volume I* (Heidelberg/London/New York: Springer Science & Business Media, 2011), 654.

468 See R. Kevin Seasoltz, *A Virtuous Church: Catholic Theology, Ethics, and Liturgy for the 21st Century* (Maryknoll, N.Y: Orbis Books, 2012), 42.

469 See Donald W. Musser and Joseph L. Price, eds., *New and Enlarged Handbook of Christian Theology* (Nashville: Abingdon Press, 2003), 304.

of society is a concrete manifestation of the implementation of the above charism into practice. For, 'the preferential option for the poor' implies working for the integral betterment of the marginalized groups or peoples that fall short of realizing a dignified standard of human living because of various levels of deprivations they might be subjugated to suffer.

In the Maratha Mission such an option has been a characteristic feature right from its beginning. Recapitulating the history of the beginning and expansion of the mission among the non-Christians by the German-Swiss Jesuits it may be pointed out that already from the time of Leo Meurin's episcopate (1867-1886) in the Bombay Archdiocese and from 1878 to be more precise, a clear option was made to work among the outcastes, the untouchables and the marginalized. It has been pointed out earlier that the first efforts to evangelize the 'outcastes' and 'untouchables' known as Mahars along with a few other smaller groups of lower caste Hindus did not meet with the expected results.[470] But there was no space for letting in discouragement and hopelessness. On the contrary, the option to work among such sections of society remained always open with even greater zeal. So much so that the Mahars eventually became the single largest group of outcastes among whom the German-Swiss Jesuits began "to work mostly"[471] even after the division of the Mission took place: the Bombay area being entrusted to the Spanish Jesuits and the Poona and adjacent areas being once again entrusted to the Southern German Province in 1929.[472] Although they did not restrict themselves to work among them, their major focus, by virtue of their larger number at the place, was among the Mahars. Hence we shall discuss in greater detail the Jesuit Mission among the Mahars to substantiate the argument that to work among the outcastes and the marginalized groups of people was a special feature of this Mission. It may be noted that "Mahars are found in almost every village of Maharashtra, constituting around 10 percent of its population."[473]

470 See Gense, *Church at the Gateway,* 299-300. See also Report to the General (13th March 1878), ARSI, Bombay. 1001-IX, 10; Report to Cardinal Simeoni, Prefect of the Propaganda Fidei (18th April 1878), ASCPF, Indie Orientali 21, 1154; Schatz, "Optionen und Prioritaten," 401.

471 Pius Geisel, "Die Mahars," IB 1/25 (January 1936): 211.

472 *SeeActRSJ,* Vol. VII, 1929, 321.

473 Narendra Jadhav, *Untouchables: My Family's Triumphant Escape from India s Caste System (hereafter; Untouchables),* (Berkeley and Los Angeles: University of California Press, 2003), 6.

The choice of the Mahars as one of the primary targets of missionary endeavour resulted not due to their docility and openness to accept Christianity alone; rather to the condition of subjugation and dehumanization that they were doomed to live in. In other words, their human condition earned them a privileged opportunity for betterment when they came into contact with the Jesuits.[474] Therefore, there was nothing arbitrary about the Mahars being a special target of evangelization. However, we cannot conclusively say that a comprehensive strategy was chalked out by the Jesuits to work among them. But certainly there is no contradiction in stating that in the course of establishing gradual contacts with the local people, the Mahars did come across as deserving a special focus of evangelization.

Although we have already pointed out who the Mahars are, it would be worthwhile to situate who the outcastes and untouchables are within the larger framework of the Hindu society. This would give us a glimpse of the 19th and 20th century socio-religious and economic condition of these people among whom the Jesuit missionaries chose to work. One of the most striking features of the Maharashtrian society, for that matter of almost the entire Indian society in these centuries, was the caste-based division and hierarchy. The caste system in India is nearly 3,500 years old. Officially it was abolished by the Indian Constitution when the country became a Republic on January 26, 1950. But in practice it is still very much prevalent in the society and manifests itself in more subtle forms with equal perniciousness. There is no denying of the fact that the situation has improved on a number of counts over the decades. Yet the fact remains that the outcastes still suffer the burden of subjugation. In order to assess the situation of the Mahars in the decades when the missionary endeavours were initiated, we need to understand some basic facts about how the caste system operated in the Mahar society. The situation as described from the vantage-point of an insider, Narendra Jadhav, a Mahar by birth, may be noted:

> Hindus believe that God created the caste system. The sacred Rig-Veda, the earliest literary source in India, dating back to around 1000 B.C. describes how human stratifications came about: a cosmic giant, *Purusha*, sacrificed parts of his body to create mankind. His mouth became the Brahmin, the priestly class; his arms the

474 See Georges De Schrij ver (ed.), *Liberation Theologies on Shifting Grounds* (Leuven: Uitgeverij Peeters, 1998), 402-103.

> *Kshatriya*, the warriors and landowners; his thighs were made into Vaishya, the merchants; and from his feet were born the Shudra, the servants. This fourfold division of society is called the Four Varnas (Chaturvarna). The untouchables have no place in the Chaturvarna, and are placed even below the lowest Shudra Varna. Ancient Hindu law books such as Manu *Smruti* and Gautama Dharma *Shashtra* did not allow the *Shudras* and Dalits to possess any wealth other than "dogs and donkeys." The doors of education were closed to them. This is what the law books prescribe for untouchables who dare to approach the sacred texts: If he listens intentionally to the Vedas, his ears shall be filled with lead. If he recites them, his tongue shall be cut out. If he remembers them, his body shall be split in twain.[475]

Where do the Mahars come under this scheme of things? The text clearly underlines the fact that the Mahars, in principal, were outside this system. But in practice it implied that they were worse than even the Shudra people, the lowest group in the caste-hierarchy. For, in spite of the fact that they did not really belong to the Hindu society, they had to bear the consequences of everything that the caste system imposed on the lower castes in society. In fact a much worse treatment was meted out to them. Precisely because of these reasons some recent authors, beginning with Bhim Rao Ambedkar himself, prefered to use the term ati-Shudra [lower than the lowest in the caste hierarchy, literally extremely low] for such people.[476] By doing so the modern writers intend to underline the fact that the condition of the outcastes and the untouchables has been worse than even those in the lowest stratum of the caste hierarchy. Therefore, it may be stated that besides political and other such factors what may possibly have contributed the most towards causing human misery in Hindu society for centuries was the caste system. The extent of injustice on account of it may be assessed from the fact that it embraced a huge chunk of human society in India. In the words of Narendra Jadhav: "Every sixth human being in the world today is an Indian, and every sixth Indian is an erstwhile untouchable, a Dalit [literally trampled underfoot]. Today there are 165 million Dalits

475 Narendra Jadhav, *Untouchables,* 1-2. Emphasis is mine.

476 Some better known names, besides B. R. Ambedkar, are the following: Aparna Devare, *History and the Making of Modern Hindu Self* (New Delhi: Routledge, 2011); Mahendra Singh, *Dalit's Inheritance in Hindu Religion* (Delhi: Kalpaz Publications, 2009); Sanjay Paswan and Paramanshi Jaideva, *Encyclopaedia of Dalits in India, Volume 13* (Delhi: Kalpaz Publications, 2003), etc.

(equal to more than half the population of the United States) and they continue to suffer under India's 3,500-year-old caste system, which remains a stigma on humanity."[477] The figures speak for themselves. The subjugation perpetuated in the Indian society for millennia in the name of a system sanctioned by a religious belief is hard to describe. But that is the bare truth. A human life outside the parameters of religion and caste system in Indian society was inconceivable. The entire existence of a person was governed by caste rules and regulations. Describing poignantly the situation of a common man in the caste-ridden society in Maharashtra in the 19th and 20th centuries, Jeevendra Jadhav, a Jesuit, writes:

> The ordinary life of [a common] man was governed by religious sanctions from birth to death. Superstition was rampant and there was no escape from it since education was limited only to the Brahmin males. The impact of the caste system was felt everywhere. The division of labour was based on the caste system. One was born in the caste and had no choice but to follow the occupation of his ancestors. The stratification of the society was based on it and there was no question of social mobility. The social, political, educational, cultural, economic aspects of life of an ordinary man were governed by pervasive religious sanctions. Society was so interwoven that it was difficult for an outsider to enter it and for an insider to come out of it.[478]

It is within this system that the Mahars suffered much subjugation and oppression. It is necessary to point out a few aspects of their dehumanization and subjugation in order to underline the fact that the option to work among the marginalized sections of the society was a priority of the Jesuit Mission in Poona. In this regard, mention may also be made of the fact that the social situation of the Mahars had a special place in the discourses of the Jesuits. It may be noted that until the opening decades of the 20th century the "Brahmanical dominance in Maharashtra [had] no parallel in the rest of the country."[479] And Mahars had been the worst sufferers of subjugation in the name of religion and religious systems.

---

477 Jadhav, *Untouchables,* 1.

478 See Jadhav, *Evangelization as Community Building,* 113.

479 Ibid., 115.

Now, to underline the plight of the Mahars one need not go to a distant past. It would suffice to have a bird's eye-view of their social condition beginning from as late as 19th century. It has already been pointed out that they were lower than even the lowest, namely the Shudras, in the caste hierarchy. Their status was reflected in the occupations they were entrusted with as a group of people. Within the traditional village administrative structure they functioned as cleaners, messengers and village servants.[480] In the larger Hindu society they were treated as untouchables. The following text gives a graphic description of their plight:

> In Pune, the capital of Maratha kingdom, Mahars were treated very badly as outcastes. A Mahar was required to have a black thread either on his wrist or around his neck so that he could easily be identified, making it easier for a high caste Hindu to keep away from him lest he touches the Mahar and be polluted; to carry a broom strung from his waist to sweep away the dust on which he treaded, lest a Hindu walking on the same road should be polluted; to carry an earthen pot hung around his neck wherever he went for holding his spit lest his spit should pollute a Hindu who might unknowingly happen to tread on it.[481]

Such an inhuman situation did not change even under the British rule in India, though it had passed several laws such as right to education including women, widow remarriage, prohibition of sati, etc. to ensure equality to the Depressed Classes as well. To a certain extent, the imposition of the British rule with its sense of equality of all before the law signaled a process of dislodging of the Brahmins from their traditional superior position in Indian society.[482] Yet, they had to depend on the upper castes for documenting and understanding of the Indian society and hence were not objective in their judgment about the low classes. For instance, the traditional British administrative manuals classified the Mahars as,

> Inferior village servant... watchman and guardian of the village and the living chronicler of its concerns. Apart from arbitrating in boundary disputes and guarding the village, their duties also

480 Jadhav, *Evangelization as Community Building,* 113-114.

481 Ibid., 118.

482 Ravinder Kumar, *Western India in the Nineteenth Century: A Study in the Social History of Maharashtra* (Abingdon: Routledge, 1968), 298.

> included carrying death notices ... sweeping the village roads, serving government officials, tracking thieves, and removing the carcasses of cattle from village.[483]

It is noteworthy to underline the fact that unlike other societies of the world the Hindu society made a division not only of labour but that of labourers as well, under the caste system. Stated otherwise, the division of labour was not based on individual's skill, intelligence or aptitude; rather on the basis of his birth in a particular caste where there was no space for mobility. Indeed it was a religiously sanctioned and hierarchically structured system. In sum "it is an institutionalized inequality."[484]

The foregoing discussion thus amply substantiates the argument that Mahars were naturally privileged to be chosen for evangelization by the missionaries. We now go into a brief discussion on how at the practical level of evangelization the missionaries perceived the Mahars as a priority target group. We shall try to identify the same in the correspondences and annual reports among the missionaries and the Superiors both in India and Europe, news reports, journals or newsletters, as well as in other literatures.

It has been pointed out earlier that the mission method, which was tried out by Bishop Leo Meurin failed to be realized. It is true that the modest but real missionary successes which were achieved in the past were mostly by sheer chances rather than meticulous planning and execution. It had been till then a general phenomenon that in the Indian missions breakthroughs were mostly achieved among the lower castes, outcastes or those not integrated in the Hindu caste system. Now came an era when the Mission applied substantially certain well planned strategies.[485] But again it must be clarified that the entire planning was not something like a written document. Yet, it is true that a considerable amount of deliberation had gone into the proposed initiatives, especially subsequent to the incident of fraud by the two Mahar catechists. The mission work basically consisted of opening schools and availing social welfare, particularly through credit societies. Besides, imparting a solid catechesis began to receive greater attention in the pastoral agenda,

483 Jadhav, *Untouchables,* 6.

484 Jadhav, *Evangelization as Community Building,* 116.

485 See Schatz, "Optionen und Missionarische Prioritaten," 401.

which was implemented through schools and regular gatherings of the people in the villages.[486]

Since we have already discussed earlier the two aspects namely how through education and social welfare the work of evangelization was further carried forward, we shall restrict ourselves here to only one aspect, i.e., catechesis. Fathers Otto Weishaupt and Leo Kraig, the first missionaries of Valan (the mission station of the Maratha Mission), for example, specifically emphasized the need of catechising the even the non-baptized people on a regular basis. To this effect they "went from there [mission stations] to the surrounding non-Christian villages to preach to the grown-ups and in Valan itself went to a Mahar and Kunbi [Farming class, much higher than Mahars in caste hierarchy] School to teach catechism to the children."[487] This initiative was further carried out by successive missionaries. The effort did bear fruit and the missionaries took pride in sharing their experiences. Although, they might sound utterly insensible to modern ears, the fact that was strongly underlined through such stories was to communicate that catechesis, so humble a work as it was, was an essential aspect of initiating the process of evangelization. An incident narrated by John Baptist Winiger, for example, has a similar import:

> Peter is a small little boy. Precisely, therefore, has he a greater honour of returning to the house of the missionary. And he knows, how the strict Father will like it to have, that not a speck of dust remains, he also knows where various things belong, and he understands what the cleanliness means - when one diligently sees it. There lay my crucifix next to my bed ... I come back to my room. My Peter has the crucifix in his hand and quietly kisses it... then places it at the wash-basin and as he looks up, sees me at the door. "What did you do with my crucifix, Peter?" I kissed it." "Why so then?" "My father had told me to do so." The little one had no crucifix of his own, that he could kiss it time and again ... But he had a good father, a pious teacher and a simple man, who was himself an uneducated man, had given to his little one, Peter.[488]

486 See Report to the Superior General (Bombay, 13th March 1878) ARSI, Bombay. 1001-XI, 10.

487 "Aus dem Leben des hohen Jubilars," IB 1/12 (October 1932): 79.

488 J. B. Winiger, "Buben der Wildnis," IB 1/18 (April 1934): 143-144.

J. B. Winiger continues his narrative to tell two more incidents wherein he came across two children in the school. Since they could not afford to buy prayer books, they had written down a set of selected prayers in their notebooks.[489] Br. Moritz Emmenecker adds his own account of his experiences of the impact of catechism among the young school children. He narrates an incident wherein a choir was formed out of the school children and taken to a place called Dhond, some 60 kms from Kendal (the second station of the Maratha Mission, where he was working) to sing in the solemn Holy Mass on the occasion of St. Sebastian's Feast (1935). After the meals and common rosary the children were sent to bed. Emmenecker further mentions: "A little later, as I along with Fr. [Ivo] Meyer and one more gentleman went to see the children, they were kneeling down by their bed side and praying their evening prayers, as they were habituated of doing the same."[490]

The significance attached to catechesis by the missionaries is evident from another account narrated from Rahata (the third mission station of Maratha Mission), wherein one more aspect of catechising is made evident, namely training children as future catechists and teachers. It was a significant development in the mission method. It is evident from the following account:

> In our 52 villages we look after 5,425 Christians. From 1st July 1935 to 1st July 1936 we had 352 baptisms. Since 95 Christians were dead the total increase in the number of Christians in the last year comes to 257. We have 37 schools wherein 39 teachers have been employed. At the mission station we look after [free of cost] 55 small boys year after year. There they can be led deeper into Christianity. They get used to receiving sacraments and attending in the liturgy regularly. From among them we identify boys for further training as future teachers and catechists. They act as dough in the villages as they return to the villages.[491]

It is interesting to note this development in the missionary method. This shows a definitive level of growth of the local church: the local people themselves acting as agents of further evangelization. Thus we come to a conclusion that as the Church grew it began to slowly move

489 Ibid., 144.

490 Moritz Emmenecker, "Eine Sangerfahrt," IB 1/27 (July 1936): 227.

491 J. B. Eichhorn, "Eins urns andere," IB 1/28 (October 1936): 233. See also "Die Fahrt ins Missionsland," IB 1/17 (January 1934): 138.

towards self-dependency. We may also state that reaching out to the local people through catechesis was certainly an effective means. A question, however, may come up here as to how the Jesuits accomplished it. Was it always an oral communication? It was both oral and written. There were already a few printed catechism books available. Probably the written catechesis became more popular after Henry Doring published a translation of the catechism in Marathi.[492]

3.6. Work among Migrants

Another distinct target group of the Jesuits was migrants. Poona, being a growing city and relatively well-connected by trains and roads, attracted a lot of migrants from other States in search of their livelihoods. The Tamils/Tamilians (people of Tamil Nadu) were one of the largest groups of people who had migrated to Poona. In many of the correspondences they are also designated as Madrasis. Maximilian Riklin described them as follows: "Madrasis are Christians from the South of India, who came mostly as camp-followers, generally very poor, ill-instructed and of low moral standard."[493] John B. Haas, on the other hand, described them as "people without homeland"[494] because of their wandering status in search of their livelihoods. Most of them had migrated to central and northern India for menial jobs as "coolies, house-servants, factory-workers,"[495] "cooks, waiters, guards and night-watches."[496] Wherever they found jobs, they normally settled there initially in small numbers, sometimes for a year and other times for longer period of time. When they lost their jobs, they looked for new ones. When they did not succeed to find the same in the same city, they migrated to some other cities. "To depart from a city was never a painful experience for them. They are at home with everyone and at the same strangers everywhere."[497] Due to the constant migratory life their families were often torn-apart. The father and the grown-up sons went out in search of jobs and the remaining members often lost contact with them for long periods of time. Often

492 See Henry Doring to the Superior General (Poona, 27th October 1932), ARSI, Poona. 1004-V, 3a.

493 Maximilian Riklin to the Superior General (Bombay, 6th September 1923), ARSI, Bombay. 1004-1, 13.

494 John B. Haas, "Volk ohne Heimat," IB 2 (March/April 1947): 27.

495 Ibid.

496 John B. Haas, "Und was geht bei den Tamil-Leuten?" IB 1/30 (April 1937): 255.

497 Haas, "Volk ohne Heimat," 27.

the children did not know where they were born. Their names had no positive connotations. They were mostly members of the lower castes known as the *pariahs*. Their status is described by John B. Haas in the following words:

> They have very few well-wishers and friends. As a cheap labour force alone, they are valued and made use of. Some of them have forgotten their language, 'sweet Tamil' ... With that their last connection with their homeland has been broken. They have become a wandering community - without a house and a home, without a foothold and group cohesiveness. They are like loose leaves that are tossed around by the wind over the fields.[498]

As for their religious affiliation, some of them were Catholics, although because of the above-mentioned grounds and more especially due to the lack of sufficient pastoral care coupled with the strong non-Christian surroundings they lived in, their family situations were often far from giving a semblance of Christian families. The number of the Catholics among them may be imagined from the fact that in Poona a church, namely St. Anne's Church, was needed to be set apart for Masses in Tamil. As for other places, they were quite thickly populated in 12 different places in the entire diocese, excepting the non-Christians among them.[499] Due to lack of Tamil-speaking chaplains, the Masses for them were often said in English, which the majority did not understand. Hence, such an arrangement was not feasible to the group as a whole. A majority of them did not feel at home with the liturgy and other services. It was imperative, therefore, that a Tamil-speaking chaplain be placed, at least in Poona, to look after their pastoral needs. This was not possible until late 1920s.[500]

---

498 Ibid.

499 See John B. Haas, "Und was geht bei den Tamil-Leuten?" IB 1/30 (April 1937): 254-255.

500 See John Haldner, "Unser erstes Antonius Fest in Puna," IB 1/19 (July 1934): 149-150. The feast of St. Anthony mentioned in the title of this article was celebrated in a church which was set apart for Masses in Tamil language. In the British period Madras (now Chennai) was the Residence of the Governor of Madras Presidency. Due to this connection, people coming from Tamil Nadu (which was a part of the erstwhile Madras Presidency) were generally, and occasionally derogatively as well, known as 'Madrasis'. Hence the Church designated for the Masses for them was known among people as 'Madrassi Church' (Madrassikirche) although the official name of the same was St. Anne's Church. See also Haas, "Volk ohne Heimat," 27.

It may be inferred from the preceding paragraph that one of the major hurdles in undertaking the ministry among the Tamils was their language, namely Tamil.[501] A majority of the Jesuits could not learn it. The primary reason for the same was: it was not the main language of the region. The natives of Poona and surrounding areas spoke Marathi. Hence, a priority of place was given to Marathi when the Jesuits first arrived in Poona. Even as late as the 1930s there were only two priests in the entire Mission who could preach fluently in Tamil, one of them being John B. Haas himself (about whom we shall discuss in greater detail in the subsequent paragraphs) and the other, a diocesan priest.[502] John B. Haas had devoted some time for learning Tamil in South India and had managed to learn it considerably well. In 1935, he took over as the first regular Jesuit chaplain to the Tamil-speaking migrant community.[503] Prior to him (probably around the end of 1920s) a Tamil speaking native priest (most likely a diocesan) was placed as a chaplain, who served in this capacity until 1934.[504] Right from the beginning, John B. Haas got wholeheartedly and "fully involved with their pastoral care."[505] As a result, he won their appreciation and acceptance instantly as noted by Geisel:

> ...He had a heart for them. He had acquired, with great patience and perseverance, an inherent sense of their language and had learnt the art of their singing, especially the hymns. Earlier they [Tamilians] invariably complained of the lack of taste for western melodies in the churches. Now it is much easier for them. The elders among them remember of their youthful days that they had spent in the South and many of them who most likely may have been away

501 Haas, "Volk ohne Heimat," 27.

502 See Haas, "Und was geht bei den Tamil-Leuten?" 255.

503 The contact of the Jesuits of the Poona Mission with the Tamil migrants is as old as the former's history in India. Bishop Alexis Canoz, originally a member of the Madurai Jesuit Mission, later Apostolic Administrator of Bombay-Poona Vicariate (1858-1861), for example, due to his previous association with the Tamilians in Madurai Mission considered them the most deserving group of people, who were in need of Jesuit pastoral care. On his personal recommendation, regular contact was maintained with them even in the later decades as well. Yet, there had been no regular Jesuit chaplain for them until John B. Haas took up this responsibility in 1935. See Gense, *Church at the Gateway,* 249-250. See also See also John B. Haas, "Das De Nobili College, Poona," (Poona, 16th January 1946), ARSI, Poona. 1004-XV, 4.

504 See Pius Geisel, "Mit dem Madrassipater in Puna," IB 1/22 (April 1935): 180.

505 "Aus der Theologie in Puna," IB 2/4 (October 1938): 46.

from the Church are coming back again due to the attraction of their native music and melodies.[506]

That he was instantly received and acknowledged by the Tamil community may be assessed also from the fact that he was fondly known as 'Madrasi-Father' (Madrassipater) among his Jesuit companions. Undoubtedly, he was the first one among the Jesuits to have established a good rapport with this community,[507] so that "the Tamilians respect[ed] him much."[508] No wonder, such an atmosphere of cordiality was created because "he loves the humble sheep and lambs of his flock."[509] When he was appointed the Rector of De Nobili College, he seems to have been highly apprehensive about his readiness to take up a new ministry. Indeed, in the words of Joseph Neuner, "he should have liked 100 times to be with his beloved people [the Tamils]."[510] In fact in his own personal testimony too he once expressed: "Almost 10 years I have spent here. And when I am asked again I shall gladly do it [ministry among the Tamils] ... It is a wonderful work here."[511]

These few instances give us an idea as to how he had earned a place in the hearts of these people. Since, after his term as their chaplain, the correspondences are virtually silent about the ministry among the Tamils, we shall restrict our present discussion to his involvement with this community and his contribution towards inculcating in them a sense of acceptance and belongingness in the larger Catholic community of Poona. Another reason for the same is this: the nature of his involvement with this community gives quite a comprehensive and broad picture of the involvement of the Jesuits with the Tamil Catholic community.

A question that may arise at this juncture is: Was the numerical strength of the Tamil migrants in Poona the sole criterion for the Jesuits to undertake the pastoral care among them? The answer to the same was undoubtedly in the affirmative. Another important reason was their lower socio-economic status and apparent poor moral standard. It has been mentioned above that due to scarcity of Tamil-speaking chaplains

506 Geisel, "Mit dem Madrassipater," 180.

507 Ibid., 179-181.

508 Jadocus Jochum, "Die Tamil-Leute," IB 1/23 (July 1935): 188.

509 Ibid.

510 Joseph Neuner to Felix A. Plattner (Dehra Dun, 28th May 1942), AMPSJ, IB. Puna-Briefe (alte).

511 John B. Haas to George (?) (Poona, 12th November 1941), AMPSJ, IB. Puna-Briefe (alte).

their spiritual and pastoral care was greatly neglected for decades and the community drifted in the practice of Christian morals. Many of the families claimed to be associated with different Churches before their migration to Poona. Yet from the religious atmosphere in their families, the Jesuit pastors perceived that they were hardly rooted in the Christian faith. Some of them were living in two religious worlds: Christian and Hindu. Some of them had statues of Hindu deities in their families, while retaining Christian names. Two cases narrated by John B. Haas reveal the situation well:

> There was a boy with a nice name, 'Jesu.' The father was unknown. I tried to trace where the boy was baptized. Every time the mother made a reference of an entirely different place. Finally, one was forced to have a doubt whether the boy was baptized at all ... The second boy is known as Moses Daniel ... He was one of the best in catechism classes and other areas. After the first Confession came the mother: "What have you done? The boy is a Hindu, we all of us are Hindus!" [I asked], "How should I know about it? He has a Christian name all the same!" [She replied] "The name was given by the Saheb [Master/Employer], under whom his father works!" What to do? I tried to persuade the mother to allow the boy to be baptized. But she was not willing to hear any more about it. Later I spoke to the boy and told him to talk to his parents ... Some days later he came back and told that his father was ready but the mother was still not. ... At last, some days later he came back again and told that the mother had consented...,[512]

The text clearly reveals a situation of borderline religious identity of the Tamil migrants. Yet, there was another side of the story too that seems to have earned the favour of the Jesuits for their pastoral care. This aspect pertains to their general communitarian trait of docility and openness towards Christian Faith. These aspects were seen quite strongly even among the non-Christians. According to John Haldner, they were "more docile than the natives of Poona"[513] in receiving the Christian Faith. Jadocus Jochum also expressed a similar view as he wrote: "The Tamils come across to me as though they are born for Christian Faith and in them the missionaries may expect to have a

512 See John B. Haas, "Meine Tamilseelsorge," IB 3 (May/June 1947): 57.

513 Geisel, "Mit dem Madrassipater," 180.

great source of spiritual joy and satisfaction."[514] John B. Haas himself was immensely taken up by their disposition: "One wonders at the piety of the Tamilians. Many acknowledge that from their very nature they are religiously oriented people. I believe that is the truth."[515] He consistently underlined these traits as he narrated his experiences with the non-Christian Tamilians. It was nothing less than a surprise when he encountered some non-Christian Tamil families, who depicted a sense of docility to the Christian teaching in spite of the reality of entangled family relationships. For example, many of them had married two or more wives. This phenomenon seems to have been quite common among the non-Christian Tamil migrants.[516] Yet, generally a remarkable atmosphere of cordiality and understanding prevailed in many of those families. Their children came across in the schools as some of the most docile children. Moreover, some of the families were even prepared to fulfill the demands of the Christian teachings on monogamy for the sake of receiving baptism in the Catholic Church.[517] Recounting an encounter with the housewife of a family (the head of the same was called Henry by his Christian employer although his real name was Krishnaswami),[518] John B. Haas expressed his astonishment:

> Father, we have long reflected and finally arrived at a decision to embrace Catholic Faith. We have decided to separate from one another. I and my children will be staying in another house. Henry will be sending me half of his earnings every month but he will be visiting me no more. Then all of us wish to come to the Church and be baptized ... This time I was speechless once again. Is such a thing possible, I asked myself ... such conversions naturally belong to the rarest cases.[519]

The woman referred to in the text above was the first wife of Henry. She was baptized at the sickbed and was re-christened as Mary. The children, altogether nine including the five from Henry's other

514 Jochum, "Die Tamil-Leute," 188.

515 Haas, "Volk ohne Heimat," 27.

516 See John B. Haas, "Und was geht bei den Tamil-Leuten?" IB 1/30 (April 1937): 254-255; Haas, "Volk ohne Heimat," 27-28.

517 See Jochum, "Die Tamil-Leute," 188; John B. Haas, "Tamil-Leute: Familie Henry," IB 2/3 (July 1938): 25-27.

518 See Jochum, "Die Tamil-Leute," 189.

519 Ibid.

wife, were baptized already prior to this event. Although Henry was at the root of this new inspiration, he could not be baptized as both of his wives were alive. Mary died shortly thereafter and thus Henry along with his second wife too was baptized. The family depicted a consistent sense of commitment to the Christian calling. Although it was an exceptional case, the disposition of the Tamilians was pretty well revealed by this incident. The incident opened a further door to the Tamilians. For, after their example, quite a few families were reported to have followed Christian moral rules with regard to married life.[520]

The foregoing discussion may give an impression that the Tamil migrants were a people without any shadow side, in the perception of the missionaries. On the contrary, the pastors realized that as in the case of any other society, they too depicted occasionally inconsistency in their disposition towards Christianity. But the positive aspects seemed to have weighed heavier on them that they decided to pastorally care for them.

As for John B. Haas' contribution in the pastoral care of the Tamilians, it may be noted that he played a pivotal role in expanding and further developing St. Anthony's School, Poona which was established primarily for the Tamil children. From raising funds to personally supervising the expansion of the infrastructure, he took up the job on his shoulders with much dedication.[521] Due to his efforts and keen interest in their education, the number of Tamil children rose to more than 260 in the year 1937, which was 166 at the time he took up as their chaplain in 1935. He himself was the in-charge of the school until he was appointed the Superior of the Mission (1944). His regular visits to the Tamil families helped awaken the need for education among them. Consequently, the school eventually became a doorway to a large number of Tamilians to step into the mainstream of society due to the education imparted to there. Their social status, too gradually grew in the subsequent decades.

---

520 See Jochum, "Die Tamil-Leute: eine Fortsetzung," IB 1/25 (January 1936): 202-203. See also Haas, "Tamil-Leute: Familie Henry," 25-26.

521 John Roder, "Puna-Stadt: Besuch in der Tamilschule," IB 2/2 (April 1938): 16. See also John B. Haas to Felix A. Planner (Poona, 13th August 1940), AMPSJ, IB. Puna-Briefe (alte).

As for the missionary objective of winning over converts to Catholic Faith from among the students, the school served as an effective means. As far as the Tamils are concerned St. Anthony's School was undoubtedly an opening to their community for pastoral care and further evangelization. Since direct evangelization was out of question, it was through catechism classes that the basic tenets of Catholic Faith were imparted to the children, who were generally very docile. In spite of the fact that there were no compulsions to come to the school, they came with much enthusiasm and showed exceptional readiness to attend catechism classes.[522] Moreover, generally, they were strongly attracted to the Christian way of life and showed their willingness to be baptized. But often their families were obstacles on the road. In such cases they were told to talk to their parents and explain that acceptance of Christianity would only make them obedient and good children. This strategy often worked. On this respect John B. Haas commented: "Often the conversion of a family begins with a child."[523]

A second aspect of his pastoral care was dealing with cases of marriage rectification. In the first two years he counselled nearly 50 marriage cases, of which some 10-15 were rectified and blessed by him. From the statistics, it may appear a meagre number. But its significance lies in the fact that such efforts were being made by John B. Haas right amidst the Hindu society. I need not elaborate on the point. Cultural and moral habits are generally hard to change in a society.[524]

Another aspect of the pastoral of Hass was his attempt at rejuvenation of Catholic life in the Tamil community. The community became more vibrant. It began to feel a greater sense of belongingness in the larger Catholic community of Poona. These changes were begun to be observed already during the first decade of his work. A very tangible expression of the same may be seen from the fact that the number of the Catholics from among them began to grow rapidly as never before, so that John B. Haas reported: "The Tamil chapel is becoming too small for the growing flock of the Tamil Christians."[525] It was not only their numerical growth but more so their quality in Christian way of life. This

---

522 See Haas, "Volk ohne Heimat," 28.

523 Haas, "Meine Tamilseelsorge," 58.

524 See Haas, "Und was geht bei den Tamil-Leuten?" 255.

525 Haas, "Meine Tamilseelsorge," 58.

seemed to have been a matter of great consolation for the Jesuits as this report says:

> Another great consolation for the priest is the faith of the Tamilians. Even when they go back to the South, hardly does anyone of them seem to go astray from the Church. Often as they come back they wish to bring back their life in order. But naturally often it does not go as they wish. Then they feel disturbed about these. ... But when there seems to be no other way, they call upon the priest and make peace with God.[526]

At the personal level, the sense of consolation and achievement experienced by John B. Haas in reaching out to the Tamil community is well captured in his own testimony:

> I have been 7 years here in Poona. When people see the externals alone, then I can say: repaired the Church, built schools, and established widow homes. The other aspects are not easy to be taken into consideration by people. But people do see the inner growth of the souls. How many of my poor Christians are exemplary in many ways that could bring joy to anyone. Of course there is a shady side of the story as well. The Christians live amidst the pagan atmosphere, which does exert influence on them.[527]

Such an experience of the inner growth of the Tamil migrants in Christian faith was marked by others as well. For example Haas has noted: "Once a European was present on the occasion of the First Holy Communion for the Tamil children. Later he testified: 'I have gone around a lot. But I have never seen the children who received their First Holy Communion with such a profound devotion.'"[528]

The foregoing survey thus reveals an important area of involvement of the Jesuits. Unfortunately the correspondences and other sources of information are conspicuously silent on the apostolate among the Tamil migrants. It seems that these were handed over to the diocesan clergy and could not be recovered for the Jesuit archives. In any case a good beginning was made by John B. Haas in according with the charism of the Society of Jesus to opt for the work among the marginalized sections of the society.

---

526 Haas, "Volk ohne Heimat," 28.

527 John B. Haas to George (?) (12th November 1941), AMPSJ, IB. Puna-Briefe (alte).

528 Haas, "Volk ohne Heimat," 27.

3.7. Conclusion

As noted above, the methods, priorities and options of the B-PM do not seem to be anything extraordinary. Practically all the methods and strategies, priorities and options seem to be falling under the common practices followed in all the Jesuit missions. Yet, what is worth noting is the peculiar geographic as well as socio-cultural contexts of the place and people. The implementation of even the conventional strategies was often not easy. An example might serve to clarify the point. We have mentioned the regular contact with the target groups as a missionary strategy. One would not be able to appreciate the real worth of it unless he has some idea of the geographical spread of the mission stations. Under the jurisdiction of the mission station at Songaon, for example, some of the villages were as far as 40 or 50 kilometers from the mission station. The condition of the roads and the means of transport, namely bullock-carts or bicycles, made their accessibility even more difficult. Yet, efforts were made to keep regular contacts with the people, which was absolutely necessary to preserve and promote the Christian community. The same argument may be applied to other strategies as well. Among the strategies of missionary service, the establishment of educational institutions certainly retains a place of priority as we have discussed elaborately. Without schools there was virtually no possibility of achieving a breakthrough in the society. Only through the application of all the methods and strategies simultaneously in various areas of operation that the objective of expansion and consolidation of the Mission could be achieved.

We also noted that there was continuity and change in the application of strategies and determining of priorities over a period of time. While education remained one of the principal strategies of missionary service, the efforts at inculturation through Christian art and paintings were newer approaches to make the message of Christianity more accessible and comprehensible to the local people. The language of images and visuals, although not entirely new as theatre and plays were already popular among people, added another dimension to presentation of the mystery of Christian faith through these media so that the people could comprehend.

Chapter-4

Collaborators, Co-workers and Helpers in the Mission

4.1. Introduction

The role of collaborators, co-workers and helpers in Jesuit missions began to be recognized more in the post-Vatican II decades. They have always played an important role in the Jesuit missions in India.[529] Ignatius of Loyola, the founder of the Jesuit Society, himself was in favour of involving more and more collaborators and helpers in the ministries. However, this ideal was not fully realized during his life-time, but was followed more earnestly by the Jesuits in the subsequent centuries, especially after the Restoration of the Society of Jesus (1814). The data on personnel at the turn of the millennium (2000), illustrate this. Some 2000 schools for both boys and girls were operating under Jesuit auspices in 56 countries worldwide, involving 10,000 Jesuits, nearly 100,000 lay collaborators, and more than 1.5 million students."[530] These figures are an indication that the Jesuits across the world not only began to draw inspiration from the charism of Ignatius of Loyola and his first companions, but also grew in awareness of the greater need of involving lay-collaborators and other co-workers in their missions. Specifically speaking of the lay-collaborators in Jesuit missions, we

529 See Peter B. Ely, "Partnership in Mission: The Future of Jesuit Higher Education," in Promise Renewed: Jesuit Higher Education for a New Millennium, ed. Martin R. Tripole (Chicago: Loyola Press, 1999), 177.

530 Roger C. Bergman, Catholic Social Learning: Educating the Faith that does Justice (New York: Fordham University Press, 2011), 21.

come across with a more authoritative articulation of this ideal, laying a special emphasis on it, only in the 34th General Congregation of the Society of Jesus (hereafter, GC 34) in its 13th Decree, under the theme "Cooperation with Laity in Mission."[531] This chapter deals with various collaborators, co-workers and helpers such as Diocesan clergy, Religious Sisters, lay catechists and so on, who were worked with the Jesuits7+ of Poona Mission.

4.2. The Coadjutor-Brothers (Lay-Brothers/*Coadjutores Temporales*)

At the very outset, I would like to discuss the role of the Jesuit Lay-Brothers (addressed simply as Brothers) in this Mission for a specific reason. First, the Jesuit Society is a clerical Order, but there have been temporal coadjutors to assist the priests in their ministries right from the beginning. A band of committed and dedicated Coadjutor Brothers, who are often described as Lay Brothers,[532] have always been a great asset to Jesuit missions across the world. They have functioned as administrators of houses, institutions, builders of buildings, agriculturalists, teachers, and as skilled men in a variety of occupations.

The Old Society had witnessed their fruitful contribution in many and varied ways. The Brothers were well-trained in various skills and trades. Consequently they were a great asset for various missions and their presence was often indispensable. One gets a glimpse into an array of their trades and skills from the following account:

> In the ranks of the lay brothers were to be found barbers, surgeons, apothecaries, turners, smiths, weavers, carpenters, tailors, metal workers, architects, cabinetmakers, bakers, cooks, sculptors, painters, bell casters, masons, locksmiths, cloth-makers, goldsmiths, organ-makers, watchmakers, fullers and tinsmiths.[533]

However, in the history of the Society, their mention has remained only in passing or within the context of some other related points. In a substantial number of books on Jesuit missions, however, one gets

531 [531] See Ely, "Partnership in Mission," 177.

532 See John W. O'Malley et al., eds., The Jesuits II: Cultures, Sciences and the Arts, 1540-1773 (Toronto/Buffalo/London: University of Toronto Press, 1999), 640. See also Malachi Martin, *Jesuits: The Society of Jesus and the Betrayal of the Roman Catholic Church* (New York: Simon & Schuster Paperbacks, 1987), 190.

533 As quoted in Eduardo C. Fernandez, La Cosecha: Harvesting Contemporary United States Hispanic Theology (1972-1998) (Minnesota: The Liturgical Press, 2000), 12.

a mention of the contribution of the Jesuit Brothers just in passing. Only a few have been generous enough to acknowledge their roles comparatively in a greater detail.[534]

It would be undermining them if they would be described only as co-workers. As members of the same Society, they need not be treated separately. They have been missionary brethren of the Jesuit Fathers. In the history narratives of B-PM, their roles have not been adequately highlighted. Hence, I deliberately earmark this section for them, because the contribution of the Brother missionaries in this Mission had been substantial. It would help the reader to get an idea of the type of missionary work they did and how they utilised their sills in this Mission. Their contribution to the Mission was in no way inferior to that of the Fathers. On the contrary every landmark in this missionary enterprise was achieved as a result of collaborative work among the Fathers and Brothers.

The Brothers of Bombay-Poona Mission shared the rich legacy of the German Coadjutor Brothers in the global mission of the Society of Jesus. The German Coadjutor Brothers had gained the reputation of

534 See for example Ignatius Echaniz, A Symphony of Love: Stories of Jesuit Brothers (Anand: Gujarat Sahitya Prakash, 1985); George J. Anderson, With Christ in Prison: Jesuits in Jail from St. Ignatius to the Present (New York: Fordham University Press, 2000), Takao Abe, The Jesuit Mission to New France: A New Interpretation in Light of the Earlier Jesuit Experience in Japan (Leiden: Koninklijke Brill NV, 2011); A Priest of the Society of Jesus, "The Jesuit Lay Brother: A Word to Young Men," Irish Messenger, 1927. These may be cited as random examples on the topic. As for a historical background on the significance of the roles played by the Coadjutor Brothers in the missions, the example of the founders of the Jesuit Reductions of Paraguay may be cited. They (the Jesuits of Paraguay) acknowledged that the great achievements in the mission would not have been possible, were it not for the most tangible contribution of the Jesuit Brothers. Such significance of their presence in the missions was not limited to the Old Society. Indeed it remained intact even in the Restored Society, barring the fact that their vocation has drastically fallen in many parts of the world. Once again the claim may be substantiated with a few examples. One of the most glorious missions of the Restored Society, related to the German Provinces has been the Zambesi Mission in Africa. The German Coadjutor Brothers made a great mark in various fields there. They were truly faithful companions to Jesuit Fathers. I sum, almost all the missions of the German Province grew into flourishing missions, largely due to the generous contribution of the Brothers. A South Dakota missionary, Fr. Florian Digmann, testified the same: "Our mission owes its prosperity in large part to the Brothers whom the old German Province had magnanimously sent to us." Rose Enochs, The Jesuit Mission to the Lakota Sioux: A Study of Pastoral Ministry, 1886-1945 (Cansas City: Sheed & Ward, 1996), 29. See also "Laienbriider in Heidenmission," IB 1/11 (July 1932): 73; Joseph Kriiinz to Karl Brust, German Assistant to the Superior General (Feldkirch, 14th June 1937), ARSI, Germ. Sup. 1012-1, 17.

disciplined, hard-working and well-trained people in various trades. Because of such a reputation, the German Provinces were receiving numerous requests for Coadjutor Brothers from their missions around the world, in beginning of the twentieth century. Precisely for this reason that "in Landsberg am Lech there was a section of the novitiate specifically meant for the Lay Brothers aspiring to go to mission lands."[535] The German Provinces did supply a substantial number of them to various missions, the Bombay-Poona Mission being one of them.[536]

The Coadjutor Brothers in this Mission have rightfully been called as the "right hands of the missionaries."[537] The presence of the Brothers was apparently much stronger before World War I broke out. Their departure from the mission field at the breaking-out of the war had created no less void than by the departure of the Professors and Priests. A series of requests followed thereafter from the Poona Mission to Germany and Switzerland to send again Coadjutor Brothers to the mission. But, until the Mission was reorganized (1921), only Brother Moritz (Maurice) Emmenecker could stay on in Kendal as only he had managed to acquire citizenship of British India. And it may be rightfully claimed that he, with his Carpet Weaving Unit, had heroically sustained the poor mission during the ten most difficult years, when the mission had to manage with only a limited number of missionaries.[538] A little later a few more Brothers arrived. But their number remained rather limited. According to an account there were just 11 Brothers during the long period from 1928 to 1988 if German and Swiss origin: "From our Assistancy there were 6 Swiss and 5 German [Brothers]. The Swiss Brothers were mostly specialized in architecture and building trade."[539] The 11 Brothers mentioned were those "who were more than 50 years in the Poona Mission"[540] implying thereby that there were still more

535 Enochs, The Jesuit Mission to the Lakota Sioux, 29.

536 See Knttnz to Brust (Feldkirch, 14th June 1937), 17.

537 Augustine Rosch to the Superior General (Munich, 20th January 1937), ARSI, Germ. Sup. 1021, 1-2. See also "Laienbriider in der Heidenmission," 72.

538 "Laienbriider in der Heidenmission," 72.

539 Anthony Herbert, "Die Jesuitenbriider aus der Schweiz und Deutschland in der Pune Mission von 1928 bis 1988," ADPSJ, *Abt. 45, Nr. 781,* 108 (38).

540 Ibid.

Brothers in the Mission who had not stayed for such a long period of time.

How did the Brothers see their call of the mission? This is an important question to consider. For, only because of their commitment to the call that they could contribute what they did. The citation below substantiates the point:

> To the question: Why be a Brother? Then one answer: To serve God with his hands. This is a fine motive. To put his skills into the service of God by helping to build the Church of God! ... The Brothers in the Puna mission are famous for their ability and solid virtue in India, and are therefore also requested by various missions. Their life epitomizes a life of sacrifices, but also of indescribable joy.[541]

It is beyond the scope of this study to discuss the activities and achievements of each and every Brother in the Mission. It is worthwhile, however, to take a look at some of the important figures among them. Their service represents a broad spectrum of the major areas and contributions as close co-workers and companions of the Jesuit Fathers in the Mission.

Brother Joseph Neukamm naturally deserves a mention in the first place. He was the first one among the Brothers to return to the mission field once the British government re-opened for the missionaries the possibility of re-entering India after World War I. The following account gives us an inkling into his life and contribution to this Mission:

> He came to India for the first time in 1906. As the First World War broke out, he was taken as a Prisoner of War ... finally in 1919 repatriated to his homeland. Br. [Joseph] Neukamm, a professional carpenter, remained faithful to the mission in his heart and was one of the first ones to return to Poona in the beginning of 1930s. There he earned much admiration not only due to his fine skills in carpentry, but more especially because of his singular contribution in extending the magnificent new wing of St. Vincent's School [in Poona].[542]

541 "Diene Gott mit deinen Handen," *Allen Alles: MICA-Sondernummer der Jndischen Bilder' September J947,* 14.

542 "Laienbrilder am Werk," IB 2/2 (March/April 1949): 139. According to another account two correctives in the above account are imperative: Firstly, the date of the second arrival of Br. Neukamm in India apparently is 1928. Secondly, it was Br. Joseph Brandle who was the first one to come back to Poona Mission after World War I. This account seems to be more authentic as it notes the related incidents clearly. For example, it notes that Br.

Br. Joseph Engel (1894-1987) too was a professional carpenter. He was trained at Schiipfheim, Switzerland. He came to India "along with Br. Neukamm in the same ship in 1929."[543] Though his training was in carpentry, he rendered his services mostly as an infirmarian and as a caretaker (minister) of the houses in the Mission. As a committed minister and caretaker of the houses, he ensured that in the kitchen and the house the provisions did not lack, so that the Fathers could carry out their work without having to worry about such things. But it would be an under-representation of the person if we restrict him to these activities alone. In fact, when a need arose, he was promptly at the disposal of the Superiors for many other works. In Harigaon, for example, he took up the work of construction of a new school building and brought it to a successful completion.[544] He was instrumental in constructing many more buildings at various other mission stations, so that Br. Herbert wrote about him: "One can without any exaggeration say that he was a great architect and builder."[545] The following account reveals his other contributions in the context:

> The many buildings he put up at Rahata, Sangamner, Songaon and the beautiful complex at Ghodegaon [a mission station in Poona city] ... are a lasting tribute. Especially if one considers them against the backdrop of the problems one had to face 30-40-50 years ago, with the lack of transport facilities, cement, hardware (I suppose even money) and what have you, then one can only stand back and admire.[546]

Such a band of dedicated Brothers also included Br. Joseph Pfiffner (1910-1961), a native of Sargans in Switzerland. He was gifted with various talents and skills. His professional skills coupled with a tireless stamina for work were exceptional in many ways. He had attained such

---

Brandle came along with Archbishop Henry Doring in 1928 in the same ship and because of the health problems he had to go back to his homeland in 1931. For these and other details, see Herbert, "Die Jesuitenbriider aus der Schweiz und Deutschland," 108 (37). See also "Brandle Joseph: 1892-1953," ABSPGJ, Pa 0025. The series '/fc'in the Archives of the Swiss Jesuits in Zurich designates the collection of personal dossier of the members of the Swiss Vice-Province and later Province.

543 [343] See Herbert, "Die Jesuitenbriider aus der Schweiz und Deutschland," 108 (39).

544 See Noel Oliver, "Br. Joseph Engel (1 Sept. 1894-31 Aug. 1987)," in Deceased Members, 119-120; "Joseph Engel: 1894-1987," ABSPGJ, Pa 0049.

545 See Herbert, "Die Jesuitenbriider aus der Schweiz und Deutschland," 108 (40).

546 See Oliver, "Br. Joseph Engel," in Deceased Members, 120.

a perfection in various skills that he was often described as a virtual architect of Poona Mission, implying thereby that he had contributed in designing a number of houses and buildings in the Mission.[547] As long as the things were within his capacity, he put up the best of his ability to accomplish them by himself. About his ability to manage the situation Pius Geisel, the then Mission Superior writes: "I have made a suggestion to Br. Pfiffner to take a clerk to assist him. But he does not want any. He is an experienced person and I must say that he is capable beyond doubt."[548]

Joseph Pfiffner had designed many buildings and brought their construction to completion, not only in the Bombay-Poona Mission but in some other Jesuit missions in India as well. He has several buildings to his credit, i.e., the novitiate in Andheri in Bombay, a small college in Jaipur (mission of the American Jesuits) and *Dnyanamata* High School, Sangamner.[549] One of his most notable achievements in the Mission has been his singular contribution in erecting the residence of De Nobili College as well as that of the Papal Seminary, Poona.[550] His imprint in the planning and execution of the plan for the building of De Nobili College may be assessed from the fact that he, along with Brothers Anthony Herbert and Joseph Neukamm, was one of the initial architects of De Nobili College. Apparently his entire plan did not get approval from the higher authorities. Yet he did contribute in conceptualising a plan which took into consideration the financial position of the Mission, future possibility of expansion of the buildings and many other such contingencies.[551]

547 "Laienbriider am Werk," 139.

548 Pius Geisel to Felix Plattner (Poona, 19th June 1951), AMPSJ, Superior Poona, P. Geisel.

549 See "Pfiffner Josef: 1910-1962," ABSPGJ, Pa 0247. "Laienbriider am Werk," 139. According to another account his first work in India was the construction of St. Xavier's High School, Jaipur, which was under the American Jesuits. See Herbert, "Die Jesuitenbrilder aus der Schweiz und Deutschland," 108 (41).

550 At present the biggest Scholasticate in Asia. It can house nearly 200 Jesuits at a time. Probably a joint venture of the South Asian Provinces, the initial effort, manpower and logistics largely came from the German-Swiss Jesuits of Bombay-Poona Mission, wherein the contribution of the Coadjutor Brothers has been remarkable. Papal Seminary, on the other hand, is a residence for the Diocesan Seminarians from across India who come to receive theological training at Jnana Deepa Vidyapeeth (Poona), the official name of the Faculty of Theology and Philosophy under the care of the Indian Jesuits.

551 See Pius Geisel to Felix Plattner (Poona, 21st July 1951), AMPSJ, Superior Poona, P. Geisel; Pius Geisel to the General (Poona, 06th July 1951), AMPSJ, Superior Poona, P.

Anthony (Anton) Herbert (1906-1991) was perhaps among the most gifted Brothers in terms of skills. In fact he was a jack of all trades. He was a carpenter, metal worker, fitter, mason, painter and builder in one person. He was probably one of the rare persons who truly deserved to be called master and expert in his field of specialization.[552] His expertise in architecture and building work, along with that of Brothers Pfiffner and Neukamm, was acknowledged in Government circles as well, so that "the Military Technical [university] College sent every year the trainee officers to our Brothers [read Brother Herbert] to learn the technicalities of planning and construction."[553]

In more than one sense he was an inventor as well, as Rudolph Schoch notes: "He was an inventor. For the horse-race track in Poona he made a start-up-machine, which was later patented in his name. He constructed a cooking stove and a water-flushing system. Everything was solid and lasting."[554] No wonder why a companion of his, namely Br. Noel Oliver called him, "a titan of the Goa-Pune Vice-province."[555] Along with Brothers Pfiffner and Neukamm, he formed a trio that accomplished a lot of works in the Mission. "The three work like a team. Externally they always appeared as a trio. Naturally they had their own opinions on certain points. But they resolved everything dialoguing with each other, so that the work never suffered,"[556] wrote Rudolph Schoch. At the cost of great hardships and personal sacrifices, he did an incredible work in Poona Mission. His meticulous planning and execution helped minimise the expenses to a large extent,[557] so that a contributor to *Indische Bilder* wrote: "No wonder, he may have saved the good Sisters from spending nearly hundred thousand Francs, including many disappointments!"[558]

Geisel; Pius Geisel to Felix Plattner (Poona, 21st July 1951) AMPSJ, Superior Poona, P. Geisel.

552 See Eugen Frei, "Nachrufe: Br. Anton Herbert," ABSPGJ, Pa 0116.

553 Ibid.

554 Ibid.

555 Noel Oliver, "A Titan of the Goa-Pune Vice-province," ABSPGJ, Pa 0116.

556 Frei, "Nachrufe: Br. Anton Herbert," ABSPGJ, Pa 0116.

557 See Herbert, "Die Jesuitenbriider aus der Schweiz und Deutschland," 108 (38); See also Frei, "Nachrufe: Br. Anton Herbert," op. cit.; Oliver, "A Titan of the Goa-Pune Vice-province," ABSPGJ, Pa 0016; "Br. Herbert," Nuntii, 2/1992, ABSPGJ, Pa 0116.

558 "Laienbriider am Werk," 139.

The variety of activities undertaken by the Brothers--both big and small--is revealed from yet some more examples. Br. Bernard Tretter (1911-1988), for example, was a trained and experienced gardener.[559] Because of his training he did much to improve the fields, irrigation and especially the milk supply in Sangamner. He possessed considerable knowledge and experience about animal husbandry as well. One of the most tangible signs of Br. Tretter's gardening expertise may be seen in the campus of De Nobili College, Poona. It is a very rocky ground. Yet he managed to grow trees and cleared grounds for cultivation. Today the campus is filled with greenery. His expertise came handy even further when he was transferred to Kendal where a section for agricultural training was opened in the school.[560]

Br. Maximilian Demmeler (1906-1978) demonstrated still another facet of the many and varied contribution of the Brothers in the Mission. He looked after the Carpet Weaving Unit at Kendal and did practically everything, i.e., operating, repairing and maintaining of the machine.[561] "This carpet manufacturing unit was instrumental in availing work and livelihood to a few dozen Christian families; which in turn made a significant contribution to raise and maintain the Christian spirit in the parish community of Kendal, while the Brother is not only the 'Director' but also an educator."[562] Br. Casimir Gatkowski (31.01.1889 - 24.11.1931), besides his regular duties as in-charge of kitchen and garden, etc., was known for his humble and unfailing service at the Mass.[563] Br. Leonard Zimmer, a native of Aachen, Germany was a humble man with not much of formal education. Yet he did marvellous jobs in the

---

559 See "Br. Bernard Tretter," HG 1983, ADPSJ, Abt. 45B-27, Nr. 686; "Laienbriider am Werk," 138-39.

560 See Hans Staffner, "Br. Bernard Tretter (01.01.1911 - 18.10.1988)," in Deceased Members, 120. For more information, see Herbert, "Die Jesuitenbruder aus der Schweiz und Deutschland," 108 (39). For still further information on the activities of Br. Tretter, see Bernhard Tretter to the Provincial, Augustine Rosch (Srirampur, 29.10.1970); Bernhard Tretter to Eugen Hillengass, Socius to the Provincial (Srirampur, 17th November 1970) ADPSJ, Abt. 45B-27, Nr. 686. For the replies of the Provincial and Eugen Hillengass to Br. Bernard Tretter, see Eugen Hillengass to Bernard Tretter (Munich, 09th November 1970); (Munich, 26th November 1970) ADPSJ, Abt. 45B-27, Nr. 686.

561 See Herbert, "Die Jesuitenbriider aus der Schweiz und Deutschland," op. cit.; "Br. Maximilian Demmeler: 22.03.1906-29.04.1978," in Deceased Members, 85.

562 "Laienbrtider am Werk," 140.

563 See Joseph Fell, "Br. Casimir Gatkowski (31.01.1889-24. 11.1931)," in Deceased Members, 10.

Mission. To his credit goes the beginning of the evangelization among a nomadic and criminal Tribe known as 'Katkaris.'[564]

Sadly his efforts did not materialize in winning them all to Christianity, yet a beginning was made. His efforts brought a lot of changes in their lives. They got settled in a place leaving behind age-old nomadic way of life. They also amended their criminal behaviour. He did so through his regular contacts and constant dialogue. He taught them handicraft and availed them job and livelihood in the Carpet Weaving Unit that he had started solely in order to help them.[565] He had earned such a place in their hearts that at his death "they kept a vigil by his body whole night and bitterly wept for him ... For he was a father to them ... 35 years long was he their best friend, their doctor and faithful father; had prayed, worked and lived for them alone."[566] A further testimony is worth noting in his case: "Bishop Alban Goodier said of this remarkable man, “He was one of the greatest missionaries I had ever met."[567]

Besides these, there were a few more Brothers in the Mission who in their humble ways made significant contributions towards the growth of the Mission. A major missionary enterprise which came into existence later, namely, St. Joseph' Technical Institute, had a huge imprint of Brothers' presence. Br. Otto Widmer (1924-1984), for example was closely associated with its growth and development. This institute has been instrumental in heralding a lot of transformation among the school drop-outs.[568]

It would be quite interesting to note as to see whether such a varied contribution of the Brothers were acknowledged by all. In general the answer would be in the affirmative. But often they remained as silent workers. Curiously Archbishop Doring did not seem to appreciate their presence in the Mission. Francis Xavier Hayler, then Provincial of Southern German Province writes: "I have offered to send always

564 Because of their nomadic life-style, they did not have a fixed source of income. Consequently they resorted to theft and burglary for their survival. Hence they had earned a notoriety and so the British Government designated as them as a “criminal tribe”. See K. S. Singh, ed., People of India: Maharashtra, Part 2, Vol. XXX (Mumbai: Popular Prakashan Pvt. Ltd., 2004), 965-969; P. K. Mohanty, Encyclopedia of Primitive Tribes in India, Volume 1 (Delhi: Kalpaz Publications, 2004), 269.

565 See ADPSJ, Abt. 45B-26, Nr. 1509.

566 Ibid.

567 [567] Deceased Members, 16.

568 See Noel Oliver, "Br. Otto Widmer," in Deceased Members, 119.

many Brothers - trained [artisans and] craftsmen, faithful and wonderful people. But Bishop [Henry Doring] does not like them, although they can render the best of services. For, [according to Archbishop Doring] they are too costly."[569] From the context of the letter it is quite apparent that the *costliness* is implied not only in monetary terms but also the entire living cost. It may be inferred thereby that in the opinion of Archbishop Doring a missionary was the one who alone was directly engaged in the work of preaching and teaching in the most conventional sense of the word.

At the end, it would be worthwhile also to examine how the presence of the Brothers contributed to the over-all missionary enterprise. As companions of the Jesuit Fathers, they were more than co-workers in the Mission. Their contributions as Brothers were not in any sense inferior to those of the Fathers. Through their skills and expertise, the natives learnt not only manual skills but the worth and dignity of manual works itself as well.[570] The visible signs of progress of the mission, i.e., churches, schools, hospitals and other buildings besides other infra-structural developments largely go to the credit of the Brothers. Moreover, inspired by the good example of these committed Brothers some local youth began to be attracted to their ideals.[571]

The above discussion shows well how beautiful and important the work of the Coadjutor Brothers in the Mission was. In the Society of Jesus, they received careful ascetic and vocational training so that they were able to work independently in every possible way later. Especially in the missions it was also granted them to develop all their skills and achieve great things for the kingdom of God.[572]

The imprint of the presence of Brothers was everywhere--from most humble works to most skilled professions. They were present alongside the Fathers at every place: from kitchen to fields, from classrooms to prayer rooms.[573] About their vocation the following tribute is fitting in this context: "It is wonderful to serve the mission as a Coadjutor Brother.

569 Francis Xavier Hayler to the General (Munich, 09.05.1934), ARSI, Germ. Sup. 1010-V, 16.

570 See Enochs, The Jesuit Mission to the Lakota Sioux, 29.

571 Herbert, "Die Jesuitenbrilder aus der Schweiz und Deutschland," 108 (37).

572 [372] "Laienbriider in der Heidenmission," 74.

573 For a similar discussion of the presence of Brothers in a specific context, see George M. Anderson, With Christ in Prison: Jesuits in Jail from St. Ignatius to the Present (New York: Fordham University Press, 2000), 65-75.

But neither is it so romantic. On the contrary it is highly challenging and demanding. Only the people, for whom the matters of God are sincerely the highest of all values, can be fitting instruments for the missions."[574]

4.3. Diocesan Clergy

The diocesan clergymen, though few in number, were valuable collaborators in the Poona Mission, especially during the interregnum when the German and Austrian Jesuits were interned. Some of the correspondences of the Superiors of the Mission and Administrators Apostolic reveal that in spite of the return of many Jesuits to the mission field by 1927, the problem of insufficient personnel still persisted even until the end of the 1920s. It will be shown in the next chapter that a number of missionaries could return to the mission field only in early 1950s. Yet, the problem persisted even later.

In a summary overview, prepared in 1959, by Maximilian Riklin, the Administrator Apostolic of Poona, one gets a picture of the situation: "In 1914, Poona was staffed by 25 Fathers S.J., 13 Secular Priests and 2 Brothers; in 1922-23 by 14 Fathers S.J., 18 Secular Priests and 2 Brothers. More than half of the clergy had been borrowed from other Dioceses or Missions ... In 1929 there were 21 [Jesuit] Fathers, 17 Secular Priests and 6 Brothers working in the Diocese."[575] A fact that clearly emerges from these figures is the collaboration between the Jesuits and the diocesan clergy. Yet, we must hasten to state that the nature of collaboration, especially in the wake of the internment and repatriation of the Jesuits, was largely in the sense of filling-up the gaps.

One of the primary reasons for the same was that a majority among the new-comers from Europe were Scholastics (Jesuits in formation for priesthood) who needed first to complete their studies before they could be sent to mission stations or institutions. That the question of personnel was acute may be concluded from a letter of Maximilian Riklin, the then Administrator Apostolic of Poona:

> What remains to be seen in the background here is the poor condition of the mission among the pagans [non-Christians] for which we need missionaries urgently, as I shall try to show it. It is true that a number of priests were sent to the mission but since they are not much of use for the purpose, it is bound to cause bitter resentments

574 "Laienbrüder in der Heidenmission," 74.

575 Maximilian Riklin, "State of the Poona Diocese," AMPSJ, Pune Alt.

> on both sides. Moreover, it would amount to a bitter mockery of the situation if one wanted to come to the help of the poor mission in such a manner. There is not the slightest doubt that the actual mission among the non-Christians has suffered a big setback during the last 12 years ... I cannot go into details here. But it is obvious that with a population of over 12,000 converts, coupled with great distances [to the villages], the small Christian communities, the poor transport system, a substantial number of new Christians who do not have a school with a catechist in the neighbourhood and entirely non-Christian surroundings, etc., make it impossible for a missionary to do justice to the work. For the purpose, in fact, not less than 12 missionaries would be required to attend to the annual pastoral care of Christians who already have been converted and to explore possibilities of further expansion of the work.[576]

A spontaneous question here is this: Did such arrangements fulfil the purpose? We come across with some correspondences dealing with the issue that seem to present the unsatisfactory situation. A letter of Maximilian Riklin may be quoted: "What help can I get? From the secular clergy of the diocese no suitable priest can be drawn. We got repeatedly priests from other dioceses and a number of them arc at present in various parishes; but, naturally, not the best are lent, and hardly any would make good missionaries."[577] Similarly Francis Schubiger was unambiguous in pinpointing the difficulties arising out of the new arrangements: "The secular clergy called instead is not enough to fill the gaps, neither in quantity nor in quality. To the latter one the less said the better."[578] Elsewhere, Archbishop Henry Doring wrote: "I begin to mark slowly among my secular clergy a spirit of freedom that causes me worry."[579]

In spite of such difficulties, a good understanding with the diocesan clergy for furthering the cause of the mission during this critical phase

---

576 Maximilian Riklin to the Provincial (Poona, 27th December 1926) AMPS J, Pune Alt.

577 Maximilian Riklin to the Superior General (Bombay, 6th September 1923), ARSI, Bombay. 1004-1, 13.

578 [378] Francis X. Schubiger to the Superior General (Sangamner, 8th February 1924), ARSI, Bombay. 1004-IX, 5.

579 Archbishop Henry Doring to the Superior General (Poona, 25th December 1930), ARSI, Poona. 1004-111, 1. See also Francis X. Schubiger to the Superior General (Sangamner, 13th November 1924), ARSI, Bombay. 1004-IX, 16; Pius Geisel to Felix A. Plattner (Poona, 26th June 1924), AMPSJ, Superior Poona P. Geisel.

was largely achieved. The contribution of the diocesan clergy was valuable, especially given the critical period when their assistance in the Mission was sought.

How far were the Jesuits successful in establishing a rapport with the diocesan clergy who came for their assistance during the period of scarcity of Jesuit personnel? In general a good understanding existed among them. But the contrary of the same was not too seldom either. The answer is undoubtedly in the affirmative to a large extent. Occasionally, however, a certain amount of dissatisfaction among the Jesuits with regard to the performance and certain aspects of the life-style of the diocesan clergy was evident. In certain cases a trust-deficit too appeared against the diocesan clergy. Their appointment as Superiors and Parish Priests, for example, were taken with apprehension by certain Jesuits. Francis Schubiger, for example, raised questions and apprehensions as regards the appointment of a diocesan clergy, Fr. Gonsalves as the Superior of the mission station at Kendal. To top it all Bishop Doring himself did not seem to have developed a trust towards the diocesan clergy as far as their leadership quality, integrity and commitment as priests, etc. were concerned. His attitude on this issue is reflected in a letter of Pius Geisel, who wrote the same in the context of his possible resignation: "His Exc[ellency] formerly said he would resign at the age of 80. During the year he told me, he considered it his duty to remain in office till the end of the war. Now he says, *he was afraid the Holy See would appoint as his successor a secular priest* and so he believes he must hold on."[580] From these instances it would not be wrong to conclude that a lack of trust towards the diocesan clergy did prevail among the Jesuits quite strongly.[581] This characteristic proves that the Jesuits often came cross with their collaborators in a proclaimed sense of superiority vis-a-vis the diocesan clergy coming from India. It is virtually impossible to assess the fact as to how the diocesan priests perceived their relationship with the Jesuits. For, once again, the correspondences in our possession originate entirely from the Jesuits.

580 Pius Geisel as Consultor of the Mission to the Superior General (Rahata, 11th May 1947), ARSI, Poona. 1004-XVI, 18. The emphasis on the text is mine.

581 See Francis X. Schubiger to the General (Sangamner, 13th November 1924) ARSI, Bombay. 1004-IX, 16b (2); Francis X. Schubiger to the General (Sangamner, 8th February 1924), ARSI, Bombay. 1004-IX, 5(2); Pius Geisel to Felix Plattner (24.6.1948), AMPSJ, Superior Poona, P. Geisel.

One of the basic complaints about the diocesan clergy that occurs rather frequently in the correspondences of the Jesuits have been the misuse of finances allotted for the purpose of maintaining the mission stations. Francis Schubiger reported of an instance: "Then I began to find out that Fr. Rodricks spent the money sent to him for the pay of the masters for other purposes and left out for what it was sent ... On my return (after 4 months' absence) I found that Fr. Rodricks had never made an entry in the account book etc., etc."[582] Occasionally, a few other problems too appear to have surfaced. To quote Schubiger again: "Rev. Fernandes because of the habit of drinking was suspended and has been sent here [Sangamner]."[583] In addition to this aspect, what seems to have earned the diocesan clergy a certain amount of displeasure of the Jesuits was their occasional lack of sense of responsibility, as may be concluded from a letter of Archbishop Henry Doring: "I only begin to mark that some of my diocesan priests begin to go about as if they were independent. This worries me a lot."[584]

A third instance, which is even more telling in its details, would illustrate that such types of cases may not have occurred in the 1920s alone. For cxample, an instance pertaining to a priest (name unknown but it becomes clear from the letter that he came from Mangalore) working at the mission station in Hubli (in the Canarese Mission in the present State of Karnataka). He claimed as his own the diocesan school attached to the mission station. While the matter was sought to be settled at the diocesan level, he went to the extent of filing of a legal petition against Bishop Andrew D'Souza (Poona), which he lost. Yet he did not give up and went for an appeal at the High Court. This may certainly be considered as an aberration. Yet, it does prove the point that the Jesuits needed to face such kind of cases as well. Similarly, there were some other cases of similar nature pertaining to the diocesan Clergy working in the Jesuit Mission.[585] Pius Geisel reported about these incidents in the following words:

---

582 Francis X. Schubiger to Archbishop Alban Goodier (Sangamner, 8th February 1924), ARSI, Bombay. 1004-1X, 5.

583 Francis X. Schubiger to the Superior General (Sangamner, 13th November 1924), ARSI, Bombay. 1004-IX, 16(b)(3).

584 Archbishop Henry Doring to the Superior General (Poona, 25th December 1930), ARSI, Poona. 1004-111, lb (8). See also Pius Geisel to the Superior General (Poona, 18th March 1953), ARSI, Poona. 1005-1, 41.

585 Pius Geisel to the Superior General (Poona, 18th March 1953), ARSI, Poona. 1005-1, 41.

> The scandal [claiming a diocesan school as one's own] is great. A second scandal is brewing up: the priest of Mahabaleshwar, also a Mangalorean, is in revolt for the last three years and His Lordship [Andrew D'Souza] asked me to intervene. Fr. Jerome D'Souza is going to Mahabaleshwar today to try a settlement, in spite of the telegram I received yesterday: visit of Fr. Jerome cancelled until Bishop pays me 700 Rs for church protection.[586]

There are indications in the same letter that Bishop Andrew D'Souza was willing to pay the amount demanded by the above-mentioned priest. He, however, was prevailed upon by Pius Geisel in order not to give in to a blackmail. In spite of paying a substantial amount of money, i.e., Rs. 300 as monthly pension and Rs. 2500 as re-imbursement for repair of the church, etc., the priest seems to have considered the church as his personal property. The case was finally resolved in the court in favour of Bishop Andrew D'Souza. But the incident was enough to reveal some of the unpleasant cases in this regard.[587]

It would be unfair to generalise such issues to include all the diocesan clergy who worked in the Poona Mission at one moment or the other. Yet, the mention of the same in the formal correspondences does communicate this reality prevalent around this time. The larger question, however, that emerges here is: how can we evaluate the aspects of collaboration between the Jesuits and the diocesan priests as co-workers in the mission? A tentative answer to the same appears to boil down to one conclusion, namely the Jesuits of this period seemed to have closed the possibility of working in collaboration. It is fairly clear that they never considered the value of working in collaboration with others till the point when the situation arrived at a dead-end. Collaboration, for the worth of it, had probably never occurred as an effective method to implement. We arrive at this conclusion also from the fact that in the peace-time, the number of diocesan priests in the mission working in close collaboration with the Jesuits was very meagre.

4.4. Religious Sisters

The Religious Sisters were an important group of collaborators in mission. Their role in this phase of the mission is well underlined by Felix Plattner as he wrote: "The Church in India and for that matter

586 Ibid.

587 Ibid.

all the missions in general cannot be imagined today without the cooperation of the Sisters. In regard to numbers they surpass the Priests and Brothers. They have taken a lead in the field of philanthropic activities and women's education."[588] The remark, although made in the general context of the presence of Women Religious in the missions in India, gives an important indication to the areas of their involvement, namely charitable works with a special focus on women's education.

The policy of fruitful co-operation with Women Religious Congregations in various missionary endeavours has been stressed since the 19th century. Prior to that, it was always believed that the hardships of sea voyages and the dangers of various descriptions in mission fields were beyond the capacity of women to overcome. The deeper reason, however, lay elsewhere, namely women Religious Life as it had developed since the Middle Ages was perceived to be strictly within the confines of cloisters. Beginning with the 19th century, this kind of perception began to change, which was the result of a general perception that conditions in the far-off mission countries had been improved due to the presence of various European colonial powers. Thus began the phase when more and more Religious Sisters, both from older and newer Congregations, appeared in mission-fields, so much so that soon missions became almost unthinkable without them.[589]

As regards the of Women Religious as co-workers in the Poona Mission, the first point that we discover is that their collaboration with the Jesuits have been rather well defined right from the beginning. As indicated above, their involvement has been in various charitable works with a special focus on women's education. Visiting homes of both the converts as well as others on a regular basis was considered as a special feature of their involvement in this Mission.

We discover that some Religious Sisters were already assisting in the Mission from around the beginning of the 20th century. For example, the St. Anne's Sisters of Hyderabad (Andhra Pradesh) were working at Sangamner mission station from the beginning of the century as we read in an article: "No wonder with such a vision a few brave and upright Italians, the St. Anne's Sisters [of Turin] ... were active

588 Felix A. Plattner, "Die Aufgaben unserer Schwestern," IB 4/5 (1955): 2. See also Felix A. Planner, Catholic Church in India: Yesterday and Today (Allahabad: St. Paul Publication, 1964), 120-21.

589 [589] Plattner, "Die Aufgaben unserer Schwestern," 1.

in the *Maratha* mission for a number of years. They had been invited from the neighbouring Diocese of Hyderabad."[590] The same becomes further apparent from another account: "For a number of years two Congregations had been doing good work in the Diocese of Poona: the Sisters of Jesus and Mary who were running a flourishing Day and Boarding School in Poona itself, and the Daughters of the Cross who had Convents in Panchgani, Hubli and Igatpuri."[591] We may notice from the two citations above, there is no mention of the time-period of their presence in this Mission. We conclude that from the dates mentioned in the articles and letters concerning this.

From the correspondences of the time we surmise that they were smaller in number: "Till then there were only a few Sisters of an Italian Congregation in the Maratha Mission working in Sangamner."[592] In any case, it is clear that the Religious Sisters eventually became invaluable co-workers in the Mission, so that describing the areas of involvement of the Sisters Felix Plattner wrote that "the missions have become almost unthinkable without them."[593]

In the decades subsequent to World War I, Francis X. Schubiger was undoubtedly one of the pillars who played a pivotal role in rescuing and maintaining the Mission. Seeing no possibility of immediate return of the German Jesuits in the mission field, he felt the need to invite coworkers and helpers, both Priests and Religious Sisters to assist in the Mission. He also clearly perceived the situation that it was beyond any possibility to get the Religious Sisters from European countries immediately. Such a condition being one of the primary reasons, besides his own way of promoting vocations among the women of the place, Schubiger decided to found a Congregation of native Sisters. He named the new congregation, *Servants of the Immaculate Conception.* His whole intention was to expand and consolidate the Mission amidst the sheer crunch of the Jesuit personnel. His sincere hope was that once the Sisters took over the work of catechism, family visits and such other pastoral works, the available number of Jesuits and diocesan priests could devote more time in visiting far-off places, besides exploring

590 "Ersehnte Hilfe," 251. See also M. Riklin, "State of the Poona Diocese," AMPSJ, Pune Alt.

591 Riklin, "State of the Poona Diocese," AMPSJ, Pune Alt.

592 "Kurze Nachrichten aus der Mission," IB 1/25 (January 1936): 203.

593 Planner, "Die Aufgaben unserer Schwestern," 2.

further possibilities of expansion of the Mission. Unfortunately the Congregation of Sisters that he had founded could not survive long. Joseph Stark narrates the story:

> The congregation consists of native Sisters called the [Servants of the] Immaculate Conception. Their number was never more than seven, at present only two are left, too little to live and too much to die. They were founded by Fr. [Francis X.] Schubiger with the help and according to the adapted rules of the St. Anne's Sisters. By calling the 3rd congregation the founder, in fact, signed the death warrant for the Native Sisters which of course he never intended or realized. A congregation who [which] is only to consist of *Mahars* will never be a success for various reasons. Their whole standard is too low, and they must have some who come from a better environment. A mission like Sangamner with so many people about is entirely unsuited for a noviceship [Novitiate]. It is almost impossible not to mix with the other women and girls. Another drawback is that there is no Marathi religious literature. Without the knowledge of English it is very difficult [to] give them the proper spiritual food ... It is only a pity that my predecessor [Francis Schubiger] took so much trouble about it. Most likely he has realized towards the end of his life that it will be a failure. He will have got his reward for his good intention and his great efforts.[594]

Thus a noble yet an effort perhaps not well foreseen by Francis X. Schubiger met with a premature death. In spite of its short-lived existence it may be said that the founder, namely Schubiger had a noble intention. It is not hard to imagine the sense of helplessness of a Jesuit left behind with a vast area for consolidation through regular pastoral care. The danger of losing the hamlets and villages already won for the Catholic Church in the absence of a sufficient number of missionaries was not something of an imaginary issue. On the contrary it was something that Schubiger not only experienced, but also lived in his person. Hence, to term his effort of founding a new Congregation of Sisters out-rightly as a failure may not be fully justified. The underlying motive was certainly not to gain a name in any sense of the term. It was purely meant for the preservation of the Mission in the first place. Secondly, it was meant for promotion of vocations among the native women and thus to foster local leadership among them. For, during his long years of working with the

594 Joseph Stark to the General (Sangamner, 1st January 1944), ARSI, Poona. 1004-XIV, 16.

Mahars, Schubiger had realized that the native community needed to be promoted not only in education and social awareness, but also in Church leadership as well and very especially among women. Apparently, it would not be wrong to conclude that he did miss the larger implications of founding a Religious Congregation for women, i.e., finance, infrastructure, personnel for training, scope of its development, etc.

About the general presence of the Religious Sisters in the Mission, one gets a better summary-overview from an annual letter of Archbishop Henry Doring to the Propaganda Fide. What appears rather strange is the absence of mention of the Congregation founded by Schubiger in the list of Congregations. There may be two explanations for the same. Firstly, Archbishop Doring may not have recognized it as a formal Congregation. Secondly, the dwindling status of the number of vocations may also have been the basis for the same. What is true, however, is that one does not find its mention in the list, for reasons best known to Archbishop Doring. Yet, from the letter of Joseph Stark to the Superior General which has been cited above, it is clear that the above-mentioned Congregation was existent till the time the annual letter of Archbishop Doring was written. Here is the list of the Congregations active in the mission until the mid-1930:

Table 4.1: Women Congregations (1935)

Religious Institutes: Women Congregations				
S. No.	**Name of the Congregation**	**No. of Houses**	**No. of Sisters of foreign origin**	**No. of Native-born Sisters**
1	Daughter Servants *(Filiae Ancis)*	3	17	8
2	Sisters of Jesus and Mary	1	7	4
3	Congregations of [the Sisters of] St. Anne's [of Providence of Turin][595] and Oblates of Mary Immaculate *(Congr. S. Annae cum Oblatis)*	1	2	1, 5 (Oblate Sisters)
4	Congregation of the Servants of Jesus	1	0	3

Source: Archbishop Henry Doring to the Prefect of Propaganda Fide (Rome, 22nd May 1935), ASCPF, *Nova Series*, *Vol. 1250*, 662.

595 Ibid.

The figures in the above table very clearly indicate that till mid-1930s there were nearly 50 Religious Sisters assisting in the Mission. This is precisely the phase when the realization of the need of incorporating more and more Religious Sisters as co-workers in the Mission became further expressed. Until this point of time the Sisters who were already present in the Mission were involved in helping out the Jesuits in the following areas: running of the hostels, orphanages and schools besides small scale health-care centres. Besides, their missionary engagements included regular visits to villages, organizing awareness programmes for women, teaching catechism, etc.[596] Thus, their collaboration was significant and counted as inestimable by the Jesuits. Besides, the Jesuits also realized that in order to make a further breakthrough among the natives, many more Religious Sisters with their characteristic feminine approach and understanding of the conditions of the mission fields like Poona were needed. As noted above, establishing a contact with the women-folk presented many challenges on account of certain aspects of societal norms of behaviour. In such circumstances, the Religious Sisters were in the best position to establish contacts with the women-folk, thereby gaining a breakthrough among the other half of society who played the most important role in their families in the right upbringing of children in faith and morals. Against such a backdrop, while drawing from their experiences of working in collaboration with the Sisters, the Jesuits considered their presence as indispensable. We draw such a conclusion from the following account:

> Invaluable services are rendered to the mission work by our Catholic nuns. They understand it well and are capable of practicing the works of Christian charity to a greater perfection [as compared to men-folk], which ultimately prepares the way for the Christian faith everywhere. Moreover, a missionary invariably encounters certain limits in the pastoral care of women in some heathen [non-Christian] countries which he cannot and must not infringe upon. In such circumstances, probably the Sisters alone can make a break-through with a greater success.[597]

Among the areas of their involvement, the second most important area was education of girls. In most of the mission stations, as the

596 See Plattner, "Die Aufgaben unserer Schwestern," 3.

597 "ErsehnteHilfe,"51.

circumstances permitted and as demands were placed on them, they rendered their services in running Primary and Middle Schools. Since the Jesuits had not been able to achieve much success in this regard, the collaboration with the Religious Sisters was thus a new beginning in the education of girls. We have a clear indication that with the passing decades the Jesuits grew ever deeper in realization of their failure in this regard and were desirous of making a start at the earliest so that a concern of such a great importance could be addressed. John B. Eichhorn's concern may be taken as representative of the Jesuits' predicament:

> A grave concern is pressing upon me now. Seven years ago [in 1927] as I returned to the mission field and came to Rahata, where Fr. Henry Diebels had fruitfully worked before the breaking out of the war and our expulsion from the land ... a lot of efforts needed to be put in order to raise the fallen state of affairs in Rahata district. Many new initiatives needed to be undertaken. But now I must take up something, which should have been done long ago, if the war with its devastating negative consequences had not intervened. In Rahata, I must have a convent for Sisters, who first of all must admit the women without any further delay.[598]

The above concern of John B. Eichhorn resulted from his experience wherein he noticed that at the Holy Masses both at the mission station as well as at the outposts, the number of women and especially young girls was always far smaller in comparison with that of men-folk. Going by his description of the state of affairs it may be concluded that he tried his best to address the issue through all the ways and means at his disposal. He himself admitted that he failed to achieve a breakthrough. He lamented therefore saying: "I do not need to explain to you what a good mother means for a Christian family ... how can I educate good Christian mothers for the families when I do not have enough opportunities to educate the girls thoroughly in their faith and morals, and above all, to train them into a truly Christian life with all its implications?"[599]

It must be noted that in the given context of the caste system education of girls was hardly encouraged. Moreover, parents stipulated that female children should practice modesty and frugality in their

598 John B. Eichhorn, "Eine schwere Sorge…," IB 1/20 (October 1934): 157.

599 Ibid.

lifestyle. From their early age they were burdened with much work in the family. As for the disposition of the parents to send their children to schools there was clearly a double standard. In the case of boys, the parents were fairly open to send them to schools, whereas in the case of girl children they were largely unwilling and not well disposed. The first reason lay in their understanding of the role of girl children in their families. For example, they took it for granted that female children were basically meant for helping out in household works, looking after their younger siblings, helping out in cooking and doing other household chores. These things apart, the more fundamental reason was their resistance to send their female children to schools with co-education system. Co-education system was not in agreement with their understanding of the social space for male-female interaction. In their perception, boys and girls needed to share separate space in order to be brought-up in right mores of behaviour.[600] Although not couched in these precise words, the remark of Joseph Stark is fitting here: "We must inculcate a deeper sense of Christianity among our girls. We need, therefore, a school for them, because the *Mahars* do not wish to send their girl children to our boys' schools. Instead they prefer to keep them back at home to look after their younger siblings or for other household works."[601]

The Jesuits were aware of the fact that a failure to address such a resistance among the *Mahars* was tantamount to neglecting the right to education for girls. This implied that they were bound to fail in imparting the message of what their mission in effect aimed at, namely bringing about transformation in the entire society. The first step towards the same was to provide education to all, which was not possible without introducing schools also for girls. Without facilities for education of girls, the possibility of imparting Christian teaching among the women-folk could not be imagined. In the context of the growth of the mission, such an aspect was a serious lacuna. Only the presence of the Religious Sisters • could alter the situation, so thought the Jesuits. It was in this context that Eichhorn insisted: "If we had Sisters here, we could admit girls here without a further delay. Then the children could also get to know Christianity properly. This in turn would lead their parents to be

600 Eichhorn, "Eine schwere Sorge 157-58. For a similar content, see also "Eine indische Mutter schreibt an unsere Freunde," IB 1/2 (1956): 2.

601 Stark, "Altes und Neues aus Kendal," 220.

positively disposed towards Christianity."[602] The opinion expressed by Eichhorn is not an isolated one. In fact in the general scenario of India, the need of Sisters in the mission fields became more intensified. This was in view of reaching out to women through various programmes. This is reflected in the text below:

> India needs still a larger number of Sisters. The education of girls and women is entirely in their hands. There is an almost limitless need for charitable works of all kinds. In order to meet these gigantic tasks, the number of our Sisters must triple, even tenfold. If the co-operation of Sisters with various missionary groups appeared indispensable in the past, the same will be twice as much in the future, in the age of equality of women.[603]

The need for Religious Sisters was not felt only by the Jesuits. In fact occasionally people themselves came forward with their wish to open schools for girl children. For example, on the occasion of the laying of the foundation stone for *Dnyanamata Vidyalaya* in Sangamner, while thanking the Jesuits for the school, a Hindu trader spoke: "Your Sisters in the mission teach the girls such beautiful things. Our children at home are not half so educated!"[604] The indication is clear that the need for schools for the girls was felt by people in general as well.

We can clearly see thus that the purpose of schools for girl children was not seen solely in terms of imparting education in the sense of what a secular institute would aim at. Rather it was perceived in terms of imparting Christian teaching. The Religious Sisters with their feminine understanding of issues such as gender-based inequality, patriarchy, etc., were understood to be in a better position to breakdown the societal resistance among the *Mahars.* Their role was even more pivotal against the background wherein the Jesuits as male members had lesser possibility of establishing contacts with women folks in the society.

The preceding paragraphs give us an idea of the factors responsible for the coming of the Sisters in this Mission. But the immediate hurdle was yet to be overcome, namely to get the Religious Sisters at the earliest time possible. Certainly there was no possibility of getting from India. Hence, the Jesuits were unambiguous as to where the Sisters

602 Eichhorn, "Eine schwere Sorge…,"158.

603 "Von unseren Schwestern," IB 6 (1954): 3.

604 Rudolph Schoch, "Dnyanamata," IB 3 (May/June 1948): 2.

must be invited from, i.e., Switzerland and Germany. We come to such a conclusion from the following description:

> And for these schools for girls we need by all means [Religious] Sisters from Switzerland and Germany, who have grown up amidst mountains and plains and along with healthy hearts, also have strong hands, possessing the energy characteristic of the westerners and imbued with Christian understanding of education.[605]

The emphasis on the need to invite the Religious Sisters from Switzerland and Germany may be seen from some other accounts as well. Since the Poona Mission was once again entrusted to the Southern German Province (1929), there was a natural tendency to bring in religious personnel from the Mother Province region. Also, this was a period of revival from the ill-effects of World War I and further expansion and consolidation of mission enterprises. Hence, inviting more co-workers in the Mission was the need of the hour. That aside, the Jesuits of this Mission did not seem to have been familiar with the Sisters in other regions, countries or nationalities. The chances of establishing a rapport in order to begin the work immediately after their arrival in the mission field would be possible only when the Jesuits shared a common socio-cultural background with them. This, no wonder, would facilitate a greater pace in the expansion and consolidation of the mission. The emphasis on the need to invite the Sisters from the above-mentioned nationalities, therefore, was a more pragmatic solution:

> In the first five years after taking over the mission, the main concerns were to accelerate the process of enrolment of young missionaries for the mission field and to revitalize the apostolates affected during and after the Great War. Now, however, more and more Sisters also need to be called in to help, if possible from one congregation, who like the missionaries have their homelands as well as their mission fields in Switzerland and southern Germany.[606]

We must hasten to add that the work of the Sisters was not perceived only as supplementary or for just filling up the gap resulting from the lack of Jesuit missionaries. On the contrary it involved a more fundamental reason. It was also seen as complementary, for the Sisters as female

605 Stark, "Altes und Neues aus Kendal," 219.

606 "Ersehnte Hilfe," 52.

missionaries could complement the work of the Jesuit missionaries. An observation by Hans Staffner is apt here:

> In the first few decades of the beginning of the [Maratha] mission there existed a serious drawback, i.e., there were no Sisters. The living Faith has its roots in the Catholic family. In India, more than anywhere else, is a mother the bearer of religion and culture. In view of a sharp gender division, which is still prevalent to a certain extent, the religious impact on women was comparatively limited, so long as the Fathers alone were employed for the same. Now the work of the Sisters in the mission is indispensable.[607]

Having discussed these issues, let us examine how the Jesuits achieved the purpose of getting more Religious Sisters. The plan of inviting more Sisters, especially from Europe, did not been materialize until Archbishop Henry Doring and other missionaries felt the need of the same. The Archbishop took upon himself the responsibility of initiating the process. As mentioned above, the major mission stations had already boarding homes for boys to look after the orphan children, which had some temporary arrangements for training of catechists as well. The Sisters were needed in order to run these establishments as well, besides doing other areas of engagement. Hence, during his *ad limina* visit in 1935, Archbishop Doring decided to make a visit to Germany and other neighbouring countries in Europe in order to make contact with some congregations of Sisters. In addition he wanted to launch a fund-raising drive along with paying courtesy visits to the benefactors and well-wishers of the Mission. He utilised the occasion for making a personal visit to Mother Catherine, the Superior General of the Franciscan Sisters of Erlenbad, Baden in order to negotiate a prospective collaboration in mission.[608] He had personally seen the nature of their work done in

---

607 Staffner, "Die Katholische Mission in Ahmednagar-Distrikt," AMPSJ, Ahmednagar Mission. See also "The Catholic Mission in Ahmednagar District: 150 Years of German Province Jesuits in Pune Province," (printed matter), PJPA, Jubilee.

608 This Congregation was begun by three women in 1859 working at a small orphanage at Schwarzach in Baden. On account of Bismarck's Kulturkampf which forced the convents to be closed down, the three women emmigrated to America. Initially they stayed for a while in Milwaukee with the German Sisters of Notre Dame (who were also known as the School Sisters of Notre Dame) and then organized their own separate congregation in 1874 in Wisconsin with the name, The School Sisters of St. Francis. The technical name they had adopted for themselves, however, seems to have been Franciscan Sisters of the Order of Penance. They grew rapidly in numbers as well as in influence and began to be recognized as an influential Association of School Sisters of St. Francis in America.

collaboration with the Jesuits of Southern German Province.[609] In his opinion, therefore, they were well-suited to the circumstances and the needs of the Mission. Eventually he succeeded in negotiating with Mother Catherine, who in turn was prompt in executing the agreement and immediately earmarked three Sisters for Poona Mission. Going by the tradition of the time, the Sisters were given a worthy farewell to undertake a challenging task ahead. Full of enthusiasm and zeal the three Sisters--"Sr. M. Helmtrudis (Elizabeth Stadler from Mannheim), Sr. M. Engelharda (Maria Silber from Freiburg/Brisgau) and Sr. M. Eustella (Emma Sauer from Neuenburg in Rheinland)"[610] --departed from their Mother House on 4th December 1936[611] and thus "in December 1936 the first batch of [three] Sisters arrived [in the mission field], followed in February 1937 by a second. They took over the Convent in Sangamner which the Hyderabad Sisters [St. Anne's Sisters] found difficult to provide with personnel. The incumbents settled in the newly built Convent in Rahata."[612] Confirming the news of their arrival John B. Eichhorn wrote on 17th December 1936: "The Sisters happily arrived in Bombay yesterday. I personally could not be away [to receive them], as I needed to prepare for their reception--as the Indians normally do--as well as for the Christmas. Therefore I have sent Fr. [Joseph] Gunter, so that he greets them on our behalf and takes care of their luggage. And the Sisters do have their word."[613] They were accommodated in the newly completed convent close to the Parish Church.[614]

Once the impact of Kulturkampf became less intense, the congregation returned to Germany. Consequently, there exists since 1907 an independent German Province of the congregation, the Motherhouse of the same being based in Erlenbad-Obersasbach, Baden. Ever since, the congregation has been rendering great service in southern Germany and Switzerland, besides in Rhineland and Holland, especially in areas of charitable works and education. See JoEllen MN. Vinyard, For Faith and Fortune: The Education of Catholic Immigrants in Detroit, 1805-1925 (Illinois: Board of Trustees of the University of Illinois, 1998), 130; Joseph Stark to the Superior General (Sangamner, 1.1.1944), ARSI, Poona. 1004-XIV, 16; "Kurze Nachrichten aus der Mission," IB 1/25 (January 1936): 203; "Ersehnte Hilfe," 252.

609 "Kurze Nachrichten aus der Mission," 203.

610 "Ersehnte Hilfe," 252.

611 Ibid.

612 Riklin, "State of the Poona Diocese," AMPSJ, Pune Alt. See also Pius Geisel to Felix Plattner (Poona, 24th July 1951), AMPSJ, Superior Poona, P. Geisel.

613 "Ersehnte Hilfe," 51-52.

614 See John B. Eichhorn, "Eins urns andere," IB 1/28 (October 1938): 232.

Subsequently followed many more Sisters from this Order until 1953 when "the Ursuline Sisters of Brig (Switzerland) came to take over the Girls' Boarding [Home) at Sangamner from the Erlenbad Nuns, who had to return to Germany for lack of personnel. In 1954 the Ursuline Sisters went to Rahata and the Nuns of Jesus and Mary succeeded them in Sangamner. In 1958 the latter also took charge of the new convent in Kendal."[615]

Next in the series came the Sisters of the Third Order of the Apostolic Carmel from Trivandrum (Kerala). They took over a small Convent in Kirkee (in the outskirts of Poona) with the purpose of running a parochial school mostly attended by Tamil children (people migrated from Tamil Nadu). They grew gradually in numbers and took over a few more parochial schools later, i.e., Ahmednagar (near Poona), Bhusaval and Solapur (395 kms north-west and 250 kms south-west of Poona respectively). Similarly the Hospitaller Sisters built a Convent in Nasik Road (206 kms north of Poona) in 1937 to run a small Boarding School and a Day-School. Besides, the above-mentioned Congregations we also come across a mention of still another Congregation basically originating from Tamil Nadu, which is named as Tamilian Sisters in an account. They came much later (1959) in the mission field and took over an orphanage in Bellary (Karnataka) which was opened initially by the then Bishop Andrew D'souza of Poona. Their steady growth in the mission is symbolized by the fact that they made the house that was given to them at their initial arrival into the headquarters and sometime later also opened a Noviciate. An aspect that is quite significant about this Congregation is that it grew in numbers chiefly from among the local candidates.[616]

Beginning with the 1940s, we notice more frequent correspondences by the Jesuits at various mission stations expressing the need for more Sisters. We come across a number of letters to this effect in various archives.[617] These efforts began to bear fruit soon. Consequently, we see a substantial presence of the Religious Sisters in the Mission, which began to be seen even more prominently from the 1950s. This phase

615 Riklin, "State of the Poona Diocese," AMPSJ, Pune Alt. See also Mother M. Catharina to Felix A. Plattner (Obersasbach, Baden, 1st September 1949), AMPSJ, Pune Alt.

616 Riklin, "State of the Poona Diocese," AMPSJ, Pune Alt.

617 See Ludwig Hassle to Felix A. Plattner (Songaon, 17th May 1942), AMPSJ, LB. Songaon-Briefe.

is symbolic of not only the growing presence of the Religious Sisters in the Mission working in collaboration with the Jesuits, but also that of their own growth towards independent existence, of course having the same objective of serving the native people. Thus, Poona began to develop as a centre for various women congregations. The objective of their arrival in Poona, though not spelled out, was quite clear: along with collaborating with the Jesuits in the Mission, they also wanted to grow in numbers so as to be able to take independent apostolates. One arrives at such a conclusion from the fact that they began to open their Noviciates in Poona. Thus "soon Poona became a favourite place for Noviciates; the Sisters of Jesus and Mary opened one in 1951, the Franciscan Missionaries of Mary in 1955."[618] Similarly the Medical Mission Sisters of Wiirzburg Germany under the guidance of their foundress, Mother Anna Dengel too opened a Noviciate in 1952.[619] As for the period until 1954, we get a good overview of the presence of the Religious Congregations of Sisters from the following account:

> In the Poona mission today there are: The Daughters of Cross Sisters in Igatpuri, Panchgani and Deolali, the Sisters of Jesus and Mary in Poona, the Sisters of the Cross in Savantwadi, the Franciscan Sisters of Goa in Nasik, the American Medical [Mission] Sisters in Puna, the Ursulines of Brig in Sangamner and Rahata, the Missionary Sisters of Wiirzburg in Shrirampur, Indian Carmelites in Poona, Kirkee, Ahmednagar, Sholapur and Bhusawal, the Indian Fatima Sisters in Puna and Manmad.[620]

A point that may be taken as relevant in the context of a general concern among the Jesuits, i.e., about promotion of indigenous vocations is strongly seen even among the Religious Sisters. Indeed they too grew awareness that one of their most important tasks was to work among the local youth. Unlike the general disposition among the boys, the number of girls who were desirous of joining the Congregations in Poona began to grow surprisingly. To avail a good training, both in Religious life and professionalism, therefore, became an important goal to be achieved. The presence of three Noviciates of the Sisters in Poona was thus a sign of the growth of the Church and lively faith among its people. All

618 M. Riklin, "State of the Poona Diocese," AMPSJ, Pune Alt.

619 See "Blitzlichter," IB 1 (January/Februar 1952): 61.

620 "Von unseren Schwestern," IB 6 (1954): 3.

these were being achieved due to the simple, yet committed life of the Sisters.[621]

We have mentioned above that the Sisters were involved in running hostels, schools and health-care units, etc. It would be important to point out a few facts about the significance of their contribution towards the general growth of the Mission. The same can be concluded by looking into the particularities of their involvement in the missionary work. Their life among people was full of challenges. But the zeal to devote their lives in the service of the people was a driving force that sustained them in spite of such challenges. Their major contribution in this regard was clearly towards forming Christian families. A vivid picture of their engagement with women and children and with families in general is presented by Hans Staffner:

> They [Sisters] not only look after the girls in the boarding at the mission station, but also manage several of the locally adapted housekeeping schools, kindergartens and maternity homes. Some Sisters ride [by bicycles] 20 to 30 km to far-off villages, often on bad roads. There, they instruct women and children in religion, teach them how to take care of children, cleanliness and hygiene to prevent disease, settle minor disputes and bring joy and love in the families. At a station in which five Sisters work, go two by two in the villages alternately from Monday to Wednesday and from Thursday to Saturday. The Sisters sleep on the floor in the mud-houses, share the food of the people, mostly rice-bread with some spices and vegetable, with no privacy, since the whole family stays in one single room, sometimes together with hens and goats. At times when a family has nothing [to eat], so do the Sisters. It is a very hard and challenging life. The Europeans and even Indians who have leamt something of the western civilization in mission boarding schools can hardly stand it.[622]

As clearly underlined in the above citation the hardships and trials were part and parcel of their missionary life. Precisely these efforts at establishing closeness with people actually gave effectiveness in their work that perhaps could not have been achieved by any other way. As for the Sisters who on health reasons or any other reasons could not

621 Ibid.

622 Staffner, "Die Katholische Mission in Ahmednagar-Distrikt," AMPSJ, Ahmednagar Mission.

travel to villages and afford to remain there day-long, they called in women from the surrounding villages and invited them to participate in the prayers with them. The women thereafter were encouraged to share their experiences. Such common experiences of their faith had very deep impact on people that perhaps would be impossible to transmit even by the best of sermon.[623] The impact of the ministries by the Sisters was not limited within the boundaries of the church. Through their regular contacts in the villages, they effected much impact on the larger society. Thus their contribution towards the general improvement of the social position of Indian woman at large, was acknowledged even by Jawaharlal Nehru, the first Prime Minister of India, in the Parliament, as "absolutely necessary and valuable".[624]

The interaction with the Sisters, in most cases, seem to have left a lasting impact on the people in general but very especially on the girls. In their later years, many of the girls found "the Christian doctrine attractive, simply because the Sisters, through their lives, testify to the purity and love of ideals that they may not have found in Hinduism or Islam or for that matter in many other religions]."[625] However, a decision to convert to Christianity was apparently not easy for them due to their family traditions and societal controls. But they did have a positive idea of what Christian faith means precisely due to the witness value of the lifestyle of the Sisters.

The reader might be curious to know at this point whether the Sisters served the mission entirely out of altruistic motives. Did they ever desire that their own efforts bore fruits in terms of new conversions? Felix Plattner argues that it would be too naive to expect that. Indeed they could not have been different from the erstwhile missionary thinking.[626] In spite of their awareness that all the areas of their involvement offered them ample opportunities for radiating the light of Christian love beyond the limits of religion or caste, it was natural to expect a tangible result in terms of conversions. In this regard, although pertaining to the general

623 Ibid. See also "The Catholic Mission in Ahmednagar District: 150 Years," (printed matter), op. cit.

624 Plattner, "Die Aufgaben unserer Schwestern," 3.

625 Plattner, Catholic Church in India, 122. For a similar content, see Plattner, "Die Aufgaben unserer Schwestern,' 10.

626 Plattner, Catholic Church in India, 127.

context of India, an observation by Felix Plattner is very apt on the role of the Sisters in this Mission:

> In a land where the caste system has held sway for thousands of years, the boundless charity of the Church makes one stop and think. The silent example of the nuns has worked like leaven on India's elite. Some nuns are trifle over anxious to make conversions which they regard as the criterion of success. A small group of Hindus has accused them of this and has even tried to bring their institutions under government control. Others have not gone so far. But they doubt the value of such charitable activities if the actual motive behind them is to effect conversions. Truly disinterested charity, which embraces the poor of all castes and creeds, is bound to have an impact on all unbiased Indians. This is the best way of bearing witness to our faith.[627]

This brief survey, thus, brings to fore that much was achieved by this Jesuit mission thanks to the collaboration of the Religious Sisters. It would be interesting, however, to examine how the relationship between the Jesuits and the Religious Sisters fared. Was it always smooth and free of misunderstandings? On the whole, the answer would be in the positive. Else the Jesuit Mission would not have achieved what it did. Indeed magnificent work was done in collaboration with the Religious Sisters. However, there were certain challenges and frictions in collaborative work. The following account points to the same, although nothing spectic can be surmised from it:

> Our mission is burdened with two Religious Congregations one consisting of German nuns calling themselves Franciscan Sisters of the Order of Penance. But you are badly mistaken if you think that their appearance conveys any idea of penance. T[h]is is already the third congregation within twenty years; the first one were Sisters of the Cross from Annecy, the second one Sisters of St. Anne's of Providence of Turin, and the 3rd one as already mentioned. That means to say that a Jesuit can get along with one congregation of Sisters only for six years. It seems that St. Ignatius anticipated something of this kind.[628]

627 Ibid. For a modified text in German, see Plattner, "Die Aufgaben unserer Schwestern," 2.

628 Joseph Stark to the Superior General (Sangamner, 1st January 1944), ARSI, Poona. 1004-XIV, 16.

Besides, there are some indications to certain occasional disputes that on property that arose between the Jesuits and the Religious Sisters. Pius Geisel, writing in the capacity as Mission Superior makes the following query to Felix Plattner, the Swiss Mission Procurator: "Whom belongs the property in Belapur, to the Jesuits as well? It seems the Mother General of the Menzingen [Sisters] came by. I am afraid that she has not come for the purpose of visit alone. You have written nothing about it in the letter of 27.12. [1948] and I hear that she is back there once again."[629]

The above instance obviously does not deserve generalization. Yet completely ignoring these facts would present only a one-sided picture. In the area of collaboration with the Religious Sisters, the Jesuits apparently had been very paternalistic and exercised male-chauvinism. It is hard to claim that all the Jesuits had genuine respect for the women Religious. Their collaboration, often appeared to have been utilitarian, meaning they wanted the Sisters only as *replacements* and *substitutes* for the tasks which they themselves could not achieve. Probably such a judgement might appear too harsh. But a deeper analysis of the issue seems to reveal precisely the same. Can it be couched in more sober terms? I leave to the reader.

What had been the approach of the European Jesuits to the native-born Religious Sisters? Had they respected and treated them as equals? One tends to think rather pessimistically on this issue. The rationale for the same is: If they were so chauvinistic in their approach to the Religious Sisters coming from their own cultural milieu, a better approach towards the native-born Religious Sisters seemed to be unlikely. My own assessment is based on on the ground that those Jesuits appeared to come across with an air of superiority vis-a-vis the Indians in general. The case of their approach towards the Indian diocesan clergy, as discussed above, re-strengthens our claim. It will be revealed in Chapter Seven that such an attitude was among the major factors for the slow progress of indigenous vocations to the Society of Jesus in Poona Mission.

Notwithstanding these drawbacks in personnel management, the collaborative mission work with the Religious Sisters may be termed as a success when judged from the overall outcome of the missionary

629 Pius Geisel to Felix Plattner (Poona, New Year 1949), AMPSJ, Superior Poona, P. Geisel.

endeavour. this Jesuit mission as far as the results of the same are considered as a criterion to judge the same. Else, the positive impact on people would not have been possible. Therefore, it can be said that the collaborative work of the Jesuits with the Sisters was quite successful at the functional level.

4.5. The Native Helpers: Catechists and School-Masters/School-Teachers[630]

Way back in 1842, a Protestant missionary in South India had acknowledged by saying that "the progress of Christianity, so far as it depends on man, depends very essentially on the catechists. A good catechist is the missionary's right hand: he cannot feed his native flock without him."[631] A Catholic journal reiterated the same in 1925: "A well-trained catechist ... can do an inestimable amount of good in spreading the Gospel."[632] Apparently these remarks are valid for all contexts, especially for rural missions.

How have the catechists been described in various sources? In some of them, they have been designated generally as 'native assistants.' However, under this category were included not only the catechist preachers but also "accountants, bookbinders, printers, washer men, cooks, as well as country priests ... school teachers and other

630 I owe the general ideas on this topic to Heike Liebau, "Country Priests, Catechists, and Schoolmasters as Cultural, Religious and Social Middlemen in the Context of the Tranquebar Mission," in Christians and Missionaries in India: Cross Cultural Communication since 1500, ed. Robert Eric Frykenberg (Grand Rapids, MI/ Cambridge, UK: Wm. B. Eerdmans, 2003), 71-92. Though Liebau has discussed the topic in a different context, yet, there are a number of meeting points on the dynamics of involvement of the catechists and schoolteachers in this Mission. As additional source of general ideas I have borrowed from Pierce Beaver, "Katechisten: Ausbildung und Anstellung," in Lexikon zur Weltmission, eds. Stephen Neill, Niels-Peter Moritzen & Ernst Schrupp (Wuppertal: Theologischer Verlag/ Erlangen: Verlag der Evang.-Luth. Mission, 1971), 271-272; Karl Heinz Schmidt, "Katechet, Katechetin;" in LTK, Vol. 5 (Freiburg/Basel/Rome/Vienna: Herder, 1996), 1304-05; Horst Rzepkowski, Lexikon der Mission: Geschichte, Theologie, Ethnologie (Graz/Vienna/Cologne: Styria, 1992), 238-39. See also "Uber die einheimische Missionshilfe durch Katechisten," MB (October 1929): 2-5.

631 TMC 10 (March 1842): 69. See also TAER 33 (1905): 238.

632 CMAPF 2 (1925): 307.

assistants."[633] In other sources, we come across with terms like "native helpers,"[634] or "native apostles"[635] and so on.

The task of tracing the history of the native helpers in this Mission is beyond the scope of this study. Yet, it may not be entirely irrelevant to point out that the missionaries across denominations heavily depended on catechists and other such helpers to play supplementary roles in mission work, due to various constraints, such as lack of priests, poor road conditions, adverse socio-political and climatic circumstances, lack of knowledge of local tongues among European missionaries, etc.[636] But more importantly, the reason for their inclusion in the missionary endeavours was their intimate experience and knowledge of the local languages and cultures of the mission areas. It was not uncommon to find missionaries, coming as they were from different linguistic traditions, not knowing the language of the people among whom they worked. Humanly speaking, it was not easy to grasp the nuances of the linguistic, religious, social, political and cultural contexts in a short time, even if some of the gifted ones managed to learn the languages in a short period of time. As may be expected, these aspects posed immense challenges to the missionaries. In such situations the native helpers were indispensable as intermediaries and interpreters. In fact, the missionaries themselves were deeply aware of the fact that the success of a mission could not be achieved without the help of native helpers.[637]

This was true of all the Jesuit missions. The catechists invariably played an important role in the Jesuit missionary endeavours. The understanding namely a catechist being a missionary's right hand became even more pronounced from around the 1920s in the Jesuit missions. In the South Dakota Mission,[638] for example, the Jesuits began to lay a special emphasis on training of catechists and teachers with

633 Liebau, "Country Priests, Catechists, and Schoolmasters," 72-73.

634 John Francis Bannon, "The Mission Frontier in Sonora: 1620-1687," in The Jesuit Missions of Northern Mexico, eds., Charles W. Polzer et al. (New York/England: Garland Publishing, 1991), 116.

635 Edward E. Andrews, Native Apostles: Black and Indian Missionaries in the British Atlantic World (Cambridge, Massachusetts/London: Harvard University Press, 2013), 92.

636 See Correia-Afonso, The Jesuits in India, 167; Liebau, "Country Priests, Catechists, and Schoolmasters," 72-73.

637 Liebau, "Country Priests, Catechists, and Schoolmasters," 84.

638 The mention is relevant because this mission is partly contemporaneous with the Poona Mission.

a view to forming an indigenous leadership among the natives. This emphasis was very much in tune with the papal mandates of the time that laid emphasis on the formation of the native clergy. The formation of the catechists was perceived as an integral dimension of promoting the indigenous clergy by the Jesuits. It was hoped that from among the native leaders such as catechists, especially the younger ones, some of the future clergy would emerge.[639]

In most of the Jesuit missions in India, the institution of catechists has been an integral part of the missionary endeavours. Along with them, other helpers and collaborators like schoolmasters have been very important co-workers of the Jesuits. They were primarily employed for the expansion and consolidation of the mission. Another important ground for their employment was the lack of sufficient number of missionaries. Secondly, it was also necessitated due to the fact that their knowledge and experience of the local contexts were invaluable for making initial contacts with the native people. Even more importantly, it has been an imitation of the charism of the early Church which had placed a special emphasis on promoting leaders from among the local people themselves.[640] Apparently this aspect has been generally ignored. They were more driven by pragmatic reasons in employing catechists so that the pastoral care of the faithful may be undertaken more effectively. For, it was impossible for the missionaries to be present all the time at all the hamlets and villages spread across miles.

In the context of this Mission, we identify two groups of native helpers, namely catechists and school-masters/school-teachers. These native helpers were mainly male members. Only in the 1950s we occasionally find the mention of female members as catechists. But it seems to be an exception.[641] This was quite a normal practice given the patriarchal structure of the society. Moreover, in the pre-Vatican II Church such a tradition was yet to emerge whereby women could be taken for such roles.

---

639 See Enochs, The Jesuit Mission to the Lokota Sioux, 84.

640 See Francis Aloysius Sullivan, From Apostles to Bishops: The Development of the Episcopacy in the Early Church (New York/Mahwah, N.J: The Newman Press, 2001), 51-53.

641 See Pius Geisel to the Superior General (Poona, 29th January 1955), ARSI, Poona. 1005-IV, 10.

How did the catechists and school-masters act as collaborators and helpers in the mission? The first aspect that may be noted is that in most cases the catechists acted both as instructors of the Catholic faith as well as school teachers. As instructors of the faith,[642] they were entrusted with the task of preparing the villagers for special occasions like Christmas and Easter. The school children were often their helpers on such occasions.[643] During the ordinary seasons of the liturgical year, they were expected to carry out the task of gathering the village community on a regular basis for the practice of prayers and instruction in the faith. Religious instruction was mostly held in the evenings, for the people in villages were generally out for work during the day. As the priests could not be available in all the villages on Sundays, the catechists were needed to conduct the liturgy of the word. The programme included, besides the recitation of regular prayers, an explanation of the Word of God in the form of homilies. They were mostly based on personal experiences of the catechists. [644] The catechists were generally instructed on the basics of the Christian faith and homiletics in the catechetical training schools. But, as may be expected, the homilies were often rudimentary in nature with regard to their theological contents. By the 1950s, in view of improving upon these aspects, they were called occasionally together at a mission station for intensive seminars that covered topics like "dogma, morals, methods of instructing children, practice of religious hymns, methods of preaching on Sundays, feast days and ordinary days, and elementary truths about Christian faith among the non-Christians ... etc."[645]

The hymns were an integral part of the catechetical instructions. Since the village communities had the tradition of singing songs based on their myths and legends while working, especially during common works undertaken by more than one family, the people found it easier to

642 The work of the catechists in the conventional sense of the term.

643 See Pius Geisel to the Benefactors in Europe (Valan, 15th March 1938), AMPSJ, LB. Valan Briefe.

644 See Otto Weishaupt, "Report on the Pagan Mission in the Ahmednagar District," in Report on the Progress of the Association in Aid of the Pagan Missions (Poona: The Albion Press, 1914), 5-6. This is a small booklet published for private circulation. A copy of the same may be found in AMPSJ, Pune Alt. See also Liebau, "Country Priests, Catechists, and Schoolmasters," 72-77.

645 Otto Faller, "Relatio Visitationis Missionis Poonensis ... a die 15 Nov. 1952 ad diem 4 febr. 1953," ARSI, Poona. 1005-1, 39.

learn the aspects of Christian mystery taught in the form of hymns than those communicated in plain languages. Since the hymns resonated the manner of communicating truths in the form of poetry, the local Christians often replaced the traditional songs with Christian hymns during certain common works. This was an innovative aspect of catechizing, thanks to the zealous catechists. The problem, however, was that initially there were not many Christian hymns in the native languages. Yet the small number of hymns that were composed by the missionaries and their helpers were effective instruments for catechetical instructions.[646]

Besides religious instruction, the catechists had a variety of other practical tasks. Firstly, they were responsible for the pastoral care of the hamlets or villages they were entrusted with. This included tasks like visiting the sick, solving problems, settling disputes, patching up disagreements.[647] They also needed to watch over the neophytes lest they relapsed into the previous faith. Occasionally their responsibility extended to the religio-cultural aspects as well, whereby they needed to watch over certain practices, rituals and customs among the neophytes. In case these contained elements that were contrary to the Christian faith, the catechists were expected to challenge them and thus rectify the situation. Over and above these, one of their most important tasks was to explore the possibilities of further evangelization through regular contacts with the non-Christians. In such cases they were often the "precursors," whereas they generally followed the missionaries to consolidate their work and carry on their instruction, and also to guide the new Christian communities and to report to them."[648] A related aspect of their task included convincing the parents to send their children to schools, teaching the children in the village schools, preparing the people for baptism and marriage, besides preparing for the liturgy on the occasion of the visitation of the Jesuit missionaries.[649] Otto Weishaupt summarizes these aspects in the following words: "They [the catechists] are so to say his [missionary's] agents who must prepare the people to listen to the Missionary, they must watch the converts and call them

646 See Weishaupt, "Report on the Pagan Mission," 5.

647 See Liebau, "Country Priests, Catechists, and Schoolmasters," 72-77.

648 Correia-Afonso, The Jesuits in India, 167. See also "Excerpta Missionis Poonensis (6th May 1953)," RLGGM. Vol. VIII, 303-304.

649 See Joseph Stark to the Superior General (Sangamner, 1st January 1944), ARSI, Poona. 1004-XIV, 16.

together for the prayers every morning and evening, and last [but] not [the] least, they must protect them against the agents of Protestant Missions."[650]

We notice from the above text an interesting peculiarity of the mission field here, namely the danger of Catholics being lured by the Protestant groups. A mention of such an issue finds place in the correspondences of the Jesuits is proof enough to claim that this danger may not have been so insignificant as to be ignored. The claim gains a further weight for the sheer reason that the Protestant presence in the area was much older than that of the Jesuits.[651] Moreover, often because of their aggressive policy, the Protestants considered even the Catholics as targets of evangelization. We must hasten to add, however, that generally the Catholics were no better in this regard either. Given such a kind of competitive atmosphere of 'sheep-stealing', the catechists were needed to be watchful of the flock under their care.[652]

As school teachers, the primary task of the catechists was to teach children how to read and write. The Christian children were taught catechism besides leading them to the daily prayers mostly before or after the normal school hours. In the mission stations, catechism classes were normally imparted to all the children irrespective of their religious affiliations. The Jesuits aside, the catechists and teachers played the most important role in teaching catechism. This was one of the most important reasons why the Jesuits laid a special emphasis on having boarding homes (student homes) alongside the schools at all the mission stations. This helped create a better atmosphere for supervision and religious instruction. In the village schools such an arrangement was not possible. Hence the catechetical instructions were imparted outside the normal school hours, i.e., generally in the evenings, often along with the parents and relatives of the children. On Sundays and holidays generally the instructions lasted longer than on normal weekdays. This took place mostly in the village chapels wherever it was available. Else it was held in the rented houses of the catechists cum teachers or at a convenient place that could accommodate a large number of villagers.

650 Weishaupt, "Report on the Pagan Mission," 5.

651 See Neill, A History of Christianity in India: 1701-1858, 116, 256-257. See also "Bischof Anastasius Hartmann O. Cap iiber die Reform des Werkes der Glaubensverbreitung," KM*4/49* (January 1921): 84-85.

652 See Liebau, "Country Priests, Catechists, and Schoolmasters," 72-77.

In most cases, the catechists who were placed at the mission stations travelled from place to place accompanying the missionaries. In such cases, they functioned as companions, advisors and helpers to the Jesuits. For every practical decision to be made with regard to the local contexts, the Jesuits often depended on their experiential knowledge. Generally speaking, thus, the catechists were a great help in making right decisions even with regard to general missionary policies.[653]

This category of specially trained catechists was chosen from among the larger group of catechists and had better qualities of leadership, piety and personal integrity as compared to others. As for the catechists placed at various outposts, hamlets and villages, it was often left to their discretion to act in a particular situation. But they were never given full autonomy with regard to making major decisions pertaining to the general policy followed by the Jesuit pastors at a particular mission station. His approval in such cases was a normal expectation placed on them. For example, if a new hamlet or village needed to be adopted for further evangelization, the approval of the Jesuit as the head of the mission station was presumed. Similarly on the question of faith and morality the advice of the Jesuit pastor was to be sought. Though a certain amount of autonomy within the village community was granted to the catechists on some issues, they generally depended on the Jesuit pastor at the mission station for their consent, approval and guidance on matters pertaining to the general policy.

Another aspect that may be mentioned here is: the Jesuits mostly tried to place the catechists in their own native villages so far it was possible. The logic behind such a step was that the catechist and teachers had a good knowledge of their village community. However, this arrangement was often not possible. Moreover, this had both advantages as well as disadvantages. The advantage, as pointed out above, was that they were already well known to the village community and they, on their part, possessed a good knowledge of the village situation. On the other hand, every aspect of their lives were known to the villagers. Hence, the Biblical saying that 'a prophet is not accepted in his own hometown' seem to have applied in their cases too. Moreover, there

653 See Swami Animananda to the Superior General (Deshnur, 1st July 1963), ARSI, Belgaum-Poona. 1006: Goa- Poona 1006 - Particulares (1963). This file does not have the page numbers as the case is with other files, i.e., Poona 1005-1, II, III etc. The corresponding reference, therefore, must be identified by the title of the sub-file and the date of the letter.

was a danger of compromising the task of the mission with their own family responsibilities, especially in those cases of the catechists who lacked zeal for the mission. In general, however, such arrangements did seem to have worked. But the practical difficulty of getting catechists to be placed in their own respective villages might not have been so easy. Overall, it can be said that without a doubt is that the presence of catechists and school-masters in the mission was an immense help to the Jesuit pastors in accelerating the process of evangelization. We get a glimpse of the same from the report of Otto Weishaupt which is cited below:

> At present over one hundred villages lying in the Talukas [sub-division of a district] of Rahuri, Nevasa, Kopargaon, Sangamner are regularly visited by the missionaries of these centres: Kendal, Valan, Sangamner, [and] Rahata. Almost every village has its school-master or catechist. Some smaller hamlets are visited by the school-master of the neighbouring village at least three times a week. The number of our Christians in these four missions exceeds at present 7,000. How great is the number of those who went already to a better life, I do not know; but no doubt, it must be very great. This I conclude from the fact the Sangamner-Mission alone counts already more than 2,000 in its Register of the dead.[654]

The preceding paragraphs might give us a good picture of a perfect mission with regard to the collaboration between the Jesuits, catechists and school-masters. It must be clarified, however, that the situation was often far from being perfect. Yet, as far as possible, the Jesuits and catechists functioned well within this framework. Let us examine what the Jesuits did in order to promote the formation of catechists and school-masters, given the recognition that the native were inevitable in a mission station. In the words of Otto Weishaupt: "For, without a schoolmaster or catechist in every village, preaching and baptizing by Priests will have no lasting effect or indeed very little. Without teachers and catechists taken from the people to whom we have to preach, the foreign Missionary will find little hearing."[655]

A curious reader might be prompted to ask as to how the Jesuits managed to get the number of such helpers that they required. Initially

---

654 Weishaupt, "Report on the Pagan Mission," 6-7. See also "Valan," IB 1/29 (January 29), 245.

655 Weishaupt, "Report on the Pagan Mission," 5.

this was certainly a difficult task. Yet the Jesuits laid special emphasis on the training of catechists and school-masters. They opened schools for catechists and schoolmasters practically at every mission station, at least those that were established in the pre-World War I decades. The Jesuits themselves had experienced that with the increasing number of school-masters and catechists, "the number of villages in which missions could be opened increased rapidly."[656]

Figure 4.1: A Group of Catechists from Maratha Mission in Ahmednagar District (1930).
Source: *IB* 1/5 (January 1931): 26.

It is significant to note here that this emphasis was generally maintained in the Mission till the end of the period of this study. However, it is also true that in the decades of the 1940s and 50s the maintenance of a bigger number of catechists and school-masters was financially not feasible.[657] We come across with the mention of these schools quite frequently in the official correspondences of successive Mission Superiors, with regard to their status, maintenance and further

656 Ibid., 6.

657 See Pius Geisel to the Superior General (Poona, 28th November 1950), ARSI, Belgaum-Poona. 1301: 1950-1959. See further in the same file, the letter of Pius Geisel dated 10th February 1953. Similarly see Richard Wasserer to Francis Xavier Hayler (Valan, 12th July 1945), AMPSJ, IB. Valan-Briefe. Hayler was the Provincial of the Southern German Province from 1928-1935. See Schatz, Geschichte, Vol V, 80. Richard Wasserer to the Benefactors (Valan, 11th July 1945), AMPSJ, IB. Valan-Briefe.

need of promoting the same. These correspondences also indicate the number of school-masters and catechists under various mission stations. Objective and impartial as these correspondences are supposed to be, they point out also certain lacunae with regard to the emphasis laid on the training of these helpers at certain mission stations.[658] As per these sources, their number in the entire Mission seems to have gone down drastically in the 1950s. For example, we may take the figures for 1953 to see the decrease in their number. The contrast may be seen from the account of Otto Weishaupt we have cited above, wherein it is clearly mentioned that "almost every village has its school-master or catechist" at all the mission stations. This was true only till late 1930s. For example, at the Sangamner mission station Francis Schubiger had employed 50 catechists-cum-teachers at various outposts. In this case the arrangement was driven by a very pragmatic reason. In other words, this unification of functions of a catechist and a teacher in one person was basically necessitated due to the lack of resources. Employing two separate persons for the purpose of catechising and teaching in the village schools would have been too heavy a burden for the mission.[659] Whatever be the case, we notice a contrasting picture with regard to the presence of catechists at various mission stations. The table clearly indicates a drastic decrease in the number of the catechists, by 1953.

Table 4.2: Presence of the Catechists cum Teachers per Mission Station[660]

S. No.	Mission Station	Number		
		Villages	Catechists/School-masters	Faithful
1	Ahmednagar	14	4	1,200
2	Kendal	45	7	5,100
3	Belapur*	?	?	?

658 See Pius Geisel to the Superior General (Poona, 4th September 1950), ARSI, Poona. 1004-XIV, 4.

659 See Joseph Stark to the Superior General (Sangamner, 1st January 1944), ARSI, Poona. 1004-XIV, 16. For a general view on this point, see Correia-Afonso, The Jesuits in India, 166.

660 At the places marked with asterisks, the number of catechists at Belapur and Nasik Road are not given because they were not mission stations in the real sense of the term. At Belapur there was a hospital. Nasik road, on the other hand was a military chaplaincy.

4	Harigaon	51	?	5,032
5	Nasik Road**	?	?	0,750
6	Rahata	59	8	7,229
7	Sangamner	30	12	7,011
8	Songaon	25	?	4,000

Source: Adapted from the letter of Otto Faller to the Superior General (Poona, 10th February 1953), ARSI, *Belgaum-Poona. 1301: 1950-1959.*

On discussing the training of the catechists, an important person who deserves a special mention is Marshal (probably Marcel) D'Souza, a diocesan priest who worked with the Jesuits at the Kendal mission station for a long time. He promoted formation of catechists and school-masters most enthusiastically through a school he founded. The initial growth of this school, indeed the very first Catholic school in the area, goes to his credit. He virtually built up the school from the scratch. While aiming at imparting general education to the local people, he devised an innovative idea of taking the assistance of the students of higher standard to teach the lower sections. This was a great help towards addressing the problem of lack of teachers and catechists. It created something of what in managerial language is called a "ripple effect"[661] at a micro level. The students teaching their own juniors was an effective method, at least in his time. This was a temporary yet a pragmatic solution to fulfil the need of the teachers required to teach in the school. The future school-masters and catechists were comprised of these students. With the passing years, their number gradually began to increase and one of the immediate needs of the mission was quite substantially addressed. Thus, in the literal sense of the term, the mission owes to him the first generation of slightly better trained school-masters and catechists. Earlier they were taken mostly from among those who depicted certain leadership qualities but lacked formal training as school-masters and catechists. Through the innovative approach and commitment, Marshal D'Souza did a great service to the mission. A tribute to him is worth quoting here:

> It is the great merit of a secular Priest, Rev. Fr. Marshal D'Souza, to have opened the first Catholic school in Kendal, in which for full 13 years (1881-1894), he himself educated a great number of boys

661 Steve Harper, The Ripple Effect: Maximizing the Power of Relationships for Your Life and Business (Austin, TX: SWOT Publishing, 2005), 133.

> and girls of Kendal and the surrounding villages. Many of these boys became later on school-masters and catechists. During the first years of existence of this school this zealous Priest taught himself the children for five hours every day beginnings of course with the lowest standard. When later on some of his boys had finished all six standards, he gave part of his work over to them as pupil-teachers and assistants. But he remained Headmaster and continued to teach his five hours every day just as in the beginning. How great a service good Fr. Marshal D'Souza rendered to the whole Mission-work by educating so many able teachers and catechists, only Missionaries can understand and appreciate. For, without a school-master or catechist in every village, preaching and baptizing by Priests will have no lasting effect or indeed very little [effect].[662]

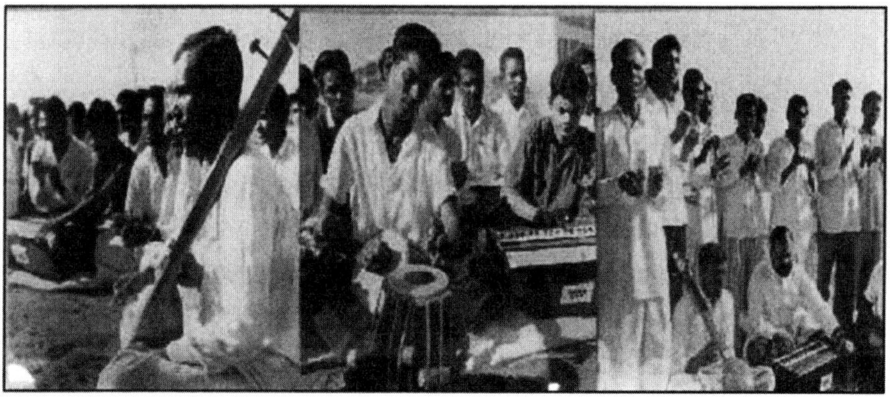

Figure 4.2: The Catechists at training at Shrirampur.
Source: AJMS, *Fotographische Belege: Katechistenschule, Shrirampur, Ahmednagar Distrikt.*

It may also be mentioned that for the purpose of their maintenance, they were paid a small salary. In most cases it was just enough for their subsistence. Often they were given support also in kind, i.e., grains, clothing or occasional medical help, etc. As for the exact figures in the form of salaries, we lack information. What emerges from our sources is the failure to make adequate arrangement for their salary hike. While on one hand, there was a consistent stress upon the need of catechists-cum-teachers in the mission, but on the other, our evidences suggest that often no sufficient efforts were put to support the families of the catechists through a reasonable hike in the salaries. We have a revealing

662 Weishaupt, "Report on the Pagan Mission," 4-5.

account from John Belser, one of the last batch of missionaries arriving in the mission:

> The pay of the catechists, school masters and servants in the mission districts is inadequate. R[upee]s. 45-R[upee]s. 75 (10-17 Dollars) per month is not a wage by which they can support their families decently ... This is hardly enough to buy the necessary clothes. This problem was discussed in many missionary meetings also in the presence of Fr. V[ice] Provincial. But some "bosses" Fathers in charge simply refuse to raise the pay. I do not dare to explain the Catholic Social principles. I would have to preach against my own brethren. All stations get very substantial help from Europe and America. They easily could raise the pay at least of those who work properly. Many expensive buildings, mostly chapels, have been erected. People see that and make their own conclusions. There is a growing discontent. Even when they get benefits as gifts, the clear teaching of the Social Encyclicals is against such practices.[663]

Lest the letter of John Belser is considered as an exceptional case, we may cite another example from a letter of Pius Geisel that seems to justify the issue raised by the former:

> H[is] Excellency] living in the olden times mentality, cannot see how things can be so dear now-a-days. Under pressure he increased the wages of the catechists and masters, but not sufficiently. Those Fathers, whose social conscience urges them, exceed the scale of pay sanctioned. It is useless to discuss this point with H[is] Excellency]. I gave him a list of prices of foodstuffs, to show that the wages sanctioned were hardly enough to buy food, not to say anything of clothing, medicine, recreation. The answer was a story of how things were formerly: One gives up discussing and proceeds.[664]

These two examples seem to suggest that in contrast to many Protestant missionary bodies, the Jesuits often failed to give adequate financial security to the catechists, which was a failure in the practice of justice preached by them. For example, Liebau mentions that the Protestant missionaries in Tranquebar mission (India) "felt a special

663 [663] John Belser to the Superior General (Harigaon, 1st May 1961), ARSI, Goa-Poonensis. 1006 - Particulares (1961).

664 Pius Geisel, "Litterae consultoris Missionis Poonensis," (Rahata, 11th May 1947), ARSI, Poona. 1004-XVI, 18.

responsibility for the material welfare of their native assistants,"[665] among whom the catechists occupied a special place. It seems to emerge from these two letters that if the Jesuits, including Archbishop Henry Doring, were to be open to see the financial situation of the catechists and teachers, probably the arrangement of the means might not have been impossible. But the lack of knowledge of the ground realities, almost bordering on insensitivity to the situation, seems to be the real reason for the state of affairs. It would be unfair to make a generalized statement in this regard. Yet, it may be assumed that partially this reason may have contributed towards the catechists often being negligent in their duties. Otto Weishaupt may have implied this reason when he said: "All missionaries agreed that the greatest drawback for the success of their Mission was the entire absence of reliable catechists and efficient school-masters."[666] We must hasten to add, however, that the statement of Weishaupt implies much more than the above reason. There might have been other reasons such as certain cultural traits and lack of disposition on the part of the catechists. Based on some instances of deception and fraud practiced by the catechists in the previous decades, during the time of Bishop Leo Meurin to be precise,[667] this kind of interpretation is not entirely unjustifiable. The crux of the matter is that the Jesuits, especially those in authority, appear to have often fallen into the trap of negligence and insensitivity so as not to ensure the financial security of the catechists. This, in turn, may have been one of the reasons for the reported "challenge" in the Mission, what Weishaupt noted: "the entire absence of reliable catechists and efficient school-masters."

This discussion leads us to another question. What was the relationship between the Jesuits and catechists-cum-teachers? Was the relationship that of a master and subjects? Were the catechists seen as

---

665 Liebau, "Country Priests, Catechists, and Schoolmasters," 74.

666 Otto Weishaupt, "Report on the Pagan Mission," 6.

667 See Hubert Sixt, "The Marathi Mission at Ahmednagar: Fr. Marcel De Souza's Account" (Poona, 1971)," ASJZ, Pune Alt, 1-2. According to this incident two catechists named Sevakrao Gaikwad and Tatyaramji, who were Protestants previously, deceived Bishop Leo Meurin telling him that if they would be admitted as catechists, they would bring their entire village as well as the surrounding villages to the Catholic fold. But they turned out to be frauds. On various pretexts they extorted a big sum of money from Leo Meurin. The promise of bringing the villagers to the Catholic fold never got realized. This remains even today as a dark chapter in the history of this Mission.

disposable objects once they failed to fulfil the demands of their call?[668] It would be unfair to make a sweeping statement on these questions. Yet, one cannot deny the fact that some of the Jesuits certainly lacked sensitivity to accord a rightful place to them as 'co-workers' in the Mission. The lower level of education among the catechists may have been one of the parameters for the same. In sum, therefore, often they were seen as mere employees to fill-up the lack of Jesuit personnel. This comes in contrast with some of the Protestant missionary bodies, who as per our sources, made conscious efforts to raise the dignity of the native assistants of every rank.[669]

Having said that we need to underline that the above conclusions are drawn mainly based on the two letters mentioned above. At the same time, there were a few Jesuit pastors who were genuinely interested in the catechists. From the examples of the Jesuits like Otto Weishaupt, Francis X. Schubiger, Pius Geisel and John Belser, etc.,[670] we conclude that there were a number of Jesuits who saw the role of the catechists in terms of co-workers and helpers of the Jesuits in the propagation of the faith. Indeed they were seen as "indigenous lay apostles"[671] who contributed in many and varied ways towards the establishment of local churches. In fact the place attributed to the catechists and teachers in the correspondences of some of the Jesuits, though not many, give us an indication that their approach to them was a virtual precursor to the Vatican Council II theology of the laity. Accordingly, the catechists, teachers and other lay leaders are to be seen as coworkers in mission. Thus we see the Jesuits in two categories: those who genuinely recognized the role of the catechists in the Mission, and others, perhaps not with malice, failed to recognize the same. The first category of Jesuits was strongly in favour of inculcating in the catechists leadership qualities. They sought not just collaboration from them, but aimed at making the catechists and schoolteachers as partners in the missionary enterprise.

668 See "Country Priests, Catechists, and Schoolmasters," 92.

669 Ibid.

670 See Geisel, "Litterae Consultoris Missionis Poonensis," ARSI, Poona. 1004-XVI, 18. Belser to the Superior General (Harigaon, lsl May 1961), ARSI, Goa-Poonensis. 1006 - Particulares (1961); Anonymous to Felix A. Plattner (Kendal, 20th January 1949), AMPSJ, Pune-Stadt Briefe.

671 See Horst Rzepkowski, Lexikon der Mission (Graz/Vienna/Cologne: Styria, 1992), 238.

Indeed they even encouraged those lay leaders to become leaders within the Church and outside in civil society.[672]

Based on the two streams of approaches of the Jesuits, we may conclude that there were Jesuits who considered the catechists as indispensable agents in the process of expansion and consolidation of the Mission. At the same time, there were other Jesuits who failed to recognize their significance. The latter, we may say, were unable to walk along with the thinking of the Church. Of course, the Church's advisory on the role of lay collaboration was not available to the Jesuits in this Mission at that time: it would come a little later, after the period of this study (1962), with Vatican Council II (Decree on the Missionary Activity of the Church--Ad Gentes). The Vatican Council II says:

> In our time, when there are so few clerics to preach the Gospel to such great numbers and to exercise the pastoral ministry, the position of catechists is of great importance. Therefore their training must be so accomplished and so adapted to advances on the cultural level that as reliable co-workers of the priestly order, they may perform their task well, though it be weighed down with new and greater burdens (AG 17. Cf. AG 15).

All said, let me point out that my assessment of Jesuit-catechist collaboration is entirely based on Jesuit sources, for there is not a single letter written by the catechists-cum-teachers in the archives that one can refer.

4.6. Conclusion

There is no doubt that the presence of the co-workers and helpers in the Poona Mission was a major factor in the overall progress of the Mission. The occasional challenges of maintaining mutual understanding must not lead one to the conclusion that the larger goal of the Mission was entirely missed out. Our discussion reveals that the overall progress of the Mission could not have been achieved were it not for the collaboration between the Jesuits and the co-workers and helpers. The role of each group of co-workers and helpers, therefore, was unique. The Jesuits alone could not have achieved many of the things without their collaboration.

672 See Ely, "Partnership in Mission," 179.

Having said that let me also add that the Jesuits of this Mission do not seem to have had the understanding of 'collaboration with co-workers and helpers' in terms of according equal importance and space to all the co-workers and helpers. In other words, the concept of 'equal partners in mission' did not seem to have been a familiar idea among them until the end of this period. The collaboration among the Jesuits and the lay workers/catechists seems to have been more at the level of availing of the help of the latter for accomplishing the task that generally fell outside the domain of what a classical clerical activity would comprise of. Besides, it is also clear that the Jesuits invariably considered themselves as superior to other collaborators.

Chapter-5

Obstacles and Challenges

5.1. Introduction

The mission field presented numerous challenges, virtually of every conceivable description. For the sake of clarity, we shall discuss these two categories here: internal and external. The distinction made here in these categories is rather arbitrary. The first category pertains to the challenges that came within the purview of the personal, societal and ecclesiastical circles implying thereby somewhat more direct implications for the lives of the Jesuits; whereas the second category implies those challenges due to the contemporary socio-economic and political developments of the country, especially of the State of Maharashtra. The latter also includes various obstacles and challenges due to the composite culture of India. Here we shall make a survey of some of such challenges.

5.2. The Western Indian Climate and Challenges to the Europeans

Doubtlessly, the Indian climate in general may be "inhospitable;"[673] and erratic to an outsider. It did pose a considerable amount of challenge to the European Jesuits, i.e., in the process of getting acclimatized. It would be a needless exercise here to engage with the theoretical questions as to whether the physiological or biological constitution of the Europeans are different from that of the Indians and that they are more susceptible to tropical diseases, etc. All the same, a few testimonies, although coming

673 Ababu Minda Yimene, *An African Indian Community in Hyderabad: Siddi Identity, Its Maintenance and Change* (Gottingen: Cuvilier, 2004), 141.

from the previous century, may help us to understand the issue because it did have a bearing on the Jesuits coming from Europe.

Reflecting on a similar issue, David Allen (a Protestant missionary), for example, wrote: "Though not so unhealthy as has been generally supposed, yet the climate [of India] will always be enervating and sickly to the European and American constitution. Not only is life shorter and health more uncertain, but they have less energy of body and mind than in their native climate."[674] Similarly another Protestant missionary wrote: "The geographical difficulties arising from the Indian climate and the vast distances to be covered by the most primitive means of transport were factors of which today we are well aware. The high death-rate from tropical diseases resulted in the loss of many Jesuits before they had been long enough in the country to begin effective work."[675]

These examples are sufficient to point out that the Jesuits in Poona Mission did face the challenges of adapting to the Indian climate. In spite of their heritage of extraordinary discipline and hard work, in many cases their optimum performance was substantially affected on account of this factor. Stated differently, it did have potentially degenerative effects on the missionaries from outside India.[676] We must hasten to add here that the purpose of discussing this point here is not to generalize the fact that every missionary who landed in India was crippled by the climate of the place. In fact a majority of them seemed to have overcome the challenge to a considerable degree. Else the achievements on record would be an imaginary tale.[677]

It may be noted that the cases of the Jesuits falling victims to tropical diseases were not few. In the context of the climate in Western India, especially that of Bombay and Poona, it may be pointed out that it

674 David Oliver Allen, *India, Ancient and Modem: Geographical, Historical, Political, Social, and Religious; with the Particular Account of the State and Prospects of Christianity* (Cleveland, Ohio: John P. Jewett and Co., 1856), 576.

675 Kenneth Ingham, *Reformers in India, 1793-1833: An Account of the Work of Christian Missionaries* (New York: The Syndics of the Cambridge University Press, n.d.), 4.

676 Marjorie Grene & David Depew, *The Philosophy of Biology: An Episodic History* (Cambridge: Cambridge University Press, 2004, reprint 2008), 120.

677 Erika Charters, *Disease, War and the Imperial State: The Welfare of the British Armed Forces during the Seven Years' War* (London: The University of Chicago Press, 2014), 144-145.

was humid yet "moderate."[678] In the words of Pius Geisel: "The climate of Poona, with an exception of some two months, is good and pleasant... in summer the heat is naturally slightly more but dry, which makes it bearable; and in rainy season we get around 80-90 cm rain."[679] In spite of such positive aspects of the climate of the mission field, the process of adaptation to the local climatic conditions was not so easy for a good number of Jesuit missionaries. As a result, some of them had to give up their missionary ambitions and return to their homelands.[680]

Although, the later correspondences of the Jesuits are conspicuously silent on the subject, we come to the conclusion, based on a few accounts in our possession, that many of the Jesuits who came to India before the close of the 19th century either lost their lives much earlier as compared to their compatriots in Europe or were forced to abandon their missionary work. We discover that during the first six years after the beginning of the mission at Kendal (during late 1870s and 1880s), seven Jesuits of German nationality had worked there. One of them, namely Antony Schumacher died in the beginning of 1880, followed by Antony Haas and Hermann Haug in 1882 and 1884 respectively.[681] In yet another account we read: "Three missionaries died within a few years, only 35-42 years old, viz., Fr. A Schumacher in 1880, Fr. A. Haas in 1883, Fr. H[ermann] Haug in 1884. Many missionaries fell sick and finally had to be sent back to Europe, as their health had broken down entirely."[682] The rest four contracted diseases like Malaria and Typhoid under the insalubrious circumstances coupled with the food with a far lower nutrition quality at their disposal than in Europe. Consequently they had to return to their homelands for health reasons.[683] Among the later Jesuits John Baptist Winiger (1897-1937) died of Typhoid at the

678 Suresh Kumar Singh, *People of India: Maharashtra*, Part 1 (Mumbai: Popular Prakashan, 2004), 651.

679 Pius Geisel to Assistant to the Superior General (Poona, 19th November 1935) ARSI, *Poona Varia 1935-1939.*

680 See Kenneth Ingham, *Reformers in India, 1793-1833: An Account of the Work of Christian Missionaries* (New York: The Syndics of the Cambridge University Press, n.d.), 4.

681 See Winiger, "Die Missionsstation Sangamner," 11.

682 Weishaupt, "Report on the Pagan Mission in the Ahmednagar District," 6.

683 See "Kendal," *IB* 1/10 (April 1932): 62-63. For an additional brief summary on the number of Jesuits who landed in India after 1867 and their consequent fate primarily on account of the of the effect of the Indian climate and other related reasons, see Vath, *Die deutschen Jesuiten*, 98.

age of 40 years[684] and John Roder at 38.[685] Francis X. Schubiger, one of the most prominent Jesuits of the Mission died at a more mature age of 61.[686] One of the latest examples of the victims of tropical diseases was Raymond Keel who died at a very young age of 41 years. Reporting on his death a necrology published in Indische Bilder reads: "Despite the best of medical efforts, once again the treacherous tropical disease has claimed another young Jesuit missionary in the person of Fr. Raymond Keel."[687] The list may be expanded adding a number of other cases. But it suffices to point out the validity of the finding.

Some of the examples cited above do go back to some four decades prior to the period of this study. Nevertheless, it does not rule out the validity of the argument in any way. On the contrary the fact that the impact of the climatic conditions on the health of the Jesuit missionaries, must be held even truer as the gradual effects of the climate changes is generally felt much stronger with every passing decade. Apparently, the development in medical sciences offers newer ways to combat the diseases and sicknesses. Precisely, this factor may be ascribed to as a possible reason for the absence of mention about these challenges in the later correspondences of the Jesuits. Besides, it may also be true that the later Jesuits, as a result of their considerably longer period of stay in India, were better able to acclimatize themselves to the climate of the region than their compatriots in the previous decades. All the same, the hardships on account of the same were a reality that did pose a hurdle to an average Jesuit missionary. In the words of Pius Geisel:

> There are people who just begin to sweat as soon as they hear the word 'India' ... In the rainy season Cholera and Malaria attacks are common. No wonder that the people fall victims to these diseases. It is surprising, however, that all of them do not succumb to these diseases ... Only a few Europeans could have sustained what these children of mother India have to bear.[688]

684 See Remigius Rauw, "Fr. John B. Winiger (1897-25 Dec. 1937)," in *Deceased Members,* 27.

685 See Pius Geisel, "Fr. John of God Roder (28th May 1912 -19th October 1950)," in *Deceased Members,* 38.

686 See "Francis X. Schubiger (3 Oct. 1878 -2 Feb. 1939)," in *Deceased Members,* 28-29. See also O'Neill & Dominguez, eds., *Diccionario Historico de La Compahia de Jesus,* 3534.

687 "f Pater Raymund Keel S.J.," *IB* 4 (1958): 16.

688 Pius Geisel, "Vom indischen Wetter," *IB* 1/18 (April 1934): 145. See also Weishaupt, "Report on the Pagan Mission," op. cit.

The above observation is very much in agreement with what a Protestant missionary, while writing on the same topic, remarked in the previous century: "It is generally believed that in this country [India], owing to the deadly climate, the average duration of missionary life is seven years ..."[689] implying thereby that the hardships on this account were much more formidable in those days. This point gains a further importance because most of the Jesuit missionaries had to travel long distances on foot, bicycles or on horseback in order to make regular pastoral visits or to explore new villages for evangelization. In order to give an idea of the geographical vastness covered by the Jesuits for regular pastoral visits, the following description may be apt:

> The Maratha Mission numbers about 11,000 low caste and very poor Neo-Christians. There are 5 independent stations: Sangamner, Rahata, Valan, Kendal and Songav [i.e., Songaon] ... The Christians live in some 180 villages, at great distance from one another, within a radius of 10 to 20 or more miles round the stations. There are, practically, no railways, very few good roads and during the rainy season unfordable rivers.[690]

Occasionally the villagers were gathered under the shades of trees. In such circumstances the exposure to heat, humidity, rain and tropical wind was unavoidable, the situation being even worse in the summer and rainy seasons.[691]

The Indian climatic factors, thus, posed great challenges to the European missionaries, and this was a matter of great concern. A missionary was expected to be keenly aware of the implications of Indian climate in order to be truly at the service of the mission. Francis Xavier Schubiger makes the following comment in this regard: "A missionary to be successful must have an intimate knowledge of the historical, social, religious, economical, climate conditions of his district and the people under his charge."[692] Obviously one sees here that Schubiger

---

689 J. J. Allies, *Per Crucem ad Lucem: The Result of a Life*. Vol. 2, Reprint, (London: Forgotten Books, 1879), 216-217.

690 Maximilian Riklin to the Superior General (Bombay, 6th September 1923), ARSI, *Bombay. 1004-1,* 13.

691 "New York Sunday-School Union Society: Arrival of Rev. William Ward, " *TCffVIUXOI* (4th November 1820): 415.

692 Francis X. Schubiger to the Superior General (Sangamner, 13th June 1925), ARSI, *Bombay. 1004-XIV,* 8a.

places all the factors on par with each other as worthy of taking note for the missionary enterprise to be successful.

The argument, all the same, will be a fallacy if we were to base the same entirely on the life-expectancy of the Jesuits in India on account of this consideration. The purpose is only to point out that the issue under consideration did pose a challenge, often reducing the working hours of the Jesuits. John B. Haas, for example, alleged the "beastly tropical climate"[693] for his inability to respond to the letters from Europe on time. The implication was that the hardships experienced on account of the rigorous climate were not imaginary.

5.3. The Two World Wars

Among the Jesuit missions in India, the B-PM was probably the worst affected in the event of the two World Wars. As discussed in chapter two, a substantial percentage of the personnel were taken into internment camps, while many others were repatriated, especially during WWI. The consequences of the breaking out of the war and eventual internment of the Jesuits posed serious challenges that had a direct bearing on this Mission. We shall discuss here two of them.

5.3.1. The Scarcity of Personnel

Lack of personnel became an acute problem for the Mission especially during the two World Wars. The situation was especially precarious in the course of WWI and the years subsequent to it. Thus the scarcity of personnel was one of the major problems that the Mission had to face from the beginning of the period under review. From the figures shown in chapter three, it is not hard to conclude that the maintenance of the mission stations and institutions emerged as a bigger challenge, leave alone the concern for the expansion of the Mission. The following figures, although occasionally differing in details, give us an idea into the abrupt change in the number of personnel.

From the figures in the table below, it is obvious that the percentage of personnel dropped nearly to 60% of its earlier strength. This percentage was maintained thanks to the presence of the diocesan priests and other personnel invited as substitutes from other Missions of the Jesuits as well as from a few other Religious Orders. It may also be noted that the number of the Scholastics was reduced to one-eighth and

693 John B. Haas to Felix A. Plattner (1st August 1941), AMPSJ, *LB. Puna-Briefe (alte).*

that of the Brothers to one quarter. Between 1916 and 1919 there were very few new arrivals from Europe. The 172 personnel available at the breakout of the war fell to 103 in 1917 in spite of the best of efforts to get substitutes.[694]

Table 5.1: An Overview of the Status of the Mission with regard to Personnel (1916)

	German Jesuits			Non-German Jesuits			Secular	Total
	Priests	**Scholastics**	**Brothers**	**Priests**	**Scholastics**	**Brothers**	**Priests**	**No.**
At the Breaking out of the war	66	16	19	25	00	04	35	165
Died	02	01	02	02	00	01	00	008
Repatriated	51	15	01	00	00	00	02	069
Interned	10	00	16	00	00	00	00	026
Remaining members	03	00	00	23	00	03	33	062
New Arrivals	00	00	00	23	04	03	15	045
Status of the Mission by the end of May 1916	03	00	00	46	04	06	48	107

Source: Alfons Vath, *Die deutschen Jesuiten in Indien: Geschichte der Mission von Bombay-Puna (1854-1920) (Regensburg: Jos. Kosel & Friedrich Pustet, 1920)*, 235.

Table 5.2: General Conspectus of shortage of men compared with the time before the war (1917)

	Staff in 1914	Old staff after Internment	Borrowed men	Staff in 1916	Men lost since	Staff in 1917
Archbishop	01	01	00	01	01	00
Bishop	01	Absent	00	00	00	00
Priests (Regular)	94	27	22	49	03	46
Scholastics	17	00	04	04	02	02
Brothers	23	02	05	07	01	06
Native Sec. Priests	36	36	14	50	01	49
Total	172	66	45	111	08	103

Source: Adapted from "The Bombay-Poona Mission in August 1917," ARSI, *Bombay. 1004-XVII*, 14; *Bombay 1004-XU.*

694 See "The Bombay-Poona Mission in August 1917," ARSI, *Bombay. 1004-XVII*, 14 (2). See also ARSI, *Bombay. 1003-XI*, 5, 18.

Taking into consideration the case of the Jesuits and other Religious priests alone, their distribution in various ministries too clearly shows that a sudden decrease in their number reached nearly 50%. There were severe difficulties as a result of this in maintaining the existing mission stations and institutions. The maintenance may be understood as normal pastoral functions such as regular pastoral visits, attending to the regular activities and many more works as the concrete situation might demand. We have the following two tables to show further that in the majority of cases the mission stations and parishes were at a greater risk of losing their impact among the people due to want of personnel.

Table 5.3: Distribution of Regular Priests (1917)

	Formerly	Now [1917]
In academic work, schools, administration, etc.	49	27
In Military Chaplaincies (full-timers)	10	07
In Civil Parishes	17	07
In Missions to heathens	18	05
Total	94	46

Source: "The Bombay-Poona Mission in August 1917," ARSI, *Bombay. 1004-XVII*, 14.

Table 5.4: Distribution of Jesuit Personnel in Colleges and Schools (1917)

Institution	Former Staff	Present Staff	Borrowed Members	Reduction of Numbers
St. Xavier's College, Bombay	14	07	00	07
St. Xavier's High School, Bombay	18	05	01	13
St. Mary's High School, Bombay	22	09	03	13
Bandra	09	06	05	03
Karachi	04	03	02	01
Poona	04	03	02	01
Hubli	01	01	00	00
Total	72	34	13	38

Source: Adapted from "The Bombay-Poona Mission in August 1917," ARSI, *Bombay. 1004-XVII*, 14.

The entire situation may be understood better by the figures above. The number of Jesuit personnel in 1917, for example, came down to 34, including the borrowed members from other Jesuit Missions in India,[695] i.e., American, Belgian, Venetian and Portuguese Missions. The Bengal Mission of the Belgian Jesuits, by far, seems to have been the most generous Mission to come to the rescue of B-PM.[696] However, as it may be expected, there were always possibilities that the members from other Missions could be recalled to their respective Missions any time according to the needs arising there. As far as schools were concerned, some of the vacancies were filled up by lay-people. A predictable consequence of the same was a perceptible decline in discipline in the schools, affecting the quality of teaching as a whole. An added challenge that emerged during this time was scarcity of Coadjutor Brothers, who were vital for the management of the schools and colleges, so far as the material aspects of the same were concerned.[697]

The sudden decline in the number of personnel affected the entire Mission. It had a greater negative impact on the mission stations as compared to the institutions and schools, because the institutions and schools were well established. However, Moreover, the vacancies in the schools could be filled-up by the lay-people, whereas such an arrangement was not possible in the case of parishes and mission stations. Francis Schubiger, hence, made an observation: "True, Bombay lost more Fathers in numbers, but they came mostly from the schools. Now schools can be managed by laymen, if need be, but not parishes and hence once more I reiterate that Poona suffered far more by the internment than Bombay."[698] Joseph Sark reiterates the same opinion on the impact of WWI: "There is plenty of work, and something more could be achieved ... And if there is only one Father to work then he is quite occupied with the school and the people on the compound. So we are always hoping for better times and as a matter of fact every year it is getting worse."[699] Thus, in general a persistent problem of the

695 Schatz, *Geschichte, Vol. II,* 249.

696 See "The Bombay-Poona Mission in August 1917," 14.

697 Ibid.

698 Francis X. Schubiger to Archbishop Alban Goodier (Sangamner, 19th December 1921), ARSI, *Bombay. 1004-IX,* 5(1).

699 See Joseph Stark to the Superior General (Sangamner, 1st January 1944), ARSI, *Poona. 1004-XIV,* 16(b).

Mission was scarcity of personnel, very especially for the expansion and consolidation of the Maratha Mission.[700]

The anxiety of Francis Schubiger expressed above was well-founded. For Poona Mission, the mission stations, outposts and parishes were of vital importance. In fact it is precisely these that signified the real reach-out to the principal target groups namely the rural masses. As may be seen from the figures in the table below, the claim of Francis Schubiger is well justified.

Table 5.5: The Apostolate-wise Distribution of the Jesuit Personnel in the Mission (1917)

A. Bombay Archdiocese	Patres	Schol.	Coadj.	Univ.
1. In Domibus S.J.				
i. In collegio Universitatis	3	0	1	4
ii. In Collegio S.F. Xaverii	4	3	1	8
iii. In Collegio S.M.V. Immacul.	5	4	5	14
iv. In Collegio Karachi	1	2	1	4
Univ (Total)				30
v. In Operibus Archidiocesis				
i. In Bandra Coll.	2	0	2	4
ii. In Missione Guzerat	2	0	1	3
iii. Capellanus Militaris	1	0	0	1
				8
B. In Poona Diocese				
i. In collegio	0	0	0	0
ii. In Missionis (a) Canara	0	0	0	0
(b) Mahratta [Maratha]	0	0	0	0
iii. In tota cetera parte Diocesis	1	0	0	1
Univ (Total)				1

Source: ARSI, *Bombay. 1004-XII*, 12.

The figures above present a clear view of the changed status of personnel in the Mission during WWI (1914 -1919).[701] It may be noted that this state of affairs continued for more than a decade, i.e., until the beginning of the return of the German Jesuits to the Mission since 1927.

700 See Schatz, *Geschichte,* Vol. Ill, 319.

701 "Der jetzige Stand der Mission (1929)," *IB,* 1/2 (April 1930): n.p.

Yet, the Mission could never regain the strength that was available in the pre-WWI era. The following table underlines the persisting personnel crunch: it never rose above 50% of the earlier strength.

Table: 5.6: The Status of the Mission Personnel (1921-1929)

Year	Bishop	Jesuits	Diocesan Priests	Coadjutor Brothers	Total
1921 End	0	13	22	2	37
1922 End	0	14	18	2	34
1923 End	0	15	18	2	35
1924 End	0	18	18	5	41
1925 End	0	17	17	6	40
1926 End	0	18	19	6 + 1 (Schol.)	44
1927 End	0	20	19	5	44
1928 End	1	23	19?	5	46
1929 End	1	21	17	6	45

Source: Adapted from ADPSJ, *Abt. 45B-26*, Nr. 1509.

The Jesuits hoped to receive newer members or to welcome back the earlier ones who were repatriated to their homelands. But the prevailing situation did not promise any of these. In his frustration, therefore, Francis Schubiger wrote[702] thus:

> Through a letter dated 23.1.24, Fr. [Maximilian] Riklin S.J., the Administrator of Poona, shared with me the reply of Fr. Assistant with regard to the return of Frs. [Henry] Diebels and [Anthony] Wessendorf to the Maratha mission in Ahmednagar district. The reply was in the negative. I do not pretend to hide [the fact] that the reply and the judgement applied therein caused me much perplexity and disappointment. I wish, therefore, to bring the ground reality to the kind notice of Your Paternity, not as a private individual but as the Vicar Forane (Vicarius Foraneus)[703] of the entire mission.

702 See also Maximilian Riklin to Assistant to the Superior General (Poona, 22nd January 1924), ARSI, *Poona. 1004-1,* 3.

703 "The institute of vicar forane is basically unchanged from the 1917 code ... [which] made it mandatory to divide the diocese into vicariates forane, deaneries, or arch-presbyterates ... The deanery was originally a grouping of ten parishes. The modern concept of the vicar forane dates back to the sixteenth century under the inspiration of St. Charles Borromeo. The term 'forane' originally meant the outlying or rural parts of the diocese where the bishop's presence and pastoral concern could be made visible by a vicar ... The vicar

> According to the catalogue I am also the 'Superior' of the mission. But as I do not have Jesuit missionaries under me, I fail to understand how I deserve these titles.[704]

A question that may arise at this juncture is: What were the further arrangements that were made by the Jesuits to address the issue of the scarcity of personnel, besides requesting for assistance from other Jesuit Missions, during this period? It was primarily done by inviting additional diocesan Priests, besides Sisters from various Congregations and employing more catechists. It may be pointed out that a few diocesan clergy were already active in the Mission even prior to WWI.[705] As compared to the earlier strength of the Jesuits, the number of the diocesan clergy could not meet the requirement, as expressed by Francis Schubiger that,

> The secular clergy by the very nature of the circumstances are very small in number and hence the majority of the parishes were in the hands of the regulars who now disappeared (in Maratha mission all but one, that is, myself) in the rest of the diocese 17 Germans were interned, only 3 Swiss and old Fr. [Martin] Durach remained together with 11 secular priests."[706]

It would have been nearly impossible for the Jesuits to maintain the Mission given such a magnitude of work, which is revealed, for example, from the following figures (1930): 21 Jesuit priests along with 17 diocesans had to reach out to 26199 Catholics, besides 129 catechumens spread across 44 parishes and mission stations. In addition there were 6 secondary schools with 230 students and a high school (St. Vincent's High School in Poona) with around 420 students that had to be directly managed by the Jesuits.[707]

---

forane is known in some countries or dioceses as the dean, archpriest, urban vicar, area vicar, etc. In the Eastern churches he is known as a protopresbyter ..." John P. Beal et al., eds., *New Commentary on the Code of Canon Law, Study Edition* (New York, N.Y./ Mahwah, N.J.: Paulist Press, 2000), 729-730.

704 Francis X. Schubiger to Archbishop Alban Goodier (Sangamner, 08th February 1924), ARSI, *Bombay. 1004-IX,* 5a.

705 See ADPSJ, *Abt. 45B-26,* Nr. 1509.

706 Francis X. Schubiger to Archbishop Alban Goodier (Sangamner, 19th December 1921), ARSI, *Bombay. 1004-IX,* 5(1).

707 "Der jetzige Stand der Mission (1929)," *IB* 1/2 (April 1930): n.p.

The missionary outreach, by no means, was to be restricted to the Catholics alone. It included not only to non-Christians, but also to other Christian denominations. The Hindus and Muslims, besides other smaller communities, were nearly 10.5 million within the jurisdiction of the Mission. The Protestants too were a formidable group numbering nearly 45000. To reach out to all these groups the Jesuits had to take the support of the Sisters and catechists besides the diocesan priests, as noted above. Thus by 1929 there were 46 European and 13 native Sisters in the Mission. They helped mainly in the running and maintenance of four High Schools for girls with 925 pupils besides seven orphanages with 490 orphans. In addition, a good number of catechists (170 male and 60 female) were inducted in order to maintain 120 primary schools with a total of 2958 children.[708] In the year 1933 "there were seven Religious Sisters, 138 catechists who looked after 117 schools with a total of 2400 children."[709] The expansion of the Mission field in the 1930s may be seen from the map #7.

It may be noted that the problem of scarcity of personnel was not peculiar to 1920s and 1930s alone. In fact a similar situation arose once again after the breaking out of World War II too. In comparison with the previous period, however, it was less acute in the sense that the duration of the internment was much shorter for the majority of the Jesuits.[710] Moreover, learning a valuable lesson from the experiences of the previous war, the Jesuits had already taken certain steps in anticipation of some of the unpleasant events, as J. B. Haas reports: "The third of September [1939] did not find us quite unprepared. During the last year it had been our policy that all the German Fathers who fulfilled the prescribed conditions became British subjects."[711] However, the scarcity of the Jesuit personnel persisted even in the post-WWII years as may be seen from the figures on the new arrivals from Europe for the period from 1930 to 1951, after which there were no new cases of arrivals. Apparently, slowly yet steadily the native vocations began to increase.

708 Ibid.

709 "Die Puna-Mission der oberdeutschen Provinz der Gesellschaft Jesu: Einige Zahlen aus der Puna-Mission vom Jahre 1933," *IB* 1/18 (April 1934): 146

710 John B. Haas to George (?) (Poona, 12th November 1941), AMPSJ, *IB. Puna-Briefe (alte).*

711 It was certainly a commendable step, which pleased the Superior General as well: "I was very pleased to hear of the foresight of the Superiors in arranging that subjects who could fulfill the conditions secured British citizenship." Wlodimir Ledochowski, Superior General to Remigius Rauw (Rome, 30* November 1939), ARSI, *RLGGM,* vol. VII, 107.

Yet until the end of the period of our study (1962) number of personnel could never reach the pre-WWI era.

Table 5.7: New Arrivals from Europe (1930-1951)

Year	New Arrivals			Total
	Scholastics	Brothers	Priests	
1930	1	0	2	03
1931	1	2	1	04
1932	5	0	0	05
1933	2	0	0	02
1934	3	0	1	04
1935	2	0	1	03
1936	2	0	0	02
1937	3	0	0	03
1938	4	1	6	11
1939	0	0	2	02
1948	4	0	1	05
1949	3	0	0	03
1951	3	1	0	04
Total	33	04	14	41

Sources: *IB* 1/4(1930): 6; 1/8 (1931): 51; 1/11 (1932): 76; 1/12 (1932): 88; 1/15 1933): 116; 1/20 (1934): 164; 1/24 (1935): 200; 1/28 (1936): 242; 1/32 (1937): 282; 2/4 (1938): 44-45; 2/5 (1939): 58-62; 2/7 (1939): 89; 3/9 (1943): 2-11; 5/4-5 (1948): 109-111; 5/4-5 (1949): 158-160; 4-5 (1951): 36-38. The source details are given in the footnote.[712]

Finally the challenge of maintaining the Mission may be assessed from the following table. It must be noted that in doing so we need to take

712 See "Drei Indienfahrer," *IB,* 1/4 (October 1930): 6; "Ausgezogen zur Missionsarbeit," *IB,* 1/8 (Oktober 1931):51; "Neue Hilfskrafte," *IB,* 1/11 (July 1932): 76; "Drei neue Missionare," *IB,* 1/12 (October 1932): 88; "Zwei junge Indienfahrer," *IB,* 1/15 (July 1933): 116; "Unsere jungen Indienfahrer des Jahres 1934," IB, 1/20 (Oktober 1934): 164; "Die Indienfahrer des Jahres 1935," *IB,* 1/24 (October 1935): 200; "Unsere Indienfahrer 1936," *IB,* 1/28 (October 1936): 242; "Unsere Indienfahrer 1937," *IB,* 1/32 (October 1937): 282; "Aussendungsfeier," *IB,* 2/4 (October 1938): 44-45; "Unsere Indienfahrer 1938," *IB,* 2/5 (January 1939): 58-62; "Die letzten Indienfahrer," *IB, 211* (July 1939): 89; "Manner der Heimat," *IB,* 3/9 (March 1943): 2-11; "Erste Ausfahrt," *IB* 5/4-5 (1948): 109-111; "Ausreise nach Indien," *IB* 5/4-5 (September 1949): 158-160; "Unsere Indienfahrer 1951," *IB* 4-5 (September-October 1951): 36-38. See also Riklin to Assistant to the Superior General (Poona, 22nd January 1924), ARSI, *Poona. 1004-1,* 3.

into consideration the entire situation of the period under consideration, namely the condition of roads, transport facilities and the like.

Having made this rather extensive survey of the status of the mission with regard to the personnel for the entire period of our study, we come to the conclusion that the challenge of acquiring a sufficient number of Jesuit missionaries from Europe was a persistent issue. The challenge of maintenance of the missions apart, the problem of scarcity of personnel partially explains the efforts to increase native vocations rather rapidly after the 1950s, although the more compelling reason was the changing national scenario of India. Moreover, the answer to the question of a slower pace of expansion of the Mission in the period under review is addressed as well to some extent.

Table 5.8: Distribution of Priests/Missionaries in Mission Stations (1934)

	Name of the Mission Station	No. of Outposts	No. of Priests/ Missionaries
a	*Maratha Mission in the North*		
	Kendal	10	1
	Valan	23	2
	Sangamner	25	2
	Rahata	46	2
	Songaon	24	1
	Ahmednagar	01	1
	Igatpuri	02	1
b	*Canarese Mission in the South*		
	Guledgud	00	1
	Assangi	09	1
	Gadag	00	1
	Tumarikop	02	1

Source: "Die Puna-Mission der oberdeutschen Provinz der Gesellschaft Jesu: Einige Zahlen aus der Puna-Mission vom Jahre 1933,"*IB* 1/18 (April 1934): 146.

A curious reader might ask whether the issue of the inadequate number of Jesuits was such an important one. The concern was not entirely unfounded given the geographical expansion of the mission field. The main consideration ultimately was not a desire to increase the number of the missionaries for its own sake, but rather to maintain the already existing mission stations and institutions. Still another concern seems to have been losing missionaries either due to death or departure from the Society.

5.3.2. The Scarcity of Resources

Another direct consequence of both the World Wars that had strained the Mission was scarcity of resources to maintain the already established institutions and schools as well as to expand the Mission. This problem was more acute in the years immediately after WW I. The "the lack of financial resources became more and more perceptible."[713] The channels for receiving the alms and donations from Europe were badly hampered on account of the effects of the war. "During the war and in the post-war period almost all other help [financial included] from the homeland also was cut off."[714] As "the alms were stopped from Germany"[715] the Mission was left to manage with its own resources. This in turn meant that the prospects of expansion of the Mission were severely curtailed.

It may be mentioned that the military chaplaincies were important sources of income for the Mission. Until 1914, nearly a dozen Jesuits were working in various military chaplaincies, from where they earned a substantial amount of money that was of a great help for the Mission that was otherwise almost entirely dependent on the funds from Europe and elsewhere. Many of the chaplains were either taken to internment camps or repatriated. The consequence of the same was a heavy reduction in the income of the Mission thereby impacting the financial position of the diocese. A letter of Francis X. Schubiger further elaborates the issue:

> When the most recent plan of cut-down heavily on the number of Military chaplains is executed, on whose income literally the existence of the [Poona] diocese depends to a large extent, then the entire diocese faces the risk of going bankrupt in a short period of time. Worse still, such a turn of events seems to come precisely when the Maratha mission is in the greatest need of support and the

713 Francis X. Schubiger to the Superior General (Sangamner, 13th November 1924), ARSI, *Bombay. 1004-IX,* 16b (2). See also Schubiger to the Superior General (Sangamner, 08th February 1924), ARSI, *Bombay. 1004-IX,* 5(a).

714 "Die Fahrt ins Missionsland," *IB* 1/17 (January 1934): 138.

715 Francis X. Schubiger to Archbishop Alban Goodier (Sangamner, 19th December 1921), ARSI, *Bombay. 1004-IX,* 5(1).

village schools need to be maintained well, that are not possible without the financial support.[716]

The worry for the whole Poona Diocese apart, the implication of Francis Schubiger was clear: if the situation of village schools were to be ignored and consequently not going to be undertaken with a sense of urgency, it was bound to have a long-run consequences impacting the future of the Mission itself. He wrote further: "Even, a minimum maintenance of the schools for about 4 to 5 years is a herculean task. If we fail to bring the standard of the school to the level that the government demands, then surely our schools are destined to be doomed and the very foundation of our missionary enterprise will be endangered."[717] It appears, thus, that the crunch of resources not only handicapped the present, but also the future of the Mission. It would be wrong to conclude, however, that the above-mentioned state of affairs was solely as a result of the declining sources of funds and donations. There were a few other factors as well.

One such factor that seems to have contributed to the poor financial state of affairs was lack of proper planning with regard to the financial management. Our sources indicate that such crises occurred in the early 1920s. The financial mismanagement may not have been a deliberate act but did have so much impact as to cause worries among some Jesuits in the later years, for Schubiger wrote: "... concedo totum, and that's why I am pressing all these many years for the declaration of [a] policy, that's why I stated that the diocese was about to get bankrupt etc., etc."[718]

It is quite apparent that certain individuals like Francis Schubiger and others were keenly aware of the implications of the lack of a proper planning in financial management. It appears that some other Jesuits were not too keen on having an idea about the financial status of the

---

716 Schubiger to the Superior General (Sangamner, 13th November 1924), op. cit.

717 Ibid.

718 Schubiger to the Superior General (Sangamner, 08th February 1924), ARSI, *Bombay. 1004-IX,* 5 (9). The pagination in this letter is peculiar. The first part of the letter originally contains 4 typed pages, wherein Schubiger gives a brief summary of the status of the Poona Mission. The second part is actually an attachment which contains an extract of Schubiger's replies and remarks to Archbishop Alban Goodier's letter. It comprises 9 pages. It touches upon various issues on the status of the Mission. The present citation is quoted in the above-indicated attachment, p. 9. Hence in the citation, the pagination has been indicated by 5 (9), thereby indicating that the content of the citation may be located on page 9 of the attachment to document number 5.

Mission. Consequently, expenses often crossed the amounts proposed in the budgets. An example might throw some more light on this issue: "From the accounts it appears that the original fund of Rs. 56, 000 had dwindled down during these last years to Rs. 35,000, a drop that may prove disastrous to those who come after you, if the same rate of consumption is long continued."[719] Lamenting the state of affairs Schubiger wrote:

> If you find that out only now then my worst fears about the ignorance of those in authority about the real state of affairs become true. That's also why when you were here with the Visitor I tried to impress you with the need of transferring the whole mission to some religious body which should have both the mind and the means to keep the mission from going to utter ruin. I have stated that over and over again.[720]

Another example further substantiates the fact that the lack of proper financial management, occasionally bordering on mismanagement was not an imaginary issue. Rather it was very realistic. In one of his correspondences Maximilian Riklin writes to Francis Schubiger: "I am horrified to find that the funds are disappearing at such a rate ... I should like to get a short and clear account of the Sangamner money ..."[721] The description pertains to the accounting of money in the mission station at Sangamner. There is sufficient indication that this mission station had received a substantial amount of funds for the purpose of relief work during the famine of 1918/1921. But the lack of clear planning and accounting were responsible for the rapidly , disappearing funds. Besides, Francis Schubiger held that the lack of foresight in channelizing and managing the sources of funds received aggravated the financial crisis:

> ...Then [Fr.] Westropp came to the rescue and Sangamner received directly or indirectly from him many ten thousands. His departure for Bombay and later for Patna (which the Superior could readily have prevented) was an awful blow financially for the [Ahmed] Nagar Mission, much worse than the war and its immediate

719 Frederick Schafer to Francis X. Schubiger (Bombay, 15th November 1921), ARSI, *Bombay. 1004-IX,* 5 (9).

720 Ibid.

721 Maximilian Riklin to Francis X. Schubiger (Poona, 17th January 1924), ARSI, *Bombay. 1004 -IX,* 5 (9).

> financial results ... so long as the present economic condition and chaos continues we have no hope of an improvement.[722]

It is quite clear that the responsible authority, i.e., the Superior Fr. Frederick Schafer had not been able to monitor the financial management. But the crisis of the 1920s continued ever later. A comment by Joseph Stark, a missionary at Sangamner after the death of Fr. Francis X. Schubiger throws some light on it, on a satirical note, he writes: "Some years ago Fr. Schubiger made another attempt to extend the Mission towards the Nasik side. He took new villages, but I had to give them up again. When I came to Sangamner we had 50 masters, now we have only 27. He trusted more in Divine Providence and I have more trust in the Bank Account as long as there is no possibility that the capitalists are smashed."[723]

These correspondences give a sufficient idea that occasionally there did exist lack of a proper planning of finance which caused serious anxiety for the maintenance of the Mission. These concerns are revealed even more strongly when the discussion about a possible division of the Mission into two: Bombay and Poona Missions. In the series of correspondences of Archbishop Henry Doring with the Superior General, a concern that was consistently underlined was lack of funds especially for the purpose of expansion and creating new foundations. Since the majority of the institutions that had almost become self-sufficient, were mostly situated in Bombay and its suburbs, the major anxiety was for further expansion of the Mission in the neighbouring district of Poona. The process of division was bound to be complicated because of the concentration of the institutions in Bombay, whereas in Poona area the schools and other institutions were fewer in numbers, besides these were situated mostly in rural areas. There were chances of leading to a disproportionate division of finance and properties, for almost all the institutions were situated in Bombay and would go to the Spanish Jesuits, while the rural institutions which were fewer in number, would come in possession of the German-Swiss Jesuits. Stated differently the German Jesuits faced the prospect of having been left with bare minimum institutions. In such a background Archbishop Doring wrote:

---

722 Francis X. Schubiger to Maximilian Riklin (Sangamner, 17th January 1924), ARSI, *Bombay. 1004-IX*, 5 (9).

723 Joseph Stark to the General (Sangamner, 1st January 1944) ARSI, *Poona. 1004-XIV*, 16a.

> I often reflect about the separation of the Poona mission from Bombay. Could I place a few points before Your Reverence, before the arrival of the Visitor, so that they could be reflected upon? The exchange of the Fathers again in Poona would be very difficult, as the Society has just one house in the diocese ... how would it be to hand-over St. Mary's along with its Villa House in Khandala to Poona. It is in Bombay, but then ... for considerably long years such a possibility does not come into question due to the financial crunch.[724]

This brief survey thus reveals that the mission had to encounter these circumstances on a regular basis. But our sources show that the situation improved much in later years as is evident from the growth of the Poona Mission.

5.4. The Conflicts on the Question of Jurisdiction

The jurisdictional conflicts related to a decree issued by Propaganda Fide on 12th August 1851. Accordingly, "the Jesuit Bishops in the missions [across the world] were supposed to assume responsibility of the office of the Mission Superiors as well. The exceptions pertained only to the 'internal' governance; what it consisted of, was unclear."[725] This decree was virtually followed during the tenures of Bishop Walter Steins (1860-1867) and Bishop Leo Meurin (1867-1876). Walter Steins was already the Superior of the Mission from 1854 onwards until he was appointed the Vicar Apostolic of West Bengal. The conflict between the Mission Superiors and the Bishops/Archbishops seems to have started during the tenure of Bishop Leo Meurin due to his strong character and self-assertiveness. Meanwhile the Propaganda Fide issued a new decree on 23rd February 1880, according to which a Vicar Apostolic could not hold the office of the Mission Superior also.

Yet, he had the last word on matters of transfer of personnel, adoption of new areas for evangelization and on matters of missionary policies, etc. As for Bishop Leo Meurin, he was not prepared to accept such a division of responsibilities. He believed that "he was not only the head of the local church, but also the Superior of his Religious members as well, who exercised his authority in the name of the Superior General

724 Henry Doring to the Superior General (Poona, 14th May 1928), ARSI, *Poona. 1004-IIA,* 3a-b.

725 Schatz, *Geschichte,* Vol. II, 223. See also Hull, *Bombay Mission History,* Vol. II, 136-39.

... This led to new conflicts, wherein the Apostolic Delegate, Archbishop [Antonio] Agliardi stood by the Mission Superior [Anthony] Willy and not by [Bishop] Mcurin."[726] It is even believed that his recall to Rome (1886), which normally never happens with a Bishop or an Archbishop except in case of grave reasons, was the result of the heightened conflict with successive Mission Superiors. Klaus Schatz cites numerous letters, reports and consultor protocols in order to trace the history of this tension-filled phase.[727]

We consider this issue here from perspective that for a missionary enterprise to be successful, a spirit of collaboration not only among the members of the same mission but also among other missionary bodies working towards the same goal, is a matter of absolute necessity. While making concessions for normal human behaviour to have differences of opinions on issues, we also need to underline the point that the missionaries had a challenge to forego certain of their pet ideas and opinions in order to achieve the common purpose of the mission. Yet, the contrary seems to have been the case here.

Before proceeding further let me explain how the Mission functioned in those days. The Jesuits who went to the mission field did have certain amount of autonomy as members of this missionary body. A few of them were raised to the dignity of Administrators Apostolic and Vicars Apostolic, by the Vatican. At the same time, for its own administration, the Society of Jesus too appointed Mission Superiors for administration of Jesuit apostolates. In principle a spirit of collaboration was imperative for furthering the common cause of the mission. But often the challenge of establishing even a working relationship was lacking. Not seldom did Bombay-Poona Mission witness this situation. It was certainly not in the interest of the Mission.

On certain occasions due to lack of clear demarcation of the exercise of jurisdiction by two authority figures in the Mission, namely the Mission Superior and the Archbishop of Bombay (later also the Bishop/Archbishop of Poona), conflicts seems to have existed. The first instance of such conflicts surfaced during the term of Alban Goodier as the Archbishop of Bombay. From his correspondences he expected more from the Jesuits in terms of availability of personnel for the

726 Schatz, *Geschichte,* Vol. II, 224.

727 Ibid., 223-226.

works assigned by him. However, often this did not Excerpt from a correspondence of Archbishop Goodier illustrate his disappointment:

> Rev. Fr. General told me he would write to the Superior of the Mission stating clearly the limits of our respective jurisdictions, and said that he would send me a copy of the letter for my guidance ... I do not in the very least care how much is taken out of my hands, but I do wish to know what is expected of me, and where my responsibilities end. It does not seem contradictory to say that I am responsible for the maintenance of the mission, and yet another authority has the complete disposition of the men; refusing them if he chooses and even removing them when it suits his purpose, without sending others in their places. It seems impossible that an Archbishop, with his vow of poverty taken from him, should have no personal means of support whatsoever, while the Jesuit Fathers, with their Vow [of poverty]; should have the means of accumulating great wealth. It seems unjust that while the Jesuit Fathers live in plenty and their Archbishop should have nothing; in fact it has been more than once hinted to him that he ought to maintain himself from his friends in England.[728]

The above correspondence reveals unambiguously that a clear demarcation of the exercise of authority was not practised. We may not judge the motivation of the letter. Moreover, it would be wrong to arrive at such a conclusion solely on the basis of one communication. But it does reveal the lack of good understanding among the authority figures of the time. We have further evidence of this—another letter that seemed to convey the Archbishop's disappointment bordering almost upon frustration:

> As you know there are many other difficulties; but I dread the future, not on account of these, or on account of the crosses connected with my work; I dread it because I have no private room which I can call my own, no means on which I can live, no authority whatsoever which the superior of the mission does not claim, entirely on some cases, ex aequo in others, for himself. I dread because I know that every time I solicit his advice and assistance, his advice will always be something for the advantage of the Society and himself, to the disadvantage of the Archbishop and Archdiocese. It has always

728 Archbishop Alban Goodier to Rudolf von Oppenraaij (London, 26th June, 1925), ARSI, *Bombay. 1004-XIII,* n.p. Rudolf v. Oppenraaij was the German Assistant to the Superior General from 1915 to 1934.

> been his consistent and unflinching policy, never even disguised except by words and silence, to leave me deserted until I have to appeal for aid, and then to offer relief in the shape of the most abject surrender to his will. I repeat, if this is what Fr. General wishes, that the Superior and not I should rule and administer the Mission, then nothing will delight me more than to surrender everything to him; it will relieve me of a great burden and give me time for other things far more according to my heart. But if this is not his wish, then Fr. Superior must somehow be shown that I am his friend, not his enemy, to be cooperated with, not to be circumvented or trapped.[729]

The conflicts on matters of administration, sharing of finance and personnel seem to have occurred quite often between Archbishop Goodier and the Mission Superiors.[730] Although the matter seems to have improved during the tenure of Archbishop Henry Doring, there were a few instances of conflicts between him and the Jesuit Mission Superior. Two main areas of contention evident in the correspondences were distribution of donations received from Europe, and division of property between the dioceses (both Bombay and Poona) and the Jesuits. When Aloysius Bertram was the Mission Superior (1919-1928) of the undivided Mission, he often found himself in disagreement with the Bishop of Poona as well as the Archbishop of Bombay. Henry Doring described him as "reserved and non-cooperative"[731] on some issues of common concern with regard to the administration of the Mission.

Maximilian Riklin, Mission Superior of Poona (1929-1935), though generally non-confrontational in his approach, often felt that Archbishop Doring had not observed the principle of equanimity with regard to the distribution of funds and properties.[732] Remigius Rauw, his successor (1935-1944), too seems to have been on uneasy terms with Archbishop Doring on a number of issues. The effect of the lack of coordination between the two was seen most conspicuously in the delayed process of acquiring a property for the De Nobili College,

---

729 Archbishop Alban Goodier to the Rudolf von Oppenraaij (London, 26th June, 1925), ARSI, *Bombay. 1004-XIII,* n.p.

730 Henry Doring to the Superior General (Poona, 31st May 1933), ARSI, *Poona. 1004-VI,* 3.

731 Henry Doring to the Superior General (Poona, 14th March 1928), ARSI, *Poona. 1004-IIA,* 2.

732 See Francis X. Hayler to the Superior General (Munich, 9th May 1934), ARSI, *Germ.-Sup. 1010-V,* 16. See also Francis X. Schubiger to Superior General (Sangamner, 26th April 1935), ARSI, *Poona. 1004-VIII,* 19.

Poona (as we shall see in chapter five, #6.2.2.1). This also happened in other areas of general administration of the mission field. The question of jurisdiction was probably most acute during the tenure of Remigius Rauw. Francis Schubiger gives us an inkling into the same:

> Now the main issue of this letter: the growing tension between His Excellency, the Archbishop Doring and the Superior Regular of the Mission, Remigius Rauw ... The question of jurisdiction - while His Excellency the Archbishop stands by the decree issued by Propaganda Fide on 8.12.[19]28, Fr. Rauw refuses to accept the same with the argument that the decree, if at all, can have a binding effect on the Poona mission as well. [In his opinion] the above-mentioned instruction was issued in relation to the Apostolic Prefectures and Vicariates.[733]

The letter quoted above reveals a few other issues of conflict as well. What emerges is the lack of clarity on the demarcation of jurisdiction between the two authorities in the Mission. Remigius Rauw seemed to take it for granted that the decisions within the jurisdiction of a Jesuit mission station was the prerogative of the Mission Superior, while the Archbishop held a contrary view. Consequently the matter reached a stage wherein the common goal of the Mission seemed to suffer. Here is an example to illustrate the point:

> The Right Reverend Bishop does not want that the Mission Superior anyway interfere in the administration with regard to the Pagan Mission. Unfortunately he can himself cannot manage to look after the affairs of the mission properly in the 80th year of his life. Thus each of the five stations is an independent unit and unfortunately lacking in the co-operation and commonality of the method.[734]

The tenure of John B. Haas (1944-1949) seems to have encountered relatively fewer number of conflicts with Archbishop Doring. But Pius Geisel as Mission Superior (1949-1956) and later as Vice-Provincial of Belgaum-Poona Vice-Province (1956-1959) had a few challenges in working with then Bishops of Poona. On some occasions the conflicts arose on account of the decisions of Bishop Andrew D'Souza (1949-

733 Francis X. Schubiger to Karl Brust, the German Assistant to the Superior General (Sangamner, 14th May 1937), ARSI, *Historia 2001- Poona.*

734 Pius Geisel to the Superior General (Valan, 2nd January 1939), ARSI, *Poona. 1004-XII,* 1. Pius Geisel was the Consultor of the Mission at this point of time.

1967) that had a direct bearing on the Canon Law. For example, according to an instruction issued by Bishop D'Souza the Priests were forbidden to administer the sacrament of matrimony to girls above 14 but below 15 years of age. According to the Canon Lay, the marriageable age was 14 years.[735] This kind of decisions were often the cause not only of conflict between the Bishop and the Mission Superior, but also tended to create pastoral problems to the priests in general. Given this kind of situation, Pius Geisel thought it wise to submit to the will of the Bishop in accordance with the charism of the Society of Jesus. He wrote: "First of all we must be convinced, that our chief task is not to build this or that, to run this institution or that, but to fulfill the most holy will of God. This is manifest to us through the voice of the Bishop of the diocese."[736]

The relationship between the Bishops and Mission Superiors (or Vice-Provincials) seems to have touched a nadir in the late 1950s. The case of Pius Geisel as Vice-Provincial and Bishop Michael Rodrigues of Belgaum Diocese (the first diocesan priest to be elevated to the dignity of a Bishop in this diocese) is in point. The seriousness of the issue may be understood from a letter of Pius Geisel where he mentions saying: "One of the troubles I have a chance to offer up to the S [acred] Heart of Jesus are the Bishops I have to deal with. I enclose a copy of a letter which I wrote--having discussed the draft of it with my consultors--to the Bishop of Belgaum."[737] The context of the conflict was an Apostolic School belonging to the diocese of Belgaum, which was entrusted to the Jesuits for its management. The two Jesuit Priests and a Coadjutor Brother assigned for this purpose often confided to Pius Geisel that Bishop Rodrigues seemingly had too much of interference in its management.[738] In order to address the issue, Pius Geisel wrote a rather strongly-worded letter to Bishop Rodrigues, a copy of which is referred to here.[739] This in turn caused much resentment in the Bishop, who in turn replied in an equally strongly worded letter. He wrote:

735 See Pius Geisel to Piet van Gestel (Poona, 30th November 1950), ARSI, *Poona. 1004-XIX,* 35. Van Gestel was the German Assistant to the Superior General from 1946-1964.

736 Pius Geisel, "Memoriale Visitationis - November 1950," (Poona, n.d.), ARSI, *Poona. 1004-XIX,* 36.

737 Pius Geisel to the Superior General (Poona, 28th June 1957), ARSI, *Poona. 1005-XI,* 26.

738 Ibid.

739 Ibid., Annex.

It is quite clear to anyone that pursues your letter of 28th ult., that you have made a most regrettable blunder, all the more to be regretted, since you hold such a high and responsible office. The blunder is that you have forgotten one of the most elementary and fundamental principles of Justice, "audi altera partem", before giving a decision."

This is a two and a half page typed letter, rebutting each and every point raised by Pius Geisel. It is difficult to assess which party possessed the truth. What is important to note, however, is that the mutual understanding necessary for achieving a common goal, namely the growth of the school, did suffer on account of this conflict. It appears that it took substantial time to resolve the same.[740]

Since there is an absence of documents to reveal the other side of the story, it would be a pure speculation to state anything. All the same, given the dignity of the See of an Archbishop the correspondences must be taken as representing a reality. Moreover, we do not intend to arrive at a general conclusion about this issue. The purpose here is to point out the fact that occasional situations of this kind did exist and that in the longer run did affect the smooth functioning of the Mission. The issue was not an insignificant one to ignore given the fact that the Jesuit Society had a long tradition of 'thinking with the Church' and obedience to the Church authority. This is evident from a fraternal admonition issued by Karl Brust, the German Assistant to the Superior General. He wrote: "Our missionaries should never forget that the Bishop is the responsible leader of our mission and therefore they owe him an Ignatian obedience."[741]

5.5. Ambedkar's Movement among the Depressed Classes

Dr. Bhimrao Ambedkar was born in a Shudra[742] caste known as Mahar at the Military Cantonment of MHOW (originally MHOW stands for

740 See Pius Geisel to the Superior General (Poona, 8th November 1958), ARSI, *Poona. 1005-XI,* 27.

741 Karl Brust to Francis X. Schubiger (Rome, 12th June 1935), ARSI, *RLGGM, Vol. VI,* 257.

742 "The *Shudras,* at the time of Dr. Ambedkar's birth were not only treated as untouchables, but were considered as those who should not be heard or seen. The degradation and indignity heaped upon them by the so-called upper castes though differed from one part of the country to another were never absent. Even in those parts or pockets of the country where there was a certain degree of tolerance towards them, they were never accepted as a part of the society. Thus at least one out of every four Hindus remained for all practical

Military Headquarters of War, but now the place is simply known as Mhow as if it were the name of the place) near Indore in Madhya Pradesh. His father at that time was posted there in the British Indian Army. His parents originally hailed from a village, Ambavade (Ambade), in the Ratnagiri District in the Konkan region of Maharashtra.[743] He spearheaded a movement among the Dalits (Depressed Classes) for their emancipation. This movement had resulted from his deep disenchantment with the Hindu caste system. After completing his studies with rare distinction he endeavoured tirelessly, almost for a decade, to create an opportunity of emancipation for his people in the Hindu society. He made every effort to refine Hinduism from within. But to no avail. Seeing no respite from caste oppressions, therefore, "he had, in 1929, advised the Untouchables to embrace any other religion that would regard them as human beings, give them an opportunity to rise in the world and enable them to act, eat, walk and live like men."[744] His exasperation with the caste oppression finally reached the breaking point by mid-1930s. Consequently, in 1935 during the event of a huge Conference of the Depressed Classes (the Dalits) he advocated a complete break-up with Hinduism, while declaring: "I solemnly assure you that I will not die a Hindu."[745] Dhananjay Keer captures the details of the entire episode in the following words:

> The Conference met, at Yeola [known, therefore, as Yeola Conference as it was held there] on October 13, 1935, and was attended by about 10,000 Untouchables of all shades of opinion ... In a tremendously feeling speech lasting over an hour and a half, Ambedkar recounted the plight of the Depressed Classes in all spheres, economic, social, educational and political, and pointed out the immense sacrifices made by them to secure the barest human rights as members of the same community under the aegis of Hinduism ... He said that it gave him a very painful realisation that the time and money spent on and efforts made to achieve those objectives had proved utterly fruitless. He, therefore, expressed his

---

purposes outside the pale of the Hindu society." M. L. Shahare, *Dr. Bhimrao Ambedkar: His Life and Work* (New Delhi: NCERT, 1987), 2.

743 Ibid., 1-5.

744 See Dhananjay Keer, *Dr. Ambedkar: Life and Mission* (Mumbai: Popular Prakashan, 1990), 251-252. For a more rudimentary presentation of this episode, see Francis X. Schubiger, "Dr. Ambedkar," 75 2/1 (January 1938): 8-10.

745 Keer, *Dr. Ambedkar,* 253.

> opinion that the time for making a final decision to settle the matter had arrived ... He inquired if it were not better for them to abjure that fold and embrace some other faith that would give them an equal status, a secure position and rightful treatment. He, then, with a rise in his voice, exhorted them to sever their connections with Hinduism and seek solace and self-respect in another religion, but warned them to be very careful in choosing the new faith and to see that equality of treatment, status and opportunities was guaranteed to them unreservedly.[746]

A deep sense of agony, frustration and helplessness on the part of Ambedkar becomes quite apparent from the preceding text. A series of experiences of caste discrimination that he had to undergo in work places or elsewhere, in spite of having acquired enviable achievements, drove him to the conclusion that there was no hope left for gaining equal status for his people while remaining within the Hindu fold. In all probability, according to him, such a possibility seemed to lie outside the Hindu fold. It is against this background that we need to continue our reflections further on the topic.

The Jesuits became naturally alarmed, yet at the same time positively surprised with unexpected hope at the news of Ambedkar's decision. A declaration of a possible mass exodus of the Dalits from the Hindu fold obviously seemed to offer a prospect for Christianity, if not alone for Catholicism. As the address made by Ambedkar at the Yeola Conference captured the headlines of the mainstream newspapers and magazines, it "rocked all circles, political parties and social institutions to the bottom."[747] The Brahmanic Hindu hegemony in Indian society was challenged headlong, probably for the first time in history, as "in a tornado of righteous rage Ambedkar hurled a very powerful weapon at the impenitent Hindu society."[748] For, given the obstinacy and rigidity of the caste Hindus, "a shock treatment was necessary to knock out the deep-rooted malady, and Ambedkar made the last bid."[749] The declaration of Ambedkar, thus, was bound to cause tremors across the Hindu society.

---

746 Ibid., 252-253. For a more detailed treatment of the topic see K. N. Kadam, *Dr. Ambedkar and the Significance of His Movement (Bombay: Popular Prakashan, 1991), 41-47. Yeola is nearly 117 kms north of Ahmednagar in Maharashtra.*

747 Ibid., 254.

748 Ibid., 257.

749 Ibid., 264.

Unlike in the case of many other movements, there was no sign of its impact receding from the public discourse. On the contrary it became even further intensified, not only nationally but also internationally.[750]

Although Ambedkar made his declaration already in 1935, the final execution of his decision came only in May 1956, when he definitively severed his allegiance to Hinduism and embraced Buddhism along with approximately 6000000 (six million) of his followers across the country.[751] A considerable span of time, thus, had elapsed. In spite of his declaration of severing his ties to Hinduism in 1935, Ambedkar was hopeful that someday an assurance of equal status to the Depressed Classes would come from the caste Hindus whose representation in the Congress Party (the national party to which Mahatma Gandhi belonged) was in a majority. Yet, nothing but disappointment was in store for him. This period of Ambedkar's decision making was a period of much speculation in socio-political and religious circles. The religious leaders, especially Muslim, Sikh and Christian, from various corners of the world tried to solicit Ambedkar to join their fold. For example, "A Christian missionary [name unknown], who had heard in Europe about Ambedkar's work and personality and was immensely charmed by the sincerity and frankness of his book What Congress and Gandhi Have Done to the Untouchables, sent forth an appeal to Ambedkar to give serious thought to the purity and radiancy of the doctrine of Christ."[752] Muslim and Sikh leaders did the same. But Ambedkar was not in a hurry. He decided to weigh the pros and cons of every possible choice. All along, however, his singular purpose was to attain equality of status to his people in all spheres of life.

The Mahars were the major target group of the Jesuit Mission in Ahmednagar District in Maharashtra. A majority of the Catholics till then had come from this group. Hence, the above question had a direct bearing on the Poona Mission. A sense of anxiety was a spontaneous consequence of the above news. The following report is illustrative of such a conclusion:

> But yet another distress weighs heavy on Fathers' heart. The movement of the Untouchables towards Catholic mission would

750 See Francis X. Schubiger, "Die Bewegung unter den ,Unberiihrbaren," *IB 212* (April 1938): 13.

751 See Keer, Dr. *Ambedkar,* 483.

752 Ibid.

> take a major turn, if - yes all kinds of obstacles are not created on the way ... The villagers from around Yeola, where about a year ago the acknowledged leader Dr. Ambedkar had advised all the Depressed Classes to abandon Hinduism, came again and again to Fr. Eichhorn to request him, in order to start the work [of evangelization] among them. It is urgently needed, therefore, to establish a few schools and a few catechists cum teachers to be placed therein.[753]

A sense of anxiety, on one hand and an urgency to act immediately in order to respond to the signs of the times, on the other were two predominant aspects that emerged. This conclusion may be formulated in the form of questions as well: Would the Jesuits be able to woe Ambedkar along with his followers to join Catholicism? Or would the existing Catholics of Mahar and other Depressed Class origin desert the fold and follow Ambedkar's advice? Thus, the anxiety was whether the people belonging to the Depressed Classes would make a choice of any other religion amidst the situation of uncertainty. At the same time would be missionaries miss that chance?

Ludwig HaBle's report throws light on the same as he writes: "If we fail to receive the people [in our fold] now, they might choose to go to Islam and then probably for a long time there would be nothing that we can do. Who knows if once again such an opportunity comes, if we miss it now?"[754] The text clearly underlines a positive disposition shown towards Catholicism on the part of the Depressed Classes from around Yeola. It was certainly an encouraging aspect and simultaneously threw a great opportunity open to the Jesuits. Ludwig HaBle, having a first-hand experience of the urgency made an urgent appeal to this effect. But from the later development of the Mission with substantial numerical growth of the Catholics around this time, it may be assumed that the Jesuits did heed to the appeal of Ludwig HaBle. Such a conclusion is drawn from the status report of the Visitor of Poona Mission, Adrian van Kalken, wherein he makes a brief mention about the progress of the mission and further need of appointing more catechists in various mission stations.[755]

753 "Ein gesegnetes neues Jahr," 244.

754 Ibid., 245.

755 See Adrian van Kalken to the General (Ahmedabad, 8th October 1936), ARSI, *1411-Visitatio Miss. Van Kalken,* 4.

It appears that the period subsequent to the announcement of Ambedkar about his decision to break-away completely from Hinduism had created a sense of uncertainty among the Depressed Classes. A section of those who had come to know about the Jesuit mission in the area did seem to be inclined towards Catholicism. The inkling of the same is gathered from the following account: "The Untouchables are getting earnest. They want to sever their connections from Hinduism ... Already now they are coming from villages at a distance of 70-80 miles and repeatedly urging that we should come and teach them our religion."[756] But a vast majority of, these groups were beyond the reach of the Jesuits. Given the limited manpower, a gradual expansion of the missionary influence was the only option available. But the circumstance at hand could not afford such a luxury. Quite naturally, therefore, this period was considered as significant in the history of the Mission: "How significant could it be for the mission, is amply clear. In the Diocese of Poona alone there are about one million such Harijans,[757] to whom a search for a new religion is recommended by their acknowledged leader [Dr. Ambedkar]."[758] The author of the text clearly implied that the opportunity was open. Yet it was a herculean task to reach out to such a big multitude at once.

On the question of Jesuit response to the situation, it may safely be concluded that the news about Ambedkar's declaration created an intense atmosphere of curiosity and optimism among the Jesuits. In fact, it appears as if they were almost given to believe that the long awaited hour of the Mission at last had arrived. The Indische Bilder, for example, published an article with the title, Eine bedeutsame Stunde fur die Punamission (a momentous hour in the history of the Poona Mission) in its January 1936 issue, underlying the aforesaid optimism and hope of the Jesuits:

> It appears as though God has now set the arid and crusted farmland of the Poona Mission out on a wonderful and great track. But who

756 "Ein gesegnetes neues Jahr," 245.

757 The term 'Harijan' was coined and popularized by Mahatma Gandhi. It may roughly be rendered as 'children of Hari (God). It was an attempt on his part to accord a respectable identity to the Depressed Classes, instead of calling them 'Untouchables'. See Mumtaz Ali Khan, *Identity formation and self-identity among Harijan elite* (Bangalore: Christian Institute for the Study of Religion and Society, 1994), 5.

758 "Eine bedeutsame Stunde fur die Punamission," *IB* 1/25 (January 1936): 202.

> would sow the seeds in the furrow? With what seeds will they be sown? On 13th October [1935] the Harijans (members of the lowest castes) held a meeting at Yeola ... some 23 kms away from Rahata ... Nearly 10000 delegates and visitors were present. The outcome of this gathering, which drew the maximum attention across India, was the speech of Professor Dr. [Bhimrao] Ambedkar, a Mahar. He spoke on the situation of the Harijans within Hinduism and discussed the issues related to the same ... i.e., the misfortune of being born in a lower caste, etc. With an utter sense of exasperation and bitterness did he demonstrate the consequences of such an unworthy treatment! ... How significant it could be for the Mission is clear. In the diocese of Poona alone there are about one million such Harijans, who are being recommended by their leader to engage in search for a new religion. At the moment, the people from around Yeola, where the meeting took place and such an echo took place, have already come repeatedly to the school and mission station of Fr. [John B.] Eichhorn in Rahata. According to our religious convictions, it is painful that larger parts of our homeland now can do little to utilize this momentous hour generously in order to spread the Kingdom of God. But all can pray that God, the source of this magnificent opportunity, to work even now with His almighty grace so that it may be utilized with the greatest efficacy. Furthermore, 'may the Lord of the harvest send workers into his vineyard!'[759]

The news article underlined the high optimism of the Jesuits in unequivocal terms. Stated differently, it underlined the fact that the Jesuits were of the opinion that they were soon going to gain a numerical strength of the Catholic community on an unprecedented scale. This sense of optimism to win the Mahars to Christianity was not lost until the end of the following decade (i.e., the 1940s) or even until the final decision made by Ambedkar in favour of Buddhism.[760]

From the text above, what emerges quite clearly were: on the one hand the opportunity was great; on the other the personnel and means of utilizing the same in favour of the progress of the mission were lacking. Simultaneously there was an apprehension as well, as to which faith would have the privilege of gaining so many adherents at the scale of a mass-movement. Did the Jesuit mission stand the chance?

759 Ibid., 201. For a similar text, see also "Ein gesegnetes neues Jahr," 244-45.

760 See John Haldner to Felix A. Plattner (Sangamner, 22nd November 1948), AMPSJ, *LB. Sangamner-Briefe.*

Such speculations were quite on expected lines. It was quite apparent that without the generous contribution of the people in the West and sufficient number of Jesuits to work in the Mission, the opportunity could not be turned in their favour. Lamenting the diminishing fervour among the Catholic supporters in the West for the promotion of missions, the author further writes: "It is painful to note that now a majority of the members of our community in our homeland can hardly contribute towards this goal so that this momentous hour may be made use of in favour of expanding the kingdom of God."[761] The goal spoken of in the foregoing text is obviously the numerical increase among the Catholics from among the Depressed Classes.

On a rather cynical note, Dhanajay Keer commented on the spontaneous reaction of the Christian missionaries, Jesuits included and that of the leaders of other missionary religions like Islam, Sikhism and Buddhism in the following words:

> Proselytizing religions with their topmost missionary zeal pricked up their ears in the hope of hearing the death-rattle of Hinduism in its national home, its birth place! Leaders of Islam cast greedy glances at Ambedkar, and promoters of Christianity turned many a holy thought in their minds at the sight of the prospective recruits who would add strength, power and support to their faith and existence. They all thought that if Ambedkar's threat was translated into action, it would definitely tilt the balance to the permanent crippling of the Hindus. The Sikhs also thought of angling for Ambedkar and of adding to their strength.[762]

Ambedkar had never clarified his position openly as to which religion might come in question after he, along with his followers, had broken away from Hinduism. Occasionally he did seem to have given a casual thought on the following religions: Christianity, Islam, Sikhism and Buddhism. His consideration in favour of Christianity was partly because of the fact that the British Government in India comprised of Christians. Certainly the British Government had maintained a policy of neutrality with regard to religions in India. But most of the higher authorities in the British Government were practising Christians. To introduce the lower caste people within the Christian fold, thus, may

761 Ibid., 202. Emphasis added.

762 Keer, *Dr. Ambedkar,* 254.

have implied a protection from the reigning power of the land. As for Islam he took into consideration the fact that the numerical strength of the Muslims across India was much bigger as compared to Christians. Moreover, a sense of unity among them too was an additional factor. The other two religions did not seem to promise these advantages. But the greatest disadvantage with Christianity and Islam was their foreign origin. As against these two, Sikhism offered a native origin which had prospered in Indian cultural tradition. The same seemed to be the case with Buddhism. For about 2200 years earlier it had succeeded in suppressing the ancient Brahmanism and ruled over India for about 600 years. Amidst such considerations, what would Ambedkar decide for, was a matter of speculation till the end of his life.[763]

Indeed, the hope of the Jesuits that the Depressed Classes under the leadership of Ambedkar may be inclined to embrace Catholicism in a mass movement was not fully unfounded. They had been working among the Mahars of Ahmednagar District for nearly five decades. They had established schools, carpet weaving units, primary health centres, etc., besides carrying out various other welfare schemes. Moreover, they had been conducting charitable works and various other ways of job creation during natural calamities like famine and plague. Around the time when Ambedkar's movement was gaining momentum, the high caste Hindu atrocities against the Depressed Classes had increased in various forms. In such a situation too, the Jesuit mission had proved itself to be a benevolent entity. Recalling an incident Francis Schubiger narrates that once a group of high caste Hindus had set the crops of the Mahars of an entire village known as Nandur-Singote on fire, destroying completely their only means of subsistence for the entire year. With the intervention of Francis Schubiger, the Collector of the district, an English man, made it sure that due compensation was paid to the Mahars by the culprits. Following the stern order of the Collector the culprits had to pay Rs. 100 to each Mahar family, which was quite a substantial amount in return for the destroyed crop. This judgment of the Collector was widely reported by the local dailies, highlighting specially the mediating role and intervention of Francis Schubiger in the entire case. This in turn had earned a good name for the Jesuit mission as a whole as a benevolent entity. No wonder Francis Schubiger emerged as a hero and a saviour

763 See Franz X. Schubiger, "Die Bewegung unter den Unberuhrbaren und das Christenturn," *IB* 2/3 (July 1938): 27-30

figure.[764] This incident subsequently proved a great opening for the Jesuit mission among the Mahars and other Depressed Classes. It well validated by Francis Schubiger himself in his report:

> Everywhere the work is going ahead so well, so that for a long time I have not experienced such a phenomenon ... We can and should actually, if we want to make use of the situation created ever since Nandur-Singote incident, open not less than twelve new schools in the villages without any further delay, each with thirty to fifty children; where, until now, we have never been able to achieve a right breakthrough. Now the people are requesting, in fact begging us for the same.[765]

Against the immense hope of the Jesuits, the Depressed Classes did not embrace Catholicism on a large scale. It is true that a substantial number of members of these groups gradually did join Catholicism in the subsequent years. As far as the personal decision of Ambedkar is concerned, it came much later. Why did the situation not turn in favour of the Jesuit mission? One of the reasons as Kher notes seems to be that "although there is a clear mention of the change of religion to achieve the status of equality in the Hindu society, the movement itself was in no way a religious one. Dr. Ambedkar stressed the same in quite unambiguous terms. It was basically a movement that aimed at achieving equality of status in social, economic and political spheres and not on the achievement of a higher level of religious consciousness."[766] Yet, V. D. Savarkar's[767] comment seems to have given a further rise to his

764 See Francis X. Schubiger, "Aus der Bewegung unter den AusgestoBenen," *IB* 1/26 (April 1936): 214-216.

765 "Ein gesegnetes neues Jahr," 244.

766 Schubiger, "Die Bewegung unter den 'Unberiihrbaren," 13. The observation of Schubiger seems to be justified to an extent. However, it is also true that Ambedkar's movement initially did emphasize the thrust on the religious aspects of equality as well. Only at a later stage the emphasis tilted more in favour of political gains, as is clear from the following comment: "The object of the temple movement is good. But you should care more for your material good than for spiritual food. You do not get food to eat, clothes to wear, opportunities of educating your children, and medical help for want of money. You should, therefore, be watchful of the political gains, and you must develop your strength and struggle for gaining material advancement in life." Keer, *Dr. Ambedkar,* 218.

767 A Hindu ideologue whose publication, namely, *Hindutva* (literally Hindu-ness) subsequently became the foundational text for the establishment of an organization known as RSS *(Rashtriya Swayamsevak Sangh,* literally National Volunteers' Organization). This organization today is spearheading various movements among Hindus. Its basic

apprehensions about joining Christianity. Dhananjay Keer notes: "On their conversion, he [V.D. Savarkar] observed, there was no possibility of their receiving treatment of equality under Christianity or Islam in India. He pointed out to the prevailing riots between touchable Christians and untouchable Christians in Travancore."[768]

The existence of caste even among the Christians, thus, proved a stumbling block. This was in spite of the fact that he had studied a number of years with Christian leaders in the West. About his dilemma about Christianity, Jan Jongeneel makes the following observation: "He [Ambedkar] confessed that both the Buddha and Christ captivated him ... But he regarded Christian missions in India, largely initiated by Westerns, as an 'instrument of de-socialization."[769] Hence his decision to embrace Buddhism.

Another important reason lay in the fact that the Hindutva lobby in the Government of Independent India did not leave a stone unturned to prohibit conversion of the Mahars either to Islam or Christianity or for that reason to any other religion other than Hinduism. For this purpose a scheme of reservation in jobs and other financial benefits were offered to them so long as they were ready to remain within the Hindu fold. "This kind of politics could bring a lot of challenges for the missionary work in the future,"[770] thought Karl Thuer after his Visitation of the mission in 1948.

To sum up this discussion let me put a hypothetical question. What would have been the trajectory of the Jesuit mission, had Ambedkar along with his followers embraced Christianity? There would have two possibilities: the numerical strength of the Catholic community would have certainly become stronger. On the other hand the qualitative strength of the community would have come under severe criticism

claim is: "Since Hindus are the majority in India, it is 'natural' and 'democratic' that their 'rights' should be promoted by the Indian state, which hitherto has been 'pseudo-secular,' indulging in the appeasement of the minorities ... Hindutva targets at influencing and controlling the Indian state and suppressing and domesticating the Muslim and Christian minorities. However, the primary goal is to transform the Hindus themselves, to 'awaken the Hindu nation." Divyesh Anand, *Hindu Nationalism in India and the Politics of Fear* (Hampshire: Palgrave Macmillan, 2011), 3.

768 Keer, *Dr. Ambedkar,* 255.

769 Jan A.B. Jongeneel, *Jesus Christ in the World History* (Frankfurt am Main: Peter Lang, 2009), 272.

770 Thuer, "Bericht liber den Besuch der Poona Mission," op.cit.

from various corners, because a multitude of people without sufficient instruction in the faith and tradition of Christianity would have joined the Catholic fold. A comment by Hubert Sixt seems to underscore the issue well:

> It was some setback for the mission when he [Ambedkar] chose Buddhism in preference to the 'selfish' and 'foreign' Christianity. But it helped also to clarify the motives of the new converts. For new catechumens now the inducements and caste concessions for employment make conversion difficult, but the older generation of Christians stand up remarkably well for their faith.[771]

There can be no doubt that Ambedkar's Movement posed a challenge to the Jesuits working right at the epicentre of the movement. Yet, the justification by Hubert Sixt seems to reflect have happened to mission later on. Ultimately what mattered was quality of the Christian community and not quantity.

5.6. Mahatma Gandhi, Hindu Renaissance and Nationalism[772]

Various theories have been proposed regarding the factors responsible for the origin and rise of Hindu cultural renaissance, communalism and nationalism in India. Some authors hold that it was the product of the growth of self-awareness of the Hindus of their centuries-old subjugation under various rulers and their consequent desire to attain self-determination and self-rule. Others hold that the immediate cause was to unite the Indian masses under the banner of Indian cultural identity in order to launch a united front against the British colonial rule. Still others maintain that it was a reactionary move to counter the growing influence of the All India Muslim League (the political party which spearheaded the move to demand a separate Muslim land subsequently, named Pakistan), which almost originated simultaneously with the Indian National Congress that was widely dominated the higher caste Hindus. The All India Muslim League leaders were anxious that the

771 Sixt, "The Ahmednagar District Mission," PJPA, *Varia.*

772 A working definition of the same is given by Jacob Kavunkal in the following words: "By nationalism we mean the political and social attitude of groups of people sharing a common culture, language, territory, as well as their common aims and purposes and thus feeling a deep seated loyalty to the group to which they belong." Jacob Kavunkal, "Conversion and Nationalism," in *Nationalism and Hindutva: A Christian Response, Papers from the 10th CMS Consultation,* Mark T. B. Laing, ed, (Delhi: ISPCK/ Pune: CMS, 2005), 231.

Indian National Congress, because of its higher caste Hindu domination, might be inclined to suppress the Muslim concerns, political and other rights, etc.[773] It can be said that both these movements were mutually opposed to each other. As for our purpose, we shall focus here mainly on two aspects, which seem to have been pertinent in our area of study: freedom struggle spearheaded by Mahatma Gandhi and the growth of nationalism, communalism and sectarian trends among Hindus and Muslims.

This gains significance for the present study because right during the heydays of freedom struggle, Christian missions in India had interaction at various levels with Mahatma Gandhi, the most towering personality of Indian politics of the time. He represented the most authoritative and critical voice of Indians. Secondly, the spirit of fundamentalism and sectarianism among the Hindus and Muslims grew simultaneously with the nationalist movement. It is not to suggest, however, that such a spirit among the afore-mentioned communities, especially the Hindus posed a grave challenge to the Christian missions during the period of our study. However, Jesuits had begun to experience fundamentalist and sectarian ideology and the currents of hostility against their presence and missionary endeavours in India. With passing decades, the same became more and more conspicuous. Some of the later generations of Jesuits appeared to be apprehensive of such currents of ideology and were concerned about the functioning of the Mission. Consequently they seem to have adopted alternative methods and strategies for evangelization.

On the stand of Mahatma Gandhi on Christian missionary activities: although he did not represent the Hindu revivalist movement

773 For a general understanding of these developments, see Prabhu Bapu, *Hindu Mahasabha in Colonial North India, 1915-1930: Constructing Nation and History* (London: Routledge, 2013), 1-2; Surendra K. Gupta, "Political Sociology in India," in *Sociology and Social Anthropology in India,* Yogesh Atal, ed., (Delhi: ICSSR, 2009), 185-236; T. K. Oommen, "Religious Nationalisms and Democratic Polity in India: Impossibility of Reconciliation," in *Nationalism and Hindutva: A Christian Response,* Mark T. B. Laing, ed, (Delhi: ISPCK, 2005), 35-52; Dawa Norbu, "The Cultural Foundations of Indian Nationalism," in *Social Science and Social Concern: Felicitation Volume in Honour of Professor B. K. Roy Burman,* S. B. Chakrabarti, ed., (Delhi: Mittal Publications, 1988), 325-343. For a comprehensive treatment of the subject, see Christophe Jaffrelot, *Religion, Caste and Politics in India* (Delhi: Primus Books, 2010), 3-70; T. K. Oommen, *Nation, Civil Society and Social Movements: Essays in Political Sociology* (New Delhi: Sage Publications, 2004), especially chapter 3.

in the classical sense of the term, his political stature in Indian scenario and the weight of his position on matters like religious conversion were significant. It may be noted that the 1920s signified the beginning of his rise as a national leader, as per our sources. However, we do not find letters directly dealing with the Hindu revivalist movements. They only allude to the experiences of the currents of opposition to Christian missions mostly within the framework of the growing nationalist consciousness, of which the Hindu cultural revivalism was an important component. Consequently, the Jesuits began to experience certain hostile attitude against them. Some of the Jesuits were already growing apprehensive that with the attainment of the independence of the country the future of the Mission too would be affected. In the words of Maximilian Riklin: "Besides, owing to the gradual introduction of Home-rule, the former English officials will be supplanted by Hindus who, as a rule, will be much less favourable, if not positively hostile, to our missions."[774]

Mahatma Gandhi, undoubtedly, was a sympathizer and admirer of Jesus Christ and Christianity in general. But he had a very clear stand vis-a-vis Christian missionary activities, especially conversion, in India. In spite of the fact that he trusted the Christian missionaries most, especially the Americans, he was unambiguous in his stand on the question of conversion and "said that America [or for that matter any other country] should send technical advice, but not money or missionaries interested primarily in conversions."[775] It is quite apparent, thus, that he was against any religious conversion and indeed on numerous occasions expressed his antipathy towards the same. He even questioned the religiosity of the missionaries who engaged in the act of conversion. Although, he did not advocate the expulsion of all the missionaries from India, he did make his stand clear on the question and expressed it by saying that missionaries were welcome in so far as they "work and serve regardless of the prospect and number of conversions."[776] In one of the interviews given to the Examiner, a monthly journal published by the Archdiocese of Bombay, on 20th January 1934, he clearly stated his position on this question:

774 Maximilian Riklin to the Superior General (Bombay, 6th September 1923), ARSI, *Bombay. 1004-1,* 13.

775 Leonard A. Gordon, "Mahatma Gandhi's Dialogues with Americans," *EPW31IA* (Jan. 26 - Feb. 1, 2002): 338.

776 Ibid., 339

> I believe in the equality of all great religions of the world and from my earliest youth, I learned to honour other religions as I do my own. I have no difficulty in inviting and accepting the collaboration of [missionary] bodies of other religions. However, removal of untouchability is one thing that concerns the Hindu religion. ... It is an attempt on the part of Hindu reformers to eradicate this disgrace. ... You can only join in, in order to achieve this purpose in accordance with the ways of the Hindus who do this work ... I need educated men and women who can do our work. In this sense, we have only a handful. We want schools for the poor wretched {Harijans) ... to bring atonement and repentance. So if anyone of you is there, ready to say: "Well, I am ready to run your schools according to your instructions," then well and good. There is a wrong way to help. Of that I am painfully aware; namely when your friends come here with an acknowledged or unacknowledged intention to convert these children. That is a wrong way. It is impossible for me to say that in this case your help will be agreeable. If you offer your help with this goal in mind, then our goal of atonement and removal of disgrace is defeated ... I think the real question is, what you think of Hinduism. If you think deeply in your heart that Hinduism is not a gift of God, but a gift of the devil, you cannot help us, and I cannot respond honestly to your offer of help.[777]

The implication of such a position is clear for the mission. Such a view expressed by a person like Mahatma Gandhi was bound to play a significant impact. No wonder, the missionaries began to entertain certain pessimistic ideas or at least a sense of uncertainty in their minds. The statement of a missionary, referring to the above mentioned interview points to the apprehensions of the Jesuits: "This speech makes it clear enough what the Catholic missions can expect from the Mahatma, and how a Catholic missionary has to face [Mahatma] Gandhi."[778]

We notice however, that such kind of anxiety and uncertainty began to appear among the Jesuits mostly after 1930, as is evident from what Francis Schubiger reported: "The Gandhian movement, though further intensifies, has till now not vexed us too much. The mission is going smoothly further on its path. For, the kingdom of God is in the world but not of the world; so that the concerns of the politicians can hardly

777 John B. Winiger, "Mahatma Gandhi," *IB* 1/19 (July 1934): 151.

778 Ibid.

afford to cause us humour."[779] It would not be wrong to conclude that a sense of insecurity did begin to creep in among the Jesuits with the rise of nationalism.

One of the manifestations of these anxieties was revealed in the incidents of hostility that the Jesuits had to encounter on a number of occasions.[780] It should be noted, however, that the hostile gestures were often subtle and indirect. They were directed against the schools and institutions rather than on persons. For example, the grants and privileges granted to the Jesuit schools began to be controlled and in some cases, even denied. Even if many, nay most of the institutions were recognized by the State, the grants-in-aid were curtailed or sometimes even completely denied.

> The grant-in-aid from the state, which is granted to a school recognized by the state, accounts for about a third of the annual expenditure. At the moment, however, a movement is in progress that aims at robbing the missions of this help. It is very clear that the movement originates from the member of the Congress. This kind of action is dictated on account of aversion, if not a hatred against Christianity. They clearly perceive that the missions effect a great impact on the lives of people through their schools. Hence they wish to stop the same by all means. Since many years, the Department of Public Instruction is in the hands of the Indians, not least the Brahmins for whom Christianity is a thorn in the eye.[781]

Sometime later in the same year (1941), it was further reported on the same issue:

> Yesterday we had an inspection of the school once again. The inspector of the school was very much satisfied. He was wondering as to why our school had not yet received an A-Grade Grant. (A school receives an A-Grade Grant when the government is satisfied with its achievements). A mission school had all the same a lot of

779 Francis X. Schubiger to Joseph Tschudi (Sangamner, 17th October 1930), AMPSJ, *Pune Alt,* 48.

780 The issue here was not exclusively a matter of concern for the German-Swiss Jesuits alone. In fact it was a matter of a general concern pertaining to the new missionaries from abroad, both Catholics and Protestants, aspiring to come to India. That the matter found mention in some letters as well as in official correspondences of the Jesuits, acquires significance in the broader context of this study.

781 Joseph Stark to Joseph M. Wiget (Sangamner, 14th February 1941), AMPSJ, *IB. Sangamner-Briefe.*

> difficulties to acquire an A-Grade Grant. The Brahmins as well as the Congress are against such a move.[782]

A reader unfamiliar with the role of schools in the Christian missions in India, might be intrigued as to ask what the implications of these steps could have been. It may be stated that the rationale behind these steps was to cut the very roots of the source of empowerment of the Depressed Classes by the Mission. In other words, the opponents of Christian missions soon realized that the Christian schools were effecting immense transformation in the lives of the people. The centuries-old higher caste hegemony was being challenged due to the increased awareness among the people. Thus controlling the grants-in-aid for the Jesuit schools implied a two pronged strategy, namely 1) to weaken financially the Jesuits themselves, who greatly depended on the grants-in-aid for further development of the school; 2) to minimize the chances of education for the poor people of the area.

It may be noted that the foreign Jesuits began to grow in anxiety in proportion to the intensification of the movement for independence of India. They were more anxious about their future when political power would be transferred from the British to the Indians, after independence.[783] By the beginning of the 1940s, the nationalist groups became much more vociferous and their tirade against Christian institutions becae unambiguously clear. Ludwig Hassle's opinion may serve as a pointer here. He wrote:

> We missionaries fear a little for the future when the English will hand over more power to the natives. The attitude of the Hindus towards Christianity is hostile. There were very ugly quarrels in the Senate of the University of Bombay about alleged proselytism, in spite of strong opposition a draft of new bill was accepted so that every teacher who brought about a change of the creed of a student can be severely punished. The bill is rather vague so that it is difficult for the accused to plead not guilty. Fr[ancis] Xfavier] College [Bombay] has to suffer from this bill. There were two Parsi [followers of Zoroastrianism] girl students, the Catholic college

782 "Aus aller Welt," *IB* 3/2 (Summer 1941): 12.

783 The German-Swiss Jesuits in Poona, on account of their personnel rapport with the British authorities on one hand, and on account of the British policy of religious neutrality, on the other had an advantage in carrying on missionary work. Such a prospect would severely be curtailed in the wake of the British colonial power leaving India. These apprehensions were certainly not without a sufficient basis.

was made responsible for the conversion although the girls stated that they acted without being influenced by the teachers.[784]

Hassle wrote in another letter: "These stories [i.e., the story of the conversion of two Parsi girls] aroused such an excitement that the newspapers presented them as if they were as important as the war events. All these signal as to what the Catholics could expect when the Indians have more power."[785] Thus the use of newspapers and other means of communication for expressing hostility against the Christian missionary activities became more and more prominent. The conversion of the aboriginals and other backward classes began to be observed carefully. The Congress supported all those stances where the conversion of such groups was refuted and missionary activities were sought to be checked.[786] Against the growing sense of insecurity on account of the incidents of hostility, it appears that the Jesuits, in some manner or the other, may have contributed towards forming an opinion among the simple Mahar Christians that the presence of British in India was a blessing in disguise. Probably this was the reason that they seem to have developed a positive attitude about the British. An instance might throw some light on it: "Here and there someone asks: Can you tell in which direction the war [i.e., WWII] is heading? Is it going on well with the English? If it is so, we can remain in peace, there is no need of anxiety."[787]

The hostility and anti-Christian missionary sentiments began to be felt more strongly from early 1950s, when missionary activities came under greater scrutiny by the higher caste Hindus, whose presence in the government too was undoubtedly strong. A caveat that Pius Geisel as Mission Superior issued to the Jesuits give us a clue into the growing under-currents of hostility against them:

Undoubtedly your ministry is under observation and suspicion and greater care than ever is required to avoid anything that might harm the

784 Ludwig Hassle to Francis X. Hayler (Songaon, 4th October 1943), AMPSJ, *LB. Songaon-Briefe.*

785 Ludwig Hassle to Adolf Gamma (Songaon, 5th October 1943), AMPSJ, *LB. Songaon-Briefe.*

786 See Ludwig Hassle to Emil Kaufmann (Songaon, 9th June 1945), AMPSJ, *LB. Songaon-Briefe.*

787 Ludwig Hassle to Felix A. Plattner (Songaon, 15th July 1944), AMPSJ, *LB. Songaon-Briefe.*

work of the Church in India. Never forget that a native of the country may say and do many a thing without causing comment, which however if said or done by a foreigner will cause resentment... Kindness is all the more necessary now-a-days when even modes of behaviour, that cannot be called exactly unkind, are easily interpreted by nationalism-inspired touchiness as show of superiority.[788]

One of the direct consequences of such sentiments prevalent even among the government officials was the refusal or indefinite pending of visa applications of foreign missionaries. "Since 1952 India has been following a definite policy of restricting the entry of foreign Christian missionaries."[789] For the purpose a definitive policy was prepared by the Government with eight-point specifically stipulated guidelines with the title: "The admission into and treatment in India of foreign missionaries should, subject to satisfactory personal record, be regulated as follows:"[790] This document reveals a deliberate control on the missionary bodies working in India by controlling the permission to enter India among other things. "Later in 1955 the Indian Government declared a definitive policy on the admittance and activities of the foreign missionaries. This in turn effectively minimized the entry of newer foreign missionaries to India after 1955 and more especially after 1960 with only very few exceptions.[791] However, it is imperative to point out that the stance of the Government of Independent India to introduce a policy of gradual restriction on the permission for new visa for missionaries from abroad

788 Pius Geisel, "Memoriale Visitationis - Stationes 1953," (Poona, 23rd November 1953), ARSI, *Poona. 1005-1,* 64.

789 Roland W. Scott, "Christian Missionary Decline in India," *PA* 30/4 (Dec. 1957): 366. See also Thomas Pothacamury, *The Church in Independent India* (Bombay: Examiner Press, 1961), especially chapters 2&3. For a polemical approach on the question within the Constitutional framework, see Ved Prakash Luthera, "Freedom of Religion under the Indian Constitution and the Foreign Missionaries," *TUPS* 16/2 (April-June 1955): 140-146. For a comparative view on the British policy on the same question, see Arthur Mayhew, *Christianity and the Government of India* (London: Faber & Gwyer, n.d.), 233-238.

790 A copy of the same may be found in ARSI, *Poona. 1005-II,* 31. This guideline included the following subjects: I. (a) Auditions, (b) Replacements, (c) Returning Missionaries, (d) Missionaries Already in India, (e) Opening of New Mission Centres. II. Border and Tribal Areas. III. Doctors, Nurses and Specialists. IV. Missionary Originations to be recognized by Government and Missionaries from Commonwealth Countries.

791 See Pothacamury, *The Church in Independent India,* 26-27.

was perceived as anti-missionary. Besides, there was a great concern as regards the future of the missions in India.

Yet, it would be unjustifiable to make a blanket statement saying that the Government of Independent India, as a whole, nurtured an anti-Christian missionary sentiment. In fact Rajendra Prasad, the first President of India, Jawaharlal Nehru, the first Prime Minister and a good number of Ministers in his cabinet were very secular minded people. Jawaharlal Nehru, "although himself not a believer in any formal religious body, is particularly outstanding for sterling qualities - nobility of mind, truth, honesty and justice"[792] and strongly supported the religious neutrality of the nation. He wrote: "It does not mean a state where religion as such is discouraged. It means freedom of religion and conscience, including freedom for those who have no religion ..."[793] Moreover, the Constitution of India itself guaranteed the rights of the citizens to practice and propagate one's religion (Cf. Articles 14, 15, 16, 19, 25, 26, 28, 29 & 30 of Indian Constitution). These have been the positive side of the story. Yet, the other side of the story is equally true that already from the time of Jawaharlal Nehru a certain section of the Ministers in his cabinet having allegiance to the ideology of radical Hinduism did entertain the idea of gradually restricting the number of new missionaries from abroad. However, the dissenting voices in the Government could not take an upper hand, thanks to the stature of Nehru. Yet, Nehru himself was not immune to the pressure of a powerful lobby headed by the Hindu hardliners in the Government. It appears that he began to give at least a tacit approval to the above mentioned lobby.

One arrives at such a conclusion given the fact that the leaders of the Church in India had to make representations concerning the issue of visa for the missionaries on a few occasions. To illustrate the point, Jerome D'Souza's letter to the General may be cited here:

> As I had mentioned in my last letter that the Bishops wanted to interview the Prime Minister and other leaders about the question of the VISA for the foreign missionaries and also about other matters of great importance to the Church in India ... The representatives of the Hierarchy came ... They were Archbishop Gracias of Bombay and Bishop Thomas of Bangalore. The Archbishop of Delhi also

792 Ibid., 2.

793 A. K. Lal, *Secularism: Concept and Practice* (New Delhi: Concept Publishing House, 1998), 106.

> joined the deputation and I was asked to be with them in order to make the introductions. The reception given to the Prelates by the Prime Minister, the President and other Ministers was very cordial and sympathetic and the representations we made were listened to and noted with every desire to help us as far as possible.[794]

Having received a cordial and sympathetic listening to the concerns brought up by the deputation, the Church in India had a respite on the issue, at least for the moment. Yet the Catholic Church in India was painfully driven to the awareness of possible unfavorable times awaiting it, so that the secretary of the Catholic Bishops' Conference of India had to issue a circular: "The Secretary of the Bishops' Conference in a circular has notified the hierarchy [of India] about the visa difficulties. He had inquired in Delhi whether this development is heading towards a policy change."[795] Yet, the expectation on the part of the Government seems to have been unequivocal at this point that the Church in India must gradually begin the process of Indianization,[796] at least beginning with the admission of native church personnel. Once again such an import emerges unambiguously from the same letter quoted above:

> First as regards the all-important question of VISAS: I had written to Your Paternity that the P[rime] Minister] had already intervened and decided that there should be no change of policy. We thanked him for his intervention and assured him that unless the church in India was in real need of assistance we would not ask for foreign help in personnel, and that the church was committed to the policy of a prudent but firm realization of putting Indian personnel as quickly as

794 Jerome D'Souza to the Superior General (Poona, 1st December 1952), ARSI, *Poona. 1403.* Jerome D'Souza has been till date probably one of the best known Indian born Jesuits. He was nominated to the Constituent Assembly which drafted the Constitution of India. The provisions on the safeguard of Minority rights, besides the freedom of religions which have great significance for the Indian Christians found their place in the Constitution, thanks to his diplomacy and statesmanship. He had won great admiration of Jawaharlal Nehru. To his credit goes the foundation of Indian Social Institute situated now in Delhi and Bangalore. As Indian and East Asian Assistancy was constituted, he was nominated its first Assistant to the Superior General in 1957. See V. Lawrence Sundaram, *A Great Indian Jesuit, Fr. Jerome D'Souza* (Anand: Gujarat Sahitya Prakash, 1986).

795 Pius Geisel to Felix A. Plattner (Poona, 31st July 1952), AMPSJ, *Superior Poona, P. Geisel.*

796 The motive of the government is unclear, at least at this stage. Whatever may have been an immediate impact, such an imperative placed on the Church in India did seem, as it would be clear from 1960 onwards, to have generated a positive result of accelerating the process of admission of the natives in the seminaries and novitiates.

> it is trained. The P[rime] M[inister] was interested in this and asked for details and figures concerning the progressive Indianization. I believe that as a result of this crisis and our subsequent talks with the officials of the Home ministry, the procedure for getting VISAS may be simplified and delays may be avoided in future ... We have explained to the Government that this is not always easy owing to the difficulties of training a priest with the discipline and the learning required in the Church.[797]

Although the above letter seems to reflect a lot of optimism, the Jesuits in Poona undeniably began to face certain challenges and uncertainties, as far as the ground reality is concerned. At the top level of the Government, thanks to the liberal and secular Prime Minster, a great hope of intervention on the question of visa was given to the church delegation. Yet, the Jesuit missionaries were not spared of anxieties about the future. Given the nature of the projects undertaken, i.e., Indian Institute of Social Order and hospital at Belapur (situated 177 kms north of Poona), in the initial years of 1950s, the policy of gradual restriction on the admission of new missionaries, seemed to cast their future in uncertainty. In spite of the openness to accelerate the process of admitting the natives to the seminaries and novitiates, the end result of ultimately handing over the Mission entirely into the hands of the native clergy was a faraway dream.

Hence, the question of immediately manning the mission with the help of native clergy was the most urgent concern of the Jesuits. Amidst such concerns, however, initially, i.e., around the beginning of 1950s the policy of restricting visas did not seem to be too formidable a hurdle in the progress of the mission. Yet, it is clear that the Jesuits had begun to experience the difficulty on account of either a slow process of getting visa or refusing the application: "It was a great consolation to see all standing bravely against the odds as well as in seeking the new solution as regards the question of visa ..."[798] But such an optimistic tone seems to have gradually changed over the months and years: "The difficulties

797 Jerome D'Souza to the General (Poona, 1st December 1952), ARSI, *Poona. 1403, Negotia Specialis.*

798 Pius Geisel (Mission Superior) to the General (Poona, 1st November 1951) ARSI, *Belgaum-Poona. 1301 (1950-1952).* This document, as may be seen, is one of the most valuable sources of information on the topic. It contains nearly 800-1000 pages. Unfortunately it is not paginated. Hence the location of the cited letter may be identified from the date mentioned in the brackets in each citation.

regarding the 'Visa' continues. We hear that Bombay has denied visa for the Sisters who have been especially invited for the work in the asylum for leprosy patients."[799] In a letter to Felix Plattner, the Mission Procurator in Zurich, repeats the situation: "Delhi keeps me waiting for the visa of [Scho. Henry] Schulz and that of Sisters."[800] Even for the existing Jesuits, a process of closer scrutiny began to be introduced, although they were never made public. The Jesuits having encountered a number of such occasions realized that things had substantially changed after the Independence of the country. Evidently the process of scrutiny of application for visa had become much stricter, as may be seen from the letter of Geisel: "The process of acquiring visa for [Henry] Volken, [Hermann] Bacher and [John] Belser is underway. I have been already twice by the police. They wish to know once again as to who has taken guarantee for them. Why and wherefore? When do they come in fact? When do the Ursulines arrive?"[801] The problem seemed to have further intensified with the passage of time. From the report of Pius Geisel in 1954, we arrive at such a conclusion:

> Since last 6 months not a single 'visa' (even after a recommendation) ... the Bishop of Delhi knows that such cases must be put under the category of 'extreme necessity' and requested as such. I am sending Br. [Otto] Widmer back to home-country (for whom visa refusal continues); nothing seems to move. But either he or anyone else will go to Delhi, if need be. Now the Fathers, for whom the visa is denied are naturalized citizens of India ... The general behavior of the officials in Bombay is indifferent; the letters under continual censure. Some of us in Bombay are watched by the Secret Police.[802]

The above account is a clear indication that the Government was on the way to introduce certain drastic measures as regards the visa policy for foreign missionaries, which eventually materialized in 1955.

---

799 Pius Geisel (Mission Superior) to the General (Poona, 11lh September 1952) ARSI, *Belgaum-Poona. 1301 (1950-1952).* See also in the same file, letters dated 23.09.1952; 18.10.1952; 27.10.1952; 27.03.1953; 28.04.1953; 30.08.1953.

800 Pius Geisel to Felix A. Plattner (Poona, 28th August 1952), AMPSJ, *Superior Poona, P. Geisel.*

801 Pius Geisel to Felix A. Plattner (Poona, 31st July 1952), AMPSJ, *Superior Poona, P. Geisel.* See also in the same file, letters dated 27th September 1952; 22nd April 1952.

802 Pius Geisel (Mission Superior) to the Superior General (Poona, 1st January 1954), ARSI, *Belgaum-Poona. 1301 (1950-1952)..*

Another aspect of the anti-missionary sentiments, which gradually gained currency among more and more people in the Government, was the state level restrictions imposed on Christian institutions by certain governments. One of the best known cases in this regard is the Report of the Christian Missionary Activities Inquiry Committee, Madhya Pradesh, 1956, popularly known as the Niyogi Committee Report, named after its Chairman Shankar Guha Niyogi, a retired High Court Judge. It was a committee of inquiry established by the Government of Madhya Pradesh state on account of the alleged conversions to Christianity taking place by force or fraud.[803] Since the matter is too complicated to be discussed here, besides it being not directly pertaining to the Poona Mission, we make only a passing reference to it same in order to underscore the point that the anti-Christian and anti-missionary sentiments were on the rise during this time.

At the functional level the Jesuits in our Mission, were beginning to experience the consequences of such sentiments more directly in their apostolate. For these developments certain Hindu organizations were responsible. Pius Geisel, for example, does not mince words indicating the fact that behind the rising anti-missionary sentiments, the Hindu Mahasabha (Great Assembly of Hindus) and similar organizations like Arya Samaj had a direct role to play. A few of his reports as Mission Superior to the General lead us to such a conclusion: "The Hindu Mahasabha has begun various actions against the mission in Poona and its suburbs ... they intend to come to the 'municipal corporation' in order to oppose the subsidies given to the Christian institutions. In Ahmednagar they placed an idol in a Hall in the campus of the 'good ladies' [Sisters]; Fr. Pius Geisel is trying to intercede with the police and other government officials."[804] Similarly he expresses his worries that under the shadow of such developments, it would not be unjustifiable to say that the future of the mission might be bleak: "In the Kkandesh District the aid to the mission schools is being denied and hostile

803 See *Vindicated by Time: The Niyogi Committee Report on Christian Missionary Activities* (New Delhi: Voice of India, 1956, this edition 1998); William Coelho et al., *The Niyogi Committee Report: A Critical Appraisal* (Varanasi: Satya Manthan Sanstha, 2000).

804 Pius Geisel, Mission Superior to the General (Poona, July 1954), ARSI, *Belgaum-Poona 1301 (1950-1959)*. See in the same document letters addressed on 11th September 1952; 1st January 1954; 27th August 1958; 15th January 1959, etc. Further see Pius Geisel to the Superior General (Poona, 18th February 1955), ARSI, 1005-IV, 12.

articles are being published in the newspapers. The future is obscure."[805] In another letter Geisel reports: "The hindoo [Hindu] Mahasabha paper 'Kesari' has every now and then articles attacking Christianity. One recent article (27-12-55) was a vicious attack on the Jesuits ... It was said, that the Jesuits were ever so often expelled from other countries and that India should beware of them. The old accusation, that we use also bad means to achieve the spread of religion was repeated."[806] What became very clear towards the end of the decade (the 1950s) was that the issuing of Visa for the missionaries from outside India was fully restricted.[807]

Another aspect of such sentiments being manifested in government policies was the move to take control of the Church properties. The matter comes to light from the letter of Jerome D'Souza: "The other matter of which we spoke to the leaders were about the Laws passed in Bombay about the supervision of church property about which we have serious difficulties…"[808] This, as may be imagined, was deemed to have multiple ramifications, i.e., an effective control over the Church, its sources of income, its expenditure, etc.

Along with the question of restriction on visa, a number of other issues began to surface with the passing of time. They were clear indications that the golden days of the missionary era were already gone. Now trying days were soon going to visit them. It is apparent that the Government was gradually going to implement certain restrictions which would have deep implications for the future of the Church in India. The issues at stake at this point of history are evident in the following letter:

> ...about concessions to Christians converted from backward classes and who ordinarily lose those financial and educational concessions when they are converted; about increasing chaplains for the Catholics in the Army, etc ... In the meantime, in spite of the

805 Geisel (Mission Superior) to the General (Poona, 1st January 1954), ARSI, *Belgaum-Poona. 1301 (1950-1952).*

806 Pius Geisel, "Litterae Superioris Missionis," (Poona, January 1956), ARSI, *Poona. 1005-VI*, 6.

807 See Joseph Übelmesser, "The Catholic Church in India: The Story of a Personal Encounter," in *Bend without Fear: Hopes and Possibilities for an Indian Church: Essays in Honour of Professor Kurian Kunnumpuram SJ,* eds., Kuruvilla Pandikattu & Rocha Rosario (Pune: Jnana Deepa Vidyapeeth/ Delhi: ISPCK, 2003), 226.

808 Jerome D'Souza to the Superior General (Poona, 1st December 1952), ARSI, *Poona. 1403.*

> propaganda by eminent persons there is still much opposition in the country to official approval of birth control. We are intensifying our own publicity against it and many Hindus and Muslims are with us in this matter.[809]

From the above discussion it is clear that a new era for the Church in India was about to dawn. The challenge of developing native leadership in spite of lot of immediate constraints seems to have helped the Church in India to take a real stock of its identity. Was it a Church with a European face or was it really Indian in its identity? These questions tended to occupy a lot of public discourse today in India. Ins sum, these difficulties and challenges did give an impetus to the Jesuits of Poona Mission toward fostering native leadership and indegenisation of mission.

5.7. Natural Calamities: Drought, Famine and Epidemic

As indicated in the maps the Jesuit mission work was more concentrated in Ahmadnagar District and surrounding regions. These areas had always been drought-prone regions and their "drought-proneness"[810] was very much related to their physical and climatic characteristics. The entire region consists of rugged hills and arid zones with below average rain year after year. Given these characteristics, the region had been witnessing frequent instances of severe famines and epidemics in the previous century too. Not seldom did the Mission witness natural calamities of various types--drought, famine, pestilence and epidemics. As for the occurrences of famines in the previous century, Pius Geisel has the following detail:

> The Ahmednagar district, where all our Marathi-speaking missions are situated, is notoriously known for its constantly recurring famines. In the last century Ahmednagar was haunted [by the same] in the years 1803, 1824, 1832-33, 1845-46, 1862, 1868, 1876-77, 1896-97, 1899 -1900. [In fact], there occurred a whole series of 'drought' years [also besides the years officially mentioned].

---

809 Ibid.

810 See Suhas Paranjpe and K. J. Joy, "An Alternative Approach to Drought and Drought-Proofing," in *Drought and Integrated Water Resource Management in South Asia: Issues, Alternatives and Futures,* eds. Jasveen Jairath & Vishva Ballabh (New Delhi: Sage Publications, 2008), 100.

[Unfortunately] they are not referred to as such by the government [in its records] and thus were not earmarked for relief efforts.[811]

About the latter instances of recurrence of famines mentioned in the above citation, another missionary adds:

> These were very difficult years for the entire mission. By the end of 1896 a terrible famine broke out followed by cholera and plague. Later, in 1899-1900 one of the severest famines broke out, probably the worst in human memory. In 1900 people could gather only a one-fifth of their normal harvest and in 1905 it was even worse when people could gather only one-sixteenth of the normal harvest.[812]

Frequent droughts and famines in the region occurred in the 20th century too; indeed right from the beginning as noted above. We are told that during the ten year span between 1911 and 1921 the western region of Maharashtra, namely Poona and Ahmednagar districts besides others, was affected by famines not less than four times.[813] Making a mention of one them, Francis X. Schubiger wrote: "There came 1917, a year of severe plague ... [Then followed] the influenza in 1918 with the subsequent famine."[814] Similarly, a study undertaken for the period 1931-1960 too reveals that a gradual decline in the average rainfall in the region had been an undeniable fact.[815] Consequently, the economic condition of the people was poor. It is hardly difficult to imagine that the people of this area were more severely hit by these natural calamities than people from other regions, very especially whenever failure of

---

811 Pius Geisel, "Hungersnot," *IB* 1/28 (October 1936): 235. The last three famines mentioned in the citation above were probably among the most devastating for the sheer fact that they collectively claimed hundreds of thousands of human lives. See Planner, "80 Jahre Mission," *WMKK* 19/1 (January 1935): 9-10; Winiger, "Die Missionsstation Sangamner," 11-14. For general information see Douglas E. Haynes, *Small Town Capitalism in Western India: Artisans, Merchants and the Making of the Informal Economy, 1870-1960* (Delhi. New York: Cambridge University Press, 2012), 175-180; John F. Riddick, *The History of British India: A Chronology* (Westport: Praeger Publishers, 2006), 84.

812 "Valan," *IB 1/29* (January 1937): 246. See also Archbp. Theodore Dalhoff to the Superior General (Bombay, 11th August 1900), *ARSI, Bombay. 1003-1,* 1. The reference to the previous century is cited precisely to show that the B-PM had to face the challenges on account of drought and famine even in the pre-World War I era as well.

813 See *Studies in Economics of Farm Management in Ahmednagar District, Maharashtra State: Report for the Year 1967* (Bombay: Directorate of Economics and Statistics, Ministry of Agriculture and Irrigation, 1967), 1; 29 & 397.

814 Francis X. Schubiger, "Unser Kleiner Guido," *IB* 1/21 (January 1935): 170.

815 See *Studies in Economics of Farm Management,* 1, 29 & 397.

monsoon caused severe famines, "for, rain is in fact the very life for Indians."[816]

When the region was hit by famines, people had hardly any alternative means of subsistence. The lack of work to earn their livelihood made the situation further tragic: "Nowhere is there any work. The work in the fields is beyond consideration as they are uncultivated ... [Besides] there are no industries around the place,"[817] wrote Pius Geisel. Apparently all means of subsistence of a majority of the people were exhausted, not only during the famine of 1935 but practically every time the region was hit by such calamities; leading the people to unspeakable miseries.[818]

The famine of 1935 was not a lone event. Indeed famines followed in the subsequent years and decades as well. For example 1936, 1937, 1939, 1943, 1945, 1953, 1960-1961 too were famine years[819] as far as the mission-field was concerned, although occasionally they were not declared officially as such. As an example, we read the following account:

> Officially, according to an instruction issued by an Indian Minister ... one may not speak of a famine; but only of an inflation. In fact, [however], the entire area of Maratha-mission is under terrible distress. It has not rained for last sixteen months ... Hundreds of wells are empty ... Last year, for months, there was not a single drop of rain ... There is no question of sowing seeds ... The prices of food items now have already gone up by more than 100%, and the people who are unemployed may earn either a little or nothing; while they do not have any fields or have no crops to harvest.[820]

The famine of 1939 hit the Mission severely, especially Songaon mission station, so much so that people talked not so much about the war [WWII) but about the famine ... The prices of grains have gone up

816 Pius Geisel, "Hungersnot," *IB* 1/28 (October 1936): 235.

817 Ibid., 236. See also Maurice Emmenecker, "Die Teppichweberei in Kendal," *IB* 1/24 (October 1935): 194.

818 See C. M. Agrawal, *Great Natural Calamities* (Delhi: Indian Publisher Distributors, 2000), 26.

819 Felix A. Plattner, "Wie Wir uns einen gesunden Bauernstand in Indien vorstellen und an seinem Aufbau mithelfen?," AMPSJ , *Varia/Felix.A. Plattner.*

820 "Ein gutes neues Jahr, 243. See also Archbishop Henry Doring to the Superior General (Poona, 2nd January 1937), ARSI, *RLGGM,* Vols. V-VI, 326. See a copy of this letter in ARSI, *1402: Visitatio Miss. Poonensis 1935-1941,* 5.

unprecedentedly ... The traders have raised the prices of other things too very high ... As a result many Christians have left their villages and settled in the areas where there are sugar factories, in order that they might get some jobs. Some of the villages are almost entirely deserted. In the schools there are so few school children left that there is hardly any sense in leaving behind a catechist.[821]

Similarly the famine of 1943 seems to have been no less severe than the earlier ones as far as the implications for the Christian population of the place was concerned. The question of survival became paramount. People had no choice but to migrate, even temporarily, to other places in search of livelihoods. This caused much anxiety to the Jesuits: "A number of villages are half deserted, two villages almost entirely so, on account of the scarcity and dearness. This means so many of our people beyond our reach and influence. Three young teachers had to be temporarily suspended, for lack of work."[822] Clearly, since a substantial number of people were moving out of the villages, the number of children in the schools was bound to drop. Consequently, a few teachers had to be temporarily suspended.

The famine and consequent breakout of pest and cholera in 1945 were even more severe and they hit especially Songaon, Hubli and other neighbouring mission stations. In these areas there was absolutely no rain from May to November 1945.[823] As a result various sicknesses broke out.

> The cholera is very strong ... followed by dysentery and small-pox. In July [1945] broke-out also bubonic plague ... in Sangamner alone died 75 people of this sickness. A man ... from Sangamner had visited his friend in Songaon and thus the sickness spread in Songaon as well. Since 5 villages here are very close to each other ... the sickness has spread here very fast. The natives of these villages have completely deserted the villages now. All have run away to the jungles and have erected small huts there, where they stay since last 4-5 months. But the pest has followed them to the jungle too, so that

821 Ludwig Hassle, "Songaon: II. Weihnachtsbericht 25. 12. 39," *IB* 2/10 (April 1940): 111-112.

822 Otto Lustig to John B. Moyersoen, Mission Superior of Calcutta Mission (Sangamner, 17th January 1944), ARSI, *Poona. 1004-XIV,* 21a.

823 See Anton Herbert to Joseph Brandle (Hubli, 30th March 1946), AMPSJ, *IB. Puna-Briefe (alte).*

> every other day some one or the other dies there. How many deaths will occur is difficult to tell.[824]

Thus the occurrence of droughts, famines and consequent epidemics was a severe challenge to the Jesuits. The later occurrences of 1953 and 1960 were equally precarious. In 1953 famine practically all the mission stations were heavily affected. Many wells at Songaon mission station completely dried up resulting in severe lack of drinking water. At Kendal mission station the Carpet Weaving Unit came to a standstill as there were no orders for carpets. Many people from Harigaon mission station deserted the villages in search of jobs.[825] Reporting about the famine of 1960, Sr. Nikolaus wrote: "The monsoon rain failed this year and the crops have failed. Most of the fields could not be cultivated. As a result, our people have no work and are on the verge of facing a difficult situation even before the real famine begins, which is evidently going to occur ... We look forward with great anxiety."[826]

Droughts and famines affected not only human lives, but also cattle, the most precious possessions of the people of the place, for farming and cultivation were impossible without cattle. Often nothing was left to graze them on and the danger of losing them was imminent: "The situation of the animals is utterly sad. They are hungry since last two months. The bigger farmers have some stock of straw left; but the poor people who own hardly a few square meters of land, have nothing left."[827] The severity of the calamities may be assessed from the fact that the people were often forced to dig the roots of plants to feed their cattle as nothing else was available on the bare grounds. Gloom and despair could be felt everywhere. Poor people had nothing left except to indulge in melancholic talks about their hardships and distress.[828]

As if the lack of food and drinks in the events of famines were not enough to drive the people into miseries, cholera and such other

---

824 Ludwig Hassle to Felix A. Plattner (Songaon, 16th November 1945), AMPSJ, *IB. Songaon-Briefe.*

825 "Hungersnot in der Puna-Mission," *IB* 3 (1953): 1-2.

826 Sr. Nikolaus, "Drohende Hungersnot?," *JHS* 5 (1959): 8. JHS began to be published from 1959 with the subtitle, *Folge von «Indische Bilder» und «Nachrichten aus Bad Schdnbrunn»* until the end of the year. From 1960 this newsletter began to be known solely as JHS.

827 Geisel, "Hungersnot," 237.

828 Ibid.

epidemics were often their necessary corollaries, although they were not always the results of famine-like situations. They were basically caused by the lack of clean drinking and washing water. Cholera, for example, was caused by the lack of clean drinking water, whereas smallpox was due to lack of clean washing water. Skin diseases were direct consequences of the lack of cleanliness: "Naturally, while the people do not have enough clean drinking water, they hardly bother about washing themselves. Thus break out skin diseases like smallpox."[829] In any case, all these implied a manifold increase in the distress level of the victims. In turn, there was a heightened sense of urgency among the Jesuits. In order to elucidate the sense of anxiety and helplessness among the Jesuits, a report of Schubiger on the epidemic of 1917 just mentioned above, which claimed around 800 lives from Sangamner alone, may be cited as an example:

> In the evenings often I really do not know, where my head lies; so much of misery invades me. In addition, whenever I am in the house, the sick and the hungry cause me botheration the entire day. Now many Marathas of all classes [both Christians and non-Christians] are coming to me who are temporarily migrating to other places in search of means of livelihood. They wish to deposit their cooking dishes and crockeries ... in the safe custody of the only reliable man - the missionary. [In fact] there is still a lot more to share, which I am utterly scared of.[830]

Based on their earlier experiences, the Jesuits in the later decades became often alarmed at a possible failure of the monsoon. Indeed it cast a deep sense of anxiety and worry among them, as may be concluded from the following text:

> Then came the official weather forecast from the government that was nothing less than a nightmare. 'We are not in a position to say anything definitive about the monsoon of this year, as the prognostic indications of a good rainfall seem to show rather unpropitious signs.' Immediately we began to fear that behind such a cautious notification, there is an unambiguous indication of imminent famine. Soon came another cautionary statement: 'The conditions

829 Francis X. Schubiger, "Aus Indien," (Sangamner, 15th April 1927), *MDPSJ,* 90 (1927): 63.

830 "Valan," *IB* 1/29 (January 1937): 247.

for a widespread and severe breaking-out of cholera epidemic are quite predictable.'[831]

The obvious questions that the Jesuit missionaries faced in such situations were: how to carry out the work of evangelization amidst such precarious conditions? How could they carry on the work of evangelization when the more pressing concern among the people was of their physical survival? How could they meet the challenge of harmonizing the physical as well as the spiritual welfare of the people?

An aspect that had consistently surfaced was that the villagers were forced to desert the villages in search of their livelihood, practically during every occurrence of famine and other natural calamities. In such situations the question was how to extend pastoral care to the Christians who were away from their villages. These and other were pressing issues were to be addressed. The Jesuit pastors, therefore, used to make extensive pastoral tours to their Christian communities, especially to the villages where the some Christians were left behind during circumstances of distress. For, their major concern was pastoral care of the Christians. Was it exclusive for Christians? It must be understood in a proper perspective. In fact it would not be unjustifiable to say that they made a compromise to cater to the Christians only as they could not have afforded to extend help to everyone around the place. Hence, it must not be interpreted as a selfish step on their part. In spite of the good will, the Jesuits had limited means of reaching out to the needy. But it would be a misrepresentation of the fact that their pastoral care was entirely and exclusively restricted to the Christians alone. They did reach out to others as well, occasionally even with financial assistance.[832]

Visits of the Jesuit pastors were always welcome to the people in distress. These were occasions when the people could share their distress with them, who were the only source of hope for them. They would place their hope entirely upon them; often much bigger hopes than could be translated into reality by the Jesuits. Apparently such expectations of the people were scary to the Jesuits given the limited

831 Geisel, "Hungersnot," 235-236.

832 See Felix A. Plattner to Gerhard Baader (Zurich, 19th July 1961), AMPSJ, *16 Superior Puna, neue - Baader, Weber, Staffner.*

means at their disposal to help them out. Pius Geisel expressed his helplessness in the following words:

> One might tell them hundreds of times: we are not omnipotent. Yet they would make incessant requests ... First of all they would wish to know exactly, the hour and the date, when it would rain. I would make sincere efforts to console them as much as possible with the suggestions that the rain might be slightly delayed, [and that they need to keep their hopes alive].[833]

The Jesuit pastors knew well that the people, especially the Christians, had none others to place their trust upon. But they too were helpless because of the lack of sufficient funds, so that Francis Schubiger lamented: "Of course the Christians look forward to the Jesuits for aid. In earlier times the priests, thanks to the generous assistance from home [Europe], were able to help many. Now they starve themselves. In addition they must painfully witness, due to cholera and plague ... the diminishing number of their hard-won Christians."[834] A similar tone is witnessed in a report of Pius Geisel: "After the nadir of the 1935 epidemic, an increase in the death-toll is to be expected. Already then we knew that something unpleasant and difficult was awaiting us. The implication was clear that we needed to be ready to help out as much as possible, nearly 3500 people [Christians] at our disposal, both materially as well as spiritually amidst such a difficulty."[835]

No doubt, these anxieties experienced by the Jesuits were realistic. Consequently, every instance of drought and famines passing-by was a moment of great relief to them.[836] Yet, in the event of the eruption of cholera and other such epidemics, the Jesuits faced great challenge because of the herculean task of providing the necessary medical care and other help. There was also the challenge of providing spiritual care to the new Christians, for often they tended to fall back to their superstitious beliefs and ascribed the tragedies of epidemics to the wrath of the un-propitiated deities. They not only needed to be rescued from such superstitions but also needed to be educated in the scientific causes of such calamities, i.e., that cholera or pest are purely natural

833 Geisel, "Hungersnot," 236.

834 "Ein gutes neues Jahr," 244.

835 Geisel, "Hungersnot," 236.

836 Archbishop Henry Doring to the Superior General (Poona, 2nd December 1936), ARSI, *Poona. 1004-IX,* 14.

phenomena. An incident may well illustrate the kind of superstition people were gripped with:

> ...but cholera is still playing a havoc in Rahata. Consequently all the paths to the villages have been blocked with stone barricades, so that the cholera-goddess Kashi could make no entry into the villages along with the car. When I recently drove over the stone barricade to enter a village, the people created a lot of commotion until I explained to them that a heathen goddess certainly could not have dared to travel in the car of a Christian missionary. Eventually they seemed to be convinced.[837]

Similarly, Joseph Winiger has noted, albeit in a sarcastic manner, the deep-seated superstition among the people:

> It concerns the cholera again... Every Tuesday hundreds of them come together - men, women and children with baskets and jugs full of offerings. They pass by the mission station. The Devi [goddess] is powerful. In Ambhore [a village close to the mission station at Valan] five Mahars were affected by the cholera. The pellets [medicinal tablets] of the missionary have saved them all. Yes, the pellets of Phader Saheb [Reverend Father] are effective; he has a good demon in it [they say]. But even if they are effective - the mother Kashi [local name for cholera goddess] ...who is our goddess is not less powerful either.[838]

It is clear that people did see the effectiveness of the medicines provided by the padre sahib. Yet, the superstition was so deeply entrenched in their psyche that they failed to see the epidemic as a natural phenomenon. The Jesuits were intrigued by the religio-cultural roots of such superstitions: "Breaking out of pest is associated with the plague of rats. Now, since the Hindus must not harm this nice creature and the government does not want to tamper with the religious sensibilities of people, nothing remains to be done."[839]

Seen against such a background, the natural calamities were among the most serious challenges faced by the Jesuits. At a very pragmatic level, therefore, the Jesuits needed to address the question by organizing

---

837 John B. Eichhorn, "Rahata," *IB* 1/32 (October 1937): 280. Taxis, cars and other vehicles seem to have been considered by the people as symbols of inauspiciousness.

838 Joseph Winiger, "Die Choleragottin," *IB* 1/29 (January 1937): 248.

839 Francis X. Schubiger, "Aus Indien," (Sangamner, 15th April 1927) *MDPSJ,* Nr. 90 (1927): 63.

support programmes for their survival first. For example, the Carpet Weaving Unit, started at Valan and later transferred to Kendal, about which we have discussed in the previous chapter, was initially visualised as a venture to make the new Christians self-reliant by creating jobs at least for some people during the situation of crisis. In more than one sense this venture was instrumental in keeping the hope of a section of the new Christians alive amidst the despair resulting from famine and epidemic situations.[840] Besides these efforts, financial help was availed to them in return for work, at least during the famine of 1961. This financial assistance was made available thanks to the 'Disaster Relief (Katastrophenhilfe), Cologne (Germany) and a private donor agency founded by a certain Mr. Stadelmann in St. Gallen (Switzerland). Apparently, priority was given to the Christian community, yet without exclusion of others, especially the homeless.[841]

Besides organizing the financial help, the Jesuit pastors took spiritual care of the new Christians. The regular pastoral visits undertaken by them seem to have been a good source of strength and hope for the people. The goodness of Christianity was thus communicated to the people through the real presence of the Jesuits amidst them no matter what the consequence might have turned out to be. An account by Francis Schubiger is worth-noting in this regard:

> Take, for example, the severe pest and epidemic of 1917 ... In October I travelled virtually whole month, day in and day out, 8 kilometres up and down by my bicycle, spent at least two hours, and often three hours and not seldom four hours with the sick and the dying and came back home along with hundreds of rodent fleas in my clothes. Once back to the house I did not go to my room, but first to the bathroom where the new clothes were ready. The soiled ones all in the laundry ... Small doses of' Ferrum Photasium' and 'Kalcium Chloratum', but every day, and nothing happened to me ... there I gave myself fully hour-long without the slightest of worry [of infection] and nothing has happened to me.[842]

840 See Maurice Emmenecker, "Die Teppichweberei in Kendal," IB 1/24 (October 1935): 194-195.

841 See Felix A. Plattner to Gerhard Baader (Zurich, 19th July 1961), AMPSJ, *16 Superior Puna, neue - Baader, Weber, Staffner.*

842 Ibid.

Such a powerful witness, just by being amidst the people in distress and without having the least of anxiety for oneself, was often a rare testimony of the pastorally-minded Jesuits in this Mission. It may be noted that in spite of the scarcity of means and personnel, they tried to do everything that was within their human capacity. We have discussed the quality of help rendered by the missionaries. But it is hard to estimate how much of material help was extended to the people, for want of statistical sources. Nevertheless, their commitment in self-giving and pastoral presence did indeed bring a sense of reassurance and restored dignity among the people.

5.8. Conclusion

The foregoing discussion has shown that the missionaries in this Mission had to face many challenges and obstacles of various types. The complexity of the situation may be imagined from the fact that several challenges and obstacles emerged simultaneously. Besides the challenges of having to face the extreme weather conditions of India, there were also challenges due to lack of personnel, resources and finances, natural calamities like epidemics, famines and droughts. The effects of the war were coupled with the intensification of the political and nationalist movements led by Gandhi and Ambedkar. It seems to me that the most formidable challenge was the growing intolerance towards Christians in general and the missionaries in particular. The challenges faced by the Mission subsequent to the wars, were often extremely difficult to address. In the case of the growing intolerance in the wake of the growing nationalist ideologies, the very future of the Mission was perceived as bleak and uncertain. As a whole, the challenges were certainly not easy to overcome.

Chapter-6

New Ventures in Missionary Service Changing Orientations and Thrusts

6.1. Introduction

The period of history of B-PM under our review can be divided into four phases. The first phase was prior to WWI which was characterized by effervescent growth. The second phase may roughly be identified with the inter-war years (1919-1939), which, as we have noted earlier, was marred by many difficulties and obstacles. The third can be identified with the post WWII years until the commencement of the Vatican Council II (1962), and the fourth phase was the post-Vatican II era.[843] Such a periodization, I am aware, can be considered arbitrary. Yet, a cursory view of the history does show certain definitive changes of approach in certain apostolic works, change of priorities and options with changing circumstances. Such changes were obviously necessitated by the existential realities, contexts and challenges. The challenges prior to WWI were undoubtedly different in nature as compared to those that emerged during the inter-war years. The same was true about the years subsequent to WWII and Vatican Council II. Besides, at every phase the changes in orientations and apostolic thrusts were induced and influenced by the contemporary theological and ideological discourses.

For the German-Swiss Jesuits of B-PM, the post WWI era marked a period of struggle for survival and consolidation of the Mission.

843 See John C. Barret, "World War I and the Decline of the First Wave of the American Protestant Missions Movement," *IBMR* 3/39 (July 2015): 122.

Similarly, the post WWII era coincided with the independence of India from the British Rule (1947) and the infancy of the world's largest democracy. Independent India implied encountering unique socio-economic and political turbulence. In sum, this chapter makes an attempt to look at the new ventures, changing orientations, major thrusts and departures in the missionary priorities and strategies of service to society in western India, in the context of the changing scenario, during the period of this study.

6.2. The Continuities and Changes

First, we need to clarify a few basic concepts about continuities and discontinuities in mission within the history of this Mission. By these terms we simply mean that the Jesuits had to adopt certain new ways of approach to the contemporary issues confronting them. Stated differently, they needed to seek new ways of approach in place of the existing options and priorities being carried on from the beginning. The sole objective behind such reconsiderations was to make the strategies more relevant to the changing times. Such reconsiderations were concrete results of a virtual compulsion that was caused by the changing situations as well as the experiences of hardships and failures in the past.[844]

What were the continuities and discontinuities in the missionary options and priorities that are identifiable here? To answer this question let me take an example. Within the broader work of developing the school system it was realized at a later stage that besides the formal education system, one required to introduce also a non-formal education system. The simple reason behind it was that formal education system could not cater to the needs of all the classes and categories of students. The school drop-outs from the formal education system, for example, had no further possibilities to make a carrier. The jobs and employments in both government as well as private sectors were almost exclusively meant for brighter students with better performance in the exams. Thus, for a section of not-so-bright students an alternative option had to be sought. The Jesuits then decided to impart technical training to such students. Subsequently they started technical training schools and institutes, which in real sense was the beginning of non-formal education. Two such institutions were St. Joseph's Technical Training

844 See Vath, *Die deutschen Jesuiten,* 100.

School, Poona and Gnanamata (Mother of Knowledge) Agricultural School, Sangamner, about which we shall discuss shortly.

This step was a clear departure from the previous period in the missionary options and priorities as far as the educational apostolate was concerned. We must hasten to add, however, that formal education did not lose its significance. On the contrary it received further and renewed emphasis. This is evident from the fact that by the beginning of WWI in 1914 " more than half the total number of Jesuits working in the mission were active in schools (43 out of 82), besides the 10 Scholastics as teachers"[845] so that the development of the school system became once again the most notable contribution of the Jesuits in Bombay-Poona Mission even in the post WWI phase.[846] It is evident, thus, that the pre-WWI phase was mostly characterized by emphasis on formal education; whereas the post-WWI and more especially post WWII phase began to give emphasis to both formal and non-formal education.

How about the options and priorities in the pastoral care of the faithful? How does one come to identify the continuities, discontinuities and new departures? It may be noted that in the pre-WWI phase a substantial number of the most experienced missionaries were placed in military chaplaincies and schools. "But they were clearly aware of the fact that a primacy of priority must be awarded to the care of the old Christians [in the far off villages and mission stations]."[847] This realization among the Jesuits is indicative of the fact that there was a need to go back to initial and original options and priorities in this regard. This plan was eventually followed and extensive pastoral apostolic involvement became once again part of the regular missionary activity.[848]

As for the strategies adopted for direct and indirect methods of evangelization, certain radical departures may be identified in the post-WWI phase of the Mission. If we take Archbishop Leo Meurin's tenure as an example, it is clear that one of his initial and most favourite projects was to work towards the conversion of the higher caste Hindus. For, he "saw in the caste system [of the Hindus] a supportive

845 Gense, *Church at the Gateway,* 394.

846 See Vath, *Die deutschen Jesuiten,* 105-106.

847 Ibid., 114.

848 See Francis X. Schubiger, "Aus Indien," (Sangamner, 15th April 1927) MDPGJ, *Nr. 90* (1927): 63.

ideology [conducive for conversion]."[849] One of the popular methods he used was organizing debates and disputations pertaining to the topics on religion, faith and morality. He was fond of such a method in the hope of influencing the Hindus. Even before he was installed as the Archbishop of Bombay, he had already employed it regularly and made efforts later in this capacity.[850] But this method did not deliver the expected results. A re-consideration on these strategies, thus, was an imperative. A radical departure was required to win over converts. Then the missionaries turned their attention to the lower caste Hindus and other socially marginalized groups, i.e., Tribals and Dalits as primary targets of evangelization.

6.3. Major Thrusts and New Departures

With the changing national and international scenarios in practically every field of life and thought,[851] especially the changing theology of mission and ecclesiology subsequent to the World Missionary Conference, Edinburgh (1910) and more especially subsequent to the WWI,[852] not only the Jesuits but also other missionary bodies began

849 Vath, *Die deutschen Jesuiten,* 117.

850 He had officially assigned Antony Bodewig in 1873 to study English, Marathi, Sanskrit, Indian Philosophy and mythology and prepare a lecture series meant for the learned non-Christians, especially Brahmins and other high caste Hindus. Besides he appointed him as the parish priest of a small parish in Igatpuri near Bombay, inhabited by numerous high caste Hindus, ordering him to adapt to the life-style of the Brahmins after the age-old method of Robert de Nobili. When the plan did not seem to work, he suggested to open a catechumenate wherein a young Brahmin convert from Madurai mission in South India and another young Brahmin about whose conversion to Christianity there seems to have been a good amount of hope being entertained by the Jesuits, but in vain. Ibid., 117-119.

851 For instance, the powerful resurgence of three world religions namely Islam, Buddhism and Hinduism besides other strands of socio-political and economic developments, i.e., the trauma of the WWI, the rise of totalitarian ideologies like Socialism, Fascism and Marxism and the anthropocentric theology of liberal Protestantism, etc. Such developments were serious challenges, which the Catholic Church could not afford to ignore. See David Bosch, *Transforming Mission: Paradigm Shifts in Theology of Mission* (Maryknoll, NY: Orbis Books, 2011), 360, 379.

852 With the developments mentioned in the footnote above, the theology of mission too began to take new orientations, especially as regards "the massive affirmations of faith which characterized the missionary enterprise of earlier times." The time had arrived when a way of humble witness to the ultimacy of God in Jesus Christ needed to be paved out. See David Bosch, *Transforming Mission: Paradigm Shift in Theology of Mission* (Maryknoll, NY: Orbis Books, 2011), 361. See also Timothy C. Tennent, *World Missions: A Trinitarian Missiology for the Twenty-First Century* (Grand Rapids, MI: Kregel, 2010), 281-282. It must be noted, however, that the Catholic Church and other Eastern

to look seriously into the existing missionary options and priorities thereby to adopt new ways of evangelization. Ultimately Theology, Ecclesiology and Missiology and other intellectual disciplines underwent re-orientation due to various historical developments. Hence it was "unthinkable that the Christian church, theology and mission would remain unscathed"[853] and stagnant against such currents. It is a known fact that the late 19th and the first half of the 20th centuries signified a massive growth of the missionary movement, whereby the participation of the lay people by way of promoting missionary vocations, fund-raising for missions and supporting of missions through prayers and donations became conspicuous features.[854] These currents of missionary expansion demanded new orientations and exploration of new thrusts for the Jesuits as well. Here we shall discuss certain new and concrete departures with respect to these options.

6.4. Emphasis on Non-formal Education

As noted above, education had been a major thrust of the B-PM right from the beginning. The orientation in the decades prior to WWI was more in line with the formal education which means teaching the students to read and write. The system itself was "institutionalized, chronologically graded, hierarchically structured ... spanning lower primary school and the upper reaches of the university levels."[855] Under this system, often enough it so happened that in the process the students were completely taken out of their context. Their minds were filled with new information and ideas and had practically no direct bearing on their existential life. Consequently, a gap was created between what was taught and learned and the day-today lived experiences. Apart from these larger problems, the formal education system normally prepared the students mostly for clerical jobs. In the British scheme of formal educational system this

Churches were not officially part of the World Missionary Conference, Edinburgh 1910; yet the wave of new missiology and ecclesiology that was slowly emerging out of the deliberations and consequent proceedings of this conference as well as the subsequent conferences were formidable enough to capture the attention of the Catholic as well as Eastern churches. See Brian Stanley, *The World Missionary Conference, Edinburgh 1910* (Grand Rapids, MI: Wm. B. Eerdmanns, 2009), 11.

853 Bosch, *Transforming Mission,* op.cit, 372.

854 See Michael Sievernich, *Die Christliche Mission: Geschichte und Gegenwart* (Darmstadt: WBG, 2009), 95-96.

855 Alan Rogers, *Non-Formal Education: Flexible Schooling or participatory education?* (New York: Springer Science and Business Media, 2005), 71.

was one of the clear and deliberate objectives, especially designed for the Indian masses. Since then the formal education system of India has not been able to detach itself from the vision of Thomas B. Macaulay, the architect of colonial education policy for India, which is pointedly summarized in the Minutes on the Education Policy presented by him in the British parliament (1835): "We must do our best to form a class who may be interpreters between us and the millions whom we govern, a class of persons Indian in blood and colour, but English in taste, in opinions, words and intellect."[856] This vision, intended at colonizing the Indian psyche, has virtually materialized itself to a point that the educationists in India have not been able to make a fundamental departure from this position.

One may, thus, well imagine the state of affairs with regard to the formal education in India in the decades immediately subsequent to Indian independence from the British Rule. In fact, the situation even today has not improved with respect to developing a fully indigenous system of education. One may fairly well imagine the situation in 1950s and 1960s when the first independent Government of India was gradually trying to formulate and implement policies on all fronts. One could not expect it to come up with a radically new education policy in India in such a short span of time. In short, thus, it may be said that the British education policy which basically emphasized the classical model of education was followed without any modification and adaptation to the needs of the Indian population. The practice of non-formal education, thus, was not very common until then.

It may not be out of place here to point out, before we go into a discussion on the missionary service through non-formal education in the context of the Poona Jesuit Mission, that in the academic circles the discourse on the issue began only in late 1960s, yet the activities to which it refers were not new.[857] In fact in many forms non-formal education was already in practice in various contexts. Indeed, among the Jesuits themselves, there were certain initiatives that can be categorized under non-formal education, though not in any systematic sense, i.e., operation of the Carpet Weaving Unit in Kendal about which

856 As quoted in V. K. Rao, *Contemporary Education* (Delhi: A.P.H. Publication, 2007), 13. See also Ali A. Abdi et al., *Citizenship Education and Social Development in Zambia* (Charlotte, North Carolina: Information Age Publishing, 2010), 24.

857 See Rogers, *Non-Formal Education,* 72.

we have already discussed in the previous chapter. Strictly speaking, however, it may be stated that until the 1930s and 1940s, the orientation to introduce technical education in the schools and colleges was rather a new aspect in the Jesuit Missions in India. As far as the facts about such initiatives are concerned, there appears to be only one Jesuit Mission in India, namely Karnataka Mission that had started a technical training institute prior to 1940s. The trend, however, began to be more common in the 1950s and 1960s. A few Jesuit Missions began to introduce even other professional courses as well, in their schools and colleges, i.e., engineering and managerial courses, with the aim to reach out to a larger number of beneficiaries.[858] An area, however, that was still rather unconventional and consequently not yet taken into consideration was training of the youth in farming and agricultural techniques. As for this Mission, the process to introduce non-formal education was already going on from around the time when WWII was coming to an end.[859]

India, at independence, was standing at the threshold of a new era. Nearly a nine-decade struggle for freedom from the British Rule had finally borne fruit when India gained the status of a free nation on 15th August 1947. The first independent Government of India needed to chart its own course of action for the development of its people. No wonder, it had a gigantic task ahead to prepare a blueprint of its plans to bring socio-economic prosperity to its citizens. Consequently, the development of industries and agriculture was uppermost in its priorities. For, in spite of India being nearly 75% agriculture-based economy, millions went hungry. A simple empirical experience, in this regard, shows that the problems of agriculture often go hand in hand with the process of industrialization and vice-versa. In the fight against hunger, displacement, overpopulation, etc., therefore, what came as a question of priority in front of the Government of India was mobilization of agricultural and industrial sectors without neglecting one or the other. The Government believed that only then the dream of bringing about

858 The Karnataka Jesuit Mission which was undertaken by the Venetian Jesuits started a technical training school namely St. Joseph's Industrial School in Ooty [Tamilnadu] in 1931. Other older Missions like Madurai and Kerala began such institutes in 1950s and 1960s respectively. See *Directory of Jesuit Schools, Colleges and Technical Institutes* 1986-1987 (New Delhi: Jesuit Educational Association of India/Indian Social Institute, 1987), 10,30, 32, 34.

859 See Rudolph Schoch to Felix A. Plattner (Sangamner, 14th October 1948), AMPSJ, *43-Dnyanamata etc. Briefe.*

public prosperity through job-creation could be realized. Precisely with this view that the Government of India in its first three (especially the Third) Five-Year Plans (1951-1956, 1956-1961, 1961-1966) kept the promotion of agricultural sector as one of the major objectives.[860] It implied not only the aim of gaining self-sufficiency with regard to food production, but also achieving growth of agricultural production to such a level that the income and life standard of the farmers in general might be brought on par with those in the industrialized areas, at least to a certain extent.[861]

Thus, the new emphasis on agricultural production seems to have influenced the Jesuits to involve in non-formal education in the 1950s. The Jesuits, by then, had come to a firm realization that formal education system alone could not sufficiently respond to the challenges of the day.[862] Therefore, while being well aware of the fact that formal schooling system (often known also as classical education system) was necessary and that it would remain as an important means for providing basic education, they began to respond to the signs of the times by going a step further, and undertook non-formal education urgently in order to reach-out to the youth, specially of the Christian community, who either lacked access to formal education or could not complete the full cycle of basic or formal education.[863] We can identify two special projects in this regard: Dnyanamata[864] High School, Sangamner and St. Joseph's Technical School, Poona.

6.4.1. Dnyanamata High School, Sangamner

The origin of Dnyanamata High School certainly marked a departure in the missionary priorities and options in the context of this Mission. Undoubtedly, this can be termed as an innovative and need-based venture that was destined to play an important role in the transformation

860 See Uma Kapila, ed., *Indian Economy since Independence,* Vol. 1 (Delhi: Academic Foundation, 1990), 28-30; S. Mukherjee & J. Chakrabarti, *Evolution of Indian Economy & Elementary Statistics* (Calcutta: Allied Publishers, 2000), 21-22.

861 See Albert Huber, "Macht Euch die Erde untertan ...!" *JHS* 3 (1961): 5.

862 Plattner, "Wie wir uns einen gesunden Bauernstand in Indien vorstellen?," AMPSJ, *Varia/ Felix.A. Plattner.*

863 See "Dnyanamata - Mutter der Weisheit," *JHS* 3 (1962): 4-5. See also Mari Yasunaga, *Non-Formal Education as a Means to Meet Learning Needs of Out-of-School Children and Adolescents* (Paris: UNESCO, 2014), 5.

864 The literal meaning of *Dnyanamata* is 'mother of knowledge'.

of the local community at various levels.[865] We shall make a brief survey here in order to identify the "mobilizing factors"[866] behind this venture, which compelled the Jesuits to expand the horizon of the education system they had followed for nearly a century in the Mission. For the sake of clarity, the related issues will be dealt with by dividing this topic under a few sub-sections.

6.4.1.1. The Background

The Jesuits were well aware of the changes taking place in the Indian scenario. They were not directly concerned with the political issues, events and developments as such since their values and interests were centered on the spiritual aspects and influence of the same on the character and lives of the people. They were not fully unmindful of the temporal needs and socio-economic prosperity of the people of the place.[867] Within their own sphere of influence, therefore, they were concerned about contributing towards the goal that the Indian Government was aiming at, namely bringing socio-economic transformation, certainly by no means sidelining the primary objective of the Mission, i.e., evangelization of the masses.

The education service being one of the priorities, the Jesuits were keen on contributing to the above-mentioned goal through this apostolate. On the other hand, it was equally clear that there was a need to explore other modes of the same, i.e., non-formal, as well. Given the emerging scenario of independent India, therefore, there couldn't have been a more opportune time to start a school offering training in farming and agricultural techniques. Thus came the decision to open the Dnyanamata Vidyalaya (school, Dnyanamata High School hereafter) in Sangamner in 1948, the foundation stone of which was laid on 28th February.[868] The school subsequently had two sections (1955): a 'classical' and an 'agricultural' section.[869]

---

865 See "Dnyanamata - Mutter der Weisheit," *JHS* 3 (1962): 4-5.

866 See Cohen, *The Missionary Strategies, 2.*

867 See Thomas Pothacamury, *The Church in Independent India* (Bombay: The Examiner Press, 1961), 2-3.

868 See Rudolph Schoch to Felix A. Plattner (Sangamner, 27.02.1950), AMPS J, *43-Dnyanamata, etc. Briefe.* The letter dated 27.02.1950 mentions the following day as being the second anniversary of laying the foundation stone.

869 Albert Huber, "Macht Euch die Erde untertan ...!" *JHS* 3 (1961): 5.

It may be pointed out here that the initial purpose of Dnyanamata School was not visualized in terms of offering non-formal education; rather, formal education in the line of the European system of "Gymnasium with classical education in Latin and Greek."[870] Taking a retrospective view of its history, Albert Huber, who was associated with the Dnyanamata High School for twenty three years (1950-1973) as a teacher and a scout-master[871] wrote much later: "During those days[872] the orientation of this school was primarily oriented towards humanities."[873] In fact the school was conducted offering only these subjects in the first year. Meanwhile the idea of introducing a section on agricultural training began to gain further currency among the Jesuits.

6.4.1.2. The Idea of Agriculture Training

The original idea of an Agricultural School was a brainchild of John Haldner, as pointed out above, who was a long time missionary in Sangamner. He expressed his concern often to his fellow Jesuits, which most likely may not have received an enthusiastic support. Finally, he found a real sympathizer and supporter of this idea in the person of Rudolph Schoch, who took a lead in implementing the plan. Hence, the real credit of introducing the non-formal education in the Mission goes to Rudolph Schoch. This plan, however, would have remained largely unrealized, were it not for the open and generous support of Felix A. Plattner, not only as the Swiss Mission Procurator, but as a person keenly interested in such an idea.[874] Both were in favour of this

---

870 Theotonius de Sales, "Institutions of the Pune Province," PJPA, *150 Jubilee Celebrations.*

871 See Noel Oliver, "Fr. Albert Huber (31.01.1916 - 11.01.2000)", in *Deceased Members,* 179. He was instrumental in introducing the Scout Movement in the area with a view to cultivating a sense of discipline and self-dependence in the students.

872 He arrived in India in 1949 and was sent to *Dnyanamata* High School in 1950. "During those days" here refers to his first encounters with this school. See Noel Oliver, "Fr. Albert Huber (31.01.1916 - 11.01.2000)," in *Deceased Members,* 179.

873 Albert Huber, "Dnyanamata: Riickblick und Ausblick (1969/70)," AMPSJ , *Varia/Felix A. Plattner.*

874 Felix A. Plattner, was probably one of the most dynamic Jesuit Mission Procurators the Swiss Jesuits ever had. He worked in this capacity for more than three decades until his death (4th August 1974). He was not only a great support behind many of the projects undertaken by the Poona Mission as far as the finance was concerned but also a dynamic spirit behind their initiative and development, including *Dnyanamata* High School. It was during one of his visits to Poona in 1947 that John Haldner came up with the idea of an Agricultural School, which he along with Rudolph Schoch instantly supported. See Felix A. Plattner to John B. Thiel (Sangamner, 13th May 1959), AMPSJ, *43-Dnyanamata,*

new idea among the Jesuits that formal education system alone was not an adequate answer to the needs of the local people, especially given the explicit emphasis of the Government on the development and promotion of agriculture and industries.[875] Besides, the Jesuits were aware, as well, of the ground realities of the people of the place who basically came from the poorer agricultural based economy.[876]

The regular occurrences of drought and famine and the consequent migrations of a huge population in the region also seem to have contributed to the evolution of this idea. While pondering on the alternatives, the Jesuits were convinced that "only through the introduction and promotion of agriculture, and not through the more enhancement of production and modernization of machines alone"[877] that "the problem of migration among the local people"[878] can be addressed effectively.

In this context, Rudolph Schoch was even more convinced about the idea of introducing a section in the school offering training in farming and agriculture. Expressing his desire already at the beginning of the second academic year of the school, he wrote:

> One of these days, I shall be writing to Rev. [Fr. Karl] Thuer in order to request him for a [Coadjutor] Brother, an agriculturist ... We need to introduce agriculture as a subject in the school here besides building a farm for ourselves. And there we need one of our own men for it. We need [to develop] a Catholic peasantry.[879]

Clearly it was not an individual decision by Rudolph Schoch. The ground reality was perceived and studied by other Jesuits as well, i.e., John Haldner, John Baptist Thiel, John of God Roder, Maximilian Zinser and others who worked at the school in its initial stage. Thus, "in

---

*etc. Briefe. H*e being the spirit behind this project along with Rudolph Schoch, a lot of communications on various matters, mostly finance, related to this venture were collected in the Swiss Jesuit Mission Procurator's Archive in Zurich (in our references we have used AMPSJ). This bears an undisputed testimony to the claim.

875 Plattner, "Wie wir uns einen gesunden Bauernstand in Indien vorstellen?," AMPSJ, *Varia/ Felix.A. Plattner.*

876 See Felix Plattner to John B. Thiel (Zurich, 13th May 1957), AMPSJ, *43-Dnyanamata, etc. Briefe.*

877 Plattner, "Wie wir uns einen gesunden Bauernstand in Indien vorstellen?," AMPSJ, *Varia/ Felix.A. Plattner.*

878 Ibid.

879 Rudolph Schoch to Felix A. Plattner (Sangamner, 24th April 1949), AMPSJ, *43-Dnyanamata, etc. Briefe.*

June 1955 an agricultural section was opened,"[880] at Dnyanamata High School with the aims and objectives mentioned above. This was the "first Agricultural High School in Ahmednagar district to be recognized by the State government as such."[881] Emil Baumann was appointed as the first director of the section.[882] We may also point out that Rudolph Schoch was already the in-charge of the entire school.[883]

As for the choice of the place and the factors contributing towards this orientation (i.e., why the training in agricultural techniques and not any other area), it may be noted that certain immediate concerns played a role in this regard. For example, Sangamner being located at the centre of the region, mostly inhabited by the peasant population, there could not have been a better choice of orientation of the new section in the school than to focus on farming and agriculture. This became even more imperative as several large sugar factories began to be erected in the region, especially in the early 1950s, along with the rise in sugar cane plantations, where thousands of people had the possibility of finding jobs. In view of these developments various Agricultural Co-operative Societies too were founded and the Irrigation Department was expanded offering quite alluring prospects of job opportunities for the aspiring youth in the State.[884] It may be concluded, thus, that these aspects played a decisive role in the choice of the place as well as the orientation.

6.4.1.3. The Vision and Objectives

What was the vision that was aimed at being achieved by this project? It included both immediate and local considerations as well as national and broader considerations. Albert Huber, for example, saw it in terms of offering "a training to a good squad of boys in order to form them into efficient farmers and cultivators."[885] In another communication

880 "History of the Poona Mission 1952-1955," ARSI, *Prov. Goa-Poonensis, Litterae Annuae 1501.*

881 Plattner, " Wie wir uns einen gesunden Bauernstand in Indien vorstellen?," AMPSJ, *Varia/ Felix.A. Plattner.*

882 *See CPGSSI (1950), 32.*

883 See Felix A. Plattner to the Vice Rector (Zurich, 13th March 1948), AMPSJ, *43-Dnyanamata, etc., Briefe.*

884 Plattner, "Wie wir uns einen gesunden Bauernstand in Indien vorstellen?," AMPSJ, *Varia/ Felix.A. Plattner.*

885 Albert Huber to *Die papstliche Missionswerke in der Schweiz,* Fribourg (Zurich, 21st March 1961), AMPSJ, *Varia/Felix A. Plattner.*

he describes it as aiming at giving "a solid professional and spiritual training particularly to the peasant youth...."[886] Describing the same Felix A. Plattner wrote:

> In order to participate in this crucial endeavour,[887] the Jesuits of Poona [Mission] have established already in 1948 the 'Dnyanamata High School' in Sangamner. The main objective of this new endeavour was in line with a serious consideration to avail to the rural population in Ahmednagar district - especially the poorer and casteless sections - a practical skill-based education.[888]

Plattner elaborated the same objective further as he wrote: "The youth of these hundreds and thousands of peasant villages must receive a general training in agricultural techniques: that was the basic objective with which we established Dnyanamata High School and developed it further in this direction."[889] A project for the expansion of the school described the same thus: "Training of the talented boys from Sangamner and surrounding areas, who generally belong to the lower castes, i.e., Mahars. They need to be brought into contact with the children coming from higher castes so that the evil of caste may be done away with."[890] Although delivered much later, a speech of the then Swiss Consul General in Bombay (1967) captures still a wider dimension of the primary objective of the school:

> Whilst I should like to invite you to make full use of these new and excellent infrastructural facilities, you are, no doubt, aware that you are not here just to lead a comfortable and well-regulated life, but

886 Huber, "Dnyanamata," AMPSJ, *Varia/Felix A. Plattner.* See also Felix Plattner to Rudolph Schoch (Zurich, 18th May 1949), AMPSJ, *43-Dnyanamata, etc. Briefe.*

887 Felix A. Plattner explains the background of what he calls the "crucial endeavour" as follows: "In recent years, the question of food-supply here in India emerging as a serious problem ... In this context, the concern about farming and peasantry has attained a greater significance. It is really strange that a country, which has nearly 75% agriculture-based economy is unable to feed its population. Very recently the Indian Prime Minister [Lai Bahadur Shastri] stated before the university students in Delhi: 'Only under the condition that the living conditions of the rural population improves that the whole country may rightfully claim of its development. The necessity of raising our agricultural production is greater and more important today than ever." Felix A. Plattner, "Wie wir uns einen gesunden Bauernstand in Indien vorstellen?," AMPSJ, *Varia/Felix.A. Plattner.*

888 Ibid.

889 Ibid.

890 Albert Huber, "Ausbau der 'Agricultural High School Dnyanamata,' Sangamner, Ahmednagar Dt, Indien," (Sangamner, 30th January 1963), AMPSJ , *Puna-Dnyanamata.*

> to prepare yourselves for a life-time of work and service not only for your own benefit but for the benefit of your community and people and--in a wider sense--for the benefit of the whole Indian nation. Students of this school are destined to be leaders of their communities.[891]

The objective thus embraces both immediate and remote dimensions: to avail skill-based education to the rural population and in the process to form future leaders who would act as catalysts of change not only in their communities but also in the entire nation.

6.4.1.4. The Growth and Progress

In our survey, we also discovered that the progress of the school had become a source of great satisfaction for the Jesuits. Apparently, the Jesuits as members of an international Religious Order did not take up an apostolate solely with the purpose of being acclaimed for the same. Their goal was much broader. Yet, as human beings they did experience great satisfaction with such positive results. This being an unconventional work, they tended to have had certain amount of apprehensions about its success. A picture of its rapid growth and the accompanying sense of satisfaction at its success almost bordering on euphoria among them emerges through various correspondences. At the end of the second year, for example, Rudolph Schoch, then Rector and Principal of the school described the achievements in the following words:

> Tomorrow is the second anniversary of the laying down of the foundation stone [of the school]. When I think about it, it seems as if a number of years have passed by. Yes, when I think of such a short period of time, I must say that something phenomenal has happened: the school has already been recognized [by the government]; it has steered clear of the initial difficulties. It's established. And that means a lot! We have received the recognition of school in these two years.[892] Then, the second recognition along

891 Speech of O. Rist, Swiss Consul General in Bombay, delivered at Sangamner (5th March 1967), AMPSJ, *Varia/Felix A. Plattner.* See also Albert Huber, "Ein Markstein Schweizerischer Entwicklungshilfe" AMPSJ, *Varia/Felix.A. Plattner.*

892 On the unexpectedly early recognition of the school, see Rudolph Schoch to Felix A. Plattner (Sangamner, 14th October 1948); Felix A. Plattner to Emil Baumann (Zurich, 22nd February 1949); Felix A. Plattner to Rudolph Schoch (Zurich, 31st December 1948), AMPSJ , *43-Dnyanamata, etc. Briefe.*

> with the permission to start the 9th standard came. Three months earlier we had sent an application for the permission to open 10th standard. That was rejected. We were very much saddened [by the same]. A week ago, however, I received [the permission] anyway. Such permission is [normally] not granted easily to a new school.[893]

In another correspondence he reported:

> About our school, thank God, I can give you only the good news! Everything is going vigorously ahead. The authorities of the Education Department are well satisfied with us. We have received the permission for this year as well, along with a rare permission to start a higher class. With the coming year, thus, we shall have all the classes. We may already conduct a class in two sections. The School Inspector had only one remark to make this year: "This is the school, I wish, I had been educated!"[894]

The remarks in the first correspondence, namely "something phenomenal has happened" and "it is established!" in connection with the status of the school after the completion of the second year of the laying down of the foundation stone are certainly significant expressions in the context of this discussion. An educational institution normally takes at least a decade or more to claim such a status.[895] Here it seems to have been different, so that Pius Geisel could report in 1955 saying "the school is doing very well."[896] It indicates its growth at an unexpected pace. As we read the second correspondence we come across with a very positive remark from the ranks of the officers like a School Inspector.

---

893 Rudolph Schoch to Felix A. Plattner (Sangamner, 27th February 1950), AMPSJ, *43-Dnyanamata, etc. Briefe.* See further in the same file Rudolph Schoch to Felix A. Plattner (Sangamner, 16th July 1949. Otto Faller, Provincial of Southern German Province too underlined the aspect of the rapid progress of the school in his remarks after his Visitation. See Otto Faller, "Elenchus Visitationis (22-27* December 1952)," ARSI, *Poona. 1005-1,* 37.

894 Rudolph Schoch to a Professor (?) (Sangamner, 18th December 1950), AMPSJ, *43-Dnyanamata, etc. Briefe.* See further in the same file, Rudolph Schoch to Felix A. Plattner (Sangamner, 27.02.1950); Rudolph Schoch to Felix A. Plattner (Sangamner, 16.07.1949). See also "Die Schule, die ich mir wUnschte," *IB* 1 (1951): 15.

895 Plattner, "Wie Wir uns einen gesunden Bauernstand in Indien vorstellen?," AMPSJ, *Varia/ Felix.A. Plattner.*

896 Pius Geisel, "Litterae Superioris Missionsis," (Poona, July 1955), ARSI, *Poona. 1005-IV,* 20.

An example may be cited from the inspection report of the Education-Inspector (1959/60):

> The arrangement for the teaching of Agriculture is very satisfactory. The equipment etc., for the teaching of the agriculture is adequate in all respects. The school continues to do good work under the able guidance of the experienced Principal Rev. Fr. [John Baptist] Thiel and claims to be among the model schools in our district. On the whole, general tone and discipline of the school are very good.[897]

An extract from the Inspection Report for the year 1962 states: "This school, run by the 'Jesuit Schools' Society' has completed 12 years of its existence and is serving the educational needs of the locality very efficiently. The consistent good S.S.C. [Secondary School Certificate] results can be cited as an important feature of the school."[898] All these may certainly be considered a sign of no mean an achievement, which was certainly a crowning of the efforts made by the Jesuits. We may assume that these results may have been quite unexpected: the quick recognition and the manner of its reception from the people as well as from the authorities of the department. For, recognition of the school by the government meant (and still means) a lot. One advantage was the validity of the certificates received from the school would carry further weight, opening more possibilities for the students. This is what Albert Huber meant when he wrote:

> The students who have done matriculation from 'Dnyanamata' (apparently also from the Agricultural Section) can study further in any higher secondary schools, technical institutes or universities, alongside but-- and that is of a much larger significance for our poor students-- the certificate from the Agricultural Section also would be recognized as a State Diploma which would be an additional advantage to get higher posts in Sugar Manufacturing Factories and State Irrigation Department, etc.[899]

---

897 Albert Huber, "Remarks from the Inspection-Report of the District Education Inspector/ Ahmednagar," AMPSJ, *Varia/Felix A. Plattner.* The report contains the remarks of the Education Inspector from 1957/58 to 1969/70, which refers to the consistent growth of the school.

898 Albert Huber, "Extracts from the Inspection-Reports (1960/61/62) given by the Educational - Inspector, Ahmednagar," (Sangamner, 30th January 1963), AMPSJ, *Puna-Dnyanamata.*

899 Albert Huber, "Macht Euch die Erde untertan ...!" *JHS* 3 (1961): 4-6.

Moreover, this implied financial security both for the school as well as the students. For, a certain amount of grant was guaranteed once a school received recognition. For a Mission that largely depended for its existence on the funds received mostly from Europe, such an achievement was a big step forward towards achieving self-sufficiency, not only in terms of financial security but also in terms of its sustainability. With regard to the financial self-sufficiency and the growth of its status, the school attained another milestone when it attained a new status in its history while being recognized by the Central Government as a 'Multi-Purpose High School'[900] in 1958-1959, which implied also an assurance of a grant from the Government:

> Dnyanamata has been selected as a Multi-Purpose High School--Agriculture by the Central Government-- with a special grant of Rs 32 000/- [Thirty two Thousand Rupees] received and 60% of the expenditure of the Agricultural Section to be borne by [the] Government in future. This is a great help and will give us a chance to make the school an all-round model institution.[901]

As for the students, it implied that the students passing out of this school had better chances and prospects for jobs as the value of their certificates, as indicated above, would carry more weight. Even if this did not happen, "the students were going to be more self-reliant on account of the skills they had learnt in the school."[902]

From the foregoing discussion, one might get an impression that the beginning and development of the school were without much problems and obstacles. On the contrary, there were many problems especially with regard to finance (in spite of the grants received from

900 It is a known fact that the students seeking admission to secondary schools have varying interests and abilities. These differences of interests and abilities are hardly taken care of in the formal education system offered in most of the schools in India. Precisely for this reason that the basic aim of the Multi-purpose schools is to offer education according to individual interests. The curriculum in such schools is designed in such a manner that the students are required to do certain amount of manual work too in the workshops in order to inculcate in them a sense of dignity of labour, besides imparting to them some vocational skills which in turn make them self-sufficient in later stage of their lives. See Ram Nath Sharma & Rajendra Sharma, *Problems of Education in India* (New Delhi: Atlantic Publishers & Distributors, 2004), 48-149.

901 Rudolph Schoch to Felix A. Plattner (Sangamner, 21st April 1958), AMPSJ, *Sangamner Briefe.*

902 See Rudolph Schoch to Felix A. Plattner (Sangamner, 16th April 1950); Albert Huber to Felix A. Plattner (Sangamner, 7th January 1959), AMPSJ, *43-Dnyanamata, etc. Briefe.*

the Government) and due to insufficient infrastructure.[903] As regards the financc, the school faced problems mostly on account of enhancing new infrastructures. The growing number of students demanded expansion of more class rooms. What appears, however, as a source of a rather long standing worry among the Jesuits was the need of enlarging the boarding facility for the students in order to accommodate more students, especially those coming from poor economic background, which could be addressed more satisfactorily only by mid 1960s.[904] Besides, the school had to face many other constraints, like lack of sufficient number of Jesuits, lack of teaching staff, etc., along with the initial difficulties of organizing the entire system,[905] about which a letter described in the following words: "The first academic year of Dnyanamata [High School], thank God, has gone by. It was really a difficult year."[906] In some other letters we read: "The hostel [boarding home] is the worst [with regard to financial status],"[907] "the boarding home is the biggest burden,"[908] etc. The financial condition of the school seems to have been "getting bad to worse"[909] even until the end of 1960s. This can be surmised from this comment:

Yet the hostel was an essential infrastructural facility for the school. Rudolph Schoch saw the need of having a hostel for non-Christians as a vital aspect for the very existence of the mission: "The hostel: In my opinion we must already begin this year the construction of a hostel. Absolutely necessary. Without a hostel for the non-Christians we cannot exist here."[910] In spite of the financial burden that incurred by the running

903 See Rudolph Schoch to Felix A. Plattner (Sangamner, 22nd February 1949); Emil Baumann to Felix A. Plattner (Sangamner, 22nd February 1949); Albert Huber to Felix A. Plattner (Sangamner, 26th August 1954), AMPSJ, *43-Dnyanamata, etc. Briefe.*

904 See Huber, "Dnyanamata," AMPSJ, *Varia/Felix A. Plattner.*

905 Albert Huber, for example, had to look after the jobs of the House Minister and Treasurer as well along with full-time teaching and administration in the school. See Albert Huber to Felix A. Plattner (Sangamner, 26th August 1954), AMPSJ, *43-Dnyanamata, etc. Briefe.*

906 Rudolph Schoch to Felix A. Plattner (Sangamner, 22nd February 1949), AMPSJ, *43-Dnyanamata, etc. Briefe.*

907 See also Rudolph Schoch to Felix A. Plattner (Sangamner, 16th July 1949), AMPSJ, *43-Dnyanamata, etc. Briefe*

908 Rudolph Schoch to Felix. A. Plattner (Sangamner, 21st May 1951), AMPSJ, *43-Dnyanamata, etc. Briefe.*

909 Anonymous to Albert Huber (Sangamner, 12th October 1969), AMPSJ, *Varia/Felix A. Plattner.*

910 Schoch to Plattner (Sangamner, 16th July 1949), AMPSJ, *43-Dnyanamata, etc. Briefe.*

of a hostel, it was necessitated by the fact that nearly 40% of the students came from very poor families, designated as "economically Backward Classes"[911] who came from the radius of 10-100 kilometers.[912]

Besides these, a problem that was faced, though mostly in the initial years, was getting a sufficient number of students, mainly due to a deliberate attempt on the part of other schools of the locality that made "heavy propaganda [against Dnyanamata High School]. [They] tried every means, fair and foul, to discourage the students from [coming to] us."[913] It looks quite tenable to hold this to be true as one of the schools in the vicinity did seem to have apprehensions of losing a number of students because of the prospect of better facilities at Dnyanamata High School:

> Out of 200 pupils 70 are Catholics. But the other school in the town has 800 and as their buildings are insufficient they have several shifts. It will take some time till more come to our school. Naturally the other school fears from ours, which is well equipped (science equipment arrived last month, which has no comparison in any district school) and well disciplined. Opposition went so far as to insult our Fathers publicly in the rival school ...Besides I am not yet sure whether the school will eventually succeed considering the opposition of the other school.[914]

Figure 6.1: Students of Dnyanamata High School/ Figure 6.2: Agriculture Section at the field for a practical session. *Source*: AJMS, *Ahmadnagar Distrikt,, Indien: Landwirtschaftsschule von Sangamner mil Schiilern bei derArbeit (1973)*

911 Huber, "Dnyanamata," AMPSJ, *Varia/Felix A. Plattner*

912 Felix A. Plattner, "Wie wir uns einen gesunden Bauernstand in Indien vorstellen?," AMPSJ, *Varia/Felix.A. Plattner.*

913 Rudolph Schoch to Felix A. Plattner (Sangamner, 24th April 1949), AMPSJ, *43-Dnyanamata, etc. Briefe.*

914 Pius Geisel, "Elenchus Visitationis: Coll. inchoatum Sangamner," (Poona, 27th November 1950), ARSI, *Poona. 1004-XIX,* 33.

It is unclear whether this problem persisted longer. The example only goes on to prove that such external factors too were not entirely absent in the history of the development of this school.

6.4.1.5. The Curriculum for Empowerment

The discussion on this school without making a mention of the curriculum would remain incomplete. The curriculum and method of dealing give us an inkling into how far the training was successful. Here is how Felix Plattner described the same:

> In our 'Agricultural High School' the students have two teaching hours on agriculture every day: theoretical and practical. The school owns approximately 30 acres (12 hectares approx.) of arable land. Each class has to cultivate a field of approximately 3 acres and prepare a report on the same. In addition, every single student has an individual piece of the field [to cultivate] and to prepare a report as well. Thus, the classes [as a whole] and students as individuals are encouraged to nurture not only a sense of a healthy competition but also to cultivate a spirit of cooperation and working together [among themselves] ... In the course of instruction of our students, thus, other skills that are closely related to farming and agriculture are also included, i.e., basic practical knowledge of animal husbandry, dairy farming ... [basic] knowledge of the soil and [the use of] fertilizers, carpentry and blacksmith's work for simple repairs in barns and fields, etc.[915]

A curious reader might wonder whether the syllabus was designed by the Jesuits themselves and whether it was arbitrarily prepared. Certainly, it was a State-approved syllabus:

> The syllabus for the school education is prepared and recommended by the Department of Education of the State Government. It is very good. It gives the students a very good and holistic education with sufficient training in practical skills. When our students leave the High School, they find quite easily jobs in sugar manufacturing factories.[916]

915 Plattner, " Wie wir uns einen gesunden Bauernstand in Indien vorstellen?," AMPSJ, *Varia/ Felix.A. Plattner.*

916 Huber, "Ein Markstein Schweizerischer Entwicklungshilfe" AMPSJ, *Varia/Felix.A. Plattner.*

In order that the students get maximum experience and exposure, various programmes were organized:

> The teachers and the students of this school do not work like in a hermitage or in a closed trial house. Often the entire class goes out with its teacher in the neighbouring villages, in order to study the situation at the spot. In addition, they go to the agricultural exhibition or visit a Model Farm.[917]

Thus this brief survey reveals that the school, within its scope, tried to offer a practical and holistic education for empowerment. Apparently, the pragmatic approach with regard to imparting need-based skills was the need of the time and context. The venture as a whole had far reaching consequences as well, which will be underlined as we take the discussion further under the subsequent sub-topics.

6.4.1.6. *The Socio-Economic and Political Impact*

The significant questions to probe into are: What was the socioeconomic impact of such a system of education? How was this objective sought to be achieved? Emil Baumann's letter throws some light on the same:

> Each boy, whether a Christian or a non-Christian, has been entrusted with a flower-bed wherein he may plant his own flowers or vegetables. We also try to make use of this opportunity to impart the basic fundamentals of Christian life and faith to non-Christian students through very practical ways. One marks already a tremendous difference between the newcomers and the old-timers. The old-timers depict more forbearance and [spirit of] teamwork.[918]

Unfortunately the above quoted letter does not elaborate on how the "basic fundamentals of Christian life and faith" were imparted. Yet, it would not be wrong to conclude that such an objective was achieved by creating an atmosphere wherein all the students, irrespective of caste and creed, could work together. Some critics might question this claim, arguing that the school children had no other choice. But one only needs to be reminded that the caste-prejudices in Ahmednagar District was so deeply entrenched in the society that even a humble act of facilitating a space to bring the children of various castes together was

---

917 Albert Huber, "Macht Euch die Erde untertan," *JHS* 3 (1961): 4.

918 Emil Baumann to Felix A. Plattner (Sangamner, 19th July 1949), AMPSJ, *43-Dnyanamata, etc. Briefe.*

of great significance, amounting to a great Christian witness.[919] This in turn was a first step towards promoting the values of coextensive and egalitarianism. Felix A. Plattner underlines this aspect as he wrote:

> What may, perhaps, be considered of even greater value [and significance] is the fact that the long-term association of the outcaste Mahars with Brahmins, Marathas and Muslims on the same school bench, working in the same field and at the same machines, etc., somehow contribute towards alleviating the ominous and the deep-rooted caste consciousness and [spirit of] communalism among them.[920]

In order to cultivate healthy growth in the spirit of communal harmony and sense of cooperation irrespective of caste differences in the students certain disciplinary norms were prescribed and sanctions for trespassing the same were recommended. The sanctions were imposed not so much with a stick in hand, neither in terms of setting a spirit of a senseless competition among the students but in terms of demanding "Shram Dhan [DaanJ [sacrifice of labour],"[921] for example, through additional hours of work in the fields. Stated differently, a student violently these disciplinary norms was sent to work in the fields for certain additional hours (besides the normal hours of practical demonstrations and experiments) as a sort of corrective measure. An immediate impact of such a measure was that the young students worked mostly to their own benefit to secure better remarks for their works in the field. For "in the agricultural section of the school, 50% marks were allotted for the practical and fieldwork."[922] The less laborious students, on the other hand, were asked to make use of the time in a productive manner through such works in the fields.[923] Testifying to the long-term impact of such measures and ways of approach to the students, Albert Huber writes: "Although the students comprise Hindus, Muslims and Christians whereby non-Christians are predominant in the

919 See K. S. Chalam, *Caste-Based Reservations and Human Development in India* (LA/ London/New Delhi/ Singapore: Sage Publications, 2007), 75-77.

920 Plattner, "Wie wir uns einen gesunden Bauernstand in Indien vorstellen?," AMPSJ, *Varia/ Felix.A. Plattner.* See also Albert Huber, "Macht Euch die Erde untertan," 4.

921 Felix A. Plattner, "Wie wir uns einen gesunden Bauernstand in Indien vorstellen?," AMPSJ, *Varia/Felix.A. Plattner.*

922 Ibid.

923 Ibid.

school -- there were hardly any student riots and strikes, which was often the case in other schools."[924] It may be noted that the students shared common classrooms, benches, fields for practical demonstrations, common refectory, dormitory, etc.

It would not be out of place here to underline once again that caste consciousness until this era (1950s-1960s) was still deep-seated in the minds of the people, in spite of the fact that 'untouchability' was outlawed in 1950 with the adoption of the Indian Constitution. In fact, in some form or the other this practice continues even today, though mostly in much more subtle and modified ways. This problem has been very prominent in Maharashtra, ever since the known history.[925] Given such a background, the impact effected through school curriculum, on a small-scale as it may be, was quite significant. The impact holds even further significance given the volatile nature of the area where 'riots and strikes' among the students due to caste rivalry were not rare, as indicated by Albert Huber above.

Another immediate impact on the students was enhanced opportunities of jobs. This aspect was of great significance given the economic background of the place. Jobs opportunities were rare, especially for those who were not trained in any skills. Against this background, the training received at the school opened new vistas of job opportunities, which Felix A. Plattner highlighted when he wrote:

> Our school offers a good general training with enough practical knowledge. When our students leave the High School, they find jobs often quite easily at the sugar manufacturing mills in various neighbouring branches. At such posts they earn Rs. 120/- [Hundred and Twenty Rupees] or more per month. The students who have agricultural enterprise at home, claim that the four-year training at Dnyanamata has brought them great benefits in their later lives ... these benefits have caused a very positive impact upon their relatives and village communities.[926]

---

924 Huber, "Dnyanamata," AMPSJ, *Varia/Felix A. Plattner.* See also Felix A. Plattner, "Wie wir uns einen gesunden Bauernstand in Indien vorstellen," AMPSJ, *Varia/Felix.A. Plattner.*

925 See Emma Tomalin, ed., *The Routledge Handbook of Religions and Global Development* (London & New York: Routledge, 2015), 193; K. S. Chalam, *Caste-Based Reservations and Human Development in India, op. cit.,* 76-77.

926 Felix A. Plattner, " Wie wir uns einen gesunden Bauernstand in Indien vorstellen," AMPSJ , *Varia/Felix A. Plattner.*

The socio-cultural impact of the school went beyond the four-walls of the school campus and student circle. A concrete instance of such a claim was the fact that the farmers from the surrounding area regularly came to seek advice and help from the teachers or to observe and learn from the practical demonstrations conducted in the fields. The farm owned by the school, in this sense, became a 'model farm' of its kind. The authorities from the District Agriculture Office too came on a regular basis to conduct experiments and practical demonstrations,[927] following a recommendation received from Firma Ruhr-Stickstoff (a German firm specialized in nitrogen fertilizers) to conduct experiments on potatoes. The students often went along with their qualified and well-experienced teachers to the surrounding villages and farms to study the properties of the soil and to ascertain relevant agricultural techniques at the spot. They often guided the farmers with suitable advice and practical tips on farming. For example, the school often helped many poorer farmers in the area in ploughing the hardest of their fields with the tractor it had received from the German Catholics from their fund under the Campaign against Hunger in the World project. This otherwise would have cost them not less than three pairs of the best of oxen, which were often hard to get even at a handsome price, especially at peak seasons of cultivation."[928]

Still other positive of the agricultural training school were the curricular activities, which had the potential to bring about a modest amount of transformation in the socio-cultural and economic spheres of the local community. Such activities included initiatives and experiments on animal husbandry, poultry farming and innovations in irrigation system. To actualize these plans the school undertook a long term study on the possibility of animal husbandry in the area to improve the local breed. On its success Plattner has the following to report: "We succeeded [in our endeavour], to a modest extent, as we undertook the process of cross-fertilization between the local sheep with merinos [Cashmere sheep]: this crossing has significantly increased the quality of wool."[929] In a similar fashion, the initiative to expand and modernize the poultry farm too was undertaken. In this regard, possibilities were

927 See Ibid.

928 Huber, "Dnyanamata," AMPSJ, *Varia/Felix A. Plattner.*

929 Plattner, " Wie wir uns einen gesunden Bauernstand in Indien vorstellen? "AMPSJ, *Varia/ Felix A. Planner.*

sought in order that eggs and other such nutritious items may be availed to the local farmers at reasonable prices. Also, given the scarcity of rain, the problem of irrigation remained one of the most acute problems for agriculture in the area; with the installation of sprinkling machines more than one-third of the water quantity could be saved. Moreover, with this technique the water quantity could be approximately measured according to the need of various types of seeds. The wastage of water, thus, could be effectively controlled. Still another dimension of these creative initiatives was the introduction of a fodder cutting machine. For, too much of fodder was lost when used without cutting, which in effect was very practical and cost effective.[930] In all these initiatives, although the success rate in terms of their immediate results appears to have been quite modest, yet what was significant in the larger context was that the local communities were shown alternative ways and means of doing things, which when effectively executed led them towards better financial self-sufficiency.

In the larger Indian context, an important impact of this model of education was inculcating the value and respect for manual labour so that the students would "regard soiled and tiresome work no more as 'coolie work."[931] The education system of India, primarily introduced by the British and essentially held intact even to this day, tends to create a dichotomy between 'physical/manual' and 'mental/clerical' works. A mason's work, for example, is considered inferior in dignity than the job of a teacher; in spite of the fact that in many cases, a teacher might earn much less than a mason. The reason for the same is unambiguous: 'mental/clerical' labour is considered superior in dignity than 'physical' labour. In fact, it can be asserted with a pretty high degree of certainty that the present state of unemployment in India is largely due to this dichotomy. The contribution of this school in this regard lies in the fact that the students who passed out from here developed a greater regard for physical labour, which is very significant.[932]

---

930 See Huber, "Dnyanamata," AMPSJ, *Varia/Felix A. Plattner.*

931 Plattner, " Wie wir uns einen gesunden Bauernstand in Indien vorstellen?," AMPSJ, *Varia/Felix A. Plattner.*

932 See Huber, "Dnyanamata," AMPSJ, *Varia/Felix A. Plattner.* See further in the same file, Plattner, "Wie wir uns einen gesunden Bauernstand in Indien vorstellen,"; Albert Huber, "A 'Multipurpose Agriculture High School: Dnyanamata Vidyalaya, Sangamner, Ahmadnagar Dt."

In addition to these, it is worth mentioning here although it may appear as a minor aspect, that the school practiced 'earn-while-you learn system' whereby many of the students in boarding home, besides some day-scholars, earned money up to one third of their personal expenses by taking up extra hours of work after the regular school hours or on holidays.[933] Such a possibility was a significant dimension of this system of education in the sense that it helped cultivate a sense of responsibility and self-sufficiency in the students, besides cultivating a personal sense of satisfaction of earning some amount of money for themselves. Moreover, it was equally important for the families of the students as well, which found it hard to afford regular fees for their children. In short, it could be said that this also was an initiative that instilled social awareness towards liberation and social transformation.[934]

6.4.1.7. Significance of Empowerment Education

As far as the significance of this strategy is concerned, the most positive point seems to lie in the fact that the image of the people of Catholic mission and missionaries changed to some extent due to the impacts created in their minds. A testimony, which is worth-quoting at some length, would suffice to underline this point:

> The main success that we can register in our school is the changed attitude of the town towards the Catholic mission. Formerly it was a constant occurrence that Fathers who went into the town, were publicly insulted and laughed at. But now we are received with the highest mark of respect. We are invited to all the public functions, are members in their committees, [and] are invited to their homes. This evening for instance, was the lamp festival of the Hindus which they call Divali feast. Two Fathers went into town in the later afternoon to admire all the decorations and house-illuminations. From all sides, so they reported, they received invitations to join them in their festive mood, come into their homes, share their sweets and honour them with a little chat. Everywhere they were told that it means a distinct pleasure and honour to them that the Fathers should grace their occasion with even the briefest call. Where there was coldness and mocking before, there is love and respect

933 Ibid.

934 See M. Thomas Thangaraj, "Indian Christian Tradition," in *Religions of South Asia: An Introduction,* eds., Sushil Mittal & Gene Thursby (London & New York: Routledge, 2006), 192.

> now. Where there was indifference towards us, there is now warm affection from every side. As the Fathers walked through the town, they couldn't help feeling like the farmer who walks steadfastly behind his plough, realizing that the soil is hard but slowly it will be broken for the seed of the divine sower.[935]

The text signifies a break-through in changing the perception of the people. It was a significant achievement, as far as the missionary strategies were concerned. Without giving a space for any pious interpretation, it may doubtlessly be termed as a rewarding experience for a missionary enterprise. The aim of empowering the weak through alternative educational service was gradually being achieved.

Figure 6.3: Students at Training
Source: AJMS, *Felix A. Plattner, Fotographische Belege-St. Joseph's Technical Institute, Pune.*

The strategic significance of this initiative was related to two other factors: the time of its opening (1948), namely immediately subsequent to the independence of India and the unconventional nature of the education service given. The opening of the Dnyanamata School, thus, can be considered a unique initiative among the Jesuit Missions of the time in India.

935 "Dnyanamata Vidyalaya Sangamner: *Historia Domus 1947-1949,*" *ARSI, Poona. 1004-XIX-4* (8).

6.4.2. St. Joseph's Technical Institute, Poona[936]

The beginning of this institute marks yet another dimension of the emphasis laid on the non-formal education by this Mission. What was the nature of the non-formal education that was intended to be offered? Who were visualized as the main beneficiaries of the same? What were the general background and major concerns that played "a discernible and significant role"[937] in the implementation of this plan? These are some of the most obvious questions here that need to be addressed in our discussion. The answers to these questions will emerge as we discuss the sub-topics under the following scheme.

6.4.2.1. The Initial Planning, Hurdles and Dilemmas

A consideration on an alternative method of education, namely technical training was already going on from late 1940s as may be inferred from the following letter:

> In addition to this a series of new works must be started: higher education of our Mahar new Christians and influence over the upper class Hindus through opening up of a school in Sangamner in their district, imminent opening of the De Nobili College, and apostolate among the elite circles of Poona ... [opening of] a technical training institute ...[938]

That such a serious consideration was already going on among the Jesuits is further revealed in the note by Joseph Meyer made elsewhere: "Plans for the future: a High School, an Industrial School, a Cooperative Society, a cottage industry."[939] Yet, before the plan was finally implemented (1959), it took nearly a decade in sorting out various hurdles and dilemmas about the nature of the institute and finalizing the entire logistics.

To implement the plan of starting the industrial school, a lot of preparation at various levels began to take place: preparation of the

936 Officially this name was given to the institute after a year of its opening. See Gerhard Baader to Felix A. Plattner (Poona, 10th May 1960), AMPSJ, *16-Superior Puna, neue: Baader, Weber, Staffner.*

937 Paul Misner, *Catholic Labour Movements in Europe: Social Thought and Action, 1914-1965* (Washington, DC: The Catholic University Press of America Press, 2015), 8-9.

938 John Baptist Haas (Sup. Reg. of Poona Mission) to Karl Thtler (Vice-Provincial) (Poona, 12th July 1947), ARSI, *Historia 2001-Poona.* Emphasis on the text mine.

939 John Joseph Meyer to Karl Thiier (Poona, 18th July 1947), ARSI, *Historia 2001-Poona.* Emphasis on the text mine.

personnel for the same, purchase of the plot of land, making a study of similar projects in other Jesuits missions in India, etc. To achieve the first aspect of the preparation, Br. Anton Herbert "departed for Europe [1950] in order that he might learn the art and techniques of [running an] industrial school."[940] This trip to Europe was planned in Switzerland, his home country as part of his home leave so that he could undertake "the preparation for the technical [training] school, which has been planned in Poona."[941] "During these holidays in Switzerland he did an internship in auto repair workshop and sometime later in electrical services."[942] The second aspect of the preparation becomes evident as we read a letter of Pius Geisel:

> Tomorrow morning I shall depart again from here. I shall be visiting the Industrial School in Trichy (Tiruchirappalli). [I] have already visited the one in Madras. Hopefully Br. [Anton] Herbert keeps his eyes open and learns what we shall be producing at the most, besides the motor repair work.[943]

Still another aspect that had to be settled before things proceeded was the selection of a suitable place, for which a consensus among the Jesuits had to be reached; but often a consensus was difficult to achieve as this note illustrates:

> Amidst all the inevitable difficulties Fr. [Hans] Staffner annoys me the most, who is a narrow-minded man, a true Tyrolean. With the Industrial School too, he is the one who creates trouble at the most. He just does not want to take risks. Without risk and without courage we come to nothing. In any venture, one must go first

940 "Historia Generalis Missionis Poonensis," ARSI, *Prov. Goa-Poonensis, Litterae Annuae 1501.*

941 Anton Herbert, "Arbeiten von 9 Mitbruder in der Pune [Poona] Mission von 1928-1987," ABSPGJ, *Pa 0116, Herbert Anton: 1906-1992.*

942 Eugen Frei, "Br. Anton Herbert (+18. Marz 1992)," ABSPGJ, *Pa 0116, Herbert Anton: 1906-1992.*

943 Pius Geisel to Felix A. Plattner (Shembaganur [Tamilnadu], 13th February 1951), AMPS J, *Superior Poona, P. Geisel.* See also in the same file, Pius Geisel to Felix A. Plattner (Poona, 15th January 1951), where he writes: "On Tuesday or Wednesday [I shall go] to Madras, Trichinopoly [Tiruchirappalli], Shembaganur ... for I want to visit the hostels and industrial schools." In another correspondence we read: "Before some days we went together [with Paul Hfifely] to an already running Vocational School and studied what we need." Pius Geisel to Felix A. Plattner (Poona, 4th December 1958), AMPS J, *Superior Poona, P. Geisel.*

through a dark tunnel, not knowing what it looks like at the other end; but one has to dare. But I am not going to give in.[944]

With regard to the choice of the place, Geisel asks: "... where? Within the city, the land prices are simply unaffordable. Besides, for a motor repair garage, one does not expect it to be too far out [in the outskirts of the city]."[945] Clearly, thus the financial implication in the selection of a good spot was undeniable. Yet, a central location was an equally important aspect of consideration. Consequently a piece of land was bought at a central location close to the Race Course (not very far away from the Jesuit-run St. Vincent's High School) in view of establishing the institute: "The race horse stables have been purchased. They cost us 100, 000 [Rupees]. I think, % of the total 5 acres and % of the rooms must be acquired for the industrial school."[946] To look after the progress of the project, "Paul Hafely will be released from his responsibilities for this purpose. He is in search of a truck for the construction that begin at the college soon."[947] Pius Geisel, the Superior of the Mission, whose brainchild this project was,[948] entertained an idea of beginning the institute at the earliest. But the lack of personnel as instructors was the main hurdle. His entire hope, therefore, was set upon Br. Anton Herbert who was on his home leave. Geisel expected him to return at the earliest: "Br. [Anton] Herbert could also come with them [Francis Kiermeier and two Scholastics], but I will have to struggle hard

944 Pius Geisel to Felix A. Plattner (Poona, 9th March 1951), AMPS J, *Superior Poona, P. Geisel.*

945 Ibid., (Poona, 14th July 1951).

946 Ibid., (Poona, 30th January 1951); Also, ibid., (Poona, 15th January 1951); ibid., (Poona, 24th February 1951). In still another letter we read: "Land for the Industrial School is bought." Pius Geisel to Felix A. Plattner (22nd March 1958); "A piece of land has been purchased sometime earlier, which obviously would be suitable for the construction of a vocational training school." Felix A. Plattner to Mr. Wider (Zurich, 12th February 1958), AMPSJ, *Gewerbeschule.* See also Gerhard Baader to Hans Breitenstein (Poona, 12th March 1958); Pius Geisel, Vice-Provincial (Zurich, 14th March, 1958), AMPSJ, *16-Superior Poona-neue: Baader, Weber, Staffner.*

947 Pius Geisel to Felix A. Plattner (Poona, 24th February 1951), AMPSJ, *Superior Poona, P. Geisel.* In another letter in the same file we read: "Hafely seems to have been entrusted with the further development. Hopefully it will go well." Pius Geisel to Felix A. Plattner (Poona, 22nd March 1958).

948 Meyer to Thuer, (Poona, 13th March 1951), AMPSJ, *Superior Poona, P. Geisel.*

in order to keep him away from the building works, in case I succeed in beginning the Industrial School immediately."[949]

It becomes thus clear that the plan was not only at the level of brainstorming; but rather certain concrete steps were already taken by way of studying similar projects in other Jesuit Missions and preparing a few Jesuit personnel as future staff. Yet, things were not as simple as they might have appeared. One of the reasons for the delay in the implementation of the plan was financial strain. For, a number of projects had to be looked after simultaneously:

> Today I wish to share with you my worries. I am afraid we have undertaken too much [at a time]...now comes the hospital... Who will build it? ...Then again the Fathers' Residence at Dnyanamata [High School] will come ...Who will build it? ... In addition comes the Industrial School. Currently I am worried about it. On the one hand it must be begun, on the other it would mean a huge loss for us if we require to take external contractors for Belapur.[950]

As pointed out above, all these implied a financial crunch that was not so easy to tackle. In the words of Pius Geisel: "From the financial point of view: can we, with all other things together on one side, take the risk of Industrial School on us now?"[951] Similarly, he expressed his worries further: "The closer the time comes to begin with this school, the more worried do I become."[952] Together with these the lack of personnel trained in building constructions and other such skills was a matter of concern:

> Br. [Joseph] Pfiffher alone cannot manage all these. He had already stressed that Br. [Anton] Herbert must be free till the end of the time of construction of the Industrial School ... I hope Br. Herbert has recovered well. With our own motor cars alone he will have a lot of work: 2 Lorries, mortar mixing machine, cement mixer and motorcycles.[953]

---

949 Pius Geisel to Felix A. Plattner (Poona, 3rd April 1951), AMPSJ, *Superior Poona, P. Geisel.*

950 Ibid., (Poona, 19th July 1951), op. cit.

951 Ibid., (Poona, 07th July 1951), op. cit.

952 Ibid., (Poona, 19th July 1951), op. cit.

953 Ibid., (Poona, 14th July 1951), *op. cit.*

Given these constraints some of the Jesuits were "of the opinion that the plan of an Industrial School could wait for the moment."[954] Pius Geisel himself perceived the impossibility of the same: "The more do I think about it, the more it becomes clear: we cannot financially afford to begin the Industrial School this year because of the hospital. With it a financial risk is attached."[955] These difficulties and challenges apart, he seems to have been determined to begin the school, sooner or later. This aspect surfaces quite consistently in his correspondences.[956]

While investigating these issues, one tends to get an impression that a section of the Jesuits may have been critical about the training of Br. Anton Herbert, which as noted above, for starting a technical institute. Since the starting of the institute needed to be postponed due to various grounds, it was clear that the plan could not be implemented immediately. It appears that in such a situation Geisel may have been criticized for his initiative to have sent Br. Anton Herbert for technical training. One arrives at such a conclusion reading one of his letters wherein he justifies his position:

> Br. Herbert is trained, which did not cost us less. Yet, his training would not be useless even when the Industrial School has to wait for a few years. We have 2 omnibuses, 2 cars, mortar mixing machine, cement mixer, a number of motor cycles, a jeep besides a mechanical oven, washing machine ... we pay a big sum to the mechanics now ... All these imply pretty heavy in terms of money. When Br. Herbert can undertake even only these works, his training would be worth the money.[957]

Besides these initial hurdles, the canonical teachings of the Church and the norms of the Society of Jesus on whether a Religious Order could run a technical training institute also needed to be considered. The Jesuits were concerned that any enterprise, however noble in its purpose, must be within these parameters. In order to seek clarification and advice on the matter, Pius Geisel had to exchange a lot of correspondences for a period of time with the Superior General, but also

954 Ibid. (19th July 1951), op. cit.

955 Ibid., (Poona, 24th July 1951), op. cit.

956 Ibid., (Poona, 24th Feb. 1951), op. cit.

957 Ibid., (Poona, 19th July 1951), op. cit.

with a few knowledgeable people.[958] It appears as though Pius Geisel faced a certain amount of dilemma about the nature and status of the intended institute, besides having a concern about raising the required funds so that the plan might be materialized into an institution proper:

> Here is what I think of the question you proposed to me concerning industrial school ... As the proposal stands in your letter of 13.10.1949 there seems to be [a] question of plain business: an institution would be started in a small way with a view to make sufficient profit from things our [B]rothers and some boys would make, to establish a bigger institution.[959]

It may safely be assumed that the apprehensions and dilemmas mentioned in the correspondences of Pius Geisel, especially regarding the funding of the intended institute, were largely because of the financial crunch in the Mission. It has been mentioned earlier that the Mission depended largely on the generosity of the benefactors in Europe. Hence, it would be unjustifiable to conclude that Pius Geisel as the Superior of the Mission may have intended to establish the institute in terms of a 'workshop in commercial lines.' However, reading between the lines of the correspondence of Jerome Sanders, this aspect comes to fore.[960]

Jerome Sanders replied to Pius Geisel:

> In your letter of 3.12.1949, the point of running the first institution to make profits is again heavily stressed: "If we started a workshop, run on commercial lines, training at the same time apprentices" ... "My chief concern is ... the question of profit accruing from the workshop. Is it according to our Institute to run workshop on commercial lines if all the profit is put first into the expansion and then into the upkeep of a school for more theoretical training and orphanage?" This last sentence again clearly shows that the intention is less a school than a workshop on commercial lines that

958 See Otto Faller, "Elenchus Visitationis [16th - 29th November 1952]," ARSI, *Poona. 1005-1,* 36.

959 Jerome Sanders to Pius Geisel (Poona, 20th March 1950), ARSI, *Poona. 1004-XIX,* 15. Jerome Sanders is mentioned as a Professor of Moral Theology and Canon Law at De Nobili College for the first time in the catalogue in 1949. See *CPGSSI (1949),* 9. 27.

960 See Jerome Sanders to Pius Geisel (Poona, 20th March 1950), ARSI, *Poona. 1004-XIX,* 15.

will produce the necessary funds for another school and even an orphanage.[961]

Since the Superior normally represented the concerns of the entire Mission, it may be concluded that Geisel's opinions on the issue were a result of the deliberations with his subordinates. Seen from this perspective, one gets an impression that a lack of consensus among the Jesuits may have existed at the initial stage, basically on the point: whether the institute was intended to be a training 'school' for boys or a 'workshop on commercial lines'. Although the rationale behind is unclear, the Superior General appears to have been in favour of the latter option: "In his letter of 15 Dec. 1949 V. R. Fr. General himself understands that the first institution will not be properly a school, but a workshop 'formaparvae fabricae."[962] Since the reference of a Roman canonist is made in the letter, it may be concluded that the General may have arrived at such a decision based on the former's opinion. For, Sanders notes that the issue under review was "also understood in the same way by the Roman canonist in his resp[onse] of 29.12.49, para 'Occasio data ... parvam Jabricam."[963] As stated earlier, a clarification on the point is not available. In all probability, however, such a decision must have been reached, based on the way the matter was presented by Pius Geisel.

Jerome Sanders, on the other hand, seems to have held that the intended institute must not be reduced to a workshop that aimed at profit-maximization alone; rather it must aim at the technical training of the local boys. Referring to the letter of the Pius Geisel he further wrote:

> In the letter of 14 Febr. 1950 to V[ery] R[ev] Fr. General the sentence "ut habemus scholam, quae cresceret ex venditione eorum quae docendo et discendo in schola tali industriali fabricarent" [as we have from the school, such as would be acquired by teaching and learning in the school [and] from the sale of such things which they would produce in the industrial school] is still very ambiguous, and the roman canonist sees it rightly, in the

961 Ibid: Texts within the inverted commas are from Pius Geisel which are quoted by Sanders in order to interpret them within the framework of Canon Law and the Norms of the Society of Jesus.

962 Ibid.

963 Ibid. "In the same way" refers to the decision of the Superior General here.

light of the English sentence he quotes in his answer of 2 March 1950, as a money making business.[964]

From the above discussion it becomes apparent that quite a few correspondences were exchanged between Pius Geisel and the Superior General, who in turn seems to have referred the matter to a canonist in Rome. Clarifying his position on the explanation sought by Pius Geisel, Sanders writes: "It still sounds as if the question were: May we erect a small industrial school to make money enough to develop it into a first rate technical school?"[965] He further summarizes the dilemma of Geisel on this question in the following words:

> So in my opinion the question comes to this: Can the Society have practical technical schools where ours are instructors, and which will be efficient enough to be self-supporting and to improve their standards according to the growing needs of the apprentices?[966]

Reading, thus, through the explanations given by Sanders, one gets the impression that the basic dilemma of Pius Geisel was: whether the clerics or religious can run an industrial school? What is the canonical position on the use of profits accruing from an institution or a school? Sanders clarifies the point further:

> It seems to me that an industrial school established and run by clerics or religious (salvispropriis constitutionibus) is perfectly in order with can. 142: if its object in itself as well as the end the clerics and religious have in view (that is the finis operis and the finis operantis) be really and sincerely the technical training of the boys ... If the finis operis and the finis operantis of the school and the Superiors is really, openly and sincerely to teach the boys, and to give them a good training so that, instead of swelling the mass of coolies, they become first rate skilled workers, the school will in fact not be an institution for business, and it will even be impossible to create the mere impression that we are after profit or doing any business. That impression is not even created by the Government or municipal industrial schools. Everyone will see that it is just a

964 Ibid.

965 Ibid.

966 Ibid. See also in the same file, Peter Abellan to Peter van Gestel, Ass. Germ. (Rome, 28th April 1950).

> question of keeping the school going at an efficient level, and of improving standards only for the boys' sake.[967]

Eventually these initial dilemmas were overcome. There are indications that the Jesuits wanted to implement the plan of establishing the institute already around 1952. Reporting on the status of the project, Pius Geisel writes to the General: "... sad to say, that 'an industrial school' could not be begun this year. It may possibly take another 2 years, [which I hope] will not be a big disappointment."[968] Ever since, the correspondences of Geisel as well as that of others on the issue are rather silent from 1954 until 957. From this it appears that the project may have been shelved due to various difficulties discussed above. At last in 1958 Geisel reports something definitive about it:

> Now we are spared of worries. Fr. General has written: "Your Reverence knows (and your successor would know as well) [that] after how much of time the mission is going to have a school of such a great importance which would be a centre of technical training in Poona." That should be a pledge to you that the dream will finally, with God's as well as your help, come to realization.[969]

Having reached this stage, another step was to undertake the architectural planning, for which first a Swiss architect was envisaged

---

967 Sanders to Geisel (Poona, 20th March 1950), op. cit. Referring to the opinion of the Holy See on the issue he writes further: "That some decent profit be made from the selling of things made in the school does not make the selling illicit. We may certainly take it for granted that the Holy See desires technical schools in the Missions to be self-supporting and to improve their standards according to needs and possibilities. Now it is impossible for an industrial school to be self-supporting if it cannot sell its products at a profit, and instead of improving and developing, it will break down. The school has to pay decently its teachers and its apprentices, must be able to cover depreciation expenses on machines and material, to appoint up to date instructors, or to provide better machines and tools according to the developing needs of the students. N.B. This is not seeking an excuse in the fact that profits are applied to a good work. It is simply saying: good management of the school requires that the school be self-supporting and efficient. That is the way in which all the Ordinaries and religious (without any dispensation) want such schools to develop, and I do not think we could say they are all wrong when they hold that this is not against the prescriptions of the Church's law."

968 Pius Geisel, "De Statu Missionis" (Poona, 1st January 1952), ARSI, *Belgaum-Poona. 1301: 1950-1959.*

969 Pius Geisel to Hans Breitenstein (Poona, 24th January 1958), AMPSJ, *Superior Poona, P. Geisel.* Further writes Geisel: "Only no worry about the Industrial School (O God). Industrial School. That will certainly come up." Pius Geisel to Hans Breitenstein (Poona, 7th December 1958), AMPSJ, *Superior Poona, P. Geisel.*

to work in collaboration with Br. Joseph Pfiffner: "I have found a brilliant architect here, a very promising (and already proven), who has already declared that he would be preparing the plans of the buildings gratuitously in collaboration with Br. [Joseph] Pfiffner ... The name of the architect is Ernst Brantschen ..."[970] In fact "architect Brantschen, who was negotiating with Br. Pfiffner, has promised me [Hans Breitenstein], to give an artist's impression of the plan till the end of the month,"[971] which he did give as planned.[972] This plan, however, had to be abandoned. Hence Br. Joseph Pfiffner, who was on holidays, was expected "to come back with the plan."[973] Accordingly "now the Industrial or Vocational Training School would be planned by Br. Pfiffner alone as the [aforementioned] Swiss architect whom he had requested seemingly did not show much interest for the same."[974] The contract (or at least an initial agreement) with the architect Brantschen, however, seems to have been broken by the Jesuits themselves, which is clear from a letter:

> I shall deliver it [artist's impression of the plan] to you, perhaps you can show it to Pfiffe [Pfiffher]. You can then thank the architect for his efforts and communicate to him that due to the urgency of the objective, the matter must be settled in Poona. Decide on the matter yourself. In any case one cannot break the head of the gentleman, in which one plans something else without communicating to him anything further.[975]

Replying to the above letter Gerhard Baader writes:

> The plans of the architect Mr. Brantschen look very good, but after studying them, Fr. [Paul] Hafely and the Brothers think that they are not very practical for our purpose here. At any rate, I am

970 Hans Breitenstein to Pius Geisel, Vice-Provincial (Zurich, 14"[1] March 1958), AMPSJ, *16-Superior Poona-Neue: Baader, Weber, Staffner.*

971 Hans Breitenstein (?) to Gerhard Baader (Zurich, 18th June 1958), AMPSJ, *16-Superior Poona-neue: Baader, Weber, Staffner.*

972 See Gerhard Baader to Felix A. Plattner (Poona, 29th July 1958), AMPSJ, *16-Superior Poona-neue: Baader, Weber, Staffner.*

973 Ibid., (Poona, 11th April 1958).

974 Ibid., (Poona, 13th June 1958).

975 Hans Breitenstein (?) to Gerhard Baader (Zurich, 18th June 1958), AMPSJ, *16-Superior Poona-neue: Baader, Weber, Staffner.* See further in the same file, Gerhard Baader to Felix A. Plattner (Poona, 29th July 1958).

writing now to the gentleman to thank him and tell him that we shall incorporate some of his ideas in the final plan.[976]

This arrangement had its own advantages: "It is also better so that the matter will be planned at the spot, where the eastern and climatic conditions may be taken into consideration at best."[977] It appears, thereafter, that Br. Joseph Pfiffner took up the preparation of the plan entirely upon himself incorporating certain ideas of architect Ernst Brantschen and got it ready so that the constructions could begin:

> The plans are ready. The vocational training school is to be built in various phases. First of all it is planned to have workshops: a carpentry with the necessary modern equipment, a metalwork unit, arc welding unit and a workshop for auto mechanics, etc. For this purpose a dormitory for the young workers and apprentices is to be constructed. Besides, a residence and a chapel are planned for the [Coadjutor] Brothers who will be working as teachers there. To undertake this venture, three Swiss Brothers are foreseen, namely Br. [Joseph] Pfiffher, Br. [Anton] Herbert, and Br. [Otto] Widmer.[978]

Yet, a final hurdle before the beginning of construction was to be overcome, which pertained to the approval of the plan from the Collector's office, which was a tedious process due to certain corrupt practices in the offices. This reveals a sad aspect of the government machinery in India that began to manifest itself already from the first decade of its independence from the British Rule. Baader describes the

---

976 Gerhard Baader to Felix A. Plattner (Poona, 19th August 1958), AMPSJ, *16-Superior Poona-neue: Baader, Weber, Staffner.*

977 Ibid., (Poona, 13th June 1958).

978 "Gewerbeschule in Poona", *IB* 6 (1957): 3. Elsewhere one reads: "Stages of the plan: 1) First Stage: in June this year, a) "Turnercourse" (Lathe-work training), etc. - 2 years, b) "Fitter course" (Schlosser und Mechaniker) - 2 years, c) "Carpenter" (General carpentry) - 2 years, d) motor-mechanic - 2 years, e) Welder (1/2 year), for those who already have certificates of a-d categories. 2) Second Stage: a) Trained Carpenters (Furniture, etc.) - 1 year more, b) Electrician (beginners Course) - 1 year, c) Smithery/Blacksmith's work - 2 years, d) Casting - 2 years, e) Auto-mechanic (complete Theory etc.) - 3 years. In this second stage we must be having also the necessary buildings, etc., in order to accommodate the Brothers of the Society of Jesus as well as those from other Missionary Societies ... 3) Third Stage: a) Complete training as electricians (3 years), b) Radio Technician (2-3 years), c) Tinsmith and Masonry (2-3 years) ... d) Further training for Turners and Fitters in la) and b) - 2 years. 4) According to the needs in the future the following courses will be included: a) Refrigerator Technicians, b) Machine Design." A Project Paper signed by Paul Hafely and Felix A. Plattner (26th March 1959), AMPSJ, *Gewerbeschule,* Appendix.

same in the following words: "We hope the Collector will soon pass the plan we submitted about two months ago. Red tape [bureaucracy] is very annoying here. Everybody seems to expect a bribe before he makes a move."[979] As hoped for, the approval seems to have been received without further delay and "the Industrial School is now under construction under the supervision of Br. Pfiffner."[980] Its "bare brickwork (Rohbau) would soon be completed, so that the machines can be installed,"[981] most of which "were expected from Aachen."[982]

Thus finally the industrial school was established. Paul Hafely was made its first in-charge. Unfortunately he suffered poor health quite recurrently, at times losing even mental balance. Gerhard Baader gives the following details on his condition:

> What Fr. Haefeli [Hafely] says there about his surprise discovery that he was in charge of the school is not quite correct. Due to his recurring abnormal condition of health and mind and great uncontrollable moodiness he is at times...completely asocial and unreliable ...We had therefore decided in our consult already in April last year to give Fr. Geisel the supreme charge and direction....[983]

Consequently he [Hafely] needed to be sent to Switzerland for the treatment, where he seems to have fared unexpectedly well in this regard, so that Felix Plattner would write: "Fr. Hafely is doing surprisingly well. Presently, it is wonderful to work with him. Hopefully it remains so. On Friday he will go to Dr. Luthold in Theodosium [a hospital in Zurich] for examination and most likely stay there till Easter. "[984] His health condition thus was an obstacle, although as an administrator he seems to have been a gifted person in the days of his better health. Even during his stay in Switzerland for his treatment he was instrumental in arranging for machines for St. Joseph's Technical Institute.[985] Precisely

979 Gerhard Baader to Felix A. Plattner (Poona, 19th August 1958), AMPSJ, *16-Superior Poona-neue: Baader, Weber, Staffner.*

980 Ibid., (Poona, 6th October 1958).

981 Ibid., (Poona, 2nd December 1958).

982 Ibid.

983 Felix A. Plattner to Gerhard Baader ((Poona, 21st January 1959), AMPSJ, *16-Superior Poona-neue: Baader, Weber, Staffner.* See further in the same file, Felix A. Plattner to Gerhard Baader (Zurich, 26th January 1959).

984 Ibid., (Zurich, 17th March 1959).

985 Ibid., (Zurich, 24th April 1959).

for this reason that he was allowed to continue in the post even after he returned from his treatment and was entrusted with the work in the school: "I am after Fr. Hafely to go ahead with the plans and sketches for the extension of the Technical School. For a long time now I have been waiting for the approval of his Paternity [Superior General] but it has not come yet,.."[986] This intended extension was possible as the Superior General "approved of the general idea of our intended extension of the Technical Institute (now with the official name),..."[987]

6.4.2.2. The Background, Need and Objectives[988]

As we discuss this point, it would be apt to mention briefly at first the prevailing general background against which the decision on this venture emerged. In the 1930s and more especially in the decades subsequent to the WWII the onslaught of atheistic communism in the wake of growing scientific and technological advancement was becoming a concern for the Jesuits, at least in the west. The significance of the problem may be gauged from the fact that three successive General Congregations (GC hereafter) of the Society of Jesus, namely 28th' 29th and 30th addressed the same issue as an urgent one to be tackled with utmost diligence.[989] GC 28 (#29 §3), for example, called upon the members of the Society of Jesus in the following words:

> Because atheistic Communism today assails nearly the entire world and threatens destruction to the very foundations of Christian society, deeply conscious of this danger Ours should gird themselves to war against it with their united strength, and should exhort and prepare everyone to ward off so great a danger. Since atheistic Communism usually draws its strength in part from agitation and antireligious propaganda and in part from shortcomings of justice in the social

986 Gerhard Baader to Felix A. Plattner (Poona, 22nd April 1960), AMPSJ, *16-Superior Poona-neue: Baader, Weber, Staffner.*

987 Ibid., (Poona, 10th May 1960)..

988 For further reading see "Schriften der Kubel-Stittung Benscheimer Preis fur Internationale Zusammenarbeit 1969: Indien, St. Joseph's Technical Institute, Poona," ADPSJ, Abt. 45B-51, Nr. 108.

989 The corresponding decrees dealing with the issue are GC 28, Decree 29, GC 29, Decree 15 and GC 30, Decree 24. See John L. McCarthy et al., eds., *For Matters of Greater Moment: The First Thirty General Congregations* (St. Louis, Missouri: Institute of Jesuit Sources, 1994), 607; 629-630; 659-660. See also Christopher Hollis, *A History of the Jesuits* (London: Weidenfeld and Nicolson, 1968), 244.

> order, Ours should zealously attempt to clearly expose the internal errors of atheistic Communism and to wisely use the correctives for it..."[990]

In India the influence of the same was not remote. Hence, it emerged as one of the urgent issues to be addressed so that the influence of the same on common people could be kept at bay. This implied that immediate efforts were needed to be made in order to raise the standard of life of the Christian workers in general. The situation of distress in any society tended to be best suited for the ideology of communism to take a toll of the masses. For, "to the poor and the downtrodden they [the proponents of Communism] hold out a messianic hope of material gain."[991] To keep the Christian workers away from such an influence, the best strategy according to the Jesuits, was to further deepen the spiritual and religious life of the Christian youth so that they would be enabled to find solutions for the problems arising out of the socio-economic relations amidst the rapidly growing process of industrialization and mechanization.[992] In view of other future objectives, technical training was visualized as suitable in the broader framework of education in Christian social values as mentioned in the previous sub-section: "the purpose of the school is excellent, namely giving technical training to the Catholic boys."[993]

While investigating the issue we discovered that the immediate objective of the proposed institute was to create better job opportunities for all such groups of beneficiaries mentioned in the previous section. The following text captures well the immediate need for such an institute:

> Our young Catholic boys now find it much more difficult to get a government job in comparison with earlier times. The same is the case with regard to private sector jobs where the employment is availed solely on the basis of better marks and certificates. Therefore, there is a general desire [among the Jesuits] since some years to open a [technical] training school.[994]

990 John L. McCarthy et al., eds., *For Matters of Greater Moment*, 607.

991 Pothacamury, *The Church in Independent India*, 15.

992 "Gewerbeschule in Poona," *IB* 6 (1957): 2-3.

993 Kester, "Goa-Poona: Visitor's Report 1963," 54.

994 A Project Paper signed by Paul Hafely and Felix Plattner (26th March 1959), AMPSJ, *Gewerbeschule*. See also Kester, "Goa-Poona: Visitor's Report 1963," 53.

It has been mentioned above that the emphasis on the welfare of Catholic students must not be understood in exclusive terms. In fact, right from the beginning, a substantial number of non-Catholic as well as non-Christian students were admitted for the courses, giving preference to Catholic students. Thus preferential option for Catholic students was in no way an indication of denominationalism or communalism.

The need and objective of including such a target group in the Institute is articulated in great detail in a report of the institute, wherein the above-mentioned aspects, besides the financial status of the year 1959 are included. The report articulates the need of the institute in five points, underlining once again the specific nature of the group visualized as a beneficiary of such an enterprise:

> 1) All cannot afford to go to a college or a university... 2) Many of them cannot afford to go for higher studies - either because of the [lack of] aptitude or finance. Many who do pass out of our High Schools and then study further have no job [opportunities], often for years. Their number is considerably high. 3) With the [offer of] technical training we can form an independent Christian community; free from the ever increasing uncertainty of government jobs for the Christians. 4) The State is encouraging small-scale industries as a means of achieving a higher standard of living. If we stay aloof when [actually] we can contribute a lot... we would be missing a great chance. Indeed, now is the time! 5) Our schools are known as the best ones in the academic circles [of the place] - in the area of technical training, however, we have hardly anything [to claim], at least for the lower classes of the population. In this regard we have always been lagging behind.[995]

It was an acute realization that the neglect with regard to the technical training was bound to deprive a substantially big number of the youth from making their lives better. The idea of offering technical training became all the more crucial as the government began to lay further emphasis on the promotion of small-scale industries in order to facilitate financial self-sufficiency among the weaker sections of society. The factor that emerged as a basic denominator in the entire

995 A Copy of the "Report of the Institute: Its Needs, Achievements and Failures," submitted to Bishop Gottfried Dossing, Secretary General of *Misereor:* Aktion Gegen Hunger und Krankheit in der Welt', Aachen (n.d.) AMPSJ, *Gewerbeschule.* See also in the same file William Clement to Felix A. Plattner (Poona, 15th April 1962).

venture was the conviction of the Jesuits that a better state of life among the local people could be ensured only through education, both formal and non-formal. Undoubtedly, the first step towards this goal was to achieve financial self-sufficiency among the people. This, in turn, would be realized once the students passing out of the Jesuit schools succeed in qualifying employment in government and private sectors. Given the prevailing socio-economic background of the local people, the prospects of employment appeared better when the possibilities of offering a non-formal education were explored. While the Catholic youth would qualify themselves for jobs, in the long run, such a process would help them not only to improve upon their financial condition but also to make them aware of the factors that contribute to their dehumanized condition. Eventually, this would lead them to live in more humane condition in their lives, achieving higher social status as well.[996]

From the discussion so far it might appear as though the objective of opening a vocational training institute was to prepare only the Catholic students for qualifying for employments and jobs alone. However, the objective was much more comprehensive embracing much wider concerns not only of the Catholic community, but also of the larger Indian society. The following text underlines such an import in more explicit terms:

> If we help these young people now ... by means of a good [non-formal] education, perhaps even to get a few prominent positions in industrial sector, they would gradually emerge out of their wretched conditions and acquire a decent existence of life with a moderate degree of prosperity. This would lead them to achieve a respectable position in the society. Besides, they would be able to overcome caste barriers, which although in the eyes of the law is non-existent, in practice, is as indomitable as before. In the process they would succeed in eradicating the fundamental evils of Indian society and economy. Such an education, thus, would be an important contribution towards eradication of the economic and social problems in the Poona mission field.[997]

As we go through the vision articulated in the above two citations, we notice two categories of objectives: short-term (immediate) and long-term. Both are interlinked. Some of the objectives were visualized

996 See Noeline Pinto, "Human Organization for Pioneering in Education," AMPSJ, *Varia*.

997 "Gewerbeschule in Poona," *IB* 6 (1957): 2.

as having more direct bearing on the Catholic community; others with implications for the larger Indian society. The long-term objectives would be attainable only in so far as the short-term objectives were attainable. It is quite obvious that the preparation of the Catholic students in order to qualify for jobs was a short-term objective. Yet, without achieving it the latter objective would be unrealizable. Formation of "an independent Christian community" and "eradication of the economic and social problems of the Poona mission field", for example, were long-term visions that would be realized only as a result of achieving the short-term objectives. These visions were significant in the larger framework of the Jesuit missions as well. For, a mission failing to aim at certain structural changes in the society would be fundamentally no different from any secular initiative or a simple philanthropic enterprise, which mostly aims at alleviation of immediate suffering and pain. Without the dimension of structural transformation, the enterprise would betray the purpose of this Jesuit Mission. After all, every single initiative undertaken was to contribute towards the afore-mentioned goals.

We need to explore here briefly as to how the Jesuits visualized the implementation of the objectives articulated above. The technical training school was visualized as not only being a place to teach technical and artisanal skills, but also to impart to the young Christians a solid spiritual education. The young Christians, thus, would be prepared for a virtual apostolate among other people with whom they would be living and working. Amidst the growing influence of materialism in the wake of the process of industrialization, the technical training institute would be a place to impart basic principles of Christian social doctrine, which promotes dignity of work, respect for human beings and equality of opportunities, etc. The vision of bringing a transformation in the Catholic community would be translated into action when the young Catholic students, strengthened in their own faith, would be representing the Christian community among their colleagues in Trade Unions, Workers' Associations, politics and other spheres of their life.[998]

---

998 See "Gewerbeschule in Poona," *IB* 6 (1957): 2-3. See also "Litterae Triennales Praepositi Viceprovinciae Belgaum-Poonensis 1956-1958," ARSI, *Goa-Poona, Litterae Annuae 1501;* "Poona Workers' Welfare Association: Private Constitution", AMPSJ , *Belege 1958 -1963.* Although the two namely technical training school and Poona Workers' Welfare Association had entirely different areas of operation, the objectives of the same were almost identical or at least shared the same common thrust.

6.4.2.3. The Beneficiaries: the Weaker Sections

By late 1940s, the Jesuits were firmly aware of the fact that something more than offering just formal education was the need of the hour. As a result, the idea of offering a non-formal education came up. Apparently, the Catholic students were envisioned as its major beneficiaries. A point, however, that calls for an immediate clarification already here is: Why were the Catholic students intended as primary beneficiaries? Why not for all the students irrespective of their caste and religious affiliations? It must be recalled that the majority of the Catholic Christians came "from the lower stratum of the Hindu society, i.e., the Mahars. Despite the abolition of the caste system, [virtually] they were still outcasts of the society ..."[999] Given the age-old experience of subjugation and dehumanization, their educational standard was undoubtedly far behind in comparison with those of the higher caste Hindus and others. Because of such a historical background, it appears that some Catholic students depicted even a lack of aptitude for this system of education. As a result they were often left behind in their performances in annual exams, which had a direct implication for their job prospects: they were going to be eligible neither for government nor for private sector jobs. The situation appeared to have been worsening for them with the passage of time in the growing atmosphere of competition for jobs. Often, such a situation caused much discouragement in the students resulting in many of them dropping-out of schools, which implied, in more than one sense, a loss of chances for betterment of their future.[1000]

Considering their background, many of the Catholic students were brought from other mission stations as well, since their number in Poona alone was not sufficient, so that they could reach out to a larger number. Since Ahmednagar District was the major centre of missionary activities of the Jesuits, arrangements were made to send a good number of Catholic students from there to Poona: "This school is also meant to give technical training to Catholic boys of Ahmednagar mission district. Among the 40 Catholic boarders practically all come from this district."[1001] From this description one more point is highlighted here,

999 "Gewerbeschule in Poona," *IB 6* (1957): 2.

1000 See "Gewerbeschule in Poona," *IB* 6 (1957): 2; Huber, " Macht Euch die Erde untertan ...!," 4-5.

1001 Gregory Kester, "Goa-Poona: Visitor's Report 1963," ARSI, *Prov. Goa-Poonensis. 1501-Litterae Annuae,* 54.

namely the Catholics coming from Ahmednagar District were perceived as more deserving of this new venture than the locals coming from Poona city itself. The reason for the same has been already indicated above, i.e., the Catholics of Ahmednagar District were mostly from among the lowest of the social group, namely the Mahars.

While discussing about the beneficiaries it is important to clarify one more point here: the increasing number of school drop-outs mentioned above must not be taken as an exclusive phenomenon among the Catholic students. It was the case with other lower groups as well. Taken together the number of students dropping out of schools was growing at a rate that was enough to draw the attention of the Jesuits.[1002]

Besides such a group of Catholic students, namely the school drop-outs who were comparatively poor in formal education, there was still another group that deserved the attention of the Jesuits in this regard: the Catholic students, financially poor could not afford or pursue their higher education. These students did possess an aptitude for higher education but mostly on account of the poor financial background of their families were not in a position to pursue the same. The Jesuits were keen on offering them as well an alternative possibility for realizing their dreams of making their lives better. Among the Catholics, a substantial number of students belonged to this group, at least in the initial phase of the development of the institute.[1003]

The last group of beneficiaries of this venture included the Brothers of various Missionary Societies working in India. Reporting on the first year of the course, Albert Huber wrote: "The first course began with 50 candidates, among whom there are a good number of Brothers from various Missionary Societies."[1004] Although in the context of the larger Indian scenario, this may appear as an insignificant aspect, the accommodation of the members of various Missionary Societies in the institute for technical training had certainly a much wider implication for the Indian Church. The enthusiasm shown by other Missionary Societies

1002 See Felix A. Plattner to Gerhard Baader ((Zurich, 24* April 1959), AMPSJ, *16-Superior Poona-neue: Baader, Weber, Staffner.*

1003 Based on an interview with Hermann Bacher (Basel, 10th November 2014, 14:00 Hour). Bacher was instrumental in implementing one of the most successful projects namely Watershed Programme in Ahmednagar District within Poona Mission. He arrived in India in 1948 and worked there until 2009 when he decided to spend his retirement in his homeland Switzerland. Ever since, he stays at the Jesuit Community Boromaum in Basel.

1004 Huber, "Macht Euch die Erde untertan ...!," 4.

to train their own members at this institute is an indication that a general perception about the value of technical training was growing among the missions. In all likelihood, the Missionary Societies were planning similar initiatives in their respective Missions. The SVD (Societatis Verbi Divini) Fathers of Indore (Madhya Pradesh), for example, seem to have been keen on starting a similar venture.[1005]

In sum, thus, a general concern for the less competent Catholic students having no possibility of pursuing higher studies and prospects for jobs and the school drop-outs in general emerged as a major factor in the consideration for the alternative system of education. Apparently, at the root of the origin of the enterprise, the aspect of "a preferential option" for the poor Catholic students was clearly present.[1006] The Jesuits, as pointed out above, were convinced that for such categories of students a need-based (vocational) educational system and learning, rather than formal education alone was a vital need of the hour in order that such students be prepared for better job prospects or at least for self-employment opportunities.

6.4.2.4. The Curriculum

We shall discuss a few aspects related to the curriculum. The nature of the non-formal education that was visualized to be offered was in the line of the technical education, whereby the students would be trained in various trades and skills according to the areas of their interest. Albert Huber explains the same: "To the future supervisors a training is offered not according to a privately designed programme...but according to the programme prescribed [and duly sanctioned] by the State...."[1007] Alongside the major trade, the curriculum was designed to include certain common subjects like the study of "languages, mathematics ... drawing, theory in the selected area of trade [and] something of book-keeping, etc."[1008]

Right from the beginning, thus, "the school began to follow a curriculum prescribed by the State government, so that the latter may

1005 Ibid. See also "Die neue Gewerbeschule," *JHS* 4 (1959): 8.

1006 See St. Joseph's Technical Institute, Pune, 1966 (Brochure), PJPA, *Varia;* Huber, "Macht Euch die Erde untertan ...!," 4-5.

1007 "Macht Euch die Erde untertan ...!," 4.

1008 [1008] Felix A. Plattner to Archbishop Gottfried Dossing (Zurich, 25th April 1962), AMPSJ, *Gewerbeschule (Attachment).* See Felix A. Plattner (?) to Gerhard Baader (Zurich, 26th January 1959), AMPSJ, *16-Superior Puna, neue: Baader, Weber, Staffner.*

give recognized diplomas. Thus it distinguished itself from many of the vocational training schools run by other Jesuit Missions."[1009] In other words, the distinction consisted in the fact that the technical institutes run by other Jesuit Missions in India followed mostly self-designed courses for a substantial number of years in the beginning.[1010] Gradually many new trades and skills were introduced, i.e., auto-repair, electricals, electronics, computer repair, fabrication, fitting, etc. besides a few others.[1011] In order to impart trainings in these skills, "the courses are planned fairly in detail ... [and] uniquely designed."[1012]

It is quite apparent that the curriculum included theoretical knowledge combined with practical knowledge as any technical training programme required. For, it helped produce not only tangible results of learning, but also contributed towards inculcating a sense of fulfillment in the learner. The State Education Department too, while accepting the proposal made by the school management, underlined the same aspect:

> The State Commission for [Public] Instructions has readily agreed and recommended thereby that the practical training, as far as possible, must be made productive and useful, which in turn contributes towards inculcating a sense of initiative and reliability among the apprentices.[1013]

In order to maintain and promote the Christian and Jesuit character it was necessary to include religious instruction alongside the training in various skills in the institute. It was, thus, visualized that the education would not be limited to technical and artisanal skills, but would include important aspects of Christian social principles with a view to prepare the students as future catalysts of change in society. Here it suffices to make just a mention of the same. We get a glimpse of the vision mentioned above from the following text:

> While the school would teach not only the technical and artisanal skills, but would convey also an intensive religious education to the young Christians; it would allow them to prepare themselves for

1009 A Project Paper signed by Paul Hafely and Felix A. Plattner (Poona, 26th March 1959), AMPSJ, *Gewerbeschule.*

1010 Ibid.

1011 See "St. Joseph's Technical Institute, Pune, 1966," (Brochure), PJPA, *Varia.*

1012 Plattner to Archbishop Gottfried Dossing (Zurich, 25th April 1962), AMPSJ, *Gewerbeschule (Attachment).*

1013 [1013] "Macht Euch die Erde untertan ...!," 3.

> the future apostolate among the industrial population. The major focus will be to teach them the basic principles of Christian Social Doctrine, which they would be transmitting among their colleagues, in trade unions, workers' associations and in politics, and thus strengthen their own faith, so that they will not be led astray amidst the complexities of materialism and technological age.[1014]

It is a matter of curiosity as to how the two goals namely teaching handicraft and artisanal skills and spiritual formation were to be met. At a practical level, therefore, "The responsibility of imparting religious and social instructions is to be undertaken by the Fathers of the Social Institute in Poona, along with Fr. Ivo Meyer, a Swiss who previously has been looking after the pastoral care of the workers.[1015]

From what we have discussed so far under this sub-section, it is clear that the curriculum was visualized within the background of the broader framework of education in Christian values. The training in skills and trades, thus, was visualized as means of formation in values having larger implications not only for the Mission but also for the Indian society at large. We shall touch upon these in detail in the following section.

6.4.2.5. The Growth and Expansion

The growth and expansion of the institute may be assessed from the fact that the permission to start the same was received comparatively much earlier and the recognition of the same was already assured within a few months of its opening, as may be concluded from the report: "Even before the completion of the first academic year the State Government of Bombay has granted the approval to our St. Joseph's Technical School in Puna."[1016] Apparently, such an achievement was a result of a close collaboration among the various individuals and agencies:

> An almost unexpected early recognition of the achievements of the Director, Fr. Paul Hafeli, the faithful Brothers who teach here and also that of the Workers' Associations of Zurich/Schaffhausen, who

1014 "Gewerbeschule in Poona," *IB* 4/6 (1957): 2. Other curricula included also participation in Marian Sodalities, "Boy Scouts" or "Boys Club", etc. See Otto Faller, "Elenchus Visitationis (22-27th December 1952)," ARSI, *Poona. 1005-1,* 37.

1015 "Gewerbeschule in Poona," 3.

1016 "Frohe Nachrichten aus Puna: Staatliche Anerkennung der Gewerbeschule," *JHS* 3 (1960): 8. See also Huber, "Macht Euch die Erde untertan ...!," 4.

by their generous contributions have made the construction of the Vocational Training School of the modern times possible.[1017]

The process of recognition of the institute was depended on the fulfillment of the minimum requirements prescribed by the Department of Technical Education with regard to its curriculum and infrastructural facilities. In our discussion on the Dnyanamata High School we have noted that the recognition received by the government implied a lot of benefits in terms of the validity of the certificates. The same applied in this case too:

> With the recognition, the government assumes the responsibility of the school partially to support the same financially, wherein the grant is estimated in proportion to the invested capital. Thus, a larger machinery operation brings a correspondingly larger annual government grant and is easier to maintain the enterprise in terms of the cost.[1018]

As one reads the correspondences on the subject, one comes across a general sense of satisfaction that emerged among the Jesuits at the quick progress of the institute. Revealing his satisfaction, for example, writes Felix Plattner: "It is gratifying to note that St. Joseph's Technical Institute in Poona has emerged well,"[1019] But such a development was not without a cost. In a rather short period of time, the Jesuits, through hard labour, had brought the institute to a level so that Huber could report: "The cleanliness, spacious campus, the sense of discipline, a presumed sense of working together among the young people of various social milieus and religions ... all that made this Industrial School well-known in Poona right up to the Central Government in Delhi."[1020] Such an accomplishment had a further impact, which was significant for its extension: "Besides, a Commission of the Central Government in Delhi[1021] has approached the management of the school and made a suggestion that the school may be enlarged, with the government aid,

1017 [1017] "Frohe Nachrichten aus Puna," 8.

1018 A project paper sjgned by Paul Hafely and Felix A. Plattner (26th March 1959), AMPSJ, *Gewerbeschule.*

1019 Felix A. Plattner to Mr. Schneider (Zurich, 30th June 1961), AMPSJ, *Gewerbeschule.*

1020 Huber, "Macht Euch die Erde untertan ...!," 4.

1021 Namely *All India Council for Technical Education* (AICTE), Delhi. See Gerhard Baader to Felix A. Plattner (Poona, 3rd April 1962), AMPSJ, *16-Superior Poona-neue: Baader, Weber, Staffner.*

to accommodate 250 apprentices."[1022] For an endeavour of this kind, a government recognition was of much significance, as noted above. That the institute was making a good impact not only in the locality, but its innovative and success story had reached the central Government becomes further evident from the following text:

> Last year, a commission of experts from the central government visited the venture: all these made an excellent impression on these gentlemen, with the result that they made a suggestion to increase the number of apprentices from 150 to 250 and to adopt the training program of the central government:[1023] the diploma issued then would apply to whole of India. [And that is] Not enough! This Commission also promised assistance with skilled teachers, with additional equipment and financial aid for the teaching staff: "You must take care of the extensions ... and above all for the order, management and a good spirit!" Truly a wonderful chance, of which one could not even dream of, three years ago.[1024]

A sense of satisfaction seems to underline all these communications. Yet, this was not the climax. The institute needed to be extended further to accommodate new students who would be coming in the succeeding academic years. It is apparent that at the time of its opening, the institute had limited infrastructure at its disposal. To this effect an approval of the Superior General was imperative: "I am after Fr. [Paul] Haefeli to go ahead with the plans and sketches for the extension of the Technical School. For a long time I have been waiting for the approval of His

1022 "Frohe Nachrichten aus Puna," *JHS* 3 (1959): 8. See also Huber, "Macht Euch die Erde untertan ...!," 4. A True Copy of the government recognition signed by J. M. Badhe, Director of Technical Education Bombay, Bombay State, Bombay states (No. RTIB 8307, Bombay 13th April 1959) reads: "This is to certify that St. Joseph's Technical School, Shankar Shet [Shankarpeth] Road, Poona of the Poona Jesuit School's Society has been granted provisional permission by this Department to start trade courses in Turning, Fitting, Welding, Motor Mechanic and Carpentry approved by the State Council of Technical Education, Bombay State from June 1959 subject to the provision of the requisite equipment necessary for the courses." AMPSJ, *Gewerbeschule.*

1023 About this programme later, however, certain apprehensions were raised for reasons unknown: "Fr. Haefeli thinks that about the Central Government Training scheme we must not be in a hurry; it is not as favourable as it looked in the beginning." Gerhard Baader to Felix A. Plattner (Poona, 16th February 1961), AMPSJ, *16-Superior Poona-neue: Baader, Weber, Staffner.*

1024 Huber, "Macht Euch die Erde untertan ...!," 5.

Paternity, but it has not come yet..."[1025] A month later he reports: "His Paternity has approved the general idea of extension of the Technical Institute (now the official name)..."[1026] Once these formalities were completed the extension of certain wings were undertaken:

> We have started on the new construction of the Garage workshop. Our garage work--the motor-mechanics' training--is going on quite splendidly ... and an excellent mechanic ... is supervising and assigning everything; so that this department seems to get on best as far as instruction and learning is concerned ... Without any advertisements we are getting known as good and reliable.[1027]

The plan of expansions implied not only addition of infrastructure, but inclusion of new trades as well, i.e., Carpentry, Masonry and the like. The training in this skill was going to be very practical and useful given the growing urbanization of Poona. But there were a few hurdles pertaining to the proposed syllabus of this trade before this plan could be implemented. The syllabus needed to be approved by the Director of Technical Education in Bombay. It may be mentioned here that by this time one begins to sense a certain amount of resistance on the part of the authorities in issuing approvals, etc., as may be concluded from this correspondence: "Fr. [Rudolph] Schoch saw the Director of Technical Education in Bombay, was promised help and encouragement, but has not yet got anything definite in writing regarding the syllabus and the recognition of the course. They said they want to study the syllabus first carefully."[1028] Such a conclusion is perceived not without certain previous experiences. In fact certain anti-missionary sentiments were gradually becoming prominent, about which we discussed earlier. All the same such cases, at least at this stage, need not be generalized. But the tempo of progress of the institute appears to have been smooth. Were it to be otherwise, the Jesuits would not have entertained the proposal

---

1025 Gerhard Baader to Felix A. Plattner (Poona, 22nd April 1960), AMPSJ, *16-Superior Poona-neue: Baader, Weber, Staffner.*

1026 Ibid., (Poona, 10th May 1960).

1027 Albert Huber to Felix A. Plattner (Poona, 26th July 1960), AMPSJ, *Gewerbeschule.*

1028 Gerhard Baader to Felix A. Plattner (Poona, 08th December 1961), AMPSJ, *16-Superior Poona-neue: Baader, Weber, Staffner.*

to open yet another technical school in the Vice-province, though eventually it had to be abandoned.[1029]

Before we conclude this sub-topic, it may not be out of place to mention that the management of the institute and extension of the same, especially in the initial years, met with difficulties, not seldom, mainly on account of lack of suitable personnel among the Jesuits:

> But I have another difficulty, which just now stands in the way of any new greater addition to the Technical Institute and that is the lack of direction. Even now the institute is too much for Fr. [Paul] Haefely to manage well. He does his best, but I do not think that he really cope with it... That may help us to get over the difficulty of direction. Among our own men we have none at present who could assist Fr. Haefeli. Everywhere we are short of suitable men...So our plans depend still much on the solution of the personnel.[1030]

Another aspect of the problem that occasionally emerged resulted from a lack of mutual understanding among the Jesuits, although such aspects are bound to surface in all innovative enterprises. Yet, since this aspect had a direct implication for the growth of the institute, we may make a mention of the same here. In order to give an inkling into the same we may quote a letter of Gerhard Baader:

> Further seeing Fr. Haefeli and listening to the Brothers working under him, I am somewhat afraid for the smooth and steady working of the extension scheme. You know that Fr. Haefeli is very much subject to moods that can make him reckless in spending money and careless in planning. The Brothers [Otto] Widmer and [Anton] Herbert are complaining that he does not procure and plan the work prudently, so that the apprentices have sometimes nothing to do in the workshops ... Some days ago Brother Herbert came in a great hurry and excitement and asked me very urgently to take him at once away from the Technical Institute, because he found impossible to work with Fr. Haefeli. Fr. H[aefeli] on the other hand says that the Brother is self-willed and too touchy, not really businesslike.[1031]

1029 See Kester, "Goa-Poona: Visitor's Report 1963," 55; Hans Breitenstein (?) to Pius Geisel (Vice-Provincial) (Zurich, 16th September 1957), AMPSJ, *Superior Poona, P. Geisel.*

1030 Gerhard Baader to Felix A. Plattner (Poona, 16th February 1961), AMPS J, *16-Superior Poona-neue: Baader, Weber, Staffner.*

1031 Gerhard Baader to Felix A. Plattner (Poona, 10th May 1960), AMPSJ, *16-Superior Poona-neue: Baader, Weber, Staffner.* See also Felix A. Plattner to Gerhard Baader (Zurich, 08th November 1962), AMPSJ, *16-Superior Poona-neue: Baader, Weber, Staffner.*

The occasional lack of team work affected the decisions even at the level of policy as well, especially with regard to finances. It is a clear indication that the management of the institute occasionally suffered on account of such aspects too. To quote Baader again: "But the Technical Institute, which has to be shorn of the building section (which causes a lot of trouble and in which Fr. [Paul] Haefeli has left us some insolvable mysteries, mainly financial) faces a financial crisis. Fr. Haefeli gave the instructors, clerks, etc. far too high salaries ...This will hit the missionaries badly ...."[1032]

The growth and expansion of the institute, later faced another hurdle on account of a new policy of the government: "only boys with matric are to be admitted to such schools if they are to get government grant."[1033] Such a policy was going to affect a substantial number of school-drop outs who had discontinued schooling often much before matriculation exam. A big number of the Catholic youth belonged to this group.[1034] In spite of such hurdles, the institute made good progress in the following decades, providing better employment prospects combined with better education in Christian as well as basic socio-cultural values.

6.4.2.6. The Socio-economic Impact

By the time the institute completed six decades of its existence, thousands of students had passed out of the institute with better prospects of jobs and self-employments, accomplishing tangible transformation in their lives as well as in their families. This had been clearly visualized in the beginning: "Over the years hundreds of master craftsmen would be leaving this school, equipped with a solid knowledge, with reliability and with healthy self-experienced social principles!"[1035] This dream seems to have been realized when hundreds of youths passed out of this institute, to the great sense of satisfaction and fulfillment of the Jesuits.

6.5. Lay Collaboration in Mission

A new departure in the missionary strategies as indicated earlier was the addition of more lay-collaborators who became partners in mission in

---

1032 Gerhard Baader to Felix A. Plattner (Poona, 09th February 1962), AMPSJ, *16-Superior Poona-neue: Baader, Weber, Staffner.*

1033 Gerhard Baader to Felix A. Plattner (Poona, 2nd May 1962), AMPSJ, *16-Superior Poona-neue: Baader, Weber, Staffner.*

1034 Ibid.

1035 Huber, " Macht Euch die Erde untertan ...!," 4-5.

Poona. Financial and technical collaborations received from associations were of great significance. An additional aspect was the collaboration and participation of the general public particularly in Switzerland. "There were usually lay people who were active and knew how to mobilize others. The aim of the enthusiasm was to promote missionary vocations and to support the missions with prayer and donations."[1036] Their response in contributing to the mission projects in this Mission was no doubt considerably generous and heartening.

6.6. Missionary Health-Care Service in Western Maharashtra

Until late 1930s, there were hardly half a dozen of Christian hospitals and dispensaries in India. Until this period, the Protestants held the lead in this area.[1037] The American Board of Commissioners for Foreign Missions, for example, were the pioneers of Christian health care in India. Other Protestant groups followed suit. Consequently, the association of the Protestant medical works in India, namely the Christian Medical Association of India (CMAI) was founded in 1905 which is an umbrella association for 330 mission hospitals and healthcare organizations across the country at the moment. The Catholic association of medical works, namely Catholic Health Association of India (CHAI) was established only in 1946. At present it has become much broader than its Protestant counterpart, with member institutions of nearly 3,400 including 484 large hospitals.[1038]

As for the Jesuits, their involvement in the health-care service sector has not been a new dimension in India. Yet it is a rather later development in practically all the Missions. The Belgian Jesuits of Bengal Mission, for example, had adopted a rather unique method of evangelization in rural areas, especially as it expanded to Ranchi area (Jharkhand). The establishment of a mission station was invariably followed by a school. Dispensaries and other such health-care establishments were added to many mission stations mostly after 1960s.[1039] These establishments

1036 Michael Sievernich, *Die christliche Mission: Geschichte und Gegenwart* (Darmstadt: WBG, 2009), 95-96.

1037 See D. Samuel Abraham, *Laws on Hospital Administration* (Chennai: B.I. Publications, 2008), ix.

1038 See Achilles Meersmann, "The Catholic Church in India," in *Christianity in India: A History in Ecumenical Perspective,* eds. H. C. Perumalil & E. R. Hambye (Allepey: Prakasham Publications, 1991), 258-260.

1039 Plattner, *Catholic Church in India,* 69.

remained as the primary health-care facilities. The Poona Mission Jesuits went a step further to establish a full-fledged hospital as a symbol of their renewed emphasis on the health-care service. It is precisely with this aspect in view that we call it a unique initiative.

6.6.1. St. Luke's Hospital, Shrirampur

Until late 1940s, the Ahmednagar District was virtually bereft of health-care facilities worth the name. In such a situation, people relied mostly upon local sorcerers and witch-doctors besides a few indigenous and ethnic methods of healing.[1040] This, as noted in a previous chapter, had serious and negative implications for the poor and uneducated people. The appalling situation with regard to the health-care facilities had a detrimental effect not only on the society in general, but also on the Jesuits. Consequently, a remedy to this effect was an immediate need of the hour. The earlier missionary policy followed the motto: "to teach, preach and heal."[1041] Under this scheme it may be stated that in the first place the promotion of medical services was intended to be aimed at relieving the poor people from their physical suffering. Yet, at the deeper level, like any other missionary service, it was "praeparatio evangelii," (preparation for evangelization)[1042] even if it was not articulated in explicit terms.

The foundation of the hospital in Shrirampur was necessitated by a very pragmatic reason in the first place. No wonder, due to utter lack of health-care facilities in Ahmednagar District as hospitals and health-care centres were virtually non-existent in the area those days, the missionaries were often exposed to the risk of losing their lives prematurely. As for the common people, even if they existed, they were beyond their reach. For example, a general hospital with bare minimum facilities was situated in Ahmednagar town, some 45 miles away from Shrirampur, making it virtually impossible for people to take the sick,

1040 See J. B. Winiger, "Die Choleragottin," *IB* 1/29 (January 1937): 248; F.X. Schubiger, "Indische Feuerprobe und ihr Ausgang," Ibid., 248-249.

1041 Ville Paivansalo, "Lutheran Perspectives on the Right to Health in a Global World," in *Lutheran Identity and Political Theology,* eds. Carl-Henric Grenholm & Goran Gunner (James Clarke & Co., 2114), 52.

1042 Ville Paivansalo, "Lutheran Perspectives on the Right to Health in a Global World," in *Lutheran Identity and Political Theology,* eds. Carl-Henric Grenholm & Goran Gunner (James Clarke & Co., 2114), 52. See also Joseph Ubelmesser, "Der Mensch, der 100 Jahre lebt!," *Indien: Arbeitsfelddeutscher Jesuiten* 3/1 (January 1957), 21.

especially given the condition of the roads and streets that were virtual reminders of medieval times. On certain stretches no vehicles could travel during the rainy season. Moreover, the cost of treatment was beyond affordable amount.[1043]

The difficulties on account of distance and condition of roads apart, the poor people were often victims of deliberate discrimination as well. In the mid-1940s, for example, when an epidemic broke out, the government tried to distribute medicines to the villages. But the agents and doctors sold out the medicines only among the richer people, clearly depriving the poor from benefitting from medical aid.[1044] Thus, the primary objective of the mission hospital was to avail medical health-care to the poor and needy people of Shrirampur and surroundings as well as to give medical aid to the missionaries working in the Ahmednagar District.[1045]

Figure 6.4: A patient being carried to a hospital from a far-off village. *Source*: AMPSJ, *Ahmednagar Distrikt, Fotographische Belege & IB 4* (August/September 1950): 212.

The lack of health-care facilities became a serious concern for the Mission. The Mission had lost a few very promising missionaries at a young age. Given the perpetual problem of lack of Jesuit personnel, every loss was a heavy blow to the Mission. Thus, the incidents which seem to have drawn the immediate attention of the Jesuits to give a serious consideration about the establishment of a hospital were:

1043 Cacilie, "Das Krankenhaus," *IB* 3 (1954): 6.

1044 See Ludwig Hassle to Francis X. Hayler (Songaon, 23rd October 1945), AMPSJ , *LB. Songaon-Briefe.*

1045 Cacilie, "Das Krankenhaus," 6.

the death of Rupert Schweigert at the very young age (37 years) and the untimely return of John Roder to Europe on account of the non-availability of medical facilities. The latter was 35 at the time of his departure from the mission field. These incidents took place in 1947.[1046] John Roder died "in a few months after his return to Europe."[1047] Both these missionaries, thus, were lost to the Mission "simply because at the epicenter of our mission there are no reliable medical treatment available and there is no mission hospital."[1048] The comment made by Rudolph Schoch that "a hospital for our mission is absolutely necessary,"[1049] therefore, was not just a personal opinion, rather a voice representing a common anxiety of other Jesuits as well. Underlining the same sense of urgency Felix Plattner wrote: "Even the consideration of our missionaries so imperatively demands the establishment of a mission medical service in Ahmednagar District. This is one of our most important duties at this hour."[1050] The imperative of implementing the plan became even stronger as a few generous individuals and agencies in Europe were keen on responding to the need of the poor masses in India:

> The Medical Mission Institute in Wurzburg is willing to cooperate. Two or three fully trained, highly qualified missionary doctors are available. From German Mission Alms the purchase of technical equipment for the operating room, etc. is assured. So it would be a matter of a terrible shame if we failed to respond to the need of the hour.[1051]

The logic that seems to have underlined the entire consideration was: the untimely death of the missionaries was not only a blow to the Jesuits alone, but had a direct impact on the expansion and consolidation of the Mission.[1052] Similarly, it appeared to be an important area to

---

1046 See *Catalogus Provinciae Germaniae Superioris 1947 & 1948.*

1047 "Historia Generalis Missionis Poonensis," ARSI, *Goa-Poona. Litterae Annuae 1501.*

1048 Felix A. Plattner, "Es muss etwas geschehen...," *IB* 4 (July-September 1950): 208.

1049 Rudolph Schoch to Felix A. Plattner (Sangamner, 21st September 1949), AMPSJ, *41-Puna Stadt Briefe.* See also Felix A. Plattner to Rudolph Schoch (Zurich, 31st December 1949), AMPSJ, *43-Dnyanamata etc. Briefe.*

1050 Felix A. Plattner, "Es muss etwas geschehen ..." *IB* 4 (July-September 1950): 208. See also Felix A. Plattner to Rudolph Schoch (Zurich, 3 1sl December 1949), AMPSJ, *43-Dnyanamata etc. Briefe.*

1051 **Felix A.** Plattner, "Es muss etwas geschehen ..." *IB* 4 (July-September 1950): 208.

1052 See Felix A. Plattner, "Es muss etwas geschehen ..." *IB* 4 (July-September 1950): 208.

concentrate as virtually the entire population of the place seemed to be at the mercy of the indigenous doctors, who were "for the most part quite ignorant of the functioning of the human body."[1053]

For the purpose, Shrirampur (earlier Belapur), 43 kilometers away from Ahmednagar was chosen as a suitable place because of its good connectivity by trains and buses.[1054] Once the negotiations were finalized with the Medical Mission Secular Institute, Wurzburg (Germany), Mother Anna Dengel, the foundress[1055] came to Poona to finalize the spot and other details, as we read in the following report:

> In 1951 Mother [Anna Maria] Dengel, the Foundress of the Medical [Mission] Sisters, paid a visit to Poona where she bought a house for her novices, and a large property in the suburbs for the erection of a hospital. Shortly afterwards Dr. Jahn, the Director of the Medical [Mission] Institute of Wurzburg, arrived [in Poona] to inspect the plot at Shrirampur which was being offered for a hospital.[1056]

The construction work was undertaken almost immediately[1057] after the above-mentioned visits of the two important figures (whose role is invaluable in the entire venture) and the permission received from the Municipality Corporation.[1058] The work of construction was taken up by Br.

1053 Samuel Jayakumar, *Dalit Consciousness and Christian Conversion: Historical Resources for a Contemporary Debate* (Oxford: Regnum International/ Delhi: ISPCK, 1999), 213.

1054 Pius Geisel to Felix A. Plattner (Poona, 31st July 1951), AMPSJ, *Superior Poona, P. Geisel.*

1055 See Achilles Meersmann, "The Catholic Church in India," op. cit., 258-260. Some of the Jesuits were not in favour of inviting the Wurzburg Sisters. See Pius Geisel to Felix A. Plattner (Poona, 24th December 1951), AMPSJ, *Superior Poona, P. Geisel.* In order to seek the possibility of working in collaboration with the Medical Mission Sisters, correspondences were started already around 1948-49. See Felix A. Plattner to Rudolph Schoch (Zurich, 1st October 1949), AMPSJ, *41-Puna-Stadt Briefe.*

1056 Hans Staffner, "Die katholische Mission im Ahmednagar-Distrikt," op.cit. See also Pius Geisel (Poona, 17* August 1951), ARSI, *RLGGM,* Vol. VIII, 144; Pius Geisel to Felix A. Plattner (Poona, 31st July 1951), AMPSJ , Superior Poona, P. Geisel. Read further Anna Dengel, "Karitas und Missionsarztlicherdienst," in *Weltkrise und Weltmission: Vortrage des IX. internationalen acedemischen Missions/congress in Wien, 3-7 Juli 1950,* pub. Johannes Thauren (Modling b.W.: St. Gabriel, 1951), 96-102; Friedrich Jahn, "Neue Wege missionsarztlicher Laienarbeit,"^M71 (1952): 39.

1057 See Pius Geisel to Felix A. Plattner (Poona, 9th August 1951), AMPSJ, *Superior Poona, P. Geisel.*

1058 Ibid., (Poona, 4th April 1952).

Figure 6.5: Plan of St. Luke's Hospital, Srirampur.
Source: IB 1 (January/February 1952): 55.

Anton Herbert.[1059] Mother Anna Dengel took a personal interest in the entire venture. After her visit to Poona, she remained there to supervise the progress of the construction of the hospital as well as to finalize "a deal for the property for the novitiate"[1060] of her Congregation. It is an indication that she desired to make an abiding contribution in the health-care sector in collaboration with the Jesuits. On the other hand, it had been a long cherished dream of Pius Geisel as Superior of the Mission too, to have a mission hospital established. Thus finally a great dream was fulfilled.

On the arrival of a doctor-couple and 5 Sisters[1061] from the above-mentioned Institute, the O.P.D. (Outdoor Patients' Department) work was started on a small scale in 1952, while the construction of the hospital had just begun, which "was completed and opened early in 1953"[1062] "with 120 beds ... [and] the necessary supply of medical equipment and medical stores."[1063] The Convent for the Sisters too was completed in the same year,[1064] followed by an apartment for the

1059 Ibid., (Poona, 18th April 1952).

1060 Ibid., (Poona, 19th July 1951).

1061 See Pius Geisel (Poona, 1st January 1952), ARSI, *Belgaum-Poona 1301 (1950-1959).* In the same file, ibid., (Poona, 1st January 1953).

1062 "History of the Poona Mission 1952-1955", ARSI, *Goa-Poona, Litterae Annuae 1501.* See also Cacilie, "Das Krankenhaus," *IB* 3 (1954): 6; Pius Geisel (Poona, 1st April 1953), ARSI, *RLGGM,* Vol. VIII, 297.

1063 Hans Staffner, "Die katholische Mission im Ahmednagar-Distrikt," op.cit.

1064 See Pius Geisel (Poona, 1st January 1953), ARSI, *Belgaum-Poona 1301 [1950-1959].* See also Pius Geisel to Felix A. Plattner (Poona, 31st July 1952), AMPSJ, *Superior Poona, P. Geisel.*

doctors, in 1955. Unfortunately it was built rather too small and needed to be enlarged later.[1065] The finance for the same was largely availed by the Swiss Jesuit Mission Procurator,[1066] besides the equipment being supplied mostly by the German Church donations.[1067] There were many other funding agencies whose generous help assisted the realization of such a significant venture.

After 6 years of fruitful work, it was necessary to extend the building. For the purpose, a larger plot comprising nearly 56 acres was already purchased in 1953.[1068] A new dispensary building was completed by December 1960. The increase in the size of the hospital and number of patients necessitated a School of Nursing with locally-trained nurses who would be in a better position to reach out to people for holistic health beyond curative service. Preventive and promotive health were stressed. The students' accommodation & classrooms were included in the new building plane, which were completed in 1961 and officially inaugurated in 1963.[1069]

The hospital grew step by step to the present capacity of 220 beds including 24 beds for private patients. It has a Medical, Surgical, Gynaec-Obstetric & Paediatric Departments. Besides, there are three operation theatres, X-Ray department, Laboratory & Pharmacy.[1070] The instant success of the hospital may be further assessed from the fact that people from distant places "mostly on the bullock-carts, carried on the backs by the relatives or occasionally walking themselves, seldom on horses or jeeps"[1071] began to come to seek medical help already within a few months after its opening. Given their financial condition they mostly visited the O.P.D. However, over the years a substantial number of people could afford to be admitted in the hospital. Moreover, in the later decades a Nursing School too was opened which benefitted thousands of native girls to avail themselves of quality nursing training.

1065 See Pius Geisel to Felix A. Plattner (Poona, 18th June 1951), AMPSJ, *Superior Poona, P. Geisel.*

1066 Pius Geisel (Poona, 17th August 1951), ARSI, *RLGGM, VIII,* 144. See also See Pius Geisel to Felix A. Plattner (Poona, 31st July 1952), AMPSJ, *Superior Poona, P. Geisel.*

1067 Plattner, "Es muss etwas geschehen ..." 208.

1068 See Geisel (Poona, 1st January 1953), op. cit.

1069 See Francis D'Souza, "Apostolates of Pune Province" (unpublished soft copy). Francis D'Souza was the Socius to the Provincial of Pune Province.

1070 Ibid.

1071 Cacilie, "Das Krankenhaus," 6.

Over the decades of its existence, it has served thousands of people in alleviating their physical suffering and helping them to live a healthy life.

6.6.2. The Socio-Cultural-Economic Impact of Medical Service

It has been mentioned earlier that the mission stations in Ahmednagar and surrounding areas had no easy access to medical facilities. In the cases of sickness and misfortunes, people were mostly dependent either on home remedies or had to take recourse to witch-doctors or magicians. Consequently, the mortality rate was invariably high. Establishment of hospitals and healthcare units thus was the need of the hour. In fact the need was felt much earlier. We have seen in the chapter four how the missionaries, often with minimum personal experience about certain basic medicines were forced to attend to the need of the people.[1072] But it was not possible to reach out to a majority of the people. Hence people's primary recourse was to sorcerers and witch-doctors which no wonder had serious implications. This meant endangering even one's own health and even one's life. Besides, the people suffered the loss of money at the hands of these manipulative witch-doctors, who took delight in extracting maximum amount of money and material from them.[1073] Consequently many poor people got into debt trap, which in many cases led them to even mortgaging their cattle and properties, the prime means of their livelihood.[1074] Thus, recourse to sorcerers or witch-doctors led not only to incurring financial debt, but also kept them under the grip of superstitious beliefs. Such practices were common among them.[1075]

Against this backdrop, was the introduction and promotion of the western system of health care and medical sciences. This in turn inculcated among the local people more health care awareness and

1072 Pius Geisel to Felix A. Plattner (Poona, 9th August 1951), AMPSJ, *Superior Poona, P. Geisel.*

1073 See J. B. Winiger, "Die Choleragottin," *IB* 1/29 (January 1937): 248; F.X. Schubiger, "Indische Feuerprobe und ihr Ausgang," op.cit., 248-249.

1074 See F. X. Schubiger, "Unser kleiner Guido," *IB* 1/21 (January 1935): 169-171. See also J. Stark, "Leichter geht ein Kamel durch ein Nadelohr...(Lk. 18, 25): II," *IB* 1/32 (October 1937): 276-277.

1075 See J. B. Winiger, "Keimende Saat," *IB* 1/22 (April 1935): 181; J.B. Winiger, "Nacht der Heidentums," *IB* 1/24 (October 1935): 198.

behavioural attitudes with regard to the health-related issues.[1076] For the people who had never seen the art of treatment in western medicine and of being "treated in a clean hospital room lying on a clean bed, etc., it was nothing less than a wonder."[1077]

Still further, the introduction of western health-care system and medicines immensely helped change the perception on sicknesses. It began to be considered no more a curse. For example, the cholera was largely considered a curse or wrath of goddess Kashi.[1078] Such perceptions began to be gradually, yet effectively done away with, so that some people began to claim that "the medicine of the missionary has saved us. Yes, the tablets of the Phader Saheb [Reverend Father] are good. He has a good demon in these tablets."[1079] Apparently, such testimonies are indicators of initial process of liberation from superstitions. Stated in the words of Amena Passah, "The medical works of the Christian Missions ... have to a great extent neutralized the superstitious beliefs of the people and introduced a more balanced and better lifestyle. It exposed them to greater vistas of learning and freed them of the shackles of superstitions."[1080]

It has been noted earlier that in the situation of illness and sickness the sole recourse of the poor people were sorcerers and witch-doctors. Needless to state that with the introduction of the western medicines and health-care system, the place and importance of indigenous medical tradition within the society was bound to be reduced. The observation of Amena Passah is apt once again here:

> [The most] important impact was the reduction of the influence of the traditional village priest. The notion that sacrifice was the only means to cure sickness was now abandoned by most people. Last but not the least, the introduction of modem systems of health care came as a great boon to empowerment of women ... In providing cure to various ailments, it was only the traditional priest who ruled the roost. But with the advent of the Christian medical mission,

1076 Amena Passah, "Christian Missions in the Khasi-Jaintia Hills: Health Care and Impact on the Society," in *Christianity and Change in Northeast India,* eds. T. B. Subba, et al. (New Delhi: Concept Publishing Co. 2006), 203.

1077 Cacilie, "Das Krankenhaus," 6.

1078 See Winiger, "Die Choleragottin," 247. See also Amena Passah, "Christian Missions in the Khasi-Jaintia Hills," 215-216.

1079 See Winiger, "Die Choleragottin," 248.

1080 Passah, "Christian Missions in the Khasi-Jaintia Hills," 215-216.

> women came into their own. It struck a chord with their inherent maternal, compassionate and nurturing character and there was no looking back ... The society desired that women stay at home and look after the family. In retrospection, when we see the changed attitude towards nursing today and the great strides made in nursing, we cannot but be filled with immense gratitude to these pioneers who persevered against great odds.[1081]

Similarly the dedicated service provided at the hospital helped in "winning the confidence of the native people very soon."[1082] An effective by-product of this consequence was that the promotion of the health-care facilities largely helped change the image of the missionaries, so that many people could be heard saying to the Sisters and Doctors: "You are my father and mother. I will do what you tell."[1083] Apparently, the critics may raise their brow at such a claim. Yet, it may not be denied that the health-care facilities availed through the hospital at Shrirampur was an important factor that had the potentiality of depicting a face of Christianity that was endearing to the poor people, whose existential experience comprised mostly the hostilities and negativities.

Initially the higher caste Hindus were against the idea that the treatment of all the patients should take place under the same roof. Many of them even rejected "water being offered by the Sisters serving in the hospital."[1084] Gradually, as the awareness grew among the people, the caste-prejudices began to wane and a greater acceptance for each other began to grow. Apparently, the credit does not go solely to this initiative as the Government too was trying to implement the provisions of the Constitutions of Independent India, wherein the caste-system had been abolished. But the campus of the hospital was a very tangible space where the experiences of caste-prejudices were effectively minimized.

6.7 Conclusion

The significance of the health care services undertaken by Poona Mission may be assessed better by taking an important aspect into consideration, namely, this service was undertaken at a time when the Mission was involved in establishing other local institutions such as the Dnyanamata

1081 As quoted in Passah, "Christian Missions in the Khasi-Jaintia Hills," 215-216.

1082 Cacilie, "Das Krankenhaus," 6.

1083 Ibid.

1084 Ibid.

Agriculture High School in Sangamner and of St. Joseph's Technical School in Poona, besides undertaking the nationally important works (such as founding of the Indian Institute of Social Order, establishing De Nobili College, Setting up the relocated Papal Seminary and establishing the Papal Athenaeum, all at Poona: see Chapter 7). The execution of all these works might not have been easy: there were difficulties on account of lack of personnel and finance. Were it not for some daring Jesuits at the helm of affairs, probably such initiatives may never have been implemented. Yet, we must hasten to add that the initiative was in no way a result of the personal interest of only a few individuals. A letter of Pius Geisel, who was at the helm of affairs reveals the constraints within which such initiatives were undertaken, underlining thereby the role of the Jesuits in the entire process of implementation of the same:

> Today I would like to share with you my worries. I am afraid we have undertaken too much. I naturally did not know as I was in Europe last year that the [Papal] Seminary too would be entrusted to us, which along with the construction of the De Nobili College is a three-million project. For these we have Brothers [Joseph] Pfiffher and [Otto] Widmer. No wonder, both them are very committed persons; yet obviously so few for such a gigantic work ... So far so good. But now comes the hospital, which means we must complete the construction within a year.[1085]

The letter clearly describes that undertaking such initiatives of such magnitude was by no means easy given the limited personnel and finances. Yet, the sheer determination to bring to completion a venture which would have deep impact on a large number of people underlines its significance. It must be said that all the missionary endeavours were ultimately aimed at giving witness to the gospel and to win over the local people to Christian faith, ideals and principles. The indirect objective of the medical help was ultimately directed towards the goal of communicating God's love to humanity through the practice of love of neighbor. Stated otherwise, we can say that the medical service of the Mission was to spread the Christian message of love.[1086]

1085 Pius Geisel to Felix A. Plattner (Poona, 19th July 1951), AMPSJ, *Superior Poona, P. Geisel.*

1086 See Joseph Ubelmesser, "Der Mensch, der 100 Jahre lebt!," *Indien: Arbeitsfelddeutscher Jesuiten* 3/1 (January 1957), 21.

The introduction and promotion of the health-care apostolate by the Jesuits was primarily because of the pressing reality of the appalling health care situation of the people. To a great extent, we have noted, that this service was immensely fruitful. Needless to say, the Jesuits, by responding to the signs of the times, were able to contribute towards one of the most fundamental aspirations of humanity, namely the aspiration for freedom from suffering, primarily from physical ailments.

The opening of the hospital was another method of evangelization. For, within the framework of missionary thinking of the time, every venture aimed at reaching out to the people was meant to act as a Christian witness articulated in the Bible.[1087] None the less, certain skeptical beneficiaries may still fail to recognize the value aspect of missionary health care and might say: "The doctrine of the Christian is bad but their medicine is good."[1088]

Finally it may be said that this venture marked a new phase in the missionary collaboration with other Religious Orders, especially Sisters on a larger scale. In this particular case the Sisters of the Medical Mission Institute was expected to carry out the work more independently. Yet, in the initial decade it appeared that "without the help of the Jesuits the Wurzburg Hospital at Sangamner cannot prosper."[1089] Even in the later decades the collaboration grew stronger and the common purpose of serving people was achieved more effectively.

1087 See Jason Mandryk, *Operation World: The Definitive Prayer Guide to Every Nation,* 7th Edition (Colorado Springs: GMI, 2010), 417.

1088 Fitzerald, "Clinical Christianity," 129 as quoted in Chad M. Bauman, *Christian Identity and Dalit Religion in Hindu India, 1868-1947* (Grand Rapids, MI/Cambridge, U.K.: William B. Eerdmans, 2008), 155.

1089 See Pius Geisel (Poona, 1st January 1953), ARSI, *Belgaum-Poona 1301 (1950-1959).*

Chapter -7

Poona Jesuits and National Contributions Establishing All-India Institutions

7.1. Introduction

Though the mandate of the Poona Jesuits was to offer missionary service in western India, the scope of their service in two spheres went beyond the geographical region of their mission area, to the whole of South Asia. These were ecclesiastical training of clerics and intellectual ministry cum social action. Actualizing their vision for national service, they established three national-level institutes, namely the De Nobili College, the Papal Seminary and the Indian Institute of Social Order, all in Poona. The first two institutes trained Jesuits in philosophy, theology and clerical ministry, which, in today's parlance, can be said to be human resource development training to enable Jesuits and others to enter into church's service in various missions. The third institute was envisaged to be a centre to facilitate modernization and development in civil society in line with the Government of India's planned schemes of development launched in early 1950s. In this chapter we focus on the contribution of the Poona Jesuits at the national level through these three national institutes.

As various Jesuit Missions developed in South Asia, there was felt the need to establish centres for training of young Jesuits in South Asia itself so that those coming from abroad as well as those recruited from South Asia could be trained within the mission area. Consequently, the Belgian Jesuits of Bengal Mission founded St. Mary's Theology

College at Kurseong, 1889, and the French Jesuits of Madurai Mission founded the Sacred Heart College in 1895 at Shembaganur. Both these institutes were later re-located to the plains: St. Mary's College (re-christened as Vidyajyoti College of Theology) to Delhi in 1972, and the Sacred Heart College (re-christened as Sathianilayam) to Chennai in 1980. All the Jesuit Missions sent their young members for ecclesiastical training to these colleges. Also, prompted by Pope Leo XIII a Papal Seminary for the training of diocesan priests in South Asia was founded in 1893, at Kandy, Ceylon (Sri Lanka) by the Belgian Jesuits then working there. Nearly forty years later, it was the turn of the German-Swiss Jesuits of Poona to establish a national level Jesuit training centre in India (De Nobili College) in 1937, at Poona. Besides, they volunteered to build up a seminary complex adjacent to De Nobili College when the Papal Seminary from Kandy was re-located to Poona in 1955. Thus these two ventures may be taken as two of the most powerful testimonies of the commitment and contribution of Poona Jesuits to clerical formation sector at the national level. It may be pointed out that the three institutions established by the Poona Mission, along with similar common institutes founded by other Missions, were subsequently placed under the management of the Jesuit Provincial of South Asia.

We must hasten to point out that the two training institutes were deemed as common ventures of the Jesuit Missions in India and not that of the Poona Mission alone.[1090] Envisioned as a common project of South Asian Missions commissioned by the Superior General of the Jesuits, the responsibility for the initial development of these institutes was almost single-handedly shouldered by the German-Swiss Jesuits, especially with regard to the formation personnel, development of infrastructure and finance. It is here that their role is most emphatically underlined. Moreover, a creative and abiding response is also thereby offered to the critics of this Mission who tend to cast aspersions on its

1090 In order to facilitate a better coordination, however, the Superior General had entrusted the venture initially to four Missions: Ahmedabad, Bombay, Poona and Goa. The initial supply of Professors and sharing of the cost of founding and running of the College by Poona Mission, was a taken for granted. See Hans Staffner, "Litterae Annuae Collegii de Nobili Poonensis, 18.09.1949," ARSI, *Prov. Goa-Poonensis, Litterae Annuae 1501*. See below, for further discussion.

commitment to this aspect.[1091] In order to appreciate these aspects better, we shall trace briefly the history of the foundation and development of these two institutions, underlining the vision and challenges involved in its implementation.

7.2. Clerical Training in Bombay-Poona Mission

Let us first take a brief retrospective view of the early contribution of the German-Swiss Jesuits to clerical training in India. Clerical training through a Seminary was an important factor for them to be invited to Bombay, by the Swiss Capuchin Bishop Anastatius Hartmann of Bombay in early 1850s. In his vision of a vibrant Catholic community, Bishop Hartmann had visualized that the Jesuits could make an important contribution in a Seminary. He believed that once the shepherds were well equipped and were led to firm conviction in their vocation, the flock would eventually be strengthened to lead a way of life worthy of a Christian calling. In his scheme of things he nurtured a dream for his Vicariate wherein a well-trained clergy would play the role of catalysts in the Catholic community. Such an objective would be achieved only when a Seminary was reorganized and a proper formation was imparted. Capturing such an import, the historian of Bishop Hartmann, Fulgentius Vanini writes:

> The reorganization of the Seminary in Bombay was part of Bishop Hartmann's plan for the general improvement of the Catholic community. He did not consider the Seminary as an isolated pocket, but as an integral part of the Mission - not an independent unit by itself, but a part of the whole. It is in the Seminary that the apostles of the morrow are moulded; the hopes of the future turn to it as to an anchor of salvation ... for there was the leaven which had to ferment the whole mass, the leven which had to lift up the fallen fortunes of the Vicariate.[1092]

Eventually the Jesuits did take up this responsibility upon themselves within a short period of their arrival in Bombay as "the diocesan Seminary, established earlier at Bandra ... [was] entrusted

1091 For example, one tends to arrive at such a conclusion by reading Gense, *Church at the Gateway,* 295-96. This question will come up for further discussion in the next chapter, wherein we shall discuss it within the framework of the totality of the period under review.

1092 Vanini, *Bishop Hartmann,* 233.

to the Society [of Jesus]."[1093] The responsibility was embraced by the Jesuits with a conviction to make the dreams of Bishop Hartmann come true. In spite of their number as the staff being very small, they made sincere efforts to give a new orientation to the Seminary formation. The commitment and dedication that they depicted in carrying out the work was beyond reproach. Yet, this apostolate was not their own project; rather it was taken up out of obedience to the Local Ordinary. At the same time the German-Swiss Jesuits did not neglect the aspect of formation in the Mission, though there were hardly any native candidates for the Society of Jesus in the Mission until 1930s.[1094] This situation changed gradually after the bifurcation of the old Bombay-Poona Mission into Bombay and Poona Missions (1929). They were earnest in contributing towards the same, not only for their own Poona Mission, but also for other Jesuit Missions in South Asia, besides the Church in India.[1095]

7.3. Founding a National Jesuit Training Centre: De Nobili College, Poona

The foundation of De Nobili College, Poona may be considered as one of "the most important works of this Mission that took place during this period"[1096] writes Klaus Schatz. Not only from the perspective of the missions of the Society of Jesus, but also from that of the Indian Church, it well deserves to be ranked among the monumental contributions of the German-Swiss Jesuits in India.[1097]

De Nobili College is a Scholasticate or a house of formation for the Jesuit Scholastics. The distinction that we notice today between De Nobili College as a house of formation and *Jnana-Deepa Vidyapeeth*[1098] as a centre of learning Philosophy and Theology came only at a

---

1093 Gense, *Church at the Gateway,* 220. This took place in 1855. Due to various factors, however, the Seminary had to be closed down in 1900. Ibid., 446.

1094 Prior to this period Gense mentions only 4 such candidates, among whom three died in the Society and the fourth probably left the Society at a later stage. See Gense, *Church at the Gateway,* 296.

1095 Formation of young missionaries aside, the Poona Jesuits also undertook other common works for the sub-continent. See below for further discussion.

1096 Schatz, *Geschichte,* Vol. Ill, 316.

1097 See Joseph Neuner, "Hundert Jahre deutsche Jesuitenmission in Indien," *KM* 1 (1954): 6.

1098 Formerly known as Pontifical Athenaeum, Poona was given a new name Jnana-Deepa Vidyapeeth under its revised statutes (1972). Its working meaning may be rendered as

Figure 7.1: De Nobili College, Poona.
Source: Letter-head of the De Nobili College, Poona. ARSI, *Belgaum-Poona. 1006-Particulares (1958)*.

later stage when the Papal Seminary and Pontifical Athenaeum, Kandy (Sri Lanka) were transferred to Poona in 1955 at a location adjacent to it.[1099] It has been indicated that it was deemed as a common venture, as the Superior General wrote in a letter, while underlining this aspect: "But as a Theologate it is also destined for other missions as well; similar to the inter-provincial study houses that we have in Europe,"[1100] Yet the task of implementation of the plan had to fall upon the shoulders of the Jesuits of Poona Mission, as it is revealed that "the College is under the jurisdiction of your mission field; certainly, therefore, it would be under the care of the respective Superior Regular of Poona Mission."[1101] Since the Mission was dependent on the Southern German Province, for every practical purpose Augustine Rosch was the "concerned Provincial, under whose care the College"[1102] had to be established and developed. Meanwhile, with the passage of time the Jesuits grew in awareness that

"The School of the Light of Wisdom." The literal meaning of *Vidyapeeth* is, 'centre of higher learning or university.

1099 The distinction may be akin to Collegium Germanicum et Hungaricum and Gregorian University in Rome.

1100 Karl Brust to Maximilian Riklin (Rome, 28th February 1935), ARSI, *RLGGM,* Vol. VI, 247.

1101 Ibid. See also "Kleine Nachrichten aus der Mission," *IB* 2/1 (January 1938): 5; Karl Brust to Maximilian Riklin (Rome, 1st March 1935), ARSI, *RLGGM,* Vol. VI, 261; Archbishop Henry Doring to Karl Brust (Poona, 13th May 1937), ARSI, *Historia 2001-Poona.*

1102 Karl Brust to Remigius Rauw (Frascati, 10th September 1937), ARSI, *RLGGM,* Vol. VII, 11. See in the same file Wlodimir Ledochowski, Superior General to Remigius Rauw (Rome, 2nd March 1940), 124.

in spite of De Nobili College deemed as a common venture, it was their (Poona Jesuits) own. In the words of Joseph Neuner: "This is the most recent foundation of our Mission, only three years old, and in a certain sense a child of sorrow [Sorgenkind]"[1103] as well.

The intention of the Superior General in consultation with the Jesuits in India was to keep the Theologate open for Seminarians and members of other Religious Congregations:

> At the moment, we consider a Theologate only for our scholastics; but it is not ruled out that later other [Religious] Orders and Congregations will come in and build small houses of their own in its vicinity in order to send their students to us. Of course, they would require to ask for the permission of the local ordinary once again in this regard.[1104]

It is noteworthy to mark that the decision to open a new Theologate was taking place in an era when the Poona Mission was still recovering from the impacts of WWI, especially with regard to the severe crunch of personnel in the Mission.[1105] Besides, the financial implications were some of the most pertinent questions to be addressed, in spite of the manifest assurance of the Superior General to help out in the initiation of the venture: "I shall try ... to avail about a half of the amount of the total cost that the construction and establishment of the College would incur. For the rest of the amount a credit must be procured and the interest of the same must be shared among the Indian Missions who would be sending their students to Poona."[1106] The truth, however, was that it was not easy to arrange for the remaining amount of the total cost.

Another factor that instantly draws the attention of the reader is: how much of preparation was undertaken before the venture was initiated? To this question E. Gales gives us a clue expressing his bewilderment as he recaptures the events leading up to the foundation of De Nobili College: "Today it seems almost beyond comprehension as to why a Seminary

1103 Josef Neuner, "De Nobili-Kolleg," *IB* 2/9 (Jaunary 1940): 109.

1104 Wlodimir Ledochowski, Superior General to Archbishop Henry Doring (Rome, 1st March 1935), ARSI, *RLGGM,* Vol. VI, 248. See also in the same file, the General to Maximilian Riklin (Rome, 28th February 1935), 247; Karl Brust to Adrian van Kalken (Rome, 22nd May 1939), ARSI, *RLGGM,* Vol. VII, 75.

1105 See Karl Brust to Archbishop Henry Doring (Rome, 7th January 1936), ARSI, *RLGGM,* Vol. V, 270.

1106 Karl Brust to Archbishop Henry Doring (Rome, 19th January 1935), ARSI, *RLGGM,* Vol. V, 241.

of the Order or much more a Faculty of Theology in Poona was taken into consideration. For, not a single aspect of planning had yet gone into ... There was no Seminary building, nay not a suitable construction site."[1107] Be that as it may, the College was established finally in spite of a considerable amount of hurdles. The entire process reveals various aspects of the challenges and commitment of the Poona Mission.

7.3.1. Mandate of the Church: Mission of the Jesuit Society

Various Missionary Societies working across the globe were urged and simultaneously challenged by the call of Benedict XV through his encyclical Maximum Mud (1919) to make a concerted effort towards the establishment of independent local churches by preparing the indigenous clergy in their respective mission fields. We shall discuss a few more aspects of this encyclical in the next chapter. Here it suffices to point out that Maximum Mud marks an important departure in the missionary thinking of the Church of the previous centuries in two basic respects: firstly it urges, wherever possible "to secure and train local candidates for the sacred ministry" {Maximum Mud, #14).[1108] Secondly, it urges to make the education of the indigenous people as the primary purpose of missionary enterprise: "If, however, the indigenous clergy is to achieve the results We hope for, it is absolutely necessary that they be well trained and well prepared" {Maximum Mud, #15).[1109] The other missionary encyclical, Rerum ecclesiae (1926) issued by Pius XI underlined once again the necessity of forming a native clergy in the missions.[1110]

Seen against this backdrop, the need of a second Jesuit Theologate in India may be viewed as an effort to respond to this call. In addition to this, it may also be mentioned that it was an earnest effort to respond to the call made by Pius XI through his Apostolic Constitution, Deus

1107 E. Gales, "Auf Felsen gegriindet," 3.

1108 Thomas J. M. Burke, ed., *Catholic Missions: Four Great Encyclicals* (New York: Fordham University Press, 1957), 13. See also Vivian H. H. Green, *A New History of Christianity* (New York: Continuum, 2000), 294.

1109 Burke, *Catholic Missions,* 14. See also Nicholas I. Omenka, *The School in the Service of Evangelization: The Catholic Educational Impact in Eastern Nigeria 1886-1950* (Leiden/New York/ Koln: E.J. Brill, 1889), 4; Patrick Taylor & Frederick I. Case, eds., *The Encyclopedia of Caribbean Religions,* Vol. 1, A-L (Urbana/Chicago/Springfeld: University of Illinois Press, 2013), 839.

1110 See Ross A. Enochs, *The Jesuit Mission to theLakota Sioux: A Study of Pastoral Ministry, 1886-1945* (Kansas City: Sheed & Ward, 1996), 73.

Scientiarum Dominus which was promulgated on 24th May 1931. One of thc most important factors behind its promulgation was a general perception prevailing at the time that there was no uniformity in seminary formation and theological education of the future priests. Pius XI, keen on addressing the issue, established a commission to carry out a survey on the state of affairs with regard to these issues. As a result, Mgr. Ernesto Ruffini as its chairman along with his colleagues discovered that the formation of the priests was marked by serious inadequacies. Through this Constitution, Pius XI desired to bring uniformity in the plan of studies in the universities and ecclesiastical faculties across the world. To this effect, Deus Scientiarum Dominus contained detailed instructions on the theological formation and all aspects of the functioning of seminaries.[1111] "With this solemn document, on the feast of Pentecost in 1931, the Church gave itself a basic principle of universality, as to how it interpreted and defended itself and its faith by means of scientific reason."[1112] The Apostolic Constitution was unique on account of its content and concern. In fact, "it was the first time that the Church had promulgated a plan of studies that would be common to all ecclesiastical faculties throughout the whole world."[1113] These specific aspects apart, given his consistent emphasis on the formation of the native clergy, i.e., in his Encyclical Rerum Ecclesiae, it would not be wrong to conclude that this aspect was inclusive in the Apostolic Constitution as well.

Coming back to the role of Poona Mission, Joseph Neuner, a veteran missionary of the Poona Mission who was associated with De Nobili College, undoubtedly for the longest period of time right from its inception and exerted perhaps the most decisive influence in its growth and orientation so that the theological "courses [could be developed]

1111 See John Pollard, *The Papacy in the Age of Totalitarianism 1914-1958* (Oxford: Oxford University Press, 2014), 172; John C. Dwyer, *Church History: Twenty Centuries of Catholic Christianity* (New York/Mahwah: Paulist Press, 1985), 366.

1112 Klaus Unterburger, *Vom Lehramt der Theologen zum Lehramt der Pdpste?: Pius XI, die Apostolische /Constitution, Deus Scientiarum Dominus, " und die Reform der Universitdtstheologie* (Freiburg/Basel/Vienna: Herder, 2010), 72.

1113 Augustine Bea, "The Apostolic Constitution *Deus Scientiarum Dominus:* Its Origin and Spirit," *TS All* (1943): 35. See also Unterburger, *Vom Lehramt der Theologen zum Lehramt der Pdpste,* 72.

against the background of, and in dialogue with Indian spiritual traditions,"[1114] has the following to say in this regard:

> Today, as more and more mission fields are being taken care of by the native clergy, the formation of the priests has become the most central missionary task. And on the training of the individuals depends even a greater task with a far-reaching implication ... This is the last and the greatest task of the mission: to lead the young Church to maturity and ripeness through its own priests.[1115]

Meanwhile, it may be stated that "since many decades the Society of Jesus in India, with its many missions, had already two study houses for Philosophy and Theology. By this time, both these houses were full to the capacity."[1116] Besides, the already existing Theologate in Kurseong in West Bengal was in the extreme north of the country making it far remote from the missions in the South. "Moreover, the cooler climate of St. Mary's in Kurseong ... was too salubrious for a number of Scholastics coming from southern India."[1117]

In the implementation of the idea of a second Jesuit Theologate, the first step goes back to early 1930s, when "the Superiors of nine Jesuit Missions in India came together time and again to discuss the matters of common concerns and needs,"[1118] the question of a second Theologate being one of them. A document reads: "In one of the last Conferences [therefore] they decided to request Very Rev. Fr. General: he may preside over the establishment of a new institution for theological education in Poona."[1119] "The [aforesaid] Conference of the Jesuit Mission Superiors [was held] in Calcutta in 1934 [wherein] it was decided that Poona would be the best suited place"[1120] for the purpose.

1114 Joseph Neuner, *Memories of my Life* (Pune: Pune Jesuit Society, 2003), 25.

1115 Joseph Neuner, "Hundert Jahre deutsche Jesuitenmission in Indien," *KM* 1 (1954): 9.

1116 Gales, "Auf Felsen gegrundet," 3. The other two study houses were: St. Mary's College, Kurseong and Satya Nilayam, Madras (Chennai), run by the Belgian and French Jesuit Missions respectively.

1117 Gales, "Auf Felsen gegrundet," 3.

1118 "Kleine Nachrichten aus der Mission," *IB 2/1* (1938): 5.

1119 Ibid.

1120 Schatz, *Geschichte,* Vol. Ill, 316. John Lauder took part in the Conference as the representative of the Poona Mission. See John J. Meyer to Karl Brust, German Assistant to the Superior General (Poona, 12th January 1935), ARSI, *Historia 2001-Poona;* Walter Brugger, "Das neue De-Nobili-Kolleg in Poona," *KM* 106 (1938): 413.

Right from the beginning, the curia of the Superior General was keenly interested in this project. In fact it seemed to have become a matter of urgency, so that Karl Brust, the German Assistant to the General wrote to Maximilian Riklin, the then Superior Regular of the Mission: "It is absolutely necessary and urgent to have a second Theologate in India."[1121] In the meantime a change of guard took place and Remigius Rauw took over as the Superior Regular of the Mission. Karl Brust emphasized the matter to him as well: "We must, by all means, establish a new Theologate in India and since according to the opinion of the concerned persons, whose opinions we sought for, are unanimous in their opinion that Poona is the most suitable place for the purpose, it must be established there."[1122]

One discovers an even greater sense of urgency as one reads a letter of M. Schurmanns, the Vicar General to Remigius Rauw, albeit in a different context yet underlining the necessity of the formation in India: "It is better even to set aside other works of the mission than to neglect or scamp the formation of our young men."[1123] The implication is clear that the curia of the Superior General was keen on the implementation of the plan at the earliest time possible.

From the information that we gather from the correspondences and other sources we arrive at a conclusion as to how the idea of a second Theologate emerged. According to the initial plan, it was intended to be "a fully developed Theologate (a second Frankfurt or Innsbruck), which later would be formed into a collegium of some Fathers who are equipped with all Indian wisdom, to deal in writing and conferences with the Indian cultural world and carry Christian ideas among the educated."[1124] At this stage, there was no consideration of a Philosophate alongside the prospective Theologate.[1125]

1121 Karl Brust to Maximilian Riklin (Rome, 28th February 1935), ARSI, *RLGGM, Vol.,* VI, 247.

1122 Karl Brust to Remigius Rauw (Rome, 15th October 1935), ARSI, *RLGGM,* Vol. VI, 262-263. See also Wlodimir Ledochowski, Superior General to Archbishop Henry Doring (Exemplar) (Rome, 1st March 1935), ARSI, *Historia 2001-Poona.*

1123 M. Schurmanns, Vicar General to Remigius Rauw (Rome, 19th March 1940), ARSI, *RLGGM,* Vol. VII, 127. See also Joseph Neuner to the Vicar General of the Society of Jesus (Khandala, 16th April 1940), ARSI, *Poona. 1004-XIII, 6.*

1124 Walter Brugger, "Das neue De-Nobili-Kolleg," *MDPGJ* 14/104-106 (1936-1938): 414.

1125 Ibid.

We have touched upon the reasons already that the central location of Poona was one of the primary considerations. This point was reiterated in the above-mentioned Conference of the Superiors of the Missions (1934): "The choice on the place fell on Poona because of its central location, its climatic advantages ..."[1126] But this concern was not limited to these aspects alone. In fact an important dimension of the missionary thinking of the time came into play quite prominently here, i.e., exploring further avenues of exercising influence among the higher castes of the Hindu society, especially the Brahmins, as "Puna is the intellectual and academic centre of Brahmanism"[1127] and therefore, "for a new venture meant for the presentation and defence of the Catholic truth, there appeared no better place than Poona."[1128] Such a contact with Hindus was intended to be established more efficaciously through regular contacts with the university students.[1129] Moreover, Poona was seen as a place of a great "cultural significance"[1130] and as the prospective capital of Independent India as well.[1131]

7.3.2. Beginning of the Theologate: A Makeshift Arrangement

While the matter about the choice of the venue was still under consideration, on being "strongly urged from Rome,"[1132] so also from

1126 Ibid. *MDPGJ* 106 (1938): 413. See also Gales, "Auf Felsen gegrundet," 3.

1127 Emil Kaufmarm, "Puncta Quaedam de Missione Punensi" (Transcript), (Zurich, 20th June 1947), ARSI, *Historia 2001-Poona.* See also "Kleine Nachrichten aus der Mission," *IB* 2/1 (1938): 5. See Emil Kaufmann, "Puncta Quaedam de Missione Punensi" (Transcript), (Zurich, 20th June 1947), ARSI, *Historia 2001-Poona;* Francis X. Schubiger (Consultor, Poona Mission) to the Superior General (Sangamner, 3rd July 1936), ARSI, *Poona. 1004-IX,* 15.

1128 "Kleine Nachrichten aus der Mission," *IB* 2/1 (1938): 5. Poona was also seen as the prospective capital of Independent India.

1129 This aspect was indeed very much taken into consideration. For example, Neuner giving his opinion on a plot of land that came in consideration once writes: "Besides, the place is situated amidst the very good quarters in the city, close to a new and big college, so that a lot of people might be expected around our college." Joseph Neuner to Karl Brust (Poona, 6th July 1938), ARSI, *Goa-Poona 1402: Visitatio,* 30.

1130 Walter Brugger, "Das neue De-Nobili-Kolleg," *MDPGJ* 14/104-106 (1936-1938): 414.

1131 See Emil Kaufmarm, "Puncta Quaedam de Missione Punensi" (Transcript), (Zurich, 20th June 1947), ARSI, *Historia 2001-Poona;* Francis X. Schubiger (Consultor, Poona Mission) to the Superior General (Sangamner, 3rd July 1936), ARSI, *Poona. 1004-IX,* 15.

1132 John B. Haas, "Das De Nobili College, Poona", (Poona, 16th January 1946), ARSI, *Poona. 1004-XV,* 4.

"various Superiors of Indian Missions,"[1133] it was decided to begin the courses on theology as Walter Brugger reports: "With God's grace, we hope to be able to begin the lectures on 11th June [1937]."[1134] The question, however, was: Where to find sufficient space to begin the Theologate? To this effect, an interim arrangement[1135] was sought to be made by Remigius Rauw, the Superior Regular whereby the new Theologate was intended to be accommodated in a new wing at St. Vincent's High School:

> You wish to know what the state of affairs with regard to our Collegium Maximum [Theologate] is. We shall be beginning it in June 1937. However, not in a beautiful and new building, but modo nostro simplici [in our simple style] in the second floor of St. Vincent's [School], if Very Rev. Fr. General allows me to construct it.[1136]

Eventually, "the new venture was accommodated at St. Vincent's [Secondary School, Poona],"[1137] wherein, "two classrooms of the

1133 Remigius Rauw to the Superior General (Poona, 7th August 1936), ARSI, *Poona. 1004-IX,* 10. See also Karl Brust to Francis X. Schubiger (Rome, 4th August 1936), ARSI, *RLGGM,* Vol., V, 315. On the other hand, Remigius Rauw too wrote quite a few letters in view of obtaining permission from the Superior General. Hence it was not solely the result of the urging of the Superior General alone. See Remigius Rauw to the Superior General (Poona, 7th August 1936), ARSI, *Poona. 1004-IX,* 10. Further in the same file (Poona, 24th August 1936), 11.

1134 Walter Brugger to the General (Poona, 1st May 1937), ARSI, *Poona. 1004-X,* 13. See also Karl Brust to Adrian van Kalken (Rome, 19th September 1936), ARSI, *RLGGM,* Vol., V, 322.

1135 Archbishop Henry Doring was of some other opinion: "As an interim arrangement Fr. Superior [Remigius Rauw] is planning to accommodate the Theologate in a new wing at St. Vincent's [High School]. In this regard have my own opinion. I have suggested to him and Fr. Visitor that the Theologate could be accommodated in Bombay in the Seminary there for a few years until the construction of the new building is complete." Archbishop Henry Doring to Karl Brust, German Assistant to the General (Poona, 20th October 1936), ARSI, *Historia 2001-Poona.*

1136 Remigius Rauw to Karl Brust (Poona, 18th September 1936), ARSI, *Historia 2001-Poona.* See also Wlodimir Ledochowski, Superior General to Adrian van Kalken (copy) (Rome, 19th September 1936), ARSI, *1411-Visitatio Miss, van Kalken, 2.* Further in the same file, Adrian van Kalken to the Superior General (Poona, 26th September 1936), 3.

1137 "Kierae Nachrichten aus der Mission," *IB* 2/1 (January 1938): 5. See also John B. Haas, "Das De Nobili College, Poona", (Poona, 16th January 1946), ARSI, *Poona. 1004-XV,* 4; Archbishop Henry Doring to Karl Brust, German Assistant to the General (Poona, 20th October 1936), ARSI, *Historia 2001-Poona.* St. Vincent's High School was one of the first schools established by the German-Swiss Jesuits in India. The School was begun by Fr. Joseph Brunner (1805-1884) in 1867 who remained its director until 1870. See Vath, *Die deutschen Jesuiten,* 91, 136-137. See also Schatz, *Geschichte,* Vol. V, 124;

adjoining school building ... were acquired, one for lectures and library, the other as the chapel."[1138] The intermediate period of its growth until the time when it was finally accommodated in the present building (1947/48) had been a virtual saga of uncertainties and hardships, the details of which does not permit space here. Coming back to its actual beginning, one finds it particularly interesting to read as E. Gales recapitulates the brief history of the College on the occasion of the Silver Jubilee (1962) of its official inauguration:

> It began on the 11th June exactly 25 years ago. In the House Chapel of St. Vincent's High School in Poona the good old Missionary Bishop Msgr. Henry Doring celebrated the Holy Mass for a group of young Jesuits. There were eight Indians, four Spaniards, two Americans, two Germans, an Austrian, a French, an Italian, altogether 19 Scholastics who were to start their theological studies in Poona. After the Holy Mass, the then Superior of the Poona mission, Fr. [Remigius] Rauw held a short introductory lecture in a classroom of the school. With this the academic year 1937/38 was officially inaugurated. The first year of the new Jesuit Seminary, which would eventually be known as De Nobili College![1139] Initially, however, it comprised of no more than a dozen students, a few professors and a mandate from the [Superior] General of the Religious Order to develop this newly opened Seminary into a second theological College of the Jesuits in India.[1140]

W.P. Krolikowski & Edward Hambye, "Brunner, Josef," in Diccinario *Historico de la Compania de Jesiis,* Vol. I, eds. O'Neill & Dominguez, 563-564.

1138 Joseph Neuner, *Memories of my Life* (Pune: Pune Jesuit Society, 2003), 9. The permission for the extension was received from the Superior General in November 1936. See Remigius Rauw to the Superior General (Poona, 27th November 1936), ARSI, *Poona. 1004-IX,* 13.

1139 The name was suggested by the Superior General himself in honour of Robert De Nobili. The reason behind this suggestion was to strive towards furthering the great tradition of inculturation introduced by De Nobili, who tried "to be an Indian to the Indians, in order that he might be able to win them over to Christianity ... His name means a real programme of action for the new institution." "Kleine Nachrichten aus der Mission," *IB* 2/1 (January 1938): 5-6. See also Joseph Neuner, *Memories of my Life* (Pune: Pune Jesuit Society, 2003), 23. Initially, however, the name for the Theologate was being suggested as "Collegium Bellarminum" by the curia of the Superior General. See Karl Brust to Remigius Rauw (Rome, 29th March 1937), ARSI, *RLGGM,* Vol. VI, 340.

1140 Gales, "Auf Felsen gegriindet," 3. See also Archbishop Henry Doring to Karl Brust (Poona, 21st June 1937), ARSI, *Historia 2001-Poona;* "Kleine Nachrichten aus der Mission," *IB* 2/1 (January 1938): 5-6; "Aus aller Welt: Indien," *KM* 12 (December 1937): 30; John B. Haas, "Das De Nobili College, Poona," (Poona, 16th January 1946), ARSI, *Poona. 1004-*

Thus, as a follow up of the resolution made at the Conference of the Superiors in Calcutta (1934) and on a persistent urge from the Superior General, at last the Theologate was opened. But the story had just begun and had a long way to go before things could be considered normal. The interim arrangement, against all expectations, lasted nearly eight years, due to some entirely unforeseen events. Thus, "from 1937 to 1945 the Seminary of the Order was conducted in a wing of St. Vincent's Secondary School and some of the houses in its neighbourhood. This was supposed to be a temporary arrangement until the College could erect its own building at a suitable location."[1141] Meanwhile, for the second scholastic year, "twelve students were expected."[1142]

Figure 7.2: After the opening of the Theologate. Front Row (sitting) from left: Fr. J.B. Haas, Fr. Richard Negre, Fr. Remigius Rauw (Mission Superior), Archbishop Henry Doring, Fr. Walter Brugger and Fr. Anicetus Deniz. *Source*: *IB* 2/4 (October 1938): 47.

XV, 4; Remigius Rauw to the General (Poona, 11th June 1937), ARSI, Poona. 1004-X, 15; Karl Brust to Remigius Rauw (Tusculi, 27th July 1937), ARSI, *RLGGM,* Vol. VII, 5-6; John B. Haas, "Das De Nobili College, Poona," (Poona, 16th January 1946), ARSI, *Poona. 1004-XV,* 4. Seen from the perspective of the Indian Missions, "The 19 Scholastics come from the following missions: Trincomali [Ceylon], Madura, Poona, Bombay and Ahmedabad [Gujarat]. Thus India and various nations of Europe are well represented and harmonize among themselves well." Remigius Rauw to the General (Poona, 11th June 1937), ARSI, *Poona. 1004-X,* 15. Initially, "22 Scholastics had applied. However, only 19 arrived on 10th June [1937]." Walter Brugger, "Das neue De-Nobili-Kolleg," *MDPGJ* 106 (1938): 414.

1141 Gales"Auf Felsen gegrundet," 3. See also John Lauder, (Consultor, Poona Mission) to Superior General (Poona, 16th November 1938), ARSI, *Poona. 1004-XII,* 11.

1142 "Aus der Theologie in Puna," *IB* 2/4 (October 1938): 46. Besides the two from Poona Mission, four from Madura, three from Calicut, two from Bombay and one from Ceylon were expected.

The question of making arrangements for accommodation became once again a big concern.[1143] For it was bound to be "more cramped... Some of them [Scholastics] needed to share the rooms, others found shelter in some out-houses..."[1144] Further still, "a big guest room was divided into four small cubicles. Moreover, a small house where earlier the teachers were staying, was cleaned up and furnished for 8 Scholastics."[1145] In general, in spite of many such inconveniences, the second year too passed by.

In the midst of these developments, the Third Year of the Theologate began. But the problem of accommodation and other constraints became even more acute on account of the increasing number of Scholastics. These constraints increased to an even greater degree in the Fourth Year. Joseph Neuner leads us again through this interesting phase of history, which is worth quoting at a length:

> This was the third year... And it was a difficult one! We rented several smaller apartments in the neighbourhood of St. Vincent's. There were about 6 houses in which our theologians lived during this period. For lectures, meals and other common programmes, they all came together; during the rainy season often with umbrella and waterproof boots ... But we had to make arrangements for a fourth year ... we began to look for a bigger house in the neighbourhood of St. Vincent's. We ... knocked at the first house in our neighbourhood. The owner of the house is a Muslim and has a beautiful house just opposite our playground. "How many?" [He asked]. "Approximately thirty. The rest can stay at St. Vincent's." "For how long?" [He further asked]. "Unfortunately, we do not know ourselves - but probably for a year at least ..." He thinks for a moment: "Should it be right now?" - "No, around the spring (1940)". And then came his proposal ... "You see, I cannot vacate this house fully. But over there ... I am constructing a new building, which you may have ..." - We took the plan of the building and studied it... Apparently, we do not have much of space ... But eventually it must suffice for the moment, even if... some may have to share the rooms. But we would come through: we have more than 50 theologians next scholastic year, some thirty will stay in the new

1143 See Joseph Neuner, "De Nobili-Kolleg," *IB* 2/10 (April 1938): 109.

1144 Neuner, "De Nobili-Kolleg," *IB* 2/9 (January 1940): 109. See also Archbishop Henry Doring to Karl Brust (Poona, 13th May 1937), ARSI, *Historia 2001-Poona.*

1145 "Aus der Theologie in Puna," *IB* 2/4 (October 1938): 46.

> house, the rest at St. Vincent's. Lectures, library, etc. would remain at St. Vincent's ... Thus far is our plan ready.[1146]

It was a big relief when the building offered in rent by the Muslim neighbour was ready. At last, they had managed to find some temporary arrangement for the growing need. The sense of optimism and determination among the Jesuits amidst such inconveniences is worth noting. Moreover, a sense of finding solace, way and means in the given situation is all too conspicuous:

> On 27th January 1940 the first Brothers moved in. After a few days the chapel was consecrated, and thus for the next year we have a shelter. We named it "Bellarmine-House" Apparently, it is a bit noisy around the place. There are lots of barking dogs and many a garrulous radio sets in the neighbourhood. Besides, it will be extremely hot in the summer season, because there is hardly any protection against the sun there. And then, during the rainy season, the road across the playground will cause some inconvenience - but we have a house, and to that extent a nice one as well. Nevertheless, we do hope not to stay too long here. At last, our College must find its own independent home sometime.[1147]

Unfortunately, the "Bellarmine House" seemed to have become a source of certain misunderstandings. Some Scholastics even complained about it to their respective Superiors, who in turn perceived the atmosphere as a hindrance for the growth of the Scholastics.[1148] What turned out, however, undoubtedly as a matter of satisfaction for the Jesuits was that in spite of numerous difficulties, the fourth year was a special year for the new Theologate, as it achieved the first milestone in its short history, as we read: "But meanwhile we are here at St. Vincent's and coming close to the first great feast of our young Theologate: On

---

1146 Neuner, "De Nobili-Kolleg," 109. See also John B. Haas, "Das De Nobili College, Poona," (Poona, 16th January 1946), ARSI, *Poona. 1004-XV,* 4.

1147 Ibid; See also Haas, ibid.

1148 See Haas, "Das De Nobili College, Poona," (Poona, 16th January 1946), op. cit. The matter was reported to the Superior General as well, following which he brought it to the attention of Adrian van Kalken, the Visitor: " Some people also reported that a good number of Scholastics seem to have been accommodated in not so suitable private homes and hence exposed to no less dangers of morality and health." Wlodimir Ledochowski, Superior General to Adrian van Kalken (Rome, 30th June 1940), ARSI, *RLGGM,* Vol. VII, 129.

Easter Monday 18 Brothers who began here their theological studies three years ago, will be ordained to the priesthood."[1149]

Apparently these arrangements were far short of being ideal for the study of theology. One can only appreciate the fact that both the Scholastics as well as the Professors were determined to do their part in carrying forward the mission entrusted to them. The duration of eight years with such a makeshift arrangement cannot be taken for granted. Yet, a general feeling of dissatisfaction among the Scholastics, especially as regards accommodation arrangements and proper atmosphere for study, cannot be ignored as is evident in an anonymous letter, most likely a Scholastic, reads:

> In the beginning, some of us stayed in the residence of the Fathers, others in the school building. Then we occupied an apartment in the neighbourhood outside the school. Finally, since the beginning of the third year of the college, we got scattered into six buildings, four of which were situated outside the boundary of the main house; the inmates of the six apartments situated outside the boundary wall need to go back and forth every day. Around the main house, the boys of the [St. Vincent's] School make noise almost every day. When we attend the lectures of professors, the boys have class intervals when they have loud recreations. Consequently we can hardly listen to the professors.[1150]

The problems became more serious when it came to certain common exercises of the community.[1151] Yet, the students were not the only ones who had to face hardships on account of these arrangements.

1149 Neuner, "De Nobili-Kolleg," 109.

1150 Anonymous, "De Studiis Nostrorum in Collegio de Nobili Poonensi" (Poona, n.d.), ARSI, *Poona. 1004-XIII,* 4. From the style of narration of the situation it appears to have been written by a Scholastic.

1151 See J. W. Lange (a representative of the Third Year Scholastics) to the General (Poona, 8th September 1939), ARSI, *Poona. 1004-XII,* 8. See also Remigius Rauw to the General (Poona, 31s* December 1939), ARSI, *Poona. 1004-XII,* 19. Some Scholastic-Priests complained of being over-burdened by the ministries. Citing a complaint, G. Bonhour, Vice-Provincial, Madura Vice-Province writes: "I think I had better communicate to Your Reverence a complaint I have received from one of my theologians at Poona ... The complainant's letter is sent herewith and give the exact situation of the Scholastic-Priests in that Theologate. Whilst I am prepared to do whatever is possible to help the brave Fathers of the Poona Mission in their dire need of men, I think the limit of the permissible has been passed and our theologians have a right to complain. No. 326 of the Epitome condemns such 'impedimenta studiorum,' I believe." ARSI, *Historia. 2001-Poona,* 177.

In fact, the professors too were under immense pressure of the demands. It is clear that the provisions for the Theologate were bare minimum at this stage. It appears that the General's curia was aware that the courses of theology along with other aspects of the training of the young Jesuits had various drawbacks. There are indications that certain anonymous letters were addressed to the General revealing the drawbacks, as may be inferred from the following content of a letter of M. Schurmanns[1152] to Remigius Rauw: "I heard recently that the training in Poona College is not satisfactory. I would ask your Reverence therefore to see to it that the studies are organized in accordance with the prescriptions of our Institute and of the Church, and to do all that you can to ensure to our Scholastics a careful training."[1153] Apparently it is not hard to comprehend the frustration of the professors themselves amidst such situations. A reply of Joseph Neuner on this issue reveals some aspects of the same:

> Reverend Father Superior Rauw sent me the letter of Your Reverence, dated 19th March 1940, containing complaints about our College ... I do not wonder in the least that there are complaints against the training in our College ... But these difficulties are necessarily connected with the conditions here in our Mission and it will be absolutely impossible to overcome them as long as we have to rely only on our resources ... Your Reverence requires that "the studies are organized in accordance with the prescriptions of the Institute and the Church." I dare say that we did our very best to fulfil these prescriptions as far as possible....[1154]

The above paragraphs suffice to indicate the kind of circumstances, the College encountered in the initial years of development.

1152 He was Superior General's Vicar at the time.

1153 Schurmanns, Vicar General to Remigius Rauw (Rome, 19th March 1940), op. cit., 127.

1154 Joseph Neuner to M. Schurmanns, Vicar General (Poona, 16th April 1940), ARSI, *Poona. 1004-XIII,* 6. The Superior General took a strong objection to such a procedure that these contents of the letters addressed to the Mission Superior were shared with his subjects in violation of the 23rd Rule of the Provincials. See Karl Brust to Remigius Rauw (Rome, 25th May 1940), ARSI, *RLGGM,* Vol. VII, 136.

7.3.3. World War II: A Period of Uncertainty

The period of WWII (1939-45) marked four major concerns of the Jesuits: a final decision on the plot of land,[1155] alternative arrangements to continue the courses on Theology, beginning of the construction of the buildings and arrangement of replacements of the existing professors in the event of their internment in camps. The decision on the venue had not been arrived at until the breaking of WWII and thus "the year under review [i.e., 1939] ended again without any progress being made towards securing a site for the Theologate."[1156] This phase, tedious and monotonous as it was, finally ended in a long process of decision-making and encountering multiple cases of failures. To bring to conclusion the negotiations to acquire a suitable plot of land for the purpose finally ended with the acquiring of the property offered by the Poona Diocese in the beginning of 1941. The work of construction of the buildings began soon thereafter. "The architect was a Belgian Jesuit. He gave the Seminary [De Nobili College] a loose but a schematic form. The construction work was taken over by the faithful Swiss Brother, Joseph Pfiffner"[1157] and others.

While tracing these events, we come across with an interesting aspect in the history of De Nobili College around this time. The effort to finalize the venue was still going on. The courses on Theology were being taught with the provisional arrangements at St. Vincent's, Poona. Meanwhile, "the war broke out. All German Fathers were interned."[1158] Thus, one of the projects of the Mission begun after WWI got once again halted.[1159] Fortunately the first period of Internment, except in a few cases, ended much earlier than it was expected.[1160] This was a great relief, seemingly turning the course of events in favour of the Jesuits.

1155 The process of final decision on a suitable plot of land for the purpose took nearly five years. The tediousness of the same may be assessed from the fact that a large quantity of correspondences, probably one of the largest on a single subject pertaining to the Poona Mission, is collected in the central archive of the Jesuits (ARSI) in Rome.

1156 Pius Geisel to the General (Poona, 28.h December 1939), ARSI, *Poona. 1004-XII,* 17.

1157 Gales, "Auf Felsen gegrtindet," 3.

1158 Neuner, "De Nobili-Kolleg," 110

1159 See John B. Haas to Mr. Schorer (Poona, 11th October 1946), AMPSJ, *LB. Puna-Brief (alte).*

1160 See Wlodimir Ledochowski, Superior General to Remigius Rauw (Rome, 2nd March 1940), ARSI, *RLGGM,* Vol. VII, 124. Among others, those who were not released were Felix zu Lowenstein and Eugene Horny (Ranchi Mission). See Neuner, *Memories,* 11.

But the situation was soon going to change once again, as Joseph Neuner writes: "The freedom lasted [only] half a year ...in June [1940] a press campaign against Germans, who were still free, set in ... we were interned again..."[1161] Yet, the Jesuits took hold of the situation, so that Neuner could further report: "The courses had to be taken over by the remaining Fathers who are stuck up in work neck-deep. What would happen to our college during this time? - But within a good quarter of a year, we are back again, almost complete in number ..."[1162] Joseph Neuner himself, along with Felix Lowenstein and Francis Xavier Hormann, was taken into the camp later where they had to stay until 1947.[1163]

No wonder the Internment of the professors was a matter of anxiety, with the implication that the Theologate itself might have to be closed: "If Frs. [Felix] Lowenstein and [Joseph] Neuner need to remain longer in the camp or cannot come back to Poona and no substitutes are sent, then the lectures in the Theologate in Poona can hardly be possible to continue any further."[1164] While such uncertainties were looming large, it was the daring decision of Remigius Rauw to keep the Theologate going with some temporary arrangements, as he writes:

> Arrangements made by Superiors to fill up the vacancies. The De Nobili College: the short course given by Fr. [Maximilian] Zinser is partly combined with the long course and partly given by Fr. [Anicetus] Deniz. The lectures of Fr. [Joseph] Neuner in the long course were taken over by Rev. Fr. Superior [Remigius Rauw] ... On the 5th of October came Fr. Rayanna from Kandy to teach Canon Law. The offices of Prefect of Studies (Fr. Neuner) and of Minister of the Scholastics (Fr. Lowenstein) were taken over by Rev. Fr. Superior himself, who is now: Professor, Prefect of Students, Minister Scholasticorum, Vice-Rector, Procurator of the house, Procurator of the Mission and Superior Regular.[1165]

1161 Neuner, *Memories,* 11.

1162 Neuner, "De Nobili-Kolleg," 110. See also ARSI, *Poona. 1004-XII,* 9; Haas, "Das De Nobili College, Poona," op. cit.

1163 See Gales, "Auf Felsen gegrtindet," 3.

1164 Karl Brust to the General (Poona, 20th October 1939), ARSI, *Poona. 1004-XII,* 10.

1165 Adrian van Kalken to the Superior General (Poona, 20th November 1939), ARSI, *1411-Visitatio Miss, van Kalken,* 59. See also Remigius Rauw to the General (Poona, 11th October 1939), ARSI, *Poona. 1004-XII,* 9.

One gets a pretty fair idea of the constraints of the situation.[1166] These arrangements of professors, in the given situation were thought to be the best possible. In fact it was considered even better than arranging the professors from other Missions, which in fact was the proposal made by the Visitor, Adrian van Kalken. This was "especially so because it [duration of Internment] was said to be only for a very short time."[1167] But contrary to the expectation it went much longer, at least in the case of some professors. Hence, the existence of the Theologate itself in Poona became a matter of apprehension, as Karl Giebens writes: "We do not even know whether we shall still be in Poona next year."[1168] With the passing years, as the number of students increased, the initial arrangements of the professors, etc., were not adequate. Hence, there was always a demand for adaptation to the emerging situation. Hence, alternative arrangements were made about which we read:

> We have borrowed some professors from some other Missions to replace the imprisoned ones. With the new scholastic year even Fr. Hans Staffner will be able to begin his lectures. Similarly a native Father. We do hope that after the end of the war we shall be able to form our own staff from among the native vocations.[1169]

Amidst these developments, the permission for the construction was obtained in September 1941 and without any further delay the work of construction began. The wells were dug some 20-30 meters deep through the hard rocks and massive roots of trees. Until mid-November 1941, the walls rose above the ground level. A massive work-force of some 230 workers were employed under the supervision of Br. Anton Herbert. The basic brickwork (under-construction) was expected to be completed until June 1942.[1170]

Meanwhile the construction work of the new building progressed, in spite of the difficulties of finance and other aspects and was completed with accommodation facilities for some 65 Scholastics: "The new College has been built up, one-storeyed, long corridors, a beautiful

---

1166 Remigius Rauw to the General (Poona, 31st December 1939), ARSI, *Poona-XII,* 18.

1167 Adrian van Kalken to the Superior General (Poona, 20th November 1939), ARSI, *1411-Visitatio Miss, van Kalken,* 59.

1168 Karl Giebens to the General (Poona, 10th January 1943), ARSI, *Poona 1004-XIV, 29.*

1169 "Der Obere berichtet aus Puna," *IB* 4/11 (September 1943): 26. See also "HH. Rauw schreibt am 18. Febr. 1943," ARSI, *Poona. 1004-XIV,* 12.

1170 See "Wir bauen: derNeubau des De Nobili-College," *IB* 3/6 (June 1942): 53.

chapel, a library, lecture rooms, etc., etc. From outside it appears very simple, which was also our idea, not to erect a palace."[1171] At this stage, while the Jesuits were looking forward to occupy the new College building, certain events unfolded in an entirely unexpected direction. The Jesuits were going to face a disappointment once again, which is revealed in the following letter: "In January 1943, thus, instead of the young Jesuits the first officer cadet [military] moved into the later De 'Nobili College'. Until 1947, the house was occupied by the military. St. Vincent's School had to give the seminarians hospitality for several more years,"[1172] following which wrote J. B. Haas: "That was a big disappointment," because "unfortunately it [De Nobili College] is being used for some other purpose, so that we cannot move in."[1173]

The sense of disappointment may be gauged also from the fact that already from around April-May 1942, there seems to have been an atmosphere of excitement among the Jesuits about moving into a new home, so that a slogan was afloat in the air: "The new scholastic year in the new home."[1174] No wonder, the persistent constraints of accommodation, the arrangements in the apartments and lack of proper atmosphere for serious study, etc., were reasons enough to make such an excitement even stronger. But the situation took an entirely different course. Hence, it was quite natural for all to have undergone such a feeling of disappointment, more specifically because a vicious circle of intriguing situations was created. Many hardships followed in succession even before the existing one was resolved. Every time a sense of security dawned, a new situation of hardship emerged.

It is amply clear that the disappointment was not on account of a sudden turn of events. Rather it was prompted more due to the seemingly unending chain of misfortunes. It is true that the Jesuits had already some indications that things might take such a turn. Stated differently, there were some information that the College would be occupied by the military:

> About the new college the situation becomes more and more hopeless. Fr. Superior has been advised orally, not to occupy it,

1171 John B. Haas to the Friends (Poona, 23.2.44), AMPSJ, *LB. Puna-Briefe (alte).*

1172 E. Gales, "Auf Felsen gegriindet," 3. See also John B. Haas, "Das De Nobili College, Poona", (Poona, 16th January 1946), ARSI, *Poona. 1004-XV,* 4.

1173 John B. Haas to the Friends (Poona, 23rd February 1944), AMPSJ, *LB. Puna-Briefe (alte).*

1174 "Wir bauen: Der Neubau des Nobili-Collegs," op. cit.

> by the highest military authority. Though they have not yet given notice that they will occupy it, but they send continually people to measure the rooms and make inquiries as to when the building will be completed.[1175]

We are told that even before the requisition of the College building by the military, certain apprehensions were being expressed by some Jesuits. The Visitor himself was at a loss to suggest something concrete as regards the possible options. Hence John B. Haas inquired:

> Then the question arises: what about the future? If I remember rightly, you were of the opinion that the Poona Theologate should be given up, if we cannot occupy the new building this year (scholastic year). I do not know whether it is not yet too early to think of this, I only mention it, in case some other arrangements have to be considered in good time.[1176]

Consequently, various rounds of consultation on the possible options took place. In case of the new building being taken over by the Military, various solutions were considered to meet the new conditions. The first solution considered was to allow the institution to die out by not admitting new students for the ensuing new scholastic year. The second solution was to transfer the college to Khandala [a hill-station on the Bombay-Poona highway]. Thirdly, the possibility of finding a sufficiently big house to accommodate all the students was suggested, which appeared next to impossible given the previous experiences. As the last solution, it was considered to close down the House and send students early in April (1943) to Kurseong.[1177]

After a long deliberation, it was decoded to have the last option. For, apparently during the period of war, it was not possible for the new Jesuit Scholastics to come from Europe to India. Besides, it was clear that St. Vincent's School could not be overburdened for an indefinite period of time. Meanwhile, some accommodations were available at St. Mary's Kurseong. Hence, in 1945 it was decided to suspend the

---

1175 John B. Haas to the Visitor (Poona, 16th November 1942), ARSI, *Historia. 2001-Poona,* 171.

1176 Ibid.

1177 Lawrence G. Fernandes to the General (Poona, 2nd January 1943), ARSI, *Poona. 1004-XIV,* 28.

Theologate in Poona for the time being and accommodate the students in Kurseong,[1178] as we read in a letter of Maximilian Riklin:

> Two months ago, it was decided by the Conference of the Superiors to close De Nobili College provisionally, as [St. Mary's] Kurseong has enough rooms (since four years no Scholastics came from Europe and after the war too, the replenishment must wait). Only the new priests would be staying here for another year...[1179]

Apparently this development threw a shadow of uncertainty whether it would be possible to bring the Theologate back to Poona again once the situation improved. Some of the Jesuits were pessimistic about it. Others, who were deeply interested in De Nobili College project, i.e., person like Joseph Neuner and others, were concerned about its future. Joseph Neuner, for example, expressed his anxiety from the Dehra Dun (present-day Uttar Pradesh) Internment camp: "The second question that preoccupies my thoughts is De Nobili College. Currently, only the Fourth Year class is preparing itself for the final examination. Then the College will die out. If, and when it could be restarted, I do not know."[1180]

An interesting aspect of the story of this phase of the history is the theological course being conducted for the Jesuit Scholastics of German origin in the internment camps wherein they virtually formed a small community:

> In the internment camp, the German companions have formed a small community. Fr. Felix Lowenstein presides over as their Superior ... The interned students continue their studies under the direction of the three professors, so that two of them are prepared for their ordinations. The imprisoned young missionaries diligently learn the languages they would require invariably and exercise also the pastoral care in the camp.[1181]

In another correspondence we read: "All are together in the Internment camp at Ahmednagar, they form a community with regular

---

1178 [1125] See also "Berichte aus unseren Missionen: Aus der Puna Mission," *MDPGJ* 17/113-117 (1953-1956): 21.

1179 Maximilian Riklin to Emil Kaufmann (Poona, 1st March 1945), AMPSJ, *LB. Puna-Briefe (alte).* See in the same file, William Clement to Felix A. Plattner (Poona, 31sl July 1945).

1180 Joseph Neuner to Felix A. Plattner (Internment Camp, Wing 1, Dehra Dun, 30th August 1945), AMPSJ , *LB. Puna-Briefe (alte).*

1181 "Der Qbere berichtet aus Puna," *IB* 4/11 (September 1943): 26. See also Wlodimir Ledochowski, Superior General to Paul Hormann (Rome, 15th February 1940), ARSI, *RLGGM,* Vol. VII, 118.

order and studies of Theology and language. They can say Mass daily and are very cheerful."[1182] Among the Scholastics who studied theology in the Internment Camp were "[Guido] Martini and [John B.] Thiel [who] did not waste time and asked to get theology classes from the beginning."[1183] No wonder it was a source of satisfaction that the Jesuits were able to enjoy a considerable degree of freedom even being in the camp, so that the General expressed his satisfaction:

> It is also a source of great consolation to me to hear that the Fathers and Brothers in the Internment camp at Ahmednagar enjoyed such freedom, and were able to hear Mass daily and to form a little community where religious discipline could be at least partially observed, and theological and language studies pursued.[1184]

The foregoing paragraphs give us an idea that the initial years were full of challenges. The story of its beginning becomes even more interesting because the Theologate was begun without having proper infrastructure and professors for the same. Yet, it emerged out of its humble existence to become an institution with great contribution towards the formation of the native clergy.

7.3.4. De Nobili College: The Second Spring[1185]

The second spring in the history of De Nobili College coincides with two other significant historical events: with regard to the history of India, the transition of India from being a British colony to an independent nation (15th August 1947), and becoming a Democratic Republic with the adoption of its own Constitution on 26th January 1950. In the context of Poona Jesuit history, the same coincides with the erection of the Swiss

1182 Remigius Rauw to the General (Poona, 11th October 1939), ARSI, *Poona. 1004-XII, 9.*

1183 [1130] Neuner, *Memories,* 11. Elsewhere do we read "The two theologians now interned, continue their theological studies in Ahmednagar with the help of Fr. Neuner and the other Fathers and together with the other three Scholastics interned." Adrian van Kalken to the Superior General (Poona, 20th November 1939), ARSI, *1411-Visitatio Miss, van Kalken,* 59.

1184 Karl Brust to Remigius Rauw (Rome, 30th November 1939), ARSI, *RLGGM,* Vol. VII, 107. The discipline in the Internment Camps, initially was rather different: "Restrictions in the beginning were stiff - e.g. scissors for cutting your nails were considered deadly weapons and were taken away. Later they were adjusted to practical needs..." Neuner, *Memories,* 10-11.

1185 The expression has been borrowed from Gales, "Auf der Felsen ..." 3.

Vice-Province (12th March 1947).[1186] Both these events were destined to play a significant impact on further orientation of the institution; i.e., the endeavour to impart contextual formation to the later generations within the larger socio-cultural context of India.

Amidst the above-mentioned developments, finally in 1948 the new De Nobili College building, which "had been rented out to the army during the war ... was taken over [by the Jesuits] for the new beginnings ..."[1187] The phase of temporary, yet comparatively longer sojourn at Vincent's School Poona (1937-1945) and St. Mary's College, Kurseong (1945-47) had finally come to an end and a new phase began, which was a pleasant surprise to the Jesuits, as we note below:

> But two years later, on 2nd February 1948 an introductory lecture was delivered and the Holy Mass was celebrated once again in Poona; this time it its own House, the "Nobili College", on the Poona-Ahmednagar road. The Theologate had awakened out of its hibernation to begin its new life in its own home. Under the leadership of Hans Staffner, its sympathetic Rector, the College began the second period of its development. The teaching staff consisted of old, experienced professors of Kurseong and some young members of the Order, who had just returned from Rome with fresh doctoral laurels.[1188]

The first 35 seminarians of the new house were partly old war veterans, for whom this type of new arrangement was just the right challenge. They created in the barren stony desert a garden full of trees. The studies were not neglected either, for it was overseen by some theologians of repute, like the "Fathers [John] Sanders, Dupont, [Charles] Giebens and [Joseph] Neuner."[1189]

Such a positive side of the story apart, a number of problems, especially with regard to the question of professors and a sufficient number of books in the library, etc., were still needed to be sorted out. Summarising the developments, writes Neuner: "This was the situation

1186 See Schatz, *Geschichte,* Vol. IV, 294.

1187 Neuner, *Memories,* 21. See also Anton Herbert to Joseph Brandle (Hubli, 30th March 1946), AMPSJ, *Pune Alt.*

1188 Gales, "Auf Felsen gegrundet," 3-4.

1189 Ibid.

when I arrived in June 1950."[1190] Hans Galli, who "was experienced in constructions and buildings"[1191] took over as its first independent Rector at the beginning of this period. Prior to this, Pius Geisel himself was the Rector besides shouldering the responsibility of the Mission Superior.[1192] In the initial years of the Second Spring, his role was most decisive, especially with regard to the development of its infrastructure. The rapid growth of the Theologate thereafter may be judged from the fact that for the academic year 1954-55, "140 theologians arrived in June 1954, so that the Theology Wing appeared too small. A few places were free only in the Philosophy Wing"[1193] of the building.

As for the library, the need of a sufficient number of books was largely fulfilled by various funding agencies, i.e., Missio Aachen and individual benefactors in Europe, thanks to the enthusiastic mediation by Felix A. Plattner.[1194] But, in the initial years, this challenge was really an acute one: "the Poona Theologate is very badly in need of books on theology."[1195] No wonder, in this regard too, the major burden was shouldered by the Poona Mission.[1196]

Added to these, the campus had to be developed gradually as it was a barren ground with virtually no vegetation. The building, when it was taken over by the army, had sufficient rooms just for accommodation of some 65 Scholastics for Theology. In 1951, therefore, when the decision was made to add a section for Philosophy to the existing Faculty of Theology, a new wing with 120 rooms needed to be constructed. The construction of these additional rooms was a new challenge, which included finalization of the plan, purchase of construction materials and other related aspects. The objective was achieved, thanks to the personal

1190 Ibid., 21. He had returned from Rome after his doctorate on the topic: "The Idea of Sacrifice in the Bhagvad Gita."

1191 Pius Geisel to Felix A. Plattner (Poona, 8th September 1951), AMPSJ, *Superior Poona, P. Geisel.*

1192 Ibid., (Poona, 3rd September 1951).

1193 Ibid., (Poona, 5th March 1954).

1194 Ibid., (Poona, 3rd September 1951)and (Poona, 2nd March 1952); Gottfried Dossing to Pius Geisel (Aachen, 17th September 1951).

1195 John B. Moyersoen to the Superior of Goa Mission (18th March 1941), ARSI, *Goa. 1003-II.*

1196 Pius Geisel to Felix A. Plattner (Poona, 1st March 1952), AMPSJ, *Superior Poona, P. Geisel.* See further in the same file, Pius Geisel to Felix A. Plattner (Poona, 2nd March 1952).

interest of Hans Galli and extraordinary zeal and efficiency of Brothers Joseph Pfiffner, Otto Widmer and Anton Herbert, who coordinated and supervised the work. It would not be an exaggeration to say that virtually every brick of De Nobili College bears the names of these committed Brothers.[1197]

Already in the First Academic Year that began in June 1951, some 50 Scholastics were expected for Philosophy from all over India.[1198] This is an indication that in spite of the many unresolved issues, the institution was growing in its reputation relatively faster. However, since the College had no academic status up to this point, it could not bestow academic degrees on its students. But since the syllabus was recognized by St. Mary's College, Kurseong, the possibility was open to continue the courses further with the minimum number of staffs available.[1199]

7.3.5. The Question of Professors: A Perennial Issue

Although certain aspects of this issue, especially pertaining to the period of WWII, has already been touched upon, we wish to complete the picture here taking a brief look at the entire period of this study. While doing the same, we found it curious to note that the question was not resolved even "until two months before the opening."[1200] For a venture of such a great significance, it is apparently difficult to comprehend that one of the most important requirements (professors) had not been met. In solving this problems the singular role played by the German-Swiss Jesuits stood out very prominently.

It may be pointed out that various possibilities had been explored in order to make an arrangement for the professors. Remigius Rauw, the Mission Superior, for example, had been making strenuous efforts to do his part, which included numerous correspondences with the Superior General as well as with the Provincial of the Southern German Province. The Superior General was equally concerned about the issue

1197 See Pius Geisel to Felix A. Plattner (Poona, 30* March 1951), (Poona, 19th June 1951), (Poona, 3rd September 1951), (Poona, 8* September 1951), (Poona, 13th September 1951), *AMPSJ, Superior Poona, P. Geisel.*

1198 Ibid., (Poona, 19th June 1951).

1199 See Neuner, *Memories,* 21.

1200 Schatz, *Geschichte,* Vol. Ill, 316. See also Francis X. Schubiger (Consultor, Poona Mission) to Karl Brust (Sangamner, 14th May 1937), ARSI, *Historia 2001-Poona.*

and wanted to see it resolved before the opening of the Theologate.[1201] To this effect he wrote:

> With regard to the professors, I will write immediately to the Superiors, so that they might prepare the Fathers appropriate for the job. Since this, I think, concerns a very important aspect [and] certainly will not be lacking in difficulties, but we do hope to overcome them with God's help ....[1202]

In view of the common venture, the Superior General took it for granted that all other Indian Jesuit Missions would be sharing the responsibility. The text above underlines the same. Hence, Adrian van Kalken was entrusted with the task of arranging for the professors from other Missions. As indicated above, the Superior General himself communicated the matter to various Superiors. The Southern German Provincial was also urged to look into the matter and to do the needful, as we read in a letter to Remigius Rauw:

> As for the professors for the theology, which should begin in June [1937], Fr. Provincial, [Augustine] Rosen has already made his suggestions and we have written to him to get in touch with Rev. Fr. Visitor, van Kalken, so that he might arrange for the still lacking professors from other Provinces.[1203]

In spite of these steps, the realization of the plan of making arrangements for professors was far from being satisfactory. It was bound to cause a worry, although "there were some young professors, who had completed their studies partly in Europe as well."[1204] The Theologate had to be started with the available manpower in the Mission; since initially the contribution from other Missions seems to have been virtually negligible, nay almost absent.[1205] In fact, it became practically the responsibility of the Poona Mission and its mother Province to do the needful. Augustine Rosch, Provincial of Southern

1201 See Gales, "Auf Felsen gegriindet," 4.

1202 Karl Brust to Maximilian Riklin (Rome, 28th February 1935), ARSI, *RLGGM,* Vol. V, 247.

1203 Karl Brust to Remigius Rauw (Rome, 13th February 1937), ARSI, *RLGGM.* Vol. V, 334.

1204 Gales, "Auf Felsen gegriindet," 3.

1205 It is not to deny the fact that certain other Missions, i.e., Bombay Mission which was then under the Spanish Jesuits of Aragon Province, did contribute towards the goal right from the beginning. We shall shortly see among the first group of professors that there were two Spanish Jesuits. See "Aus der Theologie in Puna," IB 21A (1938): 46.

German Province, expressed his grievance on the issue to the Superior General as follows:

> Since the Poona-Theologate should be a sort of central Seminary for various Indian Jesuit Missions, it seems reasonable to expect that the rest of the Missions concerned [with the venture] help out with one or the other professor and Prov. Germ. Sup. [Southern German Province] must not be left alone to carry out the responsibility.[1206]

In spite of numerous constraints, including the lack of vocations, the Southern German Province was trying to explore further possibilities within its capacity so that Augustine Rosch, was able to give a hopeful news sometime later:

> From our province, provisionally the following have been taken into consideration: For Dogma -Fr. [Walter Brugger], Fr. [Joseph] Neuner ... For Canon Law - Fr. [Alphonse] Gommenginger (now in Tertianship) ... For moral [theology] - Fr. Superior [Remigius] Rauw ... For exegesis -Fr. [Hugo] Aman ... [And] Fr. [John B.] van Hahn ... I shall see further, in case someone or the other is found suitable from Missio Helvetica [Swiss Mission for the purpose].[1207]

These arrangements apart, in any case, the assurance given by the Superior General to the Mission Superior as regards the professors seems to have been only partially fulfilled, i.e., 2 professors, were sent from Bombay Mission. Thus, the question of professors was far from being fully resolved, nay it "was acute right from the beginning."[1208] The courses on theology had to be begun with a limited number of staff. Hence, as indicated above, the inauguration of the Theologate took place (11th June 1937) with a staff of only four Professors, among whom Fr. [John Baptist] Haas, 'alongside' was a full-time chaplain to the Tamil community. By the end of August, Fr. [Walter] Brugger needed to discontinue his lectures and return to Europe in the beginning

1206 Augustine Rosch to the Superior General (Feldkirch, 20th January 1937), ARSI, *Germ. Sup. 1012-1,* 1

1207 Ibid. The last two never came to India on account of doctors' prescription. Hugo Aman was suffering from liver infection. For further information, see Schatz, *Geschichte,* Vol. Ill, 316-317.

1208 John B. Haas, "Das De Nobili College, Poona", (Poona, 16th January 1946), ARSI, *Poona. 1004-XV,* 4.

of November due to his sickness.[1209] The two Spanish Fathers from Bombay Mission, Fr. [Anicetus] Deniz and Fr. [Richard] Negre needed to share his area of work ... [Only later] on 21st May [1937] did Fr. [Josef] Neuner and Fr. [Felix] Lowenstein arrive in Puna; Fr. Neuner as Student Prefect and Professor of Dogmatic and Fr. Lowenstein as Professor of Church History.[1210]

The constraint of personnel may be well assessed from the above text. Moreover, in such a situation, the return of Walter Brugger to Europe due to ill-health within a short period of time in Poona was bound to aggravate the precariousness of the condition of the Theologate.[1211] He seems to have been suffering from a sort of depression.[1212] Sometime later Richard Negre too returned to his Mission (Bombay) for the same reason at the end of the first scholastic year. After their departure, thus, Remigius Rauw faced once again the worry about the lectures pertaining to the subjects taught by Walter Brugger and Richard Negre, which he hoped "to carry forward with the help of some substitutes."[1213] In spite of the constraints of space, library and many such other issues "the first scholastic year of the new Theologate of Puna was concluded with the

---

1209 Walter Brugger seems to have been suffering from a sort of depression. On visiting a certain Dr. Smith, a specialist in mental diseases, he was advised to travel back to Europe. See Walter Brugger to the General (Poona, 1st September 1937), *ARSI, Poona. 1004-X,* 20; Remigius Rauw to the General (Poona, 24th July 1937), ARSI, *Poona. 1004-X,* 21; Archbishop Henry Doring to Karl Brust (Poona, 15th September 1937), ARSI, *Historia 2001-Poona;* Karl Brust to Walter Brugger (Zurich, 1 1th September 1937), ARSI, *RLGGM, Vol.* VII, 13.

1210 "Aus der Theologie in Puna," *IB* 2/4 (1938): 46. See also John B. Haas, "Das De Nobili College, Poona", (Poona, 16th January 1946), ARSI, *Poona. 1004-XV,* 4; Anonymous, "De Studiis Nostrorum in Collegio de Nobili Poonensi" (Poona, n.d.), ARSI, *Poona. 1004-XIII,* 4. John B. Moyersoen, the Mission Superior of Calcutta, who was instrumental in implementing the plan of a second Theologate in India, reports the matter to the General pithily: "Poona: the Theologate goes on, but I hear that it is very poorly staffed. Something could probably be done for the duration of the war. I intend going myself to see at my earliest opportunity." "Ex litteris R. P. J. B. Moyersoen, Sup. Miss. Cal." (Calcutta, 15th November 1940), ARSI, *Poona. 1004-XIII,* 8; See also Archbishop Henry Doring to Karl Brust (Poona, 15th September 1937), ARSI, *Historia 2001-Poona.*

1211 See Remigius Rauw to the General (Poona, 24th July 1937), ARSI, *Poona. 1004-X,* 21. See also John B. Haas, "Das De Nobili College, Poona", (Poona, 16th January 1946), ARSI, *Poona. 1004-XV,* 4.

1212 Remigius Rauw to the Superior General (Poona, 24th July 1937), ARSI, *Poona. 1004-X,* 21. See also Haas, "Das De Nobili College, Poona", (Poona, 16th January 1946), op. cit.; Rauw to the Superior General (Poona, 16th June 1938), op. cit, 3.

1213 Remigius Rauw to the General (Poona, 24th July 1937), ARSI, *Poona. 1004-X,* 21.

annual examinations at the end of March [1938]. What had appeared as almost impossible for many, had become a reality."[1214] Fortunately they could begin "the second year with 3 new professors and 8 new Scholastics"[1215] besides the old-timers.

After the return of two professors at the end of the first scholastic year, the question of professors came to square one again. The Bombay Mission sent F. D'Souza to replace Richard Negre. Unfortunately, in the opinion of John B. Haas, he "was hopeless as professor and needed to stop after a year."[1216] Then "came in October 1938 [Joseph] Gachter. [According to John B. Haas, he was] a man who bred a lot of bad blood through his criticism."[1217] The first two years, thus, were constantly marked by the change of professors, including some 'unsuitable' ones as mentioned above.

The arrangement of professors for the third scholastic year was even more dramatic. Alphonse Gommenginger[1218] was expected to take over as the Professor of Canon Law after completing his studies in Rome. Meanwhile WWII broke out. Hence there was no more possibility of his coming to Poona. In such a situation,

> Fr. Felix zu Lowenstein who was destined to teach Church History and God willing, needed to make a Biennium for the same in Rome,[1219] all of a sudden needed to teach Canon Law in place of yet-to-be present Fr. Gommenginger, on which he received a news just 10 days earlier.[1220]

1214 "Aus der Theologie in Puna", *IB, 2/4* (1938): 46. See also J. W. Lange (a representative of the Third Year Scholastics) to the General (Poona, 8th September 1939), ARSI, *Poona. 1004-XII,* 8. This letter was signed by 15 Scholastics.

1215 Rauw to the Superior General (Poona, 16th June 1938), op. cit, 3. See, the copy of the same letter, ARSI, *1411-Visitatio Miss, van Kalken,* 26.

1216 John B. Haas, "Das De Nobili College, Poona", (Poona, 16th January 1946), ARSI, *Poona. 1004-XV,* 4.

1217 Ibid.

1218 He could never come to India afterwards. See Schatz, *Geschichte,* Vol. Ill, 317.

1219 "To do something of this kind [a higher study]," wrote Felix Lowenstein, "we both [Lowenstein and Neuner] considered of exceedingly great importance, not only because the College as a College of the Society of Jesus needs a set of qualified professors, but also because of its location opposite the Hindu Colleges here in Poona." Felix Lowenstein to the Superior General (Poona, 5th June 1939), ARSI, *Poona. 1004-XU,* 6.

1220 Schatz, *Geschichte,* Vol. Ill, 317.

It is not hard to imagine the dilemma that Felix Lowenstein may have undergone at this stage. Once again Remigius Rauw comes here at the centre of discussion. Felix Lowenstein had made an earnest request to him to make an arrangement for a replacement to teach the subjects taught by him before he left for Rome for his Biennium. But Remigius Rauw did not seem to have taken it seriously. At the end Felix Lowenstein had to cancel his plan of going to Rome and had to take up the teaching of an additional subject, namely Canon Law within just 8 days of preparation, interrupting his journey in north India.[1221]

This problem had remained virtually unchanged until 1946/47, so that J. B. Haas lamented the situation: "How people promised us to send personnel and did not send them; on this issue it cannot be written any further. First, we were left alone and then people hold us responsible for everything."[1222] The text seems to imply even the Superior General here. The Jesuits of the Mission had a feeling that the assurance of the General with regard to the supply of professors both from Europe and other Missions in India had not been fulfilled: "We were given an assurance from Europe that we do need not be worried about the question of professors, they would be coming. Unfortunately, the contrary is the case."[1223] It would not be an exaggeration to say that they were feeling deceived as well. In a letter, Joseph Neuner lamented the situation:

> Before coming to India I asked repeatedly who would provide professors for our College. I got constantly the answer that our province was only the in charge of it, but the professors would be provided by Rev. Fr. General. They would be taken from all the missions or the corresponding provinces. This answer was given at a time when it was still possible to get people from our own province. Now, as any supply from our own province is out of question, we remain without help, and when they consider the question to help us in a consultation (as they are actually doing in Madury [Madurai] concerning a Professor of Church history, - but apparently without

1221 See also Schatz, *Geschichte,* Vol. Ill, 317-318. The episode makes an interesting reading, revealing certain internal problems among the Jesuits. See Felix Lowenstein to the Superior General (Poona, 5th June 1939), ARSI, *Poona-XII,* 6.

1222 John B. Haas to the Superior General (Poona, 16th January 1946), ARSI, *Poona. 1004-XV,* 3.

1223 Ibid., 4.

> help) they consider it as a special act of charity. This attitude is certainly not right.[1224]

The remark made above by Joseph Neuner reveals yet another side of the story with regard to the collaboration among the Jesuit Missions in India. It is quite apparent that other Missions were not yet prepared to see the Theologate as a common venture in terms of sharing of personnel. Klaus Schatz makes the following observation in this regard: "[Every Mission] was worried about itself alone, [in other words] it was ready to give away only those with whom in any case it wanted to get rid of."[1225]

Such a situation continued even later, especially until mid-1950s.[1226] The reasons for the same were basically two-fold. Firstly, "an absence of a centrally coordinating body for the studies of the Society of Jesus in India"[1227] which was largely responsible for the failure of other Jesuit Missions to supply the professors and secondly a division of opinions among the Jesuits in Poona Mission about the establishment and development of a Theologate. A section of the Jesuits in the Mission seem to have been more inclined towards investing personnel and energy for the expansion of the Mission among the non-Christians; while the other, for the establishment and development of a Theologate. Naturally, such a division of opinion was resulted in the lack of personnel.[1228]

Going through these sources, it is quite safe to arrive at a conclusion that the College was conducted with a lot of insufficient arrangements, especially with regard to the professors.[1229] Summarizing the situation that persisted towards the end of the first decade of the beginning of the College John B. Haas writes:

> Here a general remark: The staff of the professors was 1) too inconsistent and constantly changed. 2) Very little coherence. Everyone wishes that the things should be the same way as it was

1224 Joseph Neuner to the Vicar General (Khandala, 16th April 1940), *ARSI, Poona. 1004-XIII,* 6.

1225 Schatz, *Geschichte,* Vol. Ill, 318.

1226 Once the Pontifical Athenaeum Kandy, Sri Lanka was transferred to Poona (1955), many professors too came from there making the joint strength of the staff self-sufficient to a large extent. See Carlos M. de Melo, *The Papal Seminary of Kandy-Pune* (Pune: Papal Seminary, 1993), 111.

1227 Schatz, *Geschichte,* Vol. Ill, 317.

1228 Neuner to the Vicar General (Poona, 16th April 1940), op. cit.

1229 [1176] "Wir hinken weiter: Alte Nachrichten aus Puna-Stadt," *IB* 3/16 (December 1944): 43.

> in his respective province. 3) Not prepared. That was the biggest drawback. If one requires to teach Canon Law, Church History or Holy ... But we had no professors. The only option was: to close down. And people did not wish to risk these alternatives.[1230]

Once again, on this point too, the Superior General did not mince words when he needed to communicate the truth. Quite apparently he was displeased with the way things were handled with regard to the arrangement of professors. In this regard he held both Remigius Rauw and Adrian van Kalken responsible for the inefficient management of the affairs:

> From recent correspondence I see that your college is really in a very difficult position for want of men. I am very sorry that Fr. Visitor, to whom I gave the requisite powers for dealing with this question, has made no provision and has settled nothing. It is now impossible to send professors from Europe; so you must fend for yourselves and find the best solution that you can, recommending the whole matter to the Divine Providence. When the war is over, the Province will certainly send men suitable as Professors for the Poona College.[1231]

The question of the professors, however, was still unresolved satisfactorily until 1954. It may be recalled that around this time the move of controlling the grant of visa for the foreign missionaries was even getting stricter. Hence it was becoming more and more difficult to get new professors from the West. The biggest burden of such a situation was to be borne by the Poona Mission eventually. Pius Geisel, therefore, laments:

> The foreign branch office informed me that owing to [De Nobili] College the number of foreigners in Poona had increased fourfold. The college thus has made it practically impossible for Poona Mission to get any men for its own work, and it is very difficult to move other Missions to make sacrifices for the college. I think the time has come, when Indian Scholastics must be picked for professorships and sent to Rome, but unless Your Paternity imposes on the Missions to give their best men, what will the poor

1230 John B. Haas, "Das De Nobili College, Poona", (Poona, 16th January 1946), ARSI, *Poona. 1004-XV,* 4 (2).

1231 Wlodimir Ledochowski to the Remigius Rauw (Rome, 7th June 1940), ARSI, *1402: Visitatio Missio Poonensis (1935-1941).*

> Poona Superior do, on whose neck this milestone of the college hangs, devouring our own men and preventing us from getting new ones, as our quota in the eyes of the Government is much overdrawn.[1232]

We realize from the above description of the situation that the necessity of greater cooperation among the Missions was becoming more imperative. Moreover, the question of nurturing indigenous vocations could not be treated arbitrarily any more. In any case what is revealed in the entire phase is that the question of professors was resolved to a more satisfactory level once the Pontifical Central Seminary of Kandy along with its Athenaeum was transferred to Poona (1955). For, a number of professors came along with the students to Poona.[1233] By the time De Nobili College celebrated the Silver Jubilee of its foundation (1962), the initial problems and challenges were overcome to a large extent; so that E. Gales, the then Rector could joyfully recount the achievements during 25 years of its journey.[1234]

7.3.6. The Significance of the Venture

The journey into the history of this entire phase leads us to the discovery at what cost the De Nobili College grew from its infancy to the present stage. As stated above, its establishment along with later accommodated Jnanadeepa Vidyapeeth are the symbols of an abiding contribution of the Society of Jesus, especially the German-Swiss Jesuits of Poona towards the formation of the native clergy in India. Nearly 50% of the Jesuits in India today have gone through and are still going through the formation imparted here.

Moreover, over the decades of its existence the members of various other Religious Congregations and diocesan Seminarians have benefitted from the theological and philosophical training received at Jnanadeepa Vidyapeeth. Without a doubt, therefore, De Nobili College may be ranked among the institutions that have made a singular contribution to the Church in India and to the universal Church as well. In the words of James Gense, it has "proved to have been an invaluable

---

1232 Pius Geisel to the Superior General (Poona, July 1954), ARSI, *Poona. 1005-11, 47.*

1233 Carlos Merces de Melo, *The Papal Seminary of Kandy-Pune* (Pune: Papal Seminary, 1993), 109-110.

1234 See Gales, "Auf der Felsen ..." 3-5.

investment productive of rich returns."[1235] The credit naturally goes to the Poona Jesuits who established the same with unspeakable trouble and sacrifices as the foregoing pages have revealed. The Mission that once was judged by some critics as having ignored the formation of the native clergy stood out as having made a contribution of a tremendous significance. No wonder, the vision of Joseph Neuner "to lead the young Church to maturity and ripeness through its own priests"[1236] has been achieved to a large extent due to a singular role of De Nobili College. Obviously the continual task of presenting the Christian values to the wider Indian society further remains to be carried on.

The existence and contribution of De Nobili College gains further significance because of the special challenge the Indian Church was facing at the time of its re-opening in Poona (1948 after its nearly 2 years sojourn in Kurseong). At this juncture, India was experiencing its new-gained independence. The College building was finally freed from military occupancy. It was time to move into the new campus with new hopes and aspirations. But, some of the missionaries already marked dark clouds over the Church and their missions in India. According to some, the future of the Missions seemed to be bleak. Moreover, "in some Church circles in India and especially among the foreign missionaries there was a certain amount of anxiety that the Independent India might like to see the missionaries as well along with the English officers and soldiers out of India."[1237] Yet, in the words of E. Gales, "That was the time, which 'Nobili College', could prove, that the future belongs to those who trust in God and rely on him."[1238] The Superiors of various Missions were well aware that the growth of the Church in India was directly proportional to the priestly vocations they would gain. Therefore, more and more possibilities needed to be searched and opportunities needed to be created so that more and more native vocations could be promoted. In this regard, De Nobili College was like a seed from which evolved one of the largest training centres for priests in Asia. No wonder it is for these reasons that it has been called the "Gregorian of the East."[1239]

1235 Gense, *Church at the Gateway,* 458.

1236 Neuner, "Hundert Jahre," 25.

1237 Georg Evers, *Kirche und Katholizismus seit 1945, Band 5: Die Lander Asiens* (Paderborn. Munich. Vienna. Zurich: Ferdinand Schoningh, 2003), 341.

1238 Gales, "Auf Felsen gegriindet," 4.

1239 Ibid.

7.4. The Papal Seminary, Poona

Along with the De Nobili College, the Papal Seminary of Poona marks a definitive sign of the renewed commitment of the Poona Jesuits to the formation sector. Over the decades it has served as a cradle of a large number of vocations. Founded in a critical era, it deserves to be ranked among the important centres of formation of the Diocesan Seminarians in India.

7.4.1. Papal Seminary, Kandy (Sri Lanka)

Papal Seminary was started in a small rented house in Kandy in 1893 with a group of just 11 students. The main building was completed in 1899. Students selected from the dioceses in India and Ceylon, went there to be trained, ordained and became future leaders of the Church in their own countries. By 1909, a spacious new building was erected, wherein more than 100 students could be accommodated. In 1926 the Seminary was recognized by Rome to confer degrees in philosophy and theology including the doctorate. This gave it a distinctive mark, setting it apart from the existing institutes of priestly formation in India at that time. The syllabus and the statutes of the Seminary were revised twice in order to suit its new academic status. In 1940, the revised statutes were approved by the Congregation for the Catholic Education. Consequently, it gained a status of the Pontifical Athenaeum. Truly it was an important milestone in its history.[1240]

7.4.2. The Transfer to Poona

The Papal Seminary of Kandy had established itself and earned a name by the time it celebrated the golden Jubilee of its foundation (1943). Meanwhile India was heading towards gaining self-governance and eventually did gain the status of an Independent nation in 1947, followed by Sri Lanka in the subsequent year (1948). An immediate consequence of the same was: more control of the boarders of both countries affecting thereby the free passage to either side that was available as long as the two nations were part of the larger British India. Moreover, given such political developments, the sense of the Seminary in Kandy being the Pontifical Central Seminary of India began to appear even more incongruous, as it was situated in the extreme south of the sub-continent making access to it difficult for Indians.

1240 See "Das neue papstliche Zentralseminar Indiens," *IB* 1 (1958): 2-3.

A second important factor that played an important role in the entire consideration was the gradual but steady growth of native vocations to the priesthood in the years subsequent to the independence of the nation.[1241] Apparently, this trend initially was more conspicuous in the southern states of India, which did begin to grow gradually in the northern part of the country as well. Hence, it was decided in Rome that the time had finally come to re-locate the Seminary to mainland India. As a follow up of this recommendation from Rome, the Catholic Bishops' Conference of India (CBCI) too began to give a serious consideration on the question. The following five reasons were adduced to in justification of this decision in the Conference of 1949:

> 1) Radical changes in India and Ceylon [Sri Lanka], following Independence [of the nations]. 2) Difficulties of obtaining passports; 3) Cost of living in Kandy already high; 4) Money could not be sent from India to Ceylon; 5) Too long a stay in a foreign country would deprive students of contact with their own homeland since most of the students were Indians.[1242]

The third consideration was to utilize the personnel available at Poona. Finding a sufficient number of professors was always a serious concern, as we have seen in the case of De Nobili College. In case the Seminary were to be transferred to a place other than Poona, this concern would be acute once again. Hence, Poona[1243] was chosen as the best suited place. An amalgamation of personnel both from De Nobili College as well as Papal Seminary, Kandy would address the problem to a large extent. Stated differently, the relocation of the Pontifical Central Seminary in the immediate vicinity of the existing De Nobili College was viewed as implying both intellectually as well as financially beneficial to both institutions. In spite of all these compelling reasons in favour of the transfer, the final decision on the same was pending until 1954. At any rate, given the major considerations mentioned above, the

---

1241 Ibid.

1242 De Melo, *The Papal Seminary*, 96. See also "*Souvenir: Inauguration and Solemn Blessing of the Papal Seminary Chapel, 1957*, 37," AMPSJ, *Felix Plattner Varia.*

1243 In the opinion of some higher authorities in Rome, i.e., Cardinal Fumasoni-Biondi and the then Secretary of the Sacred Congregation of Propaganda, Bangalore was being considered as the better suited place. But later the decision was made in favour of Poona when an overall assessment of both possibilities were made. See de Melo, *The Papal Seminary*, 95-97.

Seminary along with the Athenaeum was transferred to Poona in 1955. A central academic institution thus became a reality in more real terms: an Athenaeum, with lecture halls, a large and rich library, a modern and beautiful church. The amalgamation of the two faculties of Papal Athenaeum, Kandy and De Nobili College also led to an enrichment of teaching and academic pursuits, under the new institute, Jnanadeepa Vidyapeeth in 1970. Thereafter it became an autonomous academic institution, while remaining attached to the Papal Seminary.[1244]

For the sake of clarification, it is apt to make a remark here: The Papal Seminary as well as De Nobili College must be seen in close conjunction with the Jnanadeepa Vidyapeeth (Pontifical Athenaeum) after the definitive transfer of the Papal Seminary to Poona in 1955. Without the Pontifical Athenaeum, Papal Seminary would be no more than a residence and a house of formation for the Seminarians of various dioceses just like De Nobili College being the residence and a house of formation for the Jesuits in India. The inter-relation among these, i.e., De Nobili College, Papal Seminary and Jnanadeepa is akin to that among the Faculty of Theology, Jesuitenkolleg and Canisianum in Innsbruck; apparently with the difference that Jnanadeepa Vidyapeeth is entirely governed and managed by the Jesuits while the Faculty of Theology in Innsbruck is a part of the University of Innsbruck, the management of the same being under the care of the university.

7.4.3. The Initial Concerns

A process of transition, be it spatial or temporal, is always undoubtedly painful. One can easily imagine, therefore, the dilemma the Professors as well as the Seminarians might have experienced at the prospect of being transplanted, so to say, from a cosy and well-established place of Kandy to a new and barren landscape of Poona. From the perspective of the Seminary community in Kandy, there were genuinely certain crucial issues that needed to be addressed, besides the question of the transportation of the furniture and a huge bulk of books for the library, which were the property of the Jesuits. One such issue was the question of identifying and separating the ownership of the entire property in Kandy between the Jesuits and the Propaganda Fide. The immovable

---

1244 See "Das neue papstliche Zentralseminar Indiens," *IB* 1 (1958): 3. See also de Melo, *The Papal Seminary,* 97-99; *Souvenir: Inauguration and Solemn Blessing,* 11-13, AMPSJ, *Varia/ Felix A. Plattner.*

assets were mostly the Propaganda properties, while the movable ones especially a good collection of books and furniture were Jesuit properties. The safe transportation of these was not going to be too easy. The second concern was about the poor people who had been allowed to settle on the Seminary premises on an unofficial agreement. The gesture was purely out of charity towards them. How would the incumbent Religious Congregation treat the question? These and many other such issues were certainly no insignificant concerns.[1245]

After the arrival in Poona, there was the emotional baggage of attachment to the former place especially among the Professors who had resided in Kandy for decades. This could not be taken for granted. It is revealed that a "family spirit [had been] prevailing in the [Kandy] Seminary between the students and the Staff,[1246] which needed to be re-discovered in the broader context of its relationship with De Nobili College. A related aspect was the kind of relationship that existed between the Seminary and the Athenaeum in Kandy where, for example, both these formed a unity. Stated differently, the academic and community life centred around the Seminarians alone. In Poona, the students at the Athenaeum included Jesuit Scholastics besides many others.[1247] Humanly speaking, therefore, a demand for adaptation to a new situation might not have been as simple as it appeared. These aspects are well underlined in the memoriale of the visitation (1956) by Pius Geisel, Vice-Provincial:

> It was not a small sacrifice to leave Kandy with its beautiful scenery and all that you had been accustomed to for many years. Here in Poona the fact that several other institutions are attached to the Athenaeum and live in close vicinity to you, has created a number of problems. You are now more than before constrained to accommodate yourselves to the needs of others as well. We must thank God that the transition --owing to your good will-- has been smooth on the whole and it appears that happiness is not absent. The process of integration will naturally take time and you can

---

1245 *Souvenir: Inauguration and Solemn Blessing,* 11-13, AMPS J, *Varia/ Felix A. Plattner.*

1246 Gregory Koelmann to the Superior General (Poona, 1st June 1958), ARSI, *Belgaum-Poona. 1006-Particulares (1958).*

1247 See, E. F. Mann, "Report of the Visitation of the Papal Seminary, De Nobili College and Papal Athenaeum, Poona: Sept. 8 - October 6, 1961," ARSI, *Belgaum-Poona. 1006-Praep-Prov. (1961).*

> confidently hope to feel perfectly at home in the not too distant future.[1248]

A matter of even greater concern was the imperative of cultivating mutual understanding between the newly arrived staff from Kandy and that of the De Nobili College. An effort was being made from the Jesuits of both communities to "adjust themselves to the new situation."[1249] There are indications in a substantial number of correspondences that give us an impression that aspects such as these, i.e., initial challenges of establishing an understanding to achieve the common purpose, did exist in the beginning. It becomes all the more evident from the fact that Pius Geisel, the Vice-Provincial needed to take up the issue in the previously mentioned memoriale of the visitation wherein he clearly felt the need to underline the common purpose of bringing the two communities together. In his own words:

> Both the Papal Seminary and De Nobili College are Jesuit institutions. The Staff of the Professors of the Athenaeum is one, although you may live in different houses. The purpose of all institutions--include the non-Jesuits--is one and the same: to train priests for India's needs. There are thus strong bonds that unite you all. Conscious of this unity of purpose you try to live together and to work together harmoniously and thus give a shining example to the students worthy of imitation. If the staff members are one in mind and heart, the students also will be one in mutual love, which will indeed be one of the best things they can learn in Poona and one of the best promising features for the future of the Church in India. Although for obvious reasons there must be a separation between the staffs, it is highly desirable that you meet each other frequently, not only for official business, but also socially in recreation.[1250]

From the date of the above memoriale, it is clear that certain adjustment problems were bound to exist as it was the very first year after the transfer from Kandy. But there are a number of correspondences that

1248 Pius Geisel, "Elenchus Visitationis, Seminario Pontificio Poonensi: Memoriale Visitationis, 1956," ARSI, *Poona. 1005-VI,* 3.

1249 Pius Geisel, "Missio Poonensis: Litterae Superioris Missionis," ARSI, *Poona. 1005-IV,* 20.

1250 Pius Geisel, "Elenchus Visitationis," ARSI, *Poona. 1005-VI,* 3. See also, E. F. Mann, "Memorial of the Visitation: Papal Seminary Poona, Community," ARSI, *Belgaum-Poona. 1006-Praep-Prov. (1961).*

indicate that the challenge of establishing a mutual relationship between the Jesuits of the two communities was not as simple as it may appear. Among the major causes of such strained relations between the two communities, two may be mentioned here. Firstly, according to Lionel Mascarenhas, the relations were strained sometimes by considerations of what one might call 'prestige ... The Seminary Fathers are highly sensitive on the question of the connection of the 'Athenaeum' with the Seminary. Any suggestion of the separation of the two ... is apt to evoke strong reactions. Whatever the intrinsic merits or otherwise of Rev. Fr. Visitor's recommendation ... that the Athenaeum be constituted a separate legal unit ... the matter caused quite a stir among the Seminary Consultors. The reaction would doubtless have been much stronger among the rest of the Community.[1251]

The claim made above that the sentimental baggage of the old traditions of Kandy,[1252] thus, was true. From the above description, it also becomes clear that the Religious and the clergy often get too much attached to traditions and past glories. Lionel Mascarenhas makes once again a pointed remark:

> As to relations between the two Jesuit communities, one cannot help but feel that even among ours alas prejudices die hard. Only a few days ago I heard an old prejudice voiced by one of the Fathers of the Seminary: 'Of course, the Seminary is only an appendix of De Nobili College' ... With such a mentality, biased interpretations of things and events are only a matter of course ... It is a pity that ours are not always conspicuous for the broadmindedness and charity that we expect and demand from our students.[1253]

It is rather curious to note that the strained relationships were often caused, in the second place, due to certain individuals among the Jesuits. In the list of the persons, Joseph Neuner is repeatedly mentioned as being a prime cause of such a state of affairs between the two communities.

1251 Lionel Mascarenhas, "Litterae Consultoris Domus in Seminario Pontif. Poonensi in Vice-Provincia Belgaum-Poonensis," ARSI, *Belgaum-Poona. 1006-Consultores (1962).* See further in the same file, Jean de Marneffe, "Letter of Consultor in De Nobili College, Vice-Province of Belgaum-Poona,"; R. J. Cordero, "Litterae Consultoris in Collegio Maximo De Nobili in Vice-Provincia Belgaum-Poonensis."

1252 See, Pius Geisel, Vice Provincial, "Elenchus Visitationis: Seminario Pontificio, Poonensis (21st - 24th July 1957)," ARSI, *Poona. 1005-XI,* 4.

1253 Lionel Mascarenhas, "Litterae Consultoris Domus in Seminario Pontif. Poonensi in Vice-Provincia Belgaum-Poonensis," ARSI, *Belgaum-Poona. 1006-Consultores (1962).*

The following remark of Lionel Mascarenhas might give an idea of the same:

> As regards ours in the two houses ... I do not think we are very fortunate in our Prefect of Studies [Joseph Neuner]. He is a good Religious, a hardworking professor and scholar and a stimulating theologian; but he cuts a poor figure ... when it comes to human relations. The fact is he has not been liberally endowed with tact or the ability to ... see things from the other man's point of view ... this unhealthy attitude does not seem to be justifiable to me, and still less, helpful for the betterment of relations between the two houses.[1254]

Lawrence Fernandes also described the person of Joseph Neuner in even stronger terms, while hoping that the purpose of unity was not beyond reach, if the Jesuits of both the communities were disposed towards the same: "In fact, there is every hope that these relations being cordial, except for the autocratic and harsh way of acting of the Prefect of Studies, Fr. Joseph] Neuner."[1255]

It is interesting to note that in the initial years a similar kind of situation prevailed even among the students of the two communities. There may have been various other grounds for the same, besides the ones mentioned with regard to the members of the staff. What is crucial, however, was to establish an atmosphere of mutual understanding that would create a better living and learning conditions. As a concrete example, R. J. Cordero, mentions a factor responsible for the strained relations among the students of the two communities:

> As regards the tension on the side of the Seminarians: I think it is a good deal built on jealousy. The SJ disputations, dramas and performances are usually better than theirs. This inferiority, I am

1254 Lionel Mascarenhas, "Litterae Consultoris Domus in Seminario Pontif. Poonensi in Vice-Provincia Belgaum-Poonensis", ARSI, *Belgaum-Poona. 1006-Consultores (1962).* See also Gregory Koelmann to the Superior General (Poona, 1st June 1958), ARSI, *Belgaum-Poona. 1006-Particulares (1958);* E. F. Mann, "Report of the Visitation of the Papal Seminary, De Nobili College and Papal Athenaeum, Poona: Sept. 8 - October 6, 1961," ARSI, *Belgaum-Poona. 1006-Praep-Prov. (1961);* Pius Geisel, Vice Provincial, "Elenchus Visitationis: Seminario Pontificio, Poonensis (21st - 24th July 1957)," ARSI, *Poona. 1005-XI,* 4.

1255 Lawrence Fernandes to the Superior General (Poona, 1st July 1957), ARSI, *Poona. 1005-XII,* 33. See also Mascarenhas, "Litterae Consultoris Domus in Seminario Pontif. Poonensi in Vice-Provincia Belgaum-Poonensis," op. cit.; Albert Urrichio to the Superior General (Poona, 26th June 1957), ARSI, *Poona. 1005-XII,* 34.

> afraid is covered over by all sorts of reasons ... which in other circumstances would have caused no trouble whatsoever.[1256]

According to some individuals, there was no possibility of rectifying the situation "unless some members of the Seminary staff are very strongly warned or removed."[1257] Another possibility was to exchange the members of the community. The third possibility that was pondered upon was to arrange in such a way that the professors of philosophy and Theology lived separately in one of the two communities. But all these options seem to have been abandoned either on the ground that they were impracticable or possessed the potentiality of generating ill-feelings among those who might be asked to move from one community to the other.[1258]

As for its legal status, the question of the ownership of the property of the Seminary and the legal status of the Athenaeum also needed to be settled, in view of the clarity on the point in future. Pius Geisel notes a conversation with the Internuncio, Mgr. Dr. N. N. Lucas, SVD on the issue when he came for "the laying of the foundation stone of the Papal Seminary, [which was] performed on 25th March 1953."[1259] The conversation implies the fact that the issue, if unsettled, might be a point of contention in the future. He writes:

> I had a conversation with His Excellency the Internuncio which I feel I must report. He asked me in whose name the property of the Papal Seminary stood. I answered in the name of the Poona Catholic Educational Association Limited. He answered that this was not the proper thing, but it should stand in the name of the Internuncio as the representative of the Holy See ... Also the property of the Seminary and the Society should be strictly separated ....[1260]

1256 Cordero, "Litterae Consultoris in Collegio Maximo De Nobili in Vice-Provincia Belgaum-Poonensis," op. cit. See also, Mascarenhas, "Litterae Consultoris Domus in Seminario Pontif. Poonensi in Vice-Provincia Belgaum-Poonensis," op. cit.

1257 Cordero, "Litterae Consultoris in Collegio Maximo De Nobili in Vice-Provincia Belgaum-Poonensis," op. cit.

1258 Ibid. See also Mascarenhas, "Litterae Consultoris Domus in Seminario Pontif. Poonensi in Vice-Provincia Belgaum-Poonensis," op. cit.

1259 Pius Geisel, "Some Legal Questions Concerning the Papal Seminary and Athenaeum, Poona," ARSI, *Poona. 1005-1,* 1. See further, "Foundation of the Papal Seminary Poona laid by His Exc. the Apostolic Internuncio on 25th March 1953," ARSI, *Poona. 1005-1,* 43.

1260 Pius Geisel to the Superior General (Poona, 1st April 1953), ARSI, *Poona. 1005-1,* 45. See in the same file, Pius Geisel, "Some Legal Questions Concerning the Papal Seminary and

Fortunately, the aspects mentioned above were successfully settled in the subsequent years.[1261] Accordingly, it became "clear that land and buildings belong to the Society of Jesus that is the present Belgaum-Poona Vice-Province, as registered under the legal title of the Poona Catholic Educational Association Private Limited."[1262]

This, along with other aspects, gives an indication that the entire situation began to improve gradually, thanks to the concerted effort on the part of the Superiors and other staff members. During the Visitation of the Athenaeum by Edward F. Mann (Provincial of Patna Province) in 1961, the issue was emphatically addressed so that "some improvement in the mutual relations between the Seminarians and Our Scholastics"[1263] began to be more tangible. In order to address the concern, however, there was a need to tackle the issue over the space of coming years. Be that as it may, one notices a definitive improvement in this regard after the afore-mentioned Visitation: "... the Jesuits at the Papal Seminary seem to cooperate quite well with those at De Nobili College."[1264]'A tangible, expression of the improvements with regard to these aspects may be assessed from a fact that within a few years, the Seminarians too gradually began to "feel that the transfer of the Seminary to Poona has meant a solid and very definite gain from the point of view of their intellectual and apostolic formation."[1265]

7.4.4. The Architects and Builders

A young Swiss architect, Silvio Galizia was entrusted with the preparation of the plan for the Seminary. The preparatory phase of planning and execution was tedious, which became all the more so because the architect, Silvio Galizia took much longer time than it was

---

Athenaeum, Poona."

1261 Pius Geisel to the Superior General (Poona, 3rd October 1961), ARSI, *Belgaum-Poona. 1006-Particulares (1961).*

1262 Geisel, "Some Legal Questions Concerning the Papal Seminary and Athenaeum, Poona," op. cit., 1.

1263 Mascarenhas, "Litterae Consultoris Domus in Seminario Pontif. Poonensi in Vice-Provincia Belgaum-Poonensis," op. cit.

1264 E. F. Mann, "Report of the Visitation of the Papal Seminary, De Nobili College and Papal Athenaeum, Poona: Sept. 8 - October 6, 1961," ARSI, *Belgaum-Poona. 1006-Praep-Prov. (1961).*

1265 Mascarenhas, "Litterae Consultoris Domus in Seminario Pontif. Poonensi in Vice-Provincia Belgaum-Poonensi," op. cit.

anticipated due to the delay in acquiring visa for his travel to India.[1266] Meanwhile, Pius Geisel, Superior Regular of the Mission approached a few Indian architects too, besides asking two Brothers of the Mission, i.e., Joseph Pfiffner and Joseph Neukam well experienced in construction matters to prepare the sketches of the plan so that he could arrive at the decision that would be feasible with respect to the estimate and other related factors.[1267] Although, Silvio Galizia, in the eyes of the Jesuits was considered the best choice, there was no unanimity about his capability to handle a project of such a magnitude and significance. The Internuncio, for example, was of quite a different opinion. He expressed his opinion thus:

> I am under the impression that Mr. Galizia is without any experience in building and certainly with no knowledge of Indian conditions ... Should we not get an experienced and first class architect to prepare the plans? If we ask Mr. Galizia to prepare the plans he ought to agree, I think, to submit them to some local architect experienced in Indian requirements.[1268]

Figure 7.3: The builders of De Nobili College and Papal Seminary, Poona. From left: Br. Otto Widmer, Fr. Pius Geisel (Provincial), Br. Joseph Pfiffner and Br. Anton Herbert. *Source*: AMPSJ, *Fotografische Belege, Kirchliche Studienhauser.*

1266 See Pius Geisel to Felix A. Plattner (Poona, 12th January 1952), AMPSJ, *Superior Poona, P. Geisel.*

1267 [1214] The Indian architect was Mr. Tamby from Chennai. See Pius Geisel to Felix A. Plattner (Poona, 5th May 1951), AMPSJ, *Superior Poona, P. Geisel.* In the same file, Pius Geisel to Felix A. Plattner (Poona, 19th June 1951); Pius Geisel to the Superior General (Poona, 6th July 1951).

1268 Quoted in a letter of Pius Geisel to Felix A. Plattner (Poona, 15th December 195 V, AMPSJ, *Superior Poona, P. Geisel.*

In spite of the above impression, the majority view prevailed and eventually he was the one who took over the task of constructing the building along with the Brothers mentioned above. They were joined later by Brs Anton Herbert and Otto Widmer. The major portion of the planning as well as execution of the same lay with Br. Joseph Pfiffner. Other Brothers looked after various other aspects, i.e., Anton Herbert took up the task of preparing and supplying the furniture for the Athenaeum and as well Papal Seminary. It may be noted that the construction work began only in 1953. Yet, within a year and a half a portion of the building was ready for occupation, thanks to the tremendous hard work of the Brothers.[1269] The pace of the work may be assessed from the fact that "the solemn inauguration of the Papal Seminary in India and the blessing of the church was posted from 2nd, 3rd and 4th December [1957]."[1270]

7.4.5. The Significance of the Endeavour

In recent times, especially after Vatican Council II, a substantial number of Seminaries and formation houses for both men and women Congregations have come up in India. Given the proportion of the Catholics in comparison with the world-wide Catholic population, therefore, India can rightfully claim to have the highest number of vocations to the priesthood and Religious way of life.[1271] Such was, apparently, not the case even as late as mid-1950s. There were only a few Seminaries, the Papal Seminary of Kandy being one of them. Given such a background, the transfer of the Papal Seminary of Kandy was a significant step, which in the subsequent decades was going to make a contribution of great importance towards the formation of the native clergy in India.

Its contribution may be further assessed from a simple fact that nearly 7000 Seminarians from across India from both Latin, Syro-Malabar and Syro-Malankara Rites have passed through this Seminary in the six decades or so of its existence. They have worked and have been working in different capacities in numerous parishes, schools,

1269 Pius Geisel to the Superior General (Poona, January 1955), ARSI, *Poona. 1005-IV,* 5.

1270 Pius Geisel, V. Provincial, "Elenchus Visitationis: Seminario Pontificio, Poonensis (21st - 24th July 1957)," ARSI, *Poona. 1005-XI,* 4.

1271 See Georg Evers, *Kirche und Katholizismus seit 1945, Vol., 5: Die Lander Asiens* (Paderborn/Municr/Vienna/Zurich: Ferdinand Schoningh, 2003), 361.

social work and health-care centres, mission stations and many other such establishments. The combined impact of the contribution of such a big number of priests having received their training at this Seminary is not a simple thing to be discarded.[1272]

7.5. The Indian Institute of Social Order, Poona

The Indian Institute of Social Order which was later renamed as Indian Social Institute[1273] was "founded in January 1951 under the instructions from the Very Reverend Father General of the Society of Jesus as a work common to all the Jesuit Missions of India, in order to disseminate Catholic social doctrine and promote social service and social reform in India in accordance with the teaching of the Catholic Church."[1274] Thus, this venture did not belong to the Poona Mission alone. But in the absence of a central overseeing body of the Jesuits like present-day Jesuit Conference of South Asian Assistancy (JCSA), it fell within the jurisdiction of the Poona Mission for all practical purposes of administration.[1275] The topic has been included here precisely for the reason that the initiative originated in Poona and that the Poona Jesuits played not an insignificant role in its infancy and growth, at least in the first decade of its existence.

7.5.1. The Context and the Need

At the dawn of the independence of the nation, one of the major concerns of the Jesuits, as indicated earlier in the chapter, was to safeguard the Catholics as well as others, especially the poor, from the onslaught of the ideology of communism. For, the danger appeared all the more realistic as the Jesuits in the West were preoccupied with this concern in the decades subsequent to WWII.[1276] From some of the correspondences it may be concluded that the above-mentioned concern was one of the

1272 See, "Das Neue Papstliche Zentralseminar Indiens," *IB* 1 (1958): 4-5.

1273 See Jerome D'souza to the Superior General (Poona, 1.12.1952), *ARSI, Poona 1403: Indian Institute of Social Order 1952-1953.*

1274 Jerome D'Souza to Mr. Michael Cudahy, Patrick & Anna W. Cudahy Fund, (Poona, 31st January 1956), ARSI, *Poona. IX,* 19. The copies of this application were submitted to two other funding agencies, besides a copy submitted to the Superior General of the Order. See also Pius Geisel to the Superior General (Poona, 1st January 1952), ARSI, *Belgaum-Poona. 1301 [1950-1959].*

1275 "Blitzlichter: Indisches Institut Filr Soziale Ordnung," *IB* 2 (March-April 1951): 22.

1276 See Christopher Hollis, *A History of the Jesuits* (London: Weidenfeld and Nicolson, 1968), 244.

immediate contexts that necessitated the initiation of an institute of such a nature, which would promote social consciousness among the Catholics in particular, though not exclusively.

The additional reason that played a role in this regard was the perception among the educated Catholics, Jesuits included, "that India's Christian communities as a whole were not enthusiastic about the freedom movement in its earlier phase."[1277] The time had come, therefore, to make it up creatively for the same, at least by way of contributing towards cultivating social consciousness among the people.

Against such a background the need was felt of an institute that would provide a forum for a creative response to the emerging situations of the post-Independent India. The Superiors of the Missions in India, deeply aware of the worth of the kind of contribution the Jesuits could make through the instrumentality of an institute, were prompt in responding to the call. As a leading figure in the implementation of this pioneering enterprise, Jerome D'Souza played a decisive role. In his view an institute of such nature would have both an immediate as well as remote objectives. Hence, he situated the need of the institute in a larger framework that would facilitate a space for the Catholic community both in national and international scenario. He wrote: "Modest as our work is, it has, we believe, its own part to play in the preservation of freedom in India and in the Southeast Asian area and therefore in the maintenance of the world peace."[1278] He further argued that the freedom of a country is not a once-for-all reality. Therefore, it has to be nurtured, safe-guarded and preserved. That would be possible when the people of the country grow in their societal and communitarian commitments. Moreover, the sense of freedom would percolate down to every member of the society only when a spirit of societal responsibility is cultivated in the collective conscience of the people.[1279] At a very pragmatic level a beginning, according to him, in this direction was to be made, through greater participation in the implementation of the schemes introduced by the Government:

> The need for this kind of work in India is very great. The achievement of political independence and the introduction of democratic

1277 Fernando & Gispert-Sauch, *Christianity in India,* 243.

1278 Jerome D'Souza to Mr. Michael Cudahy, Patrick & Anna W. Cudahy Fund, op.cit.

1279 Ibid.

> Government with universal adult suffrage have done much for the people of India most of whom are poor and backward in many ways. It was a matter of urgency to stabilize this freedom by giving to the masses a greater degree of well-being and contentment and prevent the spread of subversive doctrines which might lead to more violent revolution. The Government of India have inaugurated a vast scheme of social and economic reform. This programme is for the greater part entirely in harmony with Catholic teaching. It was therefore necessary for the Church in India to contribute her share to this work of social and economic reform both by teaching and by practical work. The Indian Institute of Social Order was founded with this intent.[1280]

Albert Lallemand saw the need of the institute in terms of creating a structure for countering the ideological currents posing a danger to the Catholics as well as others. A letter by him highlights the above aspect well:

> The reasons particular to India which militate for social apostolate appear clearer than ever. First the relative paucity of Catholics in the national movement should be made up by a greater sharing in the social movement. Also a decided countering of communism must be made before the 1955-56 elections. Consequently priority should be given to stirring clergy and laity; talks and retreats to priests and seminarians might be directed to their heart-conversion towards social apostolate.[1281]

From the correspondences, it becomes apparent that the above-mentioned concern of countering the impact of communism, especially among the poor working class, was one of the primary motives for the founding of the Institute. To the consolation of the Jesuits, however, the impact of the same on the poor working class seems to have been less pervasive than on the other groups of people, as Albert Lallemand further reports: "In my view, communism is not making much headway among workmen; the danger is rather among the educated middle class

1280 Ibid.

1281 Albert Lallemand to the Superior General (Poona, 21st November 1953), ARSI, Poona. 1005-III, 13.

who have no job and want a change and feel like leading the workers to suit their plan."[1282] In another correspondence he adds:

> Personally I consider that the most urgent work in the near future should be to develop social mindedness in clergy and laity; a definite argument is the absolute need of anti-communist propaganda which must be developed before elections which will take place all over India in December 1955 - February 1956 and which may prove decisive for the future of the country and missions. The institute must play a part in such a propaganda.[1283]

In conclusion it may be stated that the immediate context for the foundation of the Institute was the emerging socio-economic and political situation in the post-Independent India. And the need apparently was to create a platform for research and action-based response in order to counter the ideologies like communism that had the potentiality of victimizing the poor working class of India, by spreading the Social Doctrine of the Catholic Church.

7.5.2. Vision, Aims and Objectives

The objective of the institute, at its foundation, was to render a "response to the emerging social order of an Independent India,"[1284] as noted above. Stated otherwise, the Institute was founded as a research centre to provide an ideological base for the task of social transformation. It was clearly articulated by the then Superior General of the Society of the Jesus: "The institute should be founded for the serious study of the Indian social situation in all its aspects."[1285] Hence it was unambiguous already at this stage that the Institute was deemed as a "Central Institute ... not intended [primarily] to do intensive social work in the city of Poona but to study and write and help to organize social action all over India."[1286] As for the basic option and orientation, the research was intended to be

1282 Albert Lallemand to Felix A. Plattner (Poona, 24th September 1953), AJMSZ, *41-Puna-Stadt Briefe.*

1283 Albert Lallemand to the Superior General (Poona, 12th January 1954), ARSI, *Poona. 1005-III,* 15.

1284 "Indian Social Institute: A Historical Perspective", *Indian Social Institute, New Delhi: Annual Report 2011-2012* (New Delhi: Indian Social Institute, 2012), 11.

1285 As quoted in "Indian Social Institute, New Delhi", *Indian Social Institute, New Delhi: Annual Report 2013-2014* (New Delhi: Indian Social Institute, 2014), 32.

1286 Jerome D'Souza to the Superior General (Poona, 8thJuly 1952), ARSI, *Negotia Specialia 1403-Indian Institute of Social Order (1952-9153).*

focused especially in the field of training, advocacy, social-justice and protection of human rights related to the marginalized groups, i.e., the Scheduled Tribes, Dalits, Minorities, unorganized labourers, women, children and the like.[1287]

By the end of the second year of its foundation, however, the institute realized that its sphere of operation needed to go beyond the writing tables. Consequently, it began to involve itself more directly with certain concrete social issues, which initially were focused "on charitable social works, reliefs and other such aids. With the changing times, it gradually began to accommodate development-related activities, awareness building programmes, empowerment of the weaker sections of people."[1288] The objective was further expanded to embrace various movements for human rights, social justice and equality in order that the weaker strata of the society might be empowered.[1289]

Although our focus is restricted to the first decade of the existence of the institute, it may be pointed out that its objective has often been restated and more sharply articulated in order to incorporate the emerging concerns of the wider society in its journey of some six decades. For, it is only through such a process that it discovers the relevance and meaning of its existence.[1290] The objective of the same in the present form, for instance, is expressed most comprehensively in terms of its vision and mission:

> [The] vision [of the institute is] to build a just, humane, secular, democratic and inclusive Indian society wherein the poor and marginalized communities cherish equality, dignity, freedom, justice, peace and harmony. [And the mission] is to engage in social transformation through socially relevant research, training, publication and advocacy works aimed at integral development of the marginalized communities, particularly the Dalits, Adivasis/ Tribals, women, minorities, unorganized and landless labourers in partnership with academicians, people's movements, human

---

1287 "From the Executive Director's Desk", *Indian Social Institute, New Delhi: Annual Report 2011-2012,* 3-4.

1288 "**Indian** Social Institute: A Historical Perspective", Ibid. 11.

1289 Ibid., 13.

1290 Ibid., 11.

rights organizations and ecological movements nationally and internationally.[1291]

In summary, it may be stated that "in the first decade, till [the early] 1960s, the focus was on spreading social doctrine of the Church"[1292] not only among the Catholics but also among the people of other faiths, especially among the educated masses. In the larger national scenario the objective was intended to have a wider implication. In the words of Jerome D'Souza: "Modest as our work is, it has, we believe, its own part to play in the preservation of freedom in India and in the Southeast Asian area and therefore in the maintenance of world peace."[1293]

7.5.3. Programmes and Activities

Right from its inception, various programmes and activities were planned and implemented by the Institute in order to achieve its objectives. During this first decade, for example, the Institute started implementing its vision. One of its first endeavors was to establish training centers in various parts of the country, imparting both theoretical and practical knowledge. "In the course of 1956 [for example] the members were able to help the courses of social sciences given at Loyola College, Madras, the Xavier Institute [of Labour Relations] at Jamshedpur, the Xavier Institute [of Social Sciences] of Ranchi [and] the [Xavier Institute of] Labour Relations at Bombay."[1294] These centers were visualized as training centres for professional social workers in their respective areas, which in turn responded to the demands from the field for greater professionalism needed for the many local development projects of those days, sponsored by a growing number of Development Agencies across the country.[1295] Apparently, these were just in the initial phase of implementation. In the words of Jerome D'Souza, "there are two types of courses sponsored by the Institute - courses in Social Service and

1291 *Indian Social Institute New Delhi: Annual Report 2014-2015* (New Delhi: Indian Social Institute, 2015), 6.

1292 "Indian Social Institute, New Delhi", *Indian Social Institute, New Delhi: Annual Report 2013-2014,* 32.

1293 Jerome D'Souza to Mr. Michael Cudahy, Patrick & Anna W. Cudahy Fund, op. cit.

1294 Albert Lallemand to the Superior General (Poona, 26th January 1957), ARSI, *Poona. 1005-XII,* 11.

1295 See, Albert Lallemand to the Superior General (Poona, 15th May 1956), ARSI, *Poona. 1005-IX,* 23.

Labour Relations. The greater numbers are, however, Social Service Courses."[1296]

It may be noted that there were two categories of members divided on the basis of two strands of approaches at the Institute: those supporting the idea of reaching out to the wider civil society through courses on social service and the other restricting the sphere primarily to the Catholic community. As noted above, Albert Lallemand, for instance, believed that priority should be given to train the clergy so that they might be motivated towards social services.[1297] His idea, thus, was to prepare the leaders in this area. In fact he took up the task upon himself to this effect and "organized a study camp for the theologians of De Nobili [College] and conducted two seminars for the theologians and philosophers of De Nobili and Papal Seminary."[1298]

Among the immediate endeavours of the Institute were the works in collaboration with the "Medical Guild, Nurses Association, Association of Catholic Defence Workers, Social Welfare Centre, etc."[1299] At the wider level various other programmes were organized in view of reaching out to more and more members of the Catholic community. Lallemand has the following report in this regard:

> In the same line the plan of securing the services of Fr. E[dward] De Meulder of the Ranchi Vice-Province is at last taken in hand; it is hoped that the Vice-Provincial will be prevailed upon to give the Father ample time to fostering the National Community Projects among Catholics especially.[1300]

In spite of the number of personnel in the Institute being limited, efforts were made to enlarge its sphere of action, so that every section of the Catholic community may be embraced. In view of inculcating the spirit of social-mindedness among the younger generations, for instance, various plans were visualized:

> By way of fostering the spirit of social service among High School boys, it looks preferable to set up Social Service Leagues, for

1296 Jerome D'Souza, "Diplomas of the Social Institute: Two Press Notes of the Government of India", ARSI, *Poona. 1005-IX,* 26.

1297 Albert Lallemand to the Superior General (Poona, 21st November 1953), ARSI, *Poona. 1005-III,* 13.

1298 Ibid., (Poona, 26th January 1957), ARSI, *Poona. 1005-XII,* 11.

1299 Ibid.

1300 Ibid., (Poona, 21st November 1953), op. cit.

> instance, Sodality Sections, Junior St. Vincent de Paul Societies, or more general similar associations that would devote a few hours of the weekly holiday-time to visit, and assist the poor, clean slums, distribute clothes, etc.[1301]

The Institute's domain of programmes and activities also included the hierarchy of the Catholic Church in India which is represented at the highest level by Catholic Bishops' Conference of India (CBCI). The Institute stood at the service of the CBCI to organize social conferences, "lecturing on specialized subjects in the field"[1302] and helping promote social work in all the dioceses of India. In this regard we read in a letter:

> Among the most recent activities of the institute, one must single out that under the direction of H. E. Dr. Attipetty, Secretary of the Social Section of the Bishops' Conference convened a Catholic Social Conference at Madras during the week following Christmas. It was attended by Frs. Clump, Fonseca and Rodrigues and by some 200 Catholics ...."[1303]

Besides the above-mentioned programmes, the Institute also facilitated the starting of Faculties of Social Service and Industrial Relations in several university Colleges and Institutions in India and gave to those Faculties assistance in teaching and issued diplomas to successful candidates.[1304]

> In order to expand its horizon of influence, the Indian Social Institute planned to work for the Indian students in foreign universities, especially in Europe and America. A threefold objective was envisioned as imperative in this regard: " 1) To give Catholic students facilities for study, recreation and social contacts which would preserve their faith and prevent them from falling into undesirable circles; 2) To do the same, in so far as it is possible, for non-Catholic students also. Far from the Indian environment, some of them might even be converted; 3) To contact University authorities and Foundations to secure for Catholic students in India

1301 Ibid., (Poona, 7th May 1957), ARSI, *Poona. 1005-XII,* 12.

1302 Aloysius Fonseca to the Superior General (Poona, 9th July 1957), ARSI, *Poona. 1005-XII,* 14.

1303 Albert Lallemand, Ex Officio: Social Institute, Poona (25th February 1958), ARSI, *Belgaum-Poona. 1006.*

1304 Jerome D'Souza to Mr. Michael Cudahy, Patrick & Anna W. Cudahy Fund, op.cit.

scholarships and admissions into universities."[1305] This initiative was being thought of because "many Catholic students [seem to] have lost their faith during their study in England, and the morals of some others are in grave danger."[1306]

While expanding its horizons, vision and mission with the passing decades, the Institute has been faithful to the above-stated aims and objectives. The institute, thus, has proved to be a force in the field of social service. In its approach, it has always sided with the underprivileged sections of society, especially women, Scheduled Castes, Scheduled Tribes and the poor in general. The programmes carried on in close association with activists and social scientists through seminars, workshops and various other activities make the entire exercise more experience-based. The Institute has been trying to maintain a dynamic correlation between research and action ever since its inception.[1307]

7.5.4. A Brief Assessment of its Achievements

The growth of the institute may be assessed from the fact that already by the end of the first five years it could achieve a certain degree of success, especially in terms of publications, i.e., Albert Nevett's Are we too Many?,[1308] in addition to the monthly journal Social Action. The publications were well received, especially the Social Action, as it is revealed by Pius Geisel while he makes a suggestion to search for further avenues for its distribution: "Your Review 'Social Action' is of a high standard and favourably received. To increase its influence, especially on non-Catholics, it appears, that the size should be increased and a wider circle of contributors be secured. More propaganda is advisable."[1309] He further adds that "the establishment of Social Courses in colleges, of a Labour Relations school in two places is no mean achievement."[1310]

1305 Jerome D'Souza, "Care of Asian Students in Europe and America" (Memorandum submitted to the Superior General) ARSI, *Poona. 1005-IX,* 20.

1306 Ibid.

1307 "Indian Social Institute: Checklist 2014," *Indian Social Institute, New Delhi: Annual Report 2013-2014,* 32.

1308 Jerome D'Souza to the Superior General (Poona, 8th July 1952), ARSI, *Negotia Specialia 1403 - Indian Institute of Social Order.* It was the first important publication of the institute.

1309 Pius Geisel to the Members, Indian Social Institute, Poona (Annex rel. vis. Soc), ARSI, *Poona. 1005-11,* 28.

1310 Ibid.

In general it would appear that the Institute was gradually making its mark not only in the ecclesiastical circles, but outside as well. Jerome D'Souza described the same as follows:

> The work of the Institute is appreciated both by the Church and the State. The Government of India sends us their publications, use our textbooks in different Colleges we may help prepare the personnel for some of the Schemes of the Five Year Plans of India. I have been appointed a Member of the Advisory Committee for Public Cooperation with the 'Five Year Plan of which the Prime Minister of India is the Chairman.[1311]

From the perspective of some expert laymen too, the Institute was a pioneering initiative as far as the Catholic Church in India was concerned. But it needed to expand the sphere of its engagement in certain vital aspects, like making an endeavour towards economic uplift in India. J. C. Ryan articulates the same in the following words:

> In India, in the social sphere, ecclesiastical and lay apostolate has generally been confined to charitable and educational work. While it cannot be denied that the running of schools and colleges, hospitals and dispensaries, and organizations such as the Vincent de Paul Society have immense value and are widely appreciated by Catholics and non-Catholics, there is another sphere in which very little has been done: this is the economic sphere ... So far as Catholics are concerned, although here and there an enthusiastic parish priest has devoted himself to the material uplift of his flock ... by and large, the work turned out in the economic sphere has been precious little. In any case, there is no single Catholic institution devoted exclusively to this task with a view to initiating and organizing widespread effort for the uplift of the masses of the country ... Economic backwardness often leads to neglect of religious duties, and what is worse, opens the door for communism ... It is, therefore, appropriate that in India, where communism has penetrated even to the extent of snatching away ... the Government of the State of Kerala, it will not do for the Catholic Church to leave the material improvement of its flock and its prospective adherents to the individual effort... This has to be taken up on an institutional basis, launched with vigour ... The only institution that can be thought of for the purpose is the Indian Social Institute at Poona. So

1311 Jerome D'Souza to Mr. Michael Cudahy, Patrick & Anna W. Cudahy Fund, op. cit.

> far it has done much useful work in the direction of research. Social problems are being investigated by it continuously ... It has only to spread out a little more in order to step beyond the academic realm and get into the practical field.[1312]

From a majority of correspondences in our possession, one tends to get a positive picture of its growth and achievements, yet the Institute was not without criticism. A letter from Pius Geisel as Vice-Provincial reveals an alternative perception of the entire enterprise:

> It has already been existing for several years with capable men and a lot of money sacrificed to its work, yet it is scarcely known except among priests and in a few centers and its influence is practical nil. It publishes one small periodical, which, if my impression of conversation with people and priests I meet is correct, is very little read because it is not attractive enough. One very rarely comes across articles of the Social Institute in any other paper. I feel that a lot of writing, attractive enough for the common man to take up is required for people in general to come to know the Catholic point of view of social principles and practices. Besides each member of the Institute has his own opinion as to the purpose of the Institute and the means it should adopt towards its end. Unless there can be complete unity here the Institute consists of a number of members each working along his own line, united merely by living in the same house and contributing towards the same periodical.[1313]

The text underlines a few important aspects and calls for an objective assessment of the same. The reader might be tempted to raise the question: Why such a diversity of perception on the institute? A reason for the same may be that these correspondences mostly originate from the insiders to the Institute. On the other hand it may also be said that Pius Geisel may have been too critical of its achievements, probably due to the personal issues with Jerome D'Souza as has been pointed out earlier. But a few aspects seem to have been valid, i.e., lack of teamwork and lack of common perception on the objective of the Institute.

In the chain of correspondences, even the Superior General seems to have been critical of the functioning of the institute, especially with

1312 J. C. Ryan, "Co-Operative Extension Service under the Indian Social Institute at Poona", ARSI, *Belgaum-Poona: Ex Officio (1960).*

1313 William Clement, "Ex Officio: St. Vincent's School, Poona", (15th February 1958), ARSI, *Belgaum-Poona. 1006.*

regard to the fundamental purpose of the Institute, namely to engage in serious research, study and publication. In this regard, the case of Aloysius Fonseca highlights the issue well as he tenders a clarification to the Superior General:

> He felt that I should send you this information all the more so as you had written to Fr. Lallemand to warn me that I should not forget the main purpose of the Institute which was to study ... In India there are very few books on the Labour Movement and Trade Unionism, most of the information has to be obtained by actually interviewing the people concerned ... Although I may have known something about the workers' situation in India before I joined the team, I think I learned quite a lot... Normally it is not easy to obtain such information. The books and statistics on the subject are extremely few ... Therefore there is great possibility for research even by our Institute into these various matters ... But this kind of work requires active contact with the situation as it is in reality. I don't know how one could do this by sitting and reading or studying in one's room. And that is the reason why I was surprised to receive your warning from Fr. Lallemand. Honestly I do not see what better method there could be to know the real situation in India first hand than by visiting the various centres and gathering information for oneself.[1314]

From the content of the above-cited letter, one tends to get the impression that the Superior General may have been misinformed on certain aspects of the Institute. While reading the letter in the context of its entirety, Aloysius Fonseca seems to have been justified in his approach:

> It may be Your Paternity has the European or American situation in mind where there is plenty of literature on the social situation. But here in India there is a great dearth of such material. Much research work will have to be undertaken and many books written before we can have a fairly satisfactory picture of the Indian Social background ...Certainly the Institute could do a great work in putting out a first class review and writing books on Indian social conditions. But this means a lot of spade work in the field itself.[1315]

1314 Aloysius Fonseca to the Superior General (Poona, 9th July 1957), ARSI, *Poona. 1005-XII*, 14.

1315 Ibid.

In general, we notice that the Institute, in spite of the constant crunch of personnel and finance, was making a gradual progress. Apparently, there were ever-growing demands for adaptation to the new situations endeavouring thereby to address the emerging issues. The varying views on its growth are an indication of the need for constant introspection in order to make the Institute relevant to emerging situations.

As a tangible sign of the progress of the Institute, the publication of "Social Action" might be cited. After the initial criticisms, it improved in both quality and quantity. The Diploma Courses offered by the Institute appear to have become more popular by the end of the decade. Although, the focus was invariably on research and study, in spite of the severe crunch of books, there seems to have no clarity on the method of the same. Hence a further focus on the issue was imperative.[1316]

From the foregoing discussion, it may be concluded that the Institute was a pioneering endeavour. Needless to state that the relevance of such an endeavour was immense in the context of post-Independent India. Apparently, it was imperative to make repeated course corrections along the path to its progress. But the initiative had been launched with boldness and spirit of perseverance against all odds.

An aspect, however, that demands clarification at this stage is: what was the specific role of the Jesuits of the Poona Mission in the initiation and development of the Institute, as it was deemed as a common enterprise of the Jesuit Missions in India? The answer to the question is that Poona Mission shouldered the responsibility for establishing these ventures in the early stages by making personnel and financial resources available. Moreover, the organization of various groups, i.e., Vincent de Paul Society, Social Service Leagues, Sodalities, etc., in the city of Poona in order to disseminate the vision of the Institute was solely possible due to the active participation of the Jesuits of Poona. Their commitment to the spirit of social service finally fructified in a unique enterprise called Watershed Programme which was initiated in Ahmednagar District (1961), once the Indian Social Institute was shifted to New Delhi.

7.6. Conclusion

By way of conclusion it may be said that both De Nobili College and Papal Seminary established by the Poona Jesuits at the national

1316 See, "Report of the Social Institute, Poona: November 1960", op.cit.

level, developed into huge institutions over the years and have made significant contributions to the Church in India, in offering philosophical, theological, priestly and spirituality training not only to Jesuits, but also to secular clergy, men and women religious and lay persons. So also, as we noted above, the Jesuit-run national institute, the Indian Social Institute, now located in New Delhi, which emerged from the Indian Institute of Social Order founded by the Poona Jesuits for intellectual and social ministry has made significant contributions at the national level. Credit also goes to another Poona Jesuit who later founded in 1963 a similar Indian Social Institute at Bangalore. All these institutes are presently common concerns of all the 20 Jesuit Provinces/Missions in South Asia. But the burdens of the birth pang and of the responsibility for nurturing from infancy to maturity of these institutions were borne by the Poona Mission.

Chapter-8

Some Moot-Points and Contemporary Contentious Issues

8.1. Introduction

At the outset, it may be apt to clarify what is meant by a moot-point here. In some of the sources in our possession we frequently come across with certain questions and issues, such as social status of the new converts, comparatively lesser success in winning over converts from high caste Hindus, native vocations to the Society of Jesus, constraints of moral and religious instruction in the Jesuit schools, missionary venture among non-Christians and a few other issues that seem to have been looked at either with conflicting perspectives or not addressed adequately. Such issues need further probing and evaluation in the light of the broader framework of the socio-cultural and politico-economic context of the mission field. The danger lies when these aspects are ignored or side-lined and simplistic conclusions are drawn based on arbitrary or insufficient choice of instances. As a viable and objective approach in dealing with these issues, we shall place them as moot-points or contentious issues and try to understand these against a broader framework of the contemporary context. Every decision is ultimately conditioned by the prevailing contexts. After all, the Jesuits too were products of their own culture and time.[1317]

1317 See Fidelis de Sa, *Crisis in Chota Nagpur* (Bangalore: Redemptorist Publications, 1999), 135-136.

In the following paragraphs, we shall choose some of the more significant issues having a rather representative character. Some of the issues that we shall take up for discussion have already been touched upon by certain authors. Yet, due to the relevance to the topic of this study we shall try to make a more objective assessment of the same in the light of a few more sources in our possession.

8.2. Conversion: Caste and Class Factors

Studies on conversion in India have shown that there were larger number of converts from those groups, castes or tribes who were generally marginalized in society. This has been observed across religions. This was also occurring in Christianity in the 19th and 20th centuries. The issue of the new converts to Christianity being mostly from among the people belonging to the lower castes and classes, i.e., Depressed Classes (*Dalits*) from the Hindu society or from various Tribal groups deserves a special consideration in our discussion here.[1318] It may be noted that, "of the roughly 20 million Christians in India about 14 million are of Dalit origin; that is, about 70 percent of all conversions to Christianity have occurred among Dalits."[1319] These figures speak for themselves. At the same time, they raise questions that demand response within the larger framework of the Indian Christian community as a whole. This topic is relevant in our study of the Poona Jesuit Mission, under which conversions took place mostly from the subaltern classes: the *Mahars, Mangs, Bhils* and similar smaller caste groups. In the entire history of Jesuit missions elsewhere too, it was from among the lower castes of the Hindu society that the Jesuits won the biggest number of converts. The natural questions that arise are: Were efforts not made to reach out to the higher castes? Why did the new converts come mostly from among the lower caste people?

To begin with the first question, a few facts may be stated. Firstly, it may not be irrelevant to point out that conversions from among the higher caste Hindus to Christianity--both Catholicism and Protestantism -- in general have been negligible in Maharashtra and for that matter in entire India. Leaving aside the distant past, if we take a bird's eye-

---

1318 See Kanjamala, *Future of Christian Missions*, 169. Observers outside India, i.e., Joseph Schmidlin in Munster, perceived that hardships to convert the Hindus in general as failure of the missions. See Bose, "Die katholischen Missionen,"op. cit.

1319 Fernando et al., *Journeys to Freedom: Dalit Narratives*, 69.

view on the history of Christianity in India from the beginning of the 19th century, it can be seen that this phenomenon has been consistent. The Missionary Societies, both Catholic and Protestant, who arrived in the State of Maharashtra (erstwhile Bombay Presidency during the British Rule) from around the second decade of the nineteenth century onwards, invariably made their first efforts to reach out to the urban societies (which generally comprised of higher caste Hindus and others), with explicit aims of winning over converts from among them. Such an orientation prevalent in these Missionary Societies is evident from the fact that at their arrival the missionaries settled first in towns and cities. Moreover, it is generally admitted that their first target of evangelization were Brahmins.[1320] "The rationale behind this was that if the Brahmins would follow Christ, then other castes would follow suit."[1321] In other words it was hoped that a trickling down effect would eventually follow. However, the results of these efforts did not bear much fruit. The Brahmins proved to be too resilient to the message of the Gospel. Virtually, therefore, we do not come across with any instance of a Brahmin being baptized by the Jesuits of Bombay-Poona during the period of our study. The same has been true in the case of other high caste Hindus in Maaharashta.

A brief excursus on this factor is necessary in order to give a general understanding of this issue. We may refer to Alfons Vath[1322] who argued that one of the foremost reasons for the failure to win converts from among the Brahmins has been the indissolubility of Hindu religion from its customs and cultural aspects. He explains that these aspects—

1320 See Atul Y. Aghamkar, "Christianity among the Mahars of Maharashtra," in *Christianity in India: Search for Liberation and Identity* (Delhi: CMS/ISPCK, 2000), 46; Joseph Thekkedath, *A Short History of Christianity in India* (Bangalore: Kristu Jyoti Publications, 2007), 68.

1321 Ibid., 181. See also Baumann, *Christian Identity and Dalit Religion*, 4.

1322 As Alfons Vath was a long-time missionary in Bombay, his views on the topic may be considered as a representative voice among the Jesuits. He was at the forefront among his contemporaries in dealing with such issues. Some other relevant works on this issue are: *Im Kampfe mit der Zauberwelt des Hinduismus: Upadhyaya Barahmabandhav und das Problem der Uberwindung des hoheren Hinduismus durch das Christentum* (Berlin & Bonn: Ferd. Dummlers Verlag, 1928); "Das Missionsproblem Indiens," (A brochure for private circulation only) AMPSJ, *Alte Artikel*, etc. The latter article comprises 14 pages and presents succinctly the understanding of the challenges faced by the missionaries in their attempts at converting high caste Hindus. The article maintains that the challenges arose mainly on account of the inseparability of religion, customs, caste and culture of the Hindus.

religious belief and culture--form together a formidable, cohesive unit, which is not easy to be broken. In the context of Christianity, such a link is much easier to be broken, though certain cultural elements do tend to be inseparable. The aspect of indissolubility of religion and culture in Hinduism was often incomprehensible to the missionaries in general. Some of them thought that the higher caste Hindus could be converted without interfering with their customs and cultures. In reality, however, such a proposition was a contradiction in terms. For, one could not talk of Hindu religion without at the same time implying its cultural aspects. While seeking to convert the high caste Hindus to Christianity, therefore, the Christian missionaries stood face to face with this reality. Consequently, they tended to have offered two options for converts: firstly, to discard the entire Hindu religio-cultural system and replace the same with the European Christian culture. Theoretically speaking, this may have been a pragmatic solution. At the practical level, however, it was not an easy way out. The collective societal resistance in such a situation was even more difficult to overcome. The basic difficulties facing the Jesuit missionaries may be summarized thus: of entering into the pantheistic world-view of the Hindus and at the same time detaching Christian religion from its European cultural aspects and integrating the same into the Indian culture. As may be imagined, it was certainly not an easy task. Another option was persuasion and coercion, as the Portuguese had done in Goa in the beginning their colonizing efforts. But that was the era of Portuguese colonialism. Hence Christianity began to be perceived as an agent of colonialism. Among the higher caste Hindus, this option was out of question because as religious authorities it was they who gave religious sanction to the hierarchical caste system.[1323]

The act of conversion was seen as breaking the sanctity of the caste. By the same logic a convert was seen as a rebel. Hence, in most cases, a convert was subjected to punishments like ostracization. Often, corporal punishments too were administered on them. All these aspects invariably acted as strong deterrents that hindered conversions to Christianity among the Brahmins. For, a punishment like ostracization was often worse than death.[1324] In effect, thus, "the pressure of the caste

1323 See Alfons Vath, "Das Missionsproblem Indiens," (A brochure for private circulation only) AMPSJ, *Alte Artikel*, 2-6; Neill, *A History of Christianity*, 220-221.

1324 See Vath, "Das Missionsproblem Indiens," 4-6.

system is chiefly responsible for their persistence in adhering,"[1325] to their religion. Against such a background, the only possibility was to make an attempt at converting an entire village or township inhabited by people of similar status in the caste hierarchy. As may be guessed, this option was even more difficult as collective decisions are always more difficult to arrive at than individual decisions. This kind of situation was all the more prevalent in the case of the Brahmins.[1326]

The missionaries seem to have understood that the resultant status of the higher caste Hindus as a consequence of conversion to Christianity was not as big an allurement to them as it could mean to a *Dalit*. For, the act of conversion would imply foregoing the higher status in the caste hierarchy. In other word, the attraction that the Christian faith seemingly offered to the higher castes was much less in comparison with what could imply for the *Dalits*. *That is to say,* the prospect of being freed from the sufferings of life and further possibilities of availing of the promises of the Christian faith were less attractive to the higher caste Hindus than to the *Dalits*. In addition, the sense of superiority of race and pride in their cultural heritage also had an important role to play in their resilience to conversions.[1327] This was the dynamics of what happened in the case of the later efforts at converting the higher caste Hindus. Besides, since there were many lower caste people converting to Christianity, which allows co-mingling of castes within its communities, the resistance of the higher caste Hindus became even more vehement, for they did not want to mingle at any level with the lower caste people. The sense of superiority of caste and race was at stake, they thought.[1328] These reasons partially explain the fact as to why the higher caste Hindus, in spite

---

1325 James M. Thoburn, *The Christian Conquest of India* (Philadelphia: The Westminster Press, 1906), 117.

1326 See Vath, "Das Missionsproblem Indiens," 2-6. See also Bose, "Die katholischen Missionen," op.cit.

1327 See Alfons Vath, "Die Missionsbestrebungen des neueren Hinduismus," (An off-print from *Priester und Mission: Jahrbuch der Unio cleripro Missionibus, Jahrgang 1928*), 23-25, AMPSJ, *Alte Artikel; Vath, Im Kampfe mil der Zauberwelt*, 195. Founded in 1915 in Milan (Italy), *Unio cleripro missionibus* (Missionary Union of the Clergy) was an organization of the diocesan clergy to promote missionary works in foreign countries, which eventually became a pontifical missionary society. See Floyd Keeler, "Could we have a Clerical Missionary Union?," *TER* LXII(1920): 151-152.

1328 See Thuer, "Bericht ttber den Besuch der Poona-Mission," op.cit.

of being the biggest beneficiaries of the schools, health-care facilities, social services, etc., were least inclined towards Christianity.[1329]

A final analysis of the issue, thus, leads us to two important conclusions: firstly, the higher in the caste hierarchy, the lesser the attraction towards Christianity. Secondly, the sense of racial superiority and cultural pride were significant factors in keeping them staunchly faithful to their own religious traditions.

It was against this background that the missionaries, including the Jesuits, began to look for other options. Once it was realized that winning over the higher caste Hindus was a herculean task, they opted to work among more receptive communities like the *Mahars, Mangs* and *Bhils*. In order to answer the question as to why most of the converts came from these groups of people, therefore, it would be apt to point out certain peculiar societal traits as well as other characteristics of these people. Among the groups mentioned here, since the *Mahars* comprised the largest group of converts, we shall take them as a reference point to illustrate the issue. In order to do the same a brief mention of the position of the *Dalits* within the Hindu caste hierarchy would not be out of place. They belong to the lowest stratum in the Hindu caste hierarchy. Traditionally they have been categorized as menial labourers in a village society and have largely been under the yoke of caste oppression from time immemorial. They were mostly treated as untouchables and outcastes. As for their social status in the caste hierarchy, it may be mentioned that a *Mahar* was required to have a black thread either on his wrist or neck so that he could be identified easily by the higher caste Hindus. Such a prescription was made in order to make it easier for a high caste Hindu to keep away from a *Mahar* and thus not risk the danger of being polluted. A *Mahar* was also required to carry a broom strung from his waist to sweep away the dust on which he treaded, lest an upper caste Hindu treading the same path should be polluted. Worse still, he was required to carry an earthern pot hung around his neck wherever he went for holding his spit lest it pollute a Hindu who might unknowingly happen to tread on it. In sum, it may be said that the *Mahars* were among the worst sufferers under caste oppression till the British Rule in India. For the sake of protecting their commercial interest in colonial governance, the British decided to maintain status quo with regard to

1329 See Schatz, "Optionen und missionarische Prioritaten," 395-396.

customs and religions of the subject peoples.[1330] Though the British enacted a few laws to remove caste discrimination to ensure equality of all before the law, and to free the socially and religiously oppressive customs and rites, the situation did not change much in Indian society. Precisely for these reasons, the situation of the *Mahars also* did not change substantially until the independence of India.

This leads to the question regarding the factors that aided the conversion of the *Mahars* and other Depressed Classes to Christianity. Given their historical background some of the conclusions become quite evident. Firstly, since they were victims of caste oppression and subjugation, acceptance of Christianity appeared to offer them a better status in life. This is a common sociological phenomenon, whereby a group of people subjected to a condition of dehumanization for a considerable period of time tend towards something positive. Any opportunity offering a better status of life seems alluring to them. This was what happened in their decision to embrace Christianity.

Secondly, since in most cases, the act of "conversion to another faith was a strategy adopted by Dalits to combat the wretched status accorded to them within Hinduism,"[1331] it may be inferred that the decision of the *Mahars* to convert to Christianity was an act of defiance against the caste oppression. It was an act of detaching themselves from their past history of dehumanization and suffering. The more the cultural distance from the previous one, the more they would experience being freed from the clutches of the past. Hence, a religion of a foreign origin was a better choice. The following observation elaborates the point well:

> Conversion to Christianity, by virtue of Christianity's foreign origin offers, even more than Buddhism [or any other religion of Indian origin], a break with a painful past. It aims at delivering Dalits from the strangleholds of the oppressive discourse of caste and relocating them in another [milieu] where alternative possibilities,

1330 See Vasant Moon, *Dr. Babsaheb Ambedkar, Writings and Speeches*, Vol. 1 (Bombay: Educational Department, Government of Maharashtra, 1979), 38-39. See also Jeewendra Jadhav, *Evangelization as Community Building* (Ahmednagar: Social Centre, 2006), 118-119.

1331 Franco Fernando, Jyotsna Macwan & Saguna Ramanathan, *Journeys to Freedom: Dalit Narratives* (Kolkata: Samya, 2004), 69. See also Vath, "Das Missionsproblem Indiens," 5-6.

material, psychological, social and metaphysical, all open up simultaneously.[1332]

Evidently, the above observation is general in nature. The factors mentioned above did act as stimulus towards the conversion of *Mahars* to Christianity. But there has to be something more fundamental to explain the phenomenon more comprehensively. For this we need to understand the dynamics of group conversion among the *Mahars*. An analysis of the same would show that this has been the most important factor behind their conversion to Christianity. It is a normal phenomenon that an ideology tends to spread more easily in kin groups or social units like families and villages that share common experience. As George G. Hunter maintains that "Christianity spreads most naturally and contagiously within homogeneous population units, and specifically within kinship and friendship networks ..."[1333] Donald A. McGavran states elsewhere that in "the societies ... normal way is to make religious and other decisions to convert as family or larger groups."[1334] What does it mean? In simple terms it may be explained that whenever people face a situation whereby they need to make important decisions, it becomes always easier to do so in common as a social unit. For, as a group they become a unified force to combat the opposing societal pressure. From experience the missionaries had noted that conversions occurred in groups, family lines or kin lines. This was the reason why the missionaries often made attempts to convert the entire village in a particular place.[1335]

It may not be out of place to mention as to how the *Mahars* themselves understood their decision to convert to some other religion. Each *Mahar* as an individual might not have understood the act of conversion with all related ramifications of its meanings as a personal decision. Yet at the collective level, it was perceived as departing from the past, as Fernando, Macwan and Ramanathan have stated: "One of

1332 Franco, Macwan & Ramanathan, *Journeys to Freedom*, 69. See also Vath, "Das Missionsproblem Indiens," 5-6.

1333 George G. Hunter III, "McGavran, Donald Anderson," in *Biographical Dictionary of Christian Missions*, ed. Gerald H. Anderson (Grand Rapids, Ml/Cambridge, U.K.: Wm. B. Eerdmans, 1999), 449.

1334 Donald A. McGavran, *Church Growth Bulletin, Second Consolidated Volume* (September 1969 to July 1975) (South Pasadena: William Carey Library, 1977), 98.

1335 See Vath, "Das Missionsproblem Indiens," 5. See also Bose, "Die katholischen Missionen," op.cit; Thuer, "Bericht liber den Besuch der Poona Mission," op.cit.

the strategies adopted by Dalits to deal with an oppressive history is conversion to another faith that gives them an alternative history.[1336]

As for the motives of the *Mahars* who embraced Catholicism, it remains a matter of curiosity as to what kind of motives they depicted in the initial phase of their decision making. Here below we shall engage with the question of their motives.

8.2.1. The Motives underlying Conversion to Catholicism[1337]

"The subject of motives is always difficult,"[1338] wrote J. Waskom Pickett way back in 1933. He was a Methodist missionary in India for decades and eventually became a Bishop. He had engaged extensively with the study of the phenomenon of group conversions.[1339] In fact his findings have been the basis of many other such studies that followed. One of the common features of many such studies is a general consensus that the inquiry into the religious motives is a difficult area. Daniel Potts' conclusion, in this regard, seems to summarize the issue well, as he writes that "one of the most difficult and indeed insoluble problems connected with a study of missionary enterprise is to determine as to how many of the converts ... were sincere in their resolve to become Christians."[1340] Yet the topic is significant to delve into in some detail.

One of the foremost reasons seems to be their low status in Hindu society. It is a fact that a vast majority of Christians in India have come from the lower castes of Hindu society and other oppressed groups, the *Mahars* being one of them, besides the *Tribals.*[1341] *I*t is true that the phenomenon of group conversion has come under heavy criticism ever since it has come in public discourse. Moreover, the "Criticisms ... are

---

1336 Fernando, Macwan & Ramanathan, *Journeys to Freedom*, 33.

1337 I owe the major points of arguments on this sub-topic to Ankur Barua's *Debating 'Conversion' in Hinduism and Christianity* (London and New York: Routledge, 2015), 83-114.

1338 J. Waskom Pickett, *Christian Mass Movements in India: A Study with Recommendations* (Lucknow: Lucknow Publishing House, 1933), 155.

1339 Since the conversion among the *Mahars* had taken place generally in groups, we have categorized their conversion as a 'mass movement,' or 'group movement.' The authors writing in more recent times prefer to use the latter phrase, namely 'group movement.'

1340 As quoted in Barua, *Debating 'Conversion'*, 90.

1341 John C. B. Webster, "Christian History as Indian Social History: A Review of the Literature," in *Approaches to History: Essays in Indian Historiography*, ed. Sabyasachi Bhattacharya (New Delhi: ICHR & Primus Books, 2011), 186.

so numerous and come from so many and such responsible sources that they cannot be ignored."[1342]

What is the basic point of contention? The most important reason was motive: of both converts and missionaries. While the converts sought some material benefits besides social liberation, the missionaries desired to increase the numerical strength of the their Churches. Group conversions, for example, are seen by some critics as a result of "the desire of shrewd men among the masses to secure some material benefit for themselves."[1343] Precisely due to this perception that such critics have often given a derogatory epithet to the converts, namely 'rice Christians'[1344] or its equivalents. The contention is also "that their [*Dalits* and other such groups] conversion was the product not of a reflective conscious decision on their part but of the exploitation of their poverty and ignorance by the missionaries who had employed deceptive tactics."[1345] In these discourses often a deliberate attempt is made to undermine the very capacity of the converts in making a choice with regard to religion or morals. Consequently, their act of converting to another religion is termed as a result of "fraud, force or inducement."[1346]

In addition to these, the converts had to face one more dilemma at the existential level of the politico-cultural debates in the country. Ever since the emergence of the Hindu cultural nationalist movements a myth of an exponential growth of the Christians in India wa maliciously propagated by some political parties and cultural organizations with fundamentalist ideologies. Interestingly, a good number of Hindus were gripped by a fear psychosis that they would be pushed to the wall once the minority communities like Christians and Muslims grow into majoritarian communities.[1347] The truth, however, is that it was a deliberate attempt to propagate the myth that had no correspondence to the reality. And that did not stop there. In order to put an effective check on the movements of conversion towards Christianity and other

1342 Pickett, *Christian Mass Movements*, 155.

1343 Ibid., 156. See also Richard F. Young, ed., *India and the Indianness of Christianity: Essays on Understanding - Historical, Theological, and Bibliographical - in Honour of Robert Eric Frykenberg* (Grand Rapids, MI: Wm. B. Eerdmans, 2009), 219.

1344 Pickett, *Christian Mass Movements*, 155.

1345 Barua, *Debating Conversion*', 90.

1346 As quoted in Chad M. Baumann, *Christian Identity and Dalit Religion in Hindu India, 1868-1947* (Grand Rapids, MI/Cambridge, UK: William B. Eerdmans, 2008), 16.

1347 See Barua, *Debating 'Conversion*, 90.

religions, the converted members were termed as 'anti-nationals' or 'denationalized' people, with a provocative slogan: 'change of religion is a change of nation.'[1348] What is even more curious to note was that the earlier cases of conversions too were being projected as invalid by depicting them as the results of trickery exercised on the converts by Christian missionaries.

These oppositions and criticisms from the Hindu intelligentsia and other right wing organizations apart, group movements of conversion have come under heavy criticism also from other quarters as well, whereby "many critics of mass movements, East and West, both Christians and non-Christians, appear to believe that unworthy motives predominate in making the masses therein move to a profession of Christian faith, and also in making ministers receive them into their churches."[1349] To put it in plain terms, any form of material aid extended by the missionaries to the potential converts, irrespective of their context is interpreted by the opponents of the movements as "baits,"[1350] to use Ankur Barua's expression. These are not limited to the level of political rhetoric. In fact in the academic circles too such perceptions are wide-spread. Fernando and Gispert-Sauch summarize a common line of perception of the same as follows:

> Modern writers on the conversion movements to other religions tend to see *Dalits* as victims of society, without a spiritual tradition of their own. According to them, *Dalits* just accepted the religions of those who came to them with money or power or more education for their children; presumably *Dalits* could only have converted through bribes or force or deceit.[1351]

The above observations seem to represent the views of a large number of critics in India and elsewhere. In fact some of the most prominent non-Christian figures like Mahatma Gandhi and Madan Mohan Malviya[1352] too have been unambiguous in their criticism of any

1348 Ibid., 1-2.

1349 Pickett, *Christian Mass Movements*, 155.

1350 Barua, *Debating 'Conversion,'* 93.

1351 Fernando & Gispert-Sauch, *Christianity in India*, 180.

1352 A contemporary of Mahatma Gandhi, a freedom fighter, educationist and four-time President of Indian National Congress with right-wing ideological bent, Madan Mohan Malviya was an eminent personality in Indian politics. See Chandrika P. Sharma, *Mahamana Pandit Madan Mohan Malviya* (Delhi: Parmeshwari Prakashan, 2007), 9-15.

group movement towards conversion and have held the motive behind the same as "entirely secular and mostly unworthy."[1353] In fact "Mahatma Gandhi ... was a persistent critic of conversion. Although he had many friends among the missionaries in India, Gandhi repeatedly urged them to abandon their evangelistic efforts intended to convert Hindus into Christians."[1354] He went a step further to term the evangelical efforts of the Christian missionaries as "anti-national"[1355] activities.

It would be impossible to summarize the entire gamut of implications of Gandhi's views on conversion. In gist, it may be said that he was unequivocal in denouncing 'the movements of conversions in groups,' especially those taking place among the lower caste Hindus, and termed it as an artificial change of religious allegiance. One of the underlying assumptions that dictated his judgment on the issue was: the "*Dalits*, because of their social and educational status, are not capable of making a proper judgment on matters such as the choice of religion or morals." This claim may be illustrated by an incident. On 1st March 1929, on being questioned about his views on group conversions among the *Dalits* and *Tribals* by John R. Mott, an American evangelist, Gandhi replied: "I distrust mass movements of this nature. They have as their object not the upliftment of the untouchables, but their ultimate conversion. This motive of mass proselytization lurking at the back in my opinion vitiates missionary effort."[1356] Thus in his opinion, their conversion was nothing more than a change of allegiance to another religion without going through internal transformation. Sitaram Goyal,[1357] although with a clear apologetic bent, has made a survey of the encounters of Gandhi with Christianity from his student days in South Africa (1890s) until his death in 1948. He has shown Gandhi as progressively opposing Christian missionary activities in India with ever sharper criticisms, with each passing decade.[1358] To present his position better known in the public domain, finally Gandhi dealt the issue extensively in his book, *Christian*

1353 Picket, *Christian Mass Movements*, 156.

1354 Gerald R. McDermott & Harold A. Netland, *A Trinitarian Theology of Religions: An Evangelical Proposal* (New York: Oxford University Press, 2014), 163.

1355 Baumann, *Christian Identity and Dalit Religion,* 1.

1356 As quoted in Sita Ram Goyal, *History of Hindu-Christian Encounters (AD 304 to 1996)* (New Delhi: Voice of India, 1996, second revised edition), 155.

1357 He represents the new generation of Hindu intelligentsia strongly supporting the idea of cultural nationalism among the Hindus.

1358 See Goyal, *History of Hindu-Christian Encounters*, 124-239.

Missions: Their Place in India (1941) and remained undaunted in his position until his death.[1359]

An additional brief comment on Gandhi's views on group conversions is in order here. It is clear that he seems to have understood the term 'conversion' purely in terms of an esoteric choice of a new path by an individual as a result of a long process of reflection. Apparently his position cannot be disputed. Yet it is also true that the history of conversion movements has witnessed not only individual conversions, but also and mostly group conversions. Hence taking the individual conversions alone as true conversions is flawed in its basic premise.

Since the conversion of *Mahars* falls under the category of group conversion or "people movement"[1360] as noted above, the voice of protest by Gandhi may be taken as a representative one from among the Hindu intelligentsia. From his tone and consistency of arguments in denouncing the movements of conversion, the intensity of resentment brewing among the right wing Hindus is not hard to imagine. It may be clarified, however, that the criticisms against group conversions often spring from the fact that the phenomenon is sought to be explained bereft of the socio-cultural peculiarities and constraints of the *Dalits*.

In order to understand the issue with respect to the *Mahars* a little deeper, we need to rely upon the limited sources at hand, which apparently may not give a clear picture. Yet, one can arrive at the conclusion, with a fair amount of certainty, that their initial motives behind embracing Catholicism were not purely spiritual. Drawing from the available instances, they clearly seem to fall under the group of people who took this step with mixed motives, "including the hope for temporal advantages and social security."[1361] Here below, we shall take three instances from the experiences of the Jesuits from this mission field, in order to make an objective assessment. The first one pertains to the sudden and sharp increase in the membership of the Catholic Church

1359 See Harold Coward, ed., *Indian Critiques of Gandhi* (Albany, NY: State University of New York Press, 2003), 169.

1360 Donald a. McGavran, "The People Movement Point of View," in *Church Growth and Group Conversion*, Fifth Edition, ed. Donald A. McGavran (Pasadena, California: William Carey Library, 1973), 1.

1361 Barua, Debating 'Conversion, *90*.

at the mission station at Sangamner in the event of famines and other such natural calamities, as may be read in a report:

> For the time-period from 1st July 1936 to 1st July 1937, the following figures are available: Baptism in all 474. Of them 21 were baptized at the death-bed, 107 children from Catholic parents, so that 348 are purely won over from paganism, the instance of an increase in numbers which since 1902 has been achieved only once during the famine years of 1918/19 and that too from the undivided Sangamner-Songaon mission station ... Now the total number of the Catholics who belong to this mission station is 3921. That means: ever since 1929 when Songaon was bifurcated from Sangamner, the number has been doubled and many more are waiting with a great yearning at our door.[1362]

It may be recalled that 1918, 1919, 1936 and 1937 were the famine years in Ahmednagar district.[1363] The statistics given above, thus, give a clear indication that the events of natural calamities often signalized a sharp and sudden increase in the membership to the Catholic Church from among the *Mahars*. The special context of famines apart, as we take a look at some of the personal experiences of the Jesuits, we discover that there were a few instances wherein they did feel the dilemma as regards the motive of the new or potential converts. Here is an example underlining the fact, although we need to approach the same with a clear caveat so as not to take it as a general phenomenon:

> The most disappointing feature about our people is a lack of interestedness in the demand for or acceptance of our holy religion. They all want something besides religion, and they seem to want more than they desire our religion, as a condition *sine qua non*. Though they never say so and one has to guess at their real motives, it seems to me that they always have for their real motive either financial help (alms, loans, free medicine, children fed in the boarding schools etc.) or protection against oppressors, or intercession with government officials. All these are expected from a missionary as a matter of course.[1364]

1362 "Allerlei von den Stationen: Sangamner," *IB* 1/32 (October 1937): 279.

1363 See Chapter (# 5.4.2.3).

1364 Otto Lustig to John B. Moyersoen (Kendal, 17th January 1944), ARSI, *Poona. 1004-XIV,* 21.

The initial motive of material gains is further revealed in the same letter as Otto Lustig reports:

> Another disappointing feature is lack of interest in education in the villages. True, they all are ready to send their children into boarding school. To them it means one or two months less to feed. Also all the villages desire to have their own master, but more for protection or even to watch the little children while the parents are in the fields, than for any other purpose.[1365]

Taking a closer look at these instances, there remains no doubt that the motive of temporal gains or security was not entirely absent among the new as well as the potential converts. The matter becomes even more interesting due to the time-period of its reporting, especially that of the last two examples given above. By 1944 the mission, taken from the beginning of the undivided Bombay-Poona Mission (1854), had exactly completed nine decades of its existence in the area. The encounters of the Jesuits with such experiences do give a clue to the complexity of the situation in the mission until this period.

But before passing a judgment on the converts from among the *Mahars*, we need to take a brief look also at the constraints within which their decisions were generally made. The first constraint was the condition of poverty often accentuated by frequent occurrences of famines and other natural calamities, the acuteness of which had doubtlessly an immense impact in the decision-making process. Underneath follow two vivid examples to substantiate the argument that the choice to embrace Catholicism was most likely due to social and economic security for many people in this mission. Joseph Stark narrates the same:

> Last year a boy passed out High School from Sangamner ... Now he is in search of a job corresponding to his skill and knowledge since last one year. Unfortunately he has not yet succeeded. Recently he seems to have gone to Bombay to one of the leaders of the so called Depressed Classes in connection with the search for a job. The leader seems to have suggested to him that he should describe himself as a non-Christian *Mahar* in order to get a job without any

1365 Ibid.

> further delay. Such incidents virtually force us to reflect as to what the future holds for us.[1366]

The next example seems to be even more vivid possessing a potential to exercise undoubtedly a tremendous impact on a people whose first concern was survival from physical hunger, availing of better prospects for future and other such concerns. Added to these, a few clear cases of discrimination in schools and other places on the basis of religious allegiance was not a simple concern as it may appear. The following example would illustrate the point well that the people often stood at the crossroads, from where making a decision for or *against* a position was doubtlessly a tough task:

> Although our Christians are all from the *Mahar* caste, and therefore as poor and backward as others, yet they are counted among the advanced classes. But the *Mahars*, who are still Hindus, belong to the backward classes. If a non-Christian *Mahar* boy goes to a school, from 4th standard onwards he normally receives a scholarship of 2 rupees per month (exactly the amount he requires for food and clothing); whereas a Christian *Mahar* boy gets nothing. Since our people are really very poor, this situation offers a great temptation to many of them, especially in a town like Sangamner. For example, a man from Sangamner, who himself is a Hindu but his children are Christians, has once again registered his children in the school as non-Christian *Mahars*. That is the first case of yielding to monetary gains or immediate momentary benefits. Quite a few followed this incident thereafter ... There remains no choice for us but to run the school with the bare minimum number of students which no wonder is bound to have a direct impact on the future generation of our Christians.[1367]

Having taken a brief look at the above instances, now we need to see the entire situation against the ground realities facing the *Mahars*. One of the foremost conclusions that may be drawn from these instances is: the nature and pattern of their motives were not unique. Studies on

1366 Joseph Stark to Joseph M. Wiget (Sangamner, 14th January 1941), AMPSJ, *LB. Sangamner-Briefe*. See for the similar content Thiler, "Bericht iiber den Besuch der Poona Mission," op.cit.

1367 Ibid. See also John Haldner to Felix A. Plattner (Sangamner, 22nd November 1948), AMPSJ, *LB. Sangamner-Briefe*; Pius Geisel, "Litterae Superioris Missionis," (Poona, January 1955), ARSI, *Poona*. 1005-LV, 5; Thiier, "Bericht iiber den Besuch der Poona Mission," op.cit.

conversions have shown that most of the conversion movements among the *Dalits* across India have had a similar beginning. Except for the specific aspects of the complexities of the local situation, the *Mahars* in fact largely fall under the pattern that has generally been observed in the conversion movements among other *Dalit* groups as well in India, wherein a mixture of spiritual and temporal motives have been mostly inseparable. In South India, for instane, the missionaries did not hesitate to admit that the *Dalits* initially came to Christianity out of non-spiritual considerations, i.e., for protection and aid of various descriptions.[1368] In the case of *Mahars* too, the example of the sharp rise in the membership of the Catholic Church in the event of the famines cited above is one such example.

It is here that a danger lies in the interpretation of their motives. The observers either unfamiliar with the experience of poverty and other such constraints coupled with centuries-old social subjugation under the caste system tends to ignore these aspects in order to justify their claim. They might romanticize the issue by saying that the spiritual and the material aspects must not be set on par with each other. In plain terms, some critics may claim that the temporal motives of the *Mahars* can never be justified on the ground that religion must basically be concerned with the spiritual life of its adherents. It goes without saying that at the background of such a position lies the basic understanding of the duality of body and soul. Therefore such a simplistic conclusion smacks of ignorance of the ground reality and lack of sympathy for the people whose most realistic experience of life was that of suffering and subjugation. An observation made in the context of the commentary on John's Gospel (6:26) puts the matter in a proper perspective:

> These poor cannot read, and if they have any innate ability to discuss the Torah [or for that matter the Bible] logically, they have no time or energy to spare for such pursuits. The Mahatma, Mohandas K. Gandhi, put this dilemma well: "There are people in the world so hungry that God cannot appear to them except in the form of bread." And Woodrow Wilson wrote that "No one can worship God or love

1368 See Sambaiah Gundimeda, *Dalit Politics in Contemporary India* (Abingdon/New York: Routledge, 2016), 150.

his neighbour on an empty stomach," for, said Jean de la Fontaine, "A hungry stomach cannot hear."[1369]

The parallel drawn here might seem too far-fetched and rightly so given the distance in time. The purpose of doing the same, however, is to illustrate a simple point that the situation of the *Mahars* was substantially no different from what the text implies about the situation of the society in the time of Jesus. Hence, the sayings of Gandhi, Woodrow and Fontaine quoted above are equally true today. To assert that the mixed motives of the *Mahars* was unjustifiable would be to negate the truths contained in these wisdom sayings. When the primary concern of survival and availing of basic human necessities underline the reality of a human society, the logic of dichotomizing the 'spiritual' and 'material' has no validity. Giving a book of Bible, for example, to a beggar at the road-side would amount to adding an insult to injury, in spite of the intrinsic goodness of the Bible. What a hungry man, at first, needs is the bread.

Having said that, it may also be stated in unambiguous terms that the disposition of the *Mahars* as depicted in the second example above does give a rather poor picture of theirs. The issue becomes further curious due to the fact that other groups of people elsewhere, sharing almost the same degree of depravity in terms of material poverty and societal subjugation, i.e., the Tribals of Chhotanagpur Mission (i.e., Oraon, Munda, Kharia, Ho and others),[1370] seem to have shown a much stronger docility towards the Christian faith. J. W. Pickett argues that such a dilemma in a decision-making process pertaining to matters as complex as religion is quite a natural phenomenon. Besides, none of the human motives can be unmixed at any given point of time. Also, it can be that at a given point of time, one motive may be stronger than

---

1369 James D. Audlin, ed. & trans., *The Gospel of John, Volume Two: Commentaries on the Text* (Paso Ancho, Panama: Volcan Bani, 2015), 681. See also Goyal, *History of Hindu-Christian Encounters*, 141. In light of the affirmation of Mahatma Gandhi quoted in the text, it appears to be a contradiction that he should have opposed the movements of conversion. For, in most cases the Christian missionaries have done precisely this.

1370 Largely in the south-western region of the State of Jharkhand (India) comprising Ranchi, Palamu, Garhwa, Latehar, Lohardaga, Gumla, Simdega, East and West Singhbhum, Khunti and Saraikela Kharsawan Districts. See Peter Tete, *A Short History of the Expansion of the Catholic Missions in North India* (Ranchi: St. Albert's College, 1997), 315. The name of the region is written differently in various sources. Some write *Chota Nagpur*, others *Chotanagpur* and still others *Chhotanagpur*. I prefer the latter because of its closer rendering of the original in Hindi.

others. Hence it would be unfair to conclude that the most predominant motive at a given point of time is the only motive of any group of people tending from one religion to another.[1371] In the words of J. W. Pickett:

> Religion appeals to many motives ... and it is doubtful whether any normal individual can change his beliefs, his practice, and his allegiance in religion without the operation within him of many motives. Certainly no wide movement in religion takes place without engaging numerous motives. Nevertheless, it may happen that one is so much stronger than all others that it may fairly be considered the primary cause of the action.[1372]

The issue of motives is often raised due to a misconception whereby the phenomenon of 'conversion' is considered as a one-time event, whereas the contrary is the case. The process of maturing into a new faith is a gradual one that implies a slow process of detaching oneself from the previous religious and cultural traditions.[1373] This process is decidedly much slower in the case of group movements of conversion. In fact that is a normal process in any human society as far as societal and communitarian trends are concerned. A group may take generations to evolve into a fully rooted community in the new faith. This was very true in the case of the *Mahars* too. Hence, it may be stated without any misgivings that they did embrace Christianity invariably with mixed motives, in the hope of a better future, search for dignity and respect, etc. The motives of any society or group of people undergoing a process of decision-making in favour of or against a religion are largely determined by the local circumstances, socio-cultural and politico-economic contexts.

In spite of the initial lack of clarity of motives, the *Mahars* over a few decades have grown into a substantially well-rooted Christian community. Such a claim is verified by the fact that they have gradually evolved into a more mature Christian community than the first generation of the converts. Precisely this was the hope for which the Jesuits continued their mission among them, in spite of the fact that on a number of occasions they encountered not very hopeful situations such as the ones mentioned above. A testimony of Otto Lustig is proof of

---

1371 See Pickett, *Christian Mass Movements*, 158-159.

1372 Ibid., 159.

1373 See Barua, *Debating 'Conversion'*, 94-95.

such an approach, wherein he claimed: "Well, we give them the benefit of doubt - and baptize them after suitable instruction."[1374]

To sum up, it may be claimed that in the initial stage the *Mahars*, in most cases, did lack clarity about their motives in embracing Christianity.[1375] In fact, they themselves were often "clear that the motives that had guided them towards the Christian fold were not particularly 'spiritual' but were straightforwardly material ones relating to security, dignity and self-respect."[1376] Stated differently, their motive included "a desire for social betterment"[1377] in the sense all the implications meant by this phrase. Therefore, the material aids and benefits received by them prior or subsequent to their conversion to Catholicism may not be termed categorically as 'inducements'. The point is illustrated in the approach of the Jesuit missionaries themselves in the mission. It is a known fact that the Jesuit missionaries won the hearts of the *Mahars* by reaching them out through schools, health-care facilities, relief-works during famines and other natural disasters like floods, and various other philanthropic activities. We have stated above that the critics of the conversion movement have raised questions precisely taking these aspects of mission work as a point of reference. Therefore, considering the entire gamut of the socio-cultural and politico-economic context of the *Mahars,* it is unjustifiable to interpret the material aspects of reaching out to them by the missionaries as 'force', 'fraud', 'baits' or 'inducements' offered to them.[1378]

It would be wrong to say that the temporal help extended by the missionaries to the converts as well as to the non-Christians was value neutral. Of course in the mind of the missionaries this was intended to project the goodness of Christianity. On the contrary, the tendency to see the temporal help purely as 'baits' or 'inducements', is equally wrong and a deliberate misrepresentation of the fact. According to the Jesuit way of understanding, i.e., the extension of material help to the needy forms an important aspect of its charism. Through material help, the

---

1374 Otto Lustig to John B. Moyersoen (Kendal, 17th January 1944), op.cit.

1375 See K. N. Kadam, *The Meaning of the Ambedkarite Conversion to Buddhism and Other Essays* (Mumbai: Popular Prakashan, 1997), 36-37.

1376 Barua, *Debating 'Conversion',* 84.

1377 D. Arthur Jeyakumar, "Christianity among the Nadars of Tirunelvelly," in *Christianity in India: Search for Liberation and Identity* (Delhi: CMS/ISPCK, 2000), 131.

1378 Barua, *Debating 'Conversion',* 93.

Jesuits have tried to project the goodness of Christianity to others. As a byproduct of the same, many converts to Catholicism were won. Hence, such an approach falls within a general pattern of evangelization process followed by the Jesuit and other missionaries across the centuries, which in turn springs from a particular understanding of missiology and theology, wherein the body-soul duality has no space. Seen from this perspective, the Jesuits reached out to the whole person of the *Mahars* by reaching out to them through various forms of help. The dichotomy between the spiritual and the material did not shadow their approaches.

A final comment may be made on this point by saying that so far our presentation of the story of *Mahars* has mostly been from the perspective of the missionaries. There have been studies from other perspectives and on other aspects. Fernando and Gispert-Sauch claim, on the basis of their recent studies, that often the Christian communities of *Dalit* origin have themselves initiated the movement for conversion. "Very often the movement to Christianity was initiated by the *Dalits* themselves. They were not passive victims, but agents of a liberation movement."[1379] In spite of the external impulses acting as a trigger at times, in most of the cases the inner desire of attaining self-respect, dignity and the possibility of participation in the larger egalitarian society have invariably been present among the *Dalit* groups as under-currents in the entire process of their decision-making in favour of Catholicism.[1380] No wonder, often these aspirations have been far from being translated into tangible results. In such situations, the potential converts at least "saw in conversion the possibility of gaining some freedom from at least psychological, if not social, economic and political domination."[1381] Added to these, there has been also "the desire to be freed from the fear of devils and evil spirits, and the belief that Jesus Christ would liberate them from such fears and dangers."[1382] Given the nature of their historical context, it would not be wrong to conclude that all these aspects, in some degree or the other, have been present among the *Mahars* too in the process of their conversion.

1379 Fernando & Gispert-Sauch, *Christianity in India*, 180.

1380 See Barua, *Debating 'Conversion'*, 90-91; Fernando, Macwan & Ramanathan, *Journeys to Freedom*, 120-122.

1381 Webster, "Christian History as Indian Social History," 186.

1382 Jeyakumar, "Christianity among the Nadars," 31.

8.3. The Native Vocations

"To say that every country and every nation, should as far as possible produce its own clergy, minister to its own and be ministered to by its own, is a truism so obvious that it seems almost a waste of time to state it,"[1383] so ran the opening statement of an article titled "The Development of a Native Clergy in the Foreign Missions," in the December 1922 issue of *The Messenger of the Sacred Heart for India* (MSHI hereafter).

8.3.1. The Papal Mandates

Already from around the 1630s, the Church began to place a strong emphasis on the need of promoting indigenous vocations.[1384] From the last decade of the 19th century until the end of the period of this study (1962), we discover that the several popes have laid a strong emphasis on the subject with an ever increasing sense of urgency. Pope Leo XIII (1878-1903), in his encyclical *Ad Extremas (1893),* for example, emphasized "upon raising indigenous peoples to the priesthood ... [He] called for diocesan seminaries to be established in mission territories at the earliest possible opportunity."[1385] A testimony of his earnestness on the issue can most tangibly be seen from his personal interest in founding the Pontifical Athenaeum in Ceylon (Sri Lanka) (1893). This emphasis became even more intensified in the apostolic writings and encyclicals of the successive Popes. One of the most tangible proofs of the same is the space allotted to the topic in each of the Encyclical Letter.[1386]

The successor of Leo XIII, Benedict XV (1914-1922), addressing the superiors of the missions wrote: "There is one final, and very

1383 "The Development of a Native Clergy in the Foreign Missions," *MSHI* 12/14 (December 1922), 1. *The Messenger of the Sacred Heart for India* (MSHI) was a supplement to the Irish Catholic Magazine *The Messenger of the Sacred Heart.* It was edited and published by the Jesuits for the Archdiocese of Bombay.

1384 See Thomas J. M. Burke, ed., *Catholic Missions: Four Great Encyclicals* (New York: Fordham University Press, 1957), 4. The *Four Great Encyclicals* referred to in this book are: *Maximum Illud* (1919), *Rerum Ecclesiae* (1926), *Evangelii Preacones* (1951) and *Fidei Donum* (1957). For the subsequent references to these encyclicals we shall refer to the translations from this book with the abbreviations MI, RE, EP and FD for *Maximum Illud, Rerum Ecclesiae, Evangelii Preacones* and *Fidei Donum* respectively.

1385 Christopher Harding, *Religious Transformation in South Asia: The Meaning of Conversion in Colonial Punjab* (Oxford: Oxford University Press, 2008), 64.

1386 For example, *MI* has allotted 4 paragraphs (#14-17), *RE* eleven (#10, 22-31) and *EP* seven paragraphs (#36-42). See Burke, *Catholic Missions,* 13-14, 28, 32-35; 47-48.

important, point for anyone who has charge of a mission. He must make it his special concern to secure and train local candidates for the sacred ministry. In this policy lies the great hope of the new Churches" (*MI* #14). His successor, Pius XI (1922-1939) was even more emphatic as he underlined the fact in the following words: "Let us first remind you how necessary it is that you develop a native clergy. We are convinced that, unless you provide to the very best of your ability for native priests, your apostolate will remain crippled and the establishment of a fully-organized Church in your territories will encounter still further delay" (*RE* #22, cf. #24). Although Pius XI follows the basic line of argument from his predecessor, the sense of urgency and absolute necessity emerge more strongly in *Rerum Ecclesiae.* His successor, Pius XII (1939-1958) maintained the emphasis very especially in his Encyclical Letter, *Evangelii Praecones* (1951), although the general thrust may be identified also in his Apostolic Letter *Fidei Donum* (1957).

In sum, what surfaces strongly throughout the period in consideration is the unfailing emphasis laid on the issue by succeeding Popes. This may also be seen in the efforts on the Roman curial reform and consequent internationalization of the Roman curia in this period. Apparently, the fuller realization of these ideals remains much to be desired even today. Yet, in principle these efforts may be considered as the virtual precursors of the initiatives of Pope Paul VI on the reform of the Roman curia in the post-Vatican II era. The voices of demand of the same were also more pronounced in the post-Vatican II Catholic Church.[1387]

8.3.2. The Directives of the Jesuit Superior Generals

What was the response of the successive Superior Generals of the Society of Jesus to the calls made in the papal documents? Taking a brief retrospective view on the missionary endeavours of the restored Society of Jesus (1814ff) we notice that even before the above mentioned encyclicals and apostolic writings saw the light of the day, the emphasis on the necessity of the formation of native clergy was strongly laid by the

1387 See Hans Kting, *My Struggle for Freedom: Memoir,* trans. John Bowden (London/ New York: Continuum, 2003), 415. In simple terms, 'internationalization of the Roman curia' may be defined as the incorporation of more and more non-Italians in important positions in the Roman Curia in the Vatican. See Karim Schelkens, John A. Dick & Jiirgen Mettepenningen, *Aggiornamento?: Catholicism from Gregory XVI to Benedict XVI* (Leiden/Boston: Brill, 2013), 93.

Jesuit Society. For example, John Philipp Roothaan, the 21st Superior General (1829-1853), strongly believed that a logical conclusion of a successful mission lies in the fact that a native Church is entirely handed over to the native clergy and thereby the entire ministration of the same may be undertaken by them. Indeed, he considered it as the missionary ideal of the Society of Jesus.[1388] In the context of the Chinese mission, for example, he made his views clear by declaring that "in general, the European missionaries are especially required for the formation and management of the local clergy."[1389] Elsewhere he wrote: "One cannot do something more precious and useful to a people than to give them in faith and morals well-trained priests."[1390] From these two instances, the earnestness of Roothaan on the cause of promoting native clergy becomes quite apparent.

The later successors of Roothaan, namely Wlodimir Ledochowski (1915-1942) and John Baptist Janssens (1946-1964), the 26th and 27th Superior Generals respectively too were deeply committed to the cause and promoted the same in collaboration with the contemporary popes. It is a known fact that Ledochowski was keenly interested in the missions worldwide and encouraged the Jesuits to take up the same zealously. His extraordinary zeal for missions may be imagined from the fact that the number of Jesuit missionaries across the world rose to 3, 902 in 1940 as against 1, 971 at the time when he took over as the Superior General (1915). The promotion of the cause of native clergy was an integral part of his understanding of the Jesuit mission.[1391] For example, "in a letter in 1919 he urged the Jesuits in China to develop an indigenous/native clergy both for the Jesuit Order and for the dioceses."[1392] His views on the subject are expressed even more poignantly elsewhere, as he wrote "that an indigenous clergy sufficiently numerous, well selected, and solidly established, contributes powerfully to the spread of the Gospel; that it is even indispensable if the Christian communities are to receive their definitive form and a lasting prosperity; that the efforts and co-

1388 See Plattner, *The Catholic Church in India*, 104-105. This view was strongly reiterated later by two successive Popes, i.e., Leo XIII (*MI* #16) and Pius XI (*RE* # 30).

1389 As quoted in Joseph A. Otto, *Griindung der neuen Jesuitenmission: Durch General Pater Johann Philipp Roothaan* (Freiburg i.B.: Herder & Co. G.M.B.H., 1939), 532.

1390 Ibid., 536.

1391 Witek, "Ledochowski, Wladimir (1866-1942)," 390.

1392 Ibid.

operation of all should be directed to this end, - all this is something which cannot be doubted."[1393] His successor, John B. Janssens earnestly followed in his footsteps. During his tenure, the world scenario had begun to change in a rapid pace. Numerous colonized nations, including India, were moving towards independence from the colonizing powers. Against this backdrop, he felt it of paramount importance on the need of promoting native vocations.

8.3.3. Pragmatic Reasons for the Emphasis on Native Vocations

It would be apt to point out a few factors that necessitated the emphasis on the subject. One of the first factors was the impact of certain currents of ideologies, i.e., emergence of strong nationalist ideas by the end of the 19th century and more especially from the beginning of the 20th century. These ideologies had a potential of capturing the imagination of practically all the masses that had been subjugated for centuries under one colonial power or the other. An immediate consequence of the same was a growth of the general feeling of hostility towards the white races as oppressors among the colonized people. This began to be ever more conspicuous in the form of the movements for freedom and self-rule. No wonder the Church too was going to be affected by these ideological currents and new developments in the world scenario.

One of the most basic concerns that began to be worry Rome (with sufficient grounds for the same), therefore, was the apprehension that the days of missionary enterprises in various colonized nations were soon going to end. Consequently the question, namely "what trials would the Church then suffer in those regions, unless throughout the land there were a veritable network of native priests to care for the Christian converts?," (*RE* # 26) was a crucial one to be addressed.

The second factor that played an equally decisive role was the experience drawn from the events of the past from the Chinese, Japanese and Ethiopian missions (where the missionaries from foreign lands, on numerous occasions, were either executed or expelled). The Churches in these lands were often left without their shepherds (the priests) and the hard labour of decades seemed to come to naught. A natural anxiety that Rome began to feel amidst such situations was how the Churches

1393 Quoted in "The Development of a Native Clergy in the Foreign Missions," op. cit" 1.

would be saved without priests and leaders from among the indigenous people themselves in the mission lands.[1394]

Together with the above concerns, a perennial issue that occupied Rome was the difficulty of the foreign missionaries in gaining acquaintance with the vernaculars, customs and societal norms, of the natives. Centuries-long experience of missionary enterprise of the Church was proof enough that a majority of the foreign missionaries had invariably found it difficult to familiarize with the aforementioned areas and hence could not adequately do the work of proclamation of the faith. The reason for the same may be ascribed to a common experience that one cannot enter the world of meaning system of a people unless a familiarity with their language and culture is gained. The same applies to the proclamation of the Christian faith. Due to the imperfect knowledge of the native languages, the preaching of the missionaries often 'lacked force and efficacy' (*RE* # 25). Moreover, "far better than anyone else he [indigenous clergy] knows the kind of argument they [the natives] will listen to, and as a result, he often has easy access to places where a foreign priest would not be tolerated" (*MI* # 14). Hence, the conclusion that effectiveness in the preaching of the faith would never be adequately addressed so long as the native/indigenous vocations were not promoted. This was the third important factor.

Seen from the perspective of the need of more personnel, we come across with two specific situations which necessitated promotion of native vocations in the Poona Mission, i.e., the need of replacing the Jesuits either taken into the internment camps or repatriated to their homelands in the events of the two World Wars and secondly as a result of the new political developments subsequent to the independence of the country. As for the latter case, it may be stated that in spite of Jawaharlal Nehru, the first Prime Minister of independent India, being broad-minded with regard to the secular thrust of the Constitution of the country, certain members of his Cabinet of Ministers who were deeply influenced by Hindu nationalist ideologies were often insistent that the presence of European citizens, including Christian missionaries, was a stark reminder of the colonial past. Hence the country needed to detach itself from its past history by making the visa policy for foreign missionaries stricter. It goes without saying, however, that the agenda of such a move was to get rid of the foreign missionaries so

1394 Ibid.

that the education and awareness being spread by them through various activities among the lower caste Hindus and *Tribals* may effectively be checked. Consequently a demand was placed on the Indian Church as a whole that schools, colleges, orphanages and other institutions must be manned with the indigenous clergy at the earliest date possible.

This demand was applicable even more to the Jesuits in Poona because of the presence of the Faculties of Philosophy and Theology, where the maximum numbers of professors were Europeans. A simple logic that seemed to support the position of the afore-said section of the ministers bent on implementing such a policy was that the presence of the foreign missionaries had been considerably long in India in terms of duration. Hence the demand was that native people must be able to take the charge of all the affairs of the Church, including management of faculties of Philosophy and Theology. In other words, the logic of the slow growth of the Church and the unpreparedness in taking up the formation of the indigenous clergy was often beyond the comprehension of the aforesaid section of the ministers in the government. This may be concluded from an account of Felix Plattner:

> In 1955, a delegation of Indian bishops interviewed Home Minister, Pandit Pant, to discuss certain difficulties confronting the Church. They requested him to permit the entry of some foreign missionaries who were badly needed to train an efficient body of indigenous priests. The Home Minister could not understand why the Catholic Church had not yet succeeded in training Indian priests as professors for seminaries.[1395]

Lastly, it may be said that the need of promoting the indigenous vocations became further intensified in the Poona Mission partly because of the pragmatic reason of uncertainty about the future of the Mission in the wake of the currents of communism. In the words of Francis Benz: "The call of the hour for India seems to be to have priests of the soil. We should not be surprised one moment if communism is the lawful government after the elections next year [1957]. People of the soil can minister still whilst it is impossible for us with our white skin."[1396]

1395 Plattner, *Catholic India*, 03-104.

1396 Francis Benz to the Superior General (Ahmednagar, 5th August 1956), ARSI, *Poona. 1005-IX*, 12. See further in the same file Jerome D'Souza, "Memorandum submitted to the Holy Father," (Copy to the Superior General), 17.

8.3.4. Intrinsic Reasons for the Emphasis on Native Vocations

The foregoing paragraphs show that the papal documents as well as the directives issued by the Superior Generals of the Society of Jesus adequately underlined the need-based approach to the issue of the promotion of the native/indigenous vocations. It might appear that the promotion of native vocations was necessitated mainly due to the need of more priests. Yet the purpose of the same was not just to replace foreign missionaries with native ones in order "merely to perform the humbler duties of the ministry, acting as the assistants of foreign priests." (*MI*# 15. Cf. *RE* # 24, 30). On the contrary, the purpose was to form native members to be worthy of taking up the ministry of the Church as equals in dignity with their foreign counterparts. It is in view of this ideal that the successive Popes stressed the point of a worthy formation of the native people for the dignity of the priesthood and urged those in charge of the missions, i.e., Superiors, Vicars Apostolic, etc., to take up the matter with utmost sense of urgency (Cf. *M*# 8-14; *RE*# 21, 28-30, 35, 37, 39; *EP* # 76-79, 84). Benedict XV, for example, saw the entire enterprise of promoting the native and indigenous vocations as the very essence and ultimate goal of a mission. For, only by doing this the foundation of a local Church would be possible. He wrote:

> Wherever the local clergy exist in sufficient numbers, and suitably trained and worthy of their holy vocation, there you can justly assume that the work of the missionary has been successful and that the Church has laid her foundation well. And if, after these foundations have been laid and these roots sunk, a persecution should be raised to dislodge her, there need be no reason to fear that she could not withstand the blow (MI # 16).[1397]

In his directives to his brethren, Wlodimir Ledochowski often reiterated this view.[1398] In sum we may say that the task of promoting native/indigenous vocations formed the very essence of a mission enterprise in the real sense of the term. Without achieving this objective the very purpose of a mission is defeated. Thomas Burke interprets the

1397 The same aspect has been stressed with equal or more earnestness by the successors of Benedict XV, Pius XI and XII, see RE # 24, 30; EP # 6-7, 34.

1398 See Footnote #1391.

same in terms of the nature, essence and mission of the Church. He summarizes the point well:

> The Church is eager to have each nation possess its own bishop and diocesan organizations, its own priests and religious. This eagerness is occasioned not by mere necessity as the expansion of Christianity demands more workers, nor by a mere desire to lessen the difficulty of recruiting foreign missionaries. Nor is it a merely prudent eagerness to safeguard the Church in some country from persecution in the face of an inflamed nationalism. It is an eagerness that springs from an awareness of the Church's own nature and mission. The Church can never be at home in a particular country until its full life is lived by these people who have become, as far as the Church is concerned self-governing, self-propagating and self-sustaining. Missionaries work, properly, to make themselves unnecessary in the life of a country by establishing the Church fully among the people.[1399]

The above discussion underlines the fact that the Church had been laying strong emphasis on the need of promoting native vocations. The same is true of the Superior Generals of the Society of Jesus. It is curious, against this backdrop, as to what Poona Mission had achieved in terms of vocations from among the native people.

8.3.5. Earlier Efforts at Promoting Jesuit Vocations in Poona

Our sources say that the Jesuits of undivided Bombay-Poona Mission did make efforts right from the beginning in this regard. Unfortunately, they were largely faced with misfortunes and sad experiences in the same. Following in the footsteps of other Jesuit missions, especially Madura and Calcutta-Ranchi missions, where the Jesuits had achieved a modest success in spite of great difficulties under similar conditions, Bishop Leo Meurin had founded a Jesuit novitiate on 13th November 1868. In the first year, seven candidates applied for the same; among whom four entered the novitiate, i.e., three Europeans and one native-born. In the following year three more were added to their number, among whom only one survived.[1400] Faced with many hurdles with regard to the management and owing to the dwindling number of novices, the novitiate was closed down, so that by the end of 1870, in the words of

1399 Burke, *Catholic Missions*, 4.

1400 See Gense, *Church at the Gateway*, 442.

Henry Daling (then Master of novices) "the novitiate rested in peace in the Lord."[1401] An attempt was made to revive the same in 1875/76, with John Esseiva as the Master of novices.[1402] But that brought no better results either. Between 1875 and 1876, 13 candidates entered the novitiate, among whom five were already priests.[1403] "From among these thirteen, only one Priest and two Brothers survived, Brahmin Bhausingrao being one of the latter two. After the two-year programme had ended, the novitiate was once again laid to rest in eternal peace!"[1404] Thus both these attempts novitiate programmes were abandoned.

On account of the prevailing background in Christian families, the Minor Seminary in Bombay too had undergone various difficulties and managed only to bring out very few pupils who seemed to be suitable further study of theology. Such was the situation until the first decade of the 20th century.[1405]

Bishop Henry Doring was well aware of all these. In one of his letters to the Propaganda Fide (1909), therefore, he described the situation in the following words:

> With a heavy heart, we have mentioned in the memorandum to the Propaganda Fide that we could not make a headway in promoting the training of a native clergy. On the other hand, we could not ignore the significance of the question either. In fact it did not allow us to sit back in peace. The words of the great Pope Leo XIII were a constant reminder to us: *Filii tui, India, tibi administri salutis* [Your sons, O India, shall be the ministers of your salvation]![1406]

While the previous experiences of failures were weighing down heavily on the hearts of the Jesuits, an unexpected incident in the year 1912 cast a new hope. The incident goes back to the visitation of the

---

1401 As quoted in Vath, *Die deutschen Jesuiten*, 124.

1402 See Schatz, *Geschichte*, Vol. II, 244.

1403 "Vom einheimischen Klerus," *MB* (June 1929), 2-3, AMPSJ, *Alte Nachrichten von Puna.* It may be mentioned here that *Missions-Boetl {MB)* was a typed newsletter published at Berchmanns College Pulach, Munich for private circulation for awakening missionary spirit among the Jesuits under training. It contained mostly stories of personal experiences of the missionaries in various mission fields in India and China. It was published around the end of the 1920s until the mid-1930s.

1404 Vath, *Die deutschen Jesuiten*, 124.

1405 See Vath, *Die deutschen Jesuiten*, 124.

1406 As quoted in "Vom einheimischen Klerus," *3*. See also Gense, *Church at the Gateway,* 244.

Dharwar mission in the southern part of his diocese (namely Poona) undertaken by Bishop Henry Doring. He came across some 600 old-Christians in a place called Alnavar and two other nearby places. They were the descendants of Goan migrants originally coming from the high or at least respectable Hindu castes. A native priest from Mangalore Diocese was assigned to work among them. The spirit of piety among the young boys in the school as well as in the church made such a good impression on Bishop Doring that a thought crossed his mind as to whether one or the other from among them might be suitable for the priesthood. After a short conversation with the afore-mentioned priest, he gave a homily to the assembled faithful on the virtues and blessings of the call to the ordained priesthood. It was a virtual revelation to the simple people, who gladly agreed to offer their children for the training for the priesthood. Without any further delay, five best from among the boys were chosen. As the visitation to other places continued, two more boys were subsequently chosen by the Bishop. After his return to Poona, he immediately implemented his plan. With minimal arrangements, which were gradually improved, the instructions were begun for the seven young boys who were between 10 and 13 years of age.[1407] In 1914 two of them were promoted to the 4th Grade at St. Vincent's High School, and the others followed suit in the subsequent year. Unfortunately, we lack exact information on the progress of the work thereafter. But it appears to be pretty sure that the minor seminary founded by Bishop Doring with the sole purpose of promoting vocations from among the natives was operative until the late 1930s. It is surprising, however, that most of the seminarians did not make much progress in the later stage and eventually discontinued from the seminary. After this period, most likely the minor seminary was closed, probably because the financial burden was too heavy on a single diocese and that the efforts were far from bearing satisfactory results. Secondly, it was also argued that the seminary at Mangalore (Karnataka) would be sufficient for the candidates of the entire ecclesiastical province of Bombay.[1408]

From the description above, it is clear that the fruits did not correspond to the efforts invested for the purpose. Hence when we look

1407 For the purpose, an apartment next to the Cathedral in Poona, which was earlier occupied by the military chaplain was renovated and three rooms were furnished. See "Vom einheimischen Klerus," 2-3.

1408 Ibid.

at the status of the Mission with regard to the clerical personnel presented by Archbishop Henry Doring to the Propaganda Fide (1930), we come across with the mention of 19 diocesan priests who were working in the diocese along with the Jesuits. However, they were mostly drafted from other dioceses. One of the reasons for their service in the Diocese of Poona during this period seems to have been an agreement signed with the diocese of Poona to render service of a few years in return for the cost of studies during their formation in various seminaries, which were partly borne by Bishop Doring until his departure for Europe at the breaking out of World War I and subsequently by the Administrators Apostolic of Poona. Around this period there were also some priests of European origin but not belonging to this Mission. They worked in collaboration with the Jesuits, often as their assistants, and occasionally independently too in various fields. Their main contribution consisted of pastoral care of the old-Christians.[1409] This is an overview of the progress and achievements with regard to the training of an indigenous clergy in the Mission until the beginning of the 1930s.

The above account is rather descriptive, which is a deliberate one, in order to show in the foregoing paragraphs that the Jesuits did make certain efforts to promote native/indigenous vocations. Yet, the unchanged situation until the mid-1950s does demand further investigation.

8.3.6. The Status of Native Vocations until the 1950s

It has been a point of discussion occasionally as to why native vocations were slow to emerge in the Poona Mission. In appears that not seldom did this point become a cause of embarrassment too for the Jesuits of this Mission, especially when native/indigenous vocations were growing at a much better rate in similar kind of conditions in other missions. It would be worthwhile to explore the possible factors for the same. At the outset, it would be helpful to take a brief survey of the status of the native vocations in the Mission. For the purpose we may refer to the statistics of the indigenous vocations at the beginning of the 1930s, so that we can compare Poona Mission with other contemporary Jesuit missions (see Table 7.1).

1409 See Archbishop Henry Doring, "Prospectus Status Missionis - 1930," ASCPF, *Nova Series*, *Vol. 992*, 437.

Table 8.1: An Overview of the Native Vocations (early 1930s)

Mission	Fathers		Scholastics		Brothers		Total	
	Western	Native	Western	Native	Western	Native	Western	Native
Bombay	54	0	40	19	21	0	**115**	**19**
Poona	24	0	3	0	7	0	**34**	**0**
Goa	12	6	2	11	3	2	**17**	**19**
Mangalore	33	18	11	23	13	4	**57**	**45**
Madura	119	42	28	52	3	40	**150**	**134**
Galle-Trincomaly	56	9	8	3	15	3	**79**	**15**
Calcutta-Ranchi	179	8	67	11	17	7	**263**	**26**
Patna	25	0	21	8	2	2	**48**	**10**

Source: Adapted from ARSI, *RLGGM, Vol. VI,* 183.

The table gives a good picture of the status of the native/ndigenous vocations in various contemporary Jesuit missions. It is clear that there was a good proportion of native/indigenous vocations in all other missions. What is surprising is the fact that from the same community of Christians, i.e., *Mahars,* the native-born girls were admitted as candidates in a Congregation for women founded by Francis X. Schubiger in 1925, though their number remained rather small as long as the Congregation existed.[1410] On account of all these aspects, certain apprehensions have occasionally been expressed, especially in informal conversations, as to why the status of native/indigenous vocations to the Society of Jesus in Poona Mission was so few and different from other contemporary missions.

On the situation in the following decade, i.e., the 1940s, a description by Klaus Schatz may be cited:

> Another shortcoming was the lack of indigenous [native] vocations from the mission ... The number of 23 indigenous diocesan priests (as against the 42 Jesuit missionaries), which the mission totaled in 1950 means not an appreciable growth with respect to the initial number of 18 at the time of taking over of the mission in 1929. Out

1410 A mention has been made in Chapter Five under (# 5.3.2). Unfortunately this Congregation did not survive and was subsequently closed down. See "Wie es auf einer Missionsstation aussicht," *IB* 1/14 (April 1933), 104; Joseph Stark to the Superior General (Sangamner, 1st January 1944), ARSI, *Poona. 1004-XIV,* 16.

of the 22 indigenous priests that the mission counted in 1935, only 3 hailed from among them (Mahars), the rest from the Mangalore mission or from the dioceses of Goa. The indigenous Jesuits began to come sporadically since 1933 from this mission, the pace of the same being somewhat better after 1945. With an exception of a Mahar Brother, all hailed from the old Christian families.[1411]

In the catalogue of the Southern German Province, we come across with three native novices for the first time in 1935, i.e., Lovett Dionysius D'Souza, Richard Fernandes and William Clement.[1412] Thus from the account of Klaus Schatz on the vocations to the Society of Jesus from among the *Mahars,* we come across only four cases. One of them was Br. Bernard Lohole, whose first reference is made only in 1947. Unfortunately he did not persevere in the Society and was dismissed in the same year.[1413] 'The above mentioned catalogue mentions only three names for the year 1935.

From another account, however, we learn that Lovett Dionysius D'Souza was the first Indian Jesuit for the Mission. He entered the Society on 21st November 1933 and was ordained a priest on 25th March 1948. William Clement was the second one,[1414] who joined the Society on 24th September 1934. Five years later joined Leo Dias-Ferrao (September 1939). On 17th June 1940, Hubert Machado became the fourth candidate to enter the Society. Again three years later, on 30th December 1943 joined Arthur Braganza followed by Anthony Mathias on 9th June 1946. After two months, Thomas Barco joined on 26th August 1946. In 1947 two more candidates followed-- Gregory D'Souza and Arthur Machado on 22nd June and 7th September respectively. This list was completed with Edwin Sequeira joining on 5th January and Charlie D'Lyma on 21st June 1948. From their family names it is clear that they were all of Goan/Mangalorean origin. A point must be underlined here, namely all the above candidates except Lovett D'Souza were former students of St. Vincent's School, Poona.[1415]

1411 *Schatz, Geschichte*, Vol. III, 319-320.

1412 See CPOSS/(1935), 35.

1413 See Pius Geisel to Felix A. Plattner (Poona, 27th January 1954), AMPSJ, *Superior Poona P. Geisel.*

1414 See " Neues von unseren Missionaren," *IB* 4/5 (September 1949): 157.

1415 See Hubert Machado, "Unsere indischen Mitbrader," *IB* 3 (May/June 1949): 145-146.

From this account we do see some growth with regard to the number of native vocations. Unfortunately it is not clear whether all of them persevered as Jesuits. However, it goes on to prove the fact that the Jesuits did make some efforts to promote vocations through schools. It also serves as a corrective to the perception that the Jesuits of this Mission had 'failed' to promote native vocations. But these were from the old Catholic communities of western India, not from the new convert communities.

The situation seems to have improved only by late 1960s. Concretely speaking, therefore, there was not a single vocation from among the *Mahar Christians* until 1955. We have mentioned above that some Jesuits found it disturbing to mark that "under similar conditions and with almost similar caste status of the new converts, far better results had been achieved in other contemporary Jesuit missions."[1416] This was no less than a clear indictment of the missionary methods and unflinching dedication of the Jesuits of the Poona Mission. The Ex officio letter of Gregory Conget (1955) underlines the agony and dilemma of the Jesuits on this question:

> But my surprise is that after so many years of keeping two Boarding Schools [in the Maratha Mission] there should have been not one vocation. The Christians of the Ahmedabad Mission are also untouchables and pariahs, at the same social level more or less as our Mahars of Ahmednagar District; and there in Ahmedabad, they have already one priest and several scholastics from the novitiate up to Theology and so far they are satisfied with them.[1417]

From the date of the letter and the earnestness with which the question was raised by Gregory Conget, one gets an insight into the gravity of the issue. It may be noted here that Gregory Conget was a Spaniard belonging to the Bombay Mission who previously was the Superior Regular of the same. At the time of writing the above-cited letter he was the Rector and Professor at De Nobili College, Poona. By virtue of these assignments, however, it would be unjustifiable to consider him completely as an outsider to Poona Mission. Yet, because he had come from another mission and another nation in Europe, the observation made by him may be interpreted as an objective view of

1416 Schatz, *Geschichte*, Vol. Ill, 319.

1417 Gregory Conget, "Ex Officio Letter" (De Nobili College Poona, 9th January 1955), ARSI, *Poona. 1005-V*, 3.

an outsider. His views gain a further weight while during his tenure as Superior Regular of Bombay Mission he was instrumental in founding the present novitiate, *Vinayalaya* in 1942. Besides, he strongly supported the move of promoting native vocations.[1418] Thus, it may safely be concluded that the issue was a matter of sheer surprise among other observers as well. This leads us to the conclusion that the state of affairs may have been baffling to the casual observers from other missions as well.

Taking the figures in the table as well as from the account of Klaus Schatz along with that of Hubert Machado, one gets a glimpse into the status of the native vocations until ca. 1950. Things began to change only after India became independent. We discover that after independence a general consciousness about the need of promoting Indian vocations among the Jesuit missions in India began to intensify. This cane be verified from the fact that the question was elaborately discussed in a meeting of the Major Superiors held at De Nobili College, Poona in 1959. This meeting took a statistical survey of the proportionate growth of Indian vocations in various missions. Consequently, as a measure "to promote more vocations it was considered necessary to form good Spiritual Directors, by training them in spiritual guidance, and secondly, to make fuller use of the Eucharistic Crusade, Sodality, Apostleship of Prayer and Catholic Action."[1419] This seems to have brought some positive results in the years subsequent to it so that we read in 1963: "Due to Fr. [Gerhard] Baader's constant effort the number of vocations has steadily increased [during] the last few years."[1420]

From the foregoing discussion it is clear that certain attempts were definitely made to promote Indian vocations. Yet there did exist certain factors among the Jesuits that seem to have acted as deterrents on the way to achieving the purpose fully. We shall discuss the same in the section below. Meanwhile it may be mentioned that the mid-1950s was a virtual benchmark in this regard. For, from this time around a clear sign of growth of native vocations in general is noticed. One of the important factors for the same was more intensified efforts made in this regard, as

---

1418 See Gense, *Church at the Gateway*, 443.

1419 "Minutes of the Meeting of Major Superiors of India: Held on November 23 and 24, 1959 at De Nobili College, Poona." ARSI, *Goa-Poona. 1006, Belgaum-Poonensis, Praep. Prov. (1959).*

1420 Kester, "Goa-Poona: Visitor's Report (1963)," op. cit., 9.

can be noted in a letter of Pius Geisel: "In April he [Schoch] will go to Malabar in order to personally examine the 25 applications received for the Society of Jesus. If we can select even 6 good candidates, I would be satisfied for the year. From Poona itself we are getting three vocations. 9 for one year would be good enough."[1421]

These figures are a clear indication that the situation of the native vocations to the Society of Jesus in Poona began to grow at a better pace from around the mid- 1950s. In 1954 the Poona Mission was raised to a Vice-province with the name Belgaum-Poona.[1422] As for the status of the personnel, according to the statistics provided by Felix Plattner in 1955, one marks 130 members with 60 priests, 52 Scholastics and 18 Coadjutor Brothers in the Mission. It is interesting to note that among them the majority were Indians. It would not be wrong to term the Vice-province, therefore, as truly an Indian and native Vice-province of the Society of Jesus, though this achievement came only after the 1950s.[1423] I must hasten to add that these figures must neither mislead nor give a sense of complacency. For, most of the Indian vocations during this period were either from Goa-Mangalore or from Southern India, especially Kerala. From the beginning of the 1960s, the vocations from Goa-Mangalore began to be more prominent.[1424]

What still needs to be addressed is the question of vocations from the local community of Mahars. This is worth investigating as the *Mahars* formed the principal group of the new converts in the Mission and the Catholic community of the place was almost entirely comprised of them.[1425] Klaus Schatz makes a mention of just three priests and one Brother from *Mahar* community for the period prior to 1950. The next mention of the *Mahar* candidates to the Society of Jesus is found in a letter of Pius Geisel only in 1955:

> Here are some updates about our novices. 7 of them have entered in Bombay, the eighth one comes on 30th July [1955]. 8 are in

1421 Pius Geisel to Felix A. Plattner (Poona, 8th March 1954), AMPSJ, *Superior Poona P. Geisel.*

1422 This event must be acknowledged as a milestone in the history of this mission as it acquired with this new status independence from its European mother-Province. For every practical reason it was answerable directly to the Superior General thereafter.

1423 See Felix A. Plattner, "In Puna-Belgaum," *IB* 4/5 (1955): 2.

1424 See "JHS Informationen: Eine Freude," *IB* 2 (1962): 8.

1425 Nearly all the Indian vocations were from Southern India including Mangalore and Goa.

> Alleppey, for the Pre-Novitiate. Here are the names: Sebastian Saveri Thekadam, Philipose C. Kavunkal, Philip Narikuzhayil, Zacharias Athavelil, Chako Vandakam, Agusutine Champarathiel, Chako Peedikaparambil, Cheriankunju Cherai ... Two are from Poona. Altogether we have 29 Scholastics and 2 Brother Novices. In addition we have 8 in Alleppey [Kerala].[1426]

The citation gives a sufficiently good idea of the demographic composition of the group of the novices and pre-novices. The family names of the candidates show that the majority of the candidates were from Kerala. But it is also true that among the 130 members when the Mission was raised to a Vice-Province, the larger proportion of members were from Goa and Mangalore. In sum, the policy of recruiting native vocations by the German-Swiss Jesuits of Poona began much later (in the 1950s) than all other Jesuit missions in India. Yet the question of local vocations still remained slow, whereas other Jesuits missions had made much progress in this area.

8.3.7. The Slow Progress in Local Vocations: Exploring the Factors

It has been noted that the question of native vocations was a vexing one in this Mission. The issue becomes all the more strange: that the question of recruiting local vocations from the *Mahar* and other similar caste Christians, was not seriously taken by the German-Swiss Jesuits; and even the candidates from older Christian communities of Goa or other regions who were domiciled in this Mission territory seem to have opted for other dioceses and missions. As a result, "Poona mission was the only one among 8 Jesuit missions in India, from where not a single native Jesuit had come until 1933,"[1427] even after nearly seven decades of dedicated labour of the Jesuits in the Ahmednagar District. We have seen in the foregoing paragraphs, however, that a few random cases of native vocations did come thereafter. But they were almost exclusively of either Goan/Mangalorean origin or from southern India, mainly Kerala. Hence the question of local vocations demands further probe as to the factors that may have been responsible for the same.

It may be stated that based on a few documentary evidence, it appears to be a rather difficult task to arrive at definitive conclusions.

1426 Pius Geisel to Felix A. Plattner (Poona, 10th July 1955), AMPSJ, *Superior Poona P. Geisel.*

1427 Schatz, *Geschichte*, Vol. III, 319.

Hence, it must already be anticipated that the conclusions would be tentative. To begin with, the following basic questions would be important to probe into. Was it the social traits of the *Mahars,* which dampened the inclination in them towards vocation to the priesthood in the Society of Jesus? Was there any element of a latent resistance among them for such a way of life? Or was their disposition obstructed by the external factors, i.e., lack of sufficient care in promoting the vocations, reluctance in admitting them as candidates, certain prejudices, etc. on the part of the foreign Jesuits?

Two categories of factors seem to have been responsible for the slow progress. The first category pertains to the social traits and the numerical weakness of the *Mahars* compared to the numerical strength of the older Christian communities. The second category pertains to the seeming reluctance on the part of the Jesuits themselves to admit them as candidates. As for the first category, it may be concluded without a risk of generalization that their social traits, at least to some degree, seems to have been responsible for their lack of disposition towards a life-style that did not have parallels in their own society and did not have any such Catholic tradition.[1428] Secondly, it also would not be wrong to conclude that their newer status amidst the far older Christians may have been partly responsible for the apparent diffidence. This argument seems to be supported by the following observation:

> Of the indigenous clergy: What is the status in our mission diocese Poona? Let us consider the difficulties. The first reason is the smaller number of the Catholics. The mission field counts around some 20,000 Catholic residents, out of which there are some thousand Europeans and Eurasians. There are certainly some priests from among them. But they cannot be counted as native priests. Again some of the Catholics are of Goan origin. As they are strongly attached to their homeland Goa, they normally send their children as priest candidates to the Archdiocese of Goa so that later they can work among their own near and dear ones.[1429]

It is quite natural to have such inhibitions among the newer Christians coming as they were from the lower stratum of the caste hierarchy, especially when they try to claim their rightful place amidst

1428 See Ludwig Hassle to Joseph M. Wiget (Songaon, 9th August 1941), AMPSJ, *LB. Songaon-Briefe.*

1429 "Vom einheimischen Klerus," 2.

the much older Christians. This becomes even more evident when the composition of the Christian community is as diverse as the one indicated in the citation above, with Europeans and Eurasians forming a prominent part of the same. In some cases it may also happen that the Christians coming from lower castes and tribal groups and for that matter, those from the older Indian Christian communities might have had a sort of inferiority complex in the presence of the white-skinned races, which in turn, might have undermined their aptitude for leadership roles. Narrating the events leading up to the Jesuit novitiate founded by Bishop Leo Meurin, Alfons Vath highlights this aspect well:

> With the passage of time, people are coming to a conclusion that the possibility of the natives living with the Europeans would not be easy. In addition comes the proverbial sensitivity of the natives, who in the presence of the Europeans become even more conscious of their identity as coloured people and feel themselves inferior in spite of the fact that from the other side hardly any such attitude forth comes.[1430]

Besides, speaking of native vocations in general, the Jesuits also perceived the lack of inclination, aptitude and perseverance among the boys, especially among those who came from comparatively better-off families. It may not be disputed that a better financial status often seems to have contributed towards dampening the religious spirit in most of the families with the consequence that often the younger generations are less inclined towards a life of vocation to the priesthood. In order to substantiate the claim, we may borrow an argument from the Brazilian context, which seems to be valid in most of the cases: "If one examines the sources of vocations in Brazil, they are largely from rural areas (57% in 1960), from large families ... and from the lower strata of society."[1431] This implies not only social status of the candidates, but also better economic status, were related to the lack of atmosphere in religious values in the families.

Having said that, as we turn to the experience of the Poona Jesuits on this matter, we discover that they encountered disappointments not rarely in their attempt to promote vocations among the Christians of the place. Such a conclusion may be arrived at from a description in

1430 vath, *Die deutschen Jesuiten*, 123.

1431 Thomas C. Bruneau, *The Political Transformation of the Brazilian Catholic Church* (New York: Cambridge University Press, 1974), 64.

the article cited above: "Then, still another factor is the most striking character trait of the Indians, i.e., their great instability, which renders it not advisable to get candidates for priesthood from better families who are not sufficiently rooted in the Christian life and thinking."[1432] The opinion expressed here is corroborated by certain related perceptions by some important persons in the Mission. For example, according to Walbert Biihlmann,[1433] on his arrival in Bombay (1854), Bishop Hartmann found the existing indigenous clergy as being of inferior training and upbringing. Moreover, they appeared to him as having embraced the clerical status of life purely as a career, rather than as a mission. John B. LeBmann, a Jesuit Visitor, who was sent to India in 1870 was of a similar opinion. He perceived the candidates who had joined the Seminary as mostly poorly brought-up in religious affairs, possessing weaker will power owing to the background of coming from the families of the soldiers.[1434] In fact he went to the extent of making a remark that "the Seminarians [i.e., the boys of the Minor Seminary] are a nuisance and many of them should be sent home."[1435] These examples suffice to show certain important factors contributing towards forming a particular image of the Indians among the foreign Jesuits. Over the decades, these perceptions were confirmed with the experiences of failures, i.e., in running a novitiate.

Yet, even more fundamental factor contributing towards the slow progress of Indian vocations seems to have been a certain degree of reluctance on the part of the foreign Jesuits in admitting the native-born Christians as candidates to the Society of Jesus. In fact they seem to have had a strong reservation about the suitability of Indians in general for the priesthood. Such a reluctance seems to have been even more acute in the case of the *Mahars*. It is an undeniable fact that an inclination for

---

1432 "Vom einheimischen Klerus," 3.

1433 He was one of the biographers of Bishop Anastasius Hartmann. His book is titled, *Pionier der Einheit: Bischof Anastasius Hartmann* (Zurich: Thomas Verlag/Munich/Paderborn/Vienna: Ferdinand Schoningh, 1966).

1434 Ibid. All three authors, namely Alfons Vath, James H. Gense and Ernest R. Hull dealing with the history of this Mission mention that the children of soldiers invariably came across as less inclined towards religious matters. A clear reason may have been the absence of the soldiers from their families for long periods of time during their services at different posts. See Vath, *Die deutschen Jesuiten,* 54, 60, 73, 83, 113; Gense, *Church at the Gateway,* 105; Hull, *Bombay Mission History*, 305.

1435 As quoted in Gense, *Church at the Gateway,* 428.

leadership roles among the new converts is impossible to be cultivated unless a sense of respect and acceptance as equals in the Church as a community of believers is inculcated among them, leave alone the aptitude for vocation to the priesthood. This aspect, i.e., lack of trust and confidence, seems to have been prevalent not rarely in this Mission, at least among some of the Jesuits. To be specific about the *Mahars,* there need not be any doubt in concluding that their lower status in the caste hierarchy was considered a hurdle even by the Jesuits. This may be considered as the most important factor, which until the 1940s, seems to have strongly and singularly contributed as a deterrent in the process of promotion of vocation from among the *Mahars*. We get a glimpse of the same from the following remark:

> Then there is a second difficulty: the caste system. Every member of the lower caste must be discouraged from entering the ranks of the priesthood, in order that the entire rank may not be defiled and a check on his impact on others may be applied. If most of the new Christians of the diocese come from such an unfortunate section of the society, who can fulfill the demands of the native vocations?[1436]

We notice here that in spite of the general expectation of equality towards all peoples, the Jesuits were not beyond a thinly disguised prejudice towards the people of lower caste origin. The reasons for the same might have been many and varied. Yet, it would not be wrong to conclude that their latent desire to make a breakthrough among the higher caste Hindus may have been responsible for this kind of attitude and resultant reluctance in admitting the *Mahars* even until the mid-1950s. In the words of Hans Ucko, such an approach "was a version of 'cuius regio, eius religio' adapted for the particular socio-political set up of India, e.g., aiming at the high castes, assuming that this would or might have a trickle-down effect on the low caste people."[1437]

However, what appears to be true is that there was reluctance among some of the Jesuits in admitting the *Mahars*. As an instance, the letter of Gregory Conget may be cited again, wherein he writes: "Concerning the vocations from among the Christians of our Mission stations of the Ahmednagar District, I am quite convinced that they should be admitted

1436 Ibid.

1437 Hans Ucko, *The People and the People of God: Minjung and Dalit Theology in Interaction with Jewish-Christian Dialogue* (Mtinster-Hamburg-London: LIT, 2000), 105.

with great discrimination and only if they satisfy all the requirements that must adorn any candidate for our Society."[1438]

We may conclude from the context of the letter that the caution implied in the letter was not necessarily the understanding of Gregory Conget about the *Mahars* but was a sort of preface to the more fundamental question that he had raised later in the letter. Yet it does give a clue to the fact that he too might have perceived the presence of prejudices to a certain extent, among the Jesuits towards the *Mahars*. Hence what he meant here was that a reasonable caution must be taken, or rather no concessions with regard to the demands of the Society of Jesus must be made in admitting the *Mahars*. He goes on to say that any view even indirectly implying a caste or class prejudice towards any group of people is against the spirit of the Society of Jesus or for that matter, against the entire Catholic missionary body and is out-rightly condemnable. It is against this context that he questioned: "Could the reason why there have been no vocations to the priesthood from our neophytes be that some of [the] Fathers think perhaps that untouchables or "mahars" should not be admitted to the priesthood?"[1439] The answer to this question becomes self-evident as we read elsewhere: "The Tamil migrants belong to the lowest castes and therefore by virtue of their birth in the lowest caste they are ruled out for the dignity of the priesthood."[1440] Although the citation refers to the *Tamils*, the implication of the same clearly applies likewise to the *Mahars* owing to their status in the caste hierarchy. Such reluctance in admitting not only the members of the lower castes as candidates, but also Indians in general seems to be corroborate with certain statistical data. For example, if we go once again back in history to take stock of the number of candidates admitted in the novitiate in both the attempts at running the novitiate in 1868 and 1875, we discover that 31 candidates were admitted as novices: 11 scholastics and 20 brothers ... Most of these candidates were of Irish stock; Indian applicants could be numbered on the fingers of one hand. They were just four.[1441] One can understand, without necessarily

1438 Gregory Conget, "Ex Officio Letter" (De Nobili College Poona, 9th January 1955), op. cit, 3.

1439 Ibid.

1440 "Vom einheimischen Klerus," op. cit., 2.

1441 One of the four was Bhausingrao. See Footnote 1195 in Schatz, *Geschichte*, Vol. II, 244.

endorsing, the reluctance of the German Fathers to look for recruits among lads of Indian parentage.[1442]

The reluctance on the part of the Jesuits is evident also in the article, to which we have referred frequently above, as it maintained that "with the natives one had to be extremely careful,"[1443] in the process of admitting them as candidates. Without endorsing the perception necessarily, it may also be stressed that faced by the experiences of the two consecutive failures in running a novitiate, "the Mission Consult held in 1887 came to a unanimous decision that no indigenous candidate must be admitted. The Bishops of Poona and Bangalore seem to have been of the same opinion."[1444] Consequently, it so came to be that the Jesuits of this Mission began to look "upon India as a poor recruiting ground for the novitiate."[1445] But it must be underlined that "their ultimate resolve to fight shy of admitting novices from India came at the end of a long chapter of incidents."[1446]

One hundred years prior to the period of this study (that is, 1850s) Bishop Hartmann had envisioned an Indian Church with sufficient native clergy. He was determined, therefore, to invest sufficient time and energy for the same. With the help of the Jesuits, whom he had entrusted with the care of the Seminary, he was soon able to see the fruits of his vision being actualized, especially in terms of the growing number of the native clergy, not only in his Mission (B-P M), but across India. The statistical data for early 1960s show that out of the 16 Archbishoprics, 13 were Indians; similarly, out of 50 dioceses 30 were led by Indian Bishops; out of the total of 6818 priests (in 1962), 5480 were Indians, whereas 1338 were foreigners. It was definitely a commendable rate of growth in terms of the total number of Indian priests in the all India scenario.[1447] It may be noted that the entire credit for fostering Indian clergy does not go to Hartmann alone. There was steady indianisation of ecclesiastical posts in India, especially in the Oriental Churches,

1442 Gense, *Church at the Gateway,* 442. See also Vath, *Die deutschen Jesuiten,* 241-248; Velinkar , *The German Jesuit Mission,* 129-130.

1443 "Vom einheimischen Klerus," op.cit, 3.

1444 Footnote 1195 in Schatz, *Geschichte*, Vol. II, 244.

1445 Velinkar, *German Jesuit Mission,* 129.

1446 Ibid.

1447 See Walbert Btihlmann, "Ideen, die nicht starben," *SBH, Special Issue to commemorate the Centenary Celebration of Bishop Anastasius Hartmann* (24th April 1966): 3.

after 1886, when the Indian hierarchy was established. The transfer of ecclesiastical leadership in the Latin Churches largely began due to the compulsions of the changed political situation in India after the independence.

In the case of the Jesuit missions in India, strengthening the local church by placing administrative and religious responsibility and authority to the local members had been implemented in varying degrees. Practically all the other Jesuit missions in India fostered Indian and local vocations right from the beginning of their foundation in India. The data from all the eight Jesuit missions in South Asia, and also from other Religious Congregations (Institute of the Blessed Virgin Mary, Sisters of the Mercy of the Holy Cross, Loreto Sisters, etc) show that by and large, the German-Austrian origin missions had failed in it till the 1950s. Hence one can say that it was the political compulsions in India wherein getting visas from the Indian Government for foreign missionaries became more difficult, which prompted the change in favour of fostering Indian vocations.

In fostering native vocations the responsibility of those in authority was paramount. In this regard, the figure of Archbishop Henry Doring comes up for his early initiative. But one can see a certain inconsistency in his approach. It has been indicated above that he took a personal interest in founding a minor seminary for the natives, with a specific objective of promoting native vocations. But in his letter to the Propaganda he lamented the failure in achieving tangible results with regard to the same. His great contributions to the Mission aside, there were certain instances that seem to give a different picture of the person of Archbishop Doring. It appears that in all likelihood he could not form a positive opinion about the *Mahars* so far as their aptitude and suitability for the dignity of the priesthood were concerned. This is evident in this letter:

> Since the formation of the future priests from among the new converts (even after 50 years of mission work) is still undesirable (the Right Reverend Bishop said to me: "Try it after 100 years"), it appears hardly hopeful in the foreseeable future to expand the mission work in the manner that should have been absolutely necessary and to a large extent it also appears to have been possible.[1448]

1448 Pius Geisel as Consultor of the Mission, to the Superior General (Valan, 2nd January 1939), ARSI, Poona. 1004-XII, 1. See also Ivo Meyer, "Der Gesamt Eindruck (Shrirampur, 18th

It may be stated here that Archbishop Doring's lack of a positive image about the *Mahars* almost bordering on prejudice might have been an undeniable factor behind the slow progress of vocations from among the *Mahars*. Being in the key position in the Mission, his opinion was bound to transmit an unambiguous signal across the community, in this case, an unkind one. An excerpt may be cited in order to substantiate the point:

> A remark which seemed very inappropriate to every one of us so that we needed to talk mildly, was made by Archbishop [Henry Doring] some time ago. He said that he would not come to St. Vincent's for any meals so long as a Mahar was there at the table. This statement was made in reference to Br. [Bernard] Lohole. And it has also turned out to be so that he [Archbishop Doring] has not come here ever since, although last year he did come once.[1449]

The above two sources clearly lead to the conclusion that Archbishop Henry Doring did depict occasionally a lack of not only a positive image about the *Mahars* but also a lack of sensitivity towards the natives. Quite likely he never made a positive effort towards understanding the people of his flock or their aptitude for priesthood.

The case of Archbishop Henry Doring apart, Klaus Schatz seems to have been even more critical about the role of the German-Swiss Jesuits as a whole in promoting native vocations as he makes his observation mainly on the pre-World War I period:

> For the rest, it is clear that after 1886 no Indian applied for the admission [to the Society of Jesus]. Whenever, any aspirant expressed his desire for the same, one did invite him to come and see. But there was always skepticism on the part of the Jesuits and they behaved absolutely indifferently doing nothing to encourage the admissions [to the Society]. It is only in 1914 that a native reappeared in the person of Fr. Joseph Ferreira.[1450]

Thus, the lack of concern for native leadership aside, certain prejudices towards the *Mahars* were important factors responsible for the slow progress of vocations among them. Had their social traits been

---

July 1947), ARSI, *Historia 2001- Poona; Schatz, Geschichte,* Vol. Ill, 319.

1449 Joseph Meyer to Karl Thuer (Poona, 18th July 1947), ARSI, *Historia 2001-Poona.* Karl Thuer was the first Vice-Provincial of the Swiss Vice-Province erected in 1947.

1450 Schatz, *Geschichte*, Vol. II, 244.

studied and understood, and were approached with love and respect, the possibility of gaining vocations from among them would have been much more. From the personal experience of a Jesuit, Ludwig Hassle, who had worked among them for decades we get a better understanding about them and the way of approach to them. His letter is worth quoting at length:

> It is not all easy to win over these depressed people. One must be very friendly towards them. One must show love and benevolence ... Here the friendliness is valued perhaps ten times more than anywhere else ... Here one has to do everything with great diligence. The natives are suspicious, reserved and are afraid of foreigners ... One can attract them only by love, speaking with friendliness and showing benevolence so that they have confidence on us ... One cannot get things done by coercion. Instead, they can be driven by love ... These extremely lowly people cannot resist love. There is so much to do with little things. A small gesture of friendliness can have far-reaching effects ... A little harsh word can cause an immense hurt feeling. They react immediately with hatred. Unfortunately they do not show it openly ... Once someone feels insulted even slightly, he goes around everywhere and talks against the missionary ... On account of the feeling of hatred, he invents a multitude of lies that are perceived as true by others almost without any critique ... When the missionary trusts him, he rejoices royally that he had been so clever to make a missionary bend down. But if you treat them with love, no hatred will arise and they will not do such things. However, there are always some who are not well-disposed towards us and we cannot afford to behave according to their fancies. I have tried all the ways and I have found that I cannot go through any other path except that of love. Of course, authority and prudence should never be disregarded. Some of the missionaries have disregarded these aspects altogether and hence simply have been despised.[1451]

The text is quite revealing. As it suggests, probably the Jesuits often missed these aspects on the way to winning the confidence of the people. Apparently, we do not desire to generalize the point here. From the dates of the letters we may safely assume that the Jesuits, in spite of

1451 Ludwig Hassle to Joseph M. Wiget (Songaon, 9th August 1941), AMPSJ, *LB. Songaon-Briefe. For similar content*, see further in the same file Ludwig Hassle to Emmanuel Hofer (Songaon, 25th August 1941), Ludwig Hassle to Joseph M. Wiget (Songaon, 23rd October 1941); Ludwig Hassle to Francis X. Hayler (Songaon, 2nd February 1946).

working for nearly nine decades in the area, had still to learn a lot about the social and cultural characteristics of the people in order to pave the way for the Church to take roots among them. Such a state of affairs did not facilitate getting vocations from among them.

From the foregoing paragraphs, it might appear as though the realization of the lack of native vocations was purely a concern of only the Jesuits. On the contrary, similar opinions as that of Klaus Schatz mentioned above seems to have been supported by a certain section of the laity too. Given the prevailing status of the native vocations, it would not be considered arbitrary to cite an example from the first decade of the 20th century. This is done in view of showing the consistency of the argument as well. A Certain Peter Anthony Baptista, a parishioner of the Cathedral Parish of Our Lady of Hope in Bombay, for example, in his letter to the Prefect of the Propaganda Fide, made the following remark:

> Another reason that compels me to make this appeal to your eminence is that we find the German Jesuits do not encourage or foster among our boys a vocation for priesthood. They have abolished the Seminary which existed for more than thirty years in Bombay. They do not encourage them to persevere higher studies nay they often put obstacles in their way. One instance will suffice. Out of twenty parochial stations only seven are held by native secular clergy.[1452]

Another Catholic namely Anthony De Souza, a lecturer by profession too wrote a long letter to the Cardinal Prefect of the Propaganda and addressed the issue under consideration in even more scathing terms: "... it has given me a great pain to see that a policy of repression, to keep down the Indian Catholics as much as possible, found favour with the German Jesuits for the past twenty years at least...

1452 Peter Anthony Baptista to Girolamo M. Cardinal Gotti, Prefect of the Propaganda Fide (Bombay, 13th June 1907), ASPF, *Rubrica 128, Nr. 403 (1907)*, 356. As mentioned in the text, Peter A. Baptista was a lay person, a parishioner of the Cathedral Parish of Our Lady of Hope in Bombay. His letter contains three full-typed pages. His views may appear to be exaggerated and one-sided on certain points. Yet, the veracity of his claims may not be out-rightly rejected. The claims tend to prove that the alleged failure to promote Indian vocations was not due to the clergy, but also laity.

which finds expression (1) in the complete exclusion of our young men from the Jesuit Order ...."[1453]

These instances are sufficient to illustrate the point that the issue of native vocations was a matter of public interest too. If we go by the content of these letters, it is clear that the Catholics, at least the educated ones, interpreted the failure of the German Jesuits to promote Indian vocations not only as an omission but also of commission as well.

It may not be wrong to conclude, thus, that the Indians in general and *Mahars* in particular may also have experienced, in some degree, a lack of respect and acceptance as a whole. It would be utterly unjustifiable to say that such experiences were conspicuous and common. Yet from the instances we have referred to, it clearly emerges that such an experience acted as a deterrent on the way to making a choice by the prospective aspirants for priesthood between Poona and other dioceses. Klaus Schatz makes a mention of this aspect as he writes that "in between, of course, a number of priests came from St. Vincent's School [over the years]; but a few indigenous priests from among the *Mahar* circles joined other dioceses, which indicates the fact that they felt themselves more accepted there."[1454]

All these instances are sufficient to arrive at a conclusion that in spite of the formal efforts of running a novitiate or a minor seminary the Jesuits seem to have been lacking in genuine openness to promote native vocations right from the beginning of the Mission. It does not seem to be an exaggeration to conclude that the Jesuits with tall claims to preach the Gospel of equality lacked a sense of respect for the people whom they served and did not enable them to reach clerical leadership.

For a long time there occurred no substantial changes with regard to the approach of the Jesuits until the mid-1950s. Yet it must also be stated in unambiguous terms that the entire blame must never be put on the Jesuits alone. It must be acknowledged that certain social traits of the natives too were no less peculiar so as to render the situation more complicated. Moreover, the experiences of repeated failures were not too easy to be ignored. An example might illustrate the point better that as late as the mid-1950s the responses of the native boys was often utterly

---

1453 Anthony De Souza to Girolamo M. Cardinal Gotti, Prefect of the Propaganda Fide (Bombay, 18th May 1907), ASPF, *Rubrica 128, Nr. 403 (1907),* 433. See also Schatz, *Geschichte*, Vol. II, 227.

1454 Schatz, *Geschichte*, Vol. Ill, 319-320.

unpredictable, which did make the situation difficult for the Jesuits. The example pertains to the new candidates, reported by Pius Geisel:

> Four Scholastic novices and two postulants are this year's addition so far. Alleppey pre-noviciate was not a success as far as Poona is concerned. We had 10 boys there in the beginning. In the end 2 were left and of these two one left for home the next day after reaching Poona. After two days he wired for permission to come back, but, of course I did not take him again.[1455]

8.3.8. Recruitment Policy of B-PM: A Critique

On the question of suitability or aptitude of the natives for the dignity of the priesthood, the first critique comes from the disposition of Bishop Anastasius Hartmann himself towards native population. On more than one ways, he virtually prefigures the 20th century Popes we have repeatedly referred to above, especially with regard to the attitude that the missionaries need to adopt towards native people, namely an attitude of respect and acceptance. This he considered as fundamental for the foundation of a native Church in the sense that the Church must gradually be manned with native-born bishops, priests and women religious. It was not only an ideal that he cherished at the level of good principles; but rather he practiced the same in his life. It may be recalled that one of his primary purposes behind calling the Jesuits to Bombay was the care of the Seminary in order to promote native vocations.[1456] This he desired to achieve through a good Seminary training so that the native clergy "in none of the areas of pastoral service would be as mere subsidiaries to the European counterparts."[1457] As he returned to Patna Diocese (Bihar), he widened his vision to promote the native vocations among women congregations more intensively. In fact, "he was one of the first Bishops who had the courage, even to call the Sisters for the missions. Earlier, one could not trust the 'weaker sex' for such tasks."[1458] Walbert Biihlmann further mentions that Bishop Hartmann made it a point to recommend wherever he went the admission of Indian girls in the Congregations of the Sisters. This is revealed from one of the reports

1455 Pius Geisel to the Superior General (Poona, July 1955), ARSI, *Poona. 1005-IV*, 20.

1456 See Gense, *Church at the Gateway,* 213-220.

1457 Biihlmann, "Ideen, die nicht starben," op. cit.

1458 Ibid.

of the visitation to the Convent of the Sisters at Bankipur, Patna (28th November 1865):

> All the members must strongly be admonished never to give an impression of antagonism to the native-born members so that they feel themselves taunted, hurt or despised on account of their origin or colour of their skin. Such an unchristian impression, even if they were to be communicated as jokes, would cause the saddest and most inauspicious results.[1459]

Such an opinion of Bishop Hartmann, expressed way back in 1865 may doubtlessly be taken as a path-breaking statement. While restating the fact that it is not meant here to denigrate the genuine efforts made by the German-Swiss Jesuits, the instances discussed above do appear to be antithetical to such a broad understanding of the views of a person who was instrumental in bringing in the Jesuits and shared the same cultural milieu in Europe except for the fact that he belonged to another Religious Congregation (Capuchin). Perhaps as a Swiss he was more open. This point is decidedly worth taking into consideration.

As we focus on the Jesuits, we may refer back to Gregory Conget once again. His opinion seems to be a direct critique of the attitudes occasionally depicted by Archbishop Doring, as he addresses the issue: "This opinion [i.e., that untouchables or "mahars" should not be admitted to the priesthood] cannot be held today by any Catholic missionary. Even the Indian Government is making great efforts even through legislation to break the social differences of the castes."[1460] The implication is clear that if a secular agency like the Government of India could envision a different order of things, i.e., abolition of inequality based on caste, it becomes all the more indispensable for a Religious Order to pursue the goal of realizing such a vision.

The above cited instance apart, Gregory Conget seems to have held a consistently positive view on the question of Indian vocations. His address delivered at the inauguration of the present Jesuit novitiate *(Vinayalaya)*, of which he was the founder in the capacity of the Superior Regular of the Mission, is worth quoting:

> The opening of this novitiate is destined to hasten the day when our institutions in Bombay will be chiefly manned by Jesuits who

---

1459 Ibid.

1460 Gregory Conget, "Ex Officio Letter" (De Nobili College Poona, 9th January 1955), op. cit.

> are children of India ... [Moreover] it is to the diocesan priests that the government of the Church has ultimately to be entrusted. For any Religious Order in charge of a diocese, I consider that day to be the greatest when it can hand over to an indigenous diocesan clergy the charge it once received from the Sacred Congregation of Propaganda [Fide].[1461]

The time and the content of the above address (5 April 1942) is significant to note. As for the content, it is well attuned to with the papal mandates of the time. On the other hand, the time period is ancillary to some of the most eventful endeavours of the Mission. In Poona, for example, as we have discussed in the previous chapter, a few monumental plans, i.e., establishment of De Nobili College and Papal Seminary were being implemented, which may well be described as the abiding testimonies of the commitment of the German-Swiss Jesuits to the formation of native clergy. Yet the above sources do point out the dichotomy between the avowed commitment to the cause of promotion of native vocations and the final goal of a missionary enterprise undertaken by a Religious Order as articulated by Gregory Conget, at least among a certain section of the Jesuits.

It may appear as a paradox but it is true that the strongest critique of the kind of view occasionally depicted by Archbishop Doring comes from none other than Pius XI himself in *Rerum Ecclesiae:*

> If anyone considers these locals an inferior race, endowed with only very limited intelligence, he is seriously mistaken. For experience has proved that the peoples who inhabit the remote regions of Asia and Africa acquit themselves quite well in the pursuit of learning and are, in general, our intellectual equals. If you find that students from the very heart of an undeveloped territory are slow in their studies, this is readily explained, as you can verify for yourselves, by the fact that their extremely simple mode of life has thus far made only meagre demands on their intelligence (RE # 30).

The list of critics to the position held by Archbishop Doring and probably quite a few among the Jesuits of the time can go even further. However, the critics mentioned above may be considered as representing the broader lines of criticism on the issue. An analysis of the guidelines spelled out by Pius XI above, shows that the Jesuits often fell short

1461 Quoted in Gense, *Church at the Gateway*, 443.

of the expectation on this front. Yet the later results, which brought rich harvest, would justify their positive efforts, in spite of occasional hurdles.[1462]

8.4. Attempt at Inculturation: The Jesuit *Sanyasis*[1463]/*Swamis*[1464]

Since the sub-topic is directly related to the Christian *ashram*[1465] movement, it may be worthwhile to describe the background of the same briefly. The original inspiration for adopting sanyasa way of life in India is generally ascribed to the efforts of inculturation and adaptation

---

1462 See Anton Freitag, "Die Forschritte des einheimischen Klerus und der einheimischen Hierarchie in den Missionslandern in den letzten Dreiflig Jahren (1920-1950)," in *Der einheimische Klerus in Geschichte und Gegenwart*, pub. Johannes Beckmann et al. (Schoneck-Beckenried: Administration der Neuen Zeitschrift fur Missionswissenschaft, 1950), 215-218.

1463 "The terms Sanyasi or Bairagi are generic, and mean a person who has abandoned the world and overcome his/her passions, and are therefore of general application to all religious mendicants ... Occasionally Sanyasi or Bairagi are used in a limited meaning; in that case Sanyasi means a mendicant follower of [Lord] Siva ..." J. Charles Williams, comp., *The Report on the Census of Oudh*, Vol. I, General Report (Lucknow: The Oudh Government Press, 1869), 119. In short it is a Hindi equivalent of a *monk* or *wanderer*. In different sources the word is rendered differently. For example, some sources prefer to write sannydsi, others simply write sanyasi or *sanyasi*. In the letters that we are going to refer frequently, it is written as *sanniasi*. I prefer *sanyasi* because of the closest rendering of the original word in Hindi.

1464 In simple terms 'swami' means an ascetic or a holy man.

1465 George Weckman further explains that "the *ashram* has two dimensions in Indian parlance. The usage designates a forest hermitage. It consists of an old, holy sage surrounded by a small 'family' of disciples. The second usage incorporates the forest *ashram* into a pattern for the ideal life cycle with this as one of its stages. The Sanskrit root *shram*, from which ashram is derived, means 'to exert oneself.' Thus, the *ashram* is a place of exertion, or a disciplined striving after a goal ... In summary, the *ashram*, both as a place and as a discipline of life, appears in Indian tradition as a social religious structure of a somewhat monastic type. It shares with a monastery the feature of a group of people living apart from the family or village, pursuing programmes of life for self-improvement and religious goals. However, it differs from clearly monastic institutions by being impermanent, without written rules, and casual in authority." George Weckman, "*Ashram*, Influence of," in *Encyclopedia of Monasticism: Vol. I, A-L*, ed., William M. Johnston (Chicago & London: Fitzroy Dearborn Publishers, 2000), 94-95. See also Jan Peter Schouten, *Jesus as Guru: The Image of Christ among Hindus and Christians in India*, Studies on the Contact between Christianity and other Religions, Beliefs and Cultures, vol. 36, eds. Jerald D. Gort et al., (Amsterdam/New York: Editions Rodopi B.V., 2008), 163-164. For etymological meaning of the word, *ashram*, see Paul Pattathu, *Ashram Spirituality: A Search into the Christian Ashram Movement Against its Hindu Background* (Indore: Satprakashan Sanchar Kendra, 1997), 1; S. S. Chandra and Rajendra K. Sharma, *Philosophyof Education* (New Delhi: Atlantic Publishers and Distributors, 2006), 173.

of Christianity to Indian culture initiated by Jesuit missionary Robert De Nobili, Bernard Cinnami and other Jesuit sanyasis of the 17th century. They became aware of the complexities of the Indian society. Robert De Nobili, for example, cultivated an approach towards the Indian culture that accorded due recognition and importance. For, it is a known fact that,

> the traditional policy of the mission [of the time] was to Christianize India, and they [the former missionaries] believed that the more Indians discarded their ancestral religious customs and closely adhered to Portuguese ways, the better Christians they would be. Nevertheless, De Nobili soon found that he could never come close to the people of India by living in a European lifestyle and decided to adopt the role of Hindu *sanyasi*... [He was convinced that] the only way to make Christianity acceptable to caste Hindus was to present it as a universal religion.[1466]

In principle, therefore, the *ashram* movement was a follow up of this model of De Nobili and his understanding of other religions. Based on this principle, a series of attempts were made by Christian missionaries, both Protestant as well as Catholic, to adapt to the lifestyle of Hindu monks, which included not only adaptation of food habits and clothing, but sincere efforts at emulating the entire spectrum of the meanings that a Hindu hermitage and monastic life in its essence signified. An *ashram* lifestyle appeared to be a perfect model for the same as it resembled in many ways the early Christian monastic tradition. Given the similarities in their ideals and structures, therefore, the *ashram* opened an avenue for meaningful adaptation of Christian message to Hindu culture.

As pioneers, the Protestant missionaries took the lead in the movement. "Bharat Ashram established by K. C. Sen [a Brahmin convert] near Calcutta in 1872, could be regarded as the first ashram..."[1467] Some authors, i.e., Stephen Neill and others, opine that the movement may have received the first impulse through the efforts of Sadhu Sundar

1466 K. P. Kuruvial, *The Word Became Flesh: A Christological Paradigm for Doing Theology in India* (Delhi: ISPCK, 2002), 201. See also Cyril J. Kuttiyanikkal, *Khrist Bhakta Movement: A Model for an Indian Church?* (Berlin/Zurich: LIT, 2014), 78-79; Soosai Arokiyasamy, *Dharma, Hindu and Christian According to Roberto de Nobili: Analysis of its Meaning and its Use in Hinduism and Christianity, Documenta Missionalia,* 19 (Rome: Gregorian University Press, 1986), 340.

1467 Kanjamala, *Future of Christian Mission in India*, 206.

Singh, a wandering Christian preacher of Punjab.[1468] The movement got wider currency in early 1930s with the initiatives of E. Stanley Jones (1884-1973), an American Methodist missionary in India. Drawing inspiration from the way of life in the *ashrams* established by Mahatma Gandhi and Indian poet Rabindranath Tagore, he too "set up distinctly Christian ashrams as multicultural, multiethnic, and multi-religious retreats whose participants shared an openness to the Christian gospel and a sincere desire to seek God on a basis of complete equality with one another."[1469]

As for the Catholics, Brahmabandhav (or Brahmabandhab) Upadhyay[1470] may be considered as the pioneer of this model of inculturation. He established an *ashram* in Jabalpur (Madhya Pradesh State) at the end of the 19th century, which "he called a Hindu-Catholic monastery."[1471] Unfortunately his efforts did not receive ecclesiastical approval.[1472] But beginning from the second decade of the 20th century, the movement began to flourish practically everywhere in India, which became more popular from the 1940s, with a series of efforts at establishing *ashrams* beginning with southern India.[1473] A few important names spontaneously figure as we discuss this movement owing to their pioneering efforts in this regard. They are: Jules Monchanin who took the name *Swami Param Arubi Anandam*, which in Tamil means "the Blessings of the Highest Formless One" (1895-1957), Henri Le Saux (*Swami Abhishiktananda*, in Sanskrit "the Blessing of the Anointed Lord") (1910-1973), Bede Griffiths (1906-1993), Francis Mahieu (later *Francis Acharya*) (1912-2002) and Vandana Mataji (1921-2013),

1468 Ibid.

1469 Stephen A. Graham, "Evangelism without Apology: E. Stanley Jones and the Totalitarian Kingdom of God," in *Exploring Christian Mission Beyond Christendom: United Methodist Perspectives*, ed., Michael G. Cartwright (Indianapolis: University of Indianapolis Press, 2010), 42.

1470 A Brahmin convert to Anglican Church, who later united to Catholicism (1891). See Timothy C. Tennent, *Building Christianity on Indian Foundations: The Legacy of Brahmabadhdv Upadhyay* (Delhi: ISPCK, 2005), xi, 20.

1471 Fernando and Gispert-Sauch, *Christianity in India*, 316.

1472 See Vath, *Im Kampfe mit der Zauberwelt des Hinduismus,* 137-138.

1473 For example, Saccidanand Ashram in Kulittalai (Tamil Nadu), Kurisumala Ashram (Kerala) and many others. See Fernando and Gispert-Sauch, *Christianity in India*, 316; Kanjamala, *Future of Christian Mission in India*, 208.

et al.[1474] The first two, namely Jules Monchanin and Henri Le Saux were the ones to begin the movement after Brahmabandhab Upadhyay, in independent India.[1475] The writings of all these pioneers and chroniclers of their history are fundamental to understanding the entire movement.[1476] It may be noted here that Henri Le Saux, Bede Griffiths and Francis Mahieu were all Benedictine monks, underlying their Benedictine monastic tradition in the *ashram* movement in India.[1477]

The general perception of the Hindus was that the Church being westernized had become a barrier in eliciting interest of the Hindus in Christianity. For, many Hindu elites, the Christian *ashram* movement was envisioned as an attempt to introduce a new form of Christianity that would not be alien to Indian culture and spiritual traditions.[1478] Such an objective was sought to be realized by bringing "about a synthesis of Christian monasticism and the Indian form of *sanyasa* of the classical Sanskritic tradition within the *ashram* context of solitude, silence, austerity, asceticism, Christian yoga and contemplation inspired by the Upanishads, the Gita and the like."[1479] In the words of Swami Abhishiktananda (Henri Le Saux) it is a genuine effort at living a "contemplative life, in the absolute simplicity of early Christian monasticism and at the same time in the closest possible conformity with the traditions of Indian *sannyasa*[1480] with a blend of spirituality of the

1474 See Rowena Robinson & J. Marianus Kujur, eds., *Margins of Faith: Dalit and Tribal Christianity in India* (New Delhi: Sage Publications, 2010), 69.

1475 Schouten, *Jesus as Guru*, 174.

1476 For example the writings of Bede Griffiths are *Return to the Center* (1976), *The Marriage of East and West* (1982), *The Cosmic Revelation* (1983), *A New Vision of Reality* (1989). Similarly some of the important writings of Henri Le Saux (Swami Abhishiktananda) are: *Hindu-Christian Meeting Point, within the Cave of the Heart* (1966), *Guru and Disciple* (1974), *Saccidananda* (1974), *Towards the Renewal of the Indian Church* (1970). They are very important to understand the essence of Indianization of Christianity through the ashram movement. See William M. Johnston and Christopher Kleinhenz, eds., *Encyclopedia of Monasticism, Vol. 1&2, A-Z* (London & New York: Routledge, 2000), 385; Harry Oldmeadow, *A Christian Pilgrim in India: The Spiritual Journey of Swami Abhishiktananda* (Henri Le Saux) (Bloomington, Indiana: World Wisdom, 2008), 72-100.

1477 See Gordon S. Wakefield, ed., *The Westminster Dictionary of Christian Spirituality* (Philadelphia: The Westminster Press, 1983), 29.

1478 See Bob Robinson, *Christians Meeting Hindus: An Analysis and Theological Critique of the Hindu-Christian Encounter in India* (Milton Keynes, UK/Waynesboro, GA: Regnum Books International, 2004), 55.

1479 Robinson & Kujur, *Margins of Faith*, 69.

1480 Quoted in Oldmeadow, *A Christian Pilgrim in India*, 5.

"Indian *bhakti marga* [way of devotion] and the Franciscan spirituality of poverty."[1481] Summarizing all these aspects, Oldmeadow writes that "the hope was that 'what is deepest in Christianity may be grafted on to what is deepest in India' ... The bridge between Indian spirituality and the Church was to be monasticism, 'the place whereupon they may feel themselves in consonance with other."[1482] In all these efforts, utmost care was sought to be taken so as not to fall prey to syncretism.

This is the general background, against which the Jesuit attempt at *ashram* experiment was initiated in Poona. The first Jesuit to adopt a lifestyle of a *sanyasi/swami* was Armando Alvares (who later took the name Swami Animananda Alvahi, which in Sanskrit means, "Taking Joy in the Immaculate"). From one of his letters addressed to the Superior General (1958), two things become clear: firstly, that he began to explore the possibilities of such a way of life already in 1945 and secondly that he was alone in the field for more than a decade:

Thirteen years back when I entered the village of Deshnur at the desire of Rev. Fr. A. Miranda then Superior I had neither people nor houses, nor means and personnel to help me. The little seed thrown here and there in the midst of humiliations and insults my people and I had to suffer for our Faith has given me now a decent congregation of 75 faithful people, spread in ten to twelve families, another 65 catechumens only in Deshnur, more four villages, two primary Kannada [local language of Karnataka] schools in two of them., the parents of these school children are well-disposed towards us, intense apostolate is necessary to preach to them. I do so as far as possible for one man.[1483]

Anthony Felix Mathias (who took the name Swami Amalananda) followed in his footsteps and joined him in 1957 soon after his ordination (1957). They "both traveled, dressed, and lived like *sanyasis*, complete with robes, staff, begging bowl, and all other accoutrements. Swami Animananda built a chapel at Deshnur in the style of a Hindu *mandir* or temple."[1484] These Jesuits, especially Swami Animananda, may have

1481 Kanjamala, *Future of Christian Mission in India*, 206.

1482 Oldmeadow, *A Christian Pilgrim in India, 8. See also Anthony Rehm*, "Der Puna Ashram," *IB* 2/8 (October 1939): 97.

1483 Swami Animananda Alvahi to the Superior General (Deshnur, 27th July 1958), ARSI, *Belgaum-Poona. 1006-Particulares (1958).*

1484 Malachi Martin, *The Jesuits: The Society of Jesus and the Betrayal of the Roman Catholic Church* (New York: Simon & Schuster Paperbacks, 1987), 411.

begun to draw inspiration for such a way of life around the end of 1930s. Owing to the proximity, the immediate source of the same may have been the Protestant *ashram* established in Poona in the beginning of the 1930s by the Anglican Church. Anthony Rehm, reporting on this *ashram* writes in 1939 that "people of all kinds from Poona city come there: Brahmins and *Harijans* (untouchables)."[1485] This may clearly have been a strong impulse in arriving at a decision to experiment this method by these Jesuits too.[1486]

In the late 1960s a few more Jesuits joined them. As far as the total number of such Jesuits are concerned, it never crossed a single digit. It must be stressed here, however, that by the mid-1940s a growing interest among the Jesuits about this method was noticed. This is indicated by the fact that Henry Heras, a Spanish Jesuit of the Bombay Mission and a renowned historian of Indian history, in his recommendation towards exploring new methods of evangelization in India had also included the need of experimenting with the method as a special point of concern in his report submitted to the Superior General devoting a full chapter with the title, "Our Society should undertake the foundation of a monastic Congregation of Indian sanyasis suitable to the present circumstances of India."[1487]

The *ashram* founded by Jesuit *swamis* in Deshnur (Karnataka) was a combination of features of a formal Christian mission station (with a chapel, a school, a boarding home for children and a dispensary, etc.) and a Hindu *ashram*. As a whole it formed into a self-sufficient campus, with an effort to incorporate certain symbols in the architecture of the chapel and other structures from the religious tradition of the *Lingayats* (Virasaivas).[1488]

1485 Rehm, "Der Puna Ashram," 96-97.

1486 See Rehm, "Der Puna Ashram," 96.

1487 Heras, "On the Missionary Methods in India," 136-148. See also Thiier, "Bericht iiber den Besuch der Poona Mission," op. cit.

1488 *Lingayats*, also known as *Virasaivas* believe in one of the Hindu gods, namely Shiva and generally reverence the Vedas. But in more than one sense they distinguish themselves from many Brahmanical traditions and rites. In a strict sense of the term, thus, they may be termed as "a heretical sect" or "protestant Hindus." They have renounced image worship, Brahmanical rites and caste distinctions, etc. See Julian Saldanha, *Conversion and Indian Civil Law* (Bangalore: TPI, 1981), 28-29.

8.4.1. The Rationale behind the Ashram Experiment

Drawing inspiration from the Christian *ashram* movement apart, a certain section of the Jesuits in Poona began to grow skeptical about the traditional approaches in evangelization on the ground that they had not borne sufficient results in terms of winning over converts from among the higher caste Hindus. We have discussed quite extensively (under sub-topic #7.2) that the new converts in the mission were almost exclusively from among the lower caste people, like *Mahars*. Hence, it remained always an enigma as to how a breakthrough among the higher caste Hindus (in this context *Lingayats*) could be achieved. The section of the Jesuits who were skeptical about the traditional methods were strongly in favour of the opinion that such an objective would not be achieved unless the Christian faith is presented in terms and forms more comprehensible to the Indians.[1489]

Matthew Lederle, although he himself never took to an *ashram* lifestyle, was one of the forerunners in the Mission who strongly supported the *ashram* experiment among the Jesuits, especially in the late 1950s.[1490] He believed in its potentiality in furthering the cause of Hindu-Christian dialogue, which he considered essential in establishing a rapport with the Hindus.[1491] Given a strong insistence from the Government of India to man the Christian institutions with native personnel at the earliest possible point of time, the Catholic Church too had begun to reflect on the possibility of implementing this method within the larger framework of intensifying its efforts towards inculturation and adaptation, which may be concluded from a piece of information: "Within the last few months our Catholic press had spoken very much of the need of Indian adaptation for the further progress of our church in India. For instance the Examiner of Bombay has been quite open in the matter."[1492]

1489 See Rehm, "Der Puna Ashram," 96.

1490 He was one of the last Jesuits to come to Poona from Germany. He arrived in Poona in 1951 just two years after joining the Society of Jesus in 1949. Later on he became the Provincial of the Goa-Poona Jesuit Province and died in 1985 almost exactly after one year of assuming his office (1986). See "Fr. Matthew Rainer Lederle 23 March 1926-08 June 1986)," in *Deceased Members*, 114.

1491 Harold Coward, Hindu-Christian Dialogue: Perspectives and Encounters (Delhi: Motilal Banarasidass Publishers, First Indian Edition, 1993), 125.

1492 Swami Animananda Alvahi to the Superior General (Deshnur, 14th November 1956), ARSI, *Poona. 1005-XIV, Particulares.*

Moreover, by this time (mid-1950s) it was becoming more and more evident that among the Hindus, especially among the elite, everything that appeared foreign was becoming a matter of contempt and antipathy. This was an added factor in the consideration of adopting the method, as we read in a letter of Swami Animananda which in turn underlines also the immediate need of the method:

> Besides the immediate cause why I had to take up to Indian method or rather I was allowed to do so, was the misapprehension of our Hindu people whom we wish to bring to the light of Christ Our Lord, of thinking disparagingly and acting against all that is foreign and thus making Our Blessed Lord and His work to be more and more despised ... It means a great sacrifice and humiliation to lower oneself to that state of poor Indian *sanniasi* [*sanyasi*, holy man] but it is very glorious because we show Christ Our Lord to our Indian brethren in His real state of poverty and self-abnegation. European ways in the man of God in that line cannot be understood as proper of the minister of God. On the contrary my few years of practical apostolate convinces me of the necessity of following our fore-fathers St. John de Britto and Father De Nobili.[1493]

In another letter he claims that the decision to experiment this method was the result of a long process of discernment. Moreover, he claims that the method was approved by the higher authorities as well: "After my annual retreat, which I made alone on a hill under a tree nearby at the explicit permission of Rev. Fr. P[ius Geisel], [my reflection] has confirmed me of the necessity of such an adaptation."[1494] He mentions it further elsewhere too:

> Rev. Fr. Geisel, our VP [Vice Provincial], I think is going to send Rev. Fr. Prabhu Mathias ... to work over here as a sanniasi *[sanyasi]* as soon as his studies are over next May [1957] ... He [Pius Geisel] and Rev. Fr. Superior of the District have allowed me to train the little ones who show some signs and desires to become priests, as our future sanniasis *[sanyasis]*.[1495]

The conviction about the legitimacy of the method grew even more when the Major Superiors of India were unanimous in their opinion to

1493 Ibid., (Deshnur, 28th July 1956), ARSI, *Poona. 1005-IX*, 9.

1494 Ibid.

1495 Ibid., (Deshnur, 14th November 1956), op.cit.

promote the same as we read from the minutes of the 'Meeting of the Major Superiors of India held in 1959':

> Fr. Assistant [Jerome D'Souza] asked the Superiors for their opinion on the type of apostolic approach [*ashram* experiment] adopted by Swami [Animananda] Alvahi. All agreed that the experiment should not be stopped. A successor should be found for him both for his sake, as he is getting old, and for his good work, if the experiment is found to be good.[1496]

As for the Church authorities of the place, it becomes evident that the Local Ordinary (Bishop Michael Rodrigues) as well as his Auxiliary (Fortunato da Veiga Coutinho) too were generally in favour of this method: "H[is] E[xcellency] the Bishop of Belgaum [Michael Rodrigues] has confirmed our methods and told me to try to get more *sanyasis* for this great work in Kannada Districts."[1497] In fact, he "desires this kind of work very much and he has asked our Rev. Fr. Vice-Provincial to give me a fit assistant in Kannada language for this and other works. But he has added that our humble method of adaptation must follow for the good of our ministry."[1498]

About his Auxiliary at the moment and later successor, Swami Animananda makes the following comment: "By the advent of the new Bishop Fortunato [da Veiga Coutinho] ... we feel happy that the new Bishop is a God sent pastor to see into the difficulties of this most DIFFICULT APOSTOLATE."[1499] These are indications that a general understanding in favour of this method did prevail in the beginning from every concerned Church authority as well as Religious Superior.

The general approval from the authorities apart, in so far as the account of Swami Animananda may be taken as a basis, it would seem that the *Lingayat* Hindus of the first contact village, namely Sutkati (or Suttagatti) were welcoming in their attitude towards such a method of adaptation: "The *Lingayats* of this village have provided me with

---

1496 "Minutes of the Meeting of Major Superiors of India: Held on November 23 and 24,1959 at De Nobili College, Poona." ARSI, *Goa-Poona. 1006, Belgaum-Poonensis, Praep. Prov. (1959).*

1497 Swami Animananda Alvahi to the Superior General (Deshnur, 14th November 1956), op.cit.

1498 Ibid., (Deshnur, 27th July 1958), ARSI, *Belgaum-Poona. 1006-Particulares (1958).*

1499 Ibid., (Deshnur, 1st July 1963), ARSI, *Goa Poona 1006 -Particulares (1963).*

a free shelter of their own, wherein they do not allow *Harijans*[1500] to enter, neither can I go to them."[1501] The restrictions, thus, were already drawn for the Jesuit *swamis*, which implied that they had no choice of coming into contact with the *Lingayats* without at the same time excluding the *Harijans*. This aspect became a point of severe criticism in the later stage, about which we shall come back shortly. Yet, as far as the personal testimony of Swami Animananda goes, it appears that he considered the very first impression of being accepted by the *Lingayats* as a considerable breakthrough among them: "Protestants did the work many a year in this village for the conversion of these *Lingayats*, they succeeded with the *Harijans* but not with *Lingayats*. They respect me as their own priest..."[1502]

8.4.2. A Day in the Life of the Jesuit Sanyasis/**Swamis** *in the Ashram*

Given the uniqueness of the method of adaptation, it becomes interesting to explore as to how a day in the Jesuit *ashram* was like. What were the activities of the *Swamis* in the *ashram*? How did they integrate Jesuit way of life and the spirituality of a Hindu *ashram*? We get a glimpse of the same from a description given by Swami Animananda himself:

> We both are busy daily in the following manner: As soon as the morning sacrifice [Holy Mass] is over, Swami [Amalananda] has to give directions to the teachers and other personnel of schools, boardings, dispensaries and write for financial aid. I have to go out visiting houses of the converts and non-converts and preach and teach them prayers. Then at 10.30 a.m. we both give catechism class to all the school children without any distinction and imposition, after which all the children have their meals in the *math* [monastery] daily. Then comes our noon examination of conscience], meal and one hour siesta, for me without which I am unable to recite my *matutin* and *laudes* and continue the whole office till the end ... He [Swami Amalananda] does some composing work of *Kannada* hymns ... some of them already got the necessary ecclesiastical approval. After the Divine Office and the tea for myself only our work of supervision either of *Kannada* teaching or adult women

1500 A title given to the people of *Dalit* origin by Mahatma Gandhi in an attempt to give them an intrinsic sense of dignity. *Harijan* literally means 'people of God.'

1501 Swami Animananda Alvahi to the Superior General (Deshnur, 28th July 1956), op. cit.

1502 Ibid., (Deshnur, 27th July 1958), ARSI, *Belgaum-Poona. 1006-Particulares (1958)*. The italics in the text is mine.

> catechism class or going out to one of the five villages for our weekly Mass and visiting the sick continues. All on foot or bullock [cart] Damini, a conveyance apt for our *sanniasi's [sanyasi's]* poverty and come back from such far away villages late at night about 10:00 p.m.[1503]

Besides the activities mentioned in the text above, Swami Animanand claims that they had "daily class for all the boarders mostly the converts wherein he [Swami Amalananda] teaches them prayers, singing, good manners and above all how to stand firm for their new faith before their parents and fellow villagers."[1504] In the life of the *ashram* this group was significant in the sense that it formed a core group through which the *Swamis* intended to transmit to the wider Hindu society the purpose of the lifestyle they had chosen. They made it a regular custom to have preparation for every Sunday liturgy, which was invariably preceded by preparation for confession. The confession seems to have been "made by nearly all before and during the Mass."[1505] In order to make the liturgy meaningful, attempts were made to have "the singing practice of the religious hymns for the whole congregation which is followed by the crowd very enthusiastically."[1506]

A related question that comes up for reflection here is: how far and wide had the influence of the experiment reached in some five years after the initiation of the method? The Superiors seem to have expected a rapid expansion of the same adopting more and more villages, in spite of the fact that the *Swamis* were constrained by the lack of both personnel and resources:

> But V. Rev. Fr. Visitor suggested to me that we should not be tied down to Deshnur alone and thus diminish the range of my directly spiritual and apostolic work. So I started for new villages on the eastern side about 30 to 40 miles away from Deshnur and found possibilities to open new *Math* [cloister] over one of the highly populated and centred villages, named Kadkol and informed him of the new result and asked of him to help me for my journeys up and down and staying of three persons once a month over there.[1507]

1503 Ibid., (Deshnur, 1st July 1963), op.cit.

1504 Ibid.

1505 Ibid.

1506 Ibid.

1507 Ibid.

From the reply to the above suggestion it becomes clear that the expansion in terms of adopting a larger number of villages and establishing similar *ashrams* in other places was not possible due to the constraints of personnel and finance: "He [District Mission Superior] replied to me in the following words: 'It is not possible for me to help you in anything which would involve a previous correspondence. I am taking care however to explain carefully to Fr. Provincial the situation at Deshnur and all your needs.' So there stopped our further work."[1508] The indication is clear that the area of operation was slow to increase. Yet the experiment was continued in the hope of achieving a breakthrough among the *Lingayats* even in the later decades.

8.4.3. The Impacts of the Ashram Experiment[1509]

Since the experiment was one of the newest methods employed in the mission, it was bound to take some time to show some tangible results. Yet, from the presentation of the case from the point of view of the *Swamis* themselves, we may enumerate a few areas of achievements. For example, in a letter of Swami Animananda within a year of the experiment we read: "The elders of the village Mohore who were so hard to the voice of God in the beginning, now are the most forward people to help me in every way. If Rev. Fr. Vice Provincial agrees I shall have the House of God in their midst very soon."[1510] From the perspective of a mission among non-Christians in general, this may be considered a fair achievement. Let us examine the approach adopted by Swami Animananda in order to achieve a breakthrough among the *Lingayats*. The first approach, although it might appear as syncretistic and objectionable in the eyes of the Hindu critics, was a direct approach of introducing Christian faith through prayers. Here we come across with a portion of a letter that clearly reveals the fact:

> The devotion to the Sacred Heart of Jesus and the Immaculate Heart of Mary Our Mother by their pictures have greatly facilitated my apostolate among the Hindu *Lingayat* families wherein I place those pictures and ask them to pray to them in their difficulties and needs. Through this devotion I took up in my hands a typhoid case

1508 Ibid.

1509 The conclusions are drawn mostly from the letters of Swami Animananda. No wonder, these were from the perspective of the *Swamis* alone.

1510 Swami Animananda Alvahi to the Superior General (Deshnur, 28th July 1956), op.cit.

> of small child which was practically dying. I baptized the child, which afterwards survived treatment of nursing under the guidance of Doctor continued, worse days came, the catechist and myself daily said our Holy Rosary before those pictures in that family. After one month yesterday only there is no fever and the child is now being recovered and the whole family is now much impressed by the wonder of Our Blessed Mother and Her Divine Son and very soon will be their children by the waters of the Holy Baptism too.[1511]

The second approach was reaching out to them through philanthropic works. We have mentioned in chapter six that the lack of medical facilities was a stark reality of the place. Hence an extension of medical help to the needy was a powerful means of opening the possibilities. This is how it was done:

> Our work for the sick and T. B. [Tuberculosis] patients since the appointment of a permanent physician has been considerably increased. To show to the public that it is a divine work, we do not charge anything for the medicines we supply but only the cost of the injection's tubes. We have to buy the necessary medicines and pay the D[octor]r who comes from Belgaum three time a week and gets each time 50 to 60 patients with the help through our Mass stipend ... In addition to this we are looking for the destitute families, widows and fallen women by giving them some help in the form of grain, etc.[1512]

Added to these was the attempt to reach out to the people through educational institutions. It has been mentioned above that the *Swamis* had established a school for the local people akin to a set-up that is normally found at a mission station. An attempt was made thereby to impart not only formal education, but also religious instruction in view of forming leaders from the people themselves. This was an important aspect from the point of view of the mission among non-Christians:

> I find the need very urgent to train the selected young promising boys from among the *Lingayats* who are presently only three boarding and lodging with me and attending higher classes of Kannada and English outside and receiving necessary religious instruction from me every [evening] ... and [participate in the] meditation, however short it may be, in the morning daily. They

1511 Ibid.

1512 Ibid., (Deshnur, 7th August 1961), ARSI, *Belgaum-Poona. 1006-Partulares (1961).*

> are called "Puja Sevakaru" or Mass Servers and future "Upadeshi" [namely] catechists.[1513]

The consistency of the effort made with regard to leadership formation can be inferred from Swami Animananda's reports about his regular visits to the villages after five years: "We are accompanied by the catechist, compounder and two little altar boys who are making tremendous impression upon their fellow villagers big and small by their piety, singing and serving at the Hoy Sacrifice of the Mass:"[1514] In addition to these, although in a limited manner but clearly in proportion to the possibilities available, the Jesuit **Swamis** also aimed at promoting vocations to the priesthood from among the local people. It is not clear, however, whether the candidates spoken of in the text taken from a letter of Swami Animananda could persevere in the vocation to the Society of Jesus. But the genuine effort made by the **Swamis** does seem to be commendable:

> Vocations ... One young man who is our master at Deshnur has answered to our call, he is very bright, in spite of his only one eye he has mastered his studies quite well .. ..[But] the Superior is not in favour. A brahmane [Brahmin] convert Prakash Kulkarni who is with me for the last one year after his baptism studying our big catechism and has already passed his first exam fairly well, also is desiring to join us in priesthood because brahmanes [Brahmins] generally belong to the priestly class....[1515]

These are some of the instances that lead us to the conclusion that in spite of various constraints, certain tangible results in terms of increase in membership in the Church, i.e., baptisms, were gradually coming up. Apparently the results may not have been up to the expectation of the **Swamis** as well as that of the Superiors. Yet the attempts for the same were genuine and varied, although lack of accommodation facility was one of the constraints.

> On the coming feast day 15th of August 1961 there will be a few baptisms from paganism, and first communicants ... The Sunday attendance of big and small is slowly increasing. The work of preaching the Word of God in the *math* [cloister] and on Sundays

1513 Ibid., (Deshnur, 27th July 1958), ARSI, *Belgaum-Poona. 1006-Particulares (1958).*

1514 Ibid., (Deshnur, 1st July 1963), ARSI, *Belgaum-Poona. 1006-Particulares (1961).*

1515 Ibid., (Deshnur, 14th November 1956) ARSI, *Poona. 1005-XIV, Particulares (1961).*

> in the neighbouring villages is going on but not very much to our satisfaction since there is no sufficient accommodation to shelter those who come to hear it ... Our Swami [Amalananda] has organized nicely our permanent boarding for boys and girls separately. Practically all of them are our catechumens since their parents have already given their consent to their baptisms and they themselves are disposed to hear the Word of God.[1516]

In the context of the extensive village tours undertaken by him, Swami Animananda notes: "And it has brought for the last two years 42 baptisms of children and adults."[1517] The results in terms of increasing baptisms seem to have received a stamp of approval when the Local Ordinary of the place acknowledged their contribution in bringing the *Lingayats* to the Church, not a common phenomenon to be noted in the entire mission:

> On the 2nd of the last month he [Bishop Michael Rodrigues] confirmed for the first time 30 convert children and adults with all simplicity but in the midst of dignifying appropriate Indian Kannada singing composed both the letter and music by our Swami Amalananda ... And when everything was over, we could see great joy upon his face which he could not hide but expressed in these words: Swamis I congratulate you both for this nice work.[1518]

Whatever may have been the results of the experiment with the method, one aspect does come up rather strongly is the genuine efforts made by the *Swamis*. However, the approach of the *Swamis* was constantly a matter of critique from various quarters.

8.4.4. The Critique of the Ashram Method

As indicated above, the *ashram* lifestyle as the method of adaptation was not without controversies and differences of opinions. We come across with various opposing opinions. Some of them regard the efforts of the *Swamis* as positive and deserving appreciation, while others saw the same as not in tune with the Christian principles. The efforts of adaptation were fraught with numerous challenges and the endeavour itself was very complex. Hence, arriving at a simplistic conclusion either in favour of or against any particular position would be denying these

1516 Ibid., (Deshnur, 7th August 1961), ARSI, *Belgaum-Poona. 1006-Particulares (1961).*

1517 Ibid., (Deshnur, 1st July 1963), *ARSI, Belgaum-Poona. 1006-Particulares (1961).*

1518 Ibid.

aspects. The wisdom, instead, lies in the fact that we make an attempt at seeing the entire effort more objectively. This may best be done by briefly reviewing the differences of opinions on the issue.

8.4.5. Perception of the Jesuits other than the Swamis

The positive views about the method among the Jesuits may be said to be represented by four major sources, namely a Report of the Visitation by Karl Thuer (1948) as the Vice-Provincial of the Swiss Vice-Province, the letters of Joseph Stark as representing the voices of the Jesuits working on the mission field (mid-1950s), the 'Minutes of the Meeting of Major Superiors of India' (1959) together with the 'Goa-Poona: Visitor's Report (1963),' prepared by George Kester in the capacity of the Visitor of the Mission. From the dates of these sources, one gets a good picture of the differences of opinions gradually emerging among the Jesuits themselves.

To begin with, Karl Thiier seems to have been in a tacit agreement with the method. For, he too believed that new methods needed to be tried in order to reach out to the higher caste Hindus. His report after his Visitation in 1948 gives an unambiguous impression that he was far from being satisfied with the results of nearly nine decades of missionary endeavour in India. Besides, in the course of his Visitation he came to learn that "the Indians tend to see the missionaries in European dress as '*sahebs*' (gentlemen) rather than '*swamis*' (priests)."[1519] He, therefore, seems to have favoured the method as he believed that certain innovative methods needed to be devised in order to achieve the purpose of reaching out to the higher caste Hindus.

Similarly, Joseph Stark too made the following remark on the method a few later (1957): "The personal sacrifice these Fathers are making, has to be acknowledged and appreciated."[1520] George Kester was even more generous as he noted in his report: "What is very praiseworthy in this apostolate adopted by the *Swamis* is the earnest attempt to adopt the ways of the people in the general way of living, eating and also in the way of conducting religious services, the attempt to make people feel at home with them."[1521] His enthusiasm about

1519 Thue, "Bericht tiber den Besuch der Poona Mission," op. cit.

1520 Joseph Stark, "Litterae Consultoris Viceprovinciae Belgaum-Poonensis," (Panchgani, 7th July 1957), ARSI, *Poona. 1005-XIII,* 8.

1521 Kester, "Goa-Poona, Visitor's Report 1963," op. cit., 68.

the importance of the method may be assessed from the fact that he recommended the disposition depicted by the Jesuit *Swamis* as ideals to be emulated by other Jesuits: "A similar attempt will have to be made by anyone who is seriously aiming at a religious contact with higher castes, as also the Fathers at *Shanti Bhavan* [Home of Peace] in Calcutta and at *Snehasadan* [Abode of Love] in Poona realized."[1522] Two years earlier (1959), the 'Minutes of the Meeting of Major Superiors of India' too had held a similar view as it noted: "Approach to high castes; make practical approach like *Shanti Bhavan*.,"'[1523]

These instances are sufficient to indicate that a positive disposition among the Jesuits towards this method by and large did exist. Yet, we also come across with a few strong negative criticisms of the method, in fact much more in proportion than the positive ones themselves. In sum, a section of the Jesuits were not fully in favour of the method and that they saw the same as antiquated. In the words of Joseph Stark, for example, we read:

> But it is to be questioned whether for the sake of the Gospel such sacrifices are nowadays necessary or even advisable. Through the continual contact of Indians with the west and Christianity, western and Christian ideas and customs have become so familiar that they no longer appear as strange. Why then should one return to methods for the spread of Christianity which may have been successful some hundred years agó? Why should one go about in a dress of a Hindu religious teacher, since our cassock impresses the non-Christians as a religious garment and commands their respect; some consider it even as an Indian garment?[1524]

The text clearly shows that Joseph Stark, while appreciating the effort on the one hand, was highly critical about the method on the other. The letter quoted above further shows that he was apprehensive about the general reaction of the non-Christian Indians to such an innovative method, so to say. His basic apprehension, moreover, was

1522 Ibid. Strictly speaking these two centres were dialogue centres and not comparable to the *ashrams*. But the objective of both kinds of centres was the same, namely making a breakthrough among the high caste Hindus.

1523 "Minutes of the Meeting of Major Superiors of India: Held on November 23 & 24, 1959 at De Nobili College, Poona," ARSI, *Belgaum-Poona. 1006-Praep. Prov. (1959)*.

1524 Stark, "Litterae Consultoris Vice-provinciae Belgaum-Poonensis," op. cit., 8. This opinion does seem to be on the other extreme.

with regard to the attitude of the possible reaction of the officials with whom the Jesuits had regularly something or the other to do in connection with schools and other areas of management of mission stations. He believed that those less favourably disposed towards the Jesuit missions will certainly interpret the purpose of the method as aiming at the conversion of the local people, leading thereby to an antagonism. As a result, even the functional relationship with them would be disrupted. He went so far as to state that the liberals among the Hindus too would find the method as something ridiculous, if not farcical. Narrating an incident he gives his opinion about their dress as unnecessarily creating a confusion both among the Hindus as well as Christians: "Last year one of these *Sanyasi* Fathers visited Ahmednagar District. His attire did not impress anybody, neither Hindus nor Christians. Our Christian 'Jungli' boys gave vent to their feelings by simply laughing at it."[1525] In his opinion, however, what seemed to count as ever more serious concern against implementing the method was the disproportionate results in terms of the number of conversions from among the *Lingayats*. Moreover, he considered the zeal of the Jesuits seeking to experiment with the method as prompted by a false interpretation of the traditional methods of evangelization. Here is a portion of his letter that unambiguously implied such aspects:

> There is no movement towards Christianity so far from these caste people, and it looks just as elsewhere (and this is not merely a guess, but has some foundation in facts) that the attractiveness of Christianity consists rather in financial help which one expects or experiences and in the moral support of the Father. Anyhow, the sacrifices this kind of life implies seem to me in no proportion to the success. There is also danger that a certain unhealthy ambition creeps in like this: These old Missionaries with their foreign ideas and methods could not make any headway, but we the younger ones, shall do it - After ten years of experimenting I guess, they will be just as disillusioned as the old ones.[1526]

1525 Ibid.

1526 Ibid. Unwittingly, this opinion seems to be justified to a certain extent by the experiences of Swami Animananda himself: "The old converts are not giving us the desired satisfaction. They find hard to follow the Commandments of God and the Church especially the Sunday Mass, Confession and Holy Communion. The Lingayat-mind is not quite open but reserved and hidden. Hence dangerous. Only by patience and through prayers of ours

Writing nearly six years later, George Kester, in an annex to the report referred to above, also expressed his apprehensions about the method on account of certain aspects in the approach of the *Swamis* that he perceived as counter to the Christian principles. The annex to the report may be quoted at some length in order to show his perception of the incongruities in the approach of the *Swamis*:

> My first idea was: Let these Fathers go on. They do useful preparatory work by making contacts, by removing prejudices against the Church as being western in outlook. The external way of living: Swami dress [outfit], vegetarian diet, will make them acceptable to the Hindus. Now: after visiting them twice at their place, after giving each of them one full day to talk to me, I come to realize that 1) Their approach aims at the *Lingayats* exclusively, they avoid contact with the lower castes and other people. Their Catholics do not want to mix with Catholic communities reared by other priests, who together with their flocks are considered to be 'contaminated.' What will happen if boys educated by *Swamis* go to work elsewhere in the Mission stations or parishes run by 'contaminated' Fathers? In India in general things are changing. Intercommunication between castes becomes easier and easier. 2) The Government of India and the local authorities do all they can to break down caste prejudices and encourage all social work done in this line to foster the spirit of equality and true democracy. It seems wise to follow this line of conduct as much as possible, all the more so as it is in line with natural law and Catholic doctrine. Hence it seems logical that the *Swamis* have to prove that their way of approach is the only possible way of approaching the *Lingayats* ... They are very firm that they are right. The younger Swami is almost fanatical on this point, but so far they have not been able to convince me - nor the district Superior and others - that they are right in their conviction. They appeal in a general way to the success of their work, and to some 50 baptisms in the last few years. The district Superior is not very much impressed. I have been told that a good number are children, even the majority, and not a few have fallen away again.[1527]

we hope to get them round." Swami Animananda to the Superior General (Deshnur, 7th August 1961), ARSI, *Belgaum-Poona. 1006-Particulares (1961).*

1527 George Kester, "Annexum to Litterae Visitatoris Goa-Poona 63/9," ARSI, *Prov. Goa-Poonensis, Negotia Specialia, 1408.*

In the main report itself he indicates the major points of objection in the following words:

> Yet there is a point in which the Swamis at Deshnur seem to be definitely out of date and off the right track: They think that in order to contact the Lingayats they have to conform to caste-prejudices in the sense of regarding and treating low castes and others who are eating meat as untouchables, and in consequence, in keeping aloof from them. They appeal in this to the example of Fr. De Nobili, without apparently realizing that the times have changed since then. Treating others as untouchables is certainly against the sense of Christian Brotherhood and it is equally against the trend of public opinion in the India of today.[1528]

It appears that a majority of the Jesuits nurtured such apprehensions and skepticism. The main point of contention that seems to have occupied their imagination may be put in the form of a question: Was the way of approach adopted by the *Swamis* the only possible way of approaching the *Lingayats*! The annex to the report quoted above claims that the perception of the majority of the Jesuits were otherwise:

> But what is more serious is that the District Superior and the two other Fathers in the district [Belgaum] are convinced and can prove it by facts that 'ordinary' priests are acceptable to Lingayats, even if they work among low castes at the same time, that Lingayat boys and low caste boys are mixed in the hostels and schools and that Lingayats do not object to this. The District Superior ... is convinced that he will be able to make conversions among the Lingayats even without observing caste distinctions, provided he is allowed to work in the district for two or three years, and that a priest who is working among all classes of people will ... become as little objectionable to the higher castes as a doctor or nurse or teacher who is working among all castes.[1529]

It may be noticed that the above text is basically a speculation, certainly not without a sufficient experiential knowledge of the reality of the place. However, from the force of the claim we have every reason to believe that the Jesuits working in close proximity with the *Swamis*

1528 George Kester, "Goa-Poona, Visitor's Report 1963," op. cit., 68-69.

1529 George Kester, "Annexum to Litterae Visitatoris *Goa-Poona 63/9," ARSI, Prov. Goa-Poonensis, Negotia Specialia, 1408.*

did not find the method as indispensable. This is further revealed in the same annex to the report cited above:

> I think the large majority of our Fathers working in Belgaum City and Belgaum district are of this opinion [namely the one expressed in the above citation], and most of them, if not all of them, are puzzled by the spirit of aloofness and exclusiveness of the Swamis and their Catholics. Hence the question arises whether this work has not to be discontinued as being no longer in harmony with modern developments in India and not being the only way to approach *Lingayats*.[1530]

Pius Geisel was even more critical about the Jesuit *Swamis* and their claims:

> Two Fathers are wearing the garb of sadhus [Hindu monks]. Both are eccentrics and are not taken seriously. I regret, that an earlier decision not to allow this singularity was reversed and Fr. Mathias alias Prabhu, now Swami Amalananda was allowed to take up this mode of life ... Fathers [Guy] Deleury and [Matthew] Lederle, who live in the heart of the city, leading an ordinary life, although being foreigners have achieved much more contact than these Swamis. Fathers Deleury and Lederle are accepted in the highest orthodox circles ....[1531]

Based on the above criticisms, a comment is in order here. It may be recalled that Mahatma Gandhi had launched a movement in the 1920s towards improving the condition of the untouchables in Indian society.[1532] His efforts were quite earnestly being emulated by the Government of India and local civil authorities. Undoubtedly, in view of all these, the mind of the Indian public was gradually undergoing a change. Hence, only with the purpose of achieving a breakthrough among the *Lingayats* the toleration of the caste distinction, if not the promotion of the same, did appear inconsistent with the teachings of the Church. The logic that prompted George Kester to form his opinion in this regard was the profession of the doctors, nurses and teachers, based on the opinions shared by the Jesuits working in the same district.

1530 Ibid.

1531 Pius Geisel, "Informatio de statu Vice-Provinciae Belgaum-Poonensis data a procuratore Viceprovinciae mense Septembri 1961," ARSI, *Belgaum-Poonensis, Particulares (1961).*

1532 See Barbara D. Metcalf & Thomas R. Metcalf, *A Concise History of Modern India, Second Edition* (Cambridge: Cambridge University Press, 2006), 184.

His simple take on the matter, therefore, was: if such professionals did not exclude *Harijans* from others in their profession, how the Jesuits could afford to do the same. His basic contention, thus, was that such professionals were never considered as being contaminated by the higher caste people on the ground that they served the people irrespective of their caste and class distinctions. Hence, he contested by saying that,

> It would be strange ... if caste people could not get used to the idea that a priest administering mainly to them does not exclude *Harijans* from his ministrations. As it is the Swamis would rather prefer to their people to remain without Mass for some time than to call one of the "white" and meat-eating Fathers to say Mass in their place. Thus their way of acting would introduce caste distinctions also in the Catholic community precisely now when caste-distinction in churches has been abolished with such determination also in south of India.[1533]

We may conclude from the text that George Kester was not entirely against the method *per se*. His objections were basically on certain fundamental points. For example, he saw nothing objectionable as far as the *Swamis* chose to live as they did among caste people and avoided eating meat out of politeness and respect towards the people around them. But he found it entirely unwarranted that they should treat other people who did eat meat as polluted. He refers to an incident, whereby the *Swamis* seem to have gone so far with regard to maintaining the caste-distinctions that they refused to accept a present sent to them by the Sisters on the ground that it had been brought to them by a low caste boy.[1534] Given these factors Kester gave his verdict in the following words: "As I have stated above ... I would be in favour of allowing the Swamis to continue their work in peace: making spiritual contacts, and breaking down prejudices, but I just cannot see how one could justify the spirit of separation and the lack of charity towards ordinary priests and towards other Catholics."[1535]

Similarly, he also found it incompatible with the *ashram* lifestyle that the *Swamis* should conduct schools, dispensaries and other social works. He perceived them as counter to the *ashram* lifestyle and hence

1533 Kester, "Goa-Poona, Visitor's Report 1963," 68-69.

1534 Ibid., 68.

1535 Kester, "Annexum to Litterae Visitatoris Goa-Poona 63/9," ARSI, *Prov. Goa-Poonensis, Negotia Specialia, 1408.*

remarked: "If they do this then there is really little reason to retain the external paraphernalia of Swamidom. It would be much better if they would leave school and dispensary to others to continue to wander about and preach."[1536] In addition to these, he found two more aspects going against the method. The first one was the fact that the *Swamis* were not yet well accepted by the village leaders in Deshnur and the average middle-class farmers of the district. Secondly, he also found it detrimental to the Christian witness that the two *Swamis* should live constantly at loggerheads with each other about the set-up of their apostolate. They did not seem to get on well with each other.[1537]

These sources are sufficient to illustrate the point that there were a lot of differences of opinions on the method among the Jesuits themselves. In spite of the fact that the *ashram* experiment continued even till later decades, it is clear that a lot of apprehensions were raised against it. In other words, the experiment was invariably seen with suspicion by some Jesuits.[1538] It is not hard to imagine that the *Swamis* may have been constantly confronted by differences of opinions. This becomes all the more evident from the fact that they needed to tender justifications on various occasions in favour of the lifestyle they had adopted.

8.4.6. Justification by the Jesuit Swamis

A comment made by George Kester sets a prelude to the following paragraphs pertaining to the justification given by the *Swamis* in support of their conviction about the importance of the method: "I know that they [*Swamis*] would deny this and that proves that personally they are excellent men; but it is very hard to deny the clear daily happenings of ordinary life."[1539] The comment indicates the fact that there was a lack of consensus among the Jesuits on the question of the *Swamis*. Moreover, the *Swamis* were often constrained by the criticism from various quarters. Yet they were determined to continue with the lifestyle they had chosen, with utmost zeal and unmixed motives. As far as a few letters are taken as a basis of arriving at certain conclusions, it strongly

1536 Kester, "Goa-Poona, Visitor's Report 1963," 69.

1537 Ibid., 68-69.

1538 See Bob Robinson, *Christians Meeting Hindus: An Analysis and Theological Critique of the Hindu-Christian Encounter in India* (Milton Keynes, UK: Regnum Books International, 2004), 56.

1539 George Kester, "Annexum to Litterae Visitatoris Goa-Poona 63/9," ARSI, *Prov. Goa-Poonensis, Negotia Specialia, 1408.*

emerges that their entire objective was to gain converts from among the *Lingayats*. It remains unclear, however, whether the *Swamis* realized the main point of objection raised by other Jesuits. In any case what comes up clearly is the fact that they were not prepared to look back on the choice they had made and that their entire perspective on their lifestyle was different from others. Yet, as we have noted above, it is also true that the views counter to their own were not too rare. Precisely for all these reasons, they needed to supply justifications on more than one occasion to prove their stand. In one of the letters, for example, Swami Animananda wrote:

> Of course there are prejudices in the minds of some of our Superiors which I like to mention for Y[our] P[aternity]'s information and guidance. 1) They think that a Catholic priest is respected much more in white than in saffron even by Hindus. To this I ask myself what have we done to penetrate among the Hindus, these Hindus want our white cassock only to educate their children to be big men in this world and nothing more and we priests are flattered, of course with due respect for my Superiors, with these empty honours. Whereas my little experience on the saffron garb for the last nine years has brought me much honour and success as a man of God though I know what I am by my daily meditation and examination of conscience. 2) Our Fathers will point out what is bad in the Indian (Hindu) sanniasi [*sanyasi*] namely want of cleanliness and purity in him but they will try to ignore how many good sanniasis [*sanydsis*], I mean clean and respectable, there are in Karnataka with saffron.[1540] 3) Another thing our Fathers tell me that I should not cooperate with the wrong thinking of my lingayats, regarding the non-vegetarian diet. I know how difficult it is to be vegetarian but only the love of God must take us to that for the great end we have in view and besides according to our Principle and Foundation[1541] we must consider these creatures as indifferent and use them or abstain from as far as they are means or obstacles

1540 This point is precisely underlined as one of the strongest reasons against the use of the method by Joseph Stark in his criticism of the same. See Joseph Stark, "Litterae Consultoris Viceprovinciae Belgaum-Poonensis" op.cit, 8.

1541 'The Principle and Foundation' is placed in the beginning of the classic by Ignatius of Loyola, the founder of the Society of Jesus, namely *The Spiritual Exercises of St. Ignatius of Loyola* (#23). "In the words of Karl Rahner, 'it is a preparatory testing of dispositions, already containing and explains the whole substance of the [Spiritual] Exercises." Varghese Malpan, *A Comparative Study of the Bhagavad-gita and the Spiritual Exercises*

> towards the end for which we have come to the SJ regarding the missions *ad paganos*.[1542]

In another letter, Swami Animananda tries to justify the importance of the method while countering the objection raised by other Jesuits:

> Those who have no experience of such village life, say that the life of a *sanniasi* is a mockery and scandal to the educated public, who would hoot him. This statement proves only our ignorance of our villages of our religious life. Even authorities on the contrary have shown me such respect that they are ready to grant me any favour I ask them. They have granted a big area of the Government land free and exempted me from all Government assessment and tell those who are in opposition to my plans, "why they should not be Swamis and work for the public as I do?[1543]

If the veracity of the statement above may be proved, it does show the acceptability of the method among the direct beneficiaries of the works of the *Swamis*. Hence, one tends to conclude that the difference of opinions among the Jesuits was partially a result of the lack of personal experience of the life in the villagers among some Jesuits. The details underneath taken from the same letter quoted above, seems to give an indication that the sphere of their influence was doubtlessly widening its horizons. It is here one faces a dilemma as to what the real situation may have been. For, the views of the Jesuits discussed above mostly seem to give a negative picture. On the other hand the *Swamis* continue to paint a positive picture of the response received by its direct beneficiaries. The following letter reveals something more:

> The Government of the State of Mysore, to which we belong, and of the Centre New Delhi are helping my work very much. Only the Education Department of Belgaum and Bangalore has been a little hard on me, it has not registered my three schools in spite of children's parents' request to do so for the last two years. I hold my patience and trying to see what I can do to remove the prejudices against our missionary influence by explaining our sincere and fair attitude towards the freedom, which our Indian Constitution allows

---

of St. Ignatius of Loyola on the Process of Spiritual Liberation (Rome: Editrice Pontificia Universita Gregoriana, 1992), 246.

1542 Swami Animananda to the Superior General (Deshnur, 14th November 1956), ARSI, *Poona. 1005-XIV, Particulares (1954).*

1543 Ibid., (Deshnur, 27th July 1958), ARSI, *Belgaum-Poona. 1006-Particulares (1958).*

> us. Many a village is insistently inviting us to preach the Word of God among its caste people ... The people of this village are constantly asking him to send to them a Kannada sanniasi, which request he is not able to satisfy.[1544]

8.4.7. A Brief Appraisal of the Ashram Method

Having made a brief overview of the various opinions on this method of adaptation, one does feel that the nobility of purpose, sincerity of efforts and zeal of the *Swamis* have been beyond reproach. It is an undeniable fact that the failure to win over the converts from among the higher caste Hindus (here *Lingayats*) was a serious concern. It would not be wrong, hence to state that this concern may have occupied the thoughts of many Jesuits of the younger generation. Besides, the impact of the *ashram* movement spearheaded by the Benedictines and others mentioned above, was undeniable. Hence, to throw the baby out with the bathwater would be unjustifiable. On the contrary, the effort of the *Swamis* does seem to be commendable.

The criticisms by other Jesuits in general, however, do contain certain complex questions. The first one is the challenge of keeping the demands of the Christian ethic of equality of human beings intact and at the same time to achieve a breakthrough among the *Lingayats* without neglecting the *Harijans*. Secondly, the challenge of resolving the question of the indispensability of the method, which may be stated thus: if the *Swamis* chose to relate solely with the *Lingayats*, the *Harijans* (*Dalits*) and others would be left out and vice-versa. Undoubtedly, such an approach was going to be diagonally opposed to the fundamental Christian principle, namely the basic equality of human beings. Going back to the letter of Swami Animananda, we do realize that the choice of the *Swamis* to relate exclusively with the *Lingayats* was not their choice in luxury. We have quoted the letter above wherein Swami Animananda reveals that they needed to conform to the tradition of the *Lingayats* themselves in relating to them, probably in the hope that the question of breaking caste prejudices could be addressed later once the community is brought to the Catholic Church. Such a hypothesis does not seem to be fully unfounded if we go through the letters of the *Swamis*. The tenacity vis-a-vis the adopted method shown by them gives a clue to the same.

1544 Ibid.

The second aspect that comes up for consideration here is the question of the differences of opinions. One finds it particularly difficult to understand as to why in the criticisms a middle path was not sought. This becomes all the more complex given the fact that the *ashram* lifestyle as a method of adaptation was not only seen positively but also encouraged by the Jesuits in general across India, besides the fact that the movement itself was becoming stronger in general.[1545] Hence the question comes: Why no middle path was sought to be explored to do away with the lacunae in the approach of the *Swamis* vis-a-vis the *Lingayats* and *Harijans*?

From the criticisms referred to above, it would seem that on the one hand the Jesuits in general were in favour of the method, yet the Jesuits in Poona often came across certain incongruities that seemed to go strongly against the continuation of the method. Although it is difficult to claim with certainty, yet one tends to support the idea of Swami Animananda that others may have lacked a personal experience of the complexity of the *Lingayat* village structure. While taking this position, however, there is no intention to support the caste distinctions maintained by them.

Leaving aside the inevitable incongruities in the approach of the *Swamis*, i.e., exclusively reaching out to the *Lingayats*, etc., if we make a careful analysis of the various opposing views, the matter boils down to one single issue, i.e., an implicit desire to gain a numerical increase of the Catholic community. It is an indication again that a missionary endeavour undertaken by the Jesuits was largely understood in terms of winning over converts from other religions. In fact, governed by such an understanding of the mission, the *ashram* lifestyle undertaken by the *Swamis* was often seen with skepticism. In plain terms, the Jesuits in general seemed to have had a fear of antagonizing the larger Hindu society, while at the same time they were not getting proportionate numerical increase in the membership of the Church. These experiences of the Jesuits, as well as of other Christian missionaries were the foundations for the later approaches to the issue, so that Christian missionaries in general began to see the *ashram* lifestyle not in terms of Christianizing Hinduism, rather in terms of Hinduizing Christianity "by

1545 "Minutes of the Meeting of Major Superiors of India," op. cit. See also Heras, "On the Mission Methods," 136-148.

recovering the mystical and contemplative dimension of the Christian tradition."[1546]

Finally, a brief analysis of the approach of the Jesuit *Swamis* gives us inkling into their missiological position as well. Seen in the light of Vatican II, it becomes quite apparent that they believed in the church-implantation model of missiology that lays emphasis on the numerical increase in the membership of the Church. The schools, boarding homes and dispensaries were considered as means of achieving a breakthrough amidst the high caste Hindus.[1547]

8.5. The Schools and Colleges:[1548] The Debates Pertaining to their Objectives

We have discussed at length in chapter four (Cf. 4.1.1) how education through schools and colleges was further utilized as an apostolic instrument in the mission.[1549] Here we shall discuss the debates pertaining to their primary objectives. At the outset, however, it may be apt to note the background of the same. The debate basically sprang from the fact that a section of the Church hierarchy as well as that of the Jesuits in India seemed to have grown occasionally apprehensive about the very purpose of running schools and colleges by various Catholic missions. To them, the question of minimal conversions directly resulting from educational institutions remained not only an enigma, but not seldom did it also cause pessimism among them. We come across with some instances, whereby they seem to have been of the opinion that the Catholic schools and colleges were not serving the primary purpose of their establishment, namely leading the beneficiaries to conversion to Catholicism.[1550] Hence, the critics approaching the subject from the perspective of the western countries often entertained the idea that the

1546 Harry Oldmeadow, *Journeys East: 20th Century Western Encounters with Eastern Religious Traditions* (Indiana: World Wisdom, 2004), 223.

1547 See "Minutes of the Goa-Pune Province Meeting, Xavier Training College, Deshnur [Belgaum], May 4-7, 1981," PJPA, *Varia*.

1548 Under this sub-topic, I have frequently used the term 'institutions' to indicate 'High Schools' and 'University Colleges.'

1549 It is a deliberate use to say 'further' because education through schools and colleges were utilized as apostolic instruments already from the beginning of the undivided Bombay-Poona Mission.

1550 We need not elaborate the point, yet it may be stated that this way of perception about the objective of the schools and colleges was common among the missionaries in various missions.

entire enterprise of managing educational institutions by the Catholic missions in India was a futile endeavour. Clearly such a conclusion was drawn on the ground that the tangible results of the number of converts did not seem to correspond to the magnitude of investment in terms of personnel and finance. E. R. Hull narrates an incident related to an English Jesuit Astronomer who remarked at the end of his short stay in Bombay that he would have abolished the entire educational enterprise of the Jesuits there within a week, were he to be in-charge of the mission.

The above perception by the English Jesuit Astronomer may be considered as a typical example of the critics who normally did not take into consideration the unique circumstances of India and tended to see the educational endeavour of the Jesuits purely from the western perspective. The above-mentioned English Astronomer had failed to realize that the abolition of the entire educational enterprise in a week would be equivalent to undoing a massive missionary work and a substantial indirect positive impact brought about by the same in a period of at least a decade, if not more.[1551] It is clear, thus, that he had failed to take into consideration the constraints of the prospects of direct evangelization sufficiently in the process of drawing conclusions from his perceptions. He had failed to realize that the entire educational enterprise needed to be seen more as a *preparation* rather than as a direct means of evangelization. In sum, therefore, his remark would imply "the ruin of the Catholic education in India"[1552] achieved in not less than a decade. What is surprising is the fact that this kind of perception about the objectives of the educational institutions was shared not by an insignificant number of the missionaries of the time working for decades in India.

The Jesuits being the forerunners in the area of education could not detach themselves from the debate. We gather from some of the sources that this issue had a larger significance embracing all the Jesuit missions in India. Such a conclusion is derived from the fact that the debate found its echo in the Conference of the Jesuit Educationists (1930), [hereafter Conference (1930)] too, of which we have made frequent mention in

1551 See Hull, "Some Moot-Points," op. cit, 2; E. R. Hull, "Bombay-Poona Mission: The Mixed College and School Question, 1927," ARSI, *Prov. Bombay-Poona. 1404-De Collegiis in India, 4.*

1552 Hull, "Some Moot-Points," op. cit., 2.

chapter four.[1553] The crux of the issue could be summarized in the form of the following questions: What does it gain to have a huge investment in terms of finance and personnel if the schools and colleges are seemingly failing to aid in gaining an expected number of converts? Elsewhere the questions are formulated even more sharply: "Is the Church justified in investing so largely in material and personnel in education on its various levels? ... What is the result of our educational activity in the past two centuries? 'Does it help or hinder evangelization?"[1554] These were the realistic concerns of all those observers who perceived the lesser number of converts resulting directly from the schools and colleges as going against the rationale for continuation of the entire educational enterprise of the Jesuits.[1555]

While taking the discussion further, a few basic assumptions may be underlined here. Accordingly, the first assumption that acted as a stimulus for the emergence of the debate was the differences of opinions on the understanding of the basic purpose of Catholic educational institutions. In the western set up when a school was designated as a Catholic school, it generally implied that the school was primarily meant for the Catholic students,[1556] or at least for a majority of them. Secondly, there was a perception among a section of the missionaries that the personnel working at the educational institutions were not *missionaries* in the conventional sense of the term.[1557] What was meant by this? In order to answer this question, we need to refer back to the stereotypical understanding of missionary activity whereby direct proselytism was understood to be the ultimate objective of the mission, which in other

1553 See "Educational Conference [1930]," op. cit., 2-4; 9-11; 16-19.

1554 "Perspectives on Evangelization: VIII. Education" (A booklet for private circulation only), PJPA, *Varia*.

1555 Hull mentions that in his 25 years of stay in Bombay, he came across only a couple of converts from among the direct beneficiaries of the Catholic institutions including those run by the Jesuits. See Hull, "Mixed Colleges and School Question: II. Answer of the Committee to the larger Questionnaire," ARSI, *Prov. Bombay-Poona. 1404-De Collegiis in India, 4-5.*

1556 It would be a generalization to state that such was always true. In Germany and other countries, where the population of the Protestants was often more than the Catholics, such a claim did not hold true. But in many other countries it did.

1557 "Educational Conference [1930] [Fr. Willekens]" op. cit., 3. Joseph Diihr and Henry Heras represented St. Xavier's College, Bombay.

words was "making non-Christians members of a Church."[1558] In the words of Carlos Cardoza-Orlandi, a "missionary activity consists in the proclamation of the gospel, the conversion of non-Christians ... Non-Christian territory is the location of missionary action. 'Ministries' exist within Christendom; 'missions' exist outside of Christendom."[1559] Under this scheme, a missionary is understood as one who engages in direct evangelism and proselytism. This brings us back to the basic contention in the present debate: Were it to be clearly understood that the educational institutions were primarily meant as preparation of evangelization and hence by the same logic could not be taken as direct means of evangelization?

As we analyse the central point of the debate carefully against the arguments in the foregoing paragraphs, we discover that the roots of the same ultimately go back to a particular understanding of the prevalent missiological position on the basic objectives of the Christian educational institutions. Dealing with the Indian context, M. Thomas Thangaraj, for example, makes the following distinction: "There were varying perceptions about the relationship between these educational institutions and the evangelistic task of the churches. Some missionaries ... saw the educational project as a potential way to convert Hindus to Christian faith ... Others saw the educational mission simply as a duty of love and care."[1560] Going by this distinction, there is no doubt whatsoever to identify in the entire debate that the position of the Church hierarchy and that of a good number of the Jesuits in India, by and large, had been the first one, namely perceiving the management of educational institutions as 'a potential way to convert Hindus [and others] to Christian faith.' Apparently, when the results in terms of the number of converts coming from the educational institutions did not seem to correspond to the investment of personnel and finance, the apprehensions about their objectives did begin to be raised in certain circles as indicated above.

1558 Carlos F. Cardoza-Orlandi, *Mission: An Essential Guide* (Nashville: Abingdon Press, 2002), 13.

1559 Ibid., 32.

1560 M. Thomas Thangaraj, "Indian Christian Tradition," in *Religions of South Asia: An Introduction,* eds., Sushil Mittal & Gene Thursby (London & New York: Routledge, 2006), 192. See also "Perspectives on Evangelization: VIII. Education," PJPA, *Varia.*

8.5.1. Admission to Non-Catholic Students

Another aspect that was closely related to the question of Catholic educational institutions was the question of admission to non-Catholic students on the same footing as Catholic students. A basic question that was needed to be addressed was formulated by E. R. Hull in the following words: "Can we make our Colleges and Schools exclusively Catholic by eliminating the non-Catholic pupils? And if not, why not?"[1561] At the background of the debates on this point, although there seem to have been more factors responsible for the same, we shall make a mention of just a few here. Firstly, there are indications that the Jesuits may have been alleged of doing a disservice to the Catholic Church by admitting non-Catholics to their institutions. In fact their very motive of taking this step was seen with skepticism, as being both mercenary and monetary. In any case, what becomes evident is the fact that such allegations and apprehensions may have been quite strong and hence needed to be addressed. This is revealed through a remark by E. R. Hull:

> Before starting I feel bound to address certain highly ungracious and unfair remarks which appeared in an educational journal lately, where a reproach was pointedly directed against us for 'sacrificing Catholic interests for the sake of material gains.' This mercenary motive does not enter into the case. It is not the question of gains, it is a question of securing sufficient income to run our institutions at all. It is not a question of their prosperity but of their sheer existence.[1562]

From the perspective of the Jesuits themselves who were critical about the issue, it goes back again to the western mindset of looking at the concept of a Catholic school or a college. Such a group of Jesuits were often perturbed by the fact that they had no choice but to admit non-Catholic students almost on par with the Catholics. This aspect seemed to be peculiar to them coming as they were from western countries they were accustomed to seeing Catholic schools invariably admitting Catholics exclusively or at least in a majority. Such was by no means possible in India.[1563]

1561 Hull, "Essay on Mixed Colleges and Schools," 1.

1562 Ibid.

1563 See Hull, "Some Moot-Points," op. cit., 2. See also Hull, "The Mixed College and School Question, 1927," 4-5.

Having said that, as we take a look at the history of admitting non-Catholics in Catholic institutions in India, we hardly come across with any instance of limiting admissions to Catholics alone. Hence, there is no need of elaborating the point for the simple reason that it was a matter of choice given the multi-religious and multi-cultural reality of India. Moreover the Catholic population was a tiny fraction of the total population. Hence it would be virtually preposterous even to pose a theoretical question whether Catholic institutions could have been run solely for the Catholics alone. In the concrete case of a college, for example, one of the most compelling considerations with regard to it was the question of financial viability. With a smaller number of students the financial burden of the college would have been manifold, even to the extent that eventually it would have to be closed down. This would be all the more true when the college was to consist entirely of Catholic students, a large proportion of whom needed to be subsidized due to their poor financial background. The point may be illustrated with an example. If we take the financial aspects, it would not have been feasible to manage a college exclusively for about 200 to 250 Catholic students. The income from the fees paid by the Catholic students alone would have been too small. It would thus imply a heavy financial burden on the Jesuits. Besides, they would require to dismiss all the lay-staff members due to lack of adequate finances to pay salaries and bring in Jesuit personnel in all the departments who were not remunerated financially. In spite of the reduced expenses on account of manning the college with the Jesuit personnel (which was virtually not possible), other expenses in the management of the same would remain unaltered. The inevitable solution would have been closing it down, which would ultimately mean that the desirous Catholic students who were financially capable of pursuing a university education would have been forced to go to other colleges run by either Protestants or others.[1564] The ultimate consequence of this kind of situation would mean losing all the Catholic students entirely. In the pursuit of seeking to do good to the Catholic students, thus, even the bare minimum good that was already being done in the mixed college system would not have been possible.

Although the above argument may not be justified from the present perspectives, it was a reason enough to cause much anxiety for the Jesuits as there was no other sources of financial assistance to run

1564 See Hull, "The Mixed College and School Question, 1927," 6-8.

the educational institutions. A project of the magnitude of running a college, for example, could neither be supported by the Society of Jesus nor by Rome. A remark by E. R. Hull is apt here, which may be quoted at a length:

> On financial grounds alone, leaving other questions aside, the admission of a large majority of non-Catholic pupils is absolutely necessary for the bare existence of [educational institutions like] St. Xavier's College [Bombay]. People often discuss the problem as if it were a choice between *an exclusively Catholic College* and a *Catholic College* admitting a large number of non-Catholics. But that is not the question. The real question is a choice *between a Catholic College admitting a large number of non-Catholics, and no Catholic College at all.* The choice between *giving to Catholics a University education under the care of the Fathers with the mixture of the non-Catholics both in staff and students; and sending the Catholics to seek University education in Protestant and secular institutions,* because forsooth we have not the money to run the Catholic College with so few students as the Catholic community provides, To *be or not to be, that is the question.*" Without the large majority of the non-Catholics, Catholic University is impossible.[1565]

This justification was equally applicable in the case of the High Schools too, although in some cases depending on the location of the schools the situation could be expected to be better. Taking the statistics for the year 1925, it may be shown that St. Vincent's High School, Poona, could not have existed if the number of the non-Catholic students (i.e., 156) would have been deducted from the total number of the students (i.e., 377). For the total number of the Catholic students would thus be just 221. The situation at St. Patrick's School, Karachi, was much better (i.e., only 177 non-Catholic students out of the total of 705 students). Yet the reduction of 177 non-Catholic students would have implied a substantial loss of income to manage the school and to provide for the bare necessities of the school.[1566]

While going through the foregoing paragraphs, a point does strike us, namely financial factor alone would seem too superficial a reason to justify the policy of admission of non-Catholic students. It must be stated therefore that their admission were necessitated by certain constructive

1565 Hull, "Essay on Mixed Colleges and Schools," 7. The emphasis is on the text.

1566 Ibid. See also Doring, "Prospectus Status Missionis [1929]," 403.

reasons as well.[1567] Mentioning one such reason, Fr. Willekens in the Conference 1930 stated that,

> The Catholic schools and colleges admit the non-Christians for the sake of the good they can do to and through non-Christians also; some few are converted, they all are influenced favourably with regard to their own conscience and with regard to their own attitude towards the missionaries; the non- Christian society is leavened with Christian ideas.[1568]

In the same Conference Fr. Joseph Mahe, the Superior of Madura mission expressed his opinion on the point by saying that "the good work done by Colleges [include] ... indirect help for the conversion of the Hindus ... [And] the formation of an elite."[1569] Within the framework of the two goals mentioned in the citation, it may be stated that all the ministries and services of the Society of Jesus were basically understood in terms of a preparation for further evangelization. In other words, they were not value neutral in the sense of purely extending philanthropic aids to a society lacking possibilities of gaining education.[1570]

As for the second objective articulated in the citation above, it is apt to point out that during the period of this study, the Protestants occupied eminent positions all over India chiefly in the Madras and Bombay Presidencies. Their presence in the influential positions was a symbol of their growing social status, which implied a stronger representation of their concerns in the Government for the welfare of their people. For the same reasons the Jesuits too tended to perceive the need to maintain and if possible, develop their educational institutions, in spite of the constraints in imparting moral and religious instruction (see discussion, below). After all, in spite of the humble results in terms of gaining converts, they were doing more good to the Catholic Church than any harm.[1571]

1567 We shall further elaborate on some of them under point # 7.7.3 below.

1568 "Educational Conference [1930] [Fr. Willekens]," 3.

1569 Ibid. [Fr. Mahe], 9.

1570 Under the scheme of the distinction made by M. Thomas Thangaraj, this would correspond to the second category.

1571 "Educational Conference [1930] [Fr. Willekens] & [Fr. Mahe]," 2-3, 9-10.

8.5.2. Religious and Moral Instruction in the Jesuit Institutions

Another aspect related to the Jesuit institutions was the demand for imparting moral and religious instruction. To understand the issue in its proper perspective, we need to examine the background of the debate briefly once again. It seems to have emerged from the perception of the critics that the Catholic educational institutions, including the Jesuit ones, were not serving as platforms for teaching Christian doctrine due to the mixed composition of students belonging to various religious communities. As a result there was an apprehension that the religious formation of the Catholic students was seriously hampered. Having made an analysis of this aspect one comes to realize that at the background of such an apprehension there must have been a sense of insecurity among the Catholic hierarchy, especially among those who looked at a Catholic educational institution from the western point of view. The apprehension may be expressed in simple terms thus: On account of the open door policy,[1572] the Catholic students were exposed to a risk of losing their faith. It would not be wrong to say here that the burden of supplying a response lay on the Jesuits as they were the forerunners in the area of education. Arguing against the perception that the Catholic students were exposed to the risk of losing their faith in the Jesuit institutions, therefore, E. R. Hull stated that such an apprehension was entirely unfounded for the simple reason that the people of India, sharing in the common characteristic traits of the people from the orient, generally look upon religion as a matter of birth and caste, and consider a change of religion as unnatural as a change of skin ... Hence there is no need to protect Catholics, who would no more feel any inclination to change their religion than to change their race or nationality. The other religions in India afford no attraction to Christians.[1573]

In effect, E. R. Hull's argument sought to justify the claim that no real danger lay before the Catholic students as far as the change of religion was concerned. On the other hand, however, the concern of the critics may not be considered entirely irrelevant. For, our common experience

1572 An expression used by E. R. Hull, meaning no restrictions on admission to the non-Catholic students in the Catholic institutions. See Hull, "Some Moot-Points," 4-5.

1573 Hull, "The Mixed College and School Question: II. Answers of Committee to the Large Questionnaire," op. cit., 1. Alfons Vath argues in one of his articles that this aspect may have been the strongest factor that was virtually invincible on the way to converting the Hindus to Christianity. See Vath, "Das Missionsproblem Indiens," 4.

shows that the ideological currents of the surroundings normally tend to play an important role in shaping the young minds. Hence, the claim that the Catholic students faced no direct danger of losing their faith may be true to a large extent. Yet to present them as if they were immune to any external impact on account of any negative ideological currents would be going to another extreme. Hence the argument seems slightly one sided and betrays the implicit view of superiority in comparison with the followers of other religions. In other words, arguing on the one hand, that the Catholic institutions were perceived as a preparation for evangelization and on the other, to state simultaneously that only the non-Christians shared in the general character traits of not being affected by external influences does give an impression of an implicit superiority complex. In any case, what emerges strongly in the arguments of E. R. Hull is that he vehemently sought to represent the concern of the Jesuits who strongly faced the challenge of fulfilling the demands of the Catholic Church amidst such a complex situation.

It may not be wrong to conclude that the critics such as the ones mentioned above may have been either unaware of the practical challenges of the mission field or saw the entire situation from the western perspective of a Catholic institution. As far as the decades prior to the 1920s are concerned, one of the most formidable challenges that may not have been taken into consideration was the attitude and policy of the Government with regard to religious instruction in schools and colleges. It is generally accepted that the British policy of religious neutrality was largely a boon for the Christian missions in India. But it is also undeniable that it posed certain practical difficulties too on the way. For example, the question of religious instruction was mostly viewed with apprehension by the British administration for its political expediency. It would appear that in reality there was no legislative act regulating the religious instruction in denominational schools. However, as E. R. Hull maintains, in administrative acts and deliberations there were constant allusions to certain principles implying the maintenance of religious neutrality in all Government aided schools and colleges. The implications of such principles were eventually applicable to the Catholic institutions as well, since for all practical purposes they were under Government patronage, i.e., for recognition and grant-in-aid, etc.[1574]

1574 See Hull, "The Mixed College and School Question, 1927," 15.

While elaborating on the policy of maintaining religious neutrality in educational institutions, Hull quotes a few Government Documents to show that the policy (implicit in administrative acts and deliberations), although originally coming from the previous century was strictly in vogue until the early decades of the 20th century:

> Following the policy of strictly religious neutrality, the dispatch of 1854 declared that the system of grants-in-aid should be based on entire abstinence from interference with the religious instruction conveyed in the schools assisted. Under the application of this stringent rule, aided institutions are at liberty to convey whatever religious or moral instruction they please. But the Court of Directors declared that Government institutions were founded for the benefit of the whole population of India, and that it was therefore indispensable that the education conveyed in them should be exclusively secular ... *Resolution of Government dated 8 June, 1923.* Rule 4A: No grant-in-aid will be paid to any school or college maintained by a particular religious community which, (a) being the only school or college of its class in the locality, and (b) admitting pupils of other religious communities, makes attendance at instruction in its own religion a condition for admission of such pupils.[1575]

Given the kind of restrictions noted above, the burden of maintaining neutrality towards all religions while also being expected to fulfill the demands of imparting Catholic moral and religious education may not have been too easy for the Jesuits. Indeed, it may be stated that the Jesuits may have faced a tremendous challenge in this regard. This may be illustrated with a few instances. For example, Fr. Willekens in the Conference of the Jesuit Educationists (1930) stated in unambiguous terms that "the fact that our [schools and] Colleges were founded primarily for our Catholics requires this definite policy to be kept before their eyes by those who run them: they must be organised so as to impart first and foremost a thorough Catholic education to the *'domestici fidei.'*"[1576] Similarly, in the same Conference J. Mahe added a few more aspects on the statement cited above: "Our Colleges are intended first and foremost for our Catholics. The education we impart to them must be eminently Catholic. Each of our Colleges must be an

1575 "Minutes of the Educational Conference [Fr. Mahe]," 15.

1576 Ibid. [Fr. Willekens], 3.

extension of the Catholic home. The atmosphere of the College must be all the more Catholic as that of the outer world in India is more pagan."[1577] What can be concluded from all these? Can we say that these Jesuits were utterly unaware of the demands of the Government? Since they were in key positions in the missions in India, such a conclusion would be untenable. Hence, it would be more reasonable to state that in spite of their awareness of the constraints, they could not have afforded to moderate the tone of the demands of the Church.

The citations above contain an important aspect of the question under consideration, namely the demand of imparting 'a thorough Catholic education.' We need not go into the nuances of the phrase used here. Yet, what is basically meant by the same may be understood in terms of fostering the "growth of persons towards being fully human and mature ... [while aiming] at producing a student who is both knowledgeable and wise ... [thus contributing towards] an all-round human excellence."[1578] This has been the broader framework of the vision of Catholic education. It was, therefore, a normal expectation from a Jesuit institution that it explored the avenues of actualization of the same through regular religious and moral instruction. Under such conditions, the Jesuits had two options: either to explore a middle path to introduce a programme of moral and religious instruction keeping in mind the multi-religious context or to make the catechism classes compulsory for all, implying thereby that all those parents who did not wish to expose their children to the dangers of being influenced by Catholic teachings could withdraw them from the institution.

What could have been the consequences of these steps? Before discussing this question, it may not be out of place to make a mention of a few basic facts in order to show what activities were already undertaken with regard to the moral and religious instruction to the students. It may be noted that catechism classes, sodalities, feasts, etc. were regular features of the programme of moral and religious activities for the Catholic students. As far as the common activities for the students in general (both Catholics and non-Catholics) were concerned, short prayers said both in the beginning as well as at the end of each class was a regular activity. Moreover the religious symbols like crucifix, statues

1577 Ibid. [J. Mahe], 16.

1578 John Misquitta, ed., *The Identity of the Catholic College in India* (Bombay: St. Xavier's College, 1989), 10-12.

or religious pictures were normally placed in each class room. A general sense of respect for the same was invariably marked among the non-Catholic students as well. Beyond these, apparently, nothing more was being done. It is here that E. R. Hull questioned: "Given that the present admission of non-Catholic pupils must go on, what are we doing for them from the Christian point of view? Could we do more than what we are doing?"[1579]

The implementation of the above plan was certainly not easy given the demands of the Government on one hand, and that of the Church which were diametrically opposed, on the other.[1580] Yet, the Jesuits sought to explore a middle path in order to impart Christian values, failing which the very purpose of running the educational institutions would be defeated. In the deliberations on the issue, it was strongly felt that a curriculum on moral instruction must be introduced in all higher secondary schools and colleges. For example, the Conference (1930) insisted that past failures must by no means be repeated and "some remedy must be found to save the young men of India from moral disaster, from communistic propaganda, from materialism and atheism."[1581]

The plan of introduction of a course on moral science was a kind of middle path. But the challenge was equally great so as not to give an impression that the course on moral science was a virtual replacement of the entire Christian catechism. At the same time, there was a need to clearly instruct the students that the course on moral science gave by no means the whole of Catholicism. This was the only option available to the Jesuits to discharge their duty towards the non-Christian students by giving them as much as they could in the hope that the seeds of Catholic truth sown in the form of universal moral truths would spring and grow up in their hearts.[1582]

The biggest hurdle on the way, however, was to create a standard text book for the same, which would include a syllabus of moral science topics with a clear bent towards Catholicism. Without a standard book on the course on moral science, the effort was bound to face a failure. For, a textbook would be a manual or a guide book to the teachers

1579 Hull, "Essay on Mixed Colleges and Schools," 11.

1580 See "Educational Conference [1930] [Fr. Ferroli]," 5.

1581 Ibid.

1582 Ibid. [Fr. Willekens], 4.

and would be helpful in the teaching of a complete course of Ethics. However, it was necessary that the use of discretion be made so that no charge of 'proselytism' could be levelled against the institutions on account of making references to the Catholic beliefs in moral teachings. On these points, D. Ferroli, expressed his concern thus:

> Without such a book how can the problems of sanctions of idolatry, of caste be dealt with? How can the possibility of revelation, its probability, and the duties of a man who believes in it, and suspects his religious position to be unsound, be treated fairly and serenely? In class, with the limited time at our disposal, and with the constant fear of having to face a possible outcry, it is scarcely practical. But, if a suitable text-book is prepared the boys can be referred to it; some will read it. They will then be led to seek a private talk with their teacher, or with some of the Fathers, away from the turbulent atmosphere of a class-room. Further, the book may be a safe-guide to prospective social reformers, editors of newspapers, politicians, etc. In this way the teaching of morality from a chair supplemented by a good text-book will not destroy, but will promote religious indifferentism; it will give the lie to those who accuse us of hiding Christ behind the shadow of Aristotle. For, the course of Ethics - inspired by Christ will lead to Christ - not with the directness of the Gospels, but certainly with the unambiguous allure of the *Contra Gentes.*[1583]

It was against this background of discussion that D. Ferroli published a three-volume book on Ethics in 1947/48, dealing with the general principles, personal duties and social ethics respectively.[1584] Having made this reference, we realize that the constraints of implementing the plans of imparting religious and moral education were basically of two categories: those issuing from the Government policy and the apprehension of communal tensions. It is true that not many episodes of such occurrences had been experienced in Bombay-Poona Mission, but the composition of the society in general demanded no less a precaution. Hull makes a mention of an incident of the Parsi (followers of Zoroastrianism) parents who seemed to have raised strong objection to the introduction of catechism classes for all

---

1583 Ibid. [Fr. Ferroli], 6.

1584 See D. Ferroli, *Ethica: Part I General Principles; Part II Personal Duties; Part III Social Ethics* (Ranchi: Catholic Press, 1947).

in the lower standards. This may be considered an indication that the situation may have been pretty volatile.[1585]

Now coming to the question of introducing a compulsory programme of catechism classes for all, it would be apt to point out that the tension with regard to the Government restrictions seems to have become comparatively much relaxed after around the mid-1920s. This may be concluded from the text below:

> Hence, whatever restrictions may have existed in the past down to 1921, now, within the last 5 years they have been swept away. Therefore as far as Government requirements are concerned we would be free to-morrow, if we liked, to issue a notice at St. Xavier's College, High School and elsewhere, declaring that 'in future all pupils will be obliged to attend the Catechism class with the Catholics; and those parents who object to this rule are free to take their children away and send them to some other school instead.[1586]

This brings us back to the consideration on the consequences of the two options that were available before the Jesuits, i.e., exploring a middle path or to introduce a compulsory catechism class. Going through the text above, one might be tempted to conclude instantly: why did the Jesuits not introduce a common programme of catechism classes for all then? It must be remembered, however, that the entire issue came finally to the use of discretion and expediency. It was always a dilemma as to what the consequences of such a step would be.[1587] "Would it be wise and beneficial to introduce this change, or would it be unwise, injurious and calculated to defeat its own end?"[1588] This was the fundamental question. Even a rudimentary knowledge of the context and analysis of the question would show that it would have been unwise on the part of the Jesuits. This may be explained thus: the purpose of introduction of a compulsory catechetical instruction would have been

1585 See Hull, "The Mixed College and School Question, 1927," 4.

1586 Hull "Essay on Mixed Colleges and Schools," 7. On this point there were differences of opinions among the Jesuits. For example, the Conference (1930) strongly seems to allude to the fact that the situation at the ground level may not have substantially changed. In any case, it may not be denied that certain relaxations in the Government policy may definitely have taken place by this time. This conclusion is drawn based on the strength of the high quality research normally found in the works of E. R. Hull. He may certainly have had evidences to make such a claim on the issue.

1587 Ibid., 16-18.

1588 Ibid., 11.

interpreted as having only one objective, i.e., aiming at the conversion of the students to Catholicism. It would eventually be expected that the positive results follow instantly. In the case of a failure in achieving the same, however, the second level of expectation would be to wait in the hope of achieving the same at a later stage. An unforeseen consequence of this effort would be: the catechism classes would face the danger of disintegrating into merely routine classes, failing to produce the desired results. This would eventually lead to the impression that the initiative was a failure. From the point of view of the critics, it would be considered a success when the initiative would produce tangible results in terms of a bigger number of converts. Ironically, however, this would be defeating the end of the entire effort, as Hull concludes:

> Thus the attempt to impose the Catholic message upon a non-Catholic clientele in the hope of making conversions would prove ridiculous, futile and suicidal: - (1) It would empty our institutions of just the pupils whom we hoped to convert. (2) Instead of giving us exclusively Catholic Institutions it would obliterate our Catholic institutions altogether. (3) It would deprive Catholics of Catholic education, and would force them into Protestant and secular institutions instead.[1589]

What is the rationale behind such an argument? This may be explained thus: Once the declaration would be made that the catechism classes were going to be made compulsory for all, many of the parents (say Hindus) would withdraw their children from the Jesuit institutions. For, a simple conclusion of the parents would be that the Jesuits who had depicted a remarkable tolerance towards various religions in the past were out with their real agenda of converting the Indian masses. This would invariably create tensions, because the imposition of catechism classes would be interpreted as an intrusion into the internal and familial spheres of the people. Although it was generally understood that the parents entrusted their children to the Jesuits for their formation, the interference with their faith would never be tolerated. Thus, in spite of the fact that the Jesuits were expected to take the roles of the virtual 'fathers' to the students in the institutions, no parent would give a freedom to interfere with personal matters like religion. We have mentioned above that such resilience in them sprang from their basic

1589 Ibid.

understanding of the relationship between religion and culture as forming an inseparable unity. We may read elsewhere too that "the class of pagan pupils who attend our schools are mostly of the sort which can but rarely be proselytized, on account of the racial and caste-notions which permeate their mind and character, and put the idea of becoming Christians altogether outside the horizon of their minds."[1590]

Amidst such complexities--the internal conflict on the one hand and the sense of hope on the other--experienced by the Jesuits were aptly expressed by E. R. Hull:

> When people are keen on a thing but find themselves confronted with obstacles to its attainment, it is a great relief to their feelings to know that the obstacles are inevitable and their endeavours futile. This is certainly the case in the situation before us. Attempts at proselytism among our pupils, as soon as they began to promise success, would attract the attention of the parents and cause a commotion; and if it once got abroad that we are using our schools as "instruments of propagation" the non-Christian public would fight shy of us and desert us. It is a handicap which is inevitable; but it does not make any appreciable difference to our work of evangelizing the country. For if we made our schools a proselytizing concern we should have no pupils to proselytize, because they would shun us like a plague.[1591]

In short, thus, the plan to impose compulsory catechism classes would eventually close the possibilities of maintaining educational institutions. Moreover, this would mean that even the Catholics themselves would be lost as they would be forced either to go to other institutions or to give up the pursuit of education, depending on their financial conditions.

As a conclusion, it may be stated that the entire debate posed a tremendous challenge to the Jesuits. The gravity of the same may be understood from the fact that the Jesuits found themselves caught between the demands of the Church on one hand and that of the Government, on the other. Besides, the demand of expediency at every stage was a necessary issue. In any case, the foregoing discussions have shown that the imposition of compulsory catechism classes in the name of fulfilling the demands of the Church was by no means a solution. As we

1590 Ibid., 14.

1591 Hull "Essay on Mixed Colleges and Schools," 14.

analyze the situation, it would seem, therefore, that the Jesuits could not have implemented this plan, even if there were no restrictions imposed from the Government. The reason for the same was: the prospects of proselytism were out of question on the intrinsic grounds and not due to mere external factors. Hence the use of discretion was the only way out, the imposition of compulsory catechism classes was bound to cause more harm than good, indeed endangering the very existence of the Jesuit institutions. In effect, the measure of good which was being realized through them itself risked the danger of being nullified.

8.5.3. The Wider Impacts of the Jesuit Institutions

Since a few aspects on the impact of Jesuit institutions have already been mentioned in chapter four, we need not restate them here. One central question is how far the Jesuit institutions were instrumental in bringing a transformation in the Catholic community. From the discussions in chapter four it becomes apparent that the Catholic community was lagging far behind as compared to the Protestant Churches in the area of education. The Protestant Churches were well recognized in the Government circles as the principal contributors towards educating the Indian masses, for which they received not only the appreciation but also an expressed gratitude from the Government.[1592] These aspects apart, although the results in terms of gaining converts had always been humble, yet the Jesuit institutions made significant contributions in bringing about much change among the non-Catholics. We shall mention only a select few here. It may be stated that the discussions underneath are a justification for the existence, maintenance and development of the Jesuit institutions.

To begin with, it may be mentioned that the introduction of Catholic educational institutions by the Jesuits was an important step. Indeed it was a definitive step towards raising the social status of the Catholic Church that was lagging behind due to lack of education. In the words of E. R. Hull, "it threw the Catholic clergy in the general education work of the country,"[1593] where the Protestant monopoly was unquestionable. The establishment of educational institutions attained greater reputation,

1592 By the 1850s the Protestant Churches were well-known in the area of education, whereas the Catholic Church was virtually nowhere in comparison with the Protestant Churches until the 1860s, except a few parochial and elementary schools. See Vath, *Die deutschen Jesuiten,* 58-67; Hull, "Some Moot-points," 2; *Gense, Church at the Gateway,* 198-212.

1593 Hull, "Some Moot-Points," 4.

even at times surpassing the already existing institutions of the time, due to the special effort of the Jesuits towards creating an atmosphere of discipline and hard work, which was generally valued among all sections of the society.[1594] The growing reputation of the Jesuit schools and colleges and their consequent impact in the educational circles are reflected in the text below which is taken from the reports of the Director of Public Instruction for the years 1902-1907 and 1909-1910:

> The [St. Xavier's] College [Bombay] is an admirably conducted institution. The discipline is strict, the instruction is careful and thorough ... Such schools as St. Xavier's at Bombay, St. Vincent's at Poona, and St. Patrick's at Karachi, are reported to exercise a very good influence on the non-Christian pupils, the discipline being unusually strict and the teaching careful and systematic.[1595]

Due to the raised standard of education the Catholic Church, once lacking in social status, began to appear as a sign of progress thanks to the Jesuit educational endeavours. Owing to a strong emphasis on moral instruction, in spite of all the constraints mentioned above, the Jesuit institutions began to be known better for their value-oriented approaches. The culture of discipline and the devotion to work that were imparted to the students were clearly seen as values of great worth contributing towards forming better citizens. These values were often imparted more strongly by the lives of the Jesuits themselves than by a well-prepared curriculum on the moral and value education. A tribute paid by a former Governor of Bombay Presidency, namely Lord Sandhurst to the Jesuits during one of his visits to St. Xavier's High School in Bombay (1900) underlined this:

> No one knows better than I do the life of self-abnegation which you pursue, the overwhelming industry and enthusiasm and devotion which you bring to bear on the duties which, at any rate in the commencement of your careers, were self-imposed ... Though the work may be hard and the anxieties great, you will have the satisfaction of knowing that you are doing your utmost for the rising generation ... I shall feel proud of being able to claim acquaintance with so public-spirited, so hard-working, and at the same time so

1594 See Hull, "Essay on Mixed Colleges and Schools, 1927" 3-4.

1595 Hull, "Some Moot-Points," 5.

> self-denying, modest and retiring, a body of men as I know you, Reverend Fathers, to be.[1596]

The appreciation such as this coming from a high-ranking authority of the rank of the Governor of the Presidency himself does signalize the fact that the Jesuit institutions were making a name for themselves in the educational circles. This kind of positive impact reflected in the growing recognition of the Jesuit institutions among the wider circles of society, was by no means an achievement of the Society of Jesus only. In fact through this process the entire Catholic Church in India was gaining a reputation.

A related area which had a positive influence upon the society in general was the creation of an atmosphere of communal harmony. The regular intermingling and interaction of students of different races, castes and religions helped create a positive attitude about religions other than one's own. This was an important aspect of the positive impact effected by the Jesuit institutions, especially given the volatile atmosphere of communalism and growing spirit of nationalism.[1597] Yet, what may be considered of even greater worth is the fact that at the wider level, the admission of the non-Christians was seen as effecting a positive influence among others, while at the same time, dispelling the negative perceptions about Christianity:

> The pagans themselves by their contact with us come to understand and appreciate (from a distance at least) the Catholic religion and the spirit which actuates it. Prejudices against Christianity are removed, and those who might be our enemies become our friends. In view of the future prospect of leadership passing into the hands of the Indians, it is of no small value to have had a fair proportion of them as pupils in our schools.[1598]

1596 Hull, "Essay on Mixed Colleges and Schools, 1927" 2. This document contains many more personal testimonies of the high officials who were impartial to look at the immense impact the Jesuits were effecting on the society in general not only through their schools and colleges, but through their life-style of commitment and dedication to the work

1597 See Hull, "Essay on Mixed Colleges and Schools," 3.

1598 Hull, "Some Moot Points," 6. See also "Education Conference [1930] [Fr. Willekens]," 2. Writing on the same Hull mentioned: "The pagans themselves by their contact with us come to understand and appreciate (from a distance at least) the Catholic religion and the spirit which actuates it. Prejudices against Christianity are removed, and those who might be our enemies become our friends. In view of the future prospect of leadership passing into the hands of the Indians, it is of no small value to have had a fair proportion of them as pupils in our schools." Hull, "Some Moot Points," 6.

In general, thus, we may state that though not acting as agents of direct evangelization, the Jesuit schools and colleges largely contributed in preparing the atmosphere in favour of Catholicism.

8.6. Conclusion

The foregoing discussion on a few moot-points in the history of the Poona Mission reveals that the Jesuits often found themselves amidst a number of complex issues. From their nature, we may identify two categories of the moot-points above: the first having a more general character embracing the entire Indian Church; the second, having direct implications for the Jesuit Mission in Poona. The question of native vocations and Jesuit *sanyasis,* for example, had to be addressed more locally by the Jesuits, whereas the discussion on the topics like growth of the Mission may be considered more general in nature. Similarly the question of Indian vocations to the Society of Jesus in particular and to the priesthood in general had a direct implication for the Jesuits. In the course of our discussion, it has emerged repeatedly that the Jesuits often found themselves in a situation wherein no satisfactory way out seemed to be possible. Besides, a point that is rather perturbing, is that the question did not seem to have engaged a bigger number of the Jesuits in this Mission. The last issue that we have discussed is more encompassing, as education was a major ministry of all the Churches. This service being one of the primary areas of engagement of the Jesuits, it demanded much commitment, planning and deliberations.

Chapter-9

Evaluation and Conclusions

9.1. Introduction

At the end of this study some relevant questions remain to be answered by way of concluding it. How to assess the growth and progress of the Poona Mission? What are the major achievements of this Mission? Is this Mission relevant to the 21st century Church in India? Several such questions can be added. For answering these, let me first recapitulate the main findings of this study which can be a summary overview too and can give a fairly good idea about some of the most relevant aspects of the history of this Mission.

9.2. The Progress and Growth of the Mission

A discussion on the comparative progress and growth of a mission holds a prominent space in the historical study of a mission. An issue that seems less adequately addressed is: Are there any criterion or parameter to determine the progress of a mission?[1599] Generally a mission is evaluated from the perspective of the number of conversions, number of service institutions or establishments, churches, etc in its area. It can be also evaluated from the beneficiaries' perspective in terms of the quality of their empowerment, level of upward social mobility through educational, occupational, economic development, etc. There can be

1599 Authors like J. W. Picket, Donald A. McGavran, C. Peter Wagner, Win Arn, *et. al.*, among many others have proposed various criteria in their books, *Church Growth and Group Conversion (1973), Understanding Church Growth (1970), Church Growth: State of the Art (1986) and Church Growth Ratio Book* (1987) respectively.

different criteria for different observers: church people, historians, other scholars and critics, et al. For example, a certain section of observers might judge a particular mission as successful if it was able to establish a bigger number of churches, and service institutions such as schools, technical institutes, health-care centres, orphanages, and the like. Others might take into consideration the number of converts and consequent spatial expansion of a particular mission. Still others might do the same by taking into consideration the perseverance against all odds and tenacity of the converts who contributed towards establishing a vibrant Christian community. Some even describe the growth of a church/ mission in terms of weighing the zeal and vigour of the missionaries or sluggishness and lack of zeal. Thus, such observers make simplistic conclusions saying that the number of converts was directly proportional to the zeal and energy of the missionaries in a particular mission field. And still further, some might make judgments on the missionaries saying that their failure to gain a larger number of converts was the result of the willful negligence in investing more personnel and resources in direct evangelization.[1600]

In an article published in *Kolnischen Volkszeitung* (18th December 1913), Joseph Schmidlin, Professor of Mission History in Munster presented his general impressions of Indian missions. He squarely maintained that the missions in India had failed to win over the converts largely on account of the negligence on the part of various missionary bodies in investing more personnel in the direct evangelization of peoples. Although this assessment and judgment were about missions in general, they are relevant to the Bombay-Poona Mission also.

In fact, Henry Bose as the Mission Superior of Bombay-Poona Mission considered it necessary to write a response (1914) to the above-mentioned article. This unpublished response addressed to the *Kolnischen Volkszeitung* and others concerned, was an attempt at drawing attention to a few fundamental issues pertaining to the Indian reality that one could never afford to ignore while trying to assess a mission. Quoting Schmidlin Henry Bose counters him:

> Professor [Joseph] Schmidlin claims: 1. That the process of conversion of non-Christians in India is making a very slow progress and the number of converts is vastly disproportionate to

1600 See Hull, "Some Moot-Points in the Indian Missions: With special relation to Bombay," *The Examiner* (offprint for private circulation) (January 1926), 1-2.

> that of the missionaries. 2. That the reason for such a state of affairs lies not in any external factor given the fact that missionaries enjoy the freedom of action and a large section of Indian population is receptive of the seeds of the Gospel, but much more in the fact that many individual missionary societies neglect the task of conversion of the non-Christians and in spite of the expressed desire of the Holy See do not invest enough manpower in the direct mission to the non-Christians and wish to hold fast to their monopoly at all costs, i.e., better leave the thousands of souls exposed to perish in paganism than to allow other missionary bodies to work for their salvation. 3. That the mission to the natives, who often indulge in idleness, does not incorporate them in the economic welfare programmes in order to uplift their socio-economic status....[1601]

It must be stated in unambiguous terms that Schmidlin's position is highly questionable. He had the least of idea about the complexities of the socio-cultural fabric of India. He typically represents the group of critics who, in their assessment of missionary endeavours undertaken by various missionary bodies in far-off lands, tend to ignore out-rightly the contextual realities of a particular place. More than being a matter of ignorance, this kind of approach smacks of not only a lack of sensitivity to accommodate alternative world-views but also that of a superiority complex vis-a-vis the developing countries.

A closer look at the quote reveals that many of the above-mentioned assumptions are essentially erroneous. It is also true, however, that most of these assumptions are not too uncommon either, especially in popular discourses on such issues. Hence, the plausible questions implying the above stated assumptions are: How to assess the growth of the Poona Mission? Is it possible to indicate the trajectory of its growth beyond tracing a chronology of its development? Quite naturally the answer to these questions may be as varied as the ones raising these questions. The answers may broadly be categorized in two major perspectives: spiritual and intellectual advancement and consolidation of the Christian community, and the numerical growth of the Christian community and expansion of Christianity.[1602] Besides, Christian missionary work was

1601 See Henry Bose, "Die katholischen Missionen in Indien," ARSI, *Bombay. 1003-III,* 29b.

1602 See Donald A. McGavran, "When the Church Grows," in *Church Growth and Group Conversion*, eds., J. W. Picket, et al. (California: William Carey Library, 1973), 97.

intended to give witness to the gospel values and hence make Christian impact on the wider society.

We have pointed out above that the numerical strength of the converts in a particular mission is often considered as a yardstick of its success or failure, whereas the abstract and qualitative aspect of the same remains dormant in the discourse. How to reconcile these aspects? While considering this question what is of paramount importance is to take a closer look at the specific local circumstances of the mission field. This would help us in making an objective assessment of the mission work which might have had different outcomes and impacts, namely a rapid growth in the number of converts in some places; whereas a much slower rate of growth, often appearing almost stagnant, in other places. It has been mentioned above that many observers in such cases tend to fall prey to the danger of arriving at conclusions that the factors like the lack of zeal, fervor and energy on the part of the missionaries labouring in a particular mission field were responsible for the same.[1603] However, in most of the cases such conclusions are bound to be erroneous. In fact, it would be too simplistic and also discourteous towards the missionaries, who had made immense sacrifices at the service of the mission they were entrusted with. Schmidlin's comments closely resonate such an understanding.

The first point that needs to be clearly underlined in this regard is that India is not a homogenous land. Stated differently, India is "wildly heterogeneous."[1604] Therefore every mission field must be looked at with all its peculiarities and specificities. Leaving aside these aspects and looking at India as a homogenous land exposes the observer to the danger of generalization and over simplification of facts. In order to set a general framework for understanding these questions, therefore, we may refer to Donald McGavran. In one of his books he proposes three sets of factors that need to be taken into consideration while dealing with the evaluation of a mission. In his own words:

> The first set we call contextual factors. These are political, sociological, cultural and environmental factors over which the church or the mission has no control. They may be local factors or they may extend to regions and entire nations. Church growth is slow in a country like Albania, for example, because of a national

1603 See Hull, "Some Moot-Points," 1.

1604 Ibid.

> contextual factor: religion is outlawed and offenders are severely punished. The second set is institutional factors that the church or denomination can control. Most mainline denominations in the United States suffered severe membership losses in the 1965-1990 period. This was due ... to a national institutional factor: in the mid-1960s their national leaders decided to prioritize social ministries over evangelism and church planting.[1605]

Since the numerical strength of a mission is a tangible factor and often tends to be perceived as a yardstick of its growth, we may point out briefly a few pertinent points in relation to this Mission. I have personally heard on a few occasions that the Belgian Jesuits, without malice towards anyone, came across as being proud of gaining more converts in Chhotanagpur mission (an offshoot of the Bengal Jesuit mission, which is often known as the Ranchi mission) in comparison with many other contemporary missions. As I recall those conversations (i.e., in the mid-1990s), I tend to arrive at the conclusion that the peculiarities of other mission fields were generally not taken into consideration in this case. Moreover, I also assume that such conclusions were not isolated cases either. In fact it would not be wrong to state that a substantial number of the missionaries who began their missionary carrier prior to Vatican Council II largely shared such an understanding wherein the numerical increase of the converts eventually stood as a yardstick of the growth of a mission, whereas the service of the mission for the development of the Christian community as well as the wider society should be considered as the yardstick of its success.

Moreover, the social apostolate was generally not considered as a direct means of evangelization as though it was additional extras to a missionary endeavour. On the contrary, they are an integral dimension of evangelization within the framework of evolving a theology of mission. But it is true that such a dichotomy did exist in the missionary thinking of the pre-Vatican Council II era. Apparently, such a position presents a very traditional understanding of mission.

This draws our attention to a phenomenon that instantly attracts the attention of the reader. This may be framed in the form of a question as follows: Why was the numerical growth of the converts in Poona Mission slower in comparison with certain other missions in India?

1605 McGavran, *Understanding Church Growth*, 19.

For example, the Chhotanagpur mission of the Belgian Jesuits[1606] was begun (1869) almost simultaneously[1607] as the Bombay-Poona Mission. The Chhotanagpur mission saw a phenomenal growth in terms of the number of converts from among the Tribal communities, right from its beginning. The drive of conversion gained further momentum especially when Constant Lievens realized that the most urgent need of the hour was to assist the Tribals in their struggle against the landlords and other exploiters who were snatching away their ancestral land. Lievens was convinced that he had not come to the people only "to work for their eternal happiness but also to make them happy in their earthly life."[1608] He "believed that the work of evangelization had to be accompanied by the struggle for human justice."[1609] He began, therefore, to study the customary laws of the Tribal communities and the legal provisions as safeguards in the British legal system. Subsequently, he began to mediate in the court cases in favour of the Tribals and succeeded in a number of cases. No sooner did such news spread among the Tribals, than they began to throng at his door and pleaded for instruction in Christian faith and baptism. Precisely, thus, this method produced an unprecedented result. Consequently a rare instance of an exponential growth of a Christian community was witnessed in Indian mission history, so that "instead of Lievens having to go out in search of them, they came to him."[1610] Almost a similar phenomenon was witnessed in the Telugu [Andhra Pradesh] Mission[1611] too, whereby people often converted en masse after due instruction for about a year or so.

Although making a comparison between two separate mission fields is essentially illogical given their unique characteristics, for the sake of clarity we may show some contrasting features of Poona Mission here. Accordingly, we see that the conversions among the *Mahars* and

1606 See Peter Tete, *A Short History of the Expansion of the Catholic Missions in North India* (Ranchi: St. Albert's College, 1997), 315.

1607 The Bengal Jesuit mission was begun in 1869; whereas the Bombay-Poona Mission, in 1854. See de Sa, *Crisis in Chota Nagpur, 326; Vath, Die deutschen Jesuiten,* 60.

1608 De Sa, *Crisis in Chota Nagpur,* 126.

1609 Ibid., x-xi.

1610 Ibid., xi. See also Tete, *A Short History of Christianity*, 21.

1611 In the Indian ecclesiastical history this mission is known also as *Carnatic Mission.* It was started by the French Jesuits in 1702. See S. Joseph Sebastian, *The Jesuit Carnatic Mission: A Foundation of Andhra Church* (Secunderabad: Jesuit Province Society Hyderabad, 2004), 13.

similar other caste groups did take place occasionally as groups, the phenomenon was nowhere comparable with the Chhotanagpur and Telugu missions. Thus, the momentum of conversion in this Mission was much slower than in the other two cases. This seems to have become slightly better after the 1930s. Yet, it never acquired a form of a mass movement. What is important to note in these three cases is their unique characteristics. A close look at them reveals that there is no commonality in the characteristics of these mission fields. For, every mission field is unique. And this precisely accounts for the varying degrees of momentum in the rate of conversions in all these mission fields.

Given the diversity in different mission fields, we are led back to the questions: Could one say that the Poona Mission was less successful as compared to other missions like Chhotanagpur or Telugu missions? Why such a difference in the momentum? Would it be fair to make a judgment about the success of the mission on the basis of the numerical growth of the converts alone? What about other aspects?

Underneath we shall point out only the external factors contributing for or against the numerical growth of the converts. Taking the example of Chhotanagpur mission, E. R. Hull, explains that,

> ...the [above] phenomenon was a result of the favourable conditions of the aborigines [Tribals] of Chota Nagpur ... [that] make wholesale conversions there comparatively easy and [thereby] explains abnormally large increase impossible elsewhere. [Similarly] the unfavourable conditions of the depressed classes [*Dalits*] in ... the Deccan [Poona region of the Maharashtra State] and the slow methods [i.e., schools, dispensaries, etc.] by which alone they can be brought in, would account for the slight progress of the ... Poona mission.[1612]

Hull, thus, underlines the difference in terms of the external conditions of the place and people. In Poona and Ahmednagar area, often it appeared as if nothing could be done with the adults, however friendly they may have come across. The baptisms were mostly restricted to the school children. Consequently, the cases of adult baptisms among the grown-ups were rather rare in this Mission. As a viable means of

1612 Hull, "Some Moot-Points," 1.

evangelization, therefore, the elementary and parochial schools were absolutely necessary. In the words of Hull,

> Opening of the schools was practically a contract with the parents: 'We take your children into the school on condition that we may baptize them and bring them up Christians.' Education is so valuable an asset that the parents consent. When efforts are made to convert the grown-ups their habitual reply is: 'We give you our children; but leave us our old gods.[1613]

Certainly this perception of Hull is questionable. Yet, an analysis of the same gives us a clue to a very important communitarian characteristic of the local people. It would not be unjustifiable to state here that on account of such traits, the local people appeared as less docile and open towards Christianity. While discussing the motives of conversion among the *Mahars* (for that matter all other people of similar social status) in chapter seven (see # 7.1.1), we have made a mention that the primary motive for the same appeared not seldom as a means of material gains. Yet, we have made an attempt to be objective and more generous in assessing the whole issue in relation to them with an argument that the external constraints facing them were often no less compelling. Here, at a slight risk of contradicting ourselves, therefore, we may say that a certain social and communitarian traits may certainly have been responsible for the lack of docility and receptiveness towards Christianity. Although not directly justifying our position, some of the personal testimonies of Ludwig Hassle seem to imply the same. In his own words:

> Since a few months a very serious cholera has broken out here. Many people are dying of them ... The natives are utterly helpless vis-a-vis this sickness. One could advise them what he wishes. But they would not take any precaution, so that they infect each other easily ... When it rains, the natives have always a scarcity of works ... As soon as our poor people have a good crop, they are hardly mindful of the mission. But the poverty drives them back to the mission. When a native has five sacks of grain in his hut, he will be a proud man. He has no worries whatsoever ... But when the grain runs out, all have to hunger... Then they would soon be weighed down and dejected. We always try to speak to the people, to take care of the grains and spare the same for the future. But alas, as long

1613 Ibid., 2.

> as they have the grain, they are utterly careless. They are negligent about their works. Many of them sit in their huts until their entire stock of grain has run out. Once so happens, they say that they need to work to earn their livelihood.[1614]

Hereby we get a conclusive indication about the kind of communitarian traits of the *Mahars* and other such local people. Some of the other letters of Ludwig Hassle are even more explicit in revealing the same as we have cited a few of them in chapter seven (see 7.1.1).[1615] These prove that their social and communitarian traits, to a greater degree, did contribute towards the slow momentum in their conversion to Christianity. Another aspect in understanding the growth and progress of a mission are the qualitative aspects, i.e., vibrancy of the Christian community, formation of people in Christian values and corresponding vitality in practicing their faith and morality. These aspects are non-empirical. On the growth of the mission with respect to these qualitative aspects, Hull has the following to say: "My own impression is, that the really heroic mission work in India is the work one hears nothing about--because it is a struggle against handicaps and inevitable failure."[1616]

The above observation is very much in line with what Donald A. McGavran in an article writes: "In all this consideration of church [say mission] growth, are we not forgetting that growth and perhaps the most important growth, has nothing to do with numerical increase at all?"[1617] The position of McGavran is rather extreme. The everyday discourses on the growth of a mission cannot be based fully and entirely on abstract aspects alone. One does need to see certain empirical and tangible aspects to speak on such dimensions. Our position here is a middle path between the two extremes. In other words, we consider neither the numerical increase of converts, institutions and churches etc., nor the other abstract aspects as sole parameters of the growth of a mission. Accordingly a mission must be considered as having achieved growth or progress based on both aspects--empirical and abstract. For,

1614 Ludwig Hassle to Joseph M. Wiget (Songaon, 12th July 1941), AMPSJ, IB. *Songaon-Briefe.*

1615 Ibid., (Songaon, 9th August 1941); (Songaon, 23rd October 1941), AJMS, IB. *Songaon-Briefe.* See further in the same file Ludwig Hassle to Emmanuel Hofer (Songaon, 25th August 1941), Ludwig Hassle to Francis X. Hayler (Songaon, 2nd February 1946).

1616 Hull, "Some Moot-Points," 1.

1617 Donald A. McGavran, "When the Church Grows," in *Church Growth and Group Conversion*, eds., J. W. Pickett, et al. (California: William Carey Library, 1973), 97.

it would be too naive to claim that a mission achieved growth and success without having to establish schools, institutions and churches, and winning over some converts to Christianity. The contrary is equally true. It would be meaningless to speak about progress of a mission solely based on the number of schools, institutions and churches it has managed to establish, while entirely neglecting the primary purpose of forming Christian communities. Both must go hand in hand. In fact the foundation of institutions and churches must serve as means towards the formation of a community of believers. This is precisely what had happened in the Poona Mission.

Such a judgment is possible because we are far-removed by distance in time and space. But the Jesuits working in this Mission may often have been face to face with disappointments on failing to gain a larger number of converts. Hence, it would be too mechanical a representation of the fact to say that they were not affected by such experiences and not agonized on account of the same. The disappointments and discouragements being part and partial of any human endeavour, we can easily imagine what the Jesuit missionaries may have experienced when faced with a situation in which their decades-long hard labour seemingly failed to bear fruits (in so far as it is considered in terms of gaining numerical increase of the converts). It must be remembered that one of the most prominent understandings of being sent on a mission until this period was to gain numerical increase of the Catholic Church and thereby to achieve the goal of expansion of Christianity. Stated differently, being sent on a mission certainly was not purely understood in terms of humanizing the society through schools and institutions and charitable and altruistic activities alone. Indeed the primary purpose was the expansion of Christianity, obviously through all these aspects. Be that as it may, one of their most real experiences was the disappointments on account of the reasons cited above. This was the background, which compelled Henry Heras to address the question to the Superior General, John Baptist Janssens, as he wrote:

> There is no doubt that all of us when coming to this country were moved in some way or other by the missionary spirit, by that spirit which Our Lord Jesus Christ actually gave to his disciples shortly before he sent them to preach to all the nations. To leave one's own country; to abandon forever all one's relations and friends, and even the hope of seeing them again; to break up one's own plans and

> ideals; and to go for good to an unknown country of inhospitable climate of strange customs, of unsavory food, to work among unknown people, not always well disposed towards you, are things which are not pleasant to the flesh. Yet, moved by the example of Our Lord ... we readily abandoned all that and embraced this new world when we heard the call of Holy Obedience. Yes, the missionary spirit made us to undertake courageously this difficult enterprise ... and the fact that very few conversions have up to now crowned our efforts is certainly a matter of great concern ....[1618]

Having made this comment as a preface to his reflection on the state of affairs with regard to the factors that may have contributed towards the lesser rate of conversion among the higher caste Hindus, Henry Heras further opines that the Jesuits themselves had often failed to forego an 'air of superiority'. Consequently they had failed to approach other religions and cultures of India with openness and respect. He believed that the Jesuits had often replicated a European life-style in India--be it in manners of clothing, food habits, housing. In other words, they lacked in their efforts at adapting to a genuine Indian life-style. Instead of appearing as *sanyasis*, they came across as *sahebs* (gentlemen). In effect, they had failed to project Christianity as Indian in order to win India for Christianity. He considered these as serious lacunae in their missionary endeavour, which he firmly believed that if given a serious consideration would have greatly aided towards the goal of making the Christian faith more acceptable.[1619] As an all-embracing attitude, therefore, he considered *sympathy* for everything Indian as a key to further opening among the natives in general. Quoting Mgr. Rossillon, Bishop of Vishakhapatnam, he wrote:

> Sympathy must be our general attitude with regard to India, its history, its people, its customs, its problems and various forms of religions. To condemn everything Indian and put overstress on what is wrong in the spiritual, social order of the nation, is an un-Christian attitude. Christ would not have done that ... Here I would advise a more sympathetic study of non-Christian religions and culture, to find the good that is in them, so that we might have a more sympathetic approach to the people and not to appear to them mere western iconoclasts come to destroy everything that is dear

1618 Heras "On the Mission Methods," 5.

1619 Ibid., 19-20, 85, 87-88, 123-24, 126.

> to them. We should be grateful for any truth found anywhere; we should acknowledge these truths as the foot-prints of God in this un-Christian land.[1620]

In spite of the failure to gain a larger number of converts (as was the case with a few other missions), the Jesuits have stood against all odds and contributed a great deal to the mission and to the Indian Church, in particular and the wider society in general. The establishments of educational and many other institutions that we have discussed in detail in previous chapters are testimonies of their tenacity and commitment to their call of service to society. Hence, it may be stated that the mission was a uniquely successful one. It was uniquely successful because the odds and challenges that it faced were nowhere comparable with any other Jesuit mission in India, or perhaps in the entire world. It may be noted that this was due to certain social and cultural peculiarities of the people of the place. But even more importantly it must be underlined that a missionary endeavour is never a human endeavour alone. The missionaries seem to have believed that God's Spirit not only accompanies human endeavour, but also precedes it in many and varied ways. Hence, the truth stands as what an old proverb said: "success is not one of the names of God." Therefore, genuine efforts at cooperation with God's Spirit is needed believing that ultimately it was their commitment that mattered most.

9.3. Missionary Strategies and Priorities

A cursory look at what we have discussed in the preceding chapters with regard to the strategies and priorities, a few comments are in order here. Firstly, taking the mission right from its beginning (1854), what stands out as the most significant contribution of the Jesuits of Bombay-Poona Mission was undoubtedly in the field of educational service. Since the mandate received from Bishop Anastasius Hartmann precisely implied a special focus on the educational apostolate, this achievement holds an even greater significance. In other words, the objectives visualized by Bishop Hartmann were achieved through the establishment of schools and institutions to a large extent. The communities lagging behind in education and social status acquired a place of honour in society, thanks to the unflinching dedication and commitment of the Jesuits.

1620 Ibid., 33.

We further notice that already within the first fifty years of their presence in the mission, the Jesuits had made gigantic strides in this regard. The establishment of major schools and institutions like St. Xavier's High School and College (Bombay), St. Mary's High School (Bombay), St. Vincent's High School (Poona), St. Patrick's High School (Karachi), etc. are some of the examples to substantiate this claim. Even after the episodes of internment and repatriation during the period of the World Wars, the Jesuits carried forward the mission as though there had been no interruption at all. Consequently, the later mission districts (i.e., Belgaum, Goa and Poona) too witnessed a similar fervour and zeal in their commitment to the mandate of spreading the message of the Gospel through educational service.

A distinction, however, must be made here with regard to the impacts in relation to the urban and rural Catholic communities. Apparently, the general impact of education were noticed much more tangibly in the urban communities (for example in Bombay and Poona) as compared to the rural ones. But it cannot be denied that an overall transformation began to take place gradually yet steadily even among the rural communities in the areas like Ahmednagar and Hubli. The initial resistance and lack of inclination towards education[1621] that such communities depicted earlier was largely overcome. The transformation in general could be seen more tangibly in the last four to five decades. But the foundation for the same had been laid much earlier, namely with the Jesuit mission in the area. All these were achieved solely on account of the tenacity of purpose that the Jesuits showed to the mission they were entrusted with. What seems to be a fitting tribute to their contribution in this regard is stated by E. R. Hull in the context of his effort to defend the German Jesuits from being sent to internment camps, facing the prospects of being repatriated to their home country. He wrote: "I may say without hesitation that the advent of the Jesuits in 1854-1858 was nothing short of an epoch-making event, which changed the face of history altogether."[1622]

Although we have discussed the point extensively in the third chapter (i.e., #3.1.1) that education was the most important apostolic instrument, an important point in this regard may be noted here. From

1621 See Joseph Stark to Joseph M. Wiget (Sangamner, 14th February 1941), AMPSJ, *LB. Songaon-Briefe.*

1622 Hull, *The German Jesuit Fathers,* 17-18.

the point of view of missionary strategic purpose, the schools were the most effective medium to enlighten and empower the people.

> The major problem of our mission lies in our schools. We can emphatically state that without schools, we cannot effect any impact on the people as far as the question of education and formation in Christian values and morals is concerned. In the schools one learns how to pray and thus a possibility is created so that a small percentage of them retains the prayer in the right sense. Until this point one can say only this much. As far as this mission is concerned there are no families where regular prayers are said. The exceptions are very rare. Recently I blessed a marriage in a village. The man was in our school at Sangamner till the third standard. That means he received sacraments and went for prayers regularly. At the moment he can write his name and that is all what he has retained from our schools. He could no more recite [the prayer] Our Father.[1623]

A related point that emerges at this juncture is the vision of education that Bishop Hartmann embodied. Accordingly, being entrusted with a mission implied not only engaging with direct evangelization of people in terms of preaching and administering sacraments but also engaging in the programmes aimed at uplifting the socio-political status and other spheres of human life through education. Therefore the establishment of schools and colleges was not to be reduced to a purely temporal project.

The creative approaches to education in the form of introducing non-formal education and professional training signify yet another dimension of the vision of mission. The end analysis reveals that the objective of the betterment of society through capacity building and creation of job opportunities or self-employment were ultimately symbols of a broadening vision of mission. On the pattern of the understanding of mission embodied in the approaches by Constant Lievens, the Jesuits of this mission too began to emphasize the need of addressing the here-and-now situation of the people.

The next aspect that draws our attention here is the contribution of Poona Mission in establishing institutions of national importance. There institutions were meant as training of missionary service providers of missions. In modern parlance, these were institutions for human resource development for the missions. Our discussion in chapter seven has revealed the challenges and obstacles that the Jesuits were exposed

1623 Stark to Wiget (Sangamner, 14th February 1941), op. cit.

to in setting up these institutions. Yet, the results achieved speak for themselves. The Indian Catholic Church owes its huge debt to these institutions as numerous children of hers are being trained year after year for the leadership of their respective communities. In our comment at the end of Chapter eight, we have underlined that the Jesuit mission often bearing a criticism for failing to gain native vocations, both for the Society as well as for the diocese, paved a way for the formation of numerous native candidates for priesthood.

Finally a comment is in order on the health-care apostolate undertaken by the Jesuits. The pragmatic reason of providing health-care facilities to the local people apart, this initiative too symbolizes the broadening of vision of the mission in terms of its more holistic understanding. The Jesuit mission, after all, was not meant to address the issues oriented to other-worldly concerns alone. The restoration of the physical health of the people too was an integral dimension of the mission. The scope of this service embraced all the needy, across the boundaries of caste and creed.

9.4. The Mission Theology

We need not repeat the fact that the B-P M belonged to the era prior to Vatican Council II. As far as the Catholic theology of mission is concerned, Vatican Council II is considered a benchmark for the emergence of a new and broader understanding of mission. Hence a short evaluation of the missionary understanding operative among the Jesuits is in order here. The purpose is best served when we consider the same within the framework of the development of the Catholic theology of mission during the period under review. In order to do the same we may begin by pointing out the basic propositions of the missionary understanding proposed by Gustav Warneck, the first chair of Protestant missiology founded in 1896. His understanding of mission is summarized by Henning Wrogemann in the following words:

> Therefore the mission, according to Warneck, may be characterized as follows: (1) Mission is defined in terms of *geography*. Mission is an activity of Christianity aimed at the non-Christians ... The act of sending therefore is aimed at a geographical area outside of Christian West, outside of the so called *corpus christianum*, that means outside Christian majority of Europe (North America). (2) Mission is defined in terms of *ecumenical endeavour* ... [which

> means] an act of Christianity directed at the non-Christians. (3) Mission is defined as *ecclesiocentric*... [which means] the whole missionary endeavour of Christianity implies the planting and organizing of Christian churches, while at the same time aiming at the non-Christians. (4) Mission is defined in terms of temporality... (5) Mission is defined as sending-centred. The sent [apostles/ missionaries] are understood as subjects...as against the audience [recipients/addressees] of the mission, namely the natives...as the objects of the 'mission.' (6) Mission is defined pragmatically ...That means the mission is planned and then carried out according to the same [plan] further.[1624]

Martin Uffing summarizes the same as follows: "According to Warneck, Protestants used the term mission in various ways ... It could mean (1) mission among Catholics or other (rival) Protestant groups; (2) *fnnere Mission'* (in German), that is, social service for the needy; (3) pastoral work among German Protestants who had migrated to countries outside Europe; and finally, (4) mission among non-Christians...[1625] Needless to say that the above understandings were very narrow and unilateral. Accordingly, the natives were perceived as objects and not as the subjects of their own history.

Warneck's theology of mission was further developed with greater detail by other theologians of the later decades like Karl Hartenstein and Walter Freytag. Their basic contribution to the Protestant missiology includes their understanding of mission not only in terms of this-worldly understanding but also extending beyond, including thereby also the eschatological dimension within the larger framework of the Kingdom of God and salvation history.[1626] Meanwhile, from around the beginning of the 20th century, the development of the ecumenical theology of mission also began to take place. It is embodied in the documents of the World Mission Conferences (from 1910-1958) of Edinburgh (1910), Jerusalem (1928), Tambaram (1938), Whitby (1947), Willington (1952) and Accra (1958) with key emphasis on eschatology, secularism, world-

---

1624 Henning Wrogemann, *Missionstheologien der Gegenwart: Globale Entwicklungen, kontextuelle Profile und dkumenische Herausforderungen* (Gtitersloh: Gltersloher Verlagshaus, 2013), 49-52.

1625 Martin Uffing, "Catholic Mission in Europe 1910 - 2010," in *A Century of Catholic Missions*, ed., Stephen B. Bevans (Eugene, Oregon: Wipf & Stock, 2014), 35.

1626 Ibid., 59-70.

religions, partnership, *Missio Dei* and the movements for autonomy (or independence) respectively.[1627]

What is the rationale behind the reference to the above developments in the theology of mission in our discussion? It is for the simple reason that the Catholic theology of mission had largely been influenced by these currents of theology. Our subsequent discussion will reveal that the Catholic theology of mission has borrowed substantial number of elements from the above understandings of what was meant by mission. Summarizing the major trends in the pre-Vatican Council II era, David Bosch (one of the most influential missiologists of the 20th century), in his ground breaking work (*Transforming Mission: Paradigm Shifts in Theology of Mission*), mentions four representative missiological paradigms, namely "Salvationist (School of Munster), *ecclesiocentric* (School of Louvain), *sacramentalist* (M.-J. le Guillou) and *eschatological* (Yves J. Congar)."[1628] As far as the Catholic theology of mission is concerned, we generally come across with only two representative schools, namely the *Munster School* and *Louvain School* of missiology represented by Joseph Schmidlin and Pierre Charles respectively. The *Munster School* underlines basically the proclamation of the Gospel, the conversion of individual peoples and saving the souls among non-Christians as essential aspects of missionary activities. Accordingly "the basic argument is that the primary goal of mission is the conversion of the non-Christian individuals. The Christian mission aims first and foremost at the salvation of souls (*salus animarum*)."[1629] The following text underlines the same import:

> He [Schmidlin] placed primacy on salvation of souls, describing the stages of missionary work as: 1. The proclamation of the gospel, the Christian faith, among the heathen, 2. The internal conversion, the change of heart, and the external conversion, the incorporation into the church, reception of baptism. 3. The organization of the church from the simple formation of communities to the establishment of full hierarchy.[1630]

1627 See Wrogemann, *Missionstheologien der Gegenwart,* 70-82.

1628 See Bosch, *Transforming Mission*, 380.

1629 Francis A. Oborji, "Catholic Missiology 1910-2010: Origins and Perspectives," in *A Century of Catholic Mission,* ed., Stephen B. Bevans (Eugene, Oregon: Wipf & Stock/ Regnum Books International, 2013), 135.

1630 Crajg Otto & Stephen J. Straus, *et al., Encountering Theology of Mission: Biblical Foundations, Historical Developments and Contemporary Issues* (Grand Rapids: Baker

While reading the above text, we note that Christocentric and personal dimensions are stressed more specifically here.[1631] The *Louvain School* represented by Pierre Charles and Andre Seumois, etc., on the other hand, placed more stress on the planting (or establishing) of the Church (*plantatio ecclesiae*) over individual salvation, the establishment of the hierarchy, the founding of the local churches and winning over not only the non-Christians but also the non-Catholics. In the words of Francis Oborji, "the basic thesis of the Louvain School is that the goal of the mission is the 'planting' of the church .. ,"[1632] Thus, the purpose of the mission under this scheme of understanding is to plant the church with its visible structures wherever it has not been planted. Stated differently, the purpose of the mission is to bring, through faith and the sacraments, the salvation within the reach of all people of good will, most tangibly represented by the establishment of a local church where there is none.[1633] "Therefore territorial expansion of the church is absolutely necessary"[1634] according to this school of understanding.

We notice, thus, that there is an underlying emphasis on ecclesiocentric and territorial aspects. Although the claim may be debated by some critics, a deeper analysis of this paradigm reveals that at the root of such an understanding is ultimately the dictum, '*extra ecclesiam nulla salus*' strongly operative, which in turn dictates the terms of interpretation. For, "if salvation is seen to be mediated only by the church, the church must be established everywhere as soon as possible. So ecclesiogenesis becomes the purpose of missionary activity."[1635] Both the Schools regard the Church primarily as an institution, the missionary as a foreigner, who migrates to a distant land to preach the Gospel of Christ and the natives as the targets of evangelization. Thus, "although the term 'mission' was thus sometimes used in a wider sense, mission proper meant Christian activity among 'pagans."[1636]

Publications, 2010), 114.

1631 See H. S. Brechter, "Dekret iiber die Missionstatigkeit der Kirche," in *Das Zweite Vatikanische Konzil: Dokumente undKommentare*, eds., H. S. Brechter et al. (Freiburg/Basel/Wien: Herder, 1968), 33-36.

1632 Oborji, "Catholic Missiology 1910-2010," in *A Century of Catholic Missions*, 141.

1633 Otto & Straus, *Encountering Theology of Mission*, 114.

1634 James J. Ferguson, "A Paradigm Shift in the Theology of Mission: Two Roman Catholic Perspectives," IBMR 8/3 (July 1984): 119.

1635 Ibid., 117.

1636 Uffing, "Catholic Mission in Europe 1910 - 2010," in *A Century of Catholic Missions*, 36.

This leads us to take to a brief overview of the papal encyclicals and other documents prior to Vatican Council II. Here we shall restrict our discussion to the mission encyclicals alone. It was Benedict XV who treated the issue in his encyclical *Maximum illud* (1919) for the first time in the history of the 20th century Church. This encyclical is often "called the 'Magna Carta' of modern missions and its directives have had far-reaching ramifications."[1637] The other encyclicals dealing with the subject prior to Vatican Council II are: Pius XI's *Rerum Ecclesiae* (1926), Pius XII's *Evangelii Praecones* (1951), Pius XII's *Fidei Donum* (1957) and John XXIII's *Princeps Pastorum* (1959). Against the emerging historical changes and challenges, these encyclicals emphasized various aspects of what the mission implied in a given context. In *Maximum illud*,

> Benedict XVI stated two purposes ... to encourage missionary leadership and to recommend mission methods ... He also has strong words that direct the missionary to avoid 'serving the interests of his homeland' ... The pivotal emphasis ... is the development of the indigenous clergy ...Why? 'For the local priest, one with his people by birth, by nature, by his sympathies and his aspirations, is remarkably effective in appealing to their mentality and thus attracting them to the Faith ... Mission superiors should have the founding of seminaries as a main concern ... His vision would be based on the traditional conviction *extra ecclesiam nulla salus*.[1638]

Pius XI, in *Rerum Ecclesiae*, "follows quite closely the thought of his predecessor, though some points are developed in greater detail ... In short, 'Pope Pius XI regards the planting of the visible organization of the Church and the erection of seminaries as the first duty of missionaries..."[1639] Similarly, other encyclicals laid emphasis on various other aspects ranging from human promotion, promotion of native clergy and cultures, etc., as aspects involved within the ambit of the understanding of mission. As for other religions the attitude of the aforementioned encyclicals seems to be mostly negative or at the

1637 James Kroeger, "Papal Mission Wisdom: Five Mission Encyclicals 1919-1959," *A Century of Catholic Mission*, 94.

1638 Ibid., 94-95.

1639 Ibid., 95.

most condescending.[1640] James Kroeger summarizes the pivotal topics addressed in these encyclicals in the following words:

> Based on the close reading of the material ... they are arranged according to the prominence they receive. Papal emphasis is given to the following items: (1) the missionary nature of the church; (2) the purpose of the missions; (3) the person of the missionary; (4) local churches and local clergy; (5) role of the pope and the bishops; (6) the role of the mission superiors; (7) types of mission work; (8) missionary virtues; (9) the pontifical mission aid societies; and (10) laity in the mission.[1641]

The above summary overview presents some of the most important aspects of the prevalent as well as developing theologies of mission. At the same time they also show a slow development of a new vision of mission. As we take a closer look at the Jesuit mission under review vis-avis the contemporary currents of theology of mission, we are faced with some of the general yet important questions: (1) How did the Jesuits perceive themselves as missionaries? (2) How were they perceived as missionaries among the people? (3) What was the understanding of a missionary endeavour? (4) What was the role of the laity in the mission? (5) What was the status of the native clergy? (6) What was the attitude of the Jesuits towards other religions? (7) What was the attitude of the Jesuits towards other Christian denominations? These are some of the most basic questions that give us a sufficient idea of the stream of missionary thought that was prevalent among the Jesuits, of this period.

As regards the perception about themselves as missionaries, there is no doubt that the Jesuits saw themselves as sent to a distant land to preach the Gospel to a people who had no knowledge of Jesus and his Church. By the same token, they perceived themselves as 'superior' to the people (i.e., target groups) they had been sent to. The target groups have often been designated in the Jesuit letters and documents as "pagan,"[1642] or its equivalents. The objective of a missionary endeavour

1640 See Bosch, *Transforming Mission*, 11-14.

1641 Kroeger, "Papal Mission Wisdom," in *A Century of Catholic Missions*, 99.

1642 For example see James H. Gense to the German Assistant to the Superior General (Bombay, 18th February 1922), ARSI, *Bombay. 1004-1V, 5*; Archbishop Henry Doring to the Superior General (Poona, 30th May 1929), ARSI, *Poona. 1004-IIA, 10*; Archbishop Henry Doring to the Superior General (Poona, 25th December 1925), ARSI, *Poona. 1004-111*, 1; Augustine Rosch to the Superior General (Stella Matutina, 20th January 1937),

itself was seen as "rescuing helpless 'infidels' in darkness and the shadow of death...."[1643] Under this paradigm of understanding, apparently, the Jesuits perceived themselves as chosen people possessing a higher truth than those to whom they were sent. Moreover, they understood the act of being sent as a divine obligation placed on them so that they took the act of being sent as binding on them to go and preach the Gospel. Such an understanding, in some manner or the other, was responsible for their self-understanding as being superior to the native people. Generally this attitude acted as the biggest hindrance on the way to their receptiveness and openness in accepting the socio-cultural practices of the natives as they are. In the context of our reflection on the growth and progress of the mission (cf. # 8.1) we have made a reference to a remark by Henry Heras. We may cite a further remark by him that seems apt here:

> As I shall have an occasion to remark later on, these airs of superiority have influenced our life very much in many spheres. This is a great misfortune, indeed, for besides being totally abhorrent from the spirit of the Gospel, it is absurd and illogical, and makes us thoroughly unfit for our spiritual work. Very reasonably did Prof. Jung say in this connection: "Our western air of superiority in the presence of the Indian understanding is a part of our essential barbarism."[1644]

Without making a generalization, thus, it may be said that the self-understanding among the Jesuits often resembled an attitude, which David Bosch describes in the following words: "Missionaries [read Jesuits], perhaps more than others, have tended to regard themselves as immune to the weaknesses and sins of 'ordinary' Christians [and for that matter others]...."[1645] It may be remarked, however, that such a characteristic was not unique feature among the Jesuits. On the contrary, it was shared by practically all the missionaries coming from the West.

However, without giving a space for any misinterpretation, we need to add here that the Jesuits generally tried to impart a sense of equality among all the people they served. This was, in spite of the fact that at

---

ARSI, *Germ. Sup. 1012-1*, 1; Pius Geisel to the Superior General (Poona, 25th February 1950), ARSI, *Poona. 1004-XIX*, 11.

1643 See James C. Okoye, "The Bible in Catholic Mission 1910-2010," in *A Century of Catholic Missions,* 123.

1644 Heras, "On the Mission Methods," 19.

1645 Bosch, *Transforming Mission*, 174.

the subconscious level there was certainly a sense of superiority among them. It must be acknowledged, however, that such an attitude was quite a natural human characteristic. For, given the low level of education and social backwardness of the people, the situation warranted their taking the role of teachers and guides. Therefore, their latent attitude of superiority, though negative, can be absolved.

As for the native people, it may be said that they mostly perceived themselves as recipients and beneficiaries of the benevolence embodied in the Jesuit mission. We have mentioned in chapter six (i.e., 6.2.3.1) that the medical facilities being availed to the native people through the establishment of St. Luke's Hospital in Shrirampur was one of the examples whereby the natives began to see more clearly the benevolent face of the Jesuit missionaries. This argument may be stretched to accommodate all other charitable and philanthropic activities that the Jesuits carried out for them. During the famines and epidemics, for example, the natives experienced the benevolence of the mission as a service organization. Similarly, the education imparted through schools and colleges, pastoral care extended through regular pastoral visits and caring hand extended to the widows and orphans, etc., were something unusual and extraordinary for them.[1646] Indeed all these experiences were radically in contrast with what they as people belonging to the lowest class of people in the caste hierarchy had been experiencing for ages. Although the experience below pertains to another depressed class, it resonates the fundamental experience of the *Mahar* and other Christians very well. To quote Sambaiah Gundimeda:

> It was during such times (famine) that the Dalits could truly perceive the contrast in the way that caste Hindus and the missionaries treated them. While the former dealt with them as if they were a grade lower than animals, the missionaries treated them with dignity, kindness and, most importantly, as equals. Not surprisingly, many Dalits were overwhelmed by the material help and human dignity accorded to them and eventually embraced Christianity. According to one estimate, nearly 20 percent of the Dalits in West Godavari, 32 percent in Krishna and 57 per cent in Guntur districts had converted to Christianity in 1931....[1647]

1646 See J. B. Winiger, "Die Choleragottin," *IB* 1/29 (January 1937): 248.

1647 Sambaiah Gundimeda, *Dalit Politics in Contemporary India* (Abingdon/New York: Routledge, 2016), 151.

As for the role of the laity we have discussed quite extensively in chapter four (cf. 4.3) that the catechists were among the most important group of lay helpers who contributed in the growth of the mission significantly. A lacuna in the mission history sources for this study was that they are largely from the perspective of the missionaries. This is true practically of all the mission histories of the pre-Vatican Council II era. In our case too, we lack entirely the literature from the perspective of the natives, except for the fact that through a few personal and informal talks I have tried to include certain aspects of them in our discussions. One of the good examples for the same is the interpretation of the factors responsible for the slow progress of native vocations in the Mission. Although I have not included them as references while dealing with the issue of native vocations (cf. # 7.2), the arguments in justification of the slow growth of native vocations in this Mission were articulated from my personal talks with two local clerics, namely Christopher Shelke and Ajit Lokhande.[1648]

Without further elaboration, we may say that the Jesuits showed both openness and as well as resistance to other religions they encountered in the Mission. Taking Hinduism as a reference point, it may be argued that the Jesuits, by and large, were open to dialogue with it. Three areas that we have discussed earlier, namely the *ashram* experiment, adaptation of Christian art and paintings to local sensibilities and the formation of the debate clubs during the time of Bishop Leo Meurin are indications of such an attitude. This openness was even more visibly manifested in the initiatives of Matthew Lederle who along with Guy Deleury had established a centre for formal dialogue, namely *Snehasadan*, which is still a lively centre for prayer, mediation and dialogue.

As for the dogmatic position with regard to other religions, including Hinduism, the Jesuits were staunchly faithful to the official position of the Catholic Church of this time. Yet, without deviating from the same, they did make some efforts at exploring avenues for dialoguing with other religions. In general, it would not be wrong to say that they found it no less challenging to make deliberate efforts at adopting a spirit of openness in their approach towards other religions

1648 The talks took place on 22nd May 2014 in Munich and 17th July 2014 (over telephone) with Christopher Shelke and Ajit Lokhande respectively. Both of them come from Ahmednagar District in Poona Mission. Moreover, both of them were Professors of Missiology, the former at the Gregorian University, Rome and the latter in Aachen.

and cultures. This is where Henry Heras thought it incumbent on himself to draw the attention of the Jesuits by saying: "But if the missionary on arriving in India begins his work ... with the ordinary prejudices he may have against another civilization which he may judge as inferior to his own, how many errors he will fall into, the consequences of which will be most lamentable."[1649]

It would be too presumptuous, however, to claim that their openness to other religions was a precursor to the theology of religions that we witness in post-Vatican Council II (i.e., NA 1; 8). In fact they were keen on following the traditions of their great predecessors, Robert De Nobili and Joseph Beschi. With regard to their attitude towards other Christian denominations, it would be a needless exercise to elaborate on the same. From a few instances, however, it may be assumed that the spirit of ecumenism was still an alien idea. On the contrary, a certain form of competition against other denominations operating in the mission field was not entirely absent among them. The case of accepting the former Anglicans as catechists during the time of Bishop Leo Meurin may be taken as a tacit example of this claim.[1650]

While summarizing this discussion, it may be noted that the basic missiological position of the Jesuits did not spring from a single source. In fact their missionary understanding evolved along with the new currents of the missionary thinking of the time. The foregoing discussion leads us to the conclusion that the objective of converting the people of other faiths (occasionally also from other Christian denominations) and baptizing them and eventually forming a community of believers formed the basic essence of their missionary thinking. Clearly this approach was influenced by what is called the *Munster School* (i.e., Prof. J. Schmidlin) of theology of mission, which "chiefly emphasizes the proclamation of the gospel, the conversion of humankind, the salvation of souls of non-Christians...."[1651] This, apparently, was not introduced by Schmidlin as such. Rather, such had been the tradition of the Church for many centuries.

1649 Heras, "On the Missionary Methods," 26. Heras gives a number of examples in this document, whereby the Jesuits approached the question of openness and respect towards other religions and cultures with lamentable degree of lack of sensitivity.

1650 See Appendices IA-E.

1651 Jose Madapattu, "Evangelization in a Marginalizing World: With Special Reference to the Marginalised Satnamis in the Diocese of Raipur," (Ph.D. diss., University of Bonn, 1996), 9.

Having said that, it must be noted that this position alone did not seem to have influenced the entire missionary activities that the Jesuits undertook. For, they did apply multiple strategies to accomplish their missionary objectives. Hence we need to take into account of the other streams of understanding of the theology of mission, namely the *Louvain School*, "which places the chief stress on the implantation of the Church, the establishment of the hierarchy, the foundation of particular native Churches, the winning over of non-Catholics."[1652] But a closer look at the Poona Mission history reveals that the Jesuits were not confined to either of these streams of theology. Their missionary endeavour was characterized not only by a synthesis of both these, but also went beyond to include a broader meaning of mission and evangelization. For example, the search for avenues of establishing better understanding and dialogue with Hindus through *ashram* experiment and adaptation of Christian art and paintings were certainly symbolic of a progressive stance in the missionary thinking among them. The criticisms against such initiatives, both from outside as well as inside, indicate this aspect.

As for the general dogmatic position, the Jesuits being subscribers and adherents of the contemporary theologies of the pre-Vatican II era were very much in line with the dictum 'no salvation outside the Church.' An endless debate can take place on this point. It cannot be denied that the primary concern of the Jesuits was to gain numerical growth of the Church. It is true, however, that their approach was not like the preaching of wandering preachers in those times. In short, we must understand that the Jesuits of the pre-Vatican II ear did not have the privilege of having more open and progressive theologies of mission of the post-Vatican II era.

We notice a gradual evolution in the missionary understanding among the Jesuits, which is symbolized by the new departures in the missionary strategies. In the decades roughly prior to the independence of India, we notice a relatively stronger emphasis on adopting new villages and hamlets for evangelization. After this benchmark, the indirect methods of evangelization seem to have received a greater emphasis. It is when the ashram experiment, opening of dialogue centres, promotion of Indian Christian art, etc. emerged.

1652 Ibid.

Some critics may argue that these evolving orientations in the missionary understanding were not entirely the reflections of an inner metamorphosis that the Jesuits were experiencing with regard to their missionary understanding amidst the influx of new currents of theology. They were rather the results of external contexts like the rise of nationalism and anti-missionary/Christian movements. While maintaining the position that these external contexts were certainly responsible for the rethinking of missionary strategies, we must underline that they were not the sole reasons for the same. Indeed the Jesuits were growing in the awareness of wider implications of the meaning of mission and evangelization, which eventually got spelled out most radically in their 32nd General Congregation (1975) and got redefined in the 34th General Congregation (1995). The epilogue at the end of this work precisely tries to trace this trajectory, i.e., from a traditional understanding of mission to a holistic understanding of the same in terms of faith-justice dialectical unity, which eventually culminated in the vision of evangelization spelled out in the *Evangelii Gaudium* (*EG* 160; and more specifically 176).

At the end of this discussion what seems to be a logical question to ask is: What were the challenges in incorporating the new steams of theology of mission? It would not be wrong to assume that the Jesuits often found themselves caught up between the traditional understanding of mission and the emerging new paradigms. It is true that among themselves, there were many who believed in staunchly adhering to the traditional models of mission. On the other hand, there were also members who were virtual precursors to what Vatican Council II, in *Gaudium et Spes* would emphasize later. The new understanding of evangelization included ministries covering all spheres of life--social, political, economic, cultural, etc. Conversely, it did not limit only to direct preaching of the faith and administering of sacraments (cf. GS 44, 72).[1653] In general, therefore the Jesuits had shown an openness to incorporate the broader meaning of mission and evangelization. In the later decades of this period, this changed orientation of mission work was more visible.

1653 See Avery Dulles, "Vatican II and Evangelization," in *New Evangelizations: Overcoming Obstacles,* eds., Steven Boguslawski & Ralph Martin (New York/Mahwah, NJ: Paulist Press, 2008), 10-11.

9.5. The Question of Uniqueness of the Mission

While enumerating the aims and objectives of this study, we had noted that we wished to underline the unique characteristics, if any, of this Mission, and their relevance and significance for the 21st century Church in India. What are some of those characteristics of this Mission which make it relevant to the 21st century?

i. The very first point that comes up here is the socio-cultural peculiarities and communitarian traits of the target groups. We have mentioned under the first point under this chapter that certain unique communitarian characteristics of the target groups (i.e., *Mahars* and others) accounted for the slow momentum in the conversion movement among them. It must not be denied here, however, that their social and communitarian traits, in some manner or the other, were aspects of their social status. This must be elaborated a little further. We have noted in the third chapter that the position of the *Mahars* in the Hindu caste hierarchy was right at the bottom. The other groups of people shared the same fate to a lesser or greater degree. The subjugation and deprivation that they were subjected to for centuries had certainly an imprint on their behavioural patterns. In other words, their communitarian traits were conditioned by their community history. The insights of cultural anthropology justify such a claim.[1654] Given these characteristics, therefore, the target groups presented themselves as uniquely unique, if we may use this term.
ii. Secondly, it has repeatedly surfaced that no other mission in India faced the peculiar situation in the event of the two World Wars as did the B-P M. The sudden vacuum of personnel and consequent challenges of maintaining the mission were experienced by the Jesuits of this mission in the most unique way. This aspect too deserves to be ranked among the unique features.
iii. Thirdly, the internal conflicts in the Catholic Church, i.e., Padroado-Propaganda jurisdictional conflict, largely contributed to the complexity of the situation. It must be

1654 See for example Roberta R. Greene, ed., *Human Behaviour Theory and Social Work Practice*, Second Edition (New Brunswick/London: Adline Transaction, 2009), 379-80.

pointed out, all the same, that the incisiveness of the conflict had become much less as compared to the middle of the previous century (i.e., 19th century). Yet, the challenge of restoring unity in the Catholic Church was still a major challenge, as far as the Bombay Archdiocese, torn apart by Propaganda-Padroado Conflict for centuries, was concerned.

iv. Fourthly, the nature of new initiatives that were taken, in many respects, were unconventional and by the same token very unique as well. The beginning of a national Theologate in Poona, a full-fledged hospital in Shrirampur and schools for technical education in Sangamner and Poona may be considered for this claim. The Jesuits, thus, aimed not only at increasing the numerical strength of the Catholic Church but also made efforts at leading the Church towards self-sufficiency by establishing institutions for training of the native clergy. In order to improve their socio-economic standard, besides the formal schools and colleges, they opened schools and training centres offering skill-based education. Addressing one of the most pressing needs of the place, they also established a hospital, which well deserves to be counted among the unique initiatives. All these aspects taken together do justify the claim that this Mission was unique in more than one way. On the other hand, we do not deny that other Jesuit missions in India, and those of other Religious Congregations as well as the missionary bodies of the Protestants, had similar initiatives and enterprises.

9.6. The Relevance of the Mission

This question takes us back to the rationale for the coming of the Jesuits to Bombay-Poona Mission. In order to put our argument in a proper perspective we need to mention again as to what the vision of the inviting Bishop Anastasius Hartmann implied. He clearly realized that the question of the depressing situation of the Catholic community in Bombay-Poona could be addressed solely by introducing Catholic educational institutions.[1655] The implementation of this vision by the Jesuits bore an abundant fruit subsequently. The Catholic community

1655 See Joseph Neuner, "Significance of the Advent of the Jesuits to Bombay & Poona," (Paper presented at the Workshop on Mission on the occasion of the Sesquicentennial

of Bombay and Poona emerged from a dismal and lowly state. In the words of Hermann Castelino: "Thanks to their selfless service, the Church in many parts of India, especially western India, now has a Catholic community that is second to none in many spheres of life."[1656] Elsewhere Castelino writes:

> During the last one hundred years and more, Jesuit educational work has been largely responsible for preparing an enlightened Catholic community which can hold its head high ... The impact that the Bombay [and Poona] Jesuits have had on the lives of their students through their schools is, perhaps the best testimony to the success of their efforts to realize the ideals of St. Ignatius in the field of education.[1657]

But the mention of the achievement in relation to the Catholic community alone would be tantamount to minimizing the larger impact that the Jesuits were instrumental in effecting through their schools and colleges in the long run. The impact that was effected through education in the wider society was even greater. First, the Jesuits aimed at person-oriented education in their education system, through which the teachers were encouraged to descend to the level of the students to make the subjects more comprehensible to them. Secondly, for a growing number of students of various religious affiliations attempts were made to achieve this purpose through the school counsellors. In order to make education value-based, it was attempted to make it more integral and comprehensive in nature by introducing numerous co-curricular activities besides other aspects of school curriculum. Thirdly, certain characteristics of Jesuit education included emphasis on the formation of total human person through participatory learning and faith-inspired education so that the students might be prepared to work for a just society.[1658]

It must be underlined that the Jesuits through their education system contributed a great deal not only in imparting education for certain

---

Anniversary of the Arrival of the Jesuits of the Garman- Swiss Provinces in India, Ishvani Kendra, Pune, December 27th - 29th, 2004), PJPA, *Jubilee*.

1656 Herman Castelino, "The Education Enterprise of the German Jesuit Mission," (Paper presented at the Workshop on Mission), ibid.

1657 Herman Castelino, "The Contribution of Jesuit Schools of the Bombay Province in the last Hundred Years," (For Private Circulation only), PJPA, *Varia*.

1658 Castelino, "The Contribution of Jesuit Schools of the Bombay Province," op. cit.

pragmatic purposes such as getting jobs, etc., but also in imparting education on social and human values which later fructified. In sum, the general impact on the society was the creation of awareness about the socio-political evils, rights and duties of citizens and more especially the fostering of an attitude of respect for human values. It would not be wrong to say that the process of achieving the goal of creating a more humane society with equal rights and dignity for all (the full realization of which is still a Utopian goal) was set in motion during the period of our study.

The general impacts of education apart, what takes a priority of place in our discussion here is the application of education through schools and colleges as a potent tool of mission. Today direct evangelization is virtually unthinkable in India. Our discussion on the challenges and hurdles faced by the mission (cf. chapter five) has revealed that the growing spirit of nationalism and religious fundamentalism gradually began to render the possibility of direct evangelization almost nil. Were it not for the huge network of schools and institutions, the face of the Church in India would have been entirely different. A tiny population of only 2.8% of Christians contributed nearly 70% of educational enterprises in India, even as late as in the 1960s and 70s. The mention of these figures is relevant here for one important reason. As far as the modern Catholic education is concerned, the educational institutions established by the Bombay-Poona Jesuit Mission rank among the most significant contributions of the Catholic Church in India to Indian society. Hence, the relevance of the mission in view of its contribution to educational enterprises is undeniable.

In the same way the new initiatives undertaken by the Jesuits of the B-P M in the post-World War I period and more especially in the post-World War II decades, may rightfully be considered as new departures from the missionary strategies of the earlier period (see chapter six). In this chapter we have elaborated this point extensively. As an effort to implement the papal mandates as well as the directives received from their own Superior General, the Jesuits of this Mission explored various new avenues to make mission work more meaningful to the local people. The abiding significance of their contribution may be noted in the area of formation of the native clergy through the establishment of a national Theologate and a Seminary, along with a Papal Athenaeum, for the training of members of various dioceses and Religious Orders. These establishments have greatly contributed to the realization of the vision articulated in the papal mandates and directives by the Jesuit Superior Generals.

Lastly, it may be pointed out that the efforts to impart skill-based education through technical institutions, (i.e., *Dnyanamata* Agricultural High School at Sangamner and St. Joseph's Technical Training School , Poona) were very important initiatives of the Jesuits of this Mission. The products of formal education today are facing a huge crunch of jobs and unemployment. But the initiatives of this kind have become alternatives to this problem. The Catholic Church in India needs to consider this option more seriously to make the Church more relevant in India.

Similarly it may be stated with regard to the initiative pertaining to the health-care service. Undoubtedly this initiative, managed with the collaboration of Religious Sisters, was one of the most creative ones. For the Jesuits, the healing touch extended to the people in their suffering and sickness was one of the most tangible expressions of Christian charity. For them, it revealed most tangibly what Christianity in practice meant. Hence a better image of the mission and the missionaries along with that of Christianity was projected through this service in the best way possible.

We need not elaborate each and every initiative taken by the Jesuits to justify our claim of relevance. In fact what we have discussed above is sufficient for the purpose. Not only the Jesuit missions but also the Catholic Church in India in general may draw lessons from these approaches of the Jesuits. These methods are still relevant in India, more so in the present time when the possibility of direct evangelization is considered a crime by certain fundamentalist forces. The Jesuit missions may continue to work towards the humanization of institutions and society, which in the final analysis would serve the objective set before the Church. As we conclude this discussion, we may emphatically affirm that the Poona Jesuit Mission still holds great relevance for the Church in India.

9.7. Some Critical Comments and Observations

Our foregoing discussion may aptly be closed with a few critical comments and observations. The very first point pertains to the strategies, options and priorities applied in the Bombay-Poona

Mission. A closer look reveals that educational institutions (or for that matter all other establishments, i.e., hospitals, widow houses, orphanages, etc.) and mission stations stood as symbols of two principal missionary approaches. The former may be said to represent an indirect method of evangelization, whereas the latter, the direct one. The ultimate goal of the mission in the very first place was to gain numerical strength in the Catholic Church. The basic method operative among the missionaries was first to win over the converts and then proceed to consolidation their faith through regular pastoral visits and administering of sacraments. This method was used more in the case of group conversions which implied lack of clarity with regard to the motives of the candidates to embrace Christianity. It was only when they encountered resistance from certain target groups that the priorities were reconsidered. Stated in others words, if the native people would have been readily disposed to accept Christianity at the instance of the missionary preaching to them, the establishment of schools in most likelihood would have taken place later. However, it must be stated that the reason for establishing schools, colleges and similar other institutions such as widow homes, orphanages and hospitals, etc., was to present the benevolent face of Christian missionaries so that the native people might be exposed to the benevolence and teaching of Christianity itself.

Our investigation reveals that the Jesuits of B-PM often found themselves faced with a dilemma as to whether the foundation of schools and investment in terms of personnel and resources were producing proportionate results in terms of the numerical increase of the converts. We may guess with some degree of certainty that a section of the Jesuits found it grossly disproportionate thereby raising the question of reconsidering the missionary strategy itself with regard to educational institutions. Pius Geisel, for example, saw the huge investment of personnel and resources in the schools and colleges as strategically erroneous. In his own words:

> The small mission stations in the Belgaum part of the Vice-Province are relatively speaking neglected. Although especially materially very great development has taken place in the last few years, it must be said that only tiny spots of the vast territory of the Vice-Province

> are evangelized. Perhaps too great a part of our effort goes into schools.[1659]

Yet, as we have seen, in spite of failing to produce immediate results of leading the non-Christians to the acceptance of Christianity, the establishment of schools and colleges was instrumental in effecting the impact of a much larger significance in the society in general. In fact, the education system had an immense witness value. After all, every noble enterprise springing from faith-conviction is a silent proclamation of the Good News, thereby meriting itself as an initial act of evangelization (cf. *EN* 21). Although spelt out in a much broader context of Christian witness, Paul VI's comment in his Apostolic Exhortation (i.e., *Evangelii Nuntiandi*) is meaningful here as well: "Modern man listens more willingly to witnesses than to teachers, and if he does listen to teachers, it is because they are witnesses" (*EN* 65). Obviously, we imply here the witness value imparted through education service by the Jesuits.

A second area that deserves a brief comment was the challenge of incorporating the perspective of the native people. We have noted in chapter four (i.e., #4.3) that the near absence of literary sources on the perspectives of the native people makes it virtually impossible to assess this aspect. There is a virtual absence of literature (i.e., letters, documents, reports, etc.) in the archives except for a few letters pertaining to certain controversial issues. For example, some of the educated and vocal lay people from Bombay did not hesitate to express their opinions on the lack of openness to accept the native people as candidates for the Society of Jesus (see #7.2.7). These apart, we hardly come across with any opinion of the native people on any other issue, even on the question of their decision to embrace Christianity. Thus, in spite of our initial desire to include the native perspectives to a greater degree in our discussion, it was has been unsuccessful.

A third area pertains to the slow progress of the native vocations about which we have elaborated in chapter seven. With a clear caveat of not being subjective here, I may make just one observation once again, at a slight risk of presenting an alternative (probably to some, even contradictory) view to what I have argued in chapter seven (i.e., 7.2). My reading of the issue leads us to a conclusion that among the

1659 Pius Geisel "Informatio de Statu Vice-Provinciae Belgaum-Poonensis data a procuratore Viceprovinciae mense Septembri 1961", ARSI, *Belgaum-Poona. 1006-Particulares (1961).*

Jesuits more especially among those in authority (as may be expected among any such group), there existed differences of opinions: one group supporting the promotion of native vocations, and the other, either indifferent or less articulate about it. For, it is difficult to imagine that the Jesuits of Poona working for the establishment of a National Theologate and a Seminary, where many native seminarians from other Provinces, dioceses and Congregations were being trained, would be negligent in promoting native vocations in their own Province. It might be that a majority of the German-Swiss Jesuits might have continued to think even after the experience of the two World Wars that there would be enough supply of mission personnel from Europe to sustain the Mission. Or, they might have underestimated the capability and worth of the natives to become Jesuits of their Province. With regard to the local vocations it would seem that in spite of a general opinion in favour of local vocations, probably some of the most fundamental aspects of the socio-cultural and communitarian traits of the local people especially that of the *Mahars* might not have been sufficiently understand and responded accordingly. Although we have quoted a letter by Ludwig Hassle with a similar content, we may quote here another one to emphasize the point that the socio-cultural and communitarian sensibilities of the local people were extremely vital aspects to be taken care of, especially while dealing with issues like vocation to priesthood. This letter emphasizes the need of approaching the local people with sensitivity and gentleness:

> Only by love can these highly depressed people be won. They cannot withstand love. They would be friendly once they realize that they are loved. They would emerge from their reticence and begin to talk. They will give up their deceitful attitude and will become trustful. These savages are not used to what love means. For, they had been treated like dogs by the high caste people. As soon as one shows love and respect for them, they become responsive and approachable. They are terribly proud, they cannot tolerate reproach [or rebuke]. They simply cannot accept it that they can make any mistakes. Therefore no one can say to them on the face what one thinks about them. He would be so offended and instantly become discouraged so that he would give up everything. The boys are extremely intolerant with one another. One needs only a word to say to another and he is offended ... I need to listen to all the complaints.

> If I do not ... they would say that the Father despises them. I must investigate everything exactly in order to find out as to where the injustice was done because they are very sensitive. Otherwise they would immediately say that the Father does not care for them ... Naturally one must treat everyone equally. To have favourites among them harms equally as it does in Feldkirch [Austria]. One must always speak calmly. An agitated voice can cause a big harm, while they would be anxious, become shy, deceitful and insincere. These people always live in anxiety and have fear for everything. Because of this fear one must speak very calmly and in a friendly manner. That is naturally very difficult, because these people, with their very low demeanor, are very annoying to all the Europeans. One has to be very strong and naturally it costs a lot of patience. One has to swallow a lot, ignore a lot, do not let them know that one feels tactless ... These are a few strokes from the missionary life. Nice words have no value at all here. The natives have a fine intuition to discover whether a person is friendly or inwardly has a dislike towards them.[1660]

The descriptive letter above is a good example of an admonition to fellow missionaries on the type of approach and attitude they should have had. The citation, however, does not seem to imply that the Jesuits in general were not sensitive enough or not really practicing these ideals. I only intend to stress the fact that a little more attention to these aspects might have borne better results. Without highlighting the example of Archbishop Henry Doring in relation to Br. Bernhard Lohole (cf. #7.2.6), it would not be wrong to conclude that some among the Jesuits did seem to have lacked the kind of sensitivity referred in the letter.

Finally a remark may be made on the efforts at adaptation. The issue did receive some attention. We do notice that efforts were done at various areas such as in composing of hymns in *Marathi*, introducing Christian art and paintings in Indian style, launching the ashram method, production of a few literature in *Marathi*, making attempts at dialogue with people of other faiths, etc. All these were attempts at adapting (or inculturating) the Christian faith into the cultural tradition and milieu of the local people. Moreover, through their regular pastoral visits and stay in the villages in the humble huts of the people, the Jesuit missionaries did communicate what it means to be a Christian pastor. But we do

1660 Ludwig Hassle to Emmanuel Hofer (Songaon, 25th August 1941), AMPSJ, *LB. Songaon-Briefe.*

fail to discover as to how certain cultural heritage was transformed and adopted in the Christian life and worship.

This aspect is significant to take note of for one basic reason: When a community embraces a new faith, it finds it much easier to adapt to the new ways and world-views when there is no radical break from the past. In this sense it is not completely uprooted from its cultural roots. The adaptation of positive cultural values in Christian life establishes a bridge between the present and the past. This in turn helps the process of maturity in the new faith. The official theology of the Catholic Church in this regard came to be articulated only in Vatican Council II: in the *Decree on the Missionary Activity of the Church*, i.e., *Ad Gentes* (no. 9): I give a short citation:

> Missionary activity is nothing else, and nothing less, than the manifestation of God's plan, its epiphany and realization in the world and in history; that by which God, through mission, clearly brings to its conclusion the history of salvation. Through preaching and the celebration of the sacraments, of which the holy Eucharist is the centre and summit, missionary activity makes Christ present, who is the author of salvation. It purges of evil associations those elements of truth and grace which are found among peoples, and which are, as it were, a secret presence of God; and it restores them to Christ their source who overthrows the rule of the devil and limits the manifold malice of evil. So whatever goodness is found in people's minds and hearts, or in the particular customs and cultures of peoples, far from being lost is purified, raised to the higher level and reaches its perfection, for the glory of God, the confusion of the demon and happiness of mankind.[1661]

Obviously we cannot evaluate the Jesuit missionaries of the previous era on this basis. It would seem, however, that some Jesuits (as far as the evidence goes) did seem to have lacked sufficient openness to understand and accept the positive aspects of their target people groups unlike the Jesuits elsewhere did. In the Lakota Sioux Mission they had admitted the significance of recognizing the positive aspects of a particular culture they encountered.[1662]

1661 Translation taken from Austin Flannery, *Vatican Council II: Constitutions, Decrees, Declarations* (Northport, NY: Costello Publishing Company/Dublin: Dominican Publications, 2007), 453-54. See also *LG* 11.

1662 See Enochs, *The Jesuit Mission to the Lakota Sioux*, 152-54.

It may appear as a minor point here, yet it deserves a mention at the end of this discussion. It pertains to adopting baptismal names by the new converts. Interestingly, many of the names of the converts resemble those of the Hindus. It is virtually impossible for an outsider even in India to distinguish them whether they are Christians or Hindus from their names. An interpretation is that the Jesuit missionaries in a way encouraged the converts to continue their link with their pre-conversion nominal identity and cultural heritage.

Chapter-10

Epilogue: A Retrospect and A Prospect

From Traditional Mission to 'Faith-Justice' Mandate

10.1. Introduction

Having overviewed the history of the Bombay-Poona Jesuit Mission in India I have noted that the Mission's approach to mission work during the hundred year period (roughly from 1860s to 1960) was informed by the theology of mission of the corresponding period. It is understood that missionary societies were expected to follow the official mission theology of the Catholic Church. But missiological experience and experimentation in mission fields did influence the mission theology of the Church which saw new interpretations from time to time, which in turn, brought re-orientations in mission policies and approaches of missionary societies. Such changes continued to occur in the Jesuit Order also. Obviously these changes were also reflected in the mission policies of B-P Mission. In this chapter we attempt to understand how the policies, priorities and activities of the B-PM were guided and influenced by the changing understanding of the theology of mission of both the universal Catholic Church and the universal Society of Jesus.

A closer look at the understanding of the mission of the Society of Jesus show that it began to be perceived more and more in terms of a dialectical unity between faith and justice,[1663] which in simple

1663 See Avery Dulles, "The Meaning of Faith Considered in Relationship to Justice," in *The Faith That Does Justice: Examining the Christian Sources for Social Change* (Eugene, Oregon: Wipf & Stock, 1977), 37.

terms, meant that commitment to *justice* is a constitutive element of genuine *faith*. It may be expressed in terms of a growing Christian consciousness that an authentic faith invariably involves certain social and communitarian attitudes and commitments. Faith must not be a verbal profession and an intellectual accent to a divine truth alone; rather it must flow out into a commitment to an action aimed at social and communitarian transformation.[1664] In sum, the call of St. James in his letter may be seen as an interpretation of the faith-justice relationship at the primary level: "What good is it, my brothers and sisters, if you say you have faith but do not have works? Can faith save you? If a brother or sister is naked and lacks daily food, and one of you says to them, "Go in peace; keep warm and eat your fill," and yet you do not supply their bodily needs, what is the good of that? So faith by itself, if it has no works, is dead" (James 2: 14-17). The missionaries in our field were also challenged by this scriptural verse.

We need to hasten, however, to add here that the content of the 'faith-justice' discourse is much broader than what may generally be interpreted in the text from St. James. For, here the primary emphasis is on the 'good works' which may essentially be translated as 'works of charity', which are essentially meritorious. But they are not enough. The 'faith-justice' dialectic implies much more than this. In means consciously engaging in actions that aim at addressing the causes of dehumanization, injustice and every form of evil that rob a person of his/her intrinsic human dignity. But this dialectic also demands that we as Christians are truly anchored in our faith while engaging ourselves with the justice issues. In other words, a genuine faith invariably leads us to action. We may underline the fact that an essential linkage between faith and action is evident even in the text of St. James. Indeed it "is not that works must be *added* to faith but that genuine faith *includes* works. That is its very nature."[1665]

Having made these preliminary remarks, we may dwell further on the orientation towards the faith-justice discourse that began to emerge in the understanding of mission in the Society of Jesus. It must be recalled that such an orientation signals a new understanding of mission and evangelization, which eventually got a revolutionary and an eloquent

1664 Ibid. See also Douglas J. Moo, *The Epistle of James: An Introduction and Commentary* (Grand Rapids, Ml/Cambridge, U.K.: William B. Eerdmans, 1985), 99.

1665 Moo, *The Epistle of James*, 99.

articulation in the famous decree 4, no. 2 of the General Congregation of the Society of Jesus (1975): "The mission of , the Society of Jesus today is the service of faith, of which the promotion of justice is an absolute requirement. For reconciliation with God demands the reconciliation of people with one another." The text has evoked many positive as well as critical interpretations. Indeed the radicality of the decree caused a commotion in the Society. A good number of Jesuits found themselves amidst a dilemma. Yet, the implication of the decree was clear that a direct involvement with the issues of justice would mean paying a heavy price, often with once own life. Precisely this was what happened in the following decades when a substantial number of Jesuits and their collaborators had to sacrifice their lives for the cause of justice.

Pedro Arrupe, who was elected as the 28th Superior General of the Society of Jesus during General Congregation 31 was the driving force behind this new orientation. He was firmly convinced of the linkage between the practice of faith and the promotion of justice. On various occasions he interpreted the text to his Jesuit brethren in various parts of the world. The issue of justice was a primary preoccupation, nay an obsession (used with a caveat that it is not interpreted in a negative sense). In one of his writings he wrote: "To be just, it is not enough to refrain from injustice. One must go further and refuse to play its game, substituting love for self-interest as the driving force of society."[1666] Gradually, yet firmly the meaning of mission began to be assimilated and personalized by the Jesuits with all its implications. The awareness about social problems and justice issues was not enough. Consequently many Jesuits went to the extent of sacrificing their lives for the cause of justice. The case of the martyrdom of the Jesuits of El Salvador is the best example of this. We observe, thus, that the meaning of the mission of the Society of Jesus took a radical reorientation precisely because of this new interpretation.

It must be underlined, however, that this meaning in terms of faith-justice dialectic is not a Jesuit invention. The development in this direction is a result of the Church's growing awareness of the structural evils and their direct consequences on the human society. Although it may be argued that the Church has been aware of the justice issues right from its beginning (i.e., patristic tradition of condemnation of the

1666 Pedro Arrupe, "Men and Women for Others," in *Pedro Arrupe: Essential Writings* (New York: Orbis Books, 2004), 185.

social evils), the clearer articulation of the same at least in the modern period began with Leo XIII's encyclical *Rerum Novarum.* Thereafter, the pontificate of John XXIII signified a heightened sense of urgency in addressing the issue.

The mission of the Society of Jesus today is the service of faith, of which the promotion of justice is an absolute requirement. The documents of Vatican Council II addressing the social issues have a clear imprint of this vision of a just social order. As a direct consequence of the impulses of Vatican Council II, the current of thoughts of liberation theology too began to emerge. Meanwhile Paul VI published his first encyclical, *Populorum Progressio* (1967). A year later (i.e., 1968), the Latin American Bishops published *Medellin Documents.* It is precisely these events that gave an impulse to the Society of Jesus to redefine the meaning of its mission. And it is here that the new vision of mission in terms of faith-justice dialectic emerged. In the following decades, the meaning widened its horizons side-by-side with that of the Church. It seems appropriate, therefore, to make a brief survey of the trajectory of the development of ever-widening and more comprehensive meaning of the mission. Ultimately the Society of Jesus, true to its call articulated in its foundational document (i.e., *Formula of the Institute*), namely 'defense and propagation of the faith', is committed to its pledge of *sentire cum ecclesia.* Hence, the understanding of its mission must be seen in close relation to the contemporary articulations in various Church documents. Prior to that, however, we need to describe briefly the emergence of the currents of thoughts in the world-scenario that were largely responsible for drawing the awareness of the Church towards reconsidering the meaning of mission.

10.2. The Worldwide Debates on Human Rights and Freedoms[1667]

We have indicated above that the understanding of the mission of the Society of Jesus in terms of faith-justice dialectic is not a Jesuit invention. It has a precedence both in secular history as well as in the emerging thinking of the Church. In the wake of the Industrial Revolution in the eighteenth and nineteenth centuries, a massive migration of rural

1667 The title as well as the major points of arguments under this subtopic have been borrowed from Ivan Fucek, "Justice," in *Dictionary of Fundamental Theology*, eds. Rene Latourelle & Rino Fisichella (Middlegreen, UK/Maynooth, Ireland/Manila, Philippines: St. Pauls, 1990), 573-74.

population took place to cities. This was basically driven by the need of survival. A new class, then, was born that in Marxist terminology may be termed as a new *Proletariat*. The rich people as employers exploited the skills and labours of the *Proletariat* to generate more wealth for themselves. This created a further rift between the rich and the poor. The unequal distribution of wealth became a 'social question,' raising the concern for a just and equitable distribution of wealth. Various Religious Congregations tried to address the question creatively according to the charisms they followed. The question of disparity due to unequal distribution of wealth became a serious concern from the perspective of the Catholic Church. It is there the concern for justice emerged, and consequently an official response was made by the Church.[1668]

Meanwhile, worldwide debates on human rights and freedom began to take a centre-stage in the public domain against the background of the famous slogan of the French Revolution, namely "*liberty, equality, fraternity*."' A general awareness about human rights as being innate and unalienable to a human person on the one hand, and the structures of injustice as being primary agents of violence against the same on the other, began to sharpen. These debates also influenced the Church, other religions, international laws and social systems. The cry for recognition of the basic rights of persons or groups became more prominent. Ever since the three fundamental values enshrined in the slogan of the French Revolution became popular, the awareness of the structures of injustice and aspirations for addressing the same began to be ever more prominent. Eventually, a series of powerful articulations of these aspirations found their expressions in the forms of various charters. Among them was the fundamental document of the United Nations, namely *Universal Declaration of Human Rights* (1948). Nearly two decades later followed the *Declaration on Economic, Social and Cultural Rights* (1966). The Conference on Security and Co-operation in Europe (CSCE) also promulgated the *Declaration on the Principles Regulating Relations between the Participating States* in 1975. All these are some of the most powerful declarations of the fundamental human aspirations for justice

1668 See T. Howland Sanks, "The Social Mission of the Church: Its Changing Context," in *The Gift of the Church: A Textbook Ecclesiology in Honor of Patrick Granfield O.S.B.*, ed. Peter C. Phan (Collegeville, Minnesota: The Liturgical Press, 2000), 271-72.

and peace in the world, with their core concern for protection of human rights and dignity.[1669]

10.3. Social Teaching of the Catholic Church: The Pre-Vatican Council II Era

As we take a cursory look at the historical development of the Church's teaching on social justice, we discover that the roots go as far back as the Hebrew Scripture. However, we begin our discussion from the modern period. We discover that the magisterial teaching on the question begins with Leo XIII's Encyclical *Rerum Novarum* (1891). The basic emphasis of the encyclical was on the issue of justice in the social order, placing a special stress on the fact that the voice of the Church is primarily on behalf of the poor. The theme of social justice was further developed by Pius XI in his Encyclical *Quadragesimo Anno* (1931) with emphasis on the principle of subsidiarity (nos. 70-80) and rights of the individual and family. The encyclical describes the concept of social justice as a 'directing principle' for public institutions and the economic order (nos. 88-90). While being highly critical of the Nazi Government in Germany, the next encyclical of Pius XI, i.e., *Mit Brennender Sorge* (1937) also highlighted the issue of human rights and justice. However, the social teaching of the Catholic Church began to be articulated in more unambiguous terms only since the decades subsequent to World War II. Thus, John XXIII's encyclical, *Mater et Magistra* (1961) critically reflected on the ever increasing disparity between the rich and the poor. His second encyclical, *Pacem in Terris* (1963), while making an appeal for peace in the world implicitly called attention to the need of social justice.[1670] It "put the concept of human dignity in the center of Catholic social teaching."[1671]

1669 See Ivan Fucek, "Justice," in *Dictionary of Fundamental Theology*, eds. Rene Latourelle & Rino Fisichella (Middlegreen, UK/Maynooth, Ireland/Manila, Philippines: St. Pauls, 1990), 573-74.

1670 See Thomas Rausch, "Sexual Morality and Social Justice," in *Contemporary Catholic Theology: A Reader,* eds. Michael A. Hayes & Liam Gearon (New York: Continuum, 2000), 417-20.

1671 Herminio Rico, *John Paul II and the Legacy of Dignitatis Humanae* (Washington: Georgetown University Press, 2002), 120.

10.4. Social Teaching of the Catholic Church: Conciliar Documents

Among the documents of the Vatican Council II, *Gaudium et Spes (GS)* and *Dignitatis Humanae (DH)* treat the question of human rights and justice for the first time in the history at the level of a council. *DH* underlines basically three aspects on the necessity of respecting the moral principle of personal and social responsibility by saying that "in exercising their rights individuals and social groups are bound by the moral law to have regard for the rights of others, their own duties to others and the common good of all. Everybody must be treated with justice and humanity *(DH.1)*. Besides John XXIII's *Pacem in Terris (PT),* these two are the most significant documents of Catholic doctrine on human rights, especially the rights of religious freedom.[1672] As for *Gaudium et Spes (GS)* it may undoubtedly be claimed that it was a new beginning of the Church's openness on the question of human rights and common good. The document treated the promotion of human rights and practice of social justice as part of the mission of the Church. "Christians who take an active part in present-day socio-economic development and fight for justice and charity should be convinced that they can make a great contribution to the prosperity of mankind and to the peace of the world ... Whoever in obedience to Christ seeks first the Kingdom of God, takes there from a stronger and purer love for helping all his brethren and for perfecting the work of justice under the inspiration of charity" (GS 72).

10.5. Towards a Faith-Justice Dialectic Unity: Post Conciliar Documents

Impelled by two important documents of Vatican Council II, namely *Gaudium et Spes* and *Dignitatis Humanae,* a process of serious reflection began at various levels in the Church. Pope Paul VI, in his encyclical *Populorum Progressio* (1967) laid stress on the question of land reform (no. 24), while also rejecting liberal capitalism, which he saw as one of the main factors responsible for the widening divide between the rich and the poor. One of the documents that may be said to have articulated the question more emphatically up to that point of time was the document of the Third Synod of Bishops which was published in 1971 with the title *Justice in the World.*[1673] The Synod

1672 Ibid.

1673 See Fucek, "Justice," in *Dictionary of Fundamental Theology*, 51 A.

had gathered to seek a creative response to the structural violence and injustices in the world, which create an artificial divide between the rich and the poor and robbing the majority poor of their human dignity. The most revolutionary statement of the Synod declared: "Action on behalf of justice and participation in the transformation of the world fully appear to us as a constitutive dimension of the preaching of the Gospel, or, in other words, of the Church's mission for the redemption of the human race and its liberation from every oppressive situation" (no. 6). Similarly, "It linked evangelization with a commitment to the transformation of the world."[1674] The document may be considered "the most forthright statement to date from an official collegial body in the Church on the proper response of the Church and its members to the use and abuse of political and social power."[1675] Apparently this may be seen as a definitive advancement in Church's understanding of its mission and evangelization.

Meanwhile certain currents of thought that were major driving forces behind Liberation Theology began to gain further currency. One of the most important as well as revolutionary articulations of the impact of such currents of thought found expression in the Medellin Documents (1968). The Documents raised the issue of social justice in radical terms. A few points that were significant in the conference were: structural injustice, towards a Church of the poor, option for the poor (which was given a new expression in the Puebla Document issued in 1987, i.e., *preferential option for the poor*), conscientization of people, solidarity with the victims of injustice, support of the struggle for liberty, etc. The most radical departure from the earlier thinking of the Church was on the way.[1676] The Medellin Documents "represent the first official Catholic Church articulation of, and commitment to, liberation theology; in fact, they 'serve as founding documents of Latin American Liberation Theology...."[1677] A strong imprint of these documents was

1674 Rausch, "Sexual Morality and Social Justice," 420.

1675 John C. Haughey, ed., *The Faith That Does Justice: Examining the Christian Sources for Social Change* (Eugene, Oregon: Wipf & Stock, 1977), 3.

1676 See Donal Dorr, *Option for the Poor & for the Earth: From Leo XIII to Pope Francis* (Maryknoll, New York: Orbis Books, 2012); 312-14; Edward L. Cleary, How Latin America Saved the Soul of the Catholic Church (New York/Mahwah, NJ: Paulist Press, 2009), 97-101.

1677 Thomas Oldenski, *Liberation Theology and Critical Pedagogy in Today's Catholic Schools: Social Justice in Action* (New York/Abingdon, Oxon: Routledge, 1997), 69.

also seen in the statement of the International Synod of Bishops (1971), *Justice in the World*, which we have pointed out above.

We notice a progressive broadening of the understanding of the mission of the Church, which with every new magisterial teaching or theological enunciation appears to have become more comprehensively articulated. Both in *Populorum Progressio* (1967) as well as in *Octogesimo Advdniens* (1971), Paul VI draws attention to the contemporary social problems faced by the contemporary Church and society. For our purpose, however, his call to heed to the cry of the poor (cf. *PP* 3), for justice and peace (cf. *PP* **5**), justice at every level (cfi, *PP* 59; 70; *OA* 43-44)), change not only of attitudes but also of unjust structures (cf, *OA* 45) and need of political activism in order to create a just social order (cf, *OA* 46), are significant. His genuine concern for the promotion of social justice, while at the same time being greatly influenced by the Medellin Documents and Liberation Theology, led him to a reinterpretation and enlargement of the meaning of mission and evangelization in his Apostolic Exhortation, *Evangelii Nuntiandi* (1975). In the exhortation he conceived the acts of verbal proclamation of the Word, witnessing to the Gospel through life and active participation in the process of transformation of human society as integral dimensions of Church's mission. Although the phrase "option for the poor" was not used in the document, there are repeated references implying thereby the preference for and solidarity with the poor placing the mission of the Church within the framework of Jesus' own preferential mission among the poor.[1678] Tt is not possible to include here the entire gamut of the theology of mission enshrined in the document. Yet no. 29 of the encyclical which deals with the meaning of social transformation, nay a holistic transformation, of the human society as being integral to the proclamation of the Gospel, may be cited here:

> But evangelization would not be complete if it did not take account of the unceasing interplay of the Gospel and of man's concrete life, both personal and social. This is why evangelization involves an explicit message, adapted to the different situations constantly being realized, about the rights and duties of every human being, about family life without which personal growth and development

1678 See Jon Sobrino, *The True Church and the Poor* (Eugene, Oregon: Wipf & Stock, 1985), 266-67; Alfred T. Hennelly, *Theology for a Liberating Church: The New Praxis of Freedom* (Washington: Georgetown University Press, 1989), 112-14.

> is hardly possible, about life in society, about international life, peace, justice and development--a message especially energetic today about liberation (*EN* 29).

Pope John Paul II's pontificate witnessed the publication of the maximum number of encyclicals and apostolic exhortations. A good number of his encyclicals have a strong social thrust. Indeed John Paul II deserves to be credited with the most radical articulations of the social doctrine of the Church.[1679] *Redemptor Hominis* (1979), for example, strongly underscores the need of the promotion of justice and human dignity. His next encyclical, *Laborem Exercens* (1981) is a strong articulation of his concern for the dignity of human work and rights of labour. As far as the question of social problems are concerned, the most definitive articulation of the subject is found in *Solicitudo Rei Socialis* (1987), which as the title suggests seeks to address the contemporary social problems of the world. This encyclical closely follows the spirit of John XXIII, Vatican Council II and very especially that of *Populorum Progressio* (1967).[1680] Its basic thrust is on the need of 'authentic human development' (cf. nos. 27-34). The encyclical makes a survey of the contemporary world with its emerging socio-political-economic and other aspects and devotes a considerable space for making a theological interpretation of the modern problems (cf. no. 35-40). Although John Paul II makes use of the phrase "the option or love of preference for the poor" (no. 42) only once in the entire encyclical, it is amply clear that his basic concerns included the call for creation of a just society. In order to achieve this goal, he strongly stressed the need of establishing solidarity with the poor and the victims of unjust structures. Solidarity, he believed is not just "a feeling of vague compassion or shallow distress at the misfortunes of so many people, both near and far. On the contrary, it is a firm and persevering determination to commit oneself to the common good...." (*SRS*, 38). Taking direct inspiration from his predecessors, the pontificate of John Paul II symbolized a progressive evolution of the emphasis on the need of defending the poor and advocating for social

1679 See Fucek, "Justice," in *Dictionary of Fundamental Theology*, 579; Gerard Mannion, *The Vision of John Paul II: Assessing His Thought and Influence* (Collegeville, Minnesota: Liturgical Press, 1979), 136.

1680 See Rodger Charles, *The Catholic Tradition from Genesis to Centesimus Annus, Vol. 2: Modern Christian Social Witness and Teaching/The Modern Social Teaching/Contexts (Herefordshire: Gracewing, 1998), 340-41; Hennelly, Theology for a Liberating Church,* 120-22.

justice. We have a very succinct summary of the development of the teaching on human rights by Ivan Fucek that gives us a progressive view of the subject:

> The history of the teaching on human rights can be summarized into five phases: (a) Classic teaching did not deal with human rights and freedoms, (b) The concept was used pretty cautiously both by the Catholic *magisterium* and by theologians until the 1960s, (c) The subject came to prominence with the debate on the *specijicum christianum* (the specifically Christian component) in morality (1970), (d) This teaching only enters Catholic political ethics after "signals" given by the *magisterium.* Today Catholic theology cannot ignore it any more. Thus, on this topic, the pontificate of Pius XII was still cautious; the pontificates of John XXIII and Paul VI were open, Vatican II even more so (specifically in *DH* and **GS).** But the subject comes into its own with the pontificate of John Paul II.[1681]

Among the pontificates of the 20th century, truly the legacy of John Paul II has an important place in the faith-justice discourse. He maintained his solicitude and commitment to the poor, the less privileged and the victims of injustice consistently throughout his pontificate. In the very first message of his papacy he had professed his special solicitude for all "those who are oppressed by whatever injustices or discrimination whether it has to do with economy, life in society, political life or the freedom of conscience and just religious freedom."[1682]

10.6. The 32nd General Congregation of the Society of Jesus (1975)

We have noted above that as the head of the Society of Jesus and the leading figure behind the spirit of General Congregation 32, Pedro Arrupe (28th Superior General) played the most vital role in bringing the concern for justice to the centre stage. "The plight of the poor, the disposed, the marginalized, was a constant preoccupation with Arrupe."[1683] As a missionary he had spent long years in Japan and personally witnessed the devastation that World War II had caused, "he had a profound perception of the social problems that rend mankind

---

1681 Fucek, "Justice," in *Dictionary of'Fundamental Theology,* 574-75.

1682 Rico, *Johu Paul II and the Legacy of Dignitatis Humanae*, 119.

1683 George Bishop, *Pedro Arrupe, SJ: Twenty-eighth General of the Society of Jesus* (England: Gracewing, 2000), 259.

and dehumanize the lives of the majority of men."[1684] Besides these too, he was deeply aware of the unjust structures that create a vast divide between the rich and the poor. All these acted as impulses that inspired Arrupe to convoke the 32nd General Congregation (GC). The purpose of the convocation of the GC was basically "to engage in reflection in common to experience a conversion of the whole Society."[1685] It may safely be assumed that the purpose of the GC was also to reinterpret the meaning of mission within the framework of the 'signs of the times', the impulses of Vatican Council II and that of the post-conciliar documents. In the words of John W. Padberg:

> In giving reasons for calling the congregation, the General said that the years since the 31st Congregation (1965-1966) and since Second Vatican Council (1962-1966) had brought so many changes to the Society and to the Church and to the world, he thought it incumbent upon him to present to the highest governing body of the Society its present condition for "deep, realistic and open consideration."[1686]

It must be recalled that the above-mentioned documents of Vatican Council II had condemned not only individual sins but also structural sins. It is against this background that "in 1973 he [Arrupe] had felt a new light, a conviction he was absolutely sure of the new route the Jesuits must take: their mission to serve in the name of faith in which the promotion of justice becomes an absolute consequence."[1687] The historical preface of this General Congregation reveals that there was an acute awareness among a majority of the Jesuits across the world, especially among the Jesuits from the Third World, about the existing social problems. Consequently the biggest numbers of postulates too were received on the question of promotion of justice.[1688]

From the perspective of articulation of the scope and meaning of the mission of the Society of Jesus in broader terms that took into

---

1684 Ibid., 226.

1685 John W. Padberg, ed. "Historical Preface to the Decrees of the 32nd General Congregation," in *Documents of the 31st and 32nd General Congregations of the Society of Jesus*, ed. John W. Padberg (Saint Louis: The Institute of Jesuit Sources, 1977), 346.

1686 John W. Padberg, "The Society True To Itself: A Brief History of the 32nd General Congregation of the Society of Jesus (December 2, 1974—March 7, 1975)," SSJ 15/3-4 (1983): 4.

1687 Bishop, *Pedro Arrupe*, SJ, 259.

1688 See Padberg, ed. "Historical Preface to the Decrees of the 32nd General Congregation," 363.

consideration the contemporary socio-political and economic realities, the 32nd General Congregation of the Society of Jesus may be termed as the most significant General Congregation of the 20th century. On the one hand it maintains the continuity in its understanding of the vision of mission articulated in the foundational document of the Society of Jesus, namely the *Formula of the Institute*, which spells out the same in terms of "defense and propagation of the faith." On the other, not only did it broaden and deepen its meaning, but also translated the same into a language more reflective of the modern sensibilities as well as the Society's own self-understanding after Vatican Council II.[1689]

Accordingly the mission is visualized in terms of 'service of the faith and promotion of justice.' Decree 4, no. 2 reads: "The mission of the Society of Jesus today is the service of faith, of which the promotion of justice is an absolute requirement. For, reconciliation with God demands the reconciliation of people with one another." Hereby an inseparable link is established between the service of the faith and the promotion of justice, while making the stress more emphatic by saying that the 'promotion of justice is an absolute requirement of the service of the faith.' The implication was clear. The Jesuits were called to engage in the fight against injustice and unjust structures in the world. Jesuits across the world have tried to integrate this emphasis in their ministries of whatever nature and in personal lives. As indicated in the introduction, the price of the same has been high as a number of Jesuits and collaborators have lost their lives. It is important to note, however, that the self-understanding of the Society has taken new dimensions.[1690]

10.7. The 34th General Congregation of the Society of Jesus (1995)

From the perspective of broadening of the meaning of mission, the 34th General Congregation is more relevant. Held after 30 years since the conclusion of the 32nd General Congregation, the Society of Jesus had been going through a process of reflection and internalization of the agenda it had set before it in the 32nd General Congregation, whereby it had defined the meaning of mission in terms of 'the service of faith, of which the promotion of justice is an absolute requirement.' The reflections and experiences of the Jesuits, however, led to the conclusion that the vision of mission spelt out in the GC 32 needed to be made more

1689 See Rausch, *Educating for Faith and Justice*, 76.

1690 Ibid., 76-77.

comprehensive by integrating certain important components that have become indispensable in modern discourses, i.e., cultures. While GC 34 re-emphasizes the link between faith and justice that was articulated in the GC 32, it goes beyond to include the need to enter into dialogue with cultures and religions. Martin R. Tripole points out that an explicit attempt was made in the GC 34 to enlarge the understanding of the mission of the Society of Jesus beyond that understanding set in place by GC 32 in Decree 4. GC 34 reaffirms Decree 4, but does so by going beyond it to formulate a theological and apostolic framework that notably deepens and broadens its perspective. GC 34 has taken what GC 32 has initiated, but refashioned it to produce something that is not only more theologically sound, but also more appropriate to the total mission of the Society....[1691]

In the document, the vision of mission was articulated in the following words:

> Today we realize clearly: No service of faith without promotion of justice, entry into cultures, [and] openness to other religious experiences. No promotion of justice without communicating faith, transforming cultures, collaboration with other traditions. No inculturation without communicating faith with others, dialogue with other traditions, commitment to justice. No dialogue without sharing faith with others, evaluating cultures, concern for justice" (GC 34, Decree 2, no. 19).

GC 34, Decree 2, no. 21 summarizes beautifully the content of what the mission of the Society of Jesus in today's context means: "In the light of these reflections, we can now say of our contemporary mission that the faith that does justice is, inseparably, the faith that engages other traditions in dialogue, and the faith that evangelizes culture" (GC 34, Decree 2, nos. 20-21). Doubtlessly, this broadening of meaning is very relevant. And for a context like that of India, it is all the more so. For, human rights and justice issues are so glaring that a faith-commitment worth its name can ignore the same only at the risk of losing its own meaning and significance.

1691 Martin R. Tripole, "An Assessment of the 34th General Congregation's Understanding of Justice and its Role in Jesuit Higher Education," in *Promise Renewed: Jesuit Higher Education for a New Millennium,* ed. Martin R. Tripole (Chicago: Loyola Press, 1991), 10.

10.8. Pope Francis' Evangelii Gaudium (2014)

Pope Francis's call to reinterpret the faith-commitment has clear echo of the theology of liberation originating from Latin America. His vision of mission underlines, nay further re-emphasizes the inseparability of faith and justice, which has been articulated in the 34th General Congregation of the Society of Jesus (Cf. GC 34, Decree 2, No. 2). It would not be wrong to say, thus, that the evolution of the Catholic theology of mission in terms of faith-justice unity eventually culminates in his recent encyclical, i.e., *Evangelii Gaudium* (2014). Pope Francis interprets the commitment to justice issues as an inseparable dimension of an authentic faith, which eventually expresses itself in a genuine fraternal love (Cf. *EG* 179). He writes: "An authentic faith--which is never comfortable or completely personal--always involves a deep desire to change the world, to transmit values, to leave this earth somehow better than we found it" (*EG* 183). He builds on the theology proposed by his predecessors and develops it into an articulation that doubtlessly may be called a culmination of the theology of mission up till date. The same has been spelt out poignantly in *EG* (No. 182):

> The Church's pastors, taking into account the contributions of the different sciences, have the right to offer opinions on all that affects people's lives, since the task of evangelization implies and demands the integral promotion of each human being. It is no longer possible to claim that religion should be restricted to the private sphere and that it exists only to prepare souls for heaven. We know that God wants his children to be happy in this world too, even though they are called to fulfilment in eternity, for he has created all things "for our enjoyment" (1 Tim 6:17), the enjoyment of everyone. It follows that Christian conversion demands reviewing especially those areas and aspects of life "related to the social order and the pursuit of the common good" (*EG* 182).

10.9. Concluding Remarks

What is the relevance of the foregoing discussion for Poona Jesuit Mission? First and foremost it must be underlined that Jesuit missions across the world follow a basic common charism, although the methods and strategies have to vary according to the ground realities of the place. Secondly, the relevance of the same lies in the fact that the Jesuits of this mission, while carrying out the mission entrusted to them, have been also co-pilgrims on the way to a search for newer understanding, meaning and relevance of their call. As we take a closer look at the history of this mission, we discover that in spite of their major preoccupation with the numerical increase of the membership of the Catholic Church, till about Vatican II. Since then they have been conscious of exploring a wider meaning of the mission. There is no denying of the fact that they had understood every form of social work, philanthropic activities in the form of imparting education and providing health-care, etc., as a preparation for or as indirect evangelization.[1692]

It would be entirely a misrepresentation of the fact to say that the above-mentioned enterprises were understood by them only as indirect or alternative methods of evangelization, or **because** there were no other choices left with them. On the contrary, these were understood as integral to the vision of their mission as visualized by their founder, Ignatius of Loyola, who had a clear vision of formal education. He saw it "as a special part of the work of a religious order, as a special ministry, a special means of obtaining the end of his Society: the glory of God and the salvation of souls."[1693]

The above text of Robert Schwickerath, would appear to assert that formal education was ultimately a *means to a goal*. It must be clarified here, however, that Ignatius did not interpret the meaning of *means* in terms of a pure instrumentality of an object to be used as far as it served one's purpose. On the contrary, he saw it as an integral dimension of his missionary vision, so that he included "the education of the youth as one of its [Society of Jesus] primary objects"[1694] in the Constitutions of his Order. Stated in other words, "the apostolate of Jesuit education is the expression of a mission that digs deeply into the traditions that identify Jesuit life and ministry."[1695]

Having made these observations, we may say that the Jesuits of Poona Mission were well within this parameter of thinking. Indeed, they

---

1692 See Amaladoss, *Mission Today*, 96.

1693 Robert Schwickerath, *Jesuit Education: Its History And Principles Viewed In The Light Of Modern Educational Problems,* Second Edition (St. Louis, MO: B. Herder, 1904), 73.

1694 Ibid., 69.

1695 Howard Gray, "Experience of Ignatius of Loyola: Background to Jesuit Education," in *The Jesuit Ratio Studiorum: 400th Anniversary Perspectives,* ed. Vincent J. Duminuco (New York: Fordham University Press, 2000), 18. See also H. de la Costa, "Saint Ignatius and the Jesuit School Apostolate," in *Jesuit Education in India*, ed. Gregory Naik (Anand: Gujarat Sahitya Prakash, 1987), 14.

too were moving towards a collective search for a deeper meaning of the mission. In their own concrete context, a sense of urgency for the search of a more relevant meaning of mission was growing with passing decades within the period of our study. We have ample examples to show that they have been in constant search of meaning and relevance of their mission in the given context. Especially after the 1940s we notice clearly a greater openness towards experimenting with newer methods of reaching out to the people (i.e., *ashram* experiment, adaptation of Christian art and opening of dialogue centre, etc.). These are indicative, not only of the fact that the Jesuits were keen on alternative methods of evangelization in order to gain a greater number of converts to Catholicism but also of the fact that they were experiencing the inadequacy of the scope of the existing mission. It would not be too tall a claim, therefore, that their approaches to the newer missionary methods, especially the *ashram* experiment and the search new avenues for dialogue with other religions and cultures were already some of the important precursors to the more accommodative theology of religions that emerged during and after Vatican Council II. Indeed a careful observer can identify a close connection between their orientations with that of the Church's emerging understanding of mission and evangelization.

In the decades subsequent to Vatican Council II and more especially after GC 32, the history of the missions reveals that the Jesuits have been making sincere efforts to reinterpret the meaning of their mission in terms of *preferential option for the poor* that invariably implies a 'faith-justice' dialectic unity. A greater emphasis on the ministries of social work, while in no way neglecting other apostolates, may doubtlessly be said to have gained a further emphasis solely on account of their newer understanding of mission. Moreover, in the larger framework of the Church's as well as Society's call to recognize the value of other cultures and religions, genuine efforts began to be made in the direction of making efforts at inculturation. In this direction, Pedro Arrupe had already shown a keen interest ever since his election as the Superior General (1965). In order to respond to the call of Vatican Council II more creatively, Arrupe made an appeal to the Jesuits across the world to undertake a general sociological survey of the provinces. The purpose behind the same was to make effective plans in order that the ministries of the Society of Jesus may be made more relevant to the local situations. Accordingly, Goa-Poona vice-Province (erected in 1963) too undertook the project of a sociological survey. This helped the Jesuits to understand the socio-cultural and demographic make-up of the mission field, which in turn helped them not only in the general planning of ministries and apostolates but also in working out the project of inculturation more effectively.[1696]

A comment may be made on the meaning of the phrase, *preferential option for the poor* here. The reason is that it is closely related to the *faith-justice* discourse. This is an immense leap in the understanding of what the Christian faith in its essence means, especially when one seeks to interpret faith more relevantly to the modern world. It means that the poor have been at the heart of Christianity ever since its beginning. Thus, the principle of *preferential option for the poor* is rooted in the Gospels and beatitudes as well as in the prophetic, patristic and mystical traditions within the Church. In sum, we may say that the poor have a special place in God's heart.[1697] This is precisely what Pope Francis wrote in *Evangelii Gaudium*: "God's heart has a special place for the poor, so much so that he himself became poor" (*EG* 196). The principle of *preferential option for the poor* flows from this basic affirmation.

What is the implication of this option? First, it gives "a new way of looking at the poor and their significance for the practice of our faith."[1698] Similarly it leads us to take into consideration the fact that "the poor do not merely happen to be there nor are they such because of their own lack of initiative and effort to improve their lot in life. The poor are not merely poor, but are made poor, exploited by unjust economic structures and often also oppressed by unjust political power."[1699] Hence the *preferential option for the poor* implies a deliberate commitment not only to stand with the poor but also to engage actively in the struggles of all those people who have been unjustly deprived of what rightfully belongs to them. Summarizing the stand of Pope Francis on this point, Jimmy Burns puts it more emphatically: "a radical identification with ordinary people as subjects of their own history, rather than a 'class'

1696 See Matthew Lederle, ed. "Summary Report of the General Sociological Survey of Goa-Poona Vice-province, Phase I [1967]," *ARSI,* Historia. 2001-Poona.

1697 See Dorr, *Option for the Poor and for the Earth*, 41; Thomas R. Rourke, *The Roots of Pope Francis's Social and Political Thought: From Argentina to the Vatican* (Lanham/Boulder/New York/London: Rowman & Litter field, 2016), 171-172.

1698 Amaladoss, *Mission Today*, 91.

1699 Ibid., 92.

engaged in a social and political struggle with other classes."[1700] Thus, the ultimate aim of this faith-commitment is interpreted as the creation of a just social order, leading towards a holistic vision of salvation.

On the *faith-justice* discourse, there is no need to state that the Church has always preached faith and justice in some manner or the other (cf. *EG* 186-201). But the emphasis on the promotion of justice as being an integral dimension of the service of the faith is a definitive step forward from the earlier understandings. This has a direct implication for the understanding of human salvation. The commitment to a faith-justice discourse takes into consideration the fact that salvation implies the totality of human person. In other words, faith remains no more confined to the spiritual or other-worldly domain. Rather it touches upon the very existential situation of human person. Thus the body-soul dichotomy has no space in this discourse. The salvation of the human person begins here and now in this very existence. Thus the faith-justice leads us to a more holistic and integral perspective of salvation history. Stated differently, this discourse implies the salvation of the whole human person and not only of the 'soul' alone. The discourse includes the vision of humanity that Jesus preached in Nazareth (Cf. Lk. 4, 18-19). He preached not only the Kingdom of freedom and justice, but made the same present in his person and work. The Church strives towards the establishment of the Kingdom of God. In some manner and at least partially, it prefigures this Kingdom, which implies justice for and good of all, not only in the temporal sense but rather implying all the aspects of human existence.[1701]

The study of the history of the Poona Mission, thus, reveals that the Jesuits amidst their success and failures have been moving on the path of rediscovering their own identity along with the Church under the guidance of their successive leaders (i.e., the Superior Generals, Provincials and Local Superiors). They have been making continual efforts in seeking to be ever relevant in their self-understanding and the understanding of their mission. What may undoubtedly be affirmed is the fact that the faith-justice paradigm of understanding of their mission along with the positive attitude shown by the Church towards other religions and cultures has opened up more possibilities of dialogue (Cf. *NA* 2). It must be recalled that without dialoguing with openness

1700 Jimmy Burns, *Francis: Pope of Good Promise* (New York: St. Martin's Press, 2015), 132.

1701 Amaladoss, *Mission Today*, 94-95.

and sincerity, the Church in India today faces the danger of losing its relevance. The Poona Mission has been making every effort to accommodate new developments in the Church and the society in its faith vision. Yet the challenge remains so that they are invited to look forward to make their make vision more real.

On a personal note, I feel even more convinced at the end of this study that this Jesuit Mission, in spite of its drawbacks and failures, was instrumental in setting in motion a great process of transformation among the people, it served. The Jesuits did fail sometimes in their endeavours. But the sight of the goal of bringing the Good News to the people was never lost. No human endeavour, of whatever description, can claim a linear progression. Indeed all processes of transformation move along a path passing through peaks and valleys with highs and lows as their constant features. This was what happened in the case of the Jesuits in this Mission too. Their initial failures in recognizing the innate values of other religio-cultural traditions aside, their disposition and intention were beyond reproach. Overall, the Jesuits began to incorporate more consciously every facet of life of the people within their vision of mission. This is the reason that the people, once living virtually bereft of human dignity, were led to a path where they could claim their dignity and rights. Eventually, the small group of converts in the mission became the local Church over a period of half a century. The goal of the mission, thus, was indeed achieved!

As I look back at my own history, I find a great resonance with the empowered Mahar Christian community of the Poona Mission, because as a fourth generation tribal Christian, I have experienced similar socio-religious and socio-economic changes among the Tribal Christians in my own State of Madhya Pradesh, thanks to the intervention and mediation by the Jesuit missionaries there.

Bibliography

Primary Literature: Unpublished

Unpublished primary literatures have been collected from the following archives. The entries given here correspond to the original titles on the files. In order to save space we have mentioned only the numbers of the corresponding files. For example, the entry below, Bombay. *1003-I-III, IX, X, XIII* implies that we have referred the documents under the category *Epistolae* with Serial Number 1003 under *Provincia Bombayensis*.

1. Archivum Romanum Societatis Iesu, Rome (ARSI)

A. Provincia Bombayensis

I. Epistolae

1003 1900-1921 [Missio ad Pr. Aragoniae transfer] Bombay. 1003-1-III, IX, X, XIII

1004 1918-1925 Bombay. 1004-1-

1005 1926-1929 Bombay. 1005-I-IV, VIII-X, XII, XV

1006 1929-1932 Bombay. 1006-1, II, IV – VII

II. Schedae Vicariae

1301 1950-1959 [RLGGM]

1302 1960-1969 prov.

1303 1960-1969 Ex Officio, parti.

III. Negotia Specialia

1401	1913 -1934	De proprietatibus
1402	1921-1928	Depatronatu
1403	1923-1928	De divisione
1404	1927-1930	De collegiis

1405	1927-1937	De collegiis et scholis
1406		Visite a la Mission de Bombay
1409	1933	Relatio
1010	1935	Conspectus Division is
1411	1936-1940	Visitatio Miss. Van Kalken
1416	1940-1946	Visitatio
1418	1961	Visitatio

IV. Documenta Triennalia

Litterae Annuae	1501	1936
Summaria Vitae	1701	1946
Elenchi	1901	1933

V. Varia Historica

2001	1928	Missiones Indiae orientalis
2010	1947	On the Missionary Methods in India

B. Vice-Provincia Belgaum-Poonensis

I. Epistolae

1005 1953-1957

Poona. 1005-1-Poona-XIV

1006 1958-1964

Belgaum-Poona. 1006 - Particulares (1958) Belgaum-Poona. 1006 - Consultores (1959) Belgaum-Poona. 1006 - Praep. Prov. Belgaum-Poona. 1006 - Externi (1959) Belgaum-Poona. 1006 - Ex Officio (1960) Belgaum-Poona. 1006 - Praep. Prov. (1961) Belgaum-Poona. 1006 - Consultores (1961) Belgaum-Poona. 1006 - Particulares (1961) Belgaum-Poona. 1006 - Consultores (1963) Belgaum-Poona. 1006 - Particulares (1963).

C. Provincia Goa-Poonensis

I. Epistolae

1001 1883-1918 Missio Goa + Macao et Zambia

1002 1920-1938

1004 1924-1952 Missio Poonensis

1007 1953-1957

1008 1958-1963 V. Prov. Belgaum-Poona

II. Schedae Vicariae

1301 1905-1959 Missio Poona et Vicepr. Belgaum Poona [RLGGM]

III. Negotia Specialia

1401 1930 Poona Visitatio

1402 1935-1941 Poona-Visit.+Constructio Coll. NN.

1403 1952-1953 Poona + Indian Social Inst.

1404 1954 Goa Divisio Missionis

1407 1956 Erectio Viceprov. Ind. Belgaum-Poona

1407 1963 Visitatio Patris Kester

IV. Documenta Triennalia

Litterae Annuae	1501	1946
Summaria Vitae	1701	1956
Elenchi	1901	1954

V. Varia Historica

2001 1945-1947

2. Archivio Storico Delia Congregazione De Propaganda Fide, Rome (ASCPF)

i. Nova Series, Vol. 546
ii. Nova Series, Vol. 992
iii. Nova Series, Vol. 1123
iv. Nova Series, Vol. 1251

3. Archiv Der Deutschen Provinz SJ, Miinchen (ADPSJ)

i. Abt. 45B-221 (1918)/Nr.1380 - Abt. 45B - 221 (1947)/Nr. 1408
ii. Abt. 47, Nr. 1392
iii. Abt. 45B-26, Nr. 1509
iv. Abt. 45B-51, Nr. 108

4. Archiv Und Bibliothek Der Schweizer Provinz Der Gesellschaft Jesu, Zurich (ABSPGJ)

i. Pa 0212: Oesch Alfons
ii. Pa 0286: Stockmann, Alois
iii. Pa 0112: Hegglin, Aloys

iv. Pa 0116: Herbert, Anton
v. Pa 0073: Blatter, Edelbert
vi. Pa 0025: Brandle, Josef
vii. Pa 0149: Kaufmann, Emil
viii. Pa 0049: Engel, Josef
ix. Pa 0374: Felix, Jakob
x. Pa 0275: Schubiger, Franz
xi. Pa 0086: Gaechter, Paul,
xii. Pa 0088: Gallati, Franz-Xaver
xiii. Pa 138: Gyr, Alois
xiv. Pa 0107: Haldner, Johann
xv. Pa 0247: Pfiffner, Josef
xvi. Pa 0382: Winiger, Johann Baptist
xvii. Pa 0255: Riklin, Maximilian
xviii. Pa 0182: Meyer, Ivo
xix. Pa 0104: Haefeli, Paul
xx. Pa 0272: Schoch, Rudolf
xxi. Pa 0329: Weber, Albert
xxii. Pa 0345: Zimmermann, Robert
xxiii. SJ NIE. 01.00 Sep 6
xxiv. SJ NIE. 01.00 Sep 2
xxv. SJNIE. 01.P Sep 19

5. Archiv Der Missionsprokur Der Schweizer Jesuiten, Zurich (AMPSJ)

i. 1. 13b: Prokur Briefe Erbisch. Roder
ii. 15a=Rom
iii. 16-Superior Puna, neue: Baader, Weber, Staffher
iv. 21-Schweizer Patres
v. 28-Schwestern Brig
vi. 70-Indische Bilder, Manus
vii. Alte Artikel
viii. Alte Briefe von Missionaren
ix. Belege 1930-1940
x. Belege 1941-1949

xi. Belege 1958-1963
xii. Belege 1960-1963
xiii. Belege 1964
xiv. 5 3-Briefe aus Indischen Miss.
xv. Briefe fur Liebesgaben
xvi. Briefe Pater Neuner
xvii. 43-Dnyanamata etc. Briefe
xviii. Gewerbeschule
xix. Heimat und Mission
xx. I.B. Puna Briefe (Alte)
xxi. I.B. Rahata Briefe
xxii. I.B. Sangamner Briefe
xxiii. I.B. Songaon Briefe
xxiv. I.B. Valan Briefe
xxv Indien
xxvi. Letters and Reports
xxvii. Missionare-Korrespondenz
xxviii. Missions-Predigten
xxix. Missionsvereine
xxx. 19-Papstl. Werke Schweiz
xxxi. Fotographische Belege
xxxii. Projekte der Poona Mission
xxxiii. Puna - Dnyanamata
xxxiv. Puna - Harigaon/Shevgaon
xxxv. Puna Patres in Europa
xxxvi. 41-Puna - Stadt Briefe
xxxvii. Reisebriefe, etc.
xxxviii. 48-Sangamner Briefe
xxxix. Schweiz. Missionsjahr
xl. Unio Cleri
xli. Wohltater

6. Pune Jesuit Province Archive, Pune (PJPA)

i. Diary of the Kendal Mission
ii. Walan [Valan] Diary I-XII] - Relevant Parts

iii. Pune Varia [This contains various categories of articles, generally pertaining to the history of mission stations and other related topics].

7. Heras Institute of Indian History and Culture, Bombay (HIIHC)

The materials acquired from this archive are mostly secondary in nature as they are printed materials which have appeared mainly in two publications:

i. St. Xavier's College Magazine 1908-1958

ii. *The Examiner* 1903-1919

8. Xavier Centre of Historical Research, Goa (XCHR)

The materials acquired from this archive too are mostly secondary published sources. Some of the important documents are:

i. 1st National Seminar: Jesuits in India. Sources and Problems, 1-2 December 1995

ii. Golden Jubilee of the Goa Mission - 1941 [Souvenir]

iii. J. Castets, "False Statistics of the Old Jesuit Mission Again," [Printed material]

Other Primary Sources

Castelino, Herman. "The Contribution of Jesuit Schools of the Bombay Province in the last Hundred Years [2004]." (For Private Circulation only).

Deceased Members of the Western Region of the South Asian Assis fancy of the Society of Jesus. Pune: Sanjeevan Niwas, 2008.

Die katholischen Missionen: Illustrierte Monatsschrift (1913-1960) [KM] *Zeitschriftfur Missionswissenschaft (1913-1960)* [ZM]

Directory of Jesuit Schools, Colleges and Technical Institutes 1986-1987. New Delhi: Jesuit Educational Association of India/Indian Social Institute, 1987.

Heras. Henry "On the Mission Methods in India: A Report Submitted to the Most Rev. John B. Janssens, S.J., General of the Society of Jesus - 1947." In *ARSI, Bombay. 2010-Varia Historica.* (Unpublished).

Hull, E. R. "Some Moot-Points in the Indian Missions: With special relation to Bombay." *TE* (May 1926) (offprint for private circulation only).

Hull, E. R. "The Mixed Colleges and School Question, 1927." In ARSI, *Prov. Bombay-Poona 1404-De Collegiis in India, 1927-1930.* (Offprint for private circulation only).

Indische Bilder: Nachrichten aus der oberdeutschen Jesuitenmission in Puna (1930-1963) [IB].

Kaesen, P. W. *Die Puna-Mission in Vorderindien.* (Booklet for Private Circulation only).

Misquitta, John. *The Identity of the Catholic Colleges in India.* Bombay: St. Xavier's College, 1989. [A Booklet for Private Circulation only].

Missions Entrusted to the Society of Jesus among the Heathen: Statistics and Information. Rome: Grafia, 1925.

Mitteilungen aus den deutschen Provinzen der Gesellschaft Jesu: Vol. 5-19 [MDPSJ].

Padberg, John W. "The Society True To Itself: A Brief History of the 32nd General Congregation of the Society of Jesus (December 2, 1974—March 7, 1975)." *SSJ* 15/3-4 (1983): 1-90.

Padberg, John W. "Historical Preface to the Decrees of the 32nd General Congregation." In *Documents of the 31st and 32nd General Congregations of the Society of Jesus,* edited by John W. Padberg. Saint Louis: The Institute of Jesuit Sources, 1977.

Sixt, Hubert. "The Ahmednagar District Mission: 1878-1983." In *PJPA, Varia.* [Unpublished].

Secondary Sources: Encyclopedia, Lexicons and Dictionaries

Anderson, Gerald H., ed.. *Biographical Dictionary of Christian Missions.* Grand Rapids/London: William B. Eerdmans, 1998.

Ankerberg, John & John Weldon. *Encyclopedia of New Age Beliefs.* Oregon: Harvest House Publishers, 1996.

Arens, Bernhard. *Handbuch der Katholischen Missionen.* Freiburg, i.B.: Herder & Co., 1925.

Brechter, Heinrich Suso et al., eds., "Das Zweite vatikanische Konzil-Konstitutionen, Dekrete und Erklarungen Lexikon: Kommentare, Teil 1-3." In *Lexikon fur Theologie und Kirche* Freiburg/Basel/ Vienna: Herder, 1966/1967/1968.

Chatterjee, Deen K., ed., *Encyclopedia of Global Justice: A-I, Volume I.*
Heidelberg/London/New York: Springer Science & Business Media, 2011.

D'Lima, Errol et al. ed. *A Concise Encyclopaedia of Christianity in India.* Pune: Jnana-Deepa Vidyapeeth/Mumbai: St. Pauls, 2014.

Flinn, Frank K. *Encyclopedia of Catholicism.* New York: Facts on File, 2007.

Johnston, William M. *Encyclopedia of Monasticism: Vol. I, A-L.* Chicago & London: Fitzroy Dearborn Publishers, 2000.

Jones, Tom Devonshire, ed. *The Oxford Dictionary of Christian Art and Architecture,* 2nd ed. Oxford: Oxford University Press, 2013.

Hunermann, Peter & Bernd J. Hilberath, eds., *Herders Theologischer Kommentar zum Zweiten Vatikanischen Konzil,* Vol. 4-5. Freiburg/ Basel/Vienna: Herder, 2004.

Koch, Ludwig. *Jesuiten Lexikon.* Paderborn: Bonifacius-Druckrei, 1934.

Mohanty, P. K. *Encyclopedia of Primitive Tribes in India,* Vol. 1. Delhi: Kalpaz Publications, 2004.

Neill, Stephen, et al. eds. *Lexikon zur Weltmission.* Wuppertal: Theologischer Verlag R. Brockhaus/Erlangen: Verlag der Evang.-Luth. Mission, 1975.

O'Neill, Charles E. & Joaquin M., Dominguez (eds.), *Diccionario Historico de La Compania de Jesus: Biogrdfico-Temdtico,* Vol. I-IV. Roma: Institutum Historicum S.I./Madrid: Universidad Pontificia Comillas, 2001.

Polgar, Laszlo. *Bibliographie sur Lhistoire de la Compagnie de Jesus 1901-1980, Vols. I-II.* Rome : Institutum Historicum S.I., 1986.

Rzepkowski, Horst. *Lexikon der Mission.* Graz/Vienna/Koln: Styria, 1992.

Wilhelm, Kosch, et al. eds. *Deutsches Literaturlexikon. Das 20. Jahrhundert: Band 6: Deeg-Durrenfeld.* Zurich/Miinchen: K. G. Saur, 2004.

Secondary Sources: Books

Abdi, Ali A. et al. *Citizenship Education and Social Development in Zambia.* Charlotte, North Carolina: Information Age Publishing, 2010.

Abe, Takao. *The Jesuit Mission to New France: A New Interpretation in the Light of the Earliest Jesuit Experience in Japan.* Leiden: Koninklijke Brill, 2011.

Abraham, D. Samuel. *Laws on Hospital Administration.* Chennai: B. I. Publications, 2008.

Agrawal, C. M. *Great Natural Calamities.* Delhi: Indian Publisher Distributors, 2000.

Aguiar, Benny. *Making of Mumbai: A History of Metropolis and its Catholic Past.* Mumbai: St. Paul's Publication, 2012.

Albuquerque, Teresa. *To Love is to Serve: Catholics of Bombay.* Bombay: Heras Institute of Indian History and Culture, 1986.

Aleksander, Maryks Robert and Wright Jonathan, eds. *Jesuit Survival and Restoration: A Global History, 1773-1900.* Leiden: Koninklijke Brill, 2015.

Allen, David Oliver. *India, Ancient and Modern: Geographical, Historical, Political, Social, and Religious; with the Particular Account of the State and Prospects of Christianity.* Cleveland, Ohio: John P. Jewett and Co., 1856.

Amaladass, Anand, ed. *Jesuit Presence in Indian History.* Anand: Gujarat Sahitya Prakash, 1988.

Amaladoss, Michael. *Mission Today: Reflection from an Ignatian Perspective.* Anand: Gujarat Sahitya Prakash/Rome: Centrum Ignatianum, 1989.

Anand, Divyesh. *Hindu Nationalism in India and the Politics of Fear.* Hampshire: Palgrave Macmillan, 2011.

Andrews, Edward E. *Native Apostles: Black and Indian Missionaries in the British Atlantic World.* Cambridge, Massachusetts/London: Harvard University Press, 2013.

Arbuckle, Gerald A. *From Chaos to Mission.* London: Geoffrey Chapman, 1996.

Arokiyasamy, Soosai. *Dharma, Hindu and Christian According to Roberto de Nobili: Analysis of its Meaning and its Use in Hinduism and Christianity, Documenta Missionalia, 19.* Rome: Gregorian University Press, 1986.

Asua, Miguel de. *Science in the Vanished Arcadia: Knowledge of Nature in the Jesuit Missions of Paraguay and Rio de la Plata.* Leiden: Koninklijke Brill, 2014.

Bailey, Gavin A. *The Jesuits and the Grand Mogul: Renaissance Art at the Imperial Court of India, 1580-1630.* Washington, D.C.: Smithsonian Institution, 1982.

Bapu, Prabhu. *Hindu Mahasabha in Colonial North India, 1915-1930: Constructing Nation and History.* Abingdon/New York: Routledge, 2013.

Barton, Paul. *Hispanic Methodists, Presbyterians, and Baptists in Texas.* Austin: University of Texas Press, 2006.

Barua, Ankur. Debating 'Conversion' in Hinduism and Christianity. London and New York: Routledge, 2015.

Bauman, Chad M. *Christian Identity and Dalit Religion in Hindu India, 1868-1947.* Grand Rapids, Ml/Cambridge, U.K.: William B. Eerdmans, 2008.

Beal, John P. et al., eds. *New Commentary on the Code of Canon Law, Study Edition.* New York, N.Y./Mahwah, N.J.: Paulist Press, 2000.

Benestad, J. Brian. *Church, State, and Society: An Introduction to Catholic Social Doctrine.* Washington: The Catholic University of America Press, 2011.

Bergman, Roger C. *Catholic Social Learning: Educating the Faith that does Justice.* New York: Fordham University Press, 2011.

Bevans, Stephen, ed. *A Century of Catholic Missions.* Eugene. Oregon: Wipf & Stock, 2013.

Bishop, George. *Pedro Arrupe, SJ: Twenty-eighth General of the Society of Jesus.* England: Gracewing, 2000.

Borges, Charles J. *Economics of the Goa Jesuits.* New Delhi: Concept Publishing Company, 1994.

________ et al., eds. *Goa and Portugal: History and Development.* New Delhi: Concept Publishing Company, 2000.

Bosch, David. *Transforming Mission: Paradigm Shifts in Theology of Mission.* Maryknoll, NY: Orbis Books, 2011.

Biihlmann, Walbert. *Pionier der Einheit: Bischof Anastasius Hartmann.* Zurich: Thomas Verlag/Munich/Paderborn/Vienna: Ferdinand Schoningh, 1966.

Burke, Thomas J. M., ed. *Catholic Missions: Four Great Encyclicals.* New York: Fordham University Press, 1957.

Burns, Jimmy. *Francis: Pope of Good Promise.* New York: St. Martin's Press, 2015.

Campbell, Thomas J. *The Jesuits, 1534-1901: A History of the Society of Jesus from its Foundation to the Present Time.* New York: The Encyclopedia Press, 1921.

Camps, Arnulf. *Studies in Asian Mission History: 1956-1998.* Leiden/ Boston/Koln: Brill, 2000.

Cardoza-Orlandi, Carlos F. *Mission: An Essential Guide.* Nashville: Abingdon Press, 2002.

Chalam, K. S. *Caste-Based Reservations and Human Development in India.* LA/London/New Delhi/ Singapore: Sage Publications, 2007.

Chandra, S. S. and Rajendra K. Sharma. *Philosophy of Education.* New Delhi: Atlantic Publishers and Distributors, 2006.

Charles, Rodger. *The Catholic Tradition from Genesis to Centesimus Annus, Vol. 2: Modern Christian Social Witness and Teaching/The Modern Social Teaching/Contexts.* Herefordshire: Gracewing, 1998.

Cleary, Edward L. *How Latin America Saved the Soul of the Catholic Church.* New York/Mahwah, NJ: Paulist Press, 2009.

Coelho, William, et al. *The Niyogi Committee Report: A Critical Appraisal.* Varanasi: Satya Manthan Sanstha, 2000.

Cohen, Leonardo. *The Missionary Strategies of the Jesuits in Ethiopia (1555-1632).* Wiesbaden: Harrassowitz, 2009.

Collins, Paul M. *Context, Culture and Worship: The Quest for "Indian-ness."* Delhi: ISPCK, 2006.

Correia-Afonso, John. *The Jesuits in India: 1542-1773.* Anand: Gujarat Sahitya Prakash, 1997.

Coward, Harold, ed. *Indian Critiques of Gandhi.* Albany, NY: State University of New York Press, 2003.

Dayton, Edward R. and David Allen Fraser. *Planning Strategies for World Evangelization.* Michigan: Grand Rapids, 1980.

de Melo, Carlos Merces. *The Papal Seminary of Kandy-Pune.* Pune: Papal Seminary, 1993.

de Mendonca, Delio, ed. *Jesuits in India: History and Culture.* Anand: Gujarat Sahitya Prakash/Alto Povorim, Goa: Xavier Centre of Historical Research, 2007.

________ ed. *Jesuits in India: Vision and Challenges.* Anand: Gujarat Sahitya Prakash/Alto Povorim, Goa: Xavier Centre of Historical Research, 2003.

de Sa, Fidelis. *Crisis in Chota Nagpur.* Bangalore: Redemptorist Publications, 1999.

de Souza, Teotonio R. *Discoveries, Missionary Expansion and Asian Cultures.* Goa: Xavier Centre of Historical Research, 1994.

Devare, Aparna. *History and the Making of Modern Hindu Self.* New Delhi: Routledge, 2011.

Doring, Henry. *Bilder aus deutschen Jesuitenmission Puna.* Aachen: Xaverius-Verlag, 1918.

Dorr, Donal. *Option for the Poor & for the Earth: From Leo XIII to Pope Francis.* Maryknoll, New York: Orbis Books, 2012.

Dulles, Avery. *Evangelization for the Third Millennium.* New Jersey: Paulist Press, 2009.

Duminuco, Vincent J., ed. *The Jesuit Ratio Studiorum: 400th Anniversary Perspectives.* New York: Fordham University Press, 2000.

Dunne, George H. *Generation of Giants: The Story of the Jesuits in China in the last Decades of the Ming Dynasty.* Notre Dame, Indiana: University of Notre Dame Press, 1962.

Dwyer, John C. *Church History: Twenty Centuries of Catholic Christianity.* New York/Mahwah: Paulist Press, 1985.

Dyrness, William A. *Christian Art in Asia.* Amsterdam: Editions Rodopi, 1979.

Enochs, Rose. *The Jesuit Mission to the Lakota Sioux: A Study of Pastoral Ministry, 1886-1945.* Cansas City: Sheed & Ward, 1996.

Evers, Georg. *Kirche und Katholizismus seit 1945, Band 5: Die Lander Asiens.* Paderborn/Munich/Vienna/Zurich: Ferdinand Schoningh, 2003.

Felix Wilfred, ed. *The Oxford Handbook of Christianity in Asia.* New York: Oxford University Press, 2014.

Fernando, Leonard and George Gispert-Sauch, *Christianity in India: Two Thousand Years of Faith* (New Delhi: Viking, 2004).

Fife, Erik. S. & Arthur F. Glasser. *Missions in Crisis.* London: InterVarsity Fellowship, 1961.

Flannery, Austin. *Vatican Council II: Constitutions, Decrees, Declarations*. Northport, NY: Costello Publishing Company/Dublin: Dominican Publications, 2007.

Franco, Fernando, Jyotsna Macwan, and Saguna Ramanathan. *Journeys to Freedom: Dalit Narratives*. Kolkata: Samya, 2004.

Frykenberg, Robert E. *Christianity in India: From Beginnings to the Present*. Oxford: Oxford University Press, 2008.

________ ed. *Christians and Missionaries in India: Cross-Cultural Communications since 1500*. Grand Rapids/Cambridge: William B. Eerdmans, 2003.

Gense, James H. *A History of St. Mary's: A Hundred Years of Survey*. Bombay: St. Xavier's College, 1962.

________ *The Church at the Gateway of India*. Bombay: St. Xavier's College, 1960.

Goyal, Sita Ram. *History of Hindu-Christian Encounters (AD 304 to 1996)*. 2nd revised edition New Delhi: Voice of India, 1996.

________ *Vindicated by Time: The Niyogi Committee Report on Christian Missionary Activities*. New Delhi: Voice of India, 1956, this edition 1998.

Green, Vivian H. H. *A New History of Christianity*. New York: Continuum, 2000.

Gundimeda, Sambaiah. *Dalit Politics in Contemporary India*. Abingdon/ New York: Routledge, 2016.

Harding, Christopher. *Religious Transformation in South Asia: The Meaning of Conversion in Colonial Punjab*. Oxford: Oxford University Press, 2008.

Haughey, John C, ed. *The Faith That Does Justice: Examining the Christian Sources for Social Change*. Eugene, Oregon: Wipf & Stock, 1977.

Hayes, Michael A., ed. *Mission and Evangelization*. London: Burns & Oates, 2004.

Haynes, Douglas E. *Small Town Capitalism in Western India: Artisans, Merchants and the Making of the Informal Economy, 1870-1960*. Delhi. New York: Cambridge University Press, 2012.

Hennelly, Alfred T. *Theology for a Liberating Church: The New Praxis of Freedom*. Washington: Georgetown University Press, 1989.

Hull, Ernest R. *Bombay Mission History: With a Special Study of the Padroado Question.* Bombay: Examiner Press, 1927.

Some Moot-Points in the Indian Mission. With a Special Relation to Bombay. Bombay: Examiner Press, 1926. (For Private Circulation only).

________ *The German Jesuit Fathers of Bombay: By an Englishman who knows Them.* Bombay: Examiner Press, 1915.

Ingham, Kenneth. *Reformers in India, 1793-1833: An Account of the Work of Christian Missionaries.* New York: The Syndics of the Cambridge University Press, n.d.

Jadhav, Jeevendra. *Evangelization as Community Building.* Ahmednagar: Social Centre, 2006.

Jadhav, Narendra. *Untouchables: My Family's Triumphant Escape from India's Caste System.* California: University of California Press, 1953.

Jaffrelot, Christophe. *Religion, Caste and Politics in India.* Delhi: Primus Books, 2010.

Jayakumar, Samuel. *Dalit Consciousness and Christian Conversion: Historical Resources for a Contemporary Debate.* Oxford: Regnum International/Delhi: ISPCK, 1999.

Jongeneel, Jan A. B. *Jesus Christ in the World History.* Frankfurt A. M: Peter Lang, 2009.

Josson, Henry. *History of the Bengal Mission: 1859 to 1920.* Translated by Albert Huart and Lucien Clarysse. Anand: Gujarat Sahitya Prakash, 2009.

Kadam, K. N. *The Meaning of the Ambedkarite Conversion to Buddhism and Other Essays.* Mumbai: Popular Prakashan, 1997.

Kalapura, Jose, ed. *Christian Missions in Bihar and Jharkhand till 1947 (Ranchi: Gossner Theological College & Delhi: Christian World Imprints, 2014).*

Kamath, Devadatta. *The Burning Bush: The History of Karnataka Jesuits Province,* Vols. I-II. Bangalore: Loyola Mandir, 2006.

Kane, Herbert. *Christian Mission in Biblical Perspective.* Grand Rapids, MI: Baker Book House, 1976.

Kanjamala, Augustine. *The Future of Christian Missions in India: Toward a New Paradigm for the Third Millennium.* Bombay: St. Paul's Publication, 2014.

Karanja, James. *The Missionary Movement in Colonial Kenya: The Foundation of Africa Inland Church.* Gottingen: Cuvilier, 2009.

Keer, Dhananjay. *Dr. Ambedkar: Life and Mission.* Mumbai: Popular Prakashan, 1999.

Khan, Mumtaz Ali. *Identity Formation and Self-identity among Harijan Elite.* Bangalore: Christian Institute for the Study of Religion and Society, 1994.

Klaiber, Jeffrey L. *The Jesuits in Latin America: 450 Years of Inculturation, Defense of Human Rights and Prophetic Witness.* St. Loius: The Institute of Jesuit Sources, 2009.

Kumar, Ravinder. *Western India in the Nineteenth Century: A Study in the Social History of Maharashtra.* Abingdon: Routledge, 1968.

Kiing, Hans. *My Struggle for Freedom: Memoir.* Translated by John Bowden. London/New York: Continuum, 2003.

Kuruvila, K. P. *The Word Became Flesh: A Christological Paradigm for Doing Theology in India.* Delhi: ISPCK, 2002.

Kuttiyanikkal, Cyril J. *Khrist Bhakta Movement: A Model for an Indian Church?* Berlin/Zurich: LIT, 2014.

Lai, A. K. *Secularism: Concept and Practice.* New Delhi: Concept Publishing House, 1998.

Lederle, Julia. *Mission und Okonomie der Jesuiten in Indien: Intermedials Handeln am Beispiel der Malabar-Provinz 18. Jahrhundert.* Wiesbaden: Harrassowitz Verlag, 2009.

Lederle, Matthew R. *Christian Painting in India through the Centuries.* Bombay: Heras Institute of History and Culture/Anand: Gujarat Sahitya Prakash, 1987.

Lewis, Hedwig. *The Catholic Church in Gujarat: A Historical Survey 1934-1973.* Anand: Gujarat Sahitya Prakash, 2006.

Lewis, Jonathan, ed. *World Mission: An Analysis of the World Christian Movement.* Pasadena: William Carrey Library, 1987.

Lokhande, Ajit. *Mission, Missionaries and Me.* Pune: Pune Jesuit Society, 2014.

Lowenstein, Felix. *Christliche Bilder in Altindischer Malerei.* Munster: Aschendorff, 1958.

Malpan, Varghese. *A Comparative Study of the Bhagavad-Gita and the Spiritual Exercises of St. Ignatius of Loyola on the Process of Spiritual Liberation.* Rome: Editrice Pontificia Universita Gregoriana, 1992.

Mannion, Gerard. *The Vision of John Paul II: Assessing His Thought and Influence.* Collegeville, Minnesota: Liturgical Press, 1979.

Mayhew, Arthur. *Christianity and the Government of India.* London: Faber & Gwyer, n. d.

McCoog, Thomas M., ed. *Promising Hope: Essays on the Suppression and Restoration of the English Province of the Society of Jesus.* Rome: Institutum Historicum Societatis Iesu, 2003.

McDermott, Gerald R. and Harold A. Netland. *A Trinitarian Theology of Religions: An Evangelical Proposal.* New York: Oxford University Press, 2014.

McGavran, Donald A. *Church Growth Bulletin, Second Consolidated Volume.* South Pasadena: William Carey Library, 1977.

Metcalf, Barbara D. and Thomas R. Metcalf. *A Concise History of Modern India,* Third Edition. Cambridge: Cambridge University Press, 2012.

Minj, Francis & Alexius Ekka, *Jesuit Mission Among the Adivasis of Chotanagpur (Ranchi: Xavier Publications, 2014).*

Misner, Paul. *Catholic Labour Movements in Europe: Social Thought and Action, 1914-1965.* Washington, DC: The Catholic University Press of America Press, 2015.

Moon, Vasant. *Dr. Babasaheb Ambedkar, Writings and Speeches,* Vol. 1. Bombay: Educational Department, Government of Maharashtra, 1979.

Mossa, Mark, annot. *St. Ignatius of Loyola: The Spiritual Writings.* Woodstock, Vermont: Skylight Paths, 2012.

Mukherjee, S. & J. Chakrabarti. *Evolution of Indian Economy & Elementary Statistics.* Calcutta: Allied Publishers, 2000.

Murphy, Edward P., ed. *A History of the Jesuits in Zambia: A Mission becomes a Province.* Nairobi: Pauline Publications Africa, 2003.

Musser, Donald W. & Joseph L. Price, eds. *New and Enlarged Handbook of Christian Theology.* Nashville: Abingdon Press, 2003.

Naik, Gregory, ed. *Jesuit Education in India.* Anand: Gujarat Sahitya Prakash, 1987.

Nam, Hoo-Soo Jose. *Missions Strategies of Korean Presbyterian Missionaries in Central and Southern Philippines: In Light of Paul's Missions Strategies.* Scotland: Hermit Kingdom, 2006.

Neill, Stephen. *A History of Christian Missions.* Middlesex/New York/Victoria/Auckland: Penguin Books, 1964.

________ Neill, Stephen. *A History of Christianity in India: 1707-1858.* Cambridge: Cambridge University Press, 1985.

Neuner, Joseph. *Memories of My Life.* Pune: Pune Jesuit Society, 2003.

O'Donnell, Stephen. *The Jesuit Missions of Paraguay.* Dublin: James Duffy, 1855.

O'Malley, John W. et al., eds. *The Jesuits: Cultures, Sciences and the Arts 1540-1773.* Toronto/Buffalo/London: University of Toronto Press, 1999.

________ *The First Jesuits.* Cambridge, MA: Harvard University Press, 1993.

Okwu, Augustine S. O. *Igbo Culture and the Christian Missions 1857-1957: Conversion in Theory and Practice.* Maryland: University Press of America, 2010.

Oldenski, Thomas. *Liberation Theology and Critical Pedagogy in Today's Catholic Schools: Social Justice in Action.* New York/Abingdon, Oxon: Routledge, 1997.

Oldmeadow, Harry. *A Christian Pilgrim in India: The Spiritual Journey of Swami Abhishiktananda (Henri LeSaux).* Bloomington, Indiana: World Wisdom, 2008.

Oldmeadow, Harry. *Journeys East: 20th Century Western Encounters with Eastern Religious Traditions.* Indiana: World Wisdom, 2004.

Omenka, Nicholas I. *The School in the Service of Evangelization: The Catholic Educational Impact in Eastern Nigeria 1886-1950.* Leiden/New York/Koln: E.J. Brill, 1889.

Oommen, T. K. *Nation, Civil Society and Social Movements: Essays in Political Sociology.* New Delhi: Sage Publications, 2004.

Ott, Craig, Stephen J. Straus, and Timothy C. Tennent, et al. *Encountering Theology of Mission: Biblical Foundations, Historical Developments and Contemporary Issues.* Grand Rapids, MI: Baker Publications, 2010.

Otto, Joseph A. *Griindung der Neuen Jesuitenmission: Durch General Pater Johann Philipp Roothaan.* Freiburg i. B: Herder & Co. G.M.B.H., 1939.

Parkhe, Camil. *Contribution of Christian Missionaries in India.* Anand: Gujarat Sahitya Prakash, 2007.

Pattathu, Paul. *Ashram Spirituality: A Search into the Christian Ashram Movement against its Hindu Background.* Indore: Satprakashan Sanchar Kendra, 1997.

Patton, John. *Pastoral Care: An Essential Guide.* Nashville: Abingdon Press, 2005.

Perumalil, H. C. & E. R. Hambye, eds. *Christianity in India: A History in Ecumenical Perspective.* Alleppey: Prakasam Publications, 1972.

Pickett, J. Waskom. *Christian Mass Movements in India: A Study with Recommendations.* Lucknow: Lucknow Publishing House, 1933.

Plattner, Felix A. *Catholic India: Yesterday and Today.* Allahabad: St. Paul Publication, 1964.

Pollard, John. *The Papacy in the Age of Totalitarianism 1914-1958.* Oxford: Oxford University Press, 2014.

Pothacaraury, Thomas. *The Church in Independent India.* Bombay: The Examiner Press, 1961.

Rao, V. K. *Contemporary Education.* Delhi: A.P.H. Publication, 2007.

Rico, Herminio. *John Paul II and the Legacy of Dignitatis Humanae.* Washington: Georgetown University Press, 2002.

Riddick, John F. *The History of British India: A Chronology.* Westport: Praeger Publishers, 2006.

Robinson, Bob. *Christians Meeting Hindus: An Analysis and Theological Critique of the Hindu-Christian Encounter in India.* Milton Keynes, UK/Waynesboro, GA: Regnum Books International, 2004.

Robinson, Rowena and J. Marianus Kujur, eds. *Margins of Faith: Dalit and Tribal Christianity in India.* New Delhi: Sage Publications, 2010.

Rogers, Alan. *Non-Formal Education: Flexible Schooling or Participatory Education?* New York: Springer Science and Business Media, 2005.

Rourke, Thomas R. *The Roots of Pope Francis's Social and Political Thought: From Argentina to the Vatican.* Lanham/Boulder/New York/London: Rowman & Litterfield, 2016.

Saldanha, Julian. *Conversion and Indian Civil Law.* Bangalore: TP I, 1981.

________ *Patterns of Evangelization in Mission History.* Bombay: St. Paul Publications, 1988.

Schatz, Klaus. *Geschichte der deutschen Jesuiten, Vol. I-V, 1814-1983.* Munster: Aschendorf, 2013.

Schelkens, Karim, John A. Dick & Jiirgen Mettepenningen. *Aggiornamento? Catholicism from Gregory XVI to Benedict XVI.* Leiden/Boston: Brill, 2013.

Schmidlin, Josef. *Katholische Missionslehre im Grundriss.* Mtinster: Aschendorffschen Verlagsbuchhandlung, 1919.

Schouten, Jan Peter. *Jesus as Guru: The Image of Christ among Hindus and Christians in India.* Publications of the Studies on the Contact between Christianity and other Religions, Beliefs and Cultures, eds. Jerald D. Gort, et al., no. 36. Amsterdam/New York: Editions Rodopi B.V., 2008.

Schrijver, Georges De, ed. *Liberation Theologies on Shifting Grounds.* Leuven: Uitgeverij Peeters, 1998.

Schwickerath, Robert. *Jesuit Education, Its History and Principles Viewed in the Light of Modern Educational Problems,* 2nd ed. St. Louis, MO: B. Herder, 1904.

Seasoltz, R. Kevin. *A Virtuous Church: Catholic Theology, Ethics, and Liturgy for the 21st Century.* Maryknoll, NY: Orbis Books, 2012.

Sebastian, S. Joseph. *The Jesuit Carnatic Mission: A Foundation of Andhra Church.* Secunderabad: Jesuit Province Society Hyderabad, 2004.

Shahare, M. L. *Dr. Bhimrao Ambedkar: His Life and Work.* New Delhi: NCERT, 1987.

Sharma, Chandrika P. *Mahamana Pandit Madan Mohan Malviya.* Delhi: Parmeshwari Prakashan, 2007.

Sharma, Ram Nath and Rajendra Sharma. *Problems of Education in India.* New Delhi: Atlantic Publishers & Distributors, 2004.

Sievernich, Michael. *Die Christliche Mission: Geschichte und Gegenwart.* Darmstadt: WBG, 2009.

Singh, K. S., ed. *People of India: Maharashtra, Part 2, Vol. XXX.* Mumbai: Popular Prakashan Pvt. Ltd., 2004.

Sobrino, Jon. *The True Church and the Poor.* Eugene, Oregon: Wipf & Stock, 1985.

Stanley, Brian. *The World Missionary Conference, Edinburgh 1910.* Grand Rapids, MI: Wm. B. Eerdmans, 2009.

Steenhault, Yves de. *History of the Jesuits in West Bengal: Part I, 1921-1947.* Ranchi: Catholic Press, n. d.

________ *History of the Jesuits in West Bengal Part II:* 1948-1985 (Ranchi: Catholic Press, n. d).

Stephen, M. *A Christian Theology in the Indian Context.* Delhi: ISPCK, 2001.

Streit, Robert and Johannes Dindinger, eds. *Bibliotheca Missionum: Missionsliteratur Indiens u. Indonesiens, 1800-1909.* Aachen: Internationalen Institut fur Missionswissenschaftliche Forschung, 1951.

Sundaram, V. Lawrence. *A Great Indian Jesuit, Fr. Jerome D 'Souza.* Anand: Gujarat Sahitya Prakash, 1986.

Suria, Carlos. *History of the Catholic Church in Gujarat.* Anand: Gujarat Sahitya Prakash, 1990.

Tennent, Timothy C. *Building Christianity on Indian Foundations: The Legacy of Brahmabandhav Upadhaya.* Delhi: ISPCK, 2005.

________ *World Missions: A Trinitarian Missiology for the Twenty-First Century.* Grand Rapids, MI: Kregel, 2010.

Tete, Peter. *A Short History of the Expansion of the Catholic Missions in North India.* Ranchi: St. Albert's College, 1997.

Thekkedath, Joseph. *A Short History of Christianity in India.* Bangalore: Kristu Jyoti Publications, 2007.

Thoburn, James M. *The Christian Conquest of India.* Philadelphia: The Westminster Press, 1906.

Tirkey, Agapit, et. al, *History of the Madhya Pradesh Jesuit Province,* 1905-2014 (Ranchi: Catholic Press, 2014).

Trapnell, Judson B. *Bede Griffiths: A Life in Dialogue.* Albany: State University of New York Press, 2001.

Ucko, Hans. *The People and the People of God: Minjung and Dalit Theology in Interaction.* Minister: LIT, 2002.

Unterburger, Klaus. *Vom Lehramt der Theologen zum Lehramt der Papste?: Pius XI, die Apostolische Konstitution "Deus Scientiarum Dominus," und die Reform der Universitdtstheologie.* Freiburg/ Basel/Vienna: Herder, 2010.

Vannini, Fulgentius, OFM Cap, *Bishop Hartmann* (Allahabad: St. Paul Publications, 1966).

Vath, Alfons. *Die deutschen Jesuiten in Indien: Geschichte der Mission von Bombay:-Puna (1854-1920).* Regensburg: Jos. Kosel & Friedrich Pustet, 1920.

________ *Im Kampfe mit der Zauberwelt des Hinduismus: Upadhyaya Barahmabandhav und das Problem der Uberwindung des hdheren Hinduismus durch das Christentum.* Berlin & Bonn: Ferd. Dummlers Verlag, 1928.

Velinkar, Joseph. *German Jesuits on the West Coast of India: 1854-2004.* Pune: Sanjeevan Niwas, 2004.

Vinyard, JoEllen M. N. *For Faith and Fortune: The Education of Catholic Immigrants in Detroit, 1805-1925.* Illinois: Board of Trustees of the University of Illinois, 1998.

Ward, Haruko Nawata. *Women Religious Leaders in Japan's Christian Century, 1549-1650.* Surrey, England: Ashgate Publishing Ltd., 2009.

Wrogemann, Henning. *Missionstheologien der Gegenwart: Globale Entwicklungen, kontextuelle Profile und dkumenische Herausforderungen.* Giitersloh: Gutersloher Verlagshaus, 2013.

Yasunaga, Mari. *Non-Formal Education as a Means to Meet Learning Needs of Out-of-School Children and Adolescents.* Paris: UNESCO, 2014.

Young, Richard F., ed. *India and the Indianness of Christianity: Essays on Understanding-Historical, Theological, and Bibliographical - in Honour of Robert Eric Frykenberg.* Grand Rapids, MI: Wm. B. Eerdmans, 2009.

Zupanov, Ines G. *Missionary Tropics: The Catholic Frontier in India (16th -17th Centuries).* Ann Arbor: The University of Michigan Press, 2005.

Secondary Literature: Articles In Books, Journals, Etc.

Anon, "Bischof Anastasius Hartmann O. Cap iiber die Reform des Werkes der Glaubensverbreitung," *KM4/49* (January 1921): 84-85.

Anon, "The Development of a Native Clergy in the Foreign Missions." *MSHI*12/14 (December 1922): 353-57.

Anon, "Uber die einheimische Missionshilfe durch Katechisten." *MB* (October 1929): 2-5.

Aghamkar, Atul Y. "Christianity among the Mahars of Maharashtra." In *Christianity in India: Search for Liberation and Identity.* Delhi: CMS/ISPCK, 2000.

Andrews, Paul. "The Jesuits and Education." *SIQR* 80/317 (Spring 1991); 22-30.

Arrupe, Pedro. "Men and Women for Others." In *Pedro Arrupe: Essential Writings* (New York: Orbis Books, 2004.

Bailey, Gavin A. "The Truth showing Mirror: Jesuit Catechism and the Arts in Mughal India." In *The Jesuits: Cultures, Sciences, and the Arts 1540-1773,* edited by John W. O'Malley et al. Toronto/Buffalo/Landon: University of Toronto Press, 1999.

Bannon, John Francis. "The Mission Frontier in Sonora: 1620-1687." In *The Jesuit Missions of Northern Mexico,* edited by Charles W. Polzer et al. New York/England: Garland Publishing, 1991.

Barret, John C. "World War I and the Decline of the First Wave of the American Protestant Missions Movement." *IBMR* 3/39 (July 2015): 122-126.

Bea, Augustine. "The Apostolic Constitution *Deus Scientiarum Dominus:* Its Origin and Spirit." *TS 4/1* (1943): 34-52.

Beaver, Pierce. "Katechisten: Ausbildung und Anstellung." In *Lexikon zur Weltmission,* edited by Stephen Neill, Niels-Peter Moritzen & Ernst Schrupp. Wuppertal: Theologischer Verlag/Erlangen: Verlag der Evang.-Luth. Mission, 1971.

Brechter, H. S. "Dekret iiber die Missionstatigkeit der Kirche." In *Das Zweite Vatikanische Konzil: Dokumente undKommentare,* edited by H. S. Brechter et al. Freiburg/Basel/Wien: Herder, 1968.

Biihlmann, Walbert. "Die Ideen, die nicht starben." *SBH* (24th April 1966): 2-5.

Comes, H. "Bombay Mission." In *Xavier's Footsteps 1540-1940: Jubilee Souvenir of the Centenary of the Society of Jesus.* Anand: Anand Press, 1940.

de la Costa, H. "Saint Ignatius and the Jesuit School Apostolate." In *Jesuit Education in India,* edited by Gregory Naik. Anand: Gujarat Sahitya Prakash, 1987.

de Souza, Teotonio R. "D. Jose Costa Nunes - a Patriarch who cared for more than Souls." In *Mission und Macht im Wandel politischer Orientierung: Europdische Missionsgesellschaften in politischen Spannungsfeldern in Afrika und Asien zwischen 1800 und 1945,* published by Ulrich van der Heyden & Holger Stoecker. Wiesbaden: Franz Steiner Verlag, 2005.

Dengel, Anna. "Karitas und Missionsarztlicherdienst." In *Weltkrise und Weltmission: Vortrdge des IX. Internationalen Acedemischen Missionskongress in Wien, 3-7 Juli 1950,* published by Johannes Thauren. Modling b.Wien: St. Gabriel, 1951.

Dulles, Avery. "The Meaning of Faith Considered in Relationship to Justice." In *The Faith That Does Justice: Examining the Christian Sources for Social Change,* edited by John C. Haughey. Eugene, Oregon: Wipf & Stock, 1977.

________ "Vatican II and Evangelization." In *New Evangelizations: Overcoming Obstacles,* edited by Steven Boguslawski and Ralph Martin. New York/Mahwah, NJ: Paulist Press, 2008.

Ely, Peter B. "Partnership in Mission: The Future of Jesuit Higher Education." In *Promise Renewed: Jesuit Higher Education for a New Millennium,* edited by Martin R. Tripole. Chicago: Loyola Press, 1999.

Entenmann, Robert. "The Problem of Chinese Rites in Eighteenth-Century Sichuan." In *China and Christianity: Burdened Past; Hopeful Future,* edited by Stephen Uhalley, Jr. and Xiaoxin Wu. New York: M.E. Sharpe, 2001.

Ferguson, James J. "A Paradigm Shift in the Theology of Mission: Two Roman Catholic Perspectives." *IBMR* 8/3 (July 1984): 117-119.

Freitag, Anton. "Die Forschritte des einheimischen Klerus und der einheimischen Hierarchie in den Missionslandern in den letzten dreissig Jahren (1920-1950)." In *Der einheimische Klerus in Geschichte und Gegenwart,* published by Johannes Beckmann et al. Schoneck-Beckenried: Administration der Neuen Zeitschrift fur Missionswissenschaft, 1950.

Fucek, Ivan. "Justice." In *Dictionary of Fundamental Theology,* edited by Rene Latourelle & Rino Fisichella. Middlegreen, UK/Maynooth, Ireland/Manila, Philippines: St. Pauls, 1990.

Gordon, Leonard A. "Mahatma Gandhi's Dialogues with Americans." EPWill 4 (Jan. 26 -Feb. 1, 2002): 337-352.

Graham, Stephen A. "Evangelism without Apology: E. Stanley Jones and the Totalitarian Kingdom of God." In *Exploring Christian Mission Beyond Christendom: United Methodist Perspectives,* edited by Michael G. Cartwright. Indianapolis: University of Indianapolis Press, 2010.

Gravend-Tirole, Xavier. "From Christian Ashrams to Dalit Theology - or Beyond." In *Constructing Indian Christianities: Culture, Conversion and Caste,* edited by Chad M. Bauman and Richard Fox Young (New Delhi: Routledge, 2014.

Gray, Howard. "Experience of Ignatius of Loyola: Background to Jesuit Education." In *The Jesuit Ratio Studiorum: 400th Anniversary Perspectives,* edited by Vincent J. Duminuco. New York: Fordham University Press, 2000.

Gupta, Surendra K. "Political Sociology in India." In *Sociology and Social Anthropology in India,* edited by Yogesh Atal. Delhi: ICSSR, 2009.

Heredia, Rudolph C. "Education and Mission: School as Agent of Evangelization." *EPW30/37* (September 16, 1995): 2332-2340.

Hobler, Friedrich. "Indisch-christliche Kunst: Gesprach mit Angelo da Fonseca." *KM6* (1955): 173-175.

Hunter III, George G. "McGavran, Donald Anderson." In *Biographical Dictionary of Christian Missions,* edited by Gerald H. Anderson. Grand Rapids, Michigan/Cambridge, U.K.: William B. Eerdmans, 1999.

Jeyakumar, D. Arthur. "Christianity among the Nadars of Tirunelvelly." In *Christianity in India: Search for Liberation and Identity,* edited by F. Hrankhuma. Delhi: CMS/ISPCK, 2000.

Kalapura, Jose, SJ, "Heroic Church Leadership in India: Capuchin Bishop Anastasius Hartmann (1803-1866)" in *zmr Zeitschrift fur*

Missionswissenschaft und Religionswissenschaft, (Heft 3-4, 101. Jahrgang, 2017): 226-227.

Kavunkal, Jacob. "Conversion and Nationalism." In *Nationalism and Hindutva: A Christian Response, Papers from the 10th CMS Consultation,* edited by Mark T. B. Laing. Delhi: ISPCK/Pune: CMS, 2005.

Keeler, Floyd. "Could we have a Clerical Missionary Union?," *TER* LXII (1920): 151-157.

Leonard, J. P. "Missionary Work in the New India." *RL* (Supplement) (January 1950): 12-18.

Marattukalam, C. "The Jesuits and Education in India." In *Catholic and Indian Education* Trichinopoly: St. Joseph's Industrial School Press, n. d.

McGavran, Donald A. "The People Movement Point of View." In *Church Growth and Group Conversion,* 5th ed., edited by Donald A. McGavran. Pasadena, California: William Carey Library, 1973.

________ "When the Church Grows." In *Church Growth and Group Conversion,* edited by J. W. Pickett et al. California: William Carey Library, 1973.

McKenzie, G. T. "The Royal Patronage in India: A brief History of the Portuguese Indian Empire." *TDR* 112 (1893): 32-44.

Meersmann, Achilles. "The Catholic Church in India." In *Christianity in India: A History in Ecumenical Perspective,* edited by H. C. Perumalil & E. R. Hambye. Allepey: Prakasham Publications, 1991.

Neuner, Josef. "Hundert Jahre Deutsche Jesuitenmission in Indien." *KM* 1 (1954): 4-9.

Norbu, Dawa. "The Cultural Foundations of Indian Nationalism." In *Social Science and Social Concern: Felicitation Volume in Honour of Professor B. K. Roy Burman,* edited by S. B. Chakrabarti. Delhi: Mittal Publications, 1988.

Oommen, T. K. "Religious Nationalisms and Democratic Polity in India: Impossibility of Reconciliation." In *Nationalism and Hindutva: A Christian Response,* published by Mark T. B. Laing. Delhi: ISPCK, 2005.

Pagani, Catherine. "Clockwork and the Jesuit Mission in China." In *The Jesuits II: Cultures, Sciences and the Arts, 1540-1773,* edited by John W. O'Mally et al. Toronto/Buffalo/London: University of Toronto Press, 2006.

Paranjpe, Suhas and K. J. Joy. "An Alternative Approach to Drought and Drought-Proofing." In *Drought and Integrated Water Resource Management in south Asia: Issues, Alternatives and Futures,* edited by Jasveen Jairath and Vishva Ballabh. New Delhi: Sage Publications, 2008.

Passah, Amena. "Christian Missions in the Khasi-Jaintia Hills: Health Care and Impact on the Society." In *Christianity and Change in Northeast India,* edited by T. B. Subba, et al. New Delhi: Concept Publishing Co. 2006.

Pinto, Noelline. "Human Organization for Pioneering in Education: An Attempt in Community Building and Functional Education." In *PJPA, Varia.* (Typed Material).

Plattner, Felix A. "80 Jahre Mission in 'indischen Hungersgebiet." *WMKK* (January 1935): 4-12.

________ "Achtzig Jahre deutsche Jesuiten Mission in Indien." *KM 62/S* (August 1934): 208-211.

________ "Der Alteste Deutsche Missionsbischof gestorben." *KM1M2* (1952): 40.

Raj, Solomon. "Christliche Kunst in Indien." In *Die Bilder und das Wort: Zum Verstehen christlicher Kunst in Afrika und Asien,* edited by Theo Sundermeier & Volker Kiister. Gottingen: Vandenhoeck & Ruprecht, 1999.

Rausch, Thomas. "Sexual Morality and Social Justice." In *Contemporary Catholic Theology: A Reader,* edited by Michael A. Hayes and Liam Gearon. New York: Continuum, 2000.

Rickert, Arnold. "Bocholt, Heimat der Bischofe Laurenz Boggering, Hermann Kunst, Heinrich Doring und Melchior von Diepenbrock." *UB* 19/1 (1968): 24-25.

Sanks, T. Howland. "The Social Mission of the Church: Its Changing Context." In *The Gift of the Church: A Textbook Ecclesiology in Honor of Patrick Granfield O.S.B.,* edited by Peter C. Phan. Collegeville, Minnesota: The Liturgical Press, 2000.

Schatz, Klaus. "Optionen und Prioritaten in der Bombay-Mission der Deutschen Jesuiten (1858-1916." *SM6Q* (2011): 389-407.

________ *Geschichte Der Deutschen Jesuiten (1814-1983).* Vol. I-V. Munster: Aschendorf, 2014.

________ "Gerhard Kipp (1862-1903): Ein Apostel der Maharashtra Kirche," *SM 54* (2005): 105-143.

Schneider, Rainhold. "Erzbischof Heinrich Doring J. S." *UB* 3/2 (1952): 26-29.

Sharma, Loveneesh. "A Study of Visual Interpretations of Christian Faith in Indian Art." *IJHSSS,* Vol. II, Issue VI (May 2016): 297-306.

Shelke, Christopher. "Maharashtra and Inculturation through Jesuit Apostolate: Evangelization among the Indigenous People of Bombay Presidency." *SM* 57 (2008): 147-190.

Shourie, Arun. "Missionaries in India." In *Paths of Mission in India Today,* edited by Augustine Kanjamala. Bombay: St. Pauls, 1997.

Suria, Carlos. "The German-Swiss Pioneers: 1894-1923." VJ (1979): 39-80.

Thangaraj, M. Thomas. "Indian Christian Tradition." In *Religions of South Asia: An Introduction,* edited by Sushil Mittal and Gene Thursby. London & New York: Routledge, 2006.

Tripole, Martin R. "An Assessment of the 34th General Congregation's Understanding of Justice and its Role in Jesuit Higher Education." In *Promise Renewed: Jesuit Higher Education for a New Millennium,* edited by Martin R. Tripole. Chicago: Loyola Press, 1999.

Ubelmesser, Joseph. "The Catholic Church in India: The Story of a Personal Encounter." In *Bend without Fear: Hopes and Possibilities for an Indian Church: Essays in Honour of Professor Kurian Kunnumpuram SJ,* edited by Kuruvilla Pandikattu and Rocha Rosario. Pune: Jnana-Deepa Vidyapeeth/Delhi: ISPCK, 2003.

Vath, Alfons. "Die Ereignisse der deutschen Jesuitenmissionare in Indien wahrend des Krieges."^M45 (1916/1917): 3-8.

Luthera, Ved Prakash. "Freedom of Religion under the Indian Constitution and the Foreign Missionaries." *TUPS* 16/2 (April-June 1955): 140-146.

Webster, John C. B. "Christian History as Indian Social History: A Review of the Literature." In *Approaches to History: Essays in Indian Historiography,* edited by Sabyasachi Bhattacharya. New Delhi: ICHR & Primus Books, 2011.

Theses, Souvenirs, Documents

Anon, "Father Willy: The First Principal of St. Xavier's College." *SXCM Souvenir,* 1/2 (September 1908): 54-62.

Castelino, Herman. "The Educational Enterprise of the German Jesuit Mission." (Paper presented at a Workshop on Mission on the occasion of the Sequicentennial Anniversary of the Arrival of the Jesuits of the Garman-Swiss Provinces in India, Ishvani Kendra, Pune, December 27th - 29th, 2004).

Lorimer, Michelle Marie. *Reconstructing the Past: Historical Interpretations and Native Experiences at Contemporary California Missions.* Ph.D. diss., University of California, 2013.

Madapattu, Jose. "Evangelization in a Marginalizing World: With Special Reference to the Marginalised Satnamis in the Diocese of Raipur." Ph.D. diss., University of Bonn, 1996.

Punjabi, H. T. "A Critical Study of the Contribution of German Jesuit Mission to Education in Bombay." Ph.D. Dissertation, unpublished). Bombay: Bombay University, 1984.

Reddy, Thomas. "The East Indian Catholics' Perseverance Bears Fruit: Tracking the Protagonists in the Double Jurisdiction Controversy in the Bombay Archdiocese through ARSI: 'Bombay de Patronatus 1921-1928." Ph.D. diss., Pontificia Universitas Gregoriana, 2004.

Websites for Maps

Map of India available from, https://www.google.at/'search?q=india+states+and-runion+tei'ritories+map, accessed on 17.11.2016.

Map of Maharashtra with Districts, available from http://wardha.nic.in/en/htmldocs/maps.htmh accessed on 17.11.2016.

Map available from https://en.\\ikipedia.org/'^-iki/Talukas_of_Ahmednagar_district#/media. accessed on 17.11.2016.

Thematic Index

G

H

I

J

T

U

V

W